Operating Systems
in Depth

OPERATING SYSTEMS IN DEPTH

Thomas W. Doeppner
Brown University

WILEY

JOHN WILEY & SONS, INC.

VICE-PRESIDENT & EXECUTIVE PUBLISHER	Donald Fowley
EXECUTIVE EDITOR	Beth Lang Golub
EXECUTIVE MARKETING MANAGER	Christopher Ruel
PRODUCTION EDITOR	Barbara Russiello
EDITORIAL PROGRAM ASSISTANT	Mike Berlin
SENIOR MARKETING ASSISTANT	Diana Smith
EXECUTIVE MEDIA EDITOR	Thomas Kulesa
COVER DESIGN	Wendy Lai
COVER PHOTO	Thomas W. Doeppner

Cover photo is of Banggai Cardinalfish (Pterapogon kauderni), taken in the Lembeh Strait, North Sulawesi, Indonesia.

This book was set in 10/12 Times Roman. The book was composed by MPS Limited, A Macmillan Company and printed and bound by Hamilton Printing Company.

This book is printed on acid free paper. ∞

Founded in 1807, John Wiley & Sons, Inc. has been a valued source of knowledge and understanding for more than 200 years, helping people around the world meet their needs and fulfill their aspirations. Our company is built on a foundation of principles that include responsibility to the communities we serve and where we live and work. In 2008, we launched a Corporate Citizenship Initiative, a global effort to address the environmental, social, economic, and ethical challenges we face in our business. Among the issues we are addressing are carbon impact, paper specifications and procurement, ethical conduct within our business and among our vendors, and community and charitable support. For more information, please visit our website: www.wiley.com/go/citizenship.

Library of Congress Cataloging in Publication Data:

Doeppner, Thomas W.
    Operating systems in depth / Thomas W. Doeppner.
        p. cm.
    Includes index.
        ISBN 978-0-471-68723-8 (hardback)
    1. Operating systems (Computers)   I. Title.
    QA76.76.O63D64 2010
    005.4'3—dc22

2010034669

Printed in the United States of America

10 9 8 7 6 5 4 3 2 1

To the memory of my father, Thomas W. Doeppner Sr.

Preface

The goal of this book is to bring together and explain current practice in operating systems. This includes much of what is traditionally covered in operating-system textbooks: concurrency, scheduling, linking and loading, storage management (both real and virtual), file systems, and security. However, I also cover issues that come up every day in operating-systems design and implementation but are not often taught in undergraduate courses. For example, I cover:

- *Deferred work*, which includes deferred and asynchronous procedure calls in Windows, tasklets in Linux, and interrupt threads in Solaris.

- The intricacies of *thread switching*, on both uniprocessor and multiprocessor systems.

- *Modern file systems*, such as *ZFS* and *WAFL*.

- *Distributed file systems*, including *CIFS* and *NFS* version 4.

AUDIENCE

This book is based on material I've developed over the past 30+ years for my operating-systems course at Brown University and is suitable for a one-semester course for advanced undergraduates and beginning graduate students. Students taking the course at Brown have generally had an introductory course on computer architecture and an advanced programming course. The course investigates in depth what's done in current operating systems, and its significant programming projects make students come to grips with major operating-system components and attain an intimate understanding of how they work.

But certainly not all students in an OS course want to go on to concentrate in the area, let alone work in it. A course based on this text must be accessible to these students as well. This issue is handled at Brown by letting students choose one of two projects (discussed later in this preface). The first, relatively straightforward, project involves writing a user-level threads library, a file-system cache manager, and a simple file system. The second, for the truly interested gung-ho students, is to implement a good portion of a simple but fully functional operating system. (Those portions that are not pedagogically useful for students to write are provided to them.) Students completing this latter project get a half course of additional credit (Brown's full courses and half courses are equivalent to four-credit and two-credit courses in schools using the credit system).

TOPIC COVERAGE

Part of the challenge in writing a textbook is not only choosing the topics to cover but also determining the order of presentation. There is the usual conundrum: to appreciate the individual topics one must first know how they fit together, but to appreciate how they fit together one must first know the individual topics. Compounding this problem is my belief that students must complete a comprehensive programming project in order to understand and appreciate how operating systems work. Thus the material must be presented so as to make such a project possible.

Chapter 1, Introduction, introduces the reader to what an operating system is. It discusses at an abstract level both how they're structured and what they do and provides a brief history. Then, to make things concrete and to introduce the notions of processes and files, I briefly describe early Unix (Sixth Edition, from 1975). This 35-year-old OS is attractive both because of its simplicity and elegance and because, at the level presented here, it's not all that different from either modern Unix systems or modern Windows.

Exploring the concept of a *process* has traditionally been a fundamental part of an operating systems course. However, the meaning of this term has changed over the years. As used in most of today's operating systems, a process is what was originally called a *computation*. Most systems now use the term *thread* to refer to what was originally meant by *process*. Our introduction to the process concept in Chapter 1 uses the contemporary notion of a process; we spend most of Chapter 2, Multithreaded Programming, discussing threads.

It's really important that students doing an operating-systems project understand concurrency—and by "understand" I mean not simply comprehending the concepts but also becoming proficient in multithreaded programming. Chapter 2 is a tutorial on how to write multithreaded programs, both using POSIX threads and Windows threads. Though the material covers such programming from an application-program perspective, both the concepts and the practice apply to programming within an operating system.

In this chapter, I go over the notion of deadlocks. Earlier operating-systems textbooks have spent a great deal of time on deadlocks, describing algorithms for deadlock detection and avoidance. In practice, such algorithms have little or no role in operating systems, so I simply discuss deadlock avoidance.

Chapter 3, Basic Concepts, covers a collection of topics students may have met in previous courses; they aren't all strictly operating-systems material, but they are essential for understanding operating systems. Included here is a discussion of procedure calls and various forms of context switching at an assembler-language level. We talk a lot about context switching and its cost when discussing operating systems, so students really must understand what's involved. This discussion is given both in terms of x86 assembler language and SPARC assembler language. The latter is done to balance the x86-orientation of this part of the chapter but may safely be skipped. Also included in the chapter is a rather simple discussion of I/O architectures, important both for programming projects and for understanding I/O handling in operating systems. I cover dynamic storage-allocation algorithms, following in part Knuth's classic treatment, with additional material on slab allocation. Though this topic could well be considered appropriate for an algorithms course, it doesn't seem to be taught there and it's definitely important in operating systems. I discuss linkers and loaders, concepts that also seem to be much neglected elsewhere in the curriculum. Finally, I go over how a system is booted.

Up to Chapter 4, Operating-System Design, I really haven't explained what's in an operating system, except briefly in the introduction. In Chapter 4, I go over standard operating-system components, discuss flow of control in terms of both threads and interrupt handling, and introduce structuring techniques for operating systems such as monolithic kernels, microkernels, and virtual machines. I talk about some of the layering that's used, such as the virtual file system (VFS) layer in Unix systems and its equivalent in Windows. The material in Chapter 4 is intended to be presented as students begin to design and implement their OS projects; it helps them get started writing the lower-level parts of the operating system.

Concurrency is not merely the use of threads: interrupt handling is a paramount issue, and so are the various forms of deferred processing implemented in many operating systems. I cover these in Chapter 5, Processor Management. This chapter begins by describing the various approaches to implementing threads packages, from strictly user-level approaches to kernel and hybrid approaches, including scheduler activations. It then covers the design of a simple threads implementation, first on a uniprocessor, then on a multiprocessor. I cover such concepts as preemptive and non-preemptive kernels and how they affect synchronization. This leads naturally to a discussion of scheduling, where I introduce traditional terminology and models (FIFO, SJF, etc.) and then describe approaches to scheduling used in real operating systems. I conclude with descriptions of the schedulers of Linux and Windows. I omit any mention of queuing theory, since in my experience it takes weeks to get to any non-intuitively obvious results, and it's simply not worth the time.

Chapter 6, File Systems, provides extensive coverage of an important part of operating systems. I start, as I started the book, with Sixth-Edition Unix, this time looking at its file system, which came to be called S5FS (the System 5 File System) in later Unix systems. It's amazingly simple, even simplistic, but it's easily understood and even easily implemented as part of a programming project, and it's also a good vehicle for introducing some basic file-system issues. In addition, its performance and stability limitations are inspirations to look at how later file systems have overcome them.

Then, using S5FS as motivation, I cover the basics of on-disk file-system organization, looking at such ideas as cylinder groups, extents, dynamic allocation of on-disk data structures, and log-structured systems. I then cover crash resilience and recovery, focusing on soft updates and journaling. Next comes managing the name space, including a discussion of how directories are organized. This is followed by a discussion of RAID techniques, and then a discussion of the use of flash memory to support file systems. Throughout the file-system discussion, I use examples from a number of file systems, in particular BSD's FFS, Linux's Ext3 and ReiserFS, Microsoft's NTFS, Network Appliance's WAFL, and Sun's ZFS. So that readers can appreciate how all the pieces fit together, I finish with further treatment of some of the example file systems and fill in further details of how they work. An instructor may certainly use her or his judgment in skipping some of the detailed file-system coverage, though I recommend that FFS, NTFS, and ZFS be covered.

Chapter 7, Memory Management, covers both hardware and software aspects of memory management in computer systems. Though many students take computer architecture courses before the OS course, it is still important to discuss the hardware architecture behind memory management—page tables, caches, etc. Thus I devote many pages to this here, looking at a number of representative approaches. It's useful not just to describe the architectures but to explain why they're designed as they are. So I cover the layout of address spaces, showing how support for multiple memory regions with sometimes sparse use drives the design of the memory-management system. I conclude this part of the chapter with a discussion of hardware support for virtualization. Then comes a discussion of the software issues, particularly those having to do with managing virtual memory. This includes not just the usual page-replacement strategies but also backing-store issues, such as space management, as well as handling the various forms of memory-mapped files (both shared and private, in Unix terminology). An important concern is the interplay between memory-mapped file I/O and system-call file I/O.

Chapter 8, Security, covers security as provided by operating systems. It starts with a brief discussion on the threats that modern operating systems try to handle. The bulk of the chapter talks about security architectures, starting with the access-control models developed in the 1960s and '70s. I then discuss the discretionary access-control models used in standard Windows and Unix systems. Nest I cover mandatory access control and its use in SELinux. I conclude with a discussion of capability systems.

Chapter 9, Introduction to Networking, provides a rather brief introduction to network protocols (primarily TCP/IP) and remote-procedure protocols. This is clearly a review for students who have taken a networking course. For those students who haven't, it helps form a basis for the following chapter. An instructor pressed for time may safely omit most of the discussion of network protocols, though the RPC material is assumed in the next chapter.

Chapter 10, Distributed File Systems, introduces the issues by looking at the earliest versions of NFS, using it much as S5FS was used in Chapter 6. Here I discuss stateless vs. stateful servers, single-system semantics, failure semantics, and so forth, by taking examples from OSF's DFS (which was based on CMU's AFS), Microsoft's CIFS, and the most recent version of NFS, version 4.

PROGRAMMING PROJECTS

Programming assignments are essential in an OS course. Courses using this text can use either Unix or Windows, though, as described below, we use Linux at Brown. In the past, my students did projects on a simulator that provided an architecture with simple I/O facilities and paged memory management with a software-managed TLB. One year, we had students do projects on Xen-based x86 virtual machines but found that its paravirtualization of I/O deprived students of the experience of working with actual devices. Our current projects are done on top of Bochs, an emulator for the Intel x86 architecture.

A sensitive issue is the choice of programming language. To a first approximation, all current operating systems are written in C. Attempts have been made to write operating systems in object-oriented languages—for example, Sun's Spring OS was written in C++, and in the mid-'90s I based my course's project on Spring—but such approaches never caught on. Though many CS departments (including Brown's) use managed languages, such as Java and C# in the introductory curriculum, these have yet to be used within successful operating systems (though Microsoft Research is doing interesting work on OS development with C#). It's essential that students who go on to work with real operating systems have experience with the language these systems are written in—questions about C constantly come up in job interviews. For all these reasons, all my code examples and exercises use C. For students who don't know C, a quick "introduction to C for Java programmers" at the beginning of the course has proven to be sufficient.

Though the programming projects we do at Brown are not an essential part of the text, we have made our source code and written handouts available at the book's website. As mentioned above, some of our students do more work (for more credit) than others. With that in mind, here is the list of programming assignments.

1. **Shell.** Students write a simple Unix shell in C. This is essentially a warm-up exercise to make sure they are comfortable with C. It also familiarizes them with using basic Unix system calls. What they need to know about Unix is covered in Chapter 1.

2. **Threads.** This is a rather elaborate multithreaded program in which students implement a simple database (containing names and values) as an unbalanced binary search tree. It is accessed and modified concurrently by any number of threads, which can be interrupted by signals and timeouts. The intent is to get students comfortable with concurrent program-ming (using POSIX threads, though it could be done with Win-32 threads) and with dealing with asynchronous events. The material needed for this is covered in Chapter 2.

Then, students not doing the full OS project do the following:

3. **Threads implementation.** Students implement a simple user-level threads package. They must deal with simple scheduling and synchronization. Much of this material is covered in Chapter 3, with additional topics covered in Chapter 5.

4. **VFS.** We provide a binary of a working OS, minus some features. The first feature they implement is the virtual-file-system layer, in which they provide the high-level (file-system-independent) aspects of doing I/O. This material is covered in Chapters 1 and 4.

5. **S5FS.** They implement the System 5 file system—a simple file system that is based on, if not identical to, the original Unix file system (and not that different from FAT-16 of MS-DOS). This material is covered in Chapter 6.

Students doing the full OS project (known as *Weenix*) do the following:

3. **Kernel 1.** Weenix is implemented bottom-up: students start with device drivers for the terminals and the disk. What they need to know is covered in Chapters 3 and 4.

4. **Kernel 2.** The next step is the implementation of threads and processes. This includes creation and termination, synchronization, and scheduling. This material is covered in Chapter 5.

5. **VFS.** This is identical to the VFS described above and is covered in Chapters 1 and 4.

6. **S5FS.** This is identical to the S5FS described above and is covered in Chapter 6.

7. **Virtual memory and final integration.** Students implement a simple paging system (no page-outs, just page-ins). They then get all the components to work with each other so as to support multiple user-level processes, which run the shell they implemented in the first assignment. This material is covered in Chapter 7.

We tried a few years ago to create a version of the OS project that was based on a simplification of Windows NT rather than on a simplification of Unix. Though we had what we thought was a rather elegant design, it proved to be a much larger system in terms of code size than the Unix-based system. Unix started as a small system, while Windows NT did not. Thus it is not surprising that a usable subset of Unix is much smaller than a usable subset of Windows. Our Windows subset was just large enough that it was unsuitable for a one-semester project. Therefore we continue with our Unix-based project.

ADDITIONAL MATERIALS

Much additional material is available at the book's web site: www.wiley.com/college/ Doeppner. Available to students are programming exercises, with source code, for Chapter 2 (Multithreaded Programming). Available to faculty are PowerPoint lecture slides (not just the figures from the text but the slides I use to teach my operating-systems course), answers to all exercises, and full source code, handouts, and other explanatory material for the optional semester-long operating-systems project.

EXERCISES

The end-of-chapter exercises are of three types: unstarred, starred (*), and two-starred (**). Unstarred ones are intended to be easy and are provided for quick review of the material. Starred and two-starred exercises are intended to be homework problems and exam questions. The two-starred ones are both more difficult and more valuable than the one-starred ones.

ACKNOWLEDGMENTS

A lot of people have helped me prepare this book. I particularly want to thank all the students who have been teaching assistants in my operating-systems course over the years. The following former students, all of whom were also TAs, have continued to help out, giving me useful information on the products of their employers (of which they were often principal architects): Matt Ahrens, George Cabrera, Bryan Cantrill, Kit Colbert, Peter Griess, Adam Leventhal, Dave Pacheco, and Mike Shapiro. Aaron Myers and Eric Tamura provided considerable help by writing many of the exercises. The following former students provided useful criticisms and bug reports on the text while in my course: Lucia Ballard, Sam Cates, Adam Conrad, Andrés Douglas, Colin Gordon, Alex Heitzmann, Daniel Heller, Venkatasubramanian Jayaraman, Daniel Leventhal, Chu-Chi Liu, Tim O'Donnell, Daniel Rosenberg, Allan Shortlidge, Sean Smith, Jono Spiro, Taylor Stearns, and Zhe Zhang.

The following Brown students and alums have put in significant time and effort creating and fixing up the project I use in my course at Brown, which is available on the book's web site: Keith Adams, Dimo Bounov, Michael Castelle, Adam Fenn, Alvin Kerber, Dan Kuebrich, Jason Lango, Robert Manchester, Dave Pacheco, David Powell, Eric Schrock, Chris Siden, Shaun Verch, and Joel Weinberger.

I greatly appreciate the following Microsoft employees who, with much patience, answered my frequent questions about Windows: Mark Eden, Susheel Gopalan, Dave Probert, Ravisankar Pudipeddi, Arkady Retik, Scott Williams, and Mark Zbikowski.

Bob Munck, a Brown alumnus from before I came to Brown, helped me track down historical information about virtual machines. The following Brown faculty and staff all assisted me in many ways: John Bazik, Steven Carmody, Mark Dieterich, Maurice Herlihy, John Hughes, John Jannotti, Philip Klein, Steve Reiss, Max Salvas, and Andy van Dam.

Rosemary Simpson did an amazing job of constructing the index, the URL index, and the glossary. She also checked and corrected many of my references. Any errors that remain are certainly my fault and not hers.

This book took a long time from conception to completion. During that period, I had a number of editors at Wiley, all of whom I wish to thank: Paul Crockett, Beth Golub, Dan Sayre, Bruce Spatz, and Bill Zobrist. It has been a pleasure working with Barbara Russiello, who guided the book through production at Wiley.

I wish to thank the following reviewers for their helpful comments: Bina Ramamurthy, Hugh C. Lauer, Kenneth F. Wong, Kyoungwon Suh, Tim Lin, and Euripides Montagne.

I am grateful to Microsoft for providing funding as I began the book project.

Much of the material on multithreaded programming in Chapter 2 was developed as part of training courses I have produced and taught for the Institute for Advanced Professional Studies in Boston, Massachusetts. I thank Donald French, the company's president, for his support in this.

Most of all, I couldn't have done it without my copy editor, Katrina Avery, who is also my wife.

Contents

4 Operating-System Design

5 Processor Management

6 File Systems

Introduction

We begin by explaining what an operating system is and why the field is not only worthy of study, but worthy of continued research and development. Next we delve briefly into the history of operating systems, one that combines brilliant research in both academia and industry with a colorful cast of characters. Finally we introduce the study of operating systems by looking carefully at an early version of Unix so as to understand its basic concepts and some of how it was implemented.

1.1 OPERATING SYSTEMS

What's an operating system? You might say it's what's between you and the hardware, but that would cover pretty much all software. So let's say it's the software that sits between your software and the hardware. But does that mean that the library you picked up from some web site is part of the operating system? We probably want our operating-system definition to be a bit less inclusive. So, let's say that it's that software that almost everything else depends upon. This is still vague, but then the term is used in a rather nebulous manner throughout the industry.

Perhaps we can do better by describing what an operating system is actually supposed to do. From a programmer's point of view, operating systems provide useful abstractions of the underlying hardware facilities. Since many programs can use these facilities at once, the operating system is also responsible for managing how these facilities are shared.

To be more specific, typical hardware facilities for which the operating system provides abstractions include

- processors
- RAM (random-access memory, sometimes known as *primary storage*, *primary memory*, or *physical memory*)
- disks (a particular kind of *secondary storage*)
- network interface
- display
- keyboard
- mouse

We like to think of a program as having sole use of a processor and some memory, but in reality it's sharing the processor with other programs. In addition, what the program perceives as "memory" may be partly on actual RAM and partly on disk. Rather than force the programmer to worry about all this, most operating systems provide the *process* abstraction, which captures the notions of both an execution unit (a processor) and memory.

Similarly, rather than making programmers worry about the myriad arcane details of dealing with disk storage and buffering its contents in RAM, some sort of simple *file* abstraction is provided for persistent storage.

Network interfaces provide access to computer networks such as Ethernet. The sorts of *networking* abstractions used by application programmers include *sockets*, *remote procedure calls*, and *remote method invocation*, as well as *web-oriented interactions*. Later we discuss in detail the multiple layers of abstraction used with networks.

The display, keyboard, and mouse require layers of software and hardware in order to have useful abstractions. Few programmers want to think of the display as an output device to which they send bit patterns to turn pixels on and off selectively. Instead, we use abstractions provided by drawing packages, windowing packages, and the like. A mouse provides a steady stream of position information and button-click indications. A keyboard provides indications that keys are being depressed and released. Abstractions are supplied for both devices so that, for example, we can treat mouse clicks as invocations of programs and key-down events as inputs of characters.

Some of these abstractions, usually because of their history, are considered part of fields other than operating systems. For example, file systems are generally considered part of the operating system, but databases form a field unto themselves. And though the low-level aspects of displays are considered as abstractions provided by operating systems, the higher-level graphics and windowing systems are again aspects of fields unto themselves.

Abstracting (or "virtualizing") the various components of our computing systems also makes it relatively straightforward to share them. Rather than having to worry about sharing both the sectors of a disk drive and the bandwidth through its controller, we simply deal with files. Programs create and name files, add data to them, read the data back, delete them: there's no explicit concern about actually sharing the physical disk resources (until, of course, we run out of disk space).

In addition, by using the *process* abstraction, which abstracts both processors and memory, programmers need only be concerned about the program at hand. They needn't worry about whether this program is monopolizing the processor or is using all of RAM: both the processor and RAM are multiplexed under the control of the operating system.

1.1.1 OPERATING SYSTEMS AS A FIELD OF STUDY

Why should we study operating systems? The field has been a standard part of the computer science curriculum ever since there was a computer science curriculum. One might figure that it is a solved problem and it is time to move on.

To a certain extent, it is a solved problem. We know how to build an operating system that supports a number of concurrently executing programs that, depending on our intent, can be completely oblivious of one another's existence, fully cooperating with one another, or some combination of the two. We can interact with programs running on a computer as if the entire computer were dedicated to us, even though much else is going on. Bugs in programs rarely bring down the entire system. File systems are amazingly efficient, both in time and in space. Our systems and data can survive hardware failures. Vast amounts of data can be transferred to and from our computer over networks flawlessly.

Yet things are not always so perfect, particularly when our systems are pushed to their limits. Systems are routinely attacked and succumb to their attackers. Operating systems occasionally crash due to bugs in application programs. A system might be so overloaded, perhaps due to a "denial-of-service attack," that it is effectively down. Data does occasionally get lost or corrupted.

The challenge in the field of operating systems is to continue to strive towards overcoming these problems. We like to think that our basic approaches to system design are sound and all that is required are better implementations and minor tweaking, but it may well be that completely new approaches are required. A common theme in current operating-system development is isolation: programs should be isolated from one another so that problems in one do not affect others. This has been a theme since the earliest days of operating-system development and yet continues to be a solved problem that is never solved quite well enough.

In the past isolation meant protection from bugs. A bug in one computation should not bring down another. Data was to be kept reasonably secure in file systems, but real security meant locking the file systems in vaults with no outside network connections. Today's operating systems must cope with attacks from national intelligence services, organizations that might well understand a system's limitations, bugs, and security holes far better than its designers do.

We seem to be moving towards a global computing environment in which data is stored in "the cloud." Yet this cloud resides on file systems that are not unlike those that exist on your laptop computer, managed by an operating system that might be identical to that on your laptop. Operating systems continue to be relevant, even if much of the action is moving away from personal computers.

1.2
A BRIEF
HISTORY OF
OPERATING
SYSTEMS

In this section we present a brief history of operating systems. We start with the early days, when the notion of an operating system had yet to be invented, and proceed to the systems prevalent today, concentrating on representative systems with clear relevance to today's systems.

1.2.1 THE 1950s: THE BIRTH OF THE CONCEPT

The earliest computers had no operating systems. In fact, they had very little software, period. When you ran a program on an early computer, you supplied everything — there weren't even any program libraries.

The early history of operating systems is a bit murky. The term "operating system" was probably coined sometime after the first few software systems that might be called operating systems came into existence. According to MIT's CSAIL web pages,[1] MIT's first operating system, apparently for its Whirlwind computer, was written in 1954 and was used to manage the reading of paper tapes so that the computer could run without a human operator being present.

General Motors Research Laboratories also claims to have written the first operating system, in partnership with North American Aviation, for the IBM 701 and then the IBM 704. According to (Ryckman 1983), this operating system ran on the IBM 704 in May 1956 and was simply called "Input/Output System." Its motivation was that users of the IBM 701 were allocated time in 15-minute slots, but ten minutes was needed to set up the necessary equipment, such as tapes, card readers, etc. The goal of the system was to make this setup work unnecessary. Though it may have been the precursor of the modern operating system, it apparently was not considered an important development at the time — it gets scant mention (five short lines) in just one article in a special issue of *Annals of the History of Computing* (Ryckman 1983) devoted to the IBM 701.

The earliest serious paper discussing operating systems may be the one presented at a conference in 1959 by Christopher Strachey, later of Oxford (Strachey 1959).[2] Though the title of the paper was "Time Sharing in Large Fast Computers," the subject actually was what we now call multiprogramming, and not interactive computing. ((Lee 1992) discusses this early confusion of terms.) In a January 1959 memo,[3] John McCarthy, then of MIT, proposed that MIT "time-share our expected 'transistorized IBM 709'" (referring to the IBM 7090) (McCarthy 1983). Here, "time-share" was used in its modern sense, meaning interactive computing by multiple concurrent users.

The earliest operating systems were batch systems, designed to facilitate the running of multiple jobs sequentially. A major bottleneck in the earliest computers was I/O: all computation had to stop to let an I/O operation take place. What was necessary to eliminate this problem was to enable computers to start an operation, but not wait for it to complete and, correspondingly, to find out when an operation completed. Aiding the latter is the notion of the *interrupt*. According to (Smotherman 2008), the first machine to implement interrupts was the DYSEAC, designed and built by the U.S. National Bureau of Standards in 1954. The concept was added to the Univac 1103 and in 1955 became a standard feature of the 1103a. Edsger Dijkstra, whom we encounter again in Chapter 2, designed a system with interrupts as part of his 1959 Ph.D. thesis (Dijkstra 1959). According to (Smotherman 2008), this work involved the Electrologica X-1 computer and was done in 1957–1958.

---

[1] http://www.csail.mit.edu/timeline/timeline.php/timeline.php?query=event&id=3

[2] There is some confusion about the date: Strachey himself referred to it later as being presented in 1960, but it really seems to have been presented in 1959. I have been unable to find a copy of the paper and must rely on what others have written about it.

[3] McCarthy is not entirely sure about the date; he states that it might have been in 1960.

The ability to compute and perform I/O concurrently made possible what we now call *multiprogramming* — the concurrent execution of multiple programs. Or, perhaps more precisely, multiprogramming made it possible for a system to compute and perform I/O concurrently, since while one program was doing I/O, another could be computing. While the second-generation operating systems were still batch systems, they supported multiprogramming.

Information about the actual operating systems that supported early multiprogramming is sparse, but early systems with such support include the Lincoln Labs TX-2 (1957) and the IBM Stretch computer, also known as the IBM 7030, developed in the latter half of the 1950s and first delivered in 1961. The Stretch was more expensive and slower than planned, but was nevertheless the world's fastest computer from 1961 till 1964 (Wikipedia 2009).

1.2.2 THE 1960s: THE MODERN OS TAKES FORM

While operating systems were essentially an afterthought in the 1950s, they drove computer development throughout the 1960s, perhaps the most interesting decade of operating-system development, beginning with the first systems to support virtual memory and ending with the earliest Unix system. In between came OS/360 and Multics.

As the decade began, memory devices were commonly thought of as in a hierarchy, from the fastest and most expensive — primary storage — to slower but cheaper — secondary storage — to archival storage (even slower and even cheaper). Primary storage was typically built on core memory,[4] while secondary storage was built on disks and drums.[5]

It was often not possible to fit a program in primary storage, and thus code and data had to be shuffled between primary storage and secondary storage. Doing this shuffling explicitly within a program was, at best, a nuisance. Researchers at the University of Manchester (in the United Kingdom) incorporated in the Atlas computer a *one-level store* (Kilburn, Edwards, et al. 1962): programmers wrote programs as if lots of primary storage was available, while the operating system shuffled code and data between the relatively small quantity of actual primary storage and the larger amount of secondary storage. This notion became known as *virtual memory*, a subject we take up in Chapter 7.

At roughly the same time, researchers at MIT pursued the notion of time-sharing: enabling multiple concurrent users to interact with programs running on a computer. They developed CTSS (Corbató, Daggett, et al. 1962), their compatible time-sharing system — compatible in being compatible with a standard batch system for the IBM 709/7090 computer — FMS (Fortran Monitor System). It supported three concurrent users as well as an FMS batch stream. Though CTSS was installed only at MIT, it helped prove that time-sharing made sense.

Perhaps the most influential system to come out of MIT was Multics (multiplexed information and computing service). Multics started in 1964 as a joint project of MIT, General Electric, and Bell Labs; Bell Labs dropped out in 1969 and GE's computer business was purchased in 1970 by Honeywell, who took over the commercialization of Multics. The goals of the Multics project, as stated in (Corbató, Saltzer, et al. 1972), were to build a computer utility with

1. convenient remote terminal access as the normal mode of system usage;

2. a view of continuous operation analogous to that of the electric power and telephone companies;

---

[4] "Core memory" is memory formed from magnetic toruses, called cores. Each held one bit and was the dominant technology for primary storage from the late 1950s through the early 1970s. Primary memory is still often referred to as core, as in "core dump."

[5] A drum is similar to a disk. If a disk resembles a stack of old-fashioned phonograph records, a drum resembles Edison's even older phonograph cylinder. However, drums had one head per track and could access data more quickly than disks.

3. a wide range of capacity to allow growth or contraction without either system or user reorganization;

4. an internal file system so reliable that users trust their only copy of programs and data to be stored in it;

5. sufficient control of access to allow selective sharing of information;

6. the ability to structure hierarchically both the logical storage of information as well as the administration of the system;

7. the capability of serving large and small users without inefficiency to either;

8. the ability to support different programming environments and human interfaces within a single system;

9. the flexibility and generality of system organization required for evolution through successive waves of technological improvements and the inevitable growth of user expectations.

This would be an impressive set of goals today; in 1965 it was amazing. Multics also was one of the first, if not the first, operating system to be written in a high-level language, PL/1. Operating systems had always been written in assembler language, mainly because it was thought (probably correctly) that compilers did not produce code efficient enough for an operating system.

Multics employed a one-level store, unifying the notions of file and virtual memory so that files were simply objects that were mapped into memory. Its access control system was advanced for its day; much early work in computer security was done in the context of Multics systems.

Even though Multics was highly influential and continued to be used until 2000, it was not a commercial success. Because of its importance in the secure-computing community, it was used in many environments requiring access to U.S. government secrets, but it found little application elsewhere, perhaps because it required special hardware features unavailable on other computers.

The other important operating system of the era was OS/360, which actually was commercially successful. It was designed on the premise that one operating system should run on a family of machines, from small machines of little capacity to large machines of enormous capacity. Thus applications running on it would be portable across the family of machines. The machine family was, of course, the IBM 360, which did have a wide range of performance.

Unfortunately, the project did not turn out as planned. Rather than one operating system, a family of similar operating systems was created with functionality dependent on the performance of the targeted machines.

What the OS/360 development project made painfully evident was that producing such an operating system required an enormous effort by a large group of people. Many of the lessons learned from the project were described in the 1975 book *The Mythical Man-Month* by the project's leader, Fred Brooks. The most famous of these lessons, inspiring the book's title, was that a task requiring twelve months of one person's time just could not be done in one month by twelve people.

1.2.3 MINICOMPUTERS AND UNIX

IBM, particularly in the 1960s and 1970s, was associated with *mainframe* computers — physically large computers that served entire organizations. It had a number of competitors in this market, but most fell by the wayside. In contrast to such mainframes were *minicomputers* — physically large by today's standards but puny compared to mainframes. The first, the PDP-8 from the Digital Equipment Corporation (DEC), appeared in the mid-1960s, was small and sufficiently inexpensive that it could be used by small laboratories (including those of fledgling academic computer science departments). Minicomputers became increasingly popular in the late 1960s and throughout the 1970s, with the introduction of the Nova from Data General and the PDP-11 from DEC. These, and others from a number of companies, proved useful for more general-purpose computing. A fair number of operating systems were written for them — in some cases a number of different operating systems for the same computer — making the 1970s the heyday of operating-system development.

The most famous of these minicomputer operating systems, and probably the only one still extant in any form, is Unix. Its early history is legendary. Among the people at Bell Laboratories participating in the Multics project until Bell Labs dropped out were Ken Thompson and Dennis Ritchie. In 1969 Thompson designed and implemented a simple operating system on a spare DEC PDP-7 (apparently stored in a closet). He was joined by Dennis Ritchie, and they gave the system the name Unix — punning on Multics and indicating that it was nowhere near as grandiose as Multics. It was later re-implemented on the much more capable PDP-11. A community of researchers at Bell Labs joined in, adding both systems and applications software.

An important aspect of Unix was that, except for its earliest implementations, it has been written in C. The history of C is interesting in itself. It traces its history to CPL (Combined Programming Language — "combined" because it combined efforts from Cambridge University and the University of London), among whose authors was the aforementioned Christopher Strachey. CPL begat BCPL (Basic CPL), a language intended for systems programming. BCPL begat B, a version of BCPL that was sufficiently stripped down (at Bell Labs) that its compiler could run on a minicomputer; B was used to implement some early versions of Unix. B begat C (second letter of BCPL), a version of B that was expanded so as to implement (also at Bell Labs) an early computer game ("Space Travel"). The de facto standard for C became the book *The C Programming Language*, by Brian Kernighan and Dennis Ritchie, first published in 1978, and known simply as "K&R."

Unix evolved within Bell Labs, each new version being released as a new edition. Sixth-Edition Unix was made available to universities in 1975 very inexpensively: a few hundred dollars bought the complete source code of the system, with the restriction that the source code must be treated essentially as a trade secret and that the system could not be used for administrative purposes. These were very attractive terms and a number of university computer science departments took advantage of them. Later, in 1978, Seventh-Edition Unix was released on similar terms.

At around this time, minicomputer manufacturers came out with "superminis" — even more capable minicomputers that supported virtual memory. Of particular interest was DEC's VAX-11/780, with a compatibility mode in which it could run PDP-11 code. A group at Bell Labs ported Seventh-Edition Unix to it to create a product known as Unix 32V, which was released to the academic and research communities on the same terms as Seventh-Edition Unix.

However, Unix 32V did not exploit a number of the features of the VAX-11/780, particularly virtual memory: it simply treated the VAX as a faster PDP-11. A group at the University of California, Berkeley, received an early copy of Unix 32V and from it produced a version that did take advantage of virtual memory — this was released to the academic and research communities as 3 BSD (third Berkeley Software Distribution).[6] 3 BSD did not perform very well, but the effort at Berkeley continued with the fourth Berkeley Software Distribution, which made a number of performance improvements — a major goal was for it to perform as well as VMS, DEC's operating system for the VAX-11 series. (VMS was itself an important operating system and was just as advanced for its day as Unix.) Further improvements came with 4.1 BSD. By this time the Berkeley group had received funding from DARPA (Defense Advanced Research Projects Agency, an important agency within the U.S. Department of Defense that funded much

---

[6] What were the first and second Berkeley software distributions? They were packages of application programs made available to the Unix community for PDP-11s.

computer science research) to improve the operating system so it could support research on the nascent ARPAnet (the predecessor of the Internet).

The DARPA-supported effort added much functionality to Unix, perhaps the most important of which was support for networking. This was made available through a series of releases: 4.1a, 4.1b, and 4.1c, culminating in 4.2 BSD. The project continued, producing a number of incremental improvements and ultimately 4.4 BSD (McKusick, Bostic, et al. 1996).

While the Berkeley effort was taking place, other groups within Bell Laboratories continued their own Unix development. These efforts resulted in a version that was offered as a commercial product, Unix System III, followed as a product by Unix System V (apparently System IV didn't make the cut). (Bach 1986), the first book to cover Unix internals, describes the design of early Unix System V. It was decided that Unix System V was a brand with some loyalty, and thus instead of Unix System VI, there was Unix System V Release 2, continuing through Release 4 in 1988. System V Release 4 was actually a major new release, combining aspects of 4.3 BSD and previous versions of Unix System V, as well as Xenix and SunOS.

1.2.4 THE PERSONAL COMPUTER

While the Unix saga was going on, the notion of a personal computer started to take shape. Some of the most important early work, at Xerox's Palo Alto Research Center (Xerox PARC) in the 1970s, essentially invented the whole notion of personal computing, including window-managed displays. Xerox was never able to turn the Xerox PARC work into a commercial success, but it was highly influential and set the stage for the 1980s. Below we first discuss hobbyist computing, then computer workstations. The two had essentially merged by 2000 or so.

1.2.4.1 Hobbyist Computing

The 1970s were the era of hobbyist computing. The operating systems were simple, but they had a lasting influence. One of the first and perhaps the most significant was CP/M (Kildall 1981), completed in 1974 and designed and implemented by Gary Kildall, who went on to found Digital Research to market and develop it further. Originally designed for the Intel 8080, an 8-bit processor, but eventually ported to a number of different architectures, CP/M was primitive, but so was the hardware it ran on. It handled just one application at a time and had no way to protect itself from the application. It did have a simple file system. Among its innovations (in a later release) was the clear separation of architecture-dependent code from architecture-independent code, which facilitated its adaptation to a large number of platforms. CP/M was originally structured as three components: console command processor (CCP), basic disk operating system (BDOS), and basic input/output system (BIOS). Its CCP was the component that users dealt with directly, leading to the common view that the user interface is the operating system.

Somewhat later than CP/M, but just as primitive, was Apple DOS, designed for the Apple II. The original Apple II had no disk. Later versions were given floppies, but no operating system — programs on disk were self-booting and contained their own (very primitive) OSes. Apple DOS 3.1, the first version released to customers, became available in 1978 and had similar functionality to CP/M at the time (i.e., not much). Apple introduced the Apple III computer in 1980 with a somewhat more sophisticated operating system — Apple SOS (sophisticated operating system, pronounced "apple sauce"). The system (hardware plus software) was a commercial failure, though it may have had some influence on later Apple systems.

Microsoft started as a programming-language company; its first product was a Basic interpreter, sold to MITS[7] for use on the Altair 8800 in 1975. In 1979 the company found it expedient

---

[7] Micro Instrumentation and Telemetry Systems — a small company founded by the late H. Edward Roberts with no relation to the Massachusetts Institute of Technology.

to buy its way into the operating-system business, and did so by purchasing a license for … Unix. It acquired a license for Seventh-Edition Unix from AT&T, adapted it for 16-bit microcomputers, and called its version Xenix (AT&T was extremely protective of the Unix name). It was later ported to the Intel 8086 (and still later to the 80286 and the 386) by the Santa Cruz Operation. Xenix was used internally by Microsoft throughout the 1980s and was the prevalent version of Unix during most of this period.

Microsoft is, of course, no longer known as a purveyor of Unix systems; it is more famous for another operating system for which it purchased rights. Microsoft was approached by IBM in 1980 to provide its Basic system for the forthcoming IBM PC. IBM apparently wanted to license CP/M as its operating system, but was unable to agree on terms with Digital Research. However, another company, Seattle Computer Products (SCP), had somewhat earlier produced an operating system for the 8086, QDOS (for "quick and dirty operating system"), that was similar to CP/M.[8] Microsoft, having no unencumbered operating system of its own (it had to pay royalties to AT&T for Xenix), offered to supply an operating system for the IBM PC and purchased QDOS from SCP when IBM said yes. This became known as PC-DOS when sold by IBM on their computers, and MS-DOS when licensed by Microsoft to other manufacturers for use on their computers.

CP/M, later renamed DR-DOS, was eventually offered by Digital Research as an operating system for IBM PCs and their clones, but never achieved the market share of MS-DOS.

Among the features supported by minicomputer operating systems in the 1980s, but not by operating systems for low-end personal computers, were virtual memory, multitasking, and access control for file systems. *Multitasking* is similar to multiprogramming, but emphasizes the concurrent execution of multiple programs associated with the same user. Some systems supported *cooperative multitasking*, in which the individual programs explicitly pass control to one another. Almost completely absent was any notion of *preemptive multitasking*, in which the operating system automatically preempts the execution of programs to let others execute, thus forcing all programs to share a processor. (We cover this in detail in Chapter 5.)

Access control for file systems is important when a number of people can access them. But, particularly in the early days, personal computers had floppy disks or diskettes, not hard disks. Access control was simple — people were careful with whom they shared floppies. Even with hard disks, people still considered the disk their personal property and saw no need to protect files individually. The notion that an errant program might do damage did not seem to be a concern, and the notion that a virus or other sort of malware might damage unprotected files was unheard of.

Despite its commercial success and continued development by Microsoft, MS-DOS never became as sophisticated as even the early Unix systems. It did not support any form of multitasking (though, as discussed below, the addition of early Windows provided cooperative multitasking), did not protect the operating system from applications, and did not have any form of access control in its file system.

Apple, in the meantime, began development of two new operating systems for its Lisa and Macintosh computers. The Lisa OS was relatively advanced for its time and price range — it supported multitasking, virtual memory, and a hierarchical file system, and had a very advanced graphical user interface influenced by the work at Xerox PARC. But it was completely eclipsed by the cheaper, better advertised Macintosh, which had a much less capable operating system — no multitasking, no virtual memory, and no hierarchical file system. Soon after its initial release in 1984 the Macintosh did get a hierarchical file system, but the other features did not materialize until a completely new operating system was introduced in 2000.

---

[8] Just how similar it was has been disputed both in and out of court.

1.2.4.2 Computer Workstations

While the 1980s are known for the birth of the personal computer, both IBM and Apple, also born in the decade was the computer workstation. This was essentially a personal computer as well, but much more expensive and coming more from the minicomputer tradition than the hobbyist tradition. Its operating systems were not just afterthoughts, but state of the art.

Two of the more influential systems were those of Apollo and Sun. Apollo was founded in 1980 and shipped its first workstations in 1982. Their operating system, Aegis, supported multitasking, virtual memory, and the first commercially successful distributed file system, complete with access control. It had a number of advanced features, many of them derived from Multics, and supported bit-mapped graphics and a window manager. Unfortunately for Apollo, their market began to demand Unix, so Apollo was forced to provide Unix emulation to run Unix applications. Apollo was ultimately acquired by Hewlett Packard in 1989, who integrated much of Apollo's technology into their own products.

Sun was founded in 1982 and shipped its first workstations the same year. Its operating system, SunOS, was derived from 4.2 BSD (not surprisingly, since one of its founders, Bill Joy, essentially led the 4.2 BSD development effort while a graduate student at UC Berkeley). In 1984 it introduced NFS (network file system), a distributed file system still in active use (and under active development) today. SunOS was renamed Solaris in 1992, when it was revamped to support Unix System V Release 4 as part of Sun's joint work with AT&T. (Operating-system version numbers do not necessarily follow a logical pattern. Solaris was introduced as the operating system following SunOS 4 and was called Solaris 2.0; the name Solaris 1.0 was applied retrospectively to all the previous releases of SunOS. Solaris releases followed a logical pattern for a while: Solaris 2.1, 2.2, 2.3, etc., but the version following Solaris 2.6 was called Solaris 7, apparently because 2.7 wasn't an impressive enough number.)

1.2.4.3 Microsoft Windows

Microsoft Windows started as an application running on MS-DOS. Windows 1.0, released in 1985, was not an operating system at all, but merely provided support for windows on the display. It did allow cooperative multitasking, in which a number of applications run concurrently and explicitly yield the processor to one another. Windows 2.0 provided some improvements; Windows 3.0 and 3.1 used hardware segmentation to allow programs to access more memory than in earlier versions, but it was still quite possible for one application to overwrite another, and for applications to overwrite the operating system.

Beginning with Windows 95 (released, of course, in 1995), Windows supported preemptive multitasking: concurrently executing programs could share the processor via time-slicing. It also supported something close to virtual memory, allowing programs to run in separate address spaces. However, an errant program could still crash the entire system by writing into operating-system locations. MS-DOS was still present, but much OS functionality had been subsumed by Windows. Windows 98 and Windows ME provided further improvements, but still employed the same model.

It had been apparent to both IBM and Microsoft that MS-DOS left much to be desired as an operating system, so in 1985 they jointly embarked on a project to produce a better operating system, to be called OS/2. For a variety of reasons, Microsoft dropped out of the effort in 1990. IBM continued on for a few years, but eventually discontinued it.

In its stead, Microsoft began its Windows NT project (among the various possibilities for what "NT" stands for is "new technology"). The leader of this effort was David Cutler, one of the principal architects of VMS (for the VAX-11 series) while at DEC. He modeled much of the new operating system on VMS, finally bringing the advantages of a modern operating system to Microsoft and, eventually, to most of the world. The first version of Windows NT, 3.1 (a number apparently chosen so as not to seem inferior to the current version of "normal" Windows, also 3.1 at the time) was released in 1993. Windows ME was the last of the original Windows line; after it, starting with Windows XP, there was only one Windows operating-system family, all based on Windows NT. (Russinovich and Solomon 2005) describes the design of the Windows operating system.

1.2.4.4 Unix Continues

By the late 1980s it had become apparent to much of the computer industry, particularly those whose products ran Unix, that Microsoft was beginning to dominate. Though Unix had clearly had a lot of success, different versions of it had proliferated, all of them subtly or not so subtly incompatible with the others. For example, just to name a few, there was System V Release 3, SunOS, IRIX, Xenix, Ultrix, HP-UX, AIX, and so forth. One effort to come up with a common Unix version was already mentioned — System V Release 4 (henceforth SVR4). The only major company to adopt it at the time was Sun, who was also a major contributor to it. A number of other companies formed the OSF (Open Software Foundation[9]) consortium to develop a common code base for a standard version of Unix. This system was to be called OSF/1 and, initially, was to be based on IBM's version of Unix, known as AIX.

After a short period of development, it was decided to base the OSF/1 kernel not on AIX, but on a combination of the Mach microkernel and 4.3 BSD. Mach was a research project at Carnegie Mellon University aimed at developing a very small operating-system kernel with minimal functionality, but capable of providing a great deal of functionality via user-level applications. At the time OSF picked it up, the additional functionality still had to reside in the kernel along with Mach, and this additional functionality was provided by 4.3 BSD. OSF/1 version 1 was released in 1991. It did not perform well. It was not until release 1.2 in 1993 that member companies actually used it in successful products. DEC replaced their Ultrix version of Unix with OSF/1, first calling it Digital Unix, then Tru64 Unix (since they had adapted it to support 64-bit architectures). IBM used it as the basis of AIX/ESA, which ran on mainframe computers.

All the operating systems discussed so far were owned in some sense by some corporation, which charged license fees for their use and usually imposed a large fee for source code. One of the reasons for Unix's success is that its fees for source code were relatively small, particularly for universities, and that derivative products could be developed, as long as license fees were paid. The notion of an operating system that was both completely free and useful was unheard of.

In 1987 Andrew Tanenbaum of Vrije Universiteit in Amsterdam included in his operating systems textbook (Tanenbaum 1987) the complete source code for a toy operating system called Minix, based roughly on Unix and a good pedagogical tool. In 1991, Linus Torvalds, a student in Finland, bought an Intel 386 PC. MS-DOS didn't support all the PC's features, such as memory protection and multitasking, so he ported Minix to it and added a number of features. He called his system Linux. Eventually, it was fully compliant with pretty much all specifications for Unix developed by standards organizations such as POSIX.

Linux 1.0 (released in 1994) was ported to the DEC Alpha processor and the Sun Sparc processor by 1995. In 1996 Linux 2.0 was released. By 1998 a number of major companies, including IBM and Compaq (who had acquired DEC), announced their support for Linux. In 2000 Linux 2.2 was released and IBM announced a commitment to Linux on its servers. In 2001 Linux 2.4 was released, and Linux 2.6 was released in 2004.

---

[9] Sometimes glossed as "oppose Sun forever."

In 2003 SCO,[10] which had acquired the rights to Unix, sued IBM, claiming that SCO's code was in Linux and thus SCO was owed royalties. (Suing someone with lots of money may be a good idea. Suing someone who employs really good lawyers probably isn't.) In August 2007 the judge ruled that SCO was not the rightful owner of the Unix copyright, Novell is. Novell then stated that there is no Unix source code in Linux.

Two other free versions of Unix also began development in the early 1990s (and continue to be developed): FreeBSD and NetBSD. Both are derived from the BSD project at Berkeley and are highly thought of, but neither has achieved the success of Linux.

Apple, in the meantime, was still selling a system whose operating system was derived from the original MacOS. Finally, in 2000, they released MacOS X, a Unix system. Its implementation was similar to that of OSF/1, combining both Mach and BSD Unix (in the form of NetBSD and FreeBSD) in the kernel. Apple finally had an operating system that supports virtual memory and multitasking and provides a protected file system, something it had almost achieved with Lisa OS in the early 1980s. Apple's version of Unix is now the prevalent Unix operating system.

1.3
A SIMPLE OS

In this section we examine the abstractions provided by a relatively simple operating system and delve a bit into how they are implemented. Choosing an operating system, even one to discuss in a course, is fraught with controversy. What we discuss here is an early version of Unix, as it existed in the early 1970s. We choose this partly because of its simplicity and elegance, partly because (as we saw above) it had a major influence on modern operating systems, such as modern versions of Unix (Solaris, Linux, MacOS X, etc.) as well as Windows, and primarily because it is the earliest operating system whose later versions are still in common use. (Although the descendants of IBM's OS/360 are still in use, few students in operating systems courses have direct access to them.) We call it simply Unix for now, though strictly speaking it is *Sixth-Edition Unix* (see Section 1.2.3 for why it is called this).

1.3.1 OS STRUCTURE

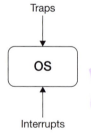

Traps

OS

Interrupts

FIGURE 1.1 Simple OS structure.

Many early operating systems were amazingly small: Sixth-Edition Unix, for instance, had to fit into 64 KB of memory. Thus it made reasonable sense to structure it as a single executable in which all parts are stored as a single file from which they are loaded into the computer's memory when it boots. This sort of structuring is known as the *monolithic approach*. As sketched in Figure 1.1, application programs call upon the operating system via *traps*; external devices, such as disks and clocks, call upon it via *interrupts*.

Almost all computers have at least two modes of execution, *user mode* (with the fewest privileges) and *privileged mode* (with the most). To limit the damage that errant programs can do to other programs and the system as a whole, the only code that runs in privileged mode is that which is part of the operating system. In simple systems such as Sixth-Edition Unix, we generally think of the whole operating system as running in privileged mode. Everything else is an application and runs in user mode. In other systems, such as modern Windows, major subsystems providing operating-system functionality run in user mode. We discuss this in Chapter 4.

We often use the word *kernel*, as in "operating-system kernel." This generally means that portion of the operating system that runs in privileged mode, but sometimes it means a subset of this — some relatively small, key portion of the privileged-mode operating-system code. We will try to make it clear which definition we're using.

---

[10] SCO nominally stands for "Santa Cruz Operation," but the original company of that name sold its Unix business to Caldera. SCO then changed its name to Tarantella, the name of the product it was now focusing on. Caldera subsequently changed its name to SCO.

1.3.1.1 Traps

Traps are the general means for invoking the kernel from user code. We usually think of a trap as an unintended request for kernel service, say that caused by a programming error such as using a bad address or dividing by zero. However, for *system calls*, an important special kind of trap discussed below, user code intentionally invokes the kernel.

Traps always elicit some sort of response. For page faults, the operating system determines the status of the faulted page and takes appropriate action (such as fetching it from secondary storage). For programming errors, what happens depends upon what the program has previously set up. If nothing, then the program is immediately terminated. A program may establish a handler to be invoked in response to the error; the handler might clean up after the error and then terminate the process, or perhaps perform some sort of corrective action and continue with normal execution.

The response to faults caused by errors is dealt with in Unix via a mechanism called *signals* (which is also used in response to other actions; see Chapter 2). Signals allow the kernel to invoke code that's part of the user program, a mechanism known as an *upcall*.

1.3.1.2 System Calls

We've already discussed the multiple layers of abstraction used in all systems. For layers implemented strictly in user code, the actual invocation of functionality within a layer is straightforward: a simple procedure call or the like. But invocation of operating-system functionality in the kernel is more complex. Since the operating system has control over everything, we need to be careful about how it is invoked. What Unix and most other operating systems do is to provide a relatively small number of *system calls* through which user code accesses the kernel. This way any necessary checking on whether the request should be permitted can be done at just these points.

A typical example of a system call is the one used to send data to a file, the *write* system call:

```
if (write(FileDescriptor, BufferAddress, BufferLength) == -1) {
    /* an error has occurred: do something appropriate */
    printf("error: %d\n", errno) /* print error message */
}
```

Here we call *write* to request the operating system to write data to the file (we discuss later the meaning of the parameters). If the call fails for some reason, *write* returns −1, and an integer identifying the cause of the error is stored in the global variable *errno*. Otherwise it returns a nonnegative value: the number of bytes that were actually written to the file.

How *write* actually invokes the operating-system kernel depends on the underlying hardware. What typically happens is that *write* itself is a normal procedure that contains a special machine instruction causing a trap. This trap transfers control to the kernel, which then figures out why it was invoked and proceeds to handle the invocation.

1.3.1.3 Interrupts

An *interrupt* is a request from an external device for a response from the processor. We discuss the mechanism in more detail in Chapter 3. Unlike a trap, which is handled as part of the program that caused it (though within the operating system in privileged mode), an interrupt is handled independently of any user program.

For example, a trap caused by dividing by zero is considered an action of the currently running program; any response directly affects that program. But the response to an interrupt from a disk controller may or may not have an indirect effect on the currently running program and definitely has no direct effect (other than slowing it down a bit as the processor deals with the interrupt).

1.3.2 PROCESSES, ADDRESS SPACES, AND THREADS

Probably the most important abstraction from the programmer's point of view is the *process*. We think of it both as an abstraction of memory — as an *address space* — and as the abstraction of one or more processors — as *threads* (or *threads of control*). The term "address space" covers both the set of all addresses that a program can generate and the storage associated with these addresses. In modern operating systems, address spaces are usually disjoint (they are always disjoint in Sixth-Edition Unix): processes generally have no direct access to one another's address spaces. How this is made to work has to do with address-translation hardware and its operating-system support, subjects we discuss in Chapter 7.

A single thread per process provides a straightforward programming model and was all that most operating systems supported until the early 1990s. We cover multithreaded processes in considerable detail in Chapter 2, but for now we use the simple model of single-threaded processes.

Note that the meaning of the term "process" has evolved over the years. The term originally meant the same thing as the current meaning of "thread" — see (Dennis and Van Horn 1966), who use the term "computation" to refer to what we now mean by "process." Though some authors still use "process" in its original sense, few if any operating systems do.

What else is there to a process? To get an idea, consider the following simple C program that implements the "Sieve of Eratosthenes" to compute the first one hundred primes. In its current form it's not very useful since, after computing these primes, it immediately terminates without doing anything with them. We'll make it more useful later.

```c
const int nprimes = 100;
int prime[nprimes];
int main() {
  int i;
  int current = 2;
  prime[0] = current;
  for (i=1; i<nprimes; i++) {
    int j;
NewCandidate:
    current++;
    for (j=0; prime[j]*prime[j] <= current; j++) {
     if (current % prime[j] == 0)
       goto NewCandidate;
    }
    prime[i] = current;
  }
  return(0);
}
```

Our concern here is not prime numbers, but what the operating system must do to make this program work. The program is compiled and linked (we explain linking in Chapter 3) and stored in a file in the file system. When we run the program, a process is created and the program is loaded from the file into the process's address space. The process's single thread of control then executes the program's code.

But how is the address space organized? The program consists of executable code and data. The code, once loaded, is never modified. Since much of the data, on the other hand, can be modified, it makes sense to segregate the two, putting the code in a special region of the address space that's protected from modification. We could simply put all the data in another readable and writable region, but we need to consider other issues too.

The variables *nprimes* and *prime* are both global, while *i*, *j*, and *current* are local. We know that the scope of global variables is the entire program, while the scope of local variables is just the block (delineated by curly braces in C) that contains them. In other words, the "lifetime" of global variables is the same as the lifetime of the program, while the lifetime of a local variable is only from when the thread enters its block to when it exits. So, we must set things up so that the portion of the address space allocated for global variables remains allocated for the lifetime of the program, but that portion allocated for a local variable remains allocated only while the thread is in the variable's scope.

Thus when the program is loaded into the address space, we'll permanently allocate space for the global variables, just beyond the space allocated for code. But there's another useful distinction to make: *nprimes* has an initial value of 100, but *prime* has no initial value, though C semantics states that its initial value is thus zero. If we group all such uninitialized variables together, we can represent them efficiently in the copy of the program stored in the file system by simply stating that we have *n* bytes of uninitialized data, which will actually be filled with zeros. For many programs, this will save a lot of space. We of course have to instantiate these variables when we load them into the address space, but there are ways to optimize this instantiation (we discuss them in Chapter 7).

The local variables can be allocated efficiently by use of a *run-time stack*: each time our thread enters a new block, it pushes a frame on the stack containing space for local variables and perhaps procedure-linkage information. Such frames are popped off the stack when the thread exits the block. So what we'll do is set up a region of the address space for the stack to reside. On most architectures, stacks range from high memory addresses to low memory addresses and thus stacks typically grown downwards.

Unix structures the address space as shown in Figure 1.2. The executable code, known as *text,* occupies the lower-addressed regions. The initialized data, known simply as *data*, follows the text. The uninitialized data is known, cryptically, as BSS (for "block started by symbol," a mnemonic from an ancient IBM 704 assembler) and comes next, followed by a dynamic region that we explain shortly. Then comes a large hole in the address space and finally a region, starting at the top and growing downwards, containing the *stack*.

Let's now modify the program a bit so that the number of primes we want to compute is passed as a parameter. Space is allocated for the primes dynamically, based on this parameter.

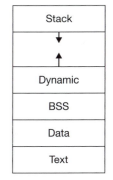

FIGURE 1.2 Unix address space.

```c
int nprimes;
int *prime;
int main(int argc, char *argv[]) {
    int i;
    int current = 2;
    nprimes = atoi(argv[1]);
    prime = (int *)malloc(nprimes*sizeof(int));
    prime[0] = current;
    for (i=1; i<nprimes; i++) {
        int j;
```

```
                NewCandidate:
                  current++;
                  for (j=0; prime[j]*prime[j] <= current; j++) {
                    if (current % prime[j] == 0)
                      goto NewCandidate;
                  }
                  prime[i] = current;
                }
                return(0);
              }
```

For readers more accustomed to Java than C or C++, things are now starting to look a bit ugly. The two arguments passed to main, *argc* and *argv*, are part of the standard C convention for passing command-line arguments to the main procedure. The first procedural argument, *argc*, indicates how many command-line arguments there are. There's always at least one such argument: the name of the program. The second procedural argument, *argv*, is a vector of strings, each of which is one of the command-line arguments. How we actually get the command-line arguments to the program is discussed in Section 1.3.4.

To invoke the *primes* program with an argument of 300, we issue the following command:

```
% primes 300
```

This causes our program *primes* to be loaded into a process and the associated thread to call the *main* procedure. The *argv* vector holds two values, "primes" and "300". Note that *argv[1]* is a character string and not an integer, so we convert it into an integer via a call to *atoi*. After doing so, *nprimes* contains the number of primes we want, so our next step is to allocate memory to hold these primes. This is done in C via a call to *malloc*, passing it the number of bytes that must be allocated. Since *prime* is an array of integers, we ask for sufficient storage to hold *nprimes* integers, where "*sizeof(int)*" returns the number of bytes in an integer.

The Java programmers will really cringe at this point, but *malloc* returns a pointer to the (typeless) block of storage allocated, which we assign to the variable *prime*. This now can be used as an array (i.e., we can refer to *prime[i]*). There is of course no bounds checking in C, so we must be careful that we don't attempt to refer to portions of *prime* that haven't actually been allocated.

Where all this leads us is to the question: where in the address space is the storage for *prime* allocated? More generally, where do storage-allocation routines such as *malloc* get their storage? The answer is: in that region of the address space called the *dynamic region* (see Figure 1.2). Its current uppermost extent is called the process's *breakpoint*. Allocation routines such as *malloc* and C++'s *new* invoke the operating system (via the system call *sbrk*) to move the breakpoint to higher addresses when necessary.

1.3.3 MANAGING PROCESSES

We've just discussed how a process is structured for running a program. How do we create a process in the first place? The only way to do so in Unix is a deceptively simple system call known as *fork*. It takes no arguments, but creates a new process that is an exact copy of the process whose thread called it (see Figure 1.3). How this copy is actually made affects performance.

In Chapter 7, we discuss some magic tricks for avoiding much of this copying. For now, we're concerned strictly with *fork*'s semantics.

Since *fork* has the effect of creating a new process containing its own thread, we need to specify where this new thread starts its execution. What happens seems a bit strange at first glance, but actually makes a lot of sense. Calls to *fork* actually return twice: once in the parent process and once in the child process.

The address space of the child contains copies of the parent's text, BSS, data, dynamic region, and stack. However, since the text is read-only, it's actually shared between the parent and child — no copying is necessary. The result of all this is a rather odd programming practice:

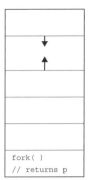

fork( )
// returns p
Parent process

```
if (fork() == 0) {
    /* the child process's thread executes here */
} else {
    /* the parent process's thread executes here */
}
```

So that the two processes can figure out which ones they are, *fork* returns something different in each: it returns zero in the child and the child's process ID (a positive value known as *PID*) in the parent. The PID and other information about a process maintained by the operating system are kept in a data structure called a *process control block* (*PCB*). Figure 1.4 shows the process control blocks of three processes.

For a process to terminate, it simply invokes the *exit* system call, passing an argument (constrained to be a nonnegative value less than 256, i.e., fitting in eight bits) that is its *return code*. The convention is that a process terminating successfully produces a zero return code, and positive return codes indicate some sort of problem. If a process simply returns from *main* (which is supposed to be an integer procedure and thus returns an integer), things still work: *main* returns to code that then calls *exit*, passing it the value returned from *main*. If no value is returned from main, *exit* is called anyway, but with an undefined (garbage) return code.

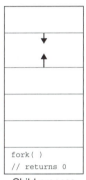

fork( )
// returns 0
Child process
(pid = p)

FIGURE 1.3   The effect of *fork*

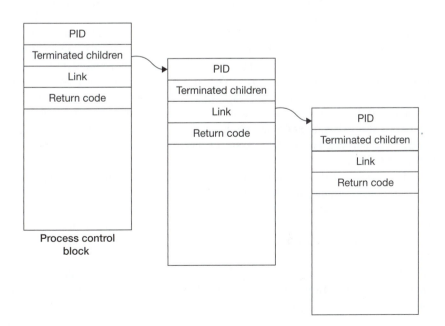

Process control block

FIGURE 1.4   Process control blocks of a parent process (on the left) and two of its terminated children

Since a process's return code actually means something, it's important for other processes to find out what it is. This is done via the *wait* system call, which allows a parent process to wait until one of its children terminates:

```
short pid;
if ((pid = fork()) == 0) {
    /* some code is here for the child to execute */
    exit(n);
} else {
    int ReturnCode;
    while(pid != wait(&ReturnCode))
        ;
    /* the child has terminated with ReturnCode as its
       return code */
}
```

Here the parent process creates a child, then waits for it to terminate. Note that *wait* returns the process ID of the child that's terminated, which might not be the one most recently created (the parent might have created others). Thus it calls *wait* repeatedly until the child it's interested in terminates. The *wait* call returns the child process's return code via its argument, which points to storage provided by the caller.

A process can wait only for its children to terminate: it has no means for waiting for the termination of other processes. This implies that the operating system must keep track of the parent-child relationships among processes.

While a process is waiting for a child to terminate, it's said to be in the "sleeping state": it won't be able to execute any further instructions until a terminating child wakes it up.

The act of termination is a bit tricky. One concern is the process ID. These are 16-bit values and thus must occasionally be reused. Suppose that when a process terminates (i.e., calls *exit*), its ID is immediately made available for assignment to new processes. It might happen that before the process's parent calls *wait*, the process ID is actually assigned to a new process. Thus there could be some ambiguity about which process is being referred to by the ID.

Another termination concern is the return code: where is it stored between the moments when a process terminates and when the code is picked up by the parent via *wait*? If all storage associated with the process is released on termination, we could have a problem.

These concerns are handled as follows. When a process calls *exit* it doesn't completely disappear, but goes into what's called the *zombie state*: it's no longer active and its address space can be relinquished, but its process ID and return value are preserved in the operating system. Thus the process still exists, though the only meaningful data associated with it are its ID and return value. When the parent eventually calls *wait*, these values are finally released and all traces of the process disappear.

But what happens if the parent terminates before the child? This could mean that, since the parent is no longer around to perform the *wait*, the child will remain forever a zombie. To deal with this problem, process number 1 (the process whose ID is 1 and which is the ancestor of all other processes with greater IDs) inherits the children (including zombies) of terminated processes. It executes a loop, continually calling *wait* and finishing the termination of all its (step) children.

As shown in Figure 1.4, a process's return code is kept in its process control block. Nothing is of course stored there until the process terminates. But when the process does terminate, its return code is copied to the PCB, which is linked to its parent's queue of terminated children. By executing the *wait* system call, the parent selects the first process from this queue, returning both the PID and return-code fields.

1.3.4 LOADING PROGRAMS INTO PROCESSES

We've briefly discussed setting up an address space to contain a program; now let's look at the user-level mechanism for doing so. A family of system calls known as *exec* is provided for this. *Exec*s are typically used shortly after *fork* creates a new process to replace the program with a new one. Here's an example of their use:

```
int pid;
if ((pid = fork()) == 0) {
    /* we'll soon discuss what might take place before exec
        is called */
    execl("/home/twd/bin/primes", "primes", "300", 0);
    exit(1);
}


/* parent continues here */


while(pid != wait(0))   /* ignore the return code */
    ;
```

Here we call *execl*, which takes a variable number of arguments — the "command-line" arguments mentioned above — and passes them to the program. The first argument is the name of the file containing the program to be loaded. The second argument is the name of the program (while this seems a bit redundant, it allows one program to do different things depending on the name by which it is called). The remaining arguments are the remaining command-line arguments, terminating with 0.

The effect of the *exec* call, as shown in Figure 1.5, is to replace the entire contents of the current process's address space with the new program: the text region is replaced with the text of *primes*. The BSS and data regions are replaced with those supplied by *primes*. The dynamic area is replaced with an empty region. The stack is replaced with the arguments that are to be passed to *main*: the total number of arguments (two in this case), followed by a vector referring to their values ("primes" and "300"). The process's thread continues execution by calling a special start routine (loaded with the *primes* program), which then calls *main* (so that on return from *main* it calls *exit*).

Note that since the prior contents of the address space are removed, there is no return from a successful call to *exec*: there's nothing to return to! However, if *exec* does return, then (since the prior contents clearly weren't removed) there must have been an error. What we do in such a case is simply call *exit* with a return code indicating an error. (This is certainly not a very helpful response, but our focus for the moment is on successful outcomes.)

The parent process waits until the child has completed (calling *wait* with an argument of zero means that the caller does not want the return code). The above code fragment shows what a command shell does in response to the command:

```
% primes 300
```

In other words, it creates a new process to run the command and waits for that process to terminate.

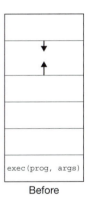

exec(prog, args)

Before

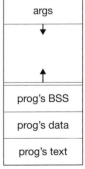

args

prog's BSS

prog's data

prog's text

After

FIGURE 1.5   The effect of *exec*.

1.3.5 FILES

As we've pointed out, our *primes* example isn't very useful since it doesn't leave the results of its computation where others (programs or people) can use them. What's needed is access to someplace outside the process that's shared with others. The notion of a *file* is our Unix system's sole abstraction for this concept of "someplace outside the process" (modern Unix systems have additional abstractions). Unix uses files both as the abstraction of persistent data storage (such as on disks) and also as the means for fetching and storing data outside a process, whether that data is stored on disk, in another process, or in some other device, such as a keyboard or display.

1.3.5.1 Naming Files

For our current discussion we're concerned about both how to refer to such "places" outside the process and how programs transfer data to and from such places. Since the place is outside the process, we need a different space from the process's address space. The nature of such spaces was an issue a number of decades ago, but pretty much all systems today use tree-structured directory systems for naming files and similar objects. These should be familiar to everyone with enough computer experience to have gotten this far in this text: a file is named by stringing together the names assigned to the edges forming a path from the root of the tree to the file.

Unix uses forward slashes as separators between the names; Windows uses back slashes. That the path starts at the root is indicated by starting the name with the separators. Such path names generally have the beginning (such as the root) at the left, though the Internet's naming scheme (Domain Name System — DNS) has it on the right.

The name space provided by the directory system is generally shared by all processes running on a computer (and perhaps by all processes running on a number of computers). Unix provides a means to restrict a process to a subtree: one simply redefines what "root" means for the process. Thus files are identified by their path names in the directory system.

Since the directory-system name space is outside the process, special means are required to access it. The usual model is that one provides the name of the desired file to the operating system, and the operating system returns a *handle* to be used to access the file. What's going on behind the scenes is that the operating system, somewhat laboriously, follows the path provided by the name, checking to make certain that the process is allowed appropriate access along the path. The returned handle provides a direct reference to the file so that such expensive path-following and access verification isn't required on subsequent accesses.

This use of a handle to refer to an object managed by the kernel is fairly important. We'll later see it generalized to the notion of a *capability* (Chapter 8). In abstract terms, possession of a handle gives the holder not only a reference to an object in the kernel, but also certain limited rights for using the object. In the case of files, as we discuss, a handle allows the holder to perform certain actions on a file.

The following code uses the *open* system call to obtain a file's handle, then uses the handle to read the file:

```c
int fd;
char buffer[1024];
int count;
if ((fd = open("/home/twd/file", O_RDWR) == -1) {
    /* the file couldn't be opened */
    perror("/home/twd/file");
    exit(1);
}
```

```
if ((count = read(fd, buffer, 1024)) == -1) {
   /* the read failed */
   perror("read");
   exit(1);
}
/* buffer now contains count bytes read from the file */
```

Here we use the *open* system call to access the directory name space to get a handle for the file whose path name is "/home/twd/file". We've indicated by the second argument that we want both read and write access to the file: if for some reason such access is not permitted, the *open* call fails. If it succeeds, *fd* contains the handle (known in Unix as a *file descriptor*) for the file.

We then use this handle as an argument to the *read* system call to identify the file and attempt to transfer its first 1024 bytes into *buffer*. *Read* returns the number of bytes that were actually transferred: it could be less than what was asked for because, for example, the file might not be that large. The *perror* routine prints, to file descriptor 2, its argument followed by a message explaining the error number currently in the global variable *errno* (recall that that's how failing system calls leave the error number).

1.3.5.2 Using File Descriptors

These handles (or *file descriptors*) form what is essentially an extension to the process's address space, allowing the process unhindered access to the associated files. This address-space extension survives *execs*. Thus files open before an *exec* takes place are open afterwards. This property is exploited as a way to pass the open files as additional parameters to the *exec*. File descriptors are small nonnegative integers that are allocated lowest-available-number first. By convention, programs expect to read their primary input from file descriptor 0, to write their primary output to file descriptor 1, and to write error messages to file descriptor 2. By default, input from file descriptor 0 comes from the keyboard and output to file descriptors 1 and 2 goes to the display (or current window).

However, as shown in the following code, different associations can be established in a process before an *exec*:

```
if (fork() == 0) {
   /* set up file descriptor 1 in the child process */
   close(1);
   if (open("/home/twd/Output", O_WRONLY) == -1) {
      perror("/home/twd/Output");
      exit(1);
   }
   execl("/home/twd/bin/primes", "primes", "300", 0);
   exit(1);
}

/* parent continues here */

while(pid != wait(0))   /* ignore the return code */
   ;
```

Once the new process is created, we close file descriptor 1, thereby removing it from the extended address space. Then we open a file; since file descriptors are allocated lowest first, the file is assigned file descriptor 1. Thus after the *exec*, the *primes* program finds the new file associated with file descriptor 1.

As it stands, our primes program doesn't use any files, so let's modify it so it does:

```
int nprimes;
int *prime;
int main(int argc, char *argv[]) {
   int i;
   int current = 2;
   nprimes = atoi(argv[1]);
   prime = (int *)malloc(nprimes*sizeof(int));
   prime[0] = current;
   for (i=1; i<nprimes; i++) {
      int j;
NewCandidate:
      current++;
      for (j=0; prime[j]*prime[j] <= current; j++) {
        if (current % prime[j] == 0)
          goto NewCandidate;
      }
      prime[i] = current;
   }
   if (write(1, prime, nprimes*sizeof(int)) == -1) {
      perror("primes output");
      exit(1);
   }
   return(0);
}
```

Now the computed set of primes, which will appear in */home/twd/Output*, can be used by others.

However, this output wouldn't be all that useful if it were written to the display, rather than the named file — the numbers are in binary, rather than expressed in decimal notation as strings of characters. So, to make our program useful in both situations, let's change it so that it writes its output as strings of decimal digits.

```
int nprimes;
int *prime;
int main(int argc, char *argv[]) {
   int i;
   int current = 2;
   nprimes = atoi(argv[1]);
   prime = (int *)malloc (nprimes*sizeof(int));
   prime[0] = current;
```

```
    for (i=1; i<nprimes; i++) {
        int j;
    NewCandidate:
        current++;
        for (j=0; prime[j]*prime[j] <= current; j++) {
            if (current % prime[j] == 0)
                goto NewCandidate;
        }
        prime[i] = current;
    }
    for (i=0; i<nprimes; i++) {
        printf("%d\n", prime[i]);
    }
    return(0);
}
```

The *printf* routine's first argument contains a format code, "%d", that instructs it to convert the next argument to a string of decimal digits suitable for printing. The "\n" instructs it to append a new-line character to the end of the string. The string is written to file descriptor 1, which we've established as our file. Note that *printf* itself calls *write* to send its output to file descriptor 1.

Our program can be invoked as follows from a command shell, with the substitution of the given output file for the display:

```
% primes 300 > /home/twd/Output
```

The ">" parameter instructs the command shell to "redirect" the output to the given file. If ">" weren't there, then the output would go to the display or window.

Let's look more deeply at how file descriptors are used. They refer not just to files, but to the process's current "context" for each file. This context includes how the file is to be accessed (recall that the second parameter of the *open* system call specifies it — read-write, read-only, or write-only) as well as the current location within the file. This latter is important since the read and write system calls don't specify this — the usual case is that files are accessed sequentially. Each read of the file returns the next specified number of bytes. Each write to the file puts data in the next locations in the file.

The context information itself must be maintained by the operating system and not directly by the user program. Some of it is important operating-system information — data that's meant only for the operating system's internal purposes. For example, when one opens a file, let's say for read-only access, the operating system checks that read-only access is indeed permitted. Rather than making this check each time the user reads the file via the returned file descriptor, the system keeps the result of the check with the context information. If the user program could modify this directly, it could change it from read-only to read-write and thus be able to write to a file without suitable permission.

So, this information is stored not in the process's address space, but in the kernel's address space (and thus is not directly accessible by the user). The user simply refers to the information using the file descriptor, which is, in effect if not in reality, an index into an array maintained for the process in the kernel's address space. This insures that the process has such indirect access only to its own file information. Thus file descriptors appear as shown in Figure 1.6.

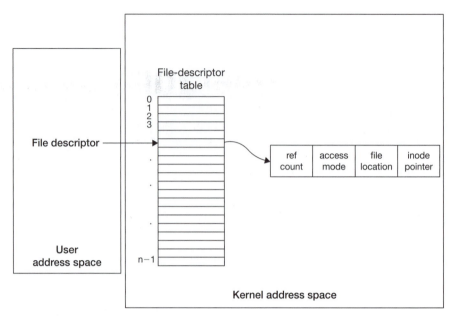

FIGURE 1.6 File-descriptor table

The context information associated with each open file is not stored directly in the file-descriptor table. For reasons explained shortly, there's another level of indirection: the file-descriptor-table entry actually points to another data structure containing this context information. This context information contains yet another pointer, this time to a data structure called an *inode* (for *index node*, a term we discuss in Chapter 6), representing the file itself.

Now we look at some file-descriptor subtleties. We know that file descriptor 1 is used for a process's normal output and file descriptor 2 for its error messages. We also know that we can redirect such output to go to specified files. Suppose we want to send both the process's normal output and its error messages to the same file, which is other than the display or current window. We might set this up with the following code, which closes file descriptors 1 and 2, then opens a file twice. Since each successful call to *open* returns the lowest available file descriptor (and since file descriptor 0 is already taken), we end up with file descriptors 1 and 2 both referring to the same file.

```
if (fork() == 0) {
    /* set up file descriptors 1 and 2 in the child process */
    close(1);
    close(2);
    if (open("/home/twd/Output", O_WRONLY) == -1) {
        exit(1);
    }
    if (open("/home/twd/Output", O_WRONLY) == -1) {
        exit(1);
    }
    execl("/home/twd/bin/program", "program", 0);
        exit(1);
}
/* parent continues here */
```

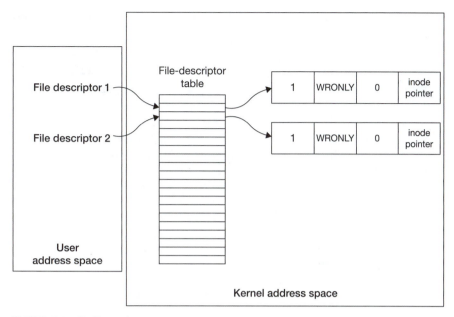

FIGURE 1.7   Redirected output

The effect of this is shown in Figure 1.7.

At this point, each of the context structures has a reference count of one (each is pointed to by exactly one file-descriptor-table entry), each has been opened write-only, each refers to the beginning of the file, and each refers to the same inode (for the same file).

Now suppose the program writes 100 bytes of normal output. The effect is shown in Figure 1.8. The context information for file descriptor 1 indicates that the next *write* will take place at location 100 in the file. But the context information for file descriptor 2 indicates that the next *write* through it will be at the beginning of the file. If the program now writes an error message (via file descriptor 2), the message will overwrite the 100 bytes of normal output that had already been written. This is probably not what's desired.

What we'd like is shown in Figure 1.9. Here both file descriptors refer to the same context information. This is accomplished with the *dup* system call:

```
if (fork() == 0) {
    /* set up file descriptors 1 and 2 in the child process */
    close(1);
    close(2);
    if (open("/home/twd/Output", O_WRONLY) == -1) {
        exit(1);
    }
    dup(1); /* set up file descriptor 2 as a duplicate of 1 */
    execl("/home/twd/bin/program", "program", 0);
    exit(1);
}
/* parent continues here */
```

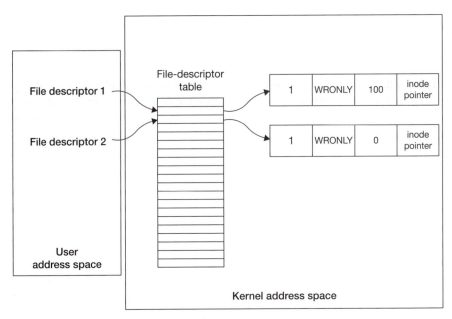

FIGURE 1.8 Redirected output after normal write

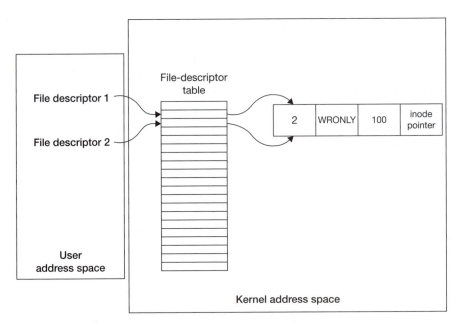

FIGURE 1.9 Redirected output with shared context information

To request such redirection using a command shell, we do the following (our example uses *csh* syntax):

```
% program >& /home/twd/Output
```

Note that in pretty much all Unix command shells, the ampersand ("&") has another use as well. At the end of a command line it means that the parent process does not wait for the child to terminate; in other words, the parent doesn't issue the *wait* system call after the *fork*, but goes on to the next command.

Finally, what should happen with the file descriptor and context information when a process forks? From what we know about *fork*, it makes sense for the child process to have a copy of the parent's file-descriptor table. But should it also have a copy of each of the context-information structures? Consider the following code:

```
int logfile = open("log", O_WRONLY);
if (fork() == 0) {
    /* child process computes something, then does: */
    write(logfile, LogEntry, strlen(LogEntry));
    ...
    exit(0);
}


/* parent process computes something, then does: */

write(logfile, LogEntry, strlen(LogEntry));
...
```

The intent here is that the "log file" contain everything written to it; thus when each process writes to it, the data goes to the current end of the file. If, however, each process had its own copy of the context information for the file descriptor corresponding to *logfile*, the writes of one process would overwrite those of the other. Instead, the two processes should share the context information. Thus the setup after a *fork* is as shown in Figure 1.10.

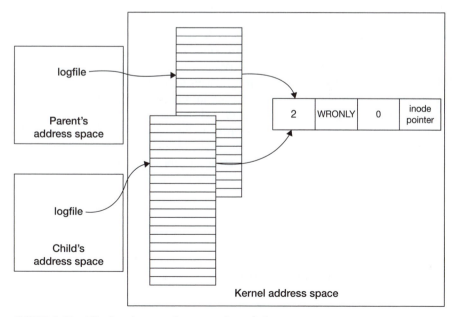

FIGURE 1.10   File descriptors and context after a *fork*

1.3.5.3 Random Access

As we've seen, the normal mode of access to files is sequential: successive reads or writes to a file are to successive locations in the file. Though this is probably what's desired in most situations, sometimes we'd like to access a file randomly, reading or writing arbitrary locations within it. This turns out to be easily done, since the *read* and *write* system calls simply look at the contents of the file-location field of the context structure and increment it after the operation.

Thus to read or write starting at an arbitrary location, all we have to do is provide a means for setting this file-location field. This is done with the *lseek* system call. The example below shows using *lseek* to print the contents of a file backwards:[11]

```
fd = open("textfile", O_RDONLY);
/* go to last char in file */
fptr = lseek(fd, (off_t)-1, SEEK_END);
while (fptr != -1) {
   read(fd, buf, 1);
   write(1, buf, 1);
   fptr = lseek(fd, (off_t)-2, SEEK_CUR);
}
```

The first argument to *lseek* is the file descriptor, the second and third arguments (of type *off_t*, an integer type) indicate the value that goes into the file-location field. The third argument specifies where we are measuring the offset from (SEEK_SET indicates the offset is interpreted as from the beginning of the file, SEEK_CUR means from the current position in the file, and SEEK_END means from the end of the file). Note that *lseek* does no actual I/O; all it does is set the file-location field.

What we've done in the example above is to start with the file location set to point to the last character in the file. After reading a byte, the location is advanced by one, so to get the previous character, we subtract two from it.

1.3.5.4 Pipes

An interesting construct based on the file notion is the *pipe*. A pipe is a means for one process to send data to another directly, as if it were writing to a file (see Figure 1.11). The process sending data behaves as if it has a file descriptor to a file that has been opened for writing. The process receiving data behaves as if it has a file descriptor referring to a file that has been opened for reading.

A pipe and the two file descriptors referring to it are set up using the *pipe* system call. This creates a pipe object in the kernel and returns, via an output parameter, the two file descriptors that refer to it: one, set for write-only, referring to the input side and the other, set for read-only, referring to the output end. Since this pipe object, though it behaves somewhat like a file, has no name, the only way for any process to refer to it is via these two file descriptors. Thus only the process that created it and its descendants (which inherit the file descriptors) can refer to the pipe.

FIGURE 1.11 Communication via a pipe

---

[11] This is definitely not a good way to print a file backwards! It simply illustrates what you can do with *lseek*.

Here's a simple pipe example:

```
int p[2];     /* array to hold pipe's file descriptors */
pipe(p);      /* create a pipe; assume no errors */
   /* p[0] refers to the output end of the pipe */
   /* p[1] refers to the input end of the pipe */
if (fork() == 0) {
   char buf[80];
   close(p[1]);     /* not needed by the child */
   while (read(p[0], buf, 80) > 0) {
      /* use data obtained from parent */

      ...
   }
} else {
   char buf[80];
   close(p[0]);         /* not needed by the parent */
   for (;;) {
      /* prepare data for child */

      ...
      write(p[1], buf, 80);
   }
}
```

1.3.5.5 Directories

A directory is essentially a file like the others we've been discussing, except that it is inter-preted by the operating system as containing references to other files (some of which may well be other directories). From a logical perspective, a directory consists of an array of pairs of *component name* and *inode number*, where the latter identifies the target file's *inode* to the operating system (recall that an inode is a data structure maintained by the operating system to represent a file).

Every directory contains two special entries, "." and "..". The former refers to the directory itself, the latter to the directory's parent. In Figure 1.12, the directory is the root directory and has no parent, and thus its ".." entry is a special case that refers to the directory itself.

Component name	Inode number

Directory entry

.	1
..	1
unix	117
etc	4
home	18
pro	36
dev	93

FIGURE 1.12   Sample directory

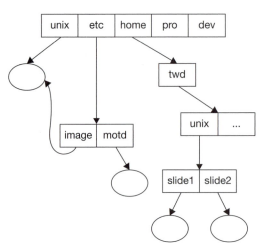

FIGURE 1.13 Directory hierarchy

.	1
..	1
unix	117
etc	4
home	18
pro	36
dev	93

.	4
..	1
image	117
motd	33

FIGURE 1.14 Directory contents

We normally think of directories as forming a tree-structured hierarchy, but Unix and many other operating systems allow limited deviations from trees in the form of hard links (we'll see the soft kind of link shortly). A *hard link* is a reference to a file in one directory that also appears in another. The only restriction is that such links may not be made to directories. Figure 1.13 and Figure 1.14 show an example. To create a hard link, one uses either the *link* system call or the *ln* shell command.

Figure 1.14, showing the logical contents of both the *root* (*/*) and */etc* directories, demonstrates that */unix* and */etc/image* are the same file. Note that if the directory entry */unix* is deleted (via the shell's *rm* command), the file (represented by inode 117) continues to exist, since there is still a directory entry referring to it. However, if */etc/image* is also deleted, then the file has no more links and is removed. To implement this, the file's inode contains a link count indicating the total number of directory entries that refer to it. A file is actually deleted only when its inode's link count reaches zero.

Note: suppose a file is open, i.e., is being used by some process, when its link count becomes zero. The file cannot be deleted while the process is using it, but must continue to exist until no process has it open. Thus the inode also contains a reference count indicating how many times it is open: in particular, how many system file table entries point to it. A file is deleted when (and only when) both the link count and this reference count become zero. The shell's *rm* command is implemented using the *unlink* system call.

A different kind of link is the *soft* or *symbolic link*, a special kind of file containing the name of another file. When the kernel processes such a file, it does not simply retrieve its contents, but replaces the portion of the directory path that it has already followed with the contents of the soft-link file and then follows the resulting path. Thus referencing */home/twd/mylink* in Figure 1.15 yields the same file as referencing */unix*. Referencing */etc/twd/unix/slide1* results in the same file as referencing */home/twd/unix/slide1*. Symbolic links are created by using the shell's *ln* command with the "*-s*" flag, which is implemented using the *symlink* system call.

Each process, as part of its kernel-maintained context, has what's called its *working directory*. A pathname that doesn't start with "/" (i.e., it doesn't start with the root directory) is considered to start at the process's current working directory. This directory is set with the *cd* shell command or the *chdir* system call. You might try to figure out how the *pwd* shell command, which prints out the pathname of the current working directory, is implemented (see Exercise 13 in this chapter).

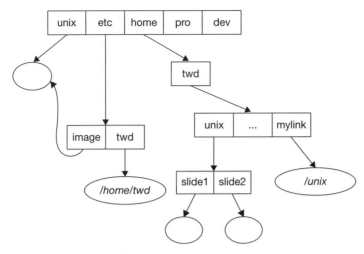

FIGURE 1.15   Symbolic links

1.3.5.6 Access Protection

Among an operating system's duties is making certain that only authorized processes are allowed access to system resources. There are various models for doing this. Unix (and many other operating systems, including Windows) associates with files (and other resources) some indication of which *security principals* are allowed access, along with what sort of access is allowed. A "security principal" is normally a user or group of users, though a "user" isn't necessarily a human but can be, say, some identity used by processes performing system functions. Each running process has potentially a number of security principals associated with it: all processes have a user identification as well as a set of group identifications (though in Sixth-Edition Unix the size of this set was exactly one).

Each file has associated with it a set of access permissions indicating, for each of three classes of principals, what sorts of operations on the file are allowed. The three classes are the owner of the file, known as *user*, the group owner of the file, known simply as *group*, and everyone else, known as *others*. The operations are grouped into the classes *read*, *write*, and *execute*, with their obvious meanings. The access permissions apply to directories as well as to ordinary files, though the meaning of *execute* for directories is not quite so obvious: one must have *execute* permission for a directory in order to follow a path through it.

The system, when checking permissions, first determines the smallest class of principals the requester belongs to: user (smallest), group, or others (largest). It then checks for appropriate permissions within the chosen class.

The permissions associated with a file are set when the file is created (see Section 1.3.5.7) and may be modified using the *chmod* system call or shell command. Consider the following example. Here we use the "ls" command to list the contents of a directory and its subdirectories, showing access permissions.

What this output says is that the current directory (indicated as ".") contains two subdirectories, *A* and *B*, each containing a file or two, all with access permissions as shown. Note that the permissions are given as a string of characters: the first character indicates whether or not the file is a directory, the next three characters are the permissions for the owner of the file, the next three are the permissions for the members of the file's group, and the last three are the permissions for the rest of the world. Also shown is the name of the file's user association (tom or trina in the example), the group association (adm in all cases), the size of the

```
% ls -lR
.:
total 2
drwxr-x--x  2 tom     adm      1024 Dec 17 13:34 A
drwxr-----  2 tom     adm      1024 Dec 17 13:34 B


./A:
total 1
-rw-rw-rw-  1 tom     adm       593 Dec 17 13:34 x


./B:
total 2
-r--rw-rw-  1 tom     adm       446 Dec 17 13:34 x
-rw----rw-  1 trina   adm       446 Dec 17 13:45 y
```

file in bytes, the time it was last modified, and the name of the file (the last component of the pathname).

Suppose users *tom* and *trina* are members of the *adm* group but *andy* is not. Consider the following access questions:

May *andy* list the contents of directory *A*?

May *andy* read *A/x*?

May *trina* list the contents of directory *B*?

May *trina* modify *B/y*?

May *tom* modify *B/x*?

May *tom* read *B/y*?

The answers are

1. No. Since *andy* fits in the category of "others" for directory *A*, his permissions for that directory are execute only. This means that though he's allowed to follow a path through that directory, he's not allowed to list its contents.

2. Yes. As mentioned above, *andy* may follow a path through directory *A*. Since he has read permission for file *x* within *A*, he may read *A/x*.

3. Yes. Since *trina* is a member of the *adm* group, *B*'s group association is adm, and the group has read permission, *trina* may list *B*'s contents.

4. No. Though *trina* does have read and write permission for file *y*, she cannot follow a path through B into it. Thus, since she can't get to *B/y*, she may not modify it.

5. No. Although *tom* may follow the path through B to *x*, *x* has a group association of *adm*, *adm* is allowed read-write access to *x*, and *tom* is a member of adm: since *tom* is listed as the user (or owner) of *x*, with only read permission for the file, *tom* may not modify the file.

6. No. Since *tom* is a member of *adm*, his permissions are given by the group category and not the others category. Since the group has no permissions, *tom* may not read the file.

1.3.5.7 Creating Files

One can create a file in Unix by using the *creat*[12] system call. This was the only way to create a file in Sixth-Edition Unix, but a separate O_CREAT flag was later given to *open* so it, too, can be used to create files. The *creat* system call fails if the file already exists. For *open*, what happens if the file already exists depends upon the use of the flags O_EXCL and O_TRUNC. If O_EXCL is included with the flags (e.g., *open("newfile", O_CREAT|O_EXCL, 0777)),* then, as with *creat*, the call fails if the file exists. Otherwise, the call succeeds and the (existing) file is opened. If O_TRUNC is included in the flags, then, if the file exists, its previous contents are eliminated and the file (whose size is now zero) is opened.

When a file is created by either *open* or *creat*, the file's initial access permissions are the bitwise AND of the mode parameter and the complement of the process's *umask*, a value that's part of each process's context and maintained by the operating system.

At first glance, this seems unnecessarily complicated, but it's less so when you understand how and why it's done. The idea is that standard programs, such as compilers and editors, create files with appropriate permissions given to everyone. For example, compilers produce executable programs whose permissions are read, write, and execute for the user, group, and others. Editors produce files whose permissions are read and write for the user, group, and others. In octal notation, these permissions are 0777 and 0666 respectively (where each octal digit encodes the permissions for one category of principals).

You typically do not want your files to be, by default, accessible to everyone in the world. Thus you set your *umask* to indicate which permissions you generally want turned off. So, for example, you might decide that, by default, files you create should not be accessible by others and should have at most read access by the file's group. You'd then set your *umask* to 0037. The rightmost octal digit (being all ones in binary) indicates that all permissions are turned off for the category others. The next octal digit has the bits set for write access (4) and execute access (1), indicating that you want these permissions turned off. Thus when a compiler creates an executable file, its permissions will be 0777 & ~(0037), which is 0740.

You set the *umask* using either a system call or a shell command.

1.4
BEYOND A
SIMPLE OS

Sixth-Edition Unix was released in 1975. What has happened with operating systems since then? Unix versions proliferated over the next two decades, but only a relatively few now survive. Though there are others, we consider Solaris as the primary example of a proprietary Unix system. Microsoft's Windows family of operating systems has come to dominate the marketplace. On the other hand, Unix implementations as open-source software, in particular the Linux and BSD operating systems, have relatively recently come out of the blue to become significant competitors. Even more recently, Chromium OS[13] is being developed as open-source software by Google, on top of a Linux base.

Our goal in this section is not to discuss the relative merits of these systems, but to introduce some of the new[14] ideas and functionality implemented in them. We first look at those items

---

[12] The story is told that someone once asked Dennis Ritchie, one of the two developers of the first Unix implementation, if he'd do anything differently if he were to do it all over again. He replied that he'd add an "e" to the end of *creat*.

[13] Since Chromium OS is built on top of Linux, isn't it really Linux and not a separate OS? Its intended use as a platform for web applications and its heavy emphasis on security stresses functionality that is not emphasized in most other Linux distributions. Though it might not be a new species of OS, it is definitely on its way to being a subspecies.

[14] "New," in many cases, means "not done in Sixth-Edition Unix." Many of the notions discussed here were first introduced in earlier systems, as we will point out.

that extend what was used in early Unix. Next we mention some areas that became important since the early days of Unix.

1.4.1 EXTENSIONS

The notions of process, file, directory, file descriptor, and so forth are seemingly simple, but amazingly useful. They weren't introduced by Unix, but Sixth-Edition Unix gave us an elegant example of their use. In this section we discuss how newer systems have elaborated these.

1.4.1.1 Multithreaded Processes

We introduced processes in Section 1.3.2. Most early operating systems provided only single-threaded processes; in fact, the term "process" was often used to mean "thread." By the late 1980s it became clear that multithreaded processes, i.e., multiple threads of control sharing the same address space, are pretty useful and important. Though a standard *API*[15] for threads in Unix wasn't accepted until 1995, various implementations with a variety of APIs were being used from 1985, if not earlier. Threads of some form were in use as early as the 1960s (Dennis and Van Horn 1966). We cover the use of threads in great detail starting in the next chapter and their implementation in Chapter 5.

1.4.1.2 Virtual Memory

Sixth-Edition Unix gave each process its own address space, but all of the currently running process had to fit into the computer's memory at once, along with the operating system. This was a major limitation back then, when memory was rather expensive (tens of thousands of dollars per megabyte). Virtual memory separates the process's view of memory — the address space — from physical resources. This allows us not only to give each process its own private address space as in early Unix, but also to assign physical memory to address spaces on an as-needed basis, allowing large address spaces to be used on machines with relatively modest amounts of physical memory.[16] It also makes possible the many other useful tricks we discuss in Chapter 7. Though the concept of virtual memory was first used in 1960 (Kilburn, Edwards, et al. 1962), it didn't make it into Unix until 1979 (and into Windows until 1993).

1.4.1.3 Naming

A major contribution of early Unix systems was their simple design. Surprisingly, even such apparently obvious ideas as tree-structured directories for file systems weren't commonplace in the operating systems of the early 1970s. Unix's designers extended the notion of naming files by their directory-system path names to naming devices, such as terminals, printers, and telephone lines, as well.

This notion of naming pretty much everything using the directory system was extended further in the early 1980s with the introduction of the */proc* file system (Killian 1984). /proc used the directory system to name operating-system objects such as processes, thus allowing programs to "open" these and then operate on them using file-related system calls (such as *read* and

---

[15] API: *Application Program Interface*, a common buzzword that means the names and arguments of the procedures, functions, methods, etc. that application programs call to access the functionality of a system. This is important to programmers because knowing the API, one can write programs that use the system without concern for its implementation details. For example, *read, write, open, close, fork,* and *wait* are all part of the API for Unix. The API is different from the *Application Binary Interface (ABI)*, the machine-language instructions necessary for accessing a system's functionality. The ABI is important to providers of software in binary form, who must be sure that their code will run without recompilation or relinking.

[16] In the late 1970s, the concern was 32-bit address spaces, a word size large enough to address up to 4 gigabytes of memory, when four gigabytes of memory cost millions of dollars. Today the concern is 64-bit address spaces, a word size large enough to address up to 2^{64} bytes of memory, an amount of memory that again costs millions of dollars.

write). This notion was extended even further in Plan 9 (Pike, Presotto, et al. 1995), an offshoot of Unix.

1.4.1.4 Object References

As we discussed in Section 1.3.5, while names are used to identify operating-system objects such as files, a process needs some sort of handle so it can perform operations on an object. Unix has pretty much only one type of object: objects on which one can use file-related system calls.

Microsoft's Win-32 interface supports a number of different types of operating-system objects, such as:

- processes
- threads
- files
- pipes
- timers
- etc.

While these different types of objects have much in common, including some of the system calls used for operating on them, they have significant differences as well. However, they are implemented and used much as Unix's file descriptors. See Microsoft's web site for details.

1.4.1.5 Security

Security wasn't a big deal back in the mid-1970s. Few computers were networked together. One could not bring down the planet's economy by launching an attack on computers. It was a simpler era. Even so, there had already been a large amount of research on computer security. The approach taken in Unix (and outlined above), though a major advance over common practice, was simple but, as always, elegant. The primary change in modern Unix systems to the basic model is that users can be in more than one group at a time. That's it.

Though this basic model suffices for most work, it's not completely general and doesn't handle all the demands of networked computers. Basic Unix security covers file access and not much more. Many modern systems, such as recent versions of Windows and, to a lesser extent, recent versions of Unix, not only allow generalizations of the file-access model but also support various sorts of *privileges* that control what a user is allowed to do, such as shut down a machine, add new software, perform backups, etc. A major emphasis in modern operating systems is the isolation of services so that the effects of successful attacks are limited. We cover much of this in Chapter 8.

1.4.2 NEW FUNCTIONALITY

Three major things have affected operating systems since 1975:

- networking
- interactive user interfaces
- software complexity

Early Unix systems were standalone computers. To get data from one to another, you wrote it to tape, then carried the tape to the other computer. A few advanced systems could communicate by low-speed telephone lines. You communicated with computers by typing commands to them. A major advance was the use of display terminals rather than teletypes (or punched cards). It's really amazing that people got any work done at all.

Adding support for networking, interactive user interfaces, and the myriad other items required to make all this usable has dramatically increased the amount of code that goes into an operating system. The Sixth-Edition Unix kernel was a few thousand lines of C code. Modern Unix systems are a few million lines of C code. Modern Windows systems are probably larger still. It's no longer feasible for the entire operating system to be a single program that sits in one file on disk. (In fact, the Solaris kernel is too large to fit in the largest file supported on Sixth Edition Unix.)

1.4.2.1 Networking

The typical modern computer is anything but a standalone device. It doesn't just connect to the Internet. It must support TCP/IP, the communication protocols. It looks up names, not just in directories on local disks but in DNS, the world-wide domain name service. It can access files not just locally but on any number of servers on the Internet. It can download code, malicious and otherwise, from other computers and execute it immediately. It can even arrange to execute on other computers and have the results sent back.

We cover a small amount of what's involved in supporting all this in Chapter 9. Covering the rest adequately requires much additional material beyond the scope of this book.

1.4.2.2 Interactive User Interfaces

An interactive user interface is not just another application, handled just like all the others. It's often what sells a computer. The entire system must be designed so the user interface (UI) works well. Sixth-Edition Unix didn't have to handle mouse events, bit-mapped displays, graphics processors, and so forth. It didn't step all over itself to make certain that the interactive user received excellent response. Though we don't explicitly address the support of user interfaces in this book, we do cover much of what an operating system must do to provide such support.

1.4.2.3 Software Complexity

In Sixth-Edition Unix, if you added a new device, such as a tape drive, to your system, you had to first obtain (or write) a "device driver" to handle the device itself. You then had to modify the operating system's source code, by adding references to the driver to a few tables. Then you recompiled the operating system and rebooted your computer. If you did it all correctly, the tape drive was now part of the system.

In a modern Windows system, if you buy a new device that's reasonably popular, odds are you can simply plug it into your computer, click a few items in some dialog boxes, and almost immediately your device is part of your system — even a reboot isn't necessary. Sometimes you may have to supply a driver from a CD, but it's read in, the operating system is automatically updated, and you can start using your device almost instantly.

To make all this possible, the operating system supports the dynamic linking of modules into a running system. We haven't covered enough to explain this in detail quite yet, but we will in Chapter 3.

An advantage of being able to add modules to an operating system dynamically is that fewer modules need to be in the initial operating system: they can be loaded in when needed. This actually provides only marginal reduction in the overall complexity; in fact, adding support for dynamic loading of modules can make the operating system even more complex.

Another approach, developed in the 1980s in the Mach (Rashid, Baron, et al. 1989) and Chorus (Zimmermann, Guillemont, et al. 1984) systems, is to pull much of an operating system's functionality out of its kernel and provide it via code running as normal applications. Thus the kernel itself, now known as a *microkernel*, doesn't have to do all that much; instead, it facilitates communication with those applications that provide the needed functionality. Though promising and interesting, the approach was never a commercial success, though a variation based on the results of some of this work is the basis of Apple's Unix implementation in MacOS X. We cover microkernels in Chapter 4.

At this point you should have a rough idea of both what operating systems are supposed to do and what goes on inside them. The rest of the book fills in the details. We return to Sixth-Edition Unix a number of times, using it as an example of simple and often naive ways of doing things — it provides motivation for what's done in recent operating systems.

1.5 CONCLUSIONS

1.6 EXERCISES

1. Explain how the notion of *interrupt* facilitated the implementation of *time sharing*.

2. A 32-bit processor can address up to 2^{32} bytes of memory. While this was an astronomical amount of memory in 1960, it is well within the means of most home-computer owners today. Virtual memory was invented partly to make it easy for one to run large programs in computers with relatively small amounts of memory. Given that one can readily afford as much real memory as virtual memory, is the concept of virtual memory relevant for 32-bit computers? Explain.

3. How might the world be different today if Microsoft was able to offer Xenix rather than DOS as the operating system for the IBM PC?

4. What might be the distinction between *time sharing* and *preemptive multitasking*?

5. Explain the difference between an interrupt and a trap.

6. If a Unix program creates a new process by calling *fork*, can a bug in the child process, such as a bad array reference, damage the parent process? Explain.

7. Most modern operating systems support multi-threaded processes. Consider Figure 1.2, which shows the Sixth-Edition-Unix address space. What would have to change in this figure for it to show an address space of a multi-threaded process?

8. Suppose, in a program that is to run on Unix, one wants to append data to the end of the file. Are the techniques given in Section 1.3.5 sufficient for doing this? In other words, using these techniques, can you write a program that is guaranteed always to append data to the current end of a file? Explain. (*Hint*: consider the case of multiple unrelated programs appending data to the same file.)

9. The program fragment shown in Section 1.3.5.3 shows how to print a file backwards. Explain why it is not a good technique for doing so. Present a program that does it better.

10. Section 1.3.5.5 mentions that hard links may not point to directories. Explain why not.

11. Symbolic links may point to directories. However, a certain restriction must be placed on their use so as to permit this. What is this restriction?

12. Most shell commands (such as *ls*, *ps*, *rm*, *cp*, etc.) are implemented by creating separate processes to run them. However, this is not the case with the *cd* (change directory) command. Explain why not.

13. Explain how the shell's *pwd* command, which prints the full path name of the current directory, might be implemented.

14. Windows lets one access files in a directory even though one is allowed no form of access to the directory's parent. Explain why this is not allowed in Unix. (Windows, as described in Chapter 8, has a different form of access control for which this makes sense.)

15. There are certain public directories, such as /tmp, in which everyone is allowed to create a file. Can one specify using the access-permission bits of Sixth-Edition Unix that only the owner of a file in such a directory can unlink it? Explain and either show how it can be done or suggest a simple modification to Sixth-Edition Unix that would make this possible.

1.7 REFERENCES

Bach, M. J. (1986). *The Design of the UNIX Operating System*, Prentice Hall.

Corbató, F. J., M. M. Daggett, R. C. Daley (1962). An experimental Time-Sharing System. *Spring Joint Computer Conference*.

Corbató, F. J., J. H. Saltzer, C. T. Clingen (1972). Multics — The First Seven Years. *Spring Joint Computer Conference*.

Dennis, J. B. and E. C. Van Horn (1966). Programming Semantics for Multiprogrammed Computations. *Communications of the ACM* **9**(3): 143–155.

Dijkstra, E. W. (1959). *Communication with an Automatic Computer*, University of Amsterdam.

Kilburn, T., D. B. G. Edwards, M. J. Lanigan, F. H. Sumner (1962). One-level Storage System. *IRE Transactions, EC-11* **2**: 223–235.

Kildall, G. A. (1981). CP/M: A Family of 8-and 16-Bit Operating Systems. *Byte Magazine*. June 1981.

Killian, T. J. (1984). Processes as Files. *USENIX Conference Proceedings*. Salt Lake City, UT, USENIX Association: 203–207.

Lee, J. A. N. (1992). Claims to the Term "Time-Sharing." *Annals of the History of Computing* **14**(1): 16–17.

McCarthy, J. (1983). Reminiscences on the History of Time Sharing. http://www-formal.stanford.edu/jmc/history/timesharing/timesharing.html.

McKusick, M. K., K. Bostic, M. J. Karels, J. S. Quarterman (1996). *The Design and Implementation of the 4.4 BSD Operating System*, Addison Wesley.

Pike, R., D. Presotto, S. Dorward, B Flandrena, K. Thompson, H. Trickey, P. Winterbottom (1995). Plan 9 from Bell Labs. *Computing Systems* **8**(3): 221–254.

Rashid, R., R. Baron, A. Forin, D. Golub, M. Jones, D. Julin, D. Orr, R. Sanzi (1989). Mach: A Foundation for Open Systems. *Proceedings of the Second Workshop on Workstation Operating Systems*.

Russinovich, M. E. and D. A. Solomon (2005). *Microsoft Windows Internals*, Microsoft Press.

Ryckman, G. F. (1983). The IBM 701 Computer at the General Motors Research Laboratories. *Annals of the History of Computing* **5**(2): 210–212.

Smotherman, M. (2008). Interrupts. http://www.cs.clemson.edu/~mark/interrupts.html.

Strachey, C. (1959). Time Sharing in Large Fast Computers. *Proceedings of International Conference on Information Processing*, UNESCO: 336–341.

Tanenbaum, A. S. (1987). *Operating Systems: Design and Implementation*, Prentice Hall.

Wikipedia. (2009). IBM 7030 Stretch. *Wikipedia*, http://en.wikipedia.org/wiki/IBM_7030.

Zimmermann, H., M. Guillemont, G. Morisett, J.-S. Banino (1984). Chorus: A Communication and Processing Architecture for Distributed Systems, INRIA, Rapports de Recherche 328.

Multithreaded Programming

In computer systems many things must go on at the same time; that is, they must be *concurrent*. Even in systems with just one processor, execution is generally multiplexed, providing at least the illusion that many things are happening at once. At any particular moment there may be a number of running programs, a disk drive that has completed an operation and requires service, packets that have just arrived from the network and also require service, characters that have been typed at the keyboard, etc. The operating system must divide processor time among the programs and arrange so that they all make progress in their execution. And while all this is going on, it must also handle all the other input/output activities and other events requiring attention as well.

This chapter covers multithreaded programming. The discussion here not only goes through the basics of using concurrency in user-level programs, but also introduces a number of concepts that are important in the operating system. We start by motivating multithreaded programming through the use of some simple, high-level examples. We introduce POSIX[1] threads and Win-32 threads, standards for multithreaded programming in C and C++ on Unix and Windows systems, respectively. As part of our discussion, we introduce synchronization, cancellation, and other threads issues.

Though this is a text on operating systems, we cover multithreaded programming from an application programmer's perspective. This is primarily to facilitate programming exercises — it is much easier to do such exercises as normal application code than as code within an operating system. Though the facilities available for multithreaded programming might be different within an operating system than on top of an operating system, the essential concepts are the same.

---

[1] POSIX stands for *portable operating system interface* and is a registered trademark of the Institute of Electrical and Electronics Engineers (IEEE).

2.1
WHY THREADS?

We are accustomed to writing single-threaded programs and to having multiple single-threaded programs running on our computers. Why do we want multiple threads running in the same program? Putting it only a bit over-dramatically, programming with multiple threads is a powerful paradigm. It is tempting to say "new paradigm," but the concept has been around since at least the 1960s — though only since the 1990s has it received serious vendor support.

So, what is so special about this paradigm? Programming with threads is a natural way both to handle and to implement concurrency. As we will see, concurrency comes up in numerous situations. A common misconception is that it is useful only on multiprocessors. Threads do let us exploit the features of a multiprocessor, but they are equally useful on uniprocessors. In many instances a multithreaded solution to a problem is simpler to write, simpler to understand, and simpler to debug than a single-threaded solution to the same problem.

To illustrate this point, let's look at some code extracted from a program *rlogind* (for "remote login daemon"), in common use on Unix systems. This program is a major component of support for remote access.[2] Figure 2.1 shows a rough sketch of how remote access works. The idea here is that as you sit at the client machine on the left you have a remote-login session on the server machine on the right. You are running applications on the server that get their keyboard input from the client and send their display output to the client.

To make this work, each character you type is transferred over the communication line to the server; it is read there by the *rlogind* program, which then simply writes the characters out to a special facility called a "pseudoterminal" that makes the characters appear as if they were typed at the server's keyboard. (We discuss pseudoterminals in detail in Section 4.1.2.1.) Similarly, characters output from applications are written to the pseudo-terminal; they are read from there by the *rlogind* program, which then writes them to the communication line. These characters are then displayed on the client.

Thus the job of the *rlogind* program is simply to process two streams of characters. It reads characters from one stream from the communication line coming from the client and writes them via the pseudoterminal to the applications running on the server. It reads characters from the other stream from the pseudoterminal and writes them to the communication line going to the client.

The C code actually used for this is:

```c
void rlogind(int r_in, int r_out, int l_in, int l_out) {
    fd_set in = 0, out;
    int want_l_write = 0, want_r_write = 0;
    int want_l_read = 1, want_r_read = 1;
```

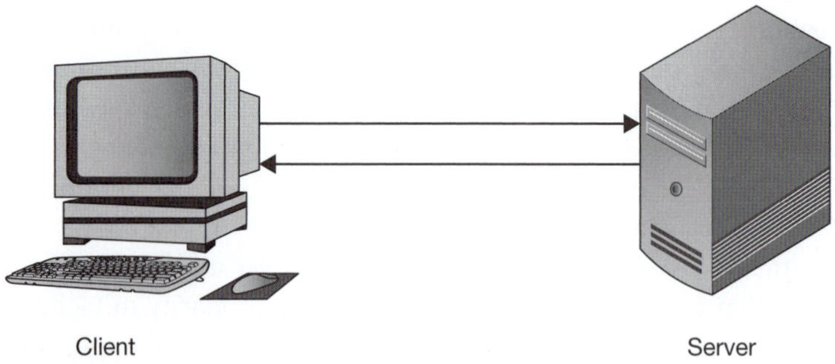

Client   Server

FIGURE 2.1   Remote login.

---

[2] It is, however, obsolete, not being secure. We discuss why in Chapter 8.

```
     int eof = 0, tsize, fsize, wret;
     char fbuf[BSIZE], tbuf[BSIZE];

     fcntl(r_in, F_SETFL, O_NONBLOCK);
     fcntl(r_out, F_SETFL, O_NONBLOCK);
     fcntl(l_in, F_SETFL, O_NONBLOCK);
     fcntl(l_out, F_SETFL, O_NONBLOCK);

while(!eof) {
   FD_ZERO(&in);
   FD_ZERO(&out);
   if (want_l_read)
    FD_SET(l_in, &in);
   if (want_r_read)
    FD_SET(r_in, &in);
   if (want_l_write)
    FD_SET(l_out, &out);
   if (want_r_write)
    FD_SET(r_out, &out);

   select(MAXFD, &in, &out, 0, 0);
   if (FD_ISSET(l_in, &in)) {
    if ((tsize = read(l_in, tbuf, BSIZE)) > 0) {
     want_l_read = 0;
     want_r_write = 1;
    } else
     eof = 1;
   }
   if (FD_ISSET(r_in, &in)) {
    if ((fsize = read(r_in, fbuf, BSIZE)) > 0) {
     want_r_read = 0;
     want_l_write = 1;
    } else
     eof = 1;
   }
   if (FD_ISSET(l_out, &out)) {
    if ((wret = write(l_out, fbuf, fsize)) == fsize) {
     want_r_read = 1;
     want_l_write = 0;
    } else if (wret >= 0)
     tsize -= wret;
    else
     eof = 1;
   }
```

```
            if (FD_ISSET(r_out, &out)) {
              if ((wret = write(r_out, tbuf, tsize)) == tsize) {
                want_l_read = 1;
                want_r_write = 0;
              } else if (wret >= 0)
                tsize -= wret;
              else
                eof = 1;
            }
          }
        }
```

It is not immediately apparent what this code does (that's the point!): after some scrutiny, you discover that it reads characters typed by the remote user (arriving on the communication line via file descriptor *r_in*), outputs these characters to local applications (via the pseudoterminal on file descriptor *l_out*), reads characters output by local applications (arriving from the pseudoterminal via file descriptor *l_in*), and sends them to the remote user (on the communication line via file descriptor *r_out*). To ensure that it never blocks indefinitely waiting for I/O on any of the four file descriptors, it makes somewhat complicated use of nonblocking I/O and the *select* system call.

Though this program is conceptually straightforward, the code definitely isn't. Look what happens when we rewrite this single-threaded program as a two-threaded program:

```
void incoming(int r_in, int l_out) {          void outgoing(int l_in, int r_out) {
  int eof = 0;                                   int eof = 0;
  char buf[BSIZE];                               char buf[BSIZE];
  int size;                                      int size;

  while (!eof) {                                 while (!eof) {
    size = read(r_in, buf, BSIZE);                 size = read(l_in, buf, BSIZE);
    if (size <= 0)                                 if (size <= 0)
      eof = 1;                                       eof = 1;
    if (write(l_out, buf, size) <= 0)              if (write(r_out, buf, size) <= 0)
      eof = 1;                                       eof = 1;
  }                                              }
}                                              }
```

One thread, running the *incoming* procedure, simply reads from *r_in* (the communication line) and writes to *l_out* (the pseudoterminal); the other, running the *outgoing* procedure, reads from *l_in* (the pseudoterminal) and writes to *r_out* (the communication line). This solution and the previous one are equivalent, but the two-threaded implementation is much easier to understand.

Figure 2.2 shows another server application, a single-threaded database server handling multiple clients. The issue here is: how does the single-threaded server handle multiple requests? The easiest approach is, of course, one at a time: it deals completely with the first request, then the second, then the third, and so on. But what if some of the requests take a long time to handle,

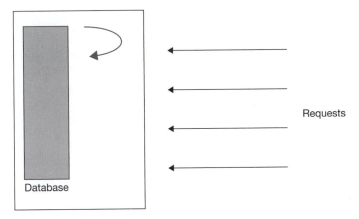

FIGURE 2.2   Single-threaded database server.

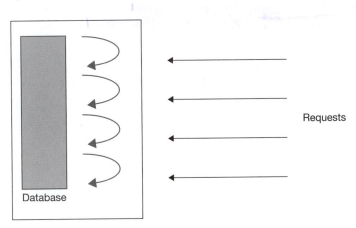

FIGURE 2.3   Multithreaded database server.

while others can be dealt with quickly? What we'd like is to handle these requests concurrently. We can do this by building a timer into the application: our thread would work on the first request for, say, a millisecond, then spend a millisecond on the next request, and so on. Once each pending request receives a millisecond of service, the thread goes back to the first and gives each another millisecond, and so forth. Thus long requests are eventually handled completely, but short requests are dealt with relatively quickly.

It wouldn't be any fun, though, to write the code for this: not only would you have to produce a correct database implementation, but you'd also have to implement the timing and multiplexing correctly. So, instead, let's look at a multithreaded implementation — see Figure 2.3. In this new version of the server, each request is handled by a separate thread. Thus any concurrency in handling the requests is provided by the threads implementation. Of course, someone has to write the code to provide this concurrency, but at least the writer of the threads package to do this didn't simultaneously have to write a correct database implementation. The resulting multithreaded database implementation should be just as efficient as the single-threaded one we did (or considered doing) ourselves. Furthermore, if we have a multiprocessor, our threads can take advantage of it without any additional work by the programmer.

2.2 PROGRAMMING WITH THREADS

Despite the advantages of programming with threads, only relatively recently have standard APIs for multithreaded programming been developed. The most important of these APIs in the Unix world is the one developed by a group originally called POSIX 1003.4a. This multi-year effort resulted in 1995 in an approved standard, now known by the number 1003.1c.

Microsoft produced as part of its Win-32 interface a threads package whose interface has little in common with that of POSIX. Moreover, there are significant differences between the Microsoft and POSIX approaches — some of the constructs of one cannot be easily implemented in terms of the constructs of the other, and vice versa. Despite these incompatibilities, both approaches are useful for multithreaded programming.

2.2.1 THREAD CREATION AND TERMINATION

Creating a thread should be a pretty straightforward operation: in response to some sort of directive, a new thread is created and proceeds to execute code independently of its creator. There are, of course, a few additional details. We may want to pass parameters to the thread. A stack of some size must be created to be the thread's execution context. Also, we need some mechanism for the thread to terminate and to make a termination value available to others.

2.2.1.1 Creating POSIX Threads

POSIX and Win-32 have similar interfaces for creating a thread. Suppose we wish to create a bunch of threads, each of which will execute code to provide some service. In POSIX, we do this as follows:

```
void start_servers( ) {
  pthread_t thread;
  int i;

  for (i=0; i<nr_of_server_threads; i++)
    pthread_create(
            &thread,         // thread ID
            0,               // default attributes
            server,          // start routine
            argument);       // argument
}

void *server(void *arg) {
  // perform service
  return (0);
}
```

Thus a thread is created by calling *pthread_create*. If it returns successfully (returns 0), a new thread has been created that is now executing independently of the caller. This thread's ID is returned via the first parameter (an output parameter that, in standard C programming style, is a pointer to where the result should be stored). The second parameter is a pointer to an attributes structure that defines various properties of the thread. Usually we can get by with the default properties, which we specify by supplying a null pointer. The third parameter is the address of the routine in which our new thread should start its execution. The last argument is the argument that is actually passed to the first procedure of the thread.

If *pthread_create* fails, it returns a positive value indicating the cause of the failure.

2.2.1.2 Creating Win-32 Threads

An equivalent program written for Windows using the Win-32 interface is:

```
void start_servers( ) {
    HANDLE thread;
    DWORD id;
    int i;

    for (i=0; i<nr_of_server_threads; i++)
        thread = CreateThread(
            0,                    // security attributes
            0,                    // default # of stack pages allocated
            server,               // start routine
            0,                    // argument
            0,                    // creation flags
            &id);                 // thread ID
}

DWORD WINAPI server(void *arg) {
    // perform service
    return(0);
}
```

Calls to *CreateThread* are used rather than *pthread_create*. A handle for the new thread is returned. A handle, as we discussed in Chapter 1, is similar to a Unix file descriptor: it refers to information belonging to the user process but maintained in the operating system. In this case, as we'll see, the handle allows the holder to perform operations on the thread.

An ID is returned via the last (output) argument. It is a means of identifying the thread that gives the holder no ability to control that thread. Thus one process can make a thread ID available to another process so as to identify the thread but not give the second process any control over it.

The first parameter is a pointer to the security attributes to be associated with the thread; we use 0 for this for now and discuss other possibilities later. The next parameter is the number of stack pages (in bytes) to allocate physical resources for (one megabyte of virtual memory is allocated; the parameter indicates how much of this initially has real memory and stack space supporting it); 0 means to use the default. The third parameter is the address of the first routine our thread executes; the next parameter is the argument that's passed to that routine. The next to the last parameter specifies various creation flags; we don't supply any here.

If *CreateThread* fails, indicated by returning a null handle, *GetLastError* can be used to determine the cause of the failure.

2.2.1.3 Handling Multiple Arguments

A problem comes up with both *pthread_create* and *CreateThread* when you want to pass more than one argument to a thread. Suppose you are creating threads for use with our two-threaded implementation of *rlogind* (Section 2.1 above). One might be tempted to use the trick outlined below:

```
typedef struct {
    int first, second;
} two_ints_t;
```

```
void rlogind(int r_in, int r_out, int l_in, int l_out) {
    pthread_t in_thread, out_thread;
    two_ints_t in={r_in, l_out}, out={l_in, r_out};
    pthread_create(&in_thread,
        0,
        incoming,
        &in);
    pthread_create(&out_thread,
        0,
        outgoing,
        &out);
}
```

Here we pack two arguments into a structure, then pass a pointer to it to *pthread_create*. This is an example of something that works in single-threaded programs but can cause disastrous failures in multithreaded programs. The variables *in* and *out* are local variables and thus are allocated on the stack of the thread that called *rlogind*. When this first thread returns from *rlogind*, these variables go out of scope — the stack locations might be used for other things. Thus when *pthread_create* is called, the addresses of *in* and *out* point to useful information. But by the time the threads created by the calls to *pthread_create* reference the data pointed to by their arguments (*in* and *out*), this data might no longer exist, since the first thread is no longer in their scope. Thus our approach works only if we can be certain that first thread does not leave the scope of the arguments while they are in use.

Is there a safe way to pass multiple arguments to a thread that works in all cases? Ideally, we'd like to copy all of a thread's arguments onto its stack. But since neither *pthread_create* nor *CreateThread* provides a means for doing this for more than one argument, we need some other technique. (Other threads packages, for example (Doeppner 1987), did provide a way to put multiple arguments on a thread's stack.) Whatever approach we use, it must involve passing a pointer or some sort of pointer-sized identifier to the thread, which then uses this identifier to refer to the actual arguments (which must reside in storage that is available while the thread is executing).

One approach might be to use static or global storage for the arguments, so that there's not a problem with them going out of scope. While this would work in some cases, suppose that in our example multiple threads are calling *rlogind* concurrently. All would use the same locations for storing the arguments to *pthread_create*, and the result would be chaos.

We might allocate storage dynamically for the arguments, using *malloc* in C or *new* in C++. This might seem to solve our problems, but who frees the storage, and when? The creating thread can do so safely only if the created thread is certain not to access the arguments at any point in the future. We can't expect the created thread to free the storage unless its arguments are always in dynamically allocated storage.

In summary, we have four approaches for passing multiple arguments to a thread:

1. copy all arguments to the thread's stack: this always works, but isn't supported in either POSIX or Win-32

2. pass a pointer to local storage containing the arguments: this works only if we are certain this storage doesn't go out of scope until the thread is finished with it

3. pass a pointer to static or global storage containing the arguments: this works only if only one thread at a time is using the storage

4. pass a pointer to dynamically allocated storage containing the arguments: this works only if we can free the storage when, and only when, the thread is finished with it (Note that this is not a problem in languages with automatic garbage collection.)

None of these approaches is suitable in all cases, so we have to figure out which is appropriate for a given situation.

2.2.1.4 Thread Termination

Terminating threads has its share of subtle issues as well. Our threads return values: which threads receive these values and how do they do it? Clearly a thread that expects to receive another's return value must wait until that thread produces it, and this happens only when the other thread terminates. Thus we need a way for one thread to wait until another terminates.[3]

Though a technique for one thread to wait for any other thread to terminate might seem useful, that threads return values makes it important to be particular about which thread (or threads) one is waiting for. Thus it's important to identify a thread uniquely. Such identification can be a bit tricky if identifiers can be reused.

POSIX provides a rather straightforward construct for waiting for a thread to terminate and retrieving its return value: *pthread_join*. We illustrate its use in a continuation of our example of passing multiple arguments to a thread:

```
void rlogind(int r_in, int r_out, int l_in, int l_out) {
    pthread_t in_thread, out_thread;
    two_ints_t in={r_in, l_out}, out={l_in, r_out};

    pthread_create(&in_thread, 0, incoming, &in);
    pthread_create(&out_thread, 0, outgoing, &out);

    pthread_join(in_thread, 0);
    pthread_join(out_thread, 0);
}
```

Here our thread uses *pthread_join* to insure that the threads it creates terminate before it leaves the scope of their arguments. The first argument to *pthread_join* indicates which thread to wait for and the second argument, if nonzero, indicates where the return value should go.

How exactly does a thread terminate? Or, more precisely, what does a thread do to cause its own termination? (In Section 2.2.5.2 we discuss how one thread can request that another terminate, but for the time being we are concerned only with self-termination.) One way for a thread to terminate is simply to return from its first procedure, returning a value of type *void* *. An alternative approach is that a thread call *pthread_exit*, supplying a *void* * argument that becomes the thread's return value.[4] The following skeletal code illustrates the two approaches:

```
void CreatorProc( ) {
    pthread_t createe;
    void *result;
```

---

[3] An alternate approach might be for a thread to check whether another has terminated and continue on regardless, rather than wait for termination. Though this might occasionally be handy, it's not considered useful enough to warrant inclusion in POSIX threads, though it can be done in Win-32 threads.

[4] Note that, although returning from the first procedure and calling *pthread_exit* are equivalent in C, they aren't in C++. In particular, calling *pthread_exit* in a C++ program terminates the thread but does not invoke the destructors of any active local objects.

```
        pthread_create(&createe, 0, CreateeProc, 0);
        ...
        pthread_join(create, &result);
        ...
}

void *CreateeProc(void *arg) {
    ...
    if (should_terminate_now)
        pthread_exit((void *)1);
    ...
    return((void *)2);
}
```

There is a big difference between *pthread_exit* and *exit*. The former terminates just the calling thread. The latter terminates the entire process, including all threads running in it. Note that if a thread returns from a program's main procedure, it calls *exit* (it actually returns to code that then calls *exit*). So, consider the following code:

```
int main(int argc, char *argv[ ]) {
    int i;
    pthread_t threads[10];

    for (i=0; i< 10; i++)
        pthread_create(&threads[i], 0, start_proc, (void *)i);

    return(0);
}
```

What happens here is that ten threads are created but the creating thread immediately returns from main, calls *exit*, and thus terminates the entire process. On a uniprocessor system, none of the ten child threads are likely to get a chance to run at all.

To create a bunch of threads and then terminate innocuously, one might do something like:

```
int main(int argc, char *argv[ ]) {
    int i;
    pthread_t threads[10];

    for (i=0; i< 10; i++)
        pthread_create(&threads[i], 0, start_proc, (void *)i);

    pthread_exit(0);
    return(0);
}
```

Here the first thread again creates ten threads, but then quietly goes away (the call to *return* is required even though it won't be executed, since *main* is defined as returning an *int*). The process terminates once all its component threads have terminated (or if one of them calls *exit*).

Let's look at thread termination and *pthread_join* a bit more closely. It's tempting to treat them as analogs of process termination and *wait*, as discussed in Chapter 1. However, *wait* can be used only to wait for the termination of a child process, while *pthread_join* can be used to wait for the termination of any thread in the process. But, as with process termination, when a thread terminates some amount of information must be left behind: its thread ID and its return value. Thus terminating threads go into a "zombie" state, just as terminating processes do. Once some other thread calls *pthread_join* on the terminated thread, then all record of it may be released and the thread ID may be reused.[5]

What happens if two threads call *pthread_join* on the same target thread? In light of our discussion above, we see that this could result in a problem. After the first thread calls *pthread_join*, the target thread's ID might be reused. Thus when the second thread calls *pthread_join*, it could well be waiting for the termination of a new thread. Since this is probably not what was desired, it's considered unsafe to make more than one call to *pthread_join* on any particular target thread.

The Win-32 approach to waiting for a thread's termination and getting its return value adds one more step. Like a POSIX thread, a Win-32 thread terminates either by returning from its first procedure or by calling an exit routine, in this case *ExitThread*. One thread can wait for another to terminate by calling either *WaitForSingleObject* or *WaitForMultipleObjects*. These routines are more general than their POSIX equivalents in that they let us wait not just for threads to terminate, but for any "kernel object" to change its state in some well defined fashion (we discuss this further in Section 2.2.3.2). However, unlike *pthread_join*, *WaitForSingleObject* and *WaitForMultipleObjects* don't affect the zombie status of the thread or yield its return value. The latter is done via a call to *GetExitCodeThread* and the former by a call to *CloseHandle*.

Thus creating a thread and performing the equivalent of *pthread_join* in Win-32 is done as follows:

```
void proc( ) {
    HANDLE thread;
    DWORD ID;

    thread = CreateThread(0, 0, thread_proc, (LPVOID)arg, 0, &id);
    WaitForSingleObject(thread, INFINITE);
    CloseHandle(thread);
}
```

The second argument to *WaitForSingleObject* is a timeout value indicating how many milliseconds to wait before giving up and returning with an error. The special value INFINITE means to wait indefinitely.

In some cases, where the value produced by a terminating thread is of no use to anyone, it might not be necessary for any other thread to wait for a thread's termination. For example, a thread might be created to service the request of a client and then quietly terminate. It's rather inconvenient to have to call *pthread_join* to remove these threads once they become zombies, so POSIX provides the *pthread_detach* routine: it marks a thread as *detached* so that when the thread terminates, its thread ID is immediately made available for reuse, and its return value is

---

[5] Exactly what the thread ID is depends on the implementation. If it's a 64-bit integer that's incremented by one every time a new thread is created, then it's highly unlikely ever to be reused. But if it's the address of a data structure that represents the thread, then reuse is likely.

ignored. Thus, so that no thread is left permanently in the zombie state, for each call to *pthread_create* there should be exactly one call to either *pthread_join* or *pthread_detach*.[6]

Win-32 uses a more general mechanism to handle whether to wait for a thread's termination. We saw above that calls to *CreateThread* return a handle to the newly created thread object. Another handle is also created that is stored as part of the newly created thread. The thread object maintains a reference count of handles referring to itself; given these two handles, this reference count is initially two. When the thread terminates, its handle to its own thread object is closed, reducing the object's handle count by one. The thread object, which contains the thread's exit code, isn't deleted until its handle count drops to zero. So, if you want a thread object to disappear once the thread terminates (that is, if you want the effect of *pthread_detach*), you simply close the handle returned by *CreateThread* after the thread is created.

2.2.1.5 Attributes and Stack Size

So far, when we've created threads using *pthread_create*, we've used the default attributes. These are normally sufficient, but in some cases we might want different attributes. First of all, what are these attributes? They are various properties of the thread itself that depend on the implementation. Rather than specifying every property as a separate argument to *pthread_create*, they are all bundled into the attributes argument, thus allowing new attributes to be added as necessary. Example attributes (or properties) are the size of the thread's stack, whether it is created as a detached thread or is joinable, and its initial scheduling priority.

We've seen that supplying a zero for the attributes argument creates a thread with default attributes. To get something other than this default, you need to create an attributes structure, then specify in it the desired attributes. To set this up, you call *pthread_attr_init* and then, via operations on the structure, specify the desired attributes. The resulting attributes structure can then be used as an argument to the creation of any number of threads.

The attributes structure affects the thread only when it is created. Modifying this structure later has no effect on already created threads, but only on threads created with it subsequently.

Storage may be allocated as a side effect of calling *pthread_attr_init*. To ensure that this storage is freed, call *pthread_attr_destroy* with the attributes structure as argument. Note that if the attributes structure goes out of scope, not all storage associated with it is necessarily released — to release this storage you must call *pthread_attr_destroy*.

One attribute that is supported by all POSIX threads implementations is the size of a thread's stack. This is a rather important attribute, though one that many programmers give little thought to. The stack that's allocated for the sole thread in single-threaded processes is so large that we're highly unlikely to need a larger one. However, if we are creating a lot of threads in a process, then we must pay more attention to stack size.

For example, suppose we are creating 1024 threads, each with an eight-megabyte stack (the default stack size in some versions of POSIX threads on Linux). This would require eight gigabytes of address space. But a 32-bit machine has only four gigabytes of address space! So if we want that many threads, each one must have a smaller stack.

Of course, we can go too far in the other direction: if we don't give a thread a large enough stack, serious problems result when the thread exceeds its stack space. This is particularly true if a thread goes beyond its allotted stack and starts clobbering other data structures, such as the stacks of other threads. Though most systems mark the last page of each thread's stack as inaccessible so that attempts to reference it are caught by hardware, a thread can jump over the last page of its stack and start writing on what follows without attracting the hardware's attention — this can

---

[6] However, one can specify in the attributes passed to *pthread_create* that the created thread is to be detached, thereby making a call to *pthread_detach* unnecessary. Note that when the process terminates, all traces of all threads are eliminated: no thread stays in the zombie state beyond the life of the process.

happen, for example, if the thread places a call to a procedure with large local variables that aren't immediately referenced. So we must be careful to give each thread a sufficiently large stack (how large is large enough depends on the program and the architecture).

To specify the stack size for a thread, one sets up an attributes structure using *pthread_attr_setstacksize* and supplies it to *pthread_create*:

```
pthread_t thread;
pthread_attr_t thr_attr;

pthread_attr_init(&thr_attr);
pthread_attr_setstacksize(&thr_attr, 20*1024*1024);

. . .

pthread_create(&thread, &thr_attr, startroutine, arg);
```

In this case we've created a thread with a twenty-megabyte stack.

How large is the default stack? This is not specified in POSIX threads. Different implementations use different values, ranging from around 20 KB in Tru64 Unix to one megabyte in Solaris and eight megabytes in some Linux implementations.

Win-32 uses a different approach to stack size: the amount of address space allocated for each thread's stack is a link-time parameter, not a run-time parameter. The "stacksize" argument to *CreateThread* indicates how many pages of primary memory are allocated to hold the stack when the thread starts execution. Additional pages of primary memory are allocated as necessary as the thread runs, up to the maximum stack size. One cannot affect this level of detail using POSIX threads.

2.2.1.6 Example

Here is a simple complete multithreaded program that computes the product of two matrices. Our approach is to create one thread for each row of the product and have these threads compute the necessary inner products. (This isn't a good way to compute the product of two matrices — it's merely an example of a multithreaded program!)

```
#include <stdio.h>
#include <pthread.h>        /* all POSIX threads declarations */
#include <string.h>         /* needed to use strerror below */

#define M        3
#define N        4
#define P        5

int A[M][N];      /* multiplier matrix */
int B[N][P];      /* multiplicand matrix */
int C[M][P];      /* product matrix */

void *matmult(void *);

int main( ) {
    int i, j;
```

```
        pthread_t thr[M];
        int error;

        /* initialize the matrices ... */

        ...

        for (i=0; i<M; i++) {        /* create the worker threads */
          if (error = pthread_create(
                  &thr[i],
                  0,
                  matmult,
                  (void *)i)) {
            fprintf(stderr, "pthread_create: %s", strerror(error));
            /* this is how one converts error codes to useful text */
            exit(1);
          }
        }

        for (i=0; i<M; i++)   /* wait for workers to finish */
          pthread_join(thr[i], 0)

        /* print the results  ... */
        ...

        return(0);
}

void *matmult(void *arg) {
    /* computes all inner products for row arg of matrix C */
    int row = (int)arg;
    int col;
    int i;
    int t;

    for (col=0; col < P; col++) {
        t = 0;
        for (i=0; i<N; i++)
          t += A[row][i] * B[i][col];
        C[row][col] = t;
    }
    return(0);
}
```

Note that we check for errors from *pthread_create*: this is important to do since it can fail (for example, because the operating system has run out of resources for representing a thread).

2.2.2 THREADS AND C++

We've introduced multithreaded programming not as part of our programming language, but as a subroutine library. We'd now like to exploit the object facilities of C++ to try to integrate multithreaded programming with the language. The result, while not a complete success, will let us take advantage of much of C++'s object orientedness to help us write multithreaded programs. We present this material in terms of POSIX threads, but it applies equally well to Win-32.

What we want to do is to treat threads as objects, so that creating a new instance of a thread object has the side effect of creating a thread. This is easy. However, combining the termination of threads with the destruction of the encapsulating object is a bit tricky. Consider the code below:

```
class Server {
public:
    Server(int in, int out): in_(in), out_(out) {
        pthread_create(&thread_, 0, start, (void*)this);
    }
private:
    int in_, out_;
    static void *start(Server*);      // it must be static!
    pthread_t thread_;
};

void *Server::start(Server* me) {
    char buf[BSIZE];
    while(!eof) {
        read(me->in_, buf, sizeof(buf));
        write(me->out_, buf, sizeof(buf));
    }
    return(0);
}
```

We have a class *Server* whose constructor creates a thread that executes a member function. Thus every time we create a new instance of *Server*, we get not only the new instance, but also a thread executing within it. We could, of course, dispense with creating a thread inside *Server*'s constructor; instead, we could simply create a thread explicitly after creating a new instance of *Server* and have this externally created thread call *Server*'s start routine. But by creating the thread in the constructor and having it call a private member function, we are absolutely certain that only one thread is active inside the object: the object and thread executing it are not two different things but the same thing. Outside *Server*, no one needs to know such details as how many threads are running inside of it; this is strictly part of *Server*'s implementation.

There are still a few details to explain and work out. The *start* routine of our thread is declared *static*.[7] This is necessary because a reference to a nonstatic member function actually requires two pieces of information: a pointer to the function's code and a pointer to the object instance. Both *pthread_create* and the thread it creates are designed to work with the only form of a reference to a function understood by C programs: a pointer to the function's code. So, by declaring *start* to be

---

[7] This is not sufficient for some C++ compilers, such as Solaris's. For them, the start routine passed to *pthread_create* must be declared as *extern "C"*.

static, we can refer to it simply with a pointer to its code. However, we still must refer to the object instance inside *start*; thus we pass to the thread as its only argument the pointer to the instance.

The object's constructor can have any number of arguments — two in this case. This gives us convenient syntax for supplying more than one argument to a thread, though we still have the storage-management issues discussed earlier: we need to make certain that the lifetime of the storage allocated to hold these arguments is the same as the lifetime of the thread. More generally, we must insure that when the thread terminates, the object is deleted, and vice versa. As we saw when we were dealing strictly with C and trying to handle the storage occupied by threads' initial arguments, there is no one way of doing this.

Nevertheless, let's try to extend our definition of *Server* to handle termination and deletion. Our first attempt is:

```
class Server {
public:
  Server(int in, int out): in_(in), out_(out) {
    pthread_create(&thread_, 0, start, (void*)this);
    pthread_detach(thread_);
  }
  ~server( ) { }
private:
  int in, out;
  static void *start(Server*);
  pthread_t thread_;
};

void *start(Server* me) {
  ...
  delete me;
  return(0);
}
```

We immediately detach the thread after creating it, so there's no need for a call to *pthread_ join*. Then just before the thread terminates, we delete the object, thus insuring that the object is deleted when the thread terminates. (Of course, we can do this only because *start* is static.)

The above approach makes sense in this example, but wouldn't work if some other thread needs to be able to wait until this one terminates, perhaps in order to receive a return value. Also, since the object is explicitly deleted by its thread, its instances cannot be local, but must be explicitly created with *new* — if they were local, then when the creating thread leaves their scope, they would be automatically deleted, even though they're also explicitly deleted.

To get around this second problem, let's turn things around a bit and put a call to *pthread_ join* in the destructor:

```
class Server {
public:
  Server(int in, int out): in_(in), out_(out) {
    pthread_create(&thread_, 0, start, (void*)this);
  }
  ~server( ) {
```

```
        pthread_join(thread_, 0);
    }
private:
    ...
};
```

Now, when any thread deletes the object, either explicitly or by going out of its scope, it invokes the destructor, which waits until the object's thread terminates.

However, since destructors cannot return values, the object's thread has no way to make a return value available to others. To get around this problem, we might do something like:

```
class Server {
public:
    Server(int in, int out): in_(in), out_(out) {
        pthread_create(&thread_, 0, start, (void*)this);
    }
    int join( ) {
        int ret;
        pthread_join(&thread_, &ret);
        return(ret);
    }
private:
    static void *start(Server*);
    ...
};
```

We've encapsulated *pthread_join* in a new member function that returns a value. However, now the programmer must call *join* and then delete the object. This makes us a bit too dependent on the object's internal details (and can cause problems if the user of the object doesn't use it correctly).

We might try to avoid this problem by:

```
class Server {
public:
    Server(int in, int out): in_(in), out_(out) {
        pthread_create(&thread_, 0, start, (void*)this);
    }
    static int join(Server *t) {
        int ret;
        pthread_join(&t->thread_, &ret);
        delete t;
        return(ret);
    }
private:
    static void *start(Server*);
    ...
};
```

We've made *join* static so that we can delete the object from within it. But now we're back to the original problem: that object instances must not be local.

The moral is that we must design the termination technique to suit the problem.

We have one final issue: subclassing thread objects. It would be convenient to design a generic thread class of which we can build subclasses. For example, consider:

```cpp
class BaseThread {
public:
    BaseThread(void *start(void *)) {
        pthread_create(&thread, 0, start, (void*)this);
    }
private:
    pthread_t thread;
};
class DerivedThread: public BaseThread {
    static void *start(void *arg) {
        cout << (DerivedThread*)arg->a;
        return(0);
    }
public:
    DerivedThread(int z):
                a(z), BaseThread((void*(*)(void*))start){ }
    int a;
};
```

What we have here is a base class, *BaseThread*, whose constructor creates a thread that calls as its first function the argument passed to the constructor. We then declare another class, *DerivedThread*, that's a subclass of *BaseThread*. *DerivedThread*'s constructor takes one argument, which is saved as an instance variable. The constructor also invokes *BaseThread*'s constructor, passing it the start routine that's part of *DerivedThread*.

Note that, according to the rules of C++, base-class constructors are called before derived-class constructors. So, despite the order of initialization given in *DerivedThread*'s constructor, *BaseThread*'s constructor is called before *a* is initialized to *z*. Thus, there's a potential race condition: suppose we create an object of type *DerivedThread*. *BaseThread*'s constructor first creates a thread, then *DerivedThread*'s constructor initializes *a*. There is a good chance that the new thread will refer to *a* before *a* is initialized.

To get around this problem, we'd really like to make certain that the thread created in the base-class constructor doesn't run until the constructors of all subclasses complete. Unfortunately, there's no convenient means for arranging this in C++.

2.2.3 SYNCHRONIZATION

Our next concern is the coordination of threads as they access common data structures. We examine this issue initially from the point of view of POSIX and Win-32 programmers, and later on from that of the operating-system developer. We start with the relatively simple concern of mutually exclusive access to data structures, then look at more complex synchronization issues.

FIGURE 2.4   World War I fighter aircraft. (*Copyright © iStockphoto.*)

2.2.3.1 Mutual Exclusion

The mutual-exclusion problem involves making certain that two things don't happen at once. A dramatic example arose in the fighter aircraft of World War I, as illustrated in Figure 2.4. Due to a number of constraints (e.g., machine guns tended to jam frequently and thus had to be near people who could unjam them), machine guns were mounted directly in front of the pilot. However, blindly shooting a machine gun through a whirling propeller was not a good idea. At the beginning of the war, pilots, being gentlemen, politely refrained from attacking fellow pilots. A bit later in the war, however, the Germans developed the tactic of gaining altitude on an opponent, diving at him, turning off the engine, then firing — without hitting the now-stationary propeller. Today this would be called *coarse-grained synchronization*. Later, the Germans developed technology that synchronized the firing of the gun with the whirling of the propeller, so that shots were fired only when the propeller blades would not be in the way. This could well be the first example of a mutual-exclusion mechanism providing *fine-grained synchronization*!

For a more computer-oriented example of the need for mutual exclusion, consider two threads, each performing the following operation:

$$x = x+1;$$

If the two threads perform the operation at the same time, what's the final value of *x* if its initial value was zero? We'd very much like the answer to be 2. However, consider the assembly-language version of the statement. It probably looks something like this:

```
ld      r1,x
add     r1,1
st      r1,x
```

Thus to add 1 to the variable *x*, the machine must first load the current contents of location *x* into a register, add 1 to the contents of the register, then store those contents back into the location containing *x*. If both threads do this at more or less the same time, the final result stored in *x* is likely to be 1!

For the concurrent execution of the two assignment statements to behave as we want it to, we somehow have to insure that the effect of executing the three assembler instructions is atomic, i.e., that all three instructions take place at once without interference.

We're not going to show how to solve this problem right away. Instead, we introduce functionality from POSIX threads and Win-32 and show how we can use it to solve the problem. In Chapter 5 we show how this functionality is implemented.

POSIX threads defines a new data type called a *mutex*, which stands for mutual exclusion. A mutex is used to insure either that only one thread is executing a particular piece of code at once (code locking) or that only one thread is accessing a particular data structure at once (data locking). A mutex belongs either to a particular thread or to no thread (i.e., it is either locked or unlocked). A thread may lock a mutex by calling *pthread_mutex_lock*. If no other thread has the mutex locked, then the calling thread obtains the lock on the mutex and returns. Otherwise it waits until no other thread has the mutex, and finally returns with the mutex locked. There may, of course, be multiple threads waiting for the mutex to be unlocked. Only one thread can lock the mutex at a time; there is no specified order for which thread gets the mutex next, though the ordering is assumed to be at least somewhat fair.

To unlock a mutex, a thread calls *pthread_mutex_unlock*. It is considered incorrect to unlock a mutex that is not held by the caller (i.e., to unlock someone else's mutex). However, checking for this is costly, so most implementations, if they check at all, do so only when certain degrees of debugging are turned on.

Like any other data structure, mutexes must be initialized. This can be done via a call to *pthread_mutex_init* or can be done statically by assigning PTHREAD_MUTEX_INITIALIZER to a mutex. The initial state of such initialized mutexes is unlocked. Of course, a mutex should be initialized only once! (That is, make certain that, for each mutex, no more than one thread calls *pthread_mutex_init*.) If a mutex is dynamically initialized, a call should be made to *pthread_mutex_destroy* when it is no longer needed.

Using mutexes, we can solve the problem of atomically adding 1 to a variable.

```
pthread_mutex_t m = PTHREAD_MUTEX_INITIALIZER;
                // shared by both threads
int x;          // ditto

    pthread_mutex_lock(&m);

    x = x+1;

    pthread_mutex_unlock(&m);
```

Using a mutex to provide mutually exclusive access to a single data structure at a time is easy. Things get a bit more involved if we need to arrange for such access to multiple data structures at once. Consider the following example in which one thread is executing *proc1* and another is executing *proc2*:

```
void proc1( ) {                          void proc2( ) {
    pthread_mutex_lock(&m1);                 pthread_mutex_lock(&m2);
    /* use object 1 */                       /* use object 2 */
    pthread_mutex_lock(&m2);                 pthread_mutex_lock(&m1);
    /* use objects 1 and 2 */                /* use objects 1 and 2 */
    pthread_mutex_unlock(&m2);               pthread_mutex_unlock(&m1);
    pthread_mutex_unlock(&m1);               pthread_mutex_unlock(&m2);
}                                        }
```

The threads are using two mutexes to control access to two different objects. Thread 1 first takes mutex 1, then, while still holding mutex 1, obtains mutex 2. Thread 2 first takes mutex 2, then, while still holding mutex 2, obtains mutex 1.

However, things do not always work out as planned. Say that thread 1 obtains mutex 1 and, at about the same time, thread 2 obtains mutex 2; then if thread 1 attempts to take mutex 2 and thread 2 attempts to take mutex 1, we're stuck: we have a *deadlock*.

Deadlock is an important concept, so let's make sure we understand it. Let's say we have a set of threads and a set of containers. Each container contains some number of items. A thread can take items from any of the containers. Threads may put the items back into the containers (and will, unless there is a deadlock). Furthermore, threads may wait until containers have the requisite number of items before taking items out. In our example, containers are mutexes and each contains at most one item. Locking a mutex corresponds to waiting until a container has an item, then taking that item — removing it from the container. Unlocking a mutex corresponds to putting the item back in the container. This is very simple, but things can get much more complicated. For example, Windows (usefully) allows threads to wait for any or all of a set of containers to have items before taking one or more of the items (see the discussion of *WaitForMultipleObjects* towards the end of Section 2.2.3.2 below).

For deadlock to be possible, the following must be true:

1. It must be possible for a thread to hold items it has removed from various containers while waiting for items to become available in other containers.

2. A thread cannot be forced to yield the items it is holding.

3. Each container has a finite capacity.

4. A *circular wait* can exist. We say that thread A is *waiting on* thread B if B is holding items from containers from which A is waiting for items. Consider all threads Z for which there is some sequence of threads B, C, D, . . . , Y, such that A is waiting on B, B is waiting on C, C is waiting on D, . . . , and Y is waiting on Z. The set of such threads Z is known as the *transitive closure* of the relation *waiting on*. If A is contained in this transitive closure, then we say that a *circular wait* exists.

In their full generality, the above conditions are necessary but not sufficient for deadlock to occur. However, in the case of simple operations on mutexes, where threads can wait on only one of them at a time (while holding locks on any number of them), these conditions are sufficient as well.

If any of the four above conditions does not hold, then deadlock cannot happen, even in the most general case. Of course the only nontrivial condition to check for is the last. Algorithms exist to determine whether a circular wait currently exists and to determine whether a particular next move will inevitably result in a circular wait. However, for most purposes, even for simple operations on mutexes, such algorithms are too expensive, since they require time quadratic in the number of threads and mutexes. Let's restrict ourselves to simple operations on mutexes and, rather than trying to solve the problem for arbitrary programs, let's simply write our code in an intelligent fashion so that circular waits, and hence deadlocks, cannot happen.

Let's represent the state of our program as a directed bipartite graph, with one type of node representing threads and the other representing mutexes (*bipartite* simply means that there are two types of nodes, and edges can go only from one type to the other). We draw an edge from a mutex to a thread if the thread has the mutex locked; and we draw an edge from a thread to a mutex if the thread is waiting to lock the mutex. A circular wait and hence deadlock are represented by the graph in Figure 2.5. It should be clear that a cycle exists in such a graph if and only if there is a circular wait. Thus to prevent deadlock, we must make certain that cycles

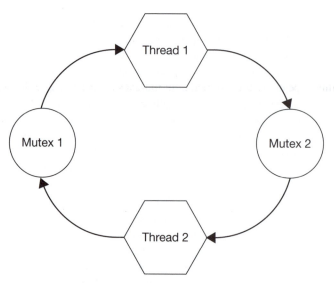

FIGURE 2.5 Thread/mutex graph.

can't possibly exist in the graph. This is easy to do: we simply arrange our mutexes in some order (for example, by assigning unique integers to them) and insist that all threads attempting to lock multiple resources do so in ascending order.

In most applications it is fairly easy to set things up so that all threads lock mutexes in ascending order. However, in some situations this is impossible, often because it is not known which mutex should be locked second until the first one is locked. An approach that often works in such situations is to use conditional lock requests, as in:

```
proc1( ) {
 pthread_mutex_lock(&m1);
 /* use object 1 */
 pthread_mutex_lock(&m2);
 /* use objects 1 and 2 */
 pthread_mutex_unlock(&m2);
 pthread_mutex_unlock(&m1);
}
```

```
proc2( ) {
  while (1) {
   pthread_mutex_lock(&m2);
   if (!pthread_mutex_trylock(&m1))
    break;
   pthread_mutex_unlock(&m2);
  }

   /* use objects 1 and 2 */

  pthread_mutex_unlock(&m1);
  pthread_mutex_unlock(&m2);
 }
```

Here thread 1, executing *proc1*, obtains the mutexes in the correct order. Thread 2, executing *proc2*, must for some reason take the mutexes out of order. If it is holding mutex 2, it must be careful about taking mutex 1. So, rather than call *pthread_mutex_lock*, it calls *pthread_mutex_trylock*, which always returns without blocking. If the mutex is available, *pthread_mutex_trylock* locks the mutex and returns 0. If the mutex is not available (that is, if it is locked by another thread), then *pthread_mutex_trylock* returns a nonzero error code (EBUSY). In the example above, if mutex 1 is not available, this is probably because it is currently held by thread 1. If thread 2 were to block waiting for the mutex, we have an excellent chance for deadlock. So, rather than block, thread 1 not only quits trying for mutex 1 but also unlocks mutex 2 (since thread 1 could well be waiting for it). It then starts all over again, first taking mutex 2, then mutex 1.

Thread 2 thus repeatedly tries to lock both mutexes (in the wrong order) until it can do so without causing any problems. This could, of course, require a fair number of iterations. When this approach is used, the assumption (which must be validated) is that contention for locks is low and thus even two iterations are unlikely to occur. If lock contention is high, another solution is necessary, perhaps one that requires all threads to honor the locking order.

2.2.3.2 Beyond Mutual Exclusion

Though mutual exclusion is the most common form of synchronization, there are numerous situations that it cannot handle. One obvious extension to mutual exclusion is what's known as the *readers-writers problem*: rather than requiring mutual exclusion for all accesses to a data structure, we can relax things a bit and insist on mutual exclusion only if the data structure is being modified. Thus any number of threads (readers) may be just looking at the data structure at once, but any thread intending to modify it must have mutually exclusive access.

Another common (at least in texts such as this) synchronization problem is the *producer-consumer problem* (sometimes called the *bounded-buffer problem*). Here we have a buffer containing a finite number of slots. As shown in Figure 2.6, a producer is a thread that wishes to put an item into the next empty slot of the buffer. A consumer is a thread that wishes to remove an item from the next occupied slot. The synchronization issue for producers is that if all slots in the buffer are occupied, then producer threads must wait until empty slots are available. Similarly, if all slots are empty, consumer threads must wait until occupied slots are available.

The next synchronization problem might seem a bit mundane, but it's particularly important in many operating systems. It doesn't have a common name; here we call it the *event* problem. A number of threads are waiting for a particular event to happen. Once the event has happened, we'd like to release all of the waiting threads. For example, a number of threads might be waiting for a read operation on a disk to complete. Once it's completed, all threads are woken up and can use the data that was just read in.

Semaphores   These problems, and many others, were first identified in the 1960s. The person who did much of the early work in identifying and elegantly solving these problems was Edsger Dijkstra. The *semaphore*, a synchronization operation (Dijkstra undated: early 1960s) he described and used in an early system (Dijkstra 1968), has proven so useful that it continues to be used in most modern operating systems.

A semaphore is a nonnegative integer on which there are exactly two operations, called by Dijkstra *P* and *V.* (What P and V stand for isn't obvious. While Dijkstra was Dutch and based his terminology on Dutch words, the mnemonic significance of P and V seems to be lost even

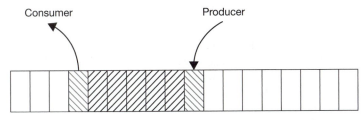

FIGURE 2.6   Producer-consumer problem.

on native Dutch speakers. According to (Dijkstra undated: early 1960s), P stands for prolagen, a made-up word derived from proberen te verlagen, "try to decrease" in Dutch. V stands for verhogen, "increase" in Dutch.) The P operation is somewhat complicated: a thread waits until it finds the value of the semaphore positive, then subtracts one from it. What's really important is that when the active part of the operation starts, the semaphore's value is definitely positive, and when this active part finishes, the value is exactly one less than when the operation started. It's often described as an *atomic* or *indivisible* operation: it has no component parts and takes place as if it were happening instantaneously.

We use the following notation to describe the semantics of P:

```
when (semaphore > 0) [
    semaphore = semaphore - 1;
]
```

This notation means that the operations in square brackets take place only when the expression following "when," known as the *guard*, is true; the statements in square brackets, known as the *command sequence,* are effectively executed instantaneously: no other operation that might interfere with it can take place while it is executing. We call the entire construct a *guarded command.*

The V operation is simpler: a thread atomically adds one to the value of the semaphore. We write this as

```
[semaphore = semaphore + 1]
```

There is no other means for manipulating the value of the semaphore (other than initializing its value in the first place). Thus if the semaphore's value is initially one and two threads concurrently execute P and V operations on it, the resulting value of the semaphore is guaranteed to be one. If its value is initially zero and the two threads concurrently execute P and V operations, the P operation must wait until the V operation makes the semaphore's value positive. Then the P operation can complete, reducing the semaphore's value to zero.

We can easily implement mutexes using semaphores:

```
semaphore S = 1;
void OneAtATime( ) {
    P(S);
    ...
    /* code executed mutually exclusively */
    ...
    V(S);
}
```

If two threads call the *OneAtATime* routine, the first one to execute the P operation finds S to be one, and so subtracts one from it, making it zero. If the second thread now attempts to execute the P operation, it finds S to be zero and thus must wait. Eventually the first thread performs the V operation, adding one back to S, which enables the second thread to continue. It subtracts one from S and eventually executes the V and adds one back to it. When semaphores are used in such a way that their values are only zero and one, as here, they are known as *binary semaphores*.

When multiple threads attempt to execute a P operation, the effect must be as if they execute it one at a time while the semaphore's value is positive. If its value is zero, they are queued up and, one at a time, they complete the P operation in response to V operations by other threads.

We can easily generalize our above example to allow up to *N* threads to execute a block of code (or access a data structure) simultaneously:

```
semaphore S = N;

void NAtATime( ) {
   P(S);
   ...
   /* No more than N threads here at once */
   ...
   V(S);
}
```

Semaphores used this way are known as *counting semaphores*.

A more interesting example of counting semaphores involves using them to solve the producer-consumer problem (see Figure 2.6 above). To keep things simple, let's assume we have one producer and one consumer. We have a buffer with B slots. We use two semaphores: *empty*, representing the number of empty slots, and *occupied*, representing the number of occupied slots. Our solution is:

```
Semaphore empty = B;
Semaphore occupied  = 0;
int nextin = 0;
int nextout = 0;
```

```
void Produce(char item) {          char Consume( ) {
   P(empty);                          char item;
   buf[nextin] = item;                P(occupied);
   nextin = nextin + 1;               item = buf[nextout];
   if (nextin == B)                   nextout = nextout + 1;
      nextin = 0;                     if (nextout == B)
   V(occupied);                          nextout = 0;
}                                     V(empty);
                                      return(item);
                                   }
```

The first P operation of *Produce* causes the thread to wait until there is at least one empty slot in the buffer; at this point the slot is "taken" and *empty*'s value is reduced by one. The producer puts its item in the buffer, then indicates there is one more occupied slot by performing a V operation on *occupied*. Similar actions take place inside of *Consume*.

POSIX provides an implementation of semaphores, but, strangely, it's not part of POSIX threads (POSIX 1003.1c) but part of the POSIX real-time specification (POSIX 1003.1b). This matters only because, depending on the system, you may need to include an additional library when you use semaphores.

The POSIX interface for semaphores is given below.

```
sem_t semaphore;
int err;
```

```
err = sem_init(&semaphore, pshared, init);
err = sem_destroy(&semaphore);
err = sem_wait(&semaphore);              // P operation
err = sem_trywait(&semaphore);           // conditional P operation
err = sem_post(&semaphore);              // V operation
```

Thus semaphores are of type *sem_t*. All operations on them return an integer error code. They must be dynamically initialized using *sem_init* (there is no static initialization such as is provided for mutexes). They take two arguments in addition to the semaphore itself: a flag, *pshared*, indicating whether the semaphore is to be used by threads of just one process (*pshared* = 0) or by threads of multiple processes (*pshared* = 1). We assume the former for now, and discuss the latter later. Once a semaphore is no longer used, *sem_destroy* should be called to free whatever storage was allocated by *sem_init*.

The *sem_wait* operation is the P operation described above. What's new is the *sem_trywait* operation, which is similar to *pthread_mutex_trylock*: if the semaphore's value is positive and thus no waiting is required, it behaves just like *sem_wait* (the value of the semaphore is immediately reduced by one). However, if the semaphore's value is zero, then, rather than waiting, the caller returns immediately with an error code (the value *EAGAIN*).

We discuss the Win-32 version of semaphores in the section on Win-32 Events, below.

POSIX Condition Variables   Semaphores are a convenient way to express solutions to a number of synchronization problems, but using them can force amazingly complex solutions for other problems. Thus most operating systems provide additional synchronization constructs. Here we describe POSIX's *condition variables;* later we discuss the *events* of Win-32.

We described the semantics of semaphores using guarded commands. A general implementation of our guarded-command construct is, however, a rather tall order. Somehow we'd have to monitor the values of all variables appearing in the guard (i.e., the expression following the *when*) so as to find out when the guard becomes true. Then we'd have to make certain it remains true when we start executing the command sequence (the code in square brackets that follows), and make certain that this execution is indivisible.

Condition variables give programmers the tools needed to implement guarded commands. A condition variable is a queue of threads waiting for some sort of notification. Threads waiting for a guard to become true join such queues. Threads that do something to change the value of a guard from false to true can then wake up the threads that were waiting.

The following code shows the general approach:

Guarded command	**POSIX implementation**

```
when (guard) [
  statement 1;
  ...
  statement n;
]
```

```
pthread_mutex_lock(&mutex);
while(!guard)
  pthread_cond_wait(
        &cond_var, &mutex));
statement 1;
...
statement n;
pthread_mutex_unlock(&mutex);
```

```
// code modifying the guard:

...
```

```
pthread_mutex_lock(&mutex);
// code modifying the guard:

...
pthread_cond_broadcast(
        &cond_var);
pthread_mutex_unlock(&mutex);
```

To evaluate the guard safely in the POSIX version, a thread must have mutually exclusive access to all of its components. This is accomplished by having it lock a mutex. If the guard is true, then, with the mutex still locked, it executes the command sequence.

The interesting part is, of course, when the guard is false and thus the thread must wait. In this case, the thread calls *pthread_cond_wait*, which has a complicated effect. What we want to happen is that the thread waits until the guard becomes true. While it's waiting, it's pretty important that it not have the mutex locked (otherwise other threads can't change the value of the guard!). So, *pthread_cond_wait* initially does two things: it unlocks the mutex given as its first argument, and puts the calling thread to sleep, queuing it on the queue represented by the condition variable (of type *pthread_cond_t*) given as its second argument.

Now, assume at least one thread is queued on the condition variable (and thus sleeping). If some other thread causes the guard to become true, we'd like to wake up the waiting threads. This guard-modifying thread first must lock the mutex protecting the guard (we must provide mutually exclusive access for all threads that examine or manipulate the guard's components). Once it makes the guard true, it notifies all threads waiting on the associated condition variable by calling *pthread_cond_broadcast*. Since it's now finished with the guard, it unlocks the mutex.[8]

The threads waiting inside *pthread_cond_wait* are woken up in response to the notification by *pthread_cond_broadcast*, which is intended to inform these threads that the guard, at least a moment ago, evaluated to true. Of course, by the time these threads get a chance to execute, the guard might evaluate to false again. For example, the code in the command sequence executed by the first of the threads to continue execution might do something to negate the guard for the others. So, to guarantee that the guard is true when a thread begins execution of the command sequence, it must reevaluate it, and of course must do so with the mutex locked.

Thus, in response to notifications from *pthread_cond_broadcast* (or from *pthread_cond_signal*, discussed soon), the threads waiting in *pthread_cond_wait* wake up and, still inside *pthread_cond_wait*, immediately call *pthread_mutex_lock* on the mutex they unlocked when they called *pthread_cond_wait* in the first place. As each thread obtains the lock on the mutex, it returns from *pthread_cond_wait*. (We said its effect was complicated!) Now with mutually exclusive access to the components of the guard, the thread can reevaluate it and go back to sleep (by calling *pthread_cond_wait*), if necessary. Thus the notification provided by *pthread_cond_broadcast* must be considered as merely a hint that the guard might now be true. A waiting thread must reevaluate the guard on its own to verify it.

If the first thread released from within *pthread_cond_wait* always makes the guard false from within its command sequence, it seems silly to wake up all the other waiting threads needlessly.

---

[8] Some argue that the mutex should be unlocked first and then the call should be made to *pthread_cond_broadcast*, since this would improve concurrency. We prefer the order shown, but both orders work fine.

Thus an alternative to *pthread_cond_broadcast* is *pthread_cond_signal*, which wakes up just the first thread waiting in the condition-variable queue.

The actual POSIX specification of *pthread_cond_wait* allows implementations to take some shortcuts. Since a thread's returning from *pthread_cond_wait* is just an indication that the guard *might* be true, POSIX allows this routine to return spontaneously, i.e., even if no call has been made to either *pthread_cond_signal* or *pthread_cond_broadcast* (though the thread must lock the mutex before returning). This causes no problems other than inefficiency when condition variables are used as described above, but does rule out other potential uses of condition variables, as we discuss below. Note that such spontaneous wakeups are intended to be rare. They don't occur in most current implementations, though there's no guarantee that they won't occur in tomorrow's implementation. See Exercise 6 for some insight on why POSIX allows such shortcuts.

Let's summarize what we've learned about the operations on condition variables:

- *pthread_cond_wait(**pthread_cond_t** *cv, **pthread_mutex_t** *m)* causes the caller to unlock mutex *m*, queue itself on condition variable *cv*, and go to sleep. When the caller wakes up, it calls *pthread_mutex_lock* on mutex *m* and returns from *pthread_cond_wait*. Wakeups occur in response to calls made by other threads to *pthread_cond_signal* and *pthread_cond_broadcast* using the same condition variable *cv*, or for no reason whatsoever.

- *pthread_cond_signal(**pthread_cond_t** *cv)* causes the first thread queued on condition variable *cv* to be woken up. If there are no such queued threads, nothing happens.

- *pthread_cond_broadcast(**pthread_cond_t** *cv)* causes all threads queued on condition variable *cv* to be woken up. If there aren't any, nothing happens.

Two more routines are needed:

- *pthread_cond_init(**pthread_cond_t** *cv, **pthread_condattr_t** *attr)* dynamically initializes condition variable *cv* according to attributes *attr*. Supplying zero for *attr* causes the default attributes to be used. An option provided by many implementations is the shared use of a condition variable by threads of different processes. Static initialization may also be used (using *PTHREAD_COND_INITIALIZER*), which establishes default attributes.

- *pthread_cond_destroy(**pthread_cond_t** *cv)* should be called for any dynamically initialized condition variable once it is no longer needed.

The readers-writers problem mentioned earlier is a good example of a conceptually simple synchronization problem that lacks a simple solution using semaphores, but can be solved easily using condition variables. Below is a solution written using guarded commands:

```
void reader( ) {                      void writer( ) {
    when (writers == 0) [                 when ((writers == 0) &&
        readers++;                            (readers == 0)) [
    ]                                         writers++;
                                          ]
    // read
                                          // write
    [readers--;]
}                                         [writers--;]
                                      }
```

Here *readers* represents the number of threads that are currently reading and *writers* represents the number of threads that are currently writing. Both are initially zero. Readers must wait until there are no writers; then they proceed, after indicating that there is one more reader. After they finish reading, they reduce the count of readers by one. Similar actions are taken by writers, but they must wait until there are both no current readers and no current writers.

Guided by our general approach to implementing guarded commands with condition variables, we implement this pseudocode with the following:

```
pthread_mutex_t m = PTHREAD_MUTEX_INITIALIZER;
pthread_cond_t readerQ = PTHREAD_COND_INITIALIZER;
pthread_cond_t writerQ = PTHREAD_COND_INITIALIZER;
int readers = 0;
int writers = 0;
```

```
void reader( ) {                          void writer( ) {
  pthread_mutex_lock(&m);                   pthread_mutex_lock(&m);
  while (!(writers == 0))                   while(!((readers == 0) &&
    pthread_cond_wait(                        (writers == 0)))
      &readerQ, &m);                         pthread_cond_wait(
  readers++;                                    &writerQ, &m);
  pthread_mutex_unlock(&m);                 writers++;
  // read                                   pthread_mutex_unlock(&m);
  pthread_mutex_lock(&m);                   // write
  if (- -readers == 0)                      pthread_mutex_lock(&m);
    pthread_cond_signal(                    writers--;
      &writerQ);                            pthread_cond_signal(
  pthread_mutex_unlock(&m);                   &writerQ);
}                                           pthread_cond_broadcast(
                                              &readerQ);
                                            pthread_mutex_unlock(&m);
                                          }
```

Here reader threads wait on the condition variable *readerQ* while *writers* is not zero, indicating the presence of an active writing thread. Writer threads wait on the condition-variable *writerQ* while *readers* and *writers* are both not zero, indicating that either some number of threads are reading or a thread is writing. When a reader thread is finished reading and discovers that it's the last, it wakes up the first waiting writer. When a writer thread is finished writing, it wakes up the first waiting writer and all the waiting readers. Depending on which of these locks the mutex first, either the readers are allowed to proceed or the next writer is allowed to proceed.

To complete our discussion of the readers-writers problem, note that the solution we've presented here might have a problem. Suppose that, whenever the last reader is just about to leave, a new reader arrives. Thus at all times there is at least one reader reading. This is unfortunate for the writers, since they will never get a chance to write.

If reading is a rare event, then such a scenario is highly unlikely. However, often reading is not a rare event but writing is. We'd really like to make certain that our writers get to write quickly, even if this means giving them favored treatment over readers. If the above solution is seen as a "readers-priority" solution, what we'd really like is a "writers-priority" solution.

Devising such a solution is fairly easy. We first solve it with guarded commands:

```
void reader( ) {                     void writer( ) {
 when (writers == 0) [               [writers++;]
  readers++;                         when((active_writers == 0) &&
 ]                                       (readers == 0)) [
                                       active_writers++;
 // read                             ]

 [readers--;]                        // write
}
                                     [writers--; active_writers--;]
                                    }
```

Here we've changed the meaning of *writers* to represent the number of threads that are either writing or waiting to write. We introduce a new variable, *active_writers*, to represent the number of threads (zero or one) that are currently writing. Reader threads must now wait until there are no threads either writing or waiting to write. Writer threads wait, as before, until no other threads are reading or writing.

Implementing this in POSIX is straightforward:

```
pthread_mutex_t m = PTHREAD_MUTEX_INITIALIZER;
pthread_cond_t readerQ = PTHREAD_COND_INITIALIZER;
pthread_cond_t writerQ = PTHREAD_COND_INITIALIZER;
int readers = 0;
int writers = 0;
int active_writers = 0;
```

```
void reader( ) {                     void writer( ) {
  pthread_mutex_lock(&m);              pthread_mutex_lock(&m);
  while (!(writers == 0))             writers++;
    pthread_cond_wait(               while(!((readers == 0) &&
      &readerQ, &m);                     (active_writers == 0)))
  readers++;                           pthread_cond_wait(
  pthread_mutex_unlock(&m);              &writerQ, &m);
  // read                             active_writers++;
  pthread_mutex_lock(&m);             pthread_mutex_unlock(&m);
  if (--readers == 0)                 // write
    pthread_cond_signal(             pthread_mutex_lock(&m);
      &writerQ);                      active_writers- -;
  pthread_mutex_unlock(&m);           if (--writers == 0)
}                                       pthread_cond_broadcast(
                                          &readerQ);
                                     else
                                       pthread_cond_signal(
                                         &writerQ);
                                     pthread_mutex_unlock(&m);
                                    }
```

In this new version, since the variable *writers* indicates whether threads are waiting to write, threads that are leaving the writing code no longer have to notify both waiting readers and the next waiting writer, but do one or the other as appropriate.

The original POSIX threads specification did not include readers-writers locks. However, a more recent version, POSIX 1003.1j, does.

We conclude our discussion of condition variables with an example showing their limitations: the *barrier problem*, a special case of the event problem mentioned above. A barrier is a synchronization construct set up for a specified number of threads, say *n*. Threads enter the barrier but cannot exit until all *n* have entered. Once all *n* threads have entered and they begin to exit, the barrier resets itself so that as threads enter again, they cannot exit until all have entered again, and so forth.

One might be tempted to solve the problem as follows:

```
int count;
pthread_mutex_t m;
pthread_cond_t BarrierQueue;

void barrier( ) {
    pthread_mutex_lock(&m);
    if (++count < n)
        pthread_cond_wait(&BarrierQueue, &m);
    else {
        count = 0;
        pthread_cond_broadcast(&BarrierQueue);
    }
    pthread_mutex_unlock(&m);
}
```

The intent here is that all but the last thread to call *barrier* wait by queuing themselves on the condition variable *BarrierQueue*, and then that the last thread wake up all the others. Thus we're using *pthread_cond_broadcast* to notify the waiting threads that a particular event has happened — all *n* threads have entered the barrier. But this is not how we're supposed to use condition variables. Returning from *pthread_cond_wait* is merely an indication that the guard we're waiting for might now be true. But since *pthread_cond_wait* might return spontaneously, we can't depend on its return to indicate that what we're interested in is true.

We might try rewriting this code so that threads evaluate a guard each time they return from *pthread_cond_wait*:

```
int count;
pthread_mutex_t m;
pthread_cond_t BarrierQueue;
void barrier( ) {
    pthread_mutex_lock(&m);
    if (++count < n)
        while(count < n)
            pthread_cond_wait(&BarrierQueue, &m);
    else {
        count = 0;
```

```
            pthread_cond_broadcast(&BarrierQueue);
       }
       pthread_mutex_unlock(&m);
   }
```

This solves the problem of a spontaneous return from *pthread_cond_wait*, but now we have a new problem: the last thread to call *barrier* resets *count* to zero. Now when the waiting threads wake up, they will find the guard false and go back to sleep.

We could try moving "count = 0" someplace else, but there really is no place to put it that makes the code work. So we're stuck — at least if we insist on using this approach. What we need is either a more appropriate synchronization construct or a guarantee that in this and all future implementations of POSIX threads, *pthread_cond_wait* never returns spontaneously. Neither is likely to happen soon (on POSIX systems).

Certainly one can solve this problem using condition variables, but the solution is far from obvious:

```
int count;
pthread_mutex_t m;
pthread_cond_t BarrierQueue;
int generation;

void barrier( ) {
   int my_generation;
   pthread_mutex_lock(&m);
   if (++count < n) {
      my_generation = generation;
      while(my_generation == generation)
         pthread_cond_wait(&BarrierQueue, &m);
   } else {
      count = 0;
      generation++;
      pthread_cond_broadcast(&BarrierQueue);
   }
   pthread_mutex_unlock(&m);
}
```

What we've done here is introduce a new guard, independent of *count*, that holds its value long enough for all threads to exit the barrier. Note that *my_generation* is a local variable and thus each thread has its own private copy on its stack. We assume that if *generation* overflows, it becomes zero without causing any exceptions.

Again, the original POSIX threads specification did not include barriers, but POSIX 1003.1j does.

Win-32 Events As might be expected, Win-32's approach to synchronization is different from POSIX's, though both provide mutexes and semaphores. We've seen that POSIX's condition variables are intended not to indicate the occurrence of an event, but to provide notification that some guard or condition might be true. The notified thread must then verify it. The approach taken in Win-32 is simply to provide an indication that some event has happened. This results in a somewhat different way to solve some synchronization problems — in many cases, a more straightforward way.

Win-32 events have to do with state changes in various sorts of kernel objects, such as the thread objects we encountered in Chapter 1. Threads may wait for events to take place in any number (within limits) of objects at once, subject to programmer-specified timeouts. A partial list of the kinds of objects that support waiting for events is given in Table 2.1.

As we saw in Chapter 1, one thread can wait for another to terminate by calling *WaitForSingleObject*:

```
HANDLE NewThread = CreateThread(…);
WaitForSingleObject(NewThread, INFINITE);
```

In general, *WaitForSingleObject* returns either because it has timed out (as specified by its second argument) or because the handle given as its first argument refers to an object in some sort of object-dependent signaled state (terminated, in the case of threads). A thread can wait for a number of threads to terminate by using *WaitForMultipleObjects*:

```
HANDLE NewThreads[n];
int i;
BOOL All;

for (i = 0; i<n; i++ )
   NewThreads[i] = CreateThread(…);

WaitForMultipleObjects(n, NewThreads, All, INFINITE);
```

Here our creating thread waits for either all or any one of the threads to terminate, depending on whether *All* is TRUE or FALSE. In the latter case, the call returns a code indicating which of the handles in the array passed as the second argument refers to a terminated thread — the index is, strangely, the return value minus the constant *WAIT_OBJECT_0*. If more than one thread has terminated, repeated calls to *WaitForMultipleObjects* are required to identify

Table 2.1 Kernel objects supporting events.

Type of Object	Events
process	termination
thread	termination
mutex	unlocked
semaphore	value is positive
event	event is "signaled"
waitable timers	timer expiration

them. As with *WaitForSingleObject*, the last argument of *WaitForMultipleObjects* indicates how many milliseconds to wait before timing out, in which case the call returns with the error code *WAIT_TIMEOUT*.

Win-32 mutexes behave like the POSIX versions, for example:

```
HANDLE mutex = CreateMutex(0, FALSE, 0);


void AccessDataStructure( ) {
    WaitForSingleObject(mutex, INFINITE);

    // code executed mutually exclusively

    ReleaseMutex(mutex);
}
```

The call to *CreateMutex* returns the handle of a newly created kernel mutex object. These objects, like other kernel objects, are either in the signaled or unsignaled state; for mutexes, signaled means unlocked and unsignaled means locked. *CreateMutex*'s first argument specifies security attributes; since these are not of concern in this chapter, we set it to zero, meaning use the default. The last argument allows one to give the object a name. This is useful if the object is to be shared by multiple processes, but since again this is not of concern in this chapter, we leave it as zero, giving the object no name. The second parameter indicates whether the mutex is created in the locked state (locked by the creator). We set it to FALSE, indicating unlocked.

To lock the mutex, a thread must first wait for it to be unlocked. Calling *WaitForSingleObject* does this, with the side effect of locking it on return. If multiple threads are waiting, they wait their turn, returning one at a time. We could also use *WaitForMultipleObjects*, where the mutex's handle is one of the elements of the handle array. In this case the mutex is locked if the call returns with an indication that the mutex was in the signaled state (meaning it was unlocked, but is now locked). To unlock a mutex, simply call *ReleaseMutex* and thus put the object into the *signaled* state.

Semaphores are supported in a similar fashion, for example

```
HANDLE semaphore = CreateSemaphore(0, 1, 1, 0);

void AccessItWithASemaphore( ) {
    WaitForSingleObject(semaphore, INFINITE);

    // code executed mutually exclusively

    ReleaseSemaphore(semaphore, 1, 0);
}
```

The call to *CreateSemaphore* returns the handle of a newly created kernel semaphore object that is considered to be in the signaled state if its value is positive and unsignaled otherwise. Its first and last arguments are the same as for *CreateMutex* — we always supply zeros. The second argument is the semaphore's initial value — a nonnegative integer. The third argument is something we don't see in POSIX: the semaphore's maximum value. This is presumably there for debugging and reliability purposes (if the program logic is such that a semaphore's value never should exceed some maximum value, this will give an error return if it does).

Dijkstra's P operation is supported using the *WaitFor* routines. When a thread returns from these routines after finding the semaphore in the signaled state, one is subtracted from the semaphore's value. If it's now zero, the semaphore changes to the unsignaled state. The V operation is performed by *ReleaseSemaphore*, which is actually a bit more general than Dijkstra's version. Its second argument indicates how much to add to the semaphore's value. The third argument, if nonzero, is a pointer to an integer that, on return, holds the semaphore's previous value.

An important aspect of *WaitForMultipleObjects* is that it can be used with different types of objects. The following solution to the producer-consumer problem mixes semaphores with mutexes to allow multiple producers and consumers:

```
HANDLE pmutex = CreateMutex(0, FALSE, 0);
HANDLE cmutex = CreateMutex(0, FALSE, 0);
HANDLE empty = CreateSemaphore(0, B, B, 0);
HANDLE occupied = CreateSemaphore(0, 0, B, 0);
int nextin = 0;
int nextout = 0;
```

```
void produce(char item) {
    HANDLE harray[2] =
        {empty, pmutex};

    WaitForMultipleObjects(
        2, harray, TRUE,
        INFINITE);
    buf[nextin] = item;
    if (++nextin >= B)
        nextin = 0;
    ReleaseMutex(pmutex);
    ReleaseSemaphore(
        filled, 1, 0);
}
```

```
char consume( ) {
    char item;
    HANDLE harray[2] =
        {filled, cmutex};

    WaitForMultipleObjects(
        2, harray, TRUE,
        INFINITE);
    item = buf[nextout];
    if (++nextout >= BSIZE)
        nextout = 0;
    ReleaseMutex(cmutex);
    ReleaseSemaphore(
        empty, 1, 0);
    return(item);
}
```

So far we haven't seen anything that is much different from what POSIX supplies. We argued earlier that additional synchronization capabilities are needed over and above mutexes and semaphores. POSIX uses condition variables; Win-32 uses yet another kind of kernel object known as *event objects*. Like the other kernel objects we've discussed in this section, threads can wait for them to enter the signaled state. However, the state these objects are in is completely under programmer control; they have no use other than their state.

Event objects come in two forms: auto-reset and manual-reset. The distinction involves what happens when a thread finds them in the signaled state and returns from one of the *WaitFor* routines. Auto-reset objects automatically revert to the unsignaled state; manual-reset objects stay in the signaled state.

As an example, let's look at two more special cases of our event problem. In the first, suppose we have a switch controlled by on and off buttons. Threads arriving at the switch must wait if it's off, but are allowed to continue if it's on. This can be handled using manual-reset events:

```
HANDLE Switch = CreateEvent(0, TRUE, FALSE, 0);
        // manual-reset event, initially unsignaled
```

```
void OnButtonPushed( ) {
    SetEvent(Switch);
}

void OffButtonPushed( ) {
    ResetEvent(Switch);
}

void WaitForSwitch( ) {
    WaitForSingleObject(Switch, INFINITE);
}
```

We create the event object by calling *CreateEvent*. Its first and last arguments are the same as in the other object-creation routines we've seen, and we supply zeros. Its second argument is TRUE if the event is to be manual-reset, FALSE if auto-reset. The third argument is the event's initial state, in this case *unsignaled*. Threads control the object's state by calling *SetEvent* to put it in the *signaled* state and *ResetEvent* to put it in the *unsignaled* state. An additional routine, *PulseEvent*, is supplied. For manual-reset event objects, *PulseEvent* sets the object's state to *signaled* just long enough to wake up all threads currently waiting for it, then resets it to *unsignaled*. For auto-reset event objects, *PulseEvent* sets the state to *signaled* just long enough to release one thread. In either case, if no thread is waiting, nothing happens.

As a simple example of auto-reset events, let's modify our button-pushing example slightly so that one button, not two, toggles between on and off each time it's pressed.

```
HANDLE Switch = CreateEvent(0, FALSE, FALSE, 0);
        // auto-reset event, initially unsignaled

void ToggleButtonPushed( ) {
    SetEvent(Switch);    // release first thread to call, or
                         // first waiting thread to have called,
                         // WaitForPermission
}

void WaitForPermission( ) {
    WaitForSingleObject(Switch, INFINITE);
}
```

We finish our discussion of Win-32 synchronization by looking again at barriers. Without additional machinery, we'll have as difficult a time implementing them as we had with POSIX constructs. For example, a naive attempt at implementing a barrier might use a single manual-reset event object to represent threads waiting for the others to enter. When the last thread does enter, it uses *PulseEvent* to wake up the others. Of course, we have to protect access to the count of the number of threads that have entered with a mutex. So our code might look like

```
HANDLE mutex = CreateMutex(0, FALSE, 0);
HANDLE queue = CreateEvent(0, TRUE, FALSE, 0);
int count = 0;
```

```
void wait( ) {
  WaitForSingleObject(mutex, INFINITE);
  if (++count < n) {
    ReleaseMutex(mutex);
    WaitForSingleObject(queue, INFINITE);
  } else {
    count = 0;
    PulseEvent(queue);
    ReleaseMutex(mutex);
  }
}
```

But this program doesn't work. Suppose the next-to-the-last thread to enter the barrier (i.e., call *wait*) has just released the mutex. Before it gets a chance to call *WaitForSingleObject* and join the queue, the last thread enters the barrier. It quickly locks the mutex, increments *count*, finds that *count* is now *n*, and executes the *PulseEvent* statement. At this point, the previous thread finally gets around to calling *WaitForSingleObject*. Unfortunately, it's too late: the *PulseEvent* call has already taken place. There won't be another call, so this thread is stuck in the queue and no other thread will ever wake it up.

We can implement barriers, with the machinery we've discussed so far, by using a different, far more complicated and rather unintuitive approach. But one further operation on object handles (added by Microsoft a few years after the introduction of the other routines) lets us use our original, intuitive approach.

We need a way to put one object into its signaled state and, without the possibility that anything else happens in between, immediately commence to wait for another object to enter the signaled state. This new operation is *SignalObjectAndWait*; its operation is shown below in a correct barrier solution.

```
HANDLE mutex = CreateMutex(0, FALSE, 0);
HANDLE queue = CreateEvent(0, TRUE, FALSE, 0);
int count = 0;

void wait( ) {
  WaitForSingleObject(mutex, INFINITE);
  if (++count < n) {
    SignalObjectAndWait(mutex, queue, INFINITE, FALSE);
  } else {
    count = 0;
    PulseEvent(queue);
    ReleaseMutex(mutex);
  }
}
```

Here, in a single operation, we unlock the mutex and join the queue, thereby eliminating the problem with the first attempt. The first argument to *SignalObjectAndWait* is the handle of the object to be signaled. The second argument is the handle of the object for which we should wait until it is signaled. The third argument is the timeout. (The last argument indicates whether the call is "alertable," a topic we discuss in Section 5.2.3.1.)

2.2.4 THREAD SAFETY

Much of the standard Unix library code was developed before multithreaded programming was common. Though the Win-32 interface in Windows has the advantage of being developed with threads in mind, the interfaces for much of the standard libraries it must support, such as that used for the socket interface to networks, were designed before the age of threads. Our concern here is that a number of practices employed in these libraries coexist badly with multithreaded programs.

Our first example of such a practice is one we've already encountered: the system-call library, providing the interface between C (and C++) programs and the Unix operating system. The culprit is the means for reporting error codes through the global variable *errno*:

```
int IOfunc( ) {
   extern int errno;
   . . .
   if (write(fd, buffer, size) == -1) {
      if (errno == EIO)
        fprintf(stderr, "IO problems ...\n");
      . . .
      return(0);
   }
   . . .
}
```

We have one global variable that is shared by all threads. Thus if two threads fail in system calls at about the same time, we'll have a conflict when each assumes *errno* holds its error code.

We might argue that the correct way to solve this problem is to change the interface, say by having system calls return their error codes, as in the POSIX threads routines, or have threads call a separate function to retrieve the error code, as in Win-32. However, so that we don't break all existing Unix programs, we must keep the interface the way it is. An imperfect approach that works well enough in this instance is to redefine *errno* as a function call:

```
#define errno    _errno( )
```

We then modify the system-call library to store a thread's error code in some nonglobal location. The _errno function would then return what's stored in that particular location. However, we still have the problem of finding a location for each thread's private instance of *errno*.

POSIX threads provides a general mechanism for doing this known as *thread-specific data*. Win-32 has essentially the same mechanism, known there as *thread-local storage*. The idea behind both is that we associate with each thread some storage for its private use. Then we provide some means so that when a thread refers to, say, *errno*, it gets the instance of *errno* stored in this private storage. Thus we have some sort of naming mechanism so that when different threads executing the same code refer to *errno*, each gets its private instance.

POSIX does not specify how this private storage is allocated. It might be pre-allocated when the thread is created or perhaps created on demand. However, to understand how the interface works, think of this storage as being implemented as an array of *void* *, one array for each thread. To implement our naming mechanism we simply agree that *errno*, for example, appears at the same index within each array, as shown in Figure 2.7. Each instance of the data item is known as a *thread-specific* data item.

To settle on such an index (or *key*, as it is called in POSIX threads), one thread should call *pthread_key_create* to get a value for the key and store it someplace accessible to other threads, such as in a global variable. Each thread may then use the key to access its instance of the thread-specific data using the routines *pthread_setspecific* to set its value and *pthread_getspecific* to get its value:

```
int errno_key;   // global

void startup ( ) {
   // executed by only one thread
   ...
   pthread_key_create(&errno_key, 0);
   ...
}

int write(...) {   // wrapper in the system-call library
   int err = syscallTrap(WRITE, ...);   // the actual trap into the
   kernel
   if (err)
      pthread_setspecific(errno_key, err);
   ...
}

#define errno pthread_getspecific(errno_key)
   // make things easy to read and type
void IOfunc( ) {
   if (write(fd, buffer, size) == -1) {
      if (errno == EIO)
         fprintf(stderr, "IO problems ...\n");
      ...
      return(0);
   }
   ...
}
```

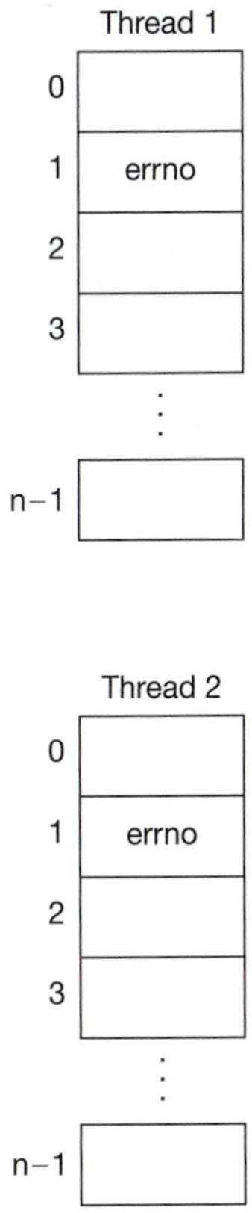

FIGURE 2.7
Thread-specific data.

Note that *pthread_key_create* takes two parameters. The first is an output parameter indicating where the key should be stored. The second, if not zero, is the address of a cleanup routine (of type *void (*)(void *)*) called when each thread terminates that has used *pthread_setspecific* on the key.

This is useful in situations similar to the following in which storage is allocated when thread-specific data is initialized:

```
#define cred      pthread_getspecific(cred_key)
pthread_key_t cred_key;

mainline( ) {
   ...
   pthread_key_create(&cred_key, free_cred);
```

```
        while (more_requests) {
          ...
          pthread_create(&thread, 0, server_start, request);
        }
    }

    void *server_start(void *req) {
      cred_t *credp;

      credp = (cred_t *)malloc(sizeof(cred_t));
      ...
      pthread_setspecific(cred_key, credp);
      ...
      handle_request(req);
      ...
      return(0);
    }

    handle_request(req_t req) {
      ...

      if (credentials_valid(req, cred))
        perform(req);

      ...
    }

    void free_cred(cred_t *credp) {
      ...
      free(credp);
    }
```

Here we have a server application in which a new thread is created to handle each incoming request. Let's assume that along with each request some sort of credentials are established. Storage is allocated to hold these credentials, and a pointer to this storage is placed in the thread-specific data item whose key is given by *cred_key*. We've defined *cred* as a shortcut for accessing this data via *pthread_getspecific*. To make certain that the storage allocated to hold the credentials is released when the thread terminates, we define *free_cred* to be the cleanup function, via the call to *pthread_key_create*. Thus when each thread terminates, it calls *free_cred*.

Win-32's *thread-local-storage* mechanism is nearly identical to POSIX's thread-specific data.

Another thread-safety issue arises in the use of static local storage in the socket library used for networking. Below is a rough outline of *gethostbyname*, the routine used to get the address of a computer on the Internet:

```
    struct hostent *gethostbyname(const char *name) {
      static struct hostent hostent;
```

```
    ... // lookup name; fill in hostent

    return(&hostent);
}
```

Here we have the same sort of problem as with *errno*: there is a conflict if multiple threads call *gethostbyname* at once, since each will expect to see its result in the same location, the static local variable *hostent*. This problem is solved in the Win-32 version of the routine by the use of thread-local storage. POSIX threads treats this differently: a new version of *gethostbyname*, called *gethostbyname_r*, is defined in which the caller passes as an output argument the location at which the result should be stored.

A final problem is the use by multiple threads of library code that has shared access to data. A good example is the C standard I/O library, comprised of such routines as *printf*, *fgets*, and so forth. These routines share data structures describing and containing I/O buffers. Thus all threads calling *printf* buffer their output in the same buffer. To avoid problems, we must provide a mutex to synchronize access. Rather than making us do this manually, POSIX-threads and Win-32 implementations supply a special thread-safe version of the standard-I/O library providing appropriate synchronization along with the threads library.

2.2.5 DEVIATIONS

In our discussion so far, a thread's execution can be directly affected by others only when it's using a synchronization construct. The only thing others can do to a thread's execution is delay it; they can't force it to do something more drastic, such as terminate. In a number of situations, however, we'd like more to be possible; in particular, forcing another thread to terminate cleanly could be very useful.

Unix programmers have traditionally used Unix's *signal* mechanism to get a thread to deviate from its normal execution path, whether to handle some sort of event or to notify it of an exception. Win-32 doesn't provide a signal mechanism, but, as we argue below, it's not really necessary.

POSIX threads includes a *cancellation* mechanism by which one thread can request the clean termination of another. Win-32 does not include such a mechanism; it does provide techniques so that programmers can implement some of this functionality, though by no means as conveniently as in POSIX.

2.2.5.1 Unix Signals

Unix signals are a mechanism by which various sorts of actions trigger the operating system to interrupt a thread and immediately terminate or suspend it (and its process) or force it to put aside what it's doing, execute a prearranged handler for the action, then go back to what it was doing earlier. This is much the way that interrupts are handled in the operating system (see Chapter 3). Typical actions that can cause signals are typing special characters on the keyboard (such as Ctrl-C), timer expirations, explicit signals sent by other threads (via the *kill* system call) and program exceptions (arithmetic and addressing errors). For all but exception handling, signals are an artifact of the days of exclusively single-threaded programs. For exception handling, they are best thought of as a means for implementing language-specific mechanisms (something that C is sorely lacking).

The original intent of signals was to force the graceful termination of a process. For example, if you type the "interrupt" key, usually Ctrl-C, a SIGINT signal is sent to the currently running process. (To be precise, it's sent to the group of processes indicated as the foreground processes for the terminal.) If this process hasn't done anything special to deal with the signal, the operating system automatically and immediately terminates it.

A process might set up a handler to be invoked when such a signal is delivered, as shown below:

```
int main( ) {
    void handler(int);
    sigset(SIGINT, handler);

    /* long-running buggy code */
    ...
}

void handler(int sig) {
    /* perform some cleanup actions */
    ...
    exit(1);
}
```

The call to *sigset* in *main* causes *handler* to be registered as the signal handler for the SIGINT signal. Thus if you run this program and decide to terminate it early by typing Ctrl-C, a SIGINT signal is delivered to the process, causing it to put aside its current state and call *handler*; *handler* performs some cleanup actions (perhaps writing some key data to a file) and then terminates the process.

Signals can also be used as a means for communicating with a process, perhaps requesting it to do something:

```
computation_state_t state;

int main( ) {
    void handler(int);

    sigset(SIGINT, handler);

    long_running_procedure( );
}

long_running_procedure( ) {
    while (a_long_time) {
        update_state(&state);
        compute_more( );
    }
}

void handler(int sig) {
    display(&state);
}
```

In this code the *main* procedure establishes a handler for SIGINT, and then calls *long_running_procedure*, which might execute for several days. Occasionally the user of the program wants to check to see what the program is doing, so she or he types Ctrl-C, which generates a signal causing the (single) thread to enter *handler*, print out that state (being maintained in *state* of some unspecified type *computation_state_t*), and then return back to *long_running_procedure*.

The above code might appear at first glance to be problem-free, but there is unsynchronized access to the data structure *state* within *update_state* and *display*. One might be tempted to use a mutex to synchronize access to *state*, but the situation here is different from what we have been assuming earlier: there is only one thread. Suppose that thread has locked the mutex within *update_state*, and then receives a signal and invokes *handler*. If it now attempts to lock the mutex within *display*, it will deadlock, since the mutex it is trying to lock is already locked (by itself).

Before we try to fix this problem, let's make sure we understand it. The issue is that the occurrence of a signal has forced the thread out of its normal flow of control and made it execute code (the signal handler) that interferes with what it was doing before the signal. This is similar to interthread synchronization issues, but we have only one thread. We discussed in Section 2.2.4 above the notion of thread-safe routines — procedures that a thread can execute without concern about interaction with other threads. Is there something analogous for signal handlers? There is, and such routines are said to be *async-signal safe*.

Operations on mutexes certainly are not async-signal safe, nor are dynamic-storage operations such as *malloc* and *free* — what if a thread in the middle of *malloc* gets interrupted by a signal whose handler calls *free*? The POSIX 1003.1 spec specifies well over sixty procedures that must be async-signal safe (including *fork*, *_exit*, *open*, *close*, *read*, *write*, and *sem_post*, but not *sem_wait*). Before reading on, you might think about what it takes for a procedure to be async-signal safe.

What can we do in our example to make *display* async-signal safe? We can make certain that any code that it might interfere with cannot be interrupted by a signal. In particular, we need to make certain that the thread cannot be interrupted by a signal while it's in *update_state*. This can be done as follows:

```
computation_state_t state;
sigset_t set;

int main( ) {
    void handler(int);

    sigemptyset(&set);
    sigaddset(&set, SIGINT);
    sigset(SIGINT, handler);

    long_running_procedure( );
}

long_running_procedure( ) {
    while (a_long_time) {
        sigset_t old_set;
        sigprocmask(SIG_BLOCK, &set, &old_set);
        update_state(&state);
        sigprocmask(SIG_SETMASK, &old_set, 0);
        compute_more( );
```

```
      }
   }

   void handler(int sig) {
      display(&state);
   }
```

Here, by using the routine *sigprocmask*, we block occurrences of SIGINT while the thread is inside *update_state*. This routine operates on signal sets, which are bit vectors representing sets of signals. We initialize such a set in *main*, first setting it to be the empty set, then adding SIGINT to it. Then, in *long_running_procedure*, we pass the set to *sigprocmask* as its second argument. The first argument, SIG_BLOCK, instructs the operating system to add the signals in the second argument to the current set of blocked signals, and to return the prior set of blocked signals in the set pointed to by the third argument. We call *sigprocmask* again to restore the set of blocked signals to its prior value.

Although this solves our problem, in many implementations of Unix *sigprocmask* is implemented as a system call and is thus somewhat expensive to use.[9] Another issue is that the notion of blocking signals so as to prevent unwanted interaction with signal handlers is completely orthogonal to thread-based synchronization and adds a fair amount to the complexity of programs, making bugs more likely.

The reason this notion of asynchronous signals and signal handlers was necessary in Unix was that processes used always to be single-threaded. With multithreaded processes, there's no need to interrupt a thread to handle the event that caused the signal: we can simply dedicate a thread to handling the event.

How are signals handled in multithreaded processes? The first issue is that signals, as used in Unix, are sent to processes, not threads. In single-threaded processes it was obvious which thread would then handle the signal. But in multithreaded processes, it's not so clear. In POSIX threads the signal is delivered to a thread chosen at random.

Another issue is the set of blocked signals. Should one such set affect all threads in a process, or should each thread have its own set? Since threads add and remove signals to and from this set to protect their own execution, it makes sense for each thread to have its own blocked-signal set.

We can now clarify the POSIX rules for delivering signal to a multithreaded process: the thread that is to receive the signal is chosen randomly from the set of threads that do not have the signal blocked. If all threads have the signal blocked, then the signal remains pending until some thread unblocks it, at which point the signal is delivered to that thread.

With this definition of how signals are handled in multithreaded processes, we revisit our example.

```
   computation_state_t state;
   sigset_t set;
   pthread_mutex_t mut = PTHREAD_MUTEX_INITIALIZER;

   int main( ) {
      pthread_t thread;
```

---

[9] Solaris implements *sigprocmask* cheaply, not as a system call, and thus our example would work well on that system. Indeed, Solaris takes this a step further and blocks signals cheaply while threads are in a number of procedures such as *printf,* making them async-signal safe, even though POSIX doesn't require it.

```
        sigemptyset(&set);
        sigaddset(&set, SIGINT);
        pthread_sigmask(SIG_BLOCK, &set, 0);
        pthread_create(&thread, 0, monitor, 0);
        long_running_procedure( );
}

long_running_procedure( ) {
    while (a_long_time) {
        sigset_t old_set;
        pthread_mutex_lock(&mut);
        update_state(&state);
        pthread_mutex_unlock(&mut);
        compute_more( );
    }
}

void *monitor( ) {
    int sig;
    while (1) {
        sigwait(&set, &sig);
        pthread_mutex_lock(&mut);
        display(&state);
        pthread_mutex_unlock(&mut);
    }
    return(0);
}
```

In this variant of our example, the first thread blocks SIGINT. It uses *pthread_sigmask* rather than *sigprocmask*. The former is nominally for use by threads in multithreaded processes, though its effect is exactly the same as that of *sigprocmask*. This first thread then calls *pthread_create* to create a new thread, which starts execution in *monitor*. One property of *pthread_create* is that the new thread's set of blocked signals is copied from its creator. Thus the new thread starts in *monitor* with SIGINT blocked.

Inside *monitor* we have something new: a call to *sigwait*. This causes the calling thread to wait until a signal mentioned in the first argument occurs.[10] Which signal did occur is then returned in storage pointed to by the second argument. This seems like (and is) a rather simple call, but it has a pretty powerful effect: signals such as SIGINT are no longer handled asynchronously, resulting in the interruption of some thread so that the handler can be called, but are now handled synchronously: a thread simply waits for the signal to delivered, then deals with it. So now we can protect access to *state* simply by using a mutex.

Let's review what we've done with signals. The signal mechanism really has two parts: the generation of a signal, caused by the occurrence of some sort of event, and the delivery of the

---

[10] There is some ambiguity about what happens if a thread is waiting for a signal within *sigwait* and other threads have the signal unblocked. To insure that the only thread that deals with the signal is the one in *sigwait*, we block the signal for all threads.

signal to a thread. We've done nothing to modify the Unix treatment of the first. What we have done is to change the second drastically. No longer does the delivery of a signal force a thread to put aside what it's doing and call a signal handler. Unless we employ the appropriate signal blocking, this can be dangerous. Instead, we treat signal handling by threads as input processing: a thread simply waits for input (the notification that a signal has been delivered to it) and then deals with the signal. This is a simple programming model and lacks the additional complexity of traditional signal handling.

This makes it clear how Microsoft was able to avoid the notion of signals in its Win-32 interface. Since Win-32 applications are multithreaded, individual threads can be dedicated to dealing with the sort of events that would cause signals in Unix.

2.2.5.2 POSIX Cancellation

An annoying aspect of many programs is that, if you mistakenly start a lengthy operation, you can't cancel it in mid-operation — you must let it run to completion. The reason for this might simply be that the developer was inconsiderate of the program's users, but it could also be that the software packages used lacked sufficient support for early termination. This is particularly likely with multithreaded programs, which might contain a number of threads whose execution we wish to terminate, perhaps in response to a request to terminate the entire program, or because the chores being performed by these threads are no longer needed.

Of course, we can't simply terminate a thread at some arbitrary point in its execution, since doing so might leave a mutex locked or leave a data structure in some indeterminate state. Consider the following procedure, executed by a thread to insert an item at the beginning of a doubly linked list:

```
void insert(list_item_t *item) {
    pthread_mutex_lock(&list_mutex);
    item->backward_link = list_head;
    item->forward_link = list_head.forward_link;
    if (list_head.forward_link != 0)
        list_head.forward_link->backward_link = item;
    list_head.forward_link = item;
    pthread_mutex_unlock(&list_mutex);
}
```

If the thread executing this procedure were forced to terminate in the middle, not only would *list_mutex* be left in the locked state, but the item being inserted would end up partially inserted, with just some of the necessary links updated. Any future operations on the list are doomed to failure: not only will no other threads be able to lock the mutex, but the list itself is now malformed. If we adopt a mechanism allowing one thread to terminate another, we need to insure that procedures such as *insert* are atomic — once their execution begins, they must be allowed to run to completion.

Suppose the thread we wish to terminate has performed some actions whose effect must be undone if the thread does not run to completion. For example, the code below is executed by a thread that's gathering data and adding it to a list, using the above *insert* procedure.

```
list_item_t list_head;

void *GatherData(void *arg) {
```

```
    list_item_t *item;
    item = (list_item_t *)malloc(sizeof(list_item_t));
    GetDataItem(&item->value);
    insert(item);
    return(0);
}
```

The *GetDataItem* routine might take a long time to execute, so it might be necessary to force the termination of the thread while it's in that routine. But if the thread is terminated, we should let it clean up after itself: in particular, it should free the storage that's been allocated for the list item.[11] Thus another requirement we must make of any termination mechanism is that it should support such cleanup.

The POSIX feature providing all this is *cancellation*. Cancellation gives us what is essentially a means for one thread to raise an exception in another that will be handled when the target thread is at a safe point in its execution. (C, of course, has no exception mechanism. C++ does, but unfortunately there is no portable means for treating the POSIX-threads notion of cancellation as a C++ exception. However, see the description of the Brown C++ Threads package (Doeppner 1995).) Though POSIX requires a thread to terminate soon after incurring such an exception, it can first execute any number of cleanup routines.

One thread may request another to terminate by calling *pthread_cancel*, with the target thread's ID as the sole argument. The target is marked as having a *pending cancel* whose effect depends on the cancellation state set up in the target. Cancellation may be either *enabled* or *disabled*. If the latter, the cancel is at least temporarily ignored, though the thread is marked as having a pending cancel. If cancellation state is *enabled*, then what happens depends on whether the *cancel type* is set to asynchronous or deferred. If it's asynchronous, then the thread immediately acts on the cancel. Otherwise (*cancel type* is deferred), the thread ignores the cancel until it reaches a *cancellation point* in its execution, when it then acts on the cancel. The intent is that such cancellation points correspond to points in the thread's execution at which it is safe to act on the cancel.

When the thread does act on a cancel, it first walks through a stack of cleanup handlers it has previously set up, invoking each of them. It then terminates. The thread that executed *pthread_cancel* in the first place does not wait for the cancel to take effect, but continues on. If desired, it may call *pthread_join* to wait for the target to terminate.

Now for the details: threads have cancellation enabled and deferred when they are created. To change the cancellation state, a thread calls *pthread_setcancelstate* with two arguments. The first, an integer, is either PTHREAD_CANCEL_DISABLE or PTHREAD_CANCEL_ENABLE. The second is a pointer that, if not null, points to an integer into which the thread's cancellation state prior to the call is stored. To change the cancellation type, a thread calls *pthread_setcanceltype*, also with two arguments. The first, an integer, is either PTHREAD_CANCEL_ASYNCHRONOUS or PTHREAD_CANCEL_DEFERRED. The second is a pointer that, if not null, points to an integer into which the thread's cancellation type prior to the call is stored.

---

[11] The alert reader might argue that we wouldn't have this cleanup problem if the storage for *item* were allocated after *GetDataItem* returns. But let's assume that *malloc* is called first to insure that the resources required to hold the item exist before the data is obtained.

POSIX specifies that following routines are cancellation points:

• aio_suspend	• open	• sigtimedwait
• close	• pause	• sigwait
• creat	• pthread_cond_wait	• sigwaitinfo
• fcntl[12]	• pthread_cond_timedwait	• sleep
• fsync	• pthread_join	• system
• mq_receive	• pthread_testcancel	• tcdrain
• mq_send	• read	• wait
• msync	• sem_wait	• waitpid
• nanosleep	• sigsuspend	• write

If a thread has a pending cancel and its cancellation type is deferred, than the cancel won't be acted upon unless the thread calls or is already in one of these cancellation points. Thus, for example, if a thread is waiting for input within *read*, on receipt of a cancel it quits the read call and immediately begins to act on the cancel.

Knowing what these cancellation points are, you should be careful with their use: you need to be certain that when a thread calls any such routine with cancellation enabled, it's safe for the thread to be terminated. Note that *pthread_mutex_lock* is not on the list. This allows you to use it freely without being certain that it's safe for the thread to terminate while it's waiting to lock a mutex. This is particularly important if a thread is holding one lock while waiting for another. Conversely, if there's a point in a program that you know is safe for cancellation, you can have the thread call *pthread_testcancel*, which does nothing if there is no pending cancel.

A thread's cancellation cleanup handlers are organized as a stack. A thread might push a cleanup handler on the stack when it enters a module for which cleanup is necessary, and then pop it off the stack on exit. When the thread acts on a cancel, it pops the handlers off the stack, invoking each one as it does, until the stack is empty, at which point the thread terminates.

To push a handler onto the stack, a thread calls *pthread_cleanup_push*, which takes two arguments. The first is a pointer to the routine being pushed as the cleanup handler, a routine whose type is *void (*)(void *)* (that is, a pointer to function with a single *void ** argument, returning *void*). The second argument is the value (of type *void **) that's passed to this routine when it's called. To pop the handler off the stack, the thread calls *pthread_cleanup_pop*, which takes one argument, called the *execute flag*. If it's zero, the handler is simply popped off the stack. If it's one, not only is it popped off the stack, but the thread also invokes it, passing it the argument registered in the original call to *pthread_cleanup_push*.

This is already a bit complicated, but there's more. The two routines *pthread_cleanup_push* and *pthread_cleanup_pop* are required to be "lexicographically scoped," meaning that each call to *pthread_cleanup_push* must have a unique matching call to *pthread_cleanup_pop*. In other words, you must treat them as if they were left and right parentheses and thus keep them balanced. The intent presumably was to make them clearly delineate their scope, but the effect can often be annoying, for instance when your module has multiple exit points at which you'd like to call *pthread_cleanup_pop* at each, but may not. Note that most implementations enforce this rule by implementing the routines as macros: *pthread_cleanup_push* contains an unmatched "{" and *pthread_cleanup_pop* contains an unmatched "}".

As an example of *pthread_cleanup_push* and *pthread_cleanup_pop*'s use, let's revisit our *GatherData* routine above. This time we add a cleanup handler.

---

[12] Only when F_SETLCKW is the command.

```
list_item_t list_head;

void *GatherData(void *arg) {
    list_item_t *item;
    item = (list_item_t *)malloc(sizeof(list_item_t));
    pthread_cleanup_push(free, item);
    GetDataItem(&item->value);
    pthread_cleanup_pop(0);
    insert(item);
    return(0);
}
```

We've added calls to *pthread_cleanup_push* and *pthread_cleanup_pop* so that, if the thread is cancelled while in *GetDataItem*, the storage it had allocated for *item* will be freed. Note that *malloc* and *insert* contain no cancellation points, so there's no danger, assuming the thread's cancellation type is deferred, of the thread acting on a cancel within them.

We know that *pthread_cond_wait* is a cancellation point. Normally a thread won't return from it until it has locked the mutex given as the second argument. What should it do if a cancel is acted upon within it? Consider the following:

```
pthread_mutex_lock(&mutex);
pthread_cleanup_push(CleanupHandler, argument);
while(should_wait)
    pthread_cond_wait(&cv, &mutex);

// . . . (code containing other cancellation points)

pthread_cleanup_pop(0);
pthread_mutex_unlock(&mutex);
```

What should *CleanupHandler* do? We want to make certain that if the thread acts on a cancel anywhere between the push and the pop, the mutex will end up unlocked. If we are assured the mutex is always locked on entry to *CleanupHandler*, we can simply unlock it there. But if, when a thread acts on a cancel within *pthread_cond_wait*, it does not lock the mutex, then there will be uncertainty within *CleanupHandler* whether the mutex is locked or unlocked. So, by insisting that a thread, when acting on a cancel within *pthread_cond_wait*, first lock the mutex, then perform its cleanup actions, we enable it to do the cleanup safely. Thus we can code our example as follows:

```
pthread_mutex_lock(&mutex);
pthread_cleanup_push(pthread_mutex_unlock, &mutex);
while(should_wait)
    pthread_cond_wait(&cv, &mutex);

// . . . (code containing other cancellation points)

pthread_cleanup_pop(1);        // unlock the mutex
```

Note that we take advantage of the execute flag to *pthread_cleanup_pop* by popping the handler off the stack and calling it at the same time.

We have one final word of caution concerning the use of cancellation in C++ programs. Consider the following C++ program fragment:

```
void tcode( ) {
    A a1;
    pthread_cleanup_push(handler, 0);
    subr( );
    pthread_cleanup_pop(0);
}

void subr( ) {
    A a2;
    pthread_testcancel( );
}
```

If the thread calling *tcode* has a pending cancel when it calls *subr*, it acts on it within *pthread_testcancel*. Since it has a cleanup handler in the calling scope (within *tcode*), it should leave *subr*, invoking the destructors for the objects local to *subr* (in particular, for *a2*). If it has no additional handlers other than the one pushed in *tcode*, it then terminates without calling the destructor for *a1*. So, the first thing to note is that if it is important for a destructor for a local object to be called as part of a thread's termination, that object must be in the scope of at least one of the cleanup handlers. You should also check to make certain that such automatic cleanup is indeed supported by the C++ system being used. If the above example is compiled and run with g++ (the Gnu C++ compiler), using a release up through at least 2.96, the destructors for neither *a1* nor *a2* are called — a result that is definitely a bug.

2.3 CONCLUSIONS

The purpose of this chapter was not just to teach you how to write a multithreaded program, but also to introduce various important operating-systems issues. The concerns include both how threads are implemented (which we cover in Chapter 5) and how multithreaded programming is used within operating systems (which we cover in Chapter 4). Experience gained from writing multithreaded programs, whether with POSIX threads, Win-32, or some other system, will help you appreciate much of what's discussed in following chapters on the inner workings of operating systems.

2.4 EXERCISES

Note: A number of programming exercises, with source code, are available at the book's web site, http://www.wiley.com/college/Doeppner.

1. Consider the following procedure, written in C:
   ```
   unsigned int count = 0;
   const int iterations = 1000000000; // one billion

   unsigned int incr(void) {
       int i;
       for (i=0; i<iterations; i++)
   ```

```
        count++;
    return count;
}
```

Suppose *incr* is executed concurrently by ten threads, all sharing the global variable *count*. Each thread calls *incr*, then prints the value returned. If the execution of threads is not time-sliced, i.e., each thread runs until it voluntarily yields the processor, what values should be printed by each thread? Can you characterize the values printed if thread execution is time-sliced? Run such a program on your own computer. Is the execution of threads time-sliced? (Make sure that heavy optimization is turned off in the C compiler, otherwise it might figure out that the *for* loop can be replaced with a simple assignment!) (If your computer has more than one processor, this simple test won't work.)

2. Assuming that the execution of threads on your computer is time-sliced, what is the cost of this time-slicing in terms of the time required for the operating system to do it? To find out, write a procedure that does a certain amount of work performing a lengthy computation, such as the repeated addition in Exercise 1 above. Then compare the time taken by one thread doing all the work with the time taken by ten threads each doing one-tenth of the work. What can you say about the cost of time-slicing? How does the number of processors on your computer affect your result?

3. Redo exercise 1, above, but this time use a mutex to synchronize access to *count*. Employ one mutex shared by all threads; lock it before incrementing count and unlock it afterwards (i.e., lock and unlock the mutex inside the loop, not outside). Compare the running time with that of Exercise 1. What can you say about the cost of mutexes?

*** 4.** The following program, from (Peterson 1981), is a means, implemented without any special hardware or operating-system support, for two threads to have mutually exclusive access to a region of data or code. Each thread calls *peterson* with its own ID, which is either 0 or 1. It assumes that each thread is running on a separate processor and that the memory holding the shared variables is *strictly coherent*, meaning that a store into a memory location by one processor will be seen by the other processor if it does a load from that location immediately thereafter.

```
unsigned int count = 0;              // shared

void *peterson(void *arg) {
    int me = (int)arg;
    static int loser;                // shared
    static int active[2] = {0, 0}; // shared
    int other = 1-me;                // private
    int i;

    for (i=0; i<iterations; i++) {
        active[me] = 1;
        loser = me;
        while (loser == me && active[other])
            ;
```

```
                count++;    // critical section
                active[me] = 0;
        }
        return(0);
}
```

The variables *loser* and *active* are shared by both threads, the other variables are private to each of the threads (i.e., each has its own copy). The idea is that the *active* array is a pair of flags, one for each thread, that the thread sets to indicate that it has entered the "critical section," in which the shared variable *count* is incremented. Each thread, before entering the critical section, sets its entry in *active*, then checks the other thread's entry to see if that thread is already in the critical section. If so, the thread waits, by repeatedly checking the array. Of course, it is possible that both threads attempt to enter at the same time. This is where the *loser* variable comes in: after setting its *active* entry to 1, a thread sets *loser* to its own ID. If both threads are attempting to enter the critical section, *loser*'s value will be the ID of just one of the two threads. That thread must yield to the other.

a. Write a program that tests whether this algorithm works. To do so, have two threads call *peterson*, with *iterations* set to a large number, such as two billion. If the code correctly provides mutual exclusion, then the final value of count will be twice the value of *iterations*. If not, it will be less. Explain why.

b. Modern shared-memory multiprocessor computers (including computers employing multicore chips) do not have strictly coherent memory. Instead, the effect of stores to memory is delayed a bit: when one processor stores a value into a memory location, loads by other processors might not retrieve the new value until after a few clock cycles (though loads by the processor performing the store will retrieve the new value, since it is in that processor's memory cache). Explain why *peterson* does not always work correctly on modern share-memory multiprocessors.

* **5.** The following solution to the producer-consumer problem is from (Lamport 1977). It works for a single producer and a single consumer, each running on a separate processor on a shared-memory multiprocessor computer.

```
char buf[BSIZE];
int in = 0;
int out = 0;

void producer(char item) {
        while(in-out == BSIZE)
                ;
        buf[in%BSIZE] = item;
        in++;
        return;
}

char consumer(void) {
```

```
        char item;
        while(in-out == 0)
                ;
        item = buf[out%BSIZE];
        out++;
        return(item);
}
```

It is easy to see how this works if you first assume that integers can be of arbitrary size. Thus *in* counts the number of bytes produced and *out* counts the number of bytes consumed. The difference between the two, *in – out*, is the number of bytes in the buffer. The solution continues to work even if integers are finite, as long as they can hold values larger than BSIZE (you might try to verify this, but you may assume it is correct for the questions below).

a. Does this solution to the producer-consumer problem work, even if memory has the delayed-store property of Exercise 4b?

b. Some shared-memory multiprocessors have even weaker memory semantics. Normally we expect that if a processor stores into location A, then into location B, and then another processor loads from A and then B, then if the second processor observes the store into B, it must also have observed the store into A. In other words, we expect the order of stores by one processor to be seen by the other processors. However, consider a system with two memory units. A is in one of them; B is in the other. It may be that the unit holding A is extremely busy, but the one holding B is not. Thus it is conceivable that the store into A will be delayed longer than the store into B, and thus other processors will see B updated before A. Suppose our computer has this "reordered store" property. Will Lamport's solution to the producer-consumer problem necessarily work on such a computer? Explain.

* **6.** Consider the following implementation of *pthread_cond_wait* and *pthread_cond_signal*. Assume that each condition variable (an item of type *pthread_cond_t*) contains a semaphore that is initialized to 0.

```
pthread_cond_wait(pthread_cond_t *c, pthread_mutex_t *m) {
    pthread_mutex_unlock(m);
    sem_wait(c->sem);
    pthread_mutex_lock(m);
}

pthread_cond_signal(pthread_cond_t *c) {
    sem_post(c->sem);
}
```

Is this implementation correct? (We are concerned only with the "normal" functioning of condition variables; we are not concerned about cancellation and interaction with signal handlers.) Explain. Does this give you any insight into why operations on condition variables are specified as they are?

2.5 REFERENCES

Dijkstra, E. W. (1968). The Structure of the "THE"-Multiprogramming System. *Communications of the ACM* **11**(5): 341–346.

Dijkstra, E. W. (undated: early 1960s). Multiprogrammering en de X8, at http://userweb.cs.utexas.edu/users/EWD/ewd00xx/EWD57.PDF

Doeppner, T. W. (1987). *Threads: A System for the Support of Concurrent Programming,* Brown University, at http://www.cs.brown.edu/~twd/ThreadsPaper.pdf

Doeppner, T. W. (1996). *The Brown C++ Threads Package,* Brown University, at http://www.cs.brown.edu/~twd/c++threads.pdf

Lamport, L. (1977). Proving the Correctness of Multiprocess Programs. *IEEE Transactions on Software Engineering* **SE-3**(2): 125–143.

Peterson, G. L. (1981). Myths About the Mutual Exclusion Problem. *Information Processing Letters* **12**(3): 115–116.

Basic Concepts

This chapter covers a number of basic concepts that, though not unique to operating systems, are essential for much of what comes later. We start with the architectural issues involved in context switching: subroutine, thread, user/privileged, and normal/interrupt-mode switching. We then discuss some other architectural issues: memory caches and basic I/O architecture. Finally, we briefly go over the software concepts of dynamic storage allocation and of program linking and loading.

We use the somewhat nebulous term "context" to mean the setting in which execution is currently taking place. This setting determines what information, in the form of storage contents, is available. For example, when a thread is executing within a procedure, it has available to it the procedure's local variables as well as all its process's global variables. When a thread has invoked a method of some object, then not only are local and global variables available, but so are instance variables. When a thread makes a system call, the processor switches from user mode to privileged mode and the thread switches from user context to system context — information within the operating system is now available to it. Note that these contexts overlap: for instance, a thread in a user context or the system context enters and exits numerous procedure contexts.

We also think of a thread itself as a context. It's the processor that's in a thread context and can switch among different contexts. If an interrupt occurs, the processor switches from the thread context (or perhaps another interrupt context) into an interrupt context. Thus when a process starts execution in *main*, the processor is running in a thread context, which is running in a user context within the context of *main*.

In the remainder of this section we examine the mechanisms for switching among contexts, focusing on switches from procedure to procedure, from thread to thread, from user to system and back, and from thread to interrupt and back.

3.1

CONTEXT SWITCHING

3.1.1 PROCEDURES

The following code illustrates a simple procedure call in C:

```
int main( ) {
    int i;
    int a;


    . . .

    i = sub(a, 1);
    . . .

    return(0);
}


int sub(int x, int y) {
  int i;
  int result = 1;
  for (i=0; i<y; i++)
   result *= x;
  return(result);
}
```

The purpose of the procedure *sub* is pretty straightforward: it computes x^y. How the context is represented and is switched from that of *main* to that of *sub* depends on the architecture. The context of *main* includes any global variables (none in this case) as well as its local variables, *i* and *a*. The context of *sub* also includes any global variables, its local variables, *i* and *result*, and its arguments, *x* and *y*. On most architectures, global variables are always found at a fixed location in the address space, while local variables and arguments are within the current stack frame.

3.1.1.1 Intel x86 Stack Frames

Figure 3.1 is a general depiction of the stack on the Intel x86 architecture. Associated with each incarnation of a subroutine is a *stack frame* that contains the arguments to the subroutine, the *instruction pointer* (in register *eip*) of the caller (i.e., the address to which control should return when the subroutine completes), a copy of the caller's *frame pointer* (in register *ebp*), which links the stack frame to the previous frame, space to save any registers modified by the subroutine, and space for *local variables* used by the subroutine. Note that these frames are of variable size — the size of the space reserved for local data depends on the subroutine, as does the size of the space reserved for registers.

The frame pointer register *ebp* points into the stack frame at a fixed position, just after the saved copy of the caller's instruction pointer (note that lower-addressed memory is towards the bottom in the figure). The subroutine does not change the value of the frame pointer, except setting it on entry to the subroutine and restoring it on exit. The stack pointer *esp* always points to the last item on the stack — new allocations, say for arguments to be passed to the next procedure, are performed here. Note that register *eax*, used for the return value of procedures, is expected to be modified across calls and is thus not saved.

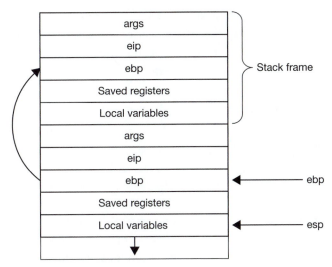

FIGURE 3.1 Intel x86 stack frames.

The picture above is idealized: not all portions of the stack frame are always used. For example, registers are not saved if the subroutine doesn't modify them, the frame pointer is not saved if it's not used, etc. For more details, see the Intel architecture manuals (http://www.intel.com/design/processor/manuals/253665.pdf).

Here's possible unoptimized assembler code for the above C code:[1]

```
main:
    ; enter main, creating a new stack frame
    pushl  %ebp              ; Push frame pointer onto the stack;
                             ; this means that the contents of the
                             ; stack-pointer register (esp) are
                             ; reduced by 4 so that esp points to
                             ; next lower word in the stack, then
                             ; the contents of the frame-pointer
                             ; register (ebp) are stored there.
    movl   %esp, %ebp        ; Set frame pointer to point to new
                             ; frame: the address of the current end
                             ; of the stack (in register esp) is
                             ; copied to the frame-pointer register.
    pushl  %esi              ; Save esi register: its contents are
                             ; pushed onto the stack.
    pushl  %edi              ; Save edi register: its contents are
                             ; pushed onto the stack.
    subl   $8, %esp          ; Create space for local variables (i
```

---

[1] We use the syntax of the Gnu assembler. It's similar to that of the Microsoft assembler (masm) except in the order of arguments: in the Gnu assembler, the first argument is the source and the second is the destination; in the Microsoft assembler, the order is reversed.

```
                                       ; and a): this is done by reducing the
                                       ; stack-pointer register (esp) by 8,
                                       ; thus lowering the end of the stack
                                       ; by 2 words.

     … ; other code that uses esi and edi registers

     ; set up the call to sub

     ; the arguments are pushed onto the stack in reverse order
     pushl  $1                         ; Push argument two onto the stack.
     movl   -4(%ebp), %eax             ; Put local variable a (argument
                                       ; number one) into eax register.
     pushl  %eax                       ; Push eax onto stack, thus pushing
                                       ; argument two onto the stack.
     call   sub                        ; Call the subroutine sub: push eip
                                       ; (instruction pointer) onto stack and
                                       ; then set eip to address of sub:
                                       ; thus the program branches to sub.
     addl   $8, %esp                   ; The call to sub has returned;
                                       ; pop arguments from stack by simply
                                       ; increasing the stack-pointer
                                       ; register's value by 8: thus the two
                                       ; words that were at the "top" of the
                                       ; stack are no longer on the stack.
     movl   %eax, -8(ebp)              ; Store sub's return value into i:
                                       ; this value was returned in register
                                       ; eax; store this value in the second
                                       ; word from the beginning of the stack
                                       ; frame (that is, 8 bytes less than
                                       ; the address contained in register
                                       ; ebp).

     …

     movl   $0, %eax                   ; Set main's return value to 0.
     ; leave main, removing stack frame
     popl   %edi                       ; Restore edi register: at this point
                                       ; the word at the end (top) of the
                                       ; stack is the saved contents of
                                       ; register edi; the popl instruction
                                       ; copies this value into register edi,
                                       ; then increases the value of esp, the
                                       ; stack-pointer register, by 4, thereby
```

```
                            ; removing the word from the stack.
    popl    %esi            ; Restore esi register.
    movl    %ebp, %esp      ; Restore stack pointer: recall that
                            ; its original value was saved in the
                            ; frame-pointer register (ebp).
    popl    %ebp            ; Restore frame pointer.
    ret                     ; Return: pop end of stack into eip
                            ; register, causing jump back to
                            ; caller.


sub:
    ; enter sub, creating new stack frame
    pushl   %ebp            ; Push frame pointer.
    movl    %esp, %ebp      ; Set frame pointer to point to new
                            ; frame.
    subl    $8, %esp        ; Allocate stack space for local
                            ; variables.

                            ; At this point the frame pointer
                            ; points into the stack at the
                            ; saved copy of itself; the two
                            ; arguments to sub are at locations
                            ; 8 and 12 bytes above this location.
    ; body of sub
    movl    $1, -4(%ebp)    ; Initialize result: the value one is
                            ; stored in the stack frame at the
                            ; location reserved for result.
    movl    $0, -8(%ebp)    ; Initialize i: the value zero is
                            ; stored in the stack frame at the
                            ; location reserved for i.
    movl    -4(%ebp), %ecx  ; Put result in ecx register.
    movl    -8(%ebp), %eax  ; Put i in eax register.
beginloop:
    cmpl    12(%ebp), %eax  ; Compare i with y (i is in the eax
                            ; register; y is in the stack 12
                            ; bytes above the location pointed
                            ; to by the frame-pointer register
                            ; (ebp)).
    jge     endloop         ; Exit loop if i >= y ("jge" means
                            ; "jump on greater than or equal"
                            ; and refers to the result of the
                            ; previous comparison).
    imull   8(%ebp), %ecx   ; Multiply result (in ecx register) by
```

```
                                    ; x ("imull" means "integer multiply").
        addl    $1, %eax            ; Add 1 to i.
        jmp     beginloop           ; Go to beginning of for loop.
endloop:
        movl    %ecx, -4(%ebp)      ; Store ecx back into result.
        movl    -4(%ebp), %eax      ; Load result in return register (eax).
        ; leave sub, removing stack frame
        movl    %ebp, %esp          ; Pop local variables off of stack.
        popl    %ebp                ; Pop frame pointer.
        ret                         ; Return: pop word at end of stack
                                    ; into eip register, causing jump
                                    ; back to caller.
```

3.1.1.2 SPARC Stack Frames

Note: this section may be skipped by readers with no interest in the SPARC architecture. It is provided as an example to show the differences between a RISC (reduced-instruction-set computer) architecture and a CISC (complex-instruction-set computer) architecture.

Sun's SPARC (Scalable Processor ARChitecture) is a RISC (reduced-instruction-set computer). Its architecture manual can be found at http://www.sparc.com/standards/V8.pdf. We cover here just the details of the SPARC architecture that are relevant to subroutine-calling conventions. As shown in Figure 3.2, the SPARC has nominally 32 registers arranged in four groups of eight — *input registers*, *local registers*, *output registers*, and *global registers*. Two of the input registers serve the special purposes of a *return address register* and a *frame pointer*, much like the corresponding registers on the Intel x86. One of the output registers is the *stack pointer*. Register 0 (of the global registers) is very special — when read it always reads 0 and when written it acts as a sink.

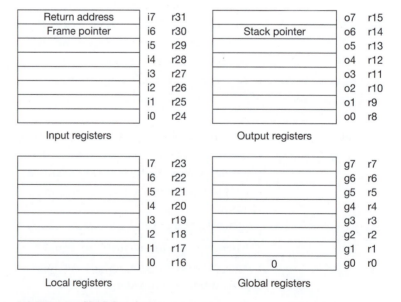

FIGURE 3.2   SPARC registers.

As its subroutine-calling technique the SPARC uses *sliding windows*: when a subroutine is called, the caller's output registers become the callee's input registers. Thus the register sets of successive subroutines overlap, as shown in Figure 3.3.

Any particular implementation of the SPARC has a fixed number of register sets (of eight registers apiece) — seven in Figure 3.3. As long as we do not exceed the number of register sets, subroutine entry and exit are very efficient — the input and local registers are effectively saved (and made unavailable to the callee) on subroutine entry, and arguments (up to six) can be efficiently passed to the callee. The caller just puts outgoing arguments in the output registers and the callee finds them in its input registers.

Returning from a subroutine involves first putting the return value in a designated input register, i0. In a single action, control transfers to the location contained in i7, the return address register, and the register windows are shifted so that the caller's registers are in place again.

However, if the nesting of subroutine calls exceeds the available number of register sets, then subroutine entry and exit are not so efficient. The register windows must be copied to an x86-like stack (see Figure 3.4). As implemented on the SPARC, when an attempt is made to nest subroutines more deeply than the register windows can handle, a *window-overflow trap* occurs and the operating system must copy the registers to the thread's stack and reset the windows (privileged instructions are required to access the complete set of on-chip registers). Similarly, when a subroutine

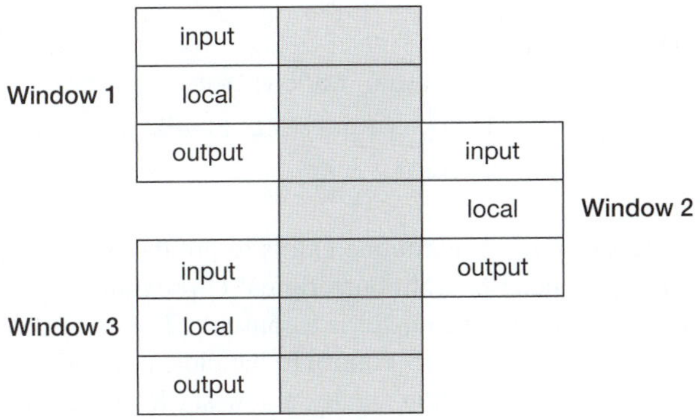

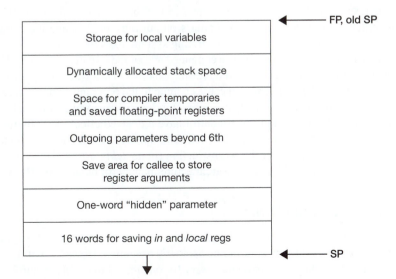

FIGURE 3.3   SPARC sliding windows.

FIGURE 3.4   SPARC stack frame.

return encounters the end of the register windows, a *window-underflow trap* occurs and the operating system loads a new set of registers from the values stored on the thread's stack.

The actual code generated for calling, entering, and exiting a procedure is:

```
main:
    ld      [%fp-8], %o0    ! Put local variable a into o0
                            ! register as 1st param.
    mov     1, %o1          ! Put 2nd parameter into o1 register.
    call    sub             ! Call sub.
    nop
    st      %o0, [%fp-4]    ! Store result into local variable i.
    ...


sub:
    save    %sp, -64, %sp   ! Push a new stack frame.

    ...


    ret                     ! Return to caller.
    restore                 ! Pop frame off stack (in delay
                            ! slot).
```

The first step in preparing for a subroutine call is to put the outgoing parameters into the output registers. The first parameter *a,* from our original C program, is a local variable and is found in the stack frame. The second parameter is a constant. The *call* instruction merely saves the program counter in *o7* and then transfers control to the indicated address.

In the subroutine, the *save* instruction creates a new stack frame and advances the register windows. It creates the new stack frame by taking the old value of the stack pointer (in the caller's *o6*), subtracting from it the amount of space that is needed (64 bytes in this example), and storing the result into the callee's stack pointer (*o6* of the callee). At the same time, it also advances the register windows, so that the caller's output registers become the callee's input registers. If there is a window overflow, the operating system takes over.

Inside the subroutine, the return value is computed and stored into the callee's *i0*. The *restore* instruction pops the stack and backs down the register windows. Thus what the callee put in *i0* is found by the caller in *o0*. The *ret* instruction causes a jump to the program counter, saved in *i7*.

Note that the order of the *ret* and *restore* instructions is reversed from what one might expect: instructions that cause a transfer of control have a delayed effect, since by the time the transfer takes place, the processor has already fetched and executed the next instruction. Thus the *restore* instruction is placed after the *ret* instruction (in its *delay slot*) and is executed before control returns to the caller. See the SPARC architecture manual for details (SPARC 1992).

3.1.2 THREADS AND COROUTINES

Our notion of threads is that they are independent of one another and, except for synchronization and cancellation, don't directly control one another's execution. However, within the implementation of a threads package it may be necessary for one thread to transfer control directly to another, yielding the processor to the other without invoking the operating system. This sort of direct transfer of control from one thread to another is known as *coroutine* linkage. A thread's context is mainly represented by its stack, but its register state is also important, such as the current value of the stack pointer. Let's assume that this and other components of its context are stored in a data structure we call the *thread control block*.

Switching between thread contexts turns out to be very straightforward, though it can't be expressed in most programming languages. We have an ordinary-looking subroutine, *switch*. A thread calls it, passing the address of the control block of the thread to whose context we wish to switch. On entry to the subroutine the caller's registers are saved. The caller saves its own stack pointer (SP) in its control block. It then fetches the target thread's stack pointers from its control block and loads it into the actual stack pointer. At this point, we have effectively switched threads, since we are now executing on the target thread's stack. All that has to be done now is to return — the return takes place on the target thread's stack.

To make this easier to follow, let's work through what happens when some thread switches to our original thread: it will switch to the original thread's stack and execute a return, in the context (on the stack) of the original thread. Thus, from the point of view of the original thread, it made a call to *switch*, which didn't appear to do much but took a long time.

Assuming that the global variable *CurrentThread* points to the control block of the current thread, the code for *switch* looks like:

```
void switch(thread_t *next_thread) {
    CurrentThread->SP = SP;
    CurrentThread = next_thread;
    SP = CurrentThread->SP;
    return;

}
```

On an Intel x86, the assembler code would be something like the following. Assume SP is the offset of the stack pointer within a thread control block.

```
switch:
    ; enter switch, creating new stack frame
    pushl   %ebp                        ; Push frame pointer.
    movl    %esp, %ebp                  ; Set frame pointer to point to new
                                        ; frame.
    pushl   %esi                        ; Save esi register
    movl    CurrentThread, %esi         ; Load address of caller's
                                        ; control block.
    movl    %esp, SP(%esi)              ; Save stack pointer in control block.
    movl    8(%ebp), CurrentThread      ; Store target thread's
                                        ; control block address
                                        ; into CurrentThread.
    movl    CurrentThread, %esi         ; Put new control-block
                                        ; address into esi.
    movl    SP(%esi), %esp              ; Restore target thread's stack pointer.
                                        ; we're now in the context of the target thread!
    popl    %esi                        ; Restore target thread's esi register.
    popl    %ebp                        ; Pop target thread's frame pointer.
    ret                                 ; Return to caller within target thread.
```

Performing such a coroutine switch on the SPARC architecture requires a bit more work, since at the moment the *switch* routine is called, the on-chip register windows contain the calling thread's registers. The operating system must be called explicitly (via a system call) to produce the effect of a window-overflow trap, forcing the register windows to be written to the calling thread's stack. Then when *switch* returns in the context of the target thread, a window-underflow trap occurs and the target thread's registers are loaded from its stack.

Thus the assembler code on the SPARC would be something like the following, assuming *CurrentThread* is kept in global register *g0*:

```
switch:
    save      %sp, -64, %sp         ! Push a new stack frame.
    t         3                     ! Trap into the OS to force window
                                    ! overflow.
    st        %sp, [%g0+SP]         ! Save CurrentThread's SP in control
                                    ! block.
    mov       %i0, %g0              ! Set CurrentThread to be target
                                    ! thread.
    ld        [%g0+SP], %sp         ! Set SP to that of target thread
    ret                             ! return to caller (in target thread's
                                    ! context).
    restore                         ! Pop frame off stack (in delay slot).
```

3.1.3 SYSTEM CALLS

System calls involve the transfer of control from user code to system (or kernel) code and back again. Keep in mind that this does not involve a switch between different threads — the original thread executing in user mode merely changes its execution mode to kernel (privileged) mode. However, it is now executing operating-system code and is effectively part of the operating system.

Most systems provide threads with two stacks, one for use in user mode and one for use in kernel mode. Thus when a thread performs a system call and switches from user mode to kernel mode, it also switches from its user-mode stack to its kernel-mode stack.

For an example, consider a C program running on a Unix system that calls *write* (see Figure 3.5). From the programmer's perspective, *write* is a system call, but a bit more work needs to be done before we enter the kernel. *Write* is actually a routine supplied in a special library of (user-level) programs, the C library. *Write* is probably written in assembler language; the heart of it is some instruction that causes a trap to occur, thereby making control enter the operating system. Prior to this point, the thread had been using the thread's user stack. After the trap, as part of entering kernel mode, the thread switches to using the thread's kernel stack. Within the kernel our thread enters a fault-handler routine that determines the nature of the fault and then calls the handler for the *write* system call.

3.1.4 INTERRUPTS

When an interrupt occurs, the processor puts aside the current context (that of a thread or another interrupt) and switches to an interrupt context. When the interrupt handler is finished, the processor generally resumes the original context. Interrupt contexts require stacks; which stack is used? There are a number of possibilities: we could allocate a new stack each time an interrupt occurs, we could have one stack that is shared by all interrupt handlers, or the interrupt handler could borrow a stack from the thread it is interrupting.

```
prog( ) {                    write( ) {
  . . .                        . . .
  write(fd, buffer, size);   trap(write_code);
  . . .                        . . .
}                            }
```

prog frame
write
↓

User stack

User
_____
Kernel

```
trap_handler(code) {

  . . .

  if(code == write_code)
    write_handler( );

  . . .

}
```

trap_handler frame
write_handler frame
↓

Kernel stack

FIGURE 3.5   System-call flow.

The first technique, allocating a stack, is ruled out for a number of reasons, not least that it is too time-consuming, though a variant is used in Solaris, as discussed below. Both the latter two approaches are used. A single system-wide interrupt stack was used on DEC's VAX computers;[2] in most other architectures the interrupt handler borrows a stack (the kernel stack) from the thread that was interrupted (see Figure 3.6). If another interrupt handler was interrupted, its context is saved on the current stack, and that stack continues to be used for the new interrupt handler.

On those systems on which multiple interrupt handlers use the same stack, perhaps one borrowed from a thread, interrupt handlers must execute differently from normal thread execution. Because there is just one shared stack, there is just one interrupt context. We cannot suspend the execution of one handler and resume the execution of another: the handler of the most recent interrupt must run to completion. Then, when it has no further need of the stack, the handler of the next-most-recent interrupt completes its execution, and so forth.

That the execution of an interrupt handler cannot be suspended is significant because it means that interrupt handling cannot yield to anything other than higher-priority interrupts. For example, on a uniprocessor system, if interrupt handler 2 interrupts interrupt handler 1 and then wakes up a high-priority thread that must immediately respond to an event, the thread cannot run until all interrupt handling completes, including that of interrupt handler 1.

If we could somehow give each interrupt handler its own stack, we wouldn't have this problem. Solaris, as well as some real-time systems, has preallocated stacks for each possible interrupt level. Thus each has its own independent context and can yield to other processing, just as threads can. We discuss this in greater detail in Chapter 5. Most other general-purpose systems do not support this style of architecture.

Another approach to getting interrupt handlers to yield to other execution is that the handler places a description of the work that must be done on a queue of some sort, then arranges for it to be done in some other context at a later time. This approach, which is used in many systems including Windows and Linux, is also discussed in Chapter 5.

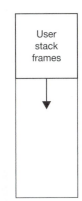

Current thread's
user stack

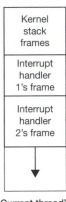

Current thread's
kernel stack

FIGURE 3.6   Interrupt handlers and stacks.

_____
[2] Multiprocessor versions of the VAX had one interrupt stack per processor.

An important property of interrupts is that they can be *masked*, i.e., temporarily blocked. If an interrupt occurs while it is masked, the interrupt indication remains pending; once it is unmasked, the processor is interrupted. How interrupts are masked is architecture-dependent, but two approaches are common. One approach is that a hardware register implements a bit vector — each bit represents a class of interrupts. If a particular bit is set, then the corresponding class of interrupts is masked. Thus the kernel masks interrupts by setting bits in the register. When an interrupt does occur, the corresponding mask bit is set in the register and cleared when the handler returns — further occurrences of that class of interrupts are masked while the handler is running.

What's more common are hierarchical interrupt levels. Each particular device issues interrupts at a particular level. The processor masks interrupts by setting an *interrupt priority level* (IPL) in a hardware register: all devices whose interrupt level is less than or equal to this value have their interrupts masked. Thus the kernel masks a class of interrupts by setting the IPL to a particular value. When an interrupt does occur and the handler is invoked, the current IPL is set to that of the device, and restored to its previous value when the handler returns.

3.2 INPUT/OUTPUT ARCHITECTURES

In this section we give a high-level, rather simplistic overview of common I/O architectures. Our intent is to provide just enough detail to discuss the responsibilities of the operating system in regard to I/O, but without covering the myriad arcane details of device management. To do this, we introduce a simple I/O architecture we have used in the past at Brown University for operating system projects.

A very simple architecture is the *memory-mapped* architecture: each device is controlled by a controller and each controller contains a set of registers for monitoring and controlling its operation (see Figure 3.7). These registers appear to the processor to occupy physical memory locations. In reality, however, each controller is connected to a *bus*. When the processor wants to access or modify a particular location, it broadcasts the address on the bus. Each controller listens for a fixed set of addresses and, when one of its addresses has been broadcast, attends to what the processor wants to have done, e.g., read the data at a particular location or modify the data at a particular location. The memory controller, a special case, passes the bus requests to the actual primary memory. The other controllers respond to far fewer addresses, and the effect of reading and writing is to access and modify the various controller registers.

There are two categories of devices, *programmed I/O* (PIO) devices and *direct memory access* (DMA) devices. PIO devices do I/O by reading or writing data in the controller registers one byte or word at a time. In DMA devices the controller itself performs the I/O: the processor puts a description of the desired I/O operation into the controller's registers, then the controller takes over and transfers data between a device and primary memory.

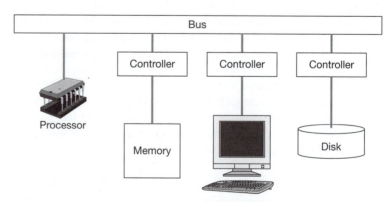

FIGURE 3.7 Simple I/O architecture.

Our architecture supports both PIO and DMA devices. The default configuration has one PIO device (a terminal) and one DMA device (a disk). Each PIO device has four registers: *Control*, *Status*, *Read*, and *Write*, each one byte in length (see Figure 3.8). Each DMA device also has four registers: *Control*, *Status*, *Memory Address*, and *Device Address* (Figure 3.9). The control and status registers are each one byte long; the others are four bytes long (they hold addresses). Certain bits of the control registers are used to start certain functions, as shown in Figure 3.8 and Figure 3.9. Bits of the status registers are used to indicate whether the associated controller is ready or busy.

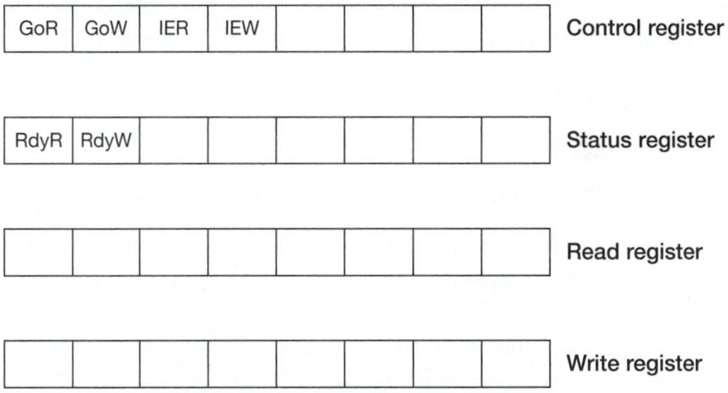

Legend: GoR Go read (start a read operation)
         GoW Go write (start a write operation)
         IER Enable read-completion interrupts
         IEW Enable write-completion interrupts
         RdyR Ready to read
         RdyW Ready to write

FIGURE 3.8 PIO registers.

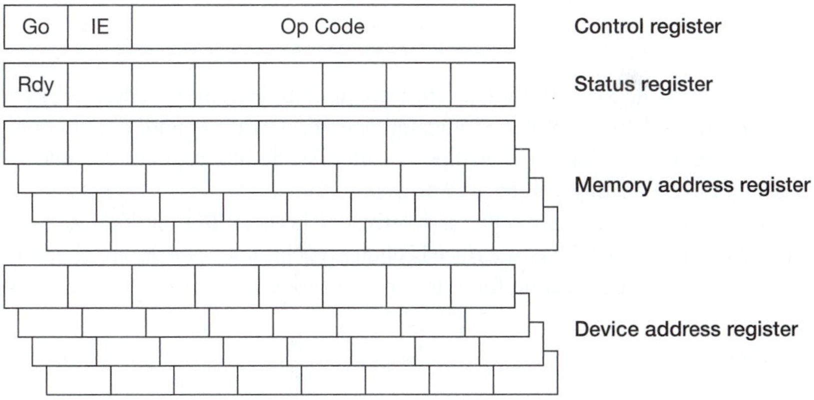

Legend: Go   Start an operation
         Op Code Operation code (identifies the operation)
         IE   Enable interrupts
         Rdy   Controller is ready

FIGURE 3.9 DMA registers.

Communicating with a PIO device is simple, though a bit laborious. For instance, to write one byte to the simulator's terminal device, you perform the following operations:

1. Store the byte in the *write register*.

2. Set the GoW bit in the *control register*.

3. Wait for RdyW bit (in the *status register*) to be set.

Rather than repeatedly checking the status register to determine if the RdyW bit has been set, you can request that an interrupt occur when it is set (indicating that the byte has been written). To do this, you set the IEW bit in the control register at the same time you set the GoW bit.

Communicating with a DMA device is a bit less laborious: the controller does the work. For example, to write the contents of a buffer to the disk you do the following:

1. Set the disk address in the *device address register*.

2. Set the buffer address in the *memory address register*.

3. Set the Op Code (Write), and the Go and IE bits in the *control register*.

The operation is complete when the IE bit is set, which it will be after the interrupt.

Most operating systems encapsulate device-specific details like those outlined above in collections of modules known as *device drivers*. These provide a standard interface to the rest of the operating system, which can then treat I/O in a device-independent manner.

If an operating system were written in C++, a device driver would be a class, with an instance for each device. We might have a base class for disks, with different types of disks being derived classes. The base class would have declarations of virtual functions for a standard disk interface, while the derived class would supply the actual definitions. A class declaration for a simple disk driver supporting a strictly synchronous interface might look like:

```
class disk {
public:
    virtual status_t read(request_t);
    virtual status_t write(request_t);
    virtual status_t interrupt( );
};
```

Within the operating system, threads (perhaps user threads in the midst of system calls) would call *read* and *write* to perform the indicated operation, waiting until completion. When an interrupt occurs, the driver's interrupt method is called in the interrupt context and, when warranted, releases a thread waiting within *read* or *write*.

Even in operating systems providing a strictly synchronous I/O interface to users, such as Sixth-Edition Unix, the internal driver interface is often asynchronous (we discuss this in Chapter 4). Thus a more realistic class declaration for a driver might look like:

```
class disk {
public:
    virtual handle_t start_read(request_t);
    virtual handle_t start_write(request_t);
    virtual status_t wait(handle_t);
    virtual status_t interrupt( );
};
```

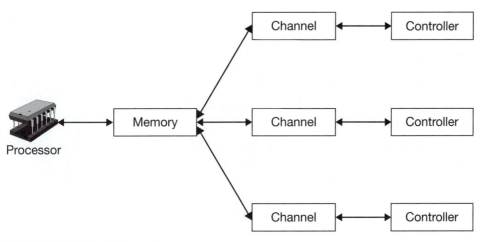

FIGURE 3.10   I/O with channels.

In this version, the *start_read* and *start_write* methods return a handle identifying the operation that has started. A thread can, at some later point, call *wait* with the handle and wait until that operation has completed. Note that multiple threads might call *wait* with the same handle if all must wait for the same operation (for example, if all need the same block from a file).

A more sophisticated approach to I/O used in what are commonly called "mainframe" computers is to employ specialized I/O processors to handle much of the I/O work. This is particularly important in large data-processing applications where I/O costs dominate computation costs. These I/O processors are traditionally called *channels* and execute programs in primary storage called *channel programs* (see Figure 3.10).

Storage allocation is a very important concern in operating systems. Whenever a thread is created, its stacks, control block, and other data structures must be allocated; whenever a thread terminates, these data structures must be freed. Since there are numerous other such dynamic data structures, both inside the operating system and within user applications, this allocation and liberation of storage must be done as quickly as possible.

The classic reference for most of this material is Donald Knuth's *The Art of Computer Programming, Vol. 1: Fundamental Algorithms*. In this section we summarize Knuth's results and discuss some additional operating-system concerns.

| **3.3** |
| **DYNAMIC** |
| **STORAGE** |
| **ALLOCATION** |

3.3.1 BEST-FIT AND FIRST-FIT ALGORITHMS

We start with the general problem of maintaining a pool of available memory and allocating variable-size quantities from it. Following Knuth (this is his example), consider the memory pool in Figure 3.11 that has two blocks of free memory, one 1300 bytes long and the other 1200 bytes long. We'll try two different algorithms to process series of allocation requests. The first is called *first fit* — an allocation request is taken from the first area of memory that is large enough to satisfy the request. The second is called *best fit* — the request is taken from the smallest area of memory that is large enough to satisfy the request.

FIGURE 3.11   Pool of free storage.

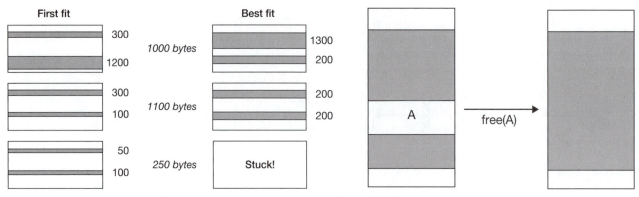

FIGURE 3.12 Allocations using first fit and best fit.

FIGURE 3.13 Liberating storage.

On the principle that whatever requires the most work must be best, one might think that best fit is the algorithm of choice. However, Figure 3.12 illustrates a case in which first fit behaves better than best fit. We first allocate 1000 bytes. Under the first-fit approach (on the left), this allocation is taken from the topmost region of free memory, leaving behind a region of 300 bytes of still unallocated memory. With the best-fit approach (right), this allocation is taken from the bottommost region of free memory, leaving behind a region of 200 bytes of still unallocated memory. The next allocation is for 1100 bytes. Under first fit, we now have two regions of 300 bytes and 100 bytes. Under best fit, we have two regions of 200 bytes. Finally, there is an allocation of 250 bytes. First fit leaves behind two regions of 50 bytes and 100 bytes, but best fit cannot handle the allocation — neither remaining region is large enough.

Clearly one can come up with examples in which best fit performs better. However, Knuth's simulation studies have shown that, on the average, first fit works best. Intuitively, the reason for this is that best fit tends to leave behind a large number of regions of memory that are too small to be useful, as in Figure 3.12.

The liberation of storage is more difficult than its allocation, for the reason shown in Figure 3.13 (another example from Knuth). Here the shaded regions are unallocated memory. The region of storage A separating the two unallocated regions is about to be liberated. We'd like this to produce one large region of unallocated storage rather than three smaller adjacent regions. Thus the liberation algorithm must be able to determine if adjacent storage regions are allocated or free. An algorithm could simply walk through the list of free storage to determine if the adjacent areas are free, but a much cheaper approach is to tag the boundaries of storage regions to indicate whether they are allocated or free. Knuth calls this the *boundary-tag* method and provides an algorithm for it.

The shortcomings of best fit illustrate a common issue in storage management: *fragmentation*. What we saw here is called *external fragmentation*, in which we end up with lots of small areas of storage that collectively are sizeable, but individually are too small to be of use. In the following sections we encounter *internal fragmentation*, in which storage is wasted because more must be allocated than is needed.

3.3.2 BUDDY SYSTEM

The buddy system is a simple dynamic storage allocation scheme that works surprisingly well. Storage is maintained in blocks whose sizes are powers of two. Requests are rounded up to the smallest such power greater than the request size. If a block of that size is free, it's taken; otherwise, the smallest free block larger than the desired size is found and split in half — the two halves are called *buddies*. If the size of either buddy is what's needed, one of them is allocated (the other remains free). Otherwise one of the buddies is split in half. This splitting continues until the appropriate size is reached.

Liberating a block is now easy: if the block's buddy is free, you join the block being liberated with its buddy, forming a larger free block. If this block's buddy is free, you join the two of them, and so forth until the largest free block possible is formed.

One bit in each block, say in its first or last byte, is used as a tag to indicate whether the block is free. Determining the address of a block's buddy is simple. If the block is of size 2^k, then the rightmost $k-1$ bits of its address are zeros. The next bit (to the left) is zero in one buddy and one in the other; so you simply complement that bit to get the buddy's address.

Turning this into a data structure and algorithm is pretty straightforward. We maintain an array of doubly linked lists of free blocks, one list for each power of two. Free blocks are linked together using fields within them (which certainly aren't being used for anything else). See (Knuth 1968) for details.

3.3.3 SLAB ALLOCATION

Many kinds of objects in operating-system kernels are allocated and liberated frequently. Allocation involves finding an appropriate-sized area of storage, then initializing it, i.e., initializing various pointers or setting up synchronization data structures. Liberation involves tearing down the data structures and freeing the storage. If, for example, the storage space is allocated using the buddy system and the size of the objects is not a power of two, there's a certain amount of loss due to internal fragmentation. Further, a fair amount of time overhead may arise from initialization and tearing down.

Slab allocation (Bonwick 1994) is a technique in which a separate cache is set up for each type of object to be managed. Contiguous sets of pages called *slabs* are allocated to hold objects. Whenever a slab is allocated, a constructor is called to initialize all the objects it holds. Then as objects are allocated, they are taken from the set of existing slabs in the cache. When objects are freed, they are simply marked as such and made available for reallocation without freeing their storage or tearing them down. Thus new objects can be allocated cheaply. When storage is given back to the kernel (either because there are too many free objects or because the kernel requests storage due to a system-wide storage shortage), entire slabs are returned and each object in them is appropriately torn down.

A further benefit of slab allocation is "cache coloring": if all instances of an object are aligned identically, then all occupy the same cache lines and thus only one (or only a few, depending on the cache) can be in the cache at once. However, we can make successive slabs start the run of objects at different offsets from the beginning of the slab. Runs starting at such different offsets are said to have different colors; thus different-colored objects can be in the cache at the same time.

Linking and loading are apparently simple concepts that involve amazing complexity. They entail piecing together programs from their various components and adjusting addresses used in the resulting program so they refer to what the programmer intended.

| 3.4 |
| **LINKING AND** |
| **LOADING** |

We discuss the basic concepts of linking and loading here; for details on specific systems see http://msdn.microsoft.com/en-us/library/ms809762.aspx for Microsoft's Portable Execution (PE) format and http://dlc.sun.com/pdf/816-1386/816-1386.pdf for Sun's version of executable and linking format (ELF). Both are supported on Linux.

3.4.1 STATIC LINKING AND LOADING

Let's examine what it takes to convert a program in C into code that is ready for execution on a computer. Consider the following simple program:

```
int main(int argc, char *[ ]) {
    return(argc);
}
```

Compiling it into x86 assembler language might produce:

```
main:
    pushl   %ebp                ; Push frame pointer.
    movl    %esp, %ebp          ; Set frame pointer to point to new
                                ; frame.
    movl    8(%ebp), %eax       ; Put argc into return register (eax).
    movl    %ebp, %esp          ; Restore stack pointer.
    popl    %ebp                ; Pop stack into frame pointer.
    ret                         ; Return: pop end of stack into eip.
```

If we run this code through an assembler and load it into our computer's memory starting at address 1000, say, we can then call it (with the stack pointer set correctly and the appropriate arguments on the stack), and it should do what was intended: return the value of *argc*. What's important is that its only reference to data was based on the value of register *ebp*, the frame pointer.

But now consider the following program:

```
int X=6;
int *aX = &X;

int main( ) {
    void subr(int);
    int y=X;
    subr(y);
    return(0);
}

void subr(int i) {
    printf("i = %d\n", i);
}
```

We don't need to look at the assembler code to see what's different: the machine code produced for it can't simply be copied to an arbitrary location in our computer's memory and executed. The location identified by the name *aX* should contain the address of the location containing *X*. But since the address of *X* is not known until the program is copied into memory, neither the compiler nor the assembler can initialize *aX* correctly. Similarly, the addresses of *subr* and *printf* are not known until the program is copied into memory — again, neither the compiler nor the assembler would know what addresses to use.

We might try solving this problem by always loading *main* at some standard location, such as 0. But suppose *subr* and the declaration for *X* are contained in a separate file. Sometime after it is compiled and assembled, the resulting code is combined with that of *main*. But it's only then, when the code is combined, that the locations of *X* and *subr* become known. Then, after we've determined the locations of *X* and *subr*, we must modify any references to them to contain their addresses. And, of course, we have to find the code for *printf* and include that in our program.

Modules such as *main* and *subr* that require modification of internal references to memory are said to be *relocatable*; the act of modifying such a module so that these references refer to the desired target is called *relocation*. The program that performs relocation is called a *loader*.

Let's now look at a slightly restructured version of our program and work things out in detail.

File *main.c*:

```
extern int X;
int *aX = &X;

int main( ) {
    void subr(int);
    int y = *aX;
    subr(y);
    return(0);
}
```

File *subr.c*:

```
#include <stdio.h>
int X;

void subr(int i) {
    printf("i = %d\n", i);
}
```

We might compile the program on Unix with the command:

```
cc -o prog main.c subr.c
```

This causes the contents of the two files to be compiled directly into machine code and placed in files *main.o* and *subr.o* (the o stands for "object file"). These files are then passed to the *ld* program (the Unix linker and loader), which combines them into an executable program that it stores in the file *prog*. Of course, it also needs the code for *printf*, which is found in a library file whose name is known to *ld*. The resulting file *prog* can be loaded into memory through the actions of one of the *exec* system calls; thus *prog* must indicate what goes into text, what goes into data, and how much space to reserve in BSS (see Section 1.3.2).

How does *ld* determine what is to be done? The file *main.c* contains references to two items defined elsewhere: *X* and *subr*. We had to declare *X* explicitly as defined elsewhere, while the fact that we've provided no definition for *subr* is an implicit indication that *subr* is defined elsewhere. As *ld* produces the executable *prog*, it must copy the code from *main.o* into it, adjusting all references to *X* and *subr* so that they refer to the ultimate locations of these things. Instructions for doing this are provided in *main.o*. What these entail is first an indication that *ld* must find definitions for *X* and *subr*. Then, once their locations are determined, the instructions must indicate which locations within *main.o* must be modified when copied to *prog*. Thus *main.o* must contain a list of external symbols, along with their type, the machine code resulting from compiling *main.c*, and instructions for updating this code.

To see what's going on, look at the result of compiling *main.c* into Intel x86 assembler code.

Offset	Op	Arguments	
0:	.data		; Initialized data follows.
0:	.globl	aX	; aX is global: it may be used by
			; others.
0:aX:			
0:	.long	X	
4:			
0:	.text		; Offset restarts; what follows
			; is text (read-only code).
0:	.globl	main	
0: main:			
0:	pushl	%ebp	; Save the frame pointer.
1:	movl	%esp,%ebp	; Set it to point to current
			; frame.
3:	subl	$4,%esp	; Make space for local variable y
			; on stack.
6:	movl	aX,%eax	; Put contents of X into register
			; eax.
11:	movl	(%eax),%eax	; Put contents of memory pointed
			; to by X into %eax.
13:	movl	%eax,-4(%ebp)	; Store *aX into y.
16:	pushl	-4(%ebp)	; Push y onto stack.
19:	call	subr	
24:	addl	$4,%esp	; Remove y from stack.
27:	movl	$0,%eax	; Set return value to 0.
31:	movl	%ebp, %esp	; Restore stack pointer.
33:	popl	%ebp	; Pop frame pointer.
35:	ret		
36:			

The code starts with an explicit directive to the assembler that what follows should be placed in the initialized data section. The *.globl* directive means that the following symbol (*aX*) is defined here, but may be used by other modules. Then we reserve four bytes of memory (a *long*), refer to it as *aX*, and indicate that its initial value is *X*, which is not further defined in this file. Next is a directive indicating that what follows should be placed in the text section, and that *main* is also a global symbol and can be used by others.

There are three locations requiring relocation. The reference to *X* in the data section must be replaced with the address where *X* is actually stored. The *movl* instruction at offset 6 in the text area contains a reference to *aX*. This must be replaced with the address of *aX*; the instruction occupies five bytes and this address goes into the upper four bytes, in other words, into the four bytes starting at offset 7. Similarly, the *call* instruction at offset 19 contains a reference to *subr*. This must be replaced with *subr*'s address: the instruction occupies five bytes and the address goes into the four bytes starting at offset 20. However, a peculiarity of the Intel x86 architecture is that such *call* instructions refer to their targets via "PC-relative" addressing. Thus what is stored at offset 20 is not the absolute address of *subr*, but its signed offset relative to the location of the instruction following the *call* (offset 24).

The result of compiling *subr.c* into Intel x86 assembler code is:

Offset	Op	Arguments	
0:	.data		; What follows is initialized data
0: printfarg:			
0:	.string "i = %d\n"		
8:			
0:	.comm	X,4	; 4 bytes in BSS is required for
			; global X.
4:			
0:	.text		; Offset restarts; what follows is
			; text (read-only code).
0:	.globl	subr	
0: subr:			
0:	pushl	%ebp	; Save the frame pointer.
1:	movl	%esp, %ebp	; Set frame pointer to point to
			; current frame.
3:	pushl	8(%ebp)	; Push *i* onto stack.
6:	pushl	$printfarg	; Push address of string onto stack.
11:	call	printf	
16:	addl	$8, %esp	; Pop arguments from stack.
19:	movl	%ebp, %esp	; Restore stack pointer.
21:	popl	%ebp	; Pop frame pointer
23:	ret		
24:			

This file specifies that one item goes into initialized data: *printfarg*, which is a constant used locally. Then *X* is defined as being *common*,[3] which means that it requires space in BSS. Within the text are the global symbol *subr* and a reference to the undefined symbol *printf*.

The object files produced by the assembler (or directly from the C code by the compiler) describe each of the three sections' data, BSS, and text. Along with each section is a list of global symbols, undefined symbols, and instructions for relocation. These instructions indicate which locations within the section must be modified and which symbol's value is used to modify the location. A symbol's value is the address that is ultimately determined for it; typically this address is added to the location being modified.

Here there are two locations requiring relocation. The *pushl* instruction at offset 6 contains a reference to *printfarg*, which must be replaced with the actual address. The instruction occupies five bytes and the address goes into the four bytes starting at offset 7. The *call* instruction at offset 11 contains a reference to *printf* that also must be replaced with the PC-relative address of *printf*'s final location. Again, the instruction occupies five bytes, and thus the address goes into the four bytes starting at offset 12.

So, in our example, *main.o*, the object file for *main*, would contain the following information.

---

[3] The term *common* originated in Fortran and meant essentially the same thing as global data in C. Initialized common was possible, but required additional syntax.

```
Data:
    Size:        4
    Global:      aX, offset 0
    Undefined:   X
    Relocation:  offset 0, size 4, value: address ofX
    Contents:    0x00000000

BSS:
    Size:        0

Text:
    Size:        36
    Global:      main, offset 0
    Undefined:   subr
    Relocation:  offset 7, size 4, value: address of aX
                 offset 20, size 4, value: PC-relative address of
                 subr
    Contents:    [machine instructions]
```

And *subr.o* would contain:

```
Data:
    Size:        8
    Contents:    "i = %d\n"

BSS:
    Size:        4
    Global:      X, offset 0

Text:
    Size:        44
    Global:      subr, offset 0
    Undefined:   printf
    Relocation:  offset 7, size 4, value: address of printfarg
                 offset 12, size 4, value: PC-relative address of
                 printf
    Contents:    [machine instructions]
```

Among the duties of *ld*, the linker-loader, is tracking down all the unresolved references. After it processes *main.o*, the unresolved references are *X* and *subr*. Its next input, *subr.o*, contains definitions for both, but has its own unresolved reference: *printf*. This and any other unresolved references are looked for in a list of libraries supplied to *ld*. We haven't supplied any libraries to it explicitly (we might, for example, have it look in the *pthreads* library if we were compiling a multithreaded program), but it always looks in the *standard C* library for anything not yet resolved. Here it finds *printf,* which, it turns out, contains its own unresolved reference: *write*. This is also in the standard C library, which is searched repeatedly for any unresolved references stemming from modules obtained from itself.

Assume the object code for *printf* is:

```
Data:
    Size:           1024
    Global:         StandardFiles
    Contents:       ...


BSS:
    Size:           256


Text:
    Size:           12000
    Global:         printf, offset 100
                    ...
    Undefined:      write
    Relocation:     offset 211, value: address of StandardFiles
                    offset 723, value: PC-relative address of write
    Contents:       [machine instructions]
```

Assume that the object code for *write* is:

```
Data:
    Size:           0


BSS:
    Size:           4
    Global:         errno, offset 0


Text:
    Size:           16
    Contents:       [machine instructions]
```

In addition, every C program contains a startup routine that is called first and then calls *main*. On return from *main*, this routine calls *exit*. Assume that its object code is:

```
Data:
    Size:           0


BSS:
    Size:           0


Text:
    Size:           36
    Undefined:      main
    Relocation:     offset 21, value main
    Contents:       [machine instructions]
```

The output of *ld* is an executable file, which is like an object file except that all references are fully resolved and no relocation is necessary. For our example, the executable file is *prog*. Based on its component object files, *ld* might set things up as follows:

Region	Symbol	Value
Text		
	main	4096
	subr	4132
	printf	4156
	write	16156
	startup	16172
Data		
	aX	16384
	printfargs	16388
	StandardFiles	16396
BSS		
	X	17420
	errno	17680

Note that *main* does not start at location 0: the first page is typically made inaccessible so that references to null pointers will fail. In order to make the text region read-only and the other regions read-write, the data region starts on the first (4096-byte) page boundary following the end of the text.

3.4.2 SHARED LIBRARIES

A drawback of the format of the executable files such as *prog* above is that they must contain everything needed for execution. This results in a fair amount of duplicate code. For example, almost every C program calls *printf*, and thus must contain a copy of it. All these copies of *printf* waste a huge amount of disk space. Furthermore, when each program is loaded into primary memory, the multiple copies of *printf* waste that memory too. What is needed is a means for programs to share a single copy of *printf* (and other routines like it).

Suppose we want just a single copy of *printf* on each computer. What is required to share it? If *printf* required no relocation, then sharing would be simple: we'd simply copy it from disk to primary memory when required, and every program using it could simply call it as needed. But *printf* does require relocation, so things aren't quite so simple.

One approach to sharing might be to have a single copy of *printf* on disk, shared by all programs. When a program using *printf* is loaded into memory, it then copies *printf* into its address space, performing the necessary relocation. This lets us reduce the disk wastage — there's just one disk copy — but every running program still has a private copy in memory.

A way to get around this problem is have all processes that use *printf* have it in the same location in their address spaces. Thus, for example, everyone might agree that if they use *printf*, they will put it at location 100,000 in their address spaces. We would "prerelocate" *printf* so that it works as long as it is placed in memory at location 100,000. This would let us have just one copy of *printf* in memory as well as on disk. Of course, if for some reason a program has something else at location 100,000, this won't work.

This technique of prerelocation has been used in some Unix systems and a form of it is currently used in Windows (see Exercise 9). If for some reason prerelocation does not work (say, because the intended location in the address space is taken), then the code is "rerelocated" to fit someplace else.

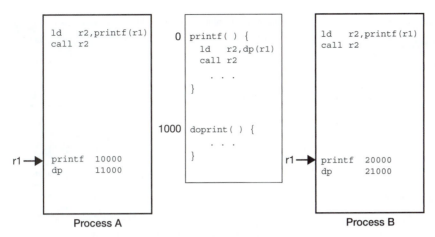

FIGURE 3.14 Position-independent code.

The final approach is to make relocation unnecessary, producing code that can be placed anywhere in memory without requiring modification. Such code is known as *position-independent code* or *PIC*. Some magic is required to make this work; the magic takes the form of indirection. PIC code does not contain any addresses; instead, it refers to process-specific tables that in turn contain addresses.

Figure 3.14 shows an example of position-independent code. Processes A and B are sharing the library containing *printf* (note that *printf* contains a call to another shared routine, *dp*), though they have it mapped into different locations. Each process maintains a private table, pointed to by register r1. In the table are the addresses of shared routines, as mapped into the process. Thus, rather than call a routine directly (via an address embedded in the code), a position-independent call is made: the address of the desired routine is stored at some fixed offset within the table. The contents of the table at this offset are loaded into register r2, and then the call is made via r2.

Shared libraries, whether implemented using prerelocation or with position-independent code, are used extensively in many modern systems. In Windows they are known as *dynamic-link libraries* (DLLs) and in Unix systems they are known as *shared objects*. An advantage of using DLLs and shared objects is that they need not be loaded when a program starts up, but can be loaded only if needed, thus reducing the start-up time of the program. A disadvantage is that their use can add to the complexity of a program, both through dependencies (DLL A uses code from DLL B, which uses code from DLL C, etc.) and from versioning (there's a new version of DLL B: is it compatible with my versions of DLLs A and C?).

We conclude this section with a detailed description of how shared objects are implemented on the x86 in ELF (executable and linking format), which is used on most Unix systems, including Linux, Solaris, FreeBSD, NetBSD, and OpenBSD, but not MacOS X. It is not used on Windows.

When a program is invoked via the *exec* system call, the code that is first given control is *ld.so* — the runtime linker. It does some initial set up of linkages, as explained shortly, and then calls the actual program code. It may be called upon later to do some further loading and linking, as explained below.

ELF requires three data structures for each dynamic executable (i.e., the program binary loaded by the *exec* system call) and shared object: the *procedure-linkage table*, the *global-offset table*, and the *dynamic structure*. To simplify discussion, we refer to dynamic executables and shared objects as *modules*. The procedure-linkage table contains the code that's actually called when control is to be transferred to an externally defined routine. It is shared by all processes using the associated executable or object, and uses data in the global-object table to link the

- **Procedure-linkage table**
  - shared, read-only executable code
  - essentially stubs for calling subroutines

- **Global-offset table**
  - private, read-write data
  - relocated dynamically for each process

- **Dynamic structure**
  - shared, read-only data
  - contains relocation info and symbol table

FIGURE 3.15 Data structures used by ELF to support shared objects.

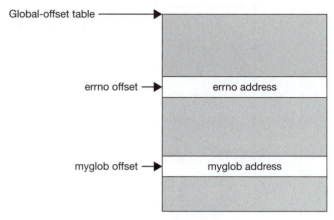

FIGURE 3.16 The global-offset table (GOT).

caller to the called program. Each process has its own private copy of each global-object table. It contains the relocated addresses of all externally defined symbols. Finally, the dynamic structure contains much information about each module. This is summarized in Figure 3.15.

To establish position-independent references to global variables, the compiler produces, for each module, a global-offset table (GOT). Modules refer to global variables indirectly by looking up their addresses in the table: a register contains the address of the table and modules refer to entries via their offsets. When the module is loaded into memory, *ld.so* is responsible for putting into it the actual addresses of all the needed global variables. When the program starts up, *ld.so* does this for the dynamic executable. As shared objects are loaded in (how and when this is done is covered soon), *ld.so* sets up their GOTs. Figure 3.16 shows an example in which *errno* and *myglob* are global variables whose locations are stored in global-offset-table entries.

Dealing with references to external procedures is considerably more complicated than dealing with references to external data. Figure 3.17 shows the procedure linkage table, global offset table, and relocation information for a module that contains references to external procedures *name1* and *name2*. Let's follow a call to procedure *name1*. The general idea is before the first call to *name1*, the actual address of the *name1* procedure is not recorded in the global-offset table. Instead, the first call to *name1* invokes *ld.so*, which is passed parameters indicating what is really wanted. It then finds *name1* and updates the global-offset table so that on subsequent calls *name1* is invoked more directly. To make this happen, references from the module to *name1* are statically linked to entry .PLT1 in the procedure-linkage table. This entry contains an unconditional jump to the address contained in the *name1* offset of the global-offset table (pointed to by register ebx). Initially this address is of the instruction following the jump instruction, which contains code that pushes onto the stack the offset of the *name1* entry in the relocation table.

The next instruction is an unconditional jump to the beginning of the procedure-linkage table, entry .PLT0. Here there's code that pushes onto the stack the contents of the second 32-bit word of the global-offset table, which contains a value identifying this module.

The following instruction is an unconditional jump to the address in the third word of the global-offset table, which is conveniently the address of *ld.so*. Thus control finally passes to *ld.so*, which looks back on the stack and determines which module has called it and what that module really wants to call. It figures this out using the module-identification word and the relocation table entry, which contains the offset of the *name1* entry in the global-offset table (which is what must be updated) and the index of *name1* in the symbol table (so it knows the name of what it must locate).

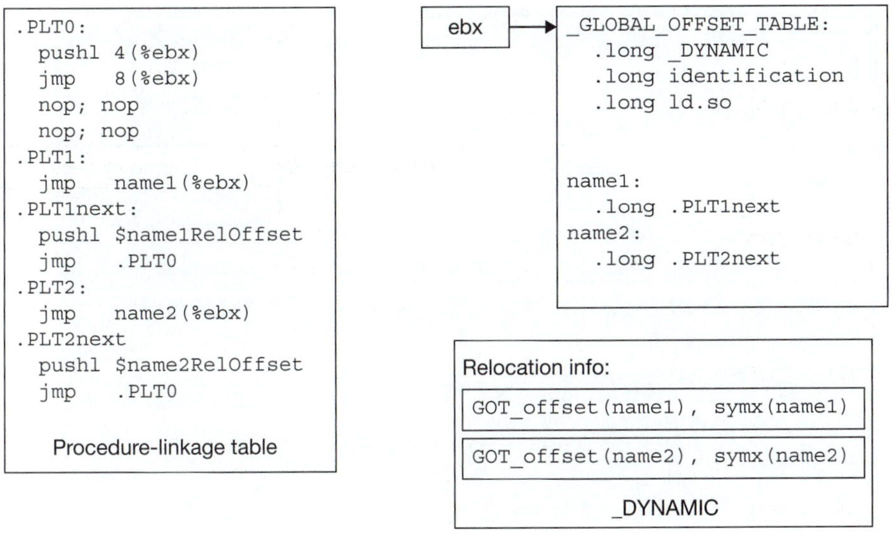

```
.PLT0:
  pushl 4(%ebx)
  jmp   8(%ebx)
  nop; nop
  nop; nop
.PLT1:
  jmp   name1(%ebx)
.PLT1next:
  pushl $name1RelOffset
  jmp    .PLT0
.PLT2:
  jmp   name2(%ebx)
.PLT2next
  pushl $name2RelOffset
  jmp    .PLT0

     Procedure-linkage table
```

```
ebx ─────────▶ _GLOBAL_OFFSET_TABLE:
                 .long _DYNAMIC
                 .long identification
                 .long ld.so


               name1:
                 .long .PLT1next
               name2:
                 .long .PLT2next
```

```
Relocation info:

  GOT_offset(name1), symx(name1)

  GOT_offset(name2), symx(name2)

              _DYNAMIC
```

FIGURE 3.17 The procedure-linkage table, global-offset table, and dynamic structure before the first call to *name1*.

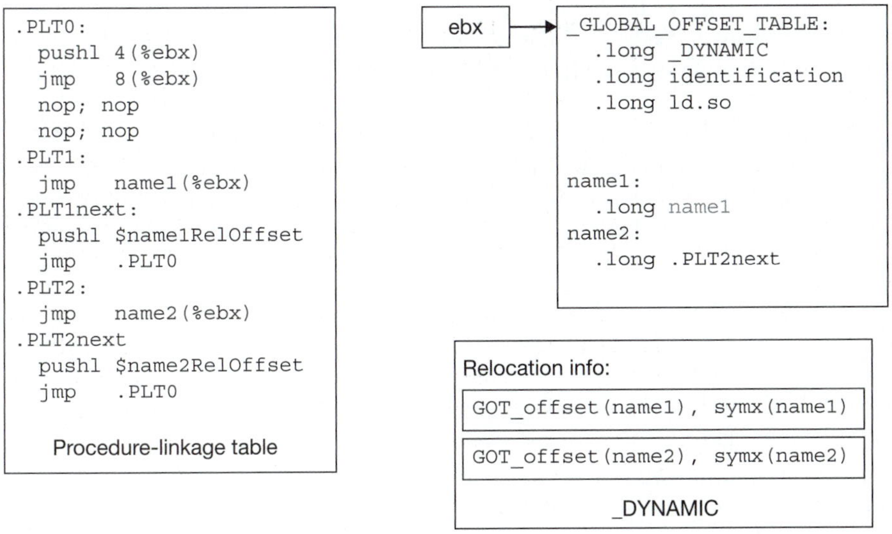

```
.PLT0:
  pushl 4(%ebx)
  jmp   8(%ebx)
  nop; nop
  nop; nop
.PLT1:
  jmp   name1(%ebx)
.PLT1next:
  pushl $name1RelOffset
  jmp    .PLT0
.PLT2:
  jmp   name2(%ebx)
.PLT2next
  pushl $name2RelOffset
  jmp    .PLT0

     Procedure-linkage table
```

```
ebx ─────────▶ _GLOBAL_OFFSET_TABLE:
                 .long _DYNAMIC
                 .long identification
                 .long ld.so


               name1:
                 .long name1
               name2:
                 .long .PLT2next
```

```
Relocation info:

  GOT_offset(name1), symx(name1)

  GOT_offset(name2), symx(name2)

              _DYNAMIC
```

FIGURE 3.18 The procedure-linkage table, global-offset table, and dynamic structure after the first call to *name1*.

Finally, *ld.so* writes the actual address of the *name1* procedure into the *name1* entry of the global-offset table and, after unwinding the stack a bit, passes control to *name1*. On subsequent calls by the module to *name1*, since the global-offset table now contains *name1*'s address, control goes to it more directly, without invoking *ld.so*. The updated tables are shown in Figure 3.18.

We finish this chapter with a discussion of booting an operating system. The term "boot" is probably derived from the idiomatic expression "to pull yourself up by your bootstraps," which means to get out of a difficult situation solely by your own efforts. The difficult situation here is that a computer must load its operating system into memory, and this task requires having

3.5
BOOTING

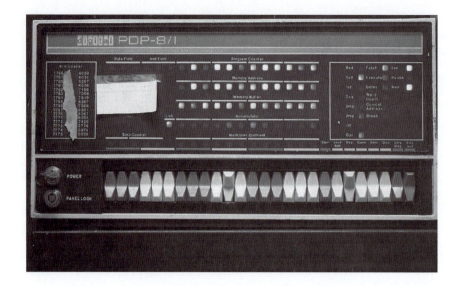

FIGURE 3.19 A DEC PDP-8.[4] Note the row of switches used to select memory addresses and insert values into memory. (*Courtesy of David Gesswein.*)

an operating system in memory. To get around this circularity, we first get a really tiny operating system into memory — the bootstrap loader — and it reads the real operating system into memory. (Or perhaps it reads a somewhat larger bootstrap loader into memory, which then fetches the real operating system.) But we still wonder: how do we get the first bootstrap loader into memory?

Early computers employed a conceptually easy approach. For example, the DEC PDP-8 (Figure 3.19) had a set of console switches through which one would manually put into memory a simple bootstrap loader, which would then read a more complicated program (perhaps an operating system) from paper tape. The code below is one such bootstrap loader that one would "toggle in" by hand:

```
07756 6032 KCC
07757 6031 KSF
07760 5357 JMP .-1
07761 6036 KRB
07762 7106 CLL RTL
07763 7006 RTL
07764 7510 SPA
07765 5357 JMP 7757
07766 7006 RTL
07767 6031 KSF
07770 5367 JMP .-1
07771 6034 KRS
07772 7420 SNL
07773 3776 DCA I 7776
07774 3376 DCA 7776
```

---

[4] The photo is from http://www.pdp8.net/pdp8i/pdp8i.shtml.

```
07775 5356 JMP 7756
07776 0000 AND 0
07777 5301 JMP 7701
```

The first column is the memory address (in octal), the second column is the code one would put into that location, and the third column gives the assembler instructions encoded.

Such an approach had obvious limitations. DEC, with its 1978 VAX-11 series, replaced the toggle switches with a separate console subsystem consisting of a specialized processor, read-only memory, a floppy-disk drive, and a hard-copy terminal. Rather than toggle in code to be deposited in the main processor's memory, one could type in commands to have the code deposited. This by itself was no improvement, but one could also type in commands to read a bootstrap program from the floppy disk into the main processor's memory. Furthermore, the computer could be configured to do this automatically when it powered up. How did one boot the specialized processor in the console subsystem? It was "hard-wired" always to run the code contained in its read-only memory when it started up.

The bootstrap loader loaded from the floppy disk would handle both the disk device and the on-disk file system (see Chapter 6) well enough to follow a directory path and read a file containing the operating system. It loaded the operating system into memory, then passed control to it. To do all this, the bootstrap code had to have the correct driver for the disk containing the file system that contained the operating system, and it had to know how that disk was set up. The latter involves both what sort of file system to expect and how the disk is partitioned — a single disk might hold multiple different file-system instances, each in a separate region of the disk.

The operating system, once loaded, had to be able to handle whatever devices were present on the system as well as however the disk was partitioned. Early Unix systems did this by having all needed device drivers statically linked in them, as well as by having the disk-partitioning information statically configured in the device drivers. Adding a new device, replacing a device, modifying disk-partitioning information, and so forth all required compiling (not just relinking) a new version of the operating system.

Later versions of Unix improved things a bit by containing all possible device drivers, then probing at boot time to determine which were actually needed. Disk-partition tables, rather than being static, were put in the first sector of each disk and read in at boot time, allowing the system to configure itself. Still later versions of Unix allowed device drivers to be dynamically loaded into a running system, thus easing the logistics of managing systems with disparate devices.

IBM introduced the IBM PC in 1981, establishing both a model and a marketplace in which a computer might include devices from any of a large number of manufacturers. The operating system (MS-DOS, from Microsoft) was distributed in binary form only. It had to be booted from a variety of devices and, once running, had to handle a large variety of devices. Not only was source code unavailable, but the typical user would not have known what to do with it. So a different approach was devised.

Included with the IBM PC is the basic input/output system (BIOS), consisting of code stored in read-only memory (ROM) and various settings stored in non-volatile memory (such as CMOS). It provides three primary functions:

- power-on self test (POST)

- load and transfer control to the boot program

- provide drivers for all devices

The provider of the computer system supplies a BIOS chip residing on the "motherboard" containing everything necessary to perform the three functions. Additional BIOS functions might reside on chips on add-on boards, providing access to additional devices.

The BIOS ROM is mapped into the last 64K of the first megabyte of address space (starting at location 0xf0000). When the system is powered on, the processor starts executing instructions at location 0xffff0 — the last sixteen bytes of this mapped region. At this location is a branch instruction that transfers control to the beginning of the BIOS code. The first thing the code does is the power-on self test, during which it initializes hardware, checks for problems, and computes the amount of primary storage.

The next step is to find a boot device. This is probably a hard disk, but could be a floppy or diskette. The list of possibilities and the order to search are in the settings stored in non-volatile RAM.

Once the boot device is found, the master boot record (MBR) is loaded from the first sector of a floppy or diskette, or from cylinder 0, head 0, sector 1 of a hard disk (see Chapter 6 for an explanation of these terms). The MBR (Figure 3.20) is 512 bytes long and contains:

- a "magic number" identifying itself

- a partition table listing up to four regions of the disk (identifying one as the *active* or boot partition)

- executable boot program

The BIOS code transfers control to the boot program. What happens next depends, of course, on the boot program. In the original version (for MS-DOS), this program would find the one active partition, load the first sector from it (containing the *volume boot program*), and pass control to that program. This program would then load the operating system from that partition.

More recent boot programs allow more flexibility. For example, both lilo (Linux Loader) and grub (Grand Unified Boot Manager), allow one to choose from multiple systems to boot, so that, for example, one can choose between booting Linux or Windows. Lilo has the sector number of the kernel images included within its code and thus must be modified if a kernel image moves. Grub understands a number of file systems and can find the image given a path name.

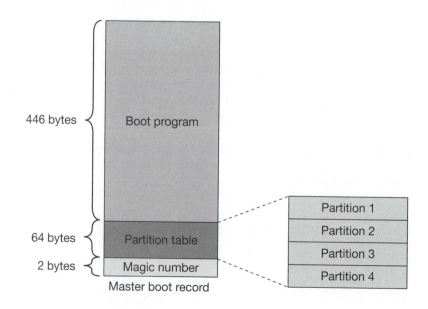

FIGURE 3.20 The master boot record, residing in the first sector of a bootable disk.

446 bytes — Boot program

64 bytes — Partition table

2 bytes — Magic number

Master boot record

Partition 1
Partition 2
Partition 3
Partition 4

The next step is for the kernel to configure itself. In Linux, most of the kernel is stored in the file system in compressed form. Here are the steps Linux goes through.

1. Performed by uncompressed code written in assembler language: set up initial stack, clear BSS, uncompress kernel, then transfer control to it.

2. Performed by newly uncompressed code, also written in assembler language: set up initial page tables and turn on address translation (see Chapter 7). At this point, process 0, which handles some aspects of paging, is created.

3. Performed by newly uncompressed code written in C: the rest of the kernel is initialized and process 1, which is the ancestor of all other user processes, is created. The scheduler is invoked, which schedules process 1.

We still need to discuss the issue of devices. One of the jobs of BIOS is to determine which devices are present. Originally, it provided drivers for all devices and the operating system would call upon BIOS-provided code whenever it required services of a device driver. But, since such drivers occupied rather slow memory and provided minimal functionality, later systems copied the BIOS drivers to primary memory, and even later ones provided their own device drivers, working through a list of devices provided by BIOS. However, BIOS drivers are still used for booting, since the operating system must be read from a disk with the aid of some sort of driver.

BIOS was designed in the 1980s for x86 computers and is not readily extensible to other architectures. Since then, Sun introduced Open Firmware, which is now used by a number of systems that don't use the x86. It is based on the language Forth, whose code is compiled into byte code and interpreted directly.

Intel developed a replacement for BIOS called extensible firmware interface (EFI) that also uses byte code, known imaginatively as EFI byte code. EFI development continues under the aegis of the UEFI forum, which is a group of a number of interested companies, including Intel and Microsoft.

3.6 CONCLUSIONS

This chapter has covered a number of topics of use throughout the rest of the book. Understanding context switching is essential to understanding the management of processors, which we cover in Chapter 5. Our brief discussion of input/output architectures prepares us to discuss file systems in Chapter 6. Dynamic storage allocation comes into play in all parts of operating systems, but most importantly in memory management, which we cover in Chapter 7. We will not have direct contact with linking and loading again, but it is clearly important for running programs. Similarly, we will not discuss booting again, but it is clearly important.

3.7 EXERCISES

1. Why does the x86 architecture require both a frame-pointer register and a stack-pointer register?

*2. Recursion, in the context of programming languages, refers to a function that calls itself. For example, the following is a simple example (assume that it's called only with appropriate argument values):

```
int factorial(int n) {
    if (n == 1)
        return n;
```

```
        else
            return n*factorial(n-1);
}
```

Tail recursion is a restriction of recursion in which the result of a recursive call is simply returned — nothing else may be done with the result. For example, here's a tail-recursive version of the factorial function:

```
int factorial(int n) {
    return f2(n, 1);
}


int f2(int a1, int a2) {
    if (a1 == 1)
        return a2;
    else
        return f2(a1-1, a1*a2);
}
```

a. Why is tail recursion a useful concept? (Hint: consider memory use.)

b. Explain how tail recursion might be implemented so as actually to be so useful.

* **3.** Section 3.1.2 describes how to switch from one thread to another. The implicit assumption is that the thread being switched to in the *switch* routine has sometime earlier yielded the processor by calling *switch* itself. Suppose, however, that this thread is newly created and is being run for the first time. Thus when its creator calls *switch* to enter the new thread's context, the new thread should start execution as if its first routine had just been called. Show what the initial contents of its stack should be to make this happen. Assume an x86-like assembler language.

4. As discussed in Chapter 1, Unix's *fork* system call creates a new process that is a child of its parent, the calling process. The thread calling *fork* returns the process ID of the new process, but in the new process the newly created thread returns 0 to the user-mode code that called *fork*. Explain how the kernel stack of the new thread is set up to make this happen.

* **5.** As discussed in Chapter 5, many systems use the clock-interrupt handler to determine if the current thread's time slice is over and, if so, force the thread to yield the processor to another thread. If the system's architecture uses the current thread's kernel stack to handle interrupts, then the current thread's context was saved on its kernel stack when the interrupt occurred and, even though the system is running in the interrupt context, the interrupt handler might simply call *switch* to switch to a different thread (it's a bit more complicated than this since we must deal with the possibility of other interrupts; we take this up in Chapter 5).

a. On architectures that have separate interrupt stacks, such as the DEC VAX-11, it does not work for an interrupt handler to call switch directly. Explain why not.

b. Explain what might be done in such an architecture for an interrupt handler to force a thread to call *switch* before normal execution resumes in the thread.

6. Assume we have a memory-mapped I/O architecture (Section 3.2) with device registers mapped into memory locations. In some situations it might be advantageous for a device driver, rather than enabling interrupts when it starts an I/O operation, to repeatedly check the ready bit until the operation completes. Describe the circumstances in which this approach would be preferable to using interrupts.

7. Despite the discussion in Section 3.3.1, there are occasions in which it makes sense to use a best-fit storage allocation algorithm. Describe a situation in which best fit would be better than first fit.

*8. Pages 112 and 113 show the assembler code in *main.s* and *subr.s*. Describe what changes are made to the corresponding machine code (in *main.o* and *subr.o*) when these routines are processed by *ld*, forming *prog*. Be specific. In particular, don't say "the address of X goes in location Y," but say, for example, "the value 11346 goes in the four-byte field starting at offset 21 in *xyz.o*." Note that for the x86 instructions used in this example, an address used in an instruction appears in the four-byte field starting with the second byte of the instruction.

9. Microsoft chose not to use position-independent code in Windows. Instead, they use the prerelocation technique (Section 3.4.2). They presumably had good technical reasons for doing so. Can you explain what they might be?

10. Why doesn't *ld.so* (Section 3.4.2) fill in the procedure-linkage tables with the actual addresses of all the procedures when the program starts up?

*11. Many C and C++ compilers allow programmers to declare thread-specific data (Section 2.2.4) as follows.

    __thread int X=6;

This declares X to be a thread-specific integer, initialized to 6. Somehow we must arrange so that each thread has its own private copy of it, initialized to 6. Doing this requires the cooperation of the compiler and the linker. Describe what must be done by both for this to work. Note that thread-specific data (TSD) items must be either global or static local variables. It makes no sense for them to be non-static local variables. You may assume that TSD items may be initialized only to values known at compile time (in particular, they may not be initialized to the results of function calls). Assume that only static linking is done — do not discuss the further work that must be done to handle dynamic linking. Note that a program might consist of a number of separately compiled modules.

12. Early versions of the Apple II computer had no operating system — many programs came with their own simple operating systems on self-booting floppy disks (see Section 1.2.4.1). Explain how such self-booting might have worked.

Bonwick, J. (1994). The Slab Allocator: An Object-Caching Kernel Memory Allocator. *Proceedings of the USENIX Summer 1994 Technical Conference*. Boston.

Knuth, D. E. (1968). *The Art of Computer Programming, Volume 1: Fundamental Algorithms*, Addison Wesley (second edition 1973, third edition 1997).

SPARC International (1992). The SPARC Architecture Manual, Version 8. from http://www.sparc.org/standards/V8.pdf.

3.8 REFERENCES

CHAPTER 4 Operating-System Design

In the previous chapter we discussed many of the concepts used in operating systems. Now we begin to examine how operating systems are constructed: what goes into them, how the components interact, how the software is structured so as to make the whole understandable and supportable, and how performance concerns are factored in. We also introduce such key components as scheduling, virtual memory, and file systems here and cover them in detail in later chapters.

Our approach is to look at a simple hardware configuration and work through the design of an equally simple operating system for it. Many of the details are covered in depth in later chapters. Similarly, we examine more sophisticated operating-system features in later chapters as well.

As far as applications are concerned, the operating system is the computer. It provides processors, memory, files, networking, interaction devices such as display and mouse, and whatever else is needed. The challenge of operating-system design is to integrate these components into a consistent whole that provides a usable interface to a secure and efficient system.

Our primary concern is a "general-purpose" operating system, one that's to run a variety of applications. Some of these applications are interactive, many of them utilize network communications, and all of them use and perhaps modify and create data on a file system. Examples of such general-purpose operating systems include Windows, Linux, FreeBSD, Solaris, and MacOS X (all but Windows are variants of Unix). Much of what we discuss applies to Chromium OS as well, since its kernel is Linux.

One way of looking at the design of such an operating system is to examine its functional components. Despite the marketing hype, Windows and most implementations of Unix are quite similar from a high-level point of view. All provide the notion of a process, which we can think of as a holder for the resources an application needs to run (Linux deviates from this a bit). All have threads, which, as we've seen, are an abstraction of the processor; they're the active agents. All provide file systems, with similar operations for working with files. All

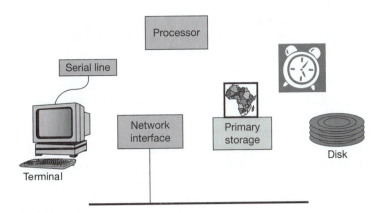

FIGURE 4.1
Hardware configuration for simple OS.

implement roughly the same set of network protocols, with pretty much the same application interface. All provide for user interaction with a display, mouse, and keyboard. All provide access control to files that is based on a notion of file ownership and is controlled by the owner of files (this is known as *discretionary access control*, a concept we cover in Chapter 8).

4.1 A SIMPLE SYSTEM

In order to look at the basics of operating-system design, we sketch the design of a simple system that incorporates many of the major components of a modern general-purpose operating system. We work with a hardware configuration that dates to the early 1980s — we omit modern display technology so as to focus on the basic OS issues. Our system, as shown in Figure 4.1, is made up of a processor with memory and memory-management hardware (to support virtual memory) along with a disk drive, a clock, a serial line to which is connected a simple terminal device made up of a display and keyboard, and an Ethernet connection for communication. The I/O architecture is the memory-mapped approach discussed in Section 3.2.

Our operating system provides functionality similar to that of current Unix and Windows systems, but without support for bit-mapped displays and mice and with a simpler but generally less efficient design. It supports multiple multithreaded processes, each with its own address space, and has a file system layered on its disks. The execution of threads is multiplexed on the single processor by a simple, time-sliced scheduler. Users interact with the system via a terminal that provides no graphics, but displays the text sent to it (typically in 24 80-character rows) and sends to the processor whatever characters are typed on the keyboard (see Figure 4.2). Communication is provided over Ethernet using the TCP/IP family of protocols (we describe these protocols in Chapter 9). This system would have been state of the art (if not then some) in the 1970s, and rather commonplace by the early to mid–1980s.

FIGURE 4.2
A computer terminal (~1980). (*Courtesy of Tom Doeppner.*)

From an application program's point of view, our system has processes with threads, a file system, terminals (with keyboards), and a network connection. Before we look at how all this is implemented, let's go over these components in a bit more detail. We need to examine how applications use them and how this affects the design of the operating system.

The purpose of a process in our system is to hold both an address space and a group of threads that execute within that address space, as well as to keep track of files and devices in current use. One definition of an address space is the set of addresses that threads of the process can usefully reference. More practically, however, it is the contents of these addressable locations. As we saw in Chapter 1, the address spaces of typical Unix processes contain text, data, BSS, dynamic, and stack regions. Thus references to the text region obtain the application's executable code, references to the data region obtain its initialized variables, and so forth.

An important design issue is how the operating system initializes these address-space regions. A simple-minded approach would be to copy their contents from the file system to the process address space as part of the *exec* operation. However, particularly for the text region, this would be unnecessarily time- and space-consuming, since what is in this region is read-only and thus can, in principle, be shared by all processes executing code from the same file. It might seem that, since a process can modify the contents of its data region, the data region really must be copied into the address space. However, if portions of it are never modified, then perhaps a savings can be achieved by sharing those portions.

Rather than copy the executable file into the address space, a better approach is to *map* it into the address space. This is an operation we cover in detail in Chapter 7. Mapping lets the operating system tie the regions of the address space to the file system. Both the address space and files are divided into pieces, typically called pages. If, for example, a number of processes are executing the same program, at most one copy of that program's text pages is in memory at once. The text regions of all the processes running this program are set up, using hardware address-translation facilities, to share these pages. The data regions of all processes running the program initially refer to pages of memory containing a copy of the initial data region.

The sort of mapping employed here is called a *private mapping*: when a process modifies something in a data-region page for the first time, it is given a new, private page containing a copy of the initial page. Thus only those pages of memory that are modified are copied. The BSS and stack regions use a special form of private mapping: their pages are initialized, with zeros, only when processes access them for the first time.

This notion of mapping is used in more modern systems by allowing additional regions to be added to the address space that are set up by mapping other files into them. In addition to private mappings, *shared mappings* are used here: when a process modifies a page for the first time, a private copy is not made for the process; instead, the original page itself is modified. Thus all processes with a shared mapping of that page share the changes to it. Furthermore, these changes are written back to the original file.[1]

Mapping files into the address space, both private and shared, is one way to perform input and output operations on files. We also need the more traditional approach using explicit system calls, such as Unix's *read* and *write*. These are necessary for interacting with devices that can't be mapped into the address space as files can, for instance receiving characters typed into the keyboard, or sending a message via a network connection. Such communication is strictly sequential: reading from the keyboard retrieves the next batch of characters; sending to the network connection transmits the next message.

---

[1] We've left out a number of details here. For example, how do we make room if more is mapped into the processes' address space than fits into memory? What happens if some processes have share-mapped a portion of a file into their address spaces while others have private-mapped the same portion into their address spaces? We cover all this, and more, in Chapter 6.

It also makes sense to use such explicit system calls when doing file I/O, even though file I/O can be done by mapping. For example, a program's input might be a sequence of commands. It makes life a lot easier to use the same code in the program to read this input from a file as to read it from the keyboard. A program that produces lines of text as output should be able to use the same code to write this output to file as to write it out to a network connection.

In the remainder of this section we focus on the design of our system. This design is relatively simple and straightforward; it makes clear what the components do and how they interact. We have to come to grips with a number of issues, including:

- What is the functionality of each of the components?

- What are the key data structures?

- How is the system broken up into modules?

- To what extent is the system extensible? That is, how easy is it to add new functionality or substitute different functionality?

- What parts run in the OS kernel in privileged mode? What parts run as library code in user applications? What parts run as separate applications?

- In which execution contexts do the various activities take place? In particular, what takes place in the context of user threads? What takes place in the context of system threads? What takes place in the interrupt context?

4.1.1 A FRAMEWORK FOR DEVICES

Before looking at how to handle individual devices, we need to devise a framework for handling them within our system. As we discussed in Chapter 3, device drivers contain the code that deals with device-level details, providing a standard interface to the rest of the system. But how do we connect the rest of the system to these device drivers? In particular, how do we make certain that, when a program reads from a keyboard, it is indeed reading from the keyboard device? How do we make certain that every time the system starts up, the file system is always associated with the same disk (or disks)? Taking this a step further, how does the system know what to do when we plug a new device into it, such as a flash drive?

In early Unix systems the kernel was statically linked to contain just the device drivers required, and each of them knew exactly the set of their devices that were physically connected to the system. There was no means for adding devices to a running system, or even for adding a device while the system is down without modifying the kernel image. If a system had two disk drives of the same sort, its kernel would have one driver for that sort of disk drive, configured to handle two instances of the drive. Each device was identified by a device number that was actually a pair: a *major device number*, identifying the driver, and a *minor device number* that was used, among other things, to identify the device among those handled by the driver. Special entries were created in the file system, usually in the /dev directory, to refer to devices. For our disk-drive example, /dev/disk1 and /dev/disk2 might be created, each marked as a *special file* — one that does not contain data, but instead refers to devices by their major and minor device numbers. If an application program opened /dev/disk2, the kernel would know to use the correct driver and the driver would now be able to identify which device, both being indicated by the device number contained in the special file.

The data structures required to support this driver framework were simple. There was a statically allocated array in the kernel called *cdevsw* (character[2] device switch) that was indexed by the major device number. Each entry in the array contained the addresses of the entry points of the indicated driver. (See Figure 4.3.) Each driver maintained its own data structures for identifying the device from the minor device number and for representing its devices. The kernel was also statically configured to contain device-specific information such as interrupt-vector locations and the locations of device-control registers on whatever bus the device was attached to.

This static approach was straightforward, but suffered from not being easily extensible. It required that a kernel be custom configured for each installation. The first approach taken to improving it was to still require that a kernel contain (i.e., be statically linked with) all necessary device drivers, but to allow the devices themselves to be found and automatically configured when the system booted. This was accomplished by having drivers include a *probe routine*, called at boot time. They would probe the relevant buses for devices and configure them, including identifying and recording interrupt-vector and device-control-register locations. This allowed one kernel image to be built that could be used for a number of similar but not identical installations.

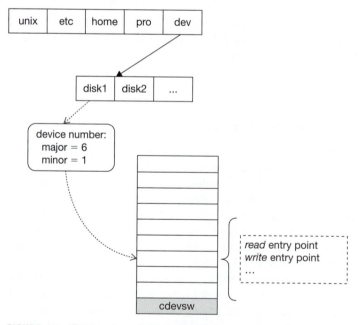

FIGURE 4.3 Devices in early Unix systems were named at the user level via special files containing the major and minor device numbers identifying the driver and the device. The major device number was an index into the *cdevsw* (character device switch), each of whose elements listed the entry points of a driver. The driver, in turn, was passed the minor device number and used it to determine the device.

---

[2] Unix drivers could support two interfaces: one for buffered I/O, called the *block* interface, and the other for nonbuffered I/O, called the *character* interface. There was also a *bdevsw* (block device switch), whose function was similar to the *cdevsw*. At the level of our discussion here, the two are identical.

There are zillions of devices available for today's systems. It is not practical to statically link all their drivers into an operating-system kernel, then check to see which devices are actually present. Instead, we must somehow discover devices without the benefit of having the relevant device driver in the kernel, then find the needed device drivers and dynamically link them into the kernel. This is a tall order, partly because identifying a device is a device-specific action.

The way around this conundrum is to allow meta-drivers that, for example, handle a particular kind of bus. Thus systems employing USB (universal serial bus) have a USB driver in addition to drivers for the various classes of devices that may be connected via USB. The USB protocol, interpreted by the USB driver, identifies the devices connected to it so that the appropriate device drivers can be selected. It is then up to system software (probably running at user level) to find the drivers and arrange for them to be loaded into the kernel.

A remaining issue is how to arrange for application programs to reference dynamically discovered devices. One approach, used until relatively recently on some Linux systems, was to list standard names for all possible devices in the /dev directory ((Kroah-Hartman 2003) reports that Red Hat 9 — a Linux distribution — has over eighteen thousand entries in its /dev directory). However, only those names associated with connected devices actually worked. Of course, if a device is added to a running system, its name would immediately be activated. An obvious improvement is to list in /dev only those names that are associated with connected devices. This was done in a later Linux distribution by having the kernel create entries in /dev as devices are discovered, getting their names from a database of names known as *devfs*. This is definitely a major advance, but it has the undesired property of imposing naming conventions that are not universally accepted. As of this writing, the current favorite Linux approach is known as *udev* (Kroah-Hartman 2003), in which a user-lever application is notified by the kernel of new devices and assigns them names based on rules provided by an administrator.

A related problem is identifying which of a class of related devices to use. For example, you might have a laptop computer that has a touchpad. You then plug in a mouse. These are very different devices but have a similar use. How should the choice be presented to applications? Windows has the notion of *interface classes*, which allow devices to register themselves as members of one or more such classes. An application can enumerate all currently connected members of such a class and choose among them (or use them all).

4.1.2 LOW-LEVEL KERNEL

We start at the lowest levels of the kernel, showing how devices are handled. Though this bottom-up approach probably isn't how you would actually design an operating system, it's a reasonable order for implementing its components. Once lower-level modules are written and debugged, higher-level ones can be built on top of them.

4.1.2.1 Terminals

Terminals are long-obsolete devices (it is a good bet that most readers of this book have never seen one, let alone used one). We include them in our simple system both because of their simplicity and because much of the processing required of them is still present in current systems. After we discuss how they are handled, we talk about why this discussion is still relevant.

How should terminals be handled? This would seem pretty straightforward: characters to be output are simply sent to the output routine of the serial-line driver. To fetch characters that have been typed at the keyboard, a call is made to its input routine. However, this turns out to be an amazing oversimplification. Here are a few concerns that must be dealt with.

1. Characters are generated by the application faster than they can be sent to the terminal. If the application is continuously generating output at this high rate, then it clearly must be made to wait until the terminal can catch up with it. But if its output is bursty, then, rather

than slow down the application so as to print the latest output burst, it makes more sense to buffer the output and send characters to the terminal from the buffer. In essence, we have here an instance of the producer-consumer problem (see Section 2.2.3.2).

2. Characters arrive from the keyboard even though there isn't a waiting read request from an application. Thus we must arrange for incoming characters to be placed in a buffer, from which they'll be given to the application once it issues a read request. Here's another instance of the producer-consumer problem.

3. Input characters may need to be processed in some way before they reach the application. For example, characters typed at the keyboard are echoed back to the display, so that you see what you type as you type it. Furthermore, characters may be grouped into lines of text and subject to simple editing (using backspace, etc.). Some applications prefer to process all characters themselves, including their editing. However, command shells and similar applications have this done for them.

To handle the first two concerns, we need two queues — one for output and one for input. Characters are placed on the output queue and taken off the input queue in the context of the application thread. A thread producing output can block if the queue is full; a thread consuming input can block if the queue is empty.

What sort of execution contexts should be used for the other ends of the queues? We might dedicate a thread to each queue. One thread would take characters from the output queue and give them to the device. Another would take characters arriving from the device and put them on the input queue. But there's a small issue: what happens if the input-queue thread blocks because the queue is full, yet characters are still arriving? The device itself cannot queue them, so some characters must necessarily be dropped. One way around this problem is to get the source of the characters (the human typist) to slow down. Alternatively, one insures that the input queue is large enough so that this problem rarely occurs.

However, the use of threads here is probably overkill and inefficient. Consider the thread handling input from the device. It initiates a read and blocks, waiting for the read-completion interrupt. When the interrupt occurs, the interrupt handler wakes the thread up. The thread moves the character to the input queue, and then starts the procedure over again by initiating another read and waiting for the interrupt.

All this seems too laborious. A simpler, more efficient technique is to have the interrupt handler do all the work. As it responds to each read-completion interrupt, it places the newly arrived character on the input queue itself. If the queue is full, it throws the character away. There is, of course, the issue of mutually exclusive access to the input queue by the interrupt handler and the application thread that's reading characters — but this is handled by having the thread mask interrupts while it is taking characters from the queue.

Similarly, the interrupt handler can also handle the transfer of characters from the output queue to the device. After each write-completion interrupt, the interrupt handler takes the next character off the queue, if any, and starts another write operation. When a thread puts a character on the queue, if an output operation isn't already in progress, it starts one.

Dealing with concern (3) above complicates things further. If incoming characters can be edited by subsequently arriving characters, then they cannot be made available to the application until there is no further chance that they might be edited — it's at the very least impolite to give the application a character, then demand it back on receipt of a backspace. However, once a complete line has been typed in, ending with a carriage-return character, no further editing of that line may take place.

So we'll have two input queues: one containing the characters in a partial line, still subject to editing, and the other containing characters from complete lines. The terminal-read interrupt handler, as before, places incoming characters on the partial-line queue. When a carriage return arrives, the interrupt handler moves the entire contents of the partial-line queue to the completed-line queue.

Next we need to handle the echoing of typed characters. When a character is typed, it should be written to the display. We can do this immediately — when an interrupt indicates that a character has arrived, the interrupt handler queues the character to be output and actually starts outputting it if it is at the head of the queue. This is how it's done on Unix systems: typed characters are always echoed immediately, even if the program that consumes them is busy doing something else.

Windows systems handle this differently: typed characters are echoed only when an application actually consumes them.[3] Thus, characters are echoed not in the interrupt context, but in the context of the thread that consumes them (the one issuing the read system call).

The next concern is modularization. Though it's tempting to put all the functionality described above into one module, there are additional concerns. One is device independence. There are many different serial-line devices, but the character processing is common to all. In fact, this character processing is performed in situations in which the source and sink of characters aren't necessarily a serial line — it can be done with bit-mapped displays, data coming from and going to network connections, etc.

It thus makes sense to separate the device-dependent part from the common, device-independent part. So, rather than put everything in the device driver, we put in it only the code that directly communicates with the device. All device drivers provide the same interface to the rest of the system. A separate module, known in some systems as the *line-discipline* module, provides the common character-handling code (see Figure 4.4). Thus the line-discipline module can interact with any device driver capable of handling terminals.

This modularization also provides a degree of extensibility. Not only is it easy to replace the serial-line device with others, but one can easily substitute different line-discipline modules that provide alternative character handling or deal with alternative character sets.

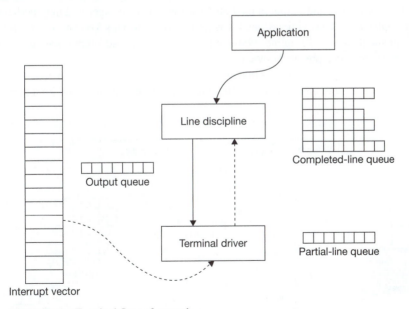

FIGURE 4.4 Terminal flow of control.

---

[3] Windows actually allows both approaches, though standard Microsoft applications echo characters as described. See Exercise 1.

The last topic in our walk-through of terminal handling is the location of the modules. The three possibilities are: in the kernel (i.e., running in privileged mode), in a separate user process, and as library routines that are linked into application processes.

Putting both modules (the device driver and the line discipline) in the kernel is the most straightforward approach. Device registers should be protected from arbitrary manipulation by application programs, so allowing only the kernel access (via the device driver) provides the necessary protection. The line-discipline module, by design, doesn't need direct access to device registers. However, it provides processing and queuing that is used by any number of user processes, all of which share the same terminal. This rules out implementing the line-discipline module as library code, though it doesn't rule out putting it into a separate process.

Putting such functionality in a separate process is intriguing. In principle, code that is outside the kernel is easier to modify, replace, and debug than code inside the kernel. We take up this topic when we discuss microkernels in Section 4.2.2 below. However, such an approach raises serious performance concerns: incoming characters must first be transferred to the line-discipline process, then transferred to other processes. Such difficulties aren't insurmountable, but it's easier to avoid them entirely by leaving the line-discipline module in the kernel. So, for now anyway, that's where we put it.

Many applications process data from the keyboard a character at a time rather than a line at a time. For example, a shell might do command completion; a document editor might correct spelling errors on the fly. This is done by turning off some of the processing of the line discipline and performing it in the application.

Modern systems do not have terminals. Instead, they might have bit-mapped display devices as well as keyboards and mice that are connected to the system via USB. A window manager implements windows on the display and determines which applications receive typed input. A server might support remote sessions in which applications receive input and send output over a network. The notion of a terminal provides a simple abstraction for input and output for many such applications, allowing them to be written as if they were interacting directly with a terminal, when in fact their input and output is mediated by a window manager and may perhaps go over a network. One way of providing this abstraction is to use what's known as a *pseudoterminal*, which implements a line discipline whose input comes from and output goes to a controlling application rather than a physical device.

Figure 4.5 shows a pseudoterminal as it might be used by a window manager to provide a terminal-like interface to an application. The operating-system kernel provides a pair of entities

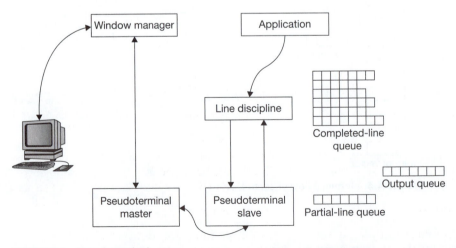

FIGURE 4.5 Pseudoterminal.

that appear to applications to be devices — the pseudoterminal *master* and *slave*. Input from the keyboard that is deemed by the window manager to belong to the application is written to the pseudoterminal master. It is transferred to the pseudoterminal slave, which appears to the rest of the operating system to be a terminal device driver. Thus it interconnects with the line discipline, from which the application can read its input just as if it were coming directly from an actual keyboard. Similarly, output from the application is written as if there were a terminal. The characters are processed by the line discipline and transferred to the pseudoterminal slave; from this they are given to the pseudoterminal master and made available to be read by the window manager, which then displays the output in the appropriate window.

How does human-computer interaction work in modern systems? In what ways are terminals still relevant? Let's assume that by "modern systems" we mean those with bit-mapped displays supporting windows (small w!), through which the user interacts using a keyboard and mouse. (It's not a big stretch to extend this model to a touch-sensitive display on a mobile device without hardware keyboard or mouse.) Application processes set up windows and indicate areas of interest via a special window-manager process. This window-manager process consumes all input from the keyboard and mouse. It is responsible for tracking the mouse and updating the cursor on the display, which it controls. Mouse events are forwarded to appropriate application processes, depending on the location of the cursor with respect to the windows. Keyboard input is also forwarded to these processes, but via pseudoterminals, so that application processes receive typed data as if they came from directly connected terminals.

4.1.2.2 Network Communication

Network communication and terminal handling have many similar aspects of architecture and implementation. In network communication there is a device, often called a network interface card (NIC), that sends and receives data. As with terminals, data arrives even if there is no outstanding read request. Entire "packets" of data, rather than single characters, arrive, but the principle is roughly the same. Incoming (and outgoing) data must be processed via network-protocol modules similar in function to the line-discipline module discussed in Section 4.1.2.1 above.

An important difference between network communication and terminal handling is that while performance is important for terminals, it's crucial in networks. Input terminal data comes in (from the keyboard) at speeds of, at best, tens of characters per second; even though output data goes out much faster, speeds over a few thousand characters per second are probably not necessary.

But consider what must be done to process data coming in from a billion-bit-per-second network. With terminal data we can afford to copy the characters from queue to queue. But merely copying data coming in from networks at such high speeds takes a fair amount of processor bandwidth. Thus, at the least, network data cannot be copied when transferred from module to module, but must be passed by reference.

Let's go over some of the basic operations required to implement network protocols; we cover them in detail in Chapter 9. As an example protocol, consider TCP (transmission control protocol), used extensively on the Internet. Data being sent by an application is organized into self-describing blocks, variously called segments, packets, and frames. TCP sends blocks *reliably*: that is, it ensures that either the blocks reach their destination or the sender is notified of the failure. To accomplish this, the receiver sends back acknowledgments of data received. If the sender does not receive an acknowledgment in due time, it retransmits the data.

Our protocol-processing modules thus need to perform the following sorts of operations:

1. Pass blocks from one module to the next without copying.

2. Append information describing a block, in the form of headers, to the beginning of outgoing data. Conversely, such headers must be removed (and interpreted) from incoming blocks.

3. Allow one module, corresponding to a layer of protocol, to hold onto outgoing blocks so they can be retransmitted if an acknowledgment is not received in due time, while passing the block to next module.

4. Be able to request and respond to time-out notifications.

To accomplish all this in our simple operating system, we use a data structure adapted from Linux. Figure 4.6 shows a pair of segments generated, say, by the TCP protocol. So that data from successive write calls can be efficiently coalesced into a single segment, and so that the headers can be efficiently appended by successive protocol modules, each segment is allocated enough memory that it can grow to some maximum size. For outgoing segments, data is copied into these segments from write calls, starting some distance from the beginning of the allocated memory so as to leave room for headers. Referring to a segment is a data structure called a *sk_buff* (socket buffer) containing pointers to the various components of the segment. Thus in Figure 4.6, *head* points to the beginning of the area containing the current header, *data* points to the beginning of the area containing the data, *tail* refers to the current end of the data (so more can be added, if necessary), and *end* points to the maximum allowable extent of data and to the beginning of a small descriptor containing a reference count, as explained in the next paragraph. The *next* field points to another *sk_buff* structure, allowing them to be queued.

Figure 4.7 shows what happens after the segments of Figure 4.6 are passed to another protocol module, say IP. So that TCP can retain a copy of the segments, yet still pass them on to IP, a new set of *sk_buff* structures is created by copying the originals, and these new ones are passed to IP. The reference count contained in the descriptor is incremented by one, thus indicating how many *sk_buff* structures refer to the segment. IP, when it is finished with the segment, simply discards it by freeing the *sk_buff* structures and decrementing the reference count by 1. The memory containing the actual segment is not freed until TCP is done with it.

Finally, support for time-outs is implemented with a callback interface to the interval-timer module. Protocol modules that must be called after a certain time interval pass the interval timer the address of the routine to be called and a time to call it. There is also a cancel routine, called, for example, if the acknowledgment actually arrives on time.

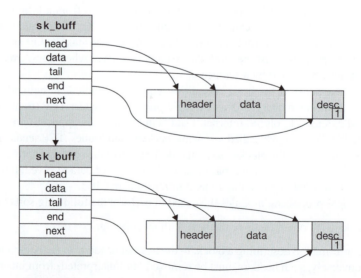

FIGURE 4.6 A queue of two segments.

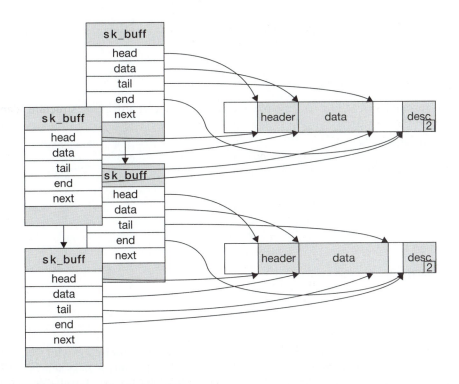

FIGURE 4.7   The segments of Figure 4-6 after being passed to the next protocol module.

4.1.3 PROCESSES AND THREADS

The next step is the design of processes and threads. A process in our system is a holder for an address space, a collection of references to open files, and other information shared by a set of threads. This definition fits Windows and most Unix systems, though, as we see in Chapter 5, things are a bit different in Linux.

To represent a process, we need a data structure, which we simply call a *process control block (PCB)*. It either contains or refers to all the per-process information mentioned above, including the address space as well as its threads. Threads also need a representation, which we call a *thread control block (TCB)*. This contains or refers to thread-specific context, such as the thread's stack and copies of important registers (e.g., the stack pointer). See Figure 4.8.

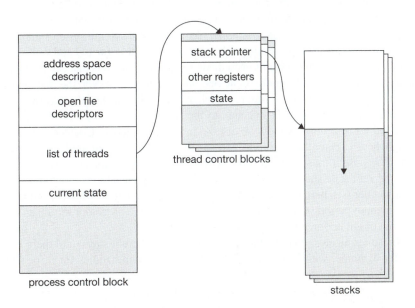

FIGURE 4.8   Process control block (PCB), thread control block (TCB), and thread stacks.

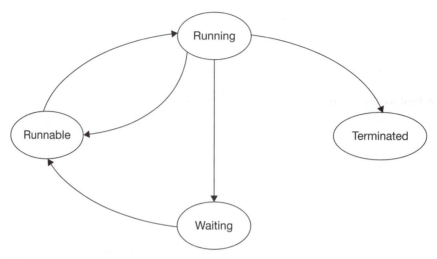

FIGURE 4.9 The states of a thread.

Operations on processes include creation and deletion, synchronization with their termination, and loading their address spaces with programs (what the Unix *exec* system call does). Creation involves setting up the address space, which we discuss in Chapter 7. Loading the program may involve relocation, as discussed in Chapter 3, as well as mapping files into memory, discussed in Chapter 7.

To allow synchronization with a process's termination, we need to keep track of the process even after it has terminated. Thus in our simple system (as in most other operating systems), we keep the process control block around after all threads in the process have terminated, indicating its current state: *active* or *terminated*. In Unix, terminated processes are known as *zombies* and are deleted by *wait* system calls. In Windows, processes are represented as kernel objects and are in the *unsignaled state* when active and the *signaled state* when terminated. These objects are deleted when there are no more handles referring to them.

The life history of threads is a bit more complicated than that of processes. A thread may be running on a processor, waiting for a processor on which to run, waiting for some synchronization event to take place, or terminated. These situations are represented as states, which we call *running*, *runnable*, *waiting*, and *terminated* (see Figure 4.9). Some systems make even finer distinctions than this, for example distinguishing between waiting for I/O and waiting for a synchronization event. Most Unix systems even distinguish between waits that can be interrupted by signals and those that cannot. For our simple operating system, however, the four states suffice.

The transitions among states deserve explanation. When a thread is created, it is in the *runnable state*. At some point it is switched to the *running state*. The code that performs this switch is called the scheduler, which we discuss in further detail in Chapter 5. A thread that's running might have to enter the *wait state*, perhaps because it must wait until an I/O operation has completed or because it must wait on some synchronization operation such as locking a mutex. A thread in the wait state stays there until released, either by the actions of another thread or by an interrupt handler (see below). If the scheduler uses time-slicing, in which running threads run for some maximum period of time but then must relinquish the processor to runnable threads, a running thread might be forced to switch to the runnable state.

If a thread terminates, it enters the *terminated state*, where it stays until there is no further use for it (for example, with Windows, until there are no open handles for it, or with POSIX threads, until some other thread performs a *pthread_join* operation on it). Note that in our system, as in most systems, a thread must be in the running state before it terminates. If we were to implement the POSIX *pthread_cancel* routine, it would set a pending-cancel bit in the target thread control block, and then make the thread runnable if necessary. When that thread runs, it would notice it has been cancelled and act accordingly.

A final issue concerning terminated threads is: how are they deleted? If, in POSIX terms, a thread is not detached, then the thread performing the *pthread_join* operation can free the thread control block and the stack. But what if a thread is detached? In this case, when the thread terminates, it should bypass the terminated state and immediately self-destruct.

In our simple operating system we avoid this issue by not supporting detached threads, but this is not an option for POSIX threads or for Windows. A problem is that a thread cannot free its own stack — since it would be using the stack when the deallocation takes place, doing so could have disastrous results. What's done to get around this is one of two things. One approach is to have a special "reaper thread" whose sole duty is to wait for detached threads to terminate and then to free their control blocks and stacks — essentially doing the equivalent of a *pthread_join* on these threads. Alternatively, terminated detached threads can be put in a list. Other running threads occasionally examine this list and, if it is nonempty, free its contents. This examination can take place whenever the scheduler puts a thread into the running state.

To summarize the above discussion: the scheduler handles transitions between the running and runnable states. Threads put themselves into the wait and terminated states. Some agent other than the thread moves it from the wait state to the runnable state. The transitions from the running to the wait states and from the wait to the runnable states are handled by synchronization routines, such as those implementing POSIX's mutexes and condition variables and Windows's events.

4.1.4 STORAGE MANAGEMENT

Storage management is a broad set of topics. In Chapter 3 we used the term in a rather narrow sense, referring strictly to what's perceived by an application as the storage comprising its address space. If we consider storage to be the physical devices that can actually store data, then we usually divide things into primary storage — what's directly addressable in the computer — and secondary storage — usually disk-based storage. However, most operating systems, including our simple system, support virtual memory, in which the application's view of memory, as presented in the address space of the process, is the result of considerable behind-the-scenes work by the operating system. In this section we briefly go over what's required to support virtual memory in our simple operating system, including the "real" memory support that's behind it.

First, what is virtual memory and why do we need it? Virtual memory both allows applications to run on computers with a different storage configurations and simplifies the application writers' job so that most of the work of managing storage is done by the operating system.

Computers have widely varying amounts of storage, both primary and secondary. Both executable code and data must be loaded into primary storage, typically by being copied from secondary storage. However, there might not be enough primary storage to hold all of it at once; also, even if there is plenty of primary storage, it might be necessary to rearrange what's in it so that a program's data occupy contiguous locations (for example, consider a stack). So, copying is required from secondary storage to primary storage, and from primary storage to secondary storage to make room for other things. If there is no other way to make data appear to be contiguous, fair amounts may need to be copied from one area of primary storage to another.

With virtual memory, most of this work is either made unnecessary or hidden from the application. The application allocates storage strictly in terms of virtual memory — its address space is strictly "virtual." Thus it might allocate one gigabyte of virtual memory, even though the computer it's running on has only 512 megabytes of RAM. As it uses this virtual memory, the operating system makes certain that real primary storage is available when necessary. If there is not enough room for everything, the operating system moves some of what's in primary storage to secondary storage to make room.

An application thread can explicitly copy data from secondary storage to primary storage. Alternatively, it can "map" the data in, by notifying the operating system that some range of virtual addresses should contain the data that's in some file (or some portion of the file). Then, when the thread references that part of its address space, the operating system makes certain that the data from the file is there.

So, how is all this made to work? We cover this question in detail in Chapter 7, so here we give only the basic structure of what our simple system does. We need to handle four things:

1. Mapping virtual addresses to real ones.

2. Determining which addresses are valid, i.e., refer to allocated memory, and which are not.

3. Keeping track of which real objects, if any, are mapped into each range of virtual addresses.

4. Deciding what to keep in primary storage (RAM) and what to fetch from elsewhere.

A valid virtual address must be ultimately resolvable by the operating system to a location in RAM. Referencing an invalid virtual address causes a fault, probably terminating the process.

The actual mechanism for converting virtual addresses into real addresses is provided by the hardware. How the mechanism works varies, as we discuss in Chapter 7. In some cases the hardware is given the complete map of virtual addresses to real addresses, in other cases just a portion of it. In either case, it's up to the operating system to provide this map, and thus also to have a data structure for representing it.

Figure 4.10 shows how our simple system represents an address space. It contains not only the portions of the address space that are in Sixth-Edition Unix, but also some data files that have been mapped into it. The process's PCB refers to an address-space structure, which in turn refers to a linked list of *as_region* structures, each representing one region of the address space. For those regions into which a file has been mapped, the *as_region* structure refers to a file object representing the file.

Each *as_region* structure indicates the bounds of the region of virtual memory it represents, along with the access permissions associated with the region and whether it is shared with other

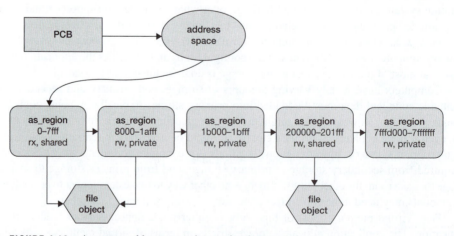

FIGURE 4.10 A process address space in our simple system.

processes. The regions shown in Figure 4.10 are, from left to right, the text region, the data region, the BSS region (i.e., the region containing uninitialized global data, as explained in Section 1.3.2), a file that has been mapped in (and is shared with other processes), and the stack region. Note that the text and data regions map portions of the same file, i.e., the one that was exec'd by the process, but the text region is read-and-execute-only, while the data region is read-write. Furthermore, the data region is marked "private," indicating that changes to it won't modify the file being exec'd and hence won't affect other processes. The mapped file is marked "shared," which means that changes made to this portion of the address space by the process will also modify the file, and hence affect any other process that uses that file.

Now we can begin to see how the operating system makes virtual memory work. As long as what the threads of an application are referencing is both in primary memory and mapped by the hardware's address map, no intervention is required. However, if a thread references something either that's not in primary storage or whose translation is not in the map, then a fault occurs and the operating system is invoked. The OS then checks the *as_region* data structures to make sure the reference is valid and, if so, does whatever is necessary to locate or create the object of the reference, find or, if necessary, make room for it in primary storage if it's not already there, and put it there.

Two issues need further discussion. How is the primary storage managed? And how are these objects managed in secondary storage? The first we cover briefly in Section 4.1.4.1, below, on managing primary storage, and then in detail in Chapter 7. The second we cover briefly in Section 4.1.4.2 below on file systems and then in detail in Chapter 6.

4.1.4.1 Managing Primary Storage

The main issue in managing primary storage is not so much keeping track of what's been allocated and what hasn't — we already know how to do this from Chapter 3 — but determining how to apportion it among the various processes and subsystems. In this brief section we discuss what the issues are, postponing how they are handled until Chapter 7.

Let's first go over who the competitors for primary memory are. Each application process can certainly use as much primary memory as it has active virtual memory. But also competing are various subsystems of the operating system. As we've seen, the terminal-handling subsystem requires memory for its character queues. But, unless we have a large number of terminals or extremely fast typists, this demand isn't that great. However, the memory requirements of the communication subsystem for handling incoming and outgoing packets are substantial. Some operating systems that manage this memory poorly have been effectively shut down by attackers who bombard them with packets so that all available memory is consumed in holding them. Last, most operating systems, including ours, cache recently accessed blocks from the file system (for a number of reasons that we cover in Chapter 6). Unless we are careful, if a lot of file-system I/O is taking place, little primary storage might be available for other subsystems and user processes.

If we eliminate the ability to map files into address spaces, then a viable, though hardly optimal, way to manage primary storage would be to give each subsystem and process a fixed fraction of primary storage, and thus not worry about competition. But it turns out that mapped files force the issue.

Suppose each process is allowed a fixed amount of primary storage, and say that a process is currently using all its allocation and must access a portion of its address space that is not currently in primary storage. In this case, some amount of primary storage that is currently holding another portion of its address space must be released so as to hold the new portion. But suppose the process is using all of its primary storage allocation, and it then maps a file into its address space and starts accessing that file. Should the primary storage required to hold the file be charged to the file subsystem or to the process? If it's charged to the file subsystem, then, if the file in question is large enough, the process might completely monopolize all the file subsystem's allocation of primary storage. But if it's charged to the process, what happens if other processes are accessing the same file, but using the read/write interface? These other processes might then take advantage of all the first process's allocation of primary memory to hold the portions of the file they are accessing, and thus deprive the first process of the primary memory required to do anything else.

We discuss solutions to this dilemma in Chapter 7. In the meantime, we take a compromise position and give each process a minimum amount of primary storage, assign the file subsystem a minimum amount of primary storage, and leave some additional storage available for which processes and the file system can compete.

4.1.4.2 File Systems

File systems control secondary storage, providing a means for the rest of the system to use it. They manage the actual space on the devices, not only keeping track of what's free and what's not, but also organizing it for efficient access. They maintain directories for finding files and provide access control, both for synchronization and security purposes. Most provide some sort of crash resiliency, so that damage is minimized when a system crashes. All of this we discuss in Chapter 6.

What we cover here is the high-level part of file systems — how they are integrated with the rest of the operating system. For the most part, this is independent of the actual low-level file systems of Chapter 6. In the Windows world the term "file system" is reserved for the low-level file system and "I/O manager" is used for the high-level portion. We use the terminology adopted in Unix systems and speak of the high-level file system as the *virtual file system* (*VFS*). From here on, "actual file system" refers to the low-level file system.

The virtual file system provides the application's view of files. We discussed this layer for Sixth-Edition Unix in Section 1.3.5. It's augmented in our system, as well as in Windows and modern Unix systems, with support for mapped files, as discussed above. In our simple system we use the roughly the same data structures as described in Section 1.3.5 for representing an open file. Figure 4.11 shows the data structures representing an open file. Note that each process has its own *file-descriptor table*, which resides in the PCB. As explained in Section 1.3.5, when a file is opened an entry is allocated in the file-descriptor table. To represent the context information for the file, an entry is also allocated in the *system file table*, and the file-descriptor entry is set to point to it. Finally, the file itself is represented in memory by a *file object* (known as an *inode* in Sixth-Edition Unix), which is pointed to by the system-file-table entry.

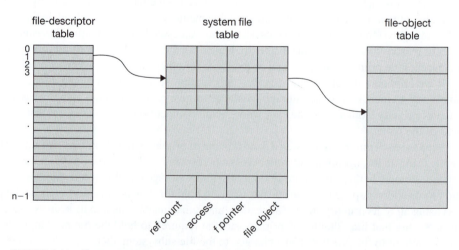

FIGURE 4.11 Data structures representing open files.

```
class FileObject {
  unsigned short refcount;
  ...
  virtual int create(const char *,
    int, FileObject **);
  virtual int read(int, void *,
    int);
  virtual int write(int,
    const void *, int);
  ...
};
```

```
typedef struct {
  unsigned short refcount;
  struct file_ops *file_op;
  /* function pointers */
} FileObject;
```

FIGURE 4.12   File object in C++ and C.

The inode of Sixth-Edition Unix described a file in terms of how its underlying file system represented it on disk. This worked fine, since there was only one kind of file system. However, our system, like all modern systems, is designed to support any number of different kinds of file system. Thus the file object forms the boundary between the virtual file system and the actual file system. To allow different kinds of actual file systems and hence different kinds of files, the kernel file object must be something that can represent any kind of file. Operations performed on the file must be directed to code that's specific for the file. If our system were written in C++ or a similar language, there might be a class *FileObject* with virtual functions for operations on files. The file object for a particular actual file system would be a subclass of the FileObject. Written in C, a FileObject contains an array of function pointers, one for each operation on a file. See Figure 4.12.

As mentioned in Section 4.1.4 above, recently accessed blocks from files are kept in a *file-system cache*. The primary storage holding these blocks might be mapped into one or more address spaces of processes that have mapped the respective files, and the blocks are also available for immediate access by read and write system calls. A simple hash function, keyed by inode number and block number, is used to locate file blocks in the cache.

The actual file system manages data on the disk or other secondary storage device. Most modern operating systems support a number of different file systems. For example, Windows systems support NTFS as their primary file system, but also support FAT-16 and FAT-32 file systems for compatibility with older Microsoft operating systems, as well as ISO 9660, which is used on CDs, and M-UDF, which is used on DVDs. Linux supports the Ext2, Ext3, and Ext4 file systems as well as a number of other systems, including those of Windows.

Layered beneath the file-system code is the device driver, which is referenced using major and minor device numbers as discussed in Section 4.1.1 above. Thus the actual file system is not concerned about the peculiarities of the device, but is written to the standard interface provided by the device driver.

Our simple operating system of Section 4.1 is a traditional monolithic system. All its components are linked together into one large module that runs in privileged mode. Its threads go from module to module via subroutine calls. Data structures are easily shared because there's just one address space. Given the set of components in the system, this is probably the most efficient means possible for running them. So, why do we want to rethink this approach?

An operating system is a large complex program. As with any such program, it makes sense to build it as a collection of modules that have well defined interfaces and interact only through these interfaces. This not only makes bugs easier to find, but also helps isolate their effect.

4.2
RETHINKING
OPERATING-
SYSTEM
STRUCTURE

This is how monolithic operating systems are designed, at least to a certain extent. Even though all components are linked into one module, the intent is that modules behave as described in Section 4.1 above. But intent doesn't necessarily translate into reality. Bugs in one component can adversely affect another. Large numbers of programmers contribute code to operating systems. Some might not be as good coders as others. Good coders have bad days.

Modern operating systems isolate applications from one another and from the operating system — bugs in one cannot directly affect others. Can this sort of isolation be provided for operating-system components without undue loss of performance?

The answer is yes, given a not-too-stringent definition of "undue." The secret is to run some of an operating-system's components as application programs and give them the standard sort of application-program protections.

The earliest and most successful example of this idea is the *virtual machine*, which behaves just like a real machine but is implemented in software and can be instantiated multiple times on one real machine. Virtual machines were invented by IBM in the 1960s as the basis for a multiuser time-sharing system (Meyer and Seawright 1970). The problem was this: it seemed difficult to design and build a monolithic multiuser time-sharing system.[4] However, a single-user time-sharing system was relatively easy. It turned out that it was also relatively easy to design and build an operating system that supported multiple virtual machines — a *virtual machine monitor*. Running multiple single-user time-sharing systems, each in a separate virtual machine yielded a multiuser time-sharing system. Voilà!

Adding to the appeal of this solution was that the single-user time-sharing system could be (and was) developed independently of the virtual machine monitor — it could be tested on a real machine, whose behavior was, of course, identical to the virtual machine's. Furthermore, there was no ambiguity about the interface the virtual machine monitor should provide to its applications — it was to behave exactly like the real machine.

Another approach with similar goals is the notion of the *microkernel*, invented in the 1980s. Rather than providing virtual-machine abstractions to their applications, microkernels provide some of the fundamental low-level pieces of an operating system, such as virtual memory, threads, and I/O devices. They then depend on servers running as applications in user mode to build user-level abstractions, such as processes and file systems, on top of these pieces and make them available to user applications. Thus what user programs see as the operating system is actually a collection of servers.

Why is the microkernel approach useful? Let's start with security. Much as we want to protect the operating system from its applications, it may also be important to protect it from some of its own components. Some components may be better tested than others. We don't want a misbehaving component to have direct access to others. If such a component fails, we want it to do so without bringing down the entire system.

Another area is debugging and testing. Let's say you are developing a new file system. The tools available to help you, such as debuggers, test generators, and the like, are probably designed for use only with user-mode application code, not privileged-mode operating-system code. Thus running your new operating-system component as a user-level application lets you take advantage of all these tools. And, of course, if it crashes, it doesn't take down the operating system.

And last, with the microkernel approach, it's relatively easy to add functionality that otherwise would have to be provided by code running in privileged mode. For example, one can add a new subsystem that needs efficient, direct access to devices, such as a file system or perhaps a database system.

---

[4] IBM was working on a monolithic multiuser time-sharing system at the time, imaginatively called TSS (time-sharing system). It had numerous development problems and ultimately failed commercially.

Two of the earliest microkernels were Mach and Chorus. Mach was initially developed at Carnegie Mellon University; later development took place at the University of Utah. Mach is currently used as part of the GNU HURD[5] project, which is building an open-source Unix implementation as a collection of servers running on Mach. Chorus was a commercial system developed by Chorus Systèmes of France (which no longer exists), providing a Unix interface along with some additional functionality.

In the following sections, we cover more of the details of virtual-machine and microkernel design and give further examples of their use.

4.2.1 VIRTUAL MACHINES

The virtual-machine concept was originally devised as a means for structuring an operating system. The virtual machine monitor (VMM) multiplexes system resources, while the OS running on the virtual machine (known as the "hosted OS" or "guest OS") provides additional functionality such as file systems, communication software, interaction support, and so forth; see Figure 4.13. This division of labor worked out well, and the concept proved to have a number of other benefits.

IBM pioneered the notion of virtual machines, having begun work in the area in 1964; almost all virtual-machine systems were from them until the mid-1990s. As mentioned above, their original motivation was to produce a viable time-sharing system quickly. Since a virtual machine behaves just like a real one, an operating system designed for a real machine can run on a virtual machine.

IBM referred to its VMM as CP 67 — CP stands for control program; the single-user time-sharing system was called CMS, which originally stood for Cambridge Monitor System but later became known as Conversational Monitor System. CP 67 was originally called CP 40 (for Control Program 40) and ran on a specially modified 360 Model 40. When the Model 67, the only 360 designed to use memory-relocation hardware, became available, the project was moved to it and renamed. The initial design of CP 40 began in late 1964, implementation of CP 40 and CMS began in mid-1965, and CP 67/CMS began production use in early 1967. An interesting and complete history of the project can be found in (Varian 1997). The entire package came to be known as VM/370 when the IBM 360 was replaced with the 370. The most recent descendants are VM/ESA and z/VM.[6]

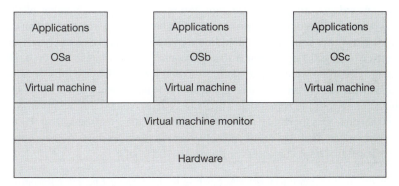

FIGURE 4.13   A system structured as a number of virtual machines.

---

[5] *HURD* stands for "hird of Unix-replacing daemons," while *hird* stands for "hurd of interfaces representing depth;" see http://www.gnu.org/software/hurd/hurd.html.

[6] See http://www.vm.ibm.com/overview/.

Though it might seem both pointless and redundant, this notion of running a complete real-machine OS on a virtual machine has proved enormously useful, so much so that it is now the dominant use of the virtual-machine concept. Here are a few examples, discovered by IBM and others, of why this is so.

1. *Debugging and testing operating systems.* Systems development in many computer installations is continuous and proceeds concurrently with production work. In the now distant past, computers were very expensive. Few places could afford to have two — one to test new releases of an operating system and another to run the current release. Instead, many places would have just one machine and reserve a few hours each night for operating-system testing. With virtual machines, one could run the current release of the operating system on one virtual machine and a test version of a new release on another, and allow people to use both operating systems around the clock.

2. *Running multiple different operating systems.* Originally this idea applied to large, "mainframe" computers. A company might need one operating system to run accounting applications and another one for general time-sharing applications. The economics of computers in the 1970s was such that it was far cheaper to have one large computer running both operating systems on different virtual machines than to dedicate a separate machine for each operating system. More recently, companies such as VMware provide virtual-machine support so that you can run both Windows and Linux concurrently on the same computer.

3. *Accommodating hardware changes.* In the 1970s and 1980s, IBM dominated the mainframe computer market. Their early competitors, in particular General Electric, NCR, and RCA, did miserably and were forced to drop out. Later Amdahl Computer Corporation (founded by Gene Amdahl, the original architect of the IBM 360) began to compete successfully with IBM by selling hardware compatible with IBM's and running IBM software (such as VM/370). IBM would introduce hardware changes (often implemented via microcode) and require such features to be present for new releases of software to work. Amdahl's customers wanted to run the latest versions of all software, but it was difficult for Amdahl to make the requisite changes to their own hardware quickly enough. However, they discovered they could make these changes quickly in the virtual machine monitor (VMM) — thus their virtual machine presented an updated version of the real machine's architecture, complete with new and modified instructions.

4. *Server consolidation and service isolation.* An organization has a number of services, each running on a different computer. Not only would it be cheaper to run them all on one computer (or, at least, on fewer computers), but it's more convenient and cheaper to create new instances of a service on an existing computer than to acquire a new computer to run it. However, the operating systems on which these services run don't do an adequate job of equitably sharing a computer's resources among all its applications. Running each server on a separate virtual machine (along with the appropriate operating system) isolates the servers from one another enough that none gets more than its fair share of the real machine's resources. Furthermore, it's safe to run services that don't trust each other on the same machine — their virtual machines are so isolated that none can access any aspect of the others.

How is this magic made to work? According to the *Oxford English Dictionary*, "virtual," as it pertains to computers, means "not physically existing as such but made by software to appear to do so from the point of view of the program or the user." The original idea was for the virtual machine to look and behave just like a real machine — an operating system running on a virtual machine (the hosted operating system) shouldn't be able to distinguish it from a real machine. This required faithful virtualization of pretty much all components: processor, memory, interval timers, and I/O devices. As the use of virtual machines has evolved, though, it's become clear that such obliviousness on the part of the OS running on the virtual machine comes at a cost. Though it's still useful to run an unmodified real-machine OS on a virtual machine, substantial improvements are gained by having the real-machine OS cooperate with the VMM.

In the paragraphs below we first discuss "pure" virtualization, in which the virtual machine behaves just like a real machine, then cover what's come to be known as "paravirtualization" — where the virtualized entity is a bit different from the real entity so as to "enhance scalability, performance, and simplicity" (Whitaker, Shaw, et al. 2002).

4.2.1.1 Processor Virtualization

Virtualizing the processor requires both multiplexing the real processor among the virtual machines and making each virtual machine behave just like a real one. Multiplexing the processor is relatively straightforward — we discuss it in Chapter 5. Reproducing the behavior of the real machine is, at least conceptually, more complicated. Not only must all instructions work identically on real and virtual machines, but the generation of and response to traps and interrupts must be the same on both as well.

For the most part, the processor in the virtual machine is the real one; that is, instructions are executed directly and not, for example, handled by an interpreter or emulator. Thus traps are generated just as they are on real machines. Interrupts are generated by both real and virtual devices, and a virtually generated interrupt must get the same sort of response that a real one does. Since it is a real processor that is executing instructions, traps and interrupts are handled by the real processor just as on the real machine. Somehow the virtual machine must be made to believe that it has just received a trap or interrupt. Since the response to both traps and interrupts on a real machine is generally established by a hardware-mandated table giving addresses of trap and interrupt handlers, the same sort of table is set up on the virtual machine. Thus, in response to a trap or interrupt, the VMM finds the address of the virtual machine's trap/interrupt handler in the table and transfers control to it.

This notion that the virtual machine's processor is real works out well, except for one problem: if the virtual machine is in privileged mode and thus can execute privileged instructions, it may seem to have full control over all resources, not just the virtual resources assigned to it. For example, the VMM uses privileged instructions to set up memory-mapping resources so that virtual machines are isolated from one another as well as from the VMM itself. An operating system or one of its applications in one virtual machine cannot access memory belonging to another. But if the operating system running in the virtual machine is executing instructions in privileged mode, what is to prevent it from changing how the memory-mapping resources have been set up?

Popek and Goldberg treat this problem formally in a 1974 paper (Popek and Goldberg 1974), in which they define a virtual machine as "an *efficient, isolated duplicate* of the real machine." They distinguish *sensitive instructions* from *privileged instructions*. The latter are simply those that execute fully when the processor is in privileged mode, but cause some sort of privileged-instruction trap when executed in non-privileged mode. The former are those instructions that affect the allocation of (real) system resources or whose effect depends upon such allocation or on the current processor mode. Instructions that change the mapping of virtual to real memory are an example of affecting the allocation of system resources. An instruction that returns the real address of a location in virtual memory is an example of one that depends on such an allocation. An instruction, such as the x86's *popf* instruction, that sets a set of processor flags when run in privileged mode but sets a smaller set of flags when run in non-privileged mode, is an example of one whose effect depends on processor mode.

Popek and Goldberg prove as a theorem that if a computer's set of sensitive instructions is a subset of its privileged instructions, then a virtual machine monitor can be constructed for it.

The actual proof involves a lot of notation but no deep concepts — we treat it here as intuitively obvious.[7] Though the theorem's converse is not true, when the theorem's premise does not hold constructing a virtual machine monitor is sufficiently challenging that for a couple of decades no one did so.

Fortunately for the developers of CP 67, the theorem does hold for the IBM 360 — all of its sensitive instructions are privileged instructions. For it and other architectures for which the theorem holds, the following strategy can be used. (See Figure 4.14.)

Only the VMM runs in privileged mode; all other software runs in user mode. For each virtual machine, the VMM keeps track of whether it is in "virtual privileged mode" or "virtual user mode." Whenever a virtual machine is in privileged mode, the VMM represents the virtual machine's state as being virtual privileged mode, even though the (real) processor is in user mode. When a sensitive (and thus privileged) instruction is executed on a virtual machine, the real processor traps to the virtual machine monitor. The VMM then checks the state of the virtual machine: if the virtual machine is in virtual user mode, then this attempt to execute a sensitive instruction should result in a trap on the virtual machine. However, if the virtual machine is in virtual privileged mode, then the effect of the sensitive instruction is emulated by the VMM, subject to whatever constraints are placed on the virtual machine. For example, if the virtual machine attempts to access an I/O device that hasn't been assigned to it, then the instruction is made to fail as it would on a real machine that attempts to access a non-existent device (which probably causes the operating system running on the virtual machine to crash). The virtual machine might be allowed to modify how memory-mapping resources are configured, but only to the extent of modifying resources already assigned to it (we discuss this in more detail in Chapter 7).

If the execution of sensitive instructions doesn't cause traps in user mode, processor virtualization is more difficult. Things are especially complex on the Intel x86 and its descendants. Though its architecture employs four processor modes, known as rings 0 through 3, the full effect of all instructions is available only in ring 0. Most operating systems utilize only rings 0, for privileged code, and 3, for user code. What complicates things is that, though some of its sensitive instructions are privileged and hence user-mode execution (i.e., in rings 1 through 3) causes a trap, some of its sensitive instructions are not privileged but execute differently in ring 0 than in the other rings. For example, the x86 *popf* instruction sets various flags in a processor control register. If executed in ring 0, all the flags are set, but if executed in ring 1, 2, or 3, only certain

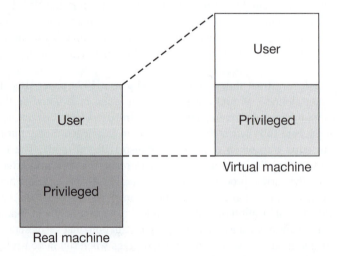

FIGURE 4.14 Both user and privileged modes of the virtual machine run in user mode of the real machine.

User

Privileged

Virtual machine

User

Privileged

Real machine

---

[7] This is known as "proof by obviousness." If you don't think it's obvious, then it's "proof by intimidation."

flags are set and the intended settings for the others are quietly ignored. In particular, in ring 0 the instruction can be used to enable and disable interrupts, while in the other rings it cannot. So if a virtual machine executes *popf* in virtual privileged mode, intending to enable interrupts, the attempt will go unnoticed by both the hardware and the VMM.

The first truly successful approach towards virtual machines on a non-Popek-and-Goldberg-friendly architecture was developed by VMware (U.S. patent 6397242) and involves a machine-code translator. When a virtual machine is in virtual privileged mode, its instructions are handled by a "binary translation subsystem" that generates, from the code the virtual machine was trying to run, code that is safe to run in real privileged mode. So if, for example, such code contained a *popf* instruction, the generated code would invoke the VMM, which would enable or disable interrupts if appropriate. Such sequences of translated code are cached so that future executions can be done quickly.

More recently, both Intel and AMD have recognized the importance of virtualization and have independently enhanced the x86 architecture to support it. Intel's enhancement, known as VT-x, provides two modes of operation orthogonal to the four rings known as root and non-root. In root mode, in which a VMM would run, the processor behaves pretty much as it does without the enhancement. In non-root mode the processor still appears to behave that way to code running within it, but certain operations and events make it exit non-root mode and, effectively, trap back to the VMM running in root mode. Which operations and events are affected is specified by the VMM. Thus, for example, the VMM can arrange to receive control when privileged instructions and page faults occur, but the virtual machine handles arithmetic exceptions directly. We discuss additional enhancements affecting address translation in Chapter 7.

Sharing the real processor among virtual machines is a scheduling problem that's not much different from the scheduling used by a normal OS to multiplex the processor among its threads. In the original CP 67/CMS system, the processor was multiplexed among the virtual machines by CP 67. CMS was single-threaded and thus did no further multiplexing of the processor. This was a sensible division of labor and simplified the design of CMS.

The mechanism for multiplexing the processor was fairly straightforward. At any moment of time the real processor might be assigned to a particular virtual machine, executing instructions on its behalf. But if the virtual machine's processor was idle, the real processor could safely be assigned to another virtual machine. Thus whenever the virtual machine's processor entered the idle state (an operation that required a privileged instruction), the VMM came into play and transferred the real processor to another virtual machine. Of course, this assumes that the OS on the virtual machine actually bothers to put its processor in the idle state. Many operating systems instead employ an *idle loop* in which a tight loop of instructions repeatedly checks for something to do. This is probably not a desirable behavior on a virtual machine, but if an OS is to be run unmodified, it must be supported.

For this and other reasons, a virtual machine might remain active indefinitely. Thus CP 67 also employed time-slicing: each virtual machine was given the processor for no more than some finite period before it was another processor's turn (Chapter 5 discusses processor scheduling in detail). Time slicing is implemented with the help of an *interval timer*, hardware that causes an interrupt after a specified period of time.

For a simple operating system such as CMS, there was no need to virtualize the interval timer. However, other operating systems that were run on CP 67 were multithreaded and thus did multiplex the processor. How did such double multiplexing work? While the real processor was assigned to a virtual machine, the virtual machine's operating system would multiplex the processor among its threads: when a thread yielded the processor, the operating system simply assigned it to another of its threads. If the operating system time-sliced its threads, it gave each some amount of time to run, say x seconds. However, the x seconds was of course not real time, but virtual time — the virtual clock would advance only when the virtual machine was assigned the real processor; i.e., the virtualized interval timer measured virtual time.

But does it always make sense for a virtualized interval timer to measure virtual time? Suppose the need is to provide a time-out mechanism. This might be used to give a user 60 seconds to type in a password. Or it might be used by a communications protocol to wait, say, 10 milliseconds before retransmitting a packet. In these cases, it seems clear that we want the virtualized interval timer to measure real time.

One can't transparently provide both virtual and real interval timing through the same virtualized interval timer. CP 67 provided the former, thus facilitating time-slicing within a virtual machine. When both are needed it's necessary to break from the strict notion that the virtual machine behaves just like the real machine and have the VMM explicitly provide both kinds of timers. On CP 67, a special *hypervisor* call (see the discussion of paravirtualization in Section 4.2.1.3, below) was provided so that the operating system running on the virtual machine could request (real) time information.

4.2.1.2 I/O Virtualization

I/O devices provide additional challenges. It is pretty clear, at least conceptually, how to share a single real processor among a number of virtual processors: some sort of scheduler multiplexes the real processor among the virtual ones. A real disk might be divided into a number of virtual disks — each behaving similarly to a real disk, but providing a fraction of the real disk's storage. A virtual display might be a window on a real display. In implementing virtual disks and virtual displays, care must be taken to make sure that the virtual processor cannot access beyond the bounds of the virtual device; the virtual device must appear to be a real device of reduced size.

A virtual network interface provides an even greater challenge. One real Ethernet device can support a number of virtual Ethernet devices by giving each virtual device a separate (real and unique) MAC address, and handling the frames addressed to all the virtual devices. Thus the effect is that each of the virtual Ethernet devices is on the same network as the real one.

Ideally, an operating system on a virtual machine is oblivious to the fact that its devices are not real. It performs operations and receives notifications using the same code it would use when running directly on a real machine. These operations must be vetted by the VMM and mapped into operations on real devices, which the VMM then performs. Notifications from devices, such as interrupts and status changes, must first be handled by the VMM, then passed on to the appropriate virtual machine.

Starting an I/O operation (see Section 3.2) involves the use of privileged instructions or access to special areas of the address space into which device registers are mapped, both of which should generate a trap to the VMM when done on a virtual machine.

Vetting an I/O request is conceptually straightforward. The VMM must simply check that the request is within the bounds of the virtual device. Thus, for example, if a virtual disk is assigned 20 cylinders (see Section 6.1.2) from the 1000 supported by the real disk to which it is mapped, the VMM must make certain that no operation on the virtual disk will attempt to access any cylinders other than those assigned to it.

A properly vetted I/O request is then mapped by the VMM into a request to the real device. This mapping can be simple; in the case of the 20-cylinder virtual disk, the disk location in the request is simply mapped to the area where the virtual disk has been allocated on the real disk. The VMM can now apply the mapped operation to the real device. Resulting interrupts are applied to the virtual machine.

Figure 4.15, a very rough schematic of an operating system on a real machine, shows the logical location of the device drivers. In Figure 4.16, this operating system is moved to a virtual machine. Both the operating system on the virtual machine and VMM must have device drivers (see Section 3.2) encapsulating the interfaces to devices, whether virtual or real. Even if a virtual device has identical characteristics to the real device, the virtual device driver might well differ considerably from the real device driver, since the virtual-machine OS's interface to device

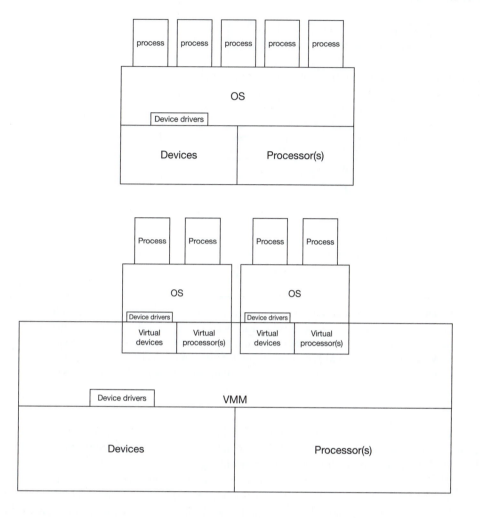

FIGURE 4.15
A high-level schematic of an operating system, showing its device drivers.

FIGURE 4.16
The operating system of Figure 4.15 moved to a virtual machine.

drivers is likely to be different from the VMM's. This is unfortunate, because it may mean that two different device drivers must be supported for each device. For disks and displays, the virtual device might well have different characteristics from the real device. In such cases we would clearly need two different device drivers.

The need for two drivers per device is a real problem in practice. Vendors of devices supply drivers for the major operating systems, but are unlikely to supply drivers for VMMs (though this could change if VMMs become a more important source of sales). One way around this problem is for the VMM to coexist on the real machine with a major operating system, such as Linux or Windows. This is the approach taken in VMware Workstation and in Xen. We discuss the former here and the latter in the next section on paravirtualization.

In VMware Workstation (Sugerman, Venkitachalam, et al. 2001), virtual-machine support is an add-on to a normal operating system, called the *host operating system*. Processor virtualization is provided by a module — VMDriver, providing the VMM functionality — that is installed in the system as if it were a device driver. Virtual machines appear to the host OS as if they were processes. They are scheduled like ordinary processes and memory resources are assigned to them as if they were ordinary processes. Of course, the OS within the virtual machine (the *guest OS*) schedules its own virtual processes and manages the memory assigned to it. I/O virtualization is provided with the help of another module, VMApp, that runs as a user-level application on the host operating system.

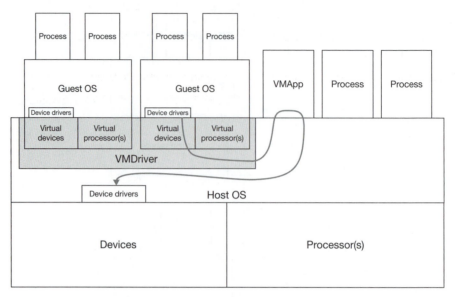

FIGURE 4.17 The VMware-workstation approach to virtualizing I/O. The device driver in the guest OS starts an I/O operation, which results in a privileged-operation trap that is handled by the VMM, which is implemented within the VMDriver module. This module forwards the request to VMApp, running within a user process on the host operating system. It performs a normal I/O system call, which is eventually handled by the (real) device driver on the host operating system.

Each virtual machine is equipped with a collection of relatively standard (virtual) devices, including keyboard, mouse, speakers, disks, and network interface cards. Since they are standard devices, their drivers come with the standard operating systems.

The guest OS's device drivers perform operations as if they were on a real machine. In the case of writes, the VMM code in VMDriver forwards requests to the user-level VMApp, which then places a system call to have the request performed by the host OS. Reads proceed analogously, with data read by VMApp, then transferred to the guest OS by VMApp's writing it to VMDriver, which then posts an interrupt to the virtual machine. See Figure 4.17.

This approach clearly has a cost. There is considerable overhead in switching between the VMM environment (in VMDriver) and the host OS environment, and to and from the user process running VMApp. However, (Sugerman, Venkitachalam, et al. 2001) reports that an application running on a virtual machine hosted on a 733 MHz PC can transmit data at a rate that saturates a 100 million bit/second Ethernet, despite the overhead of the virtual-machine implementation (though see Exercise 10). Nevertheless, for servers VMware does not use this approach, but instead uses the more direct approach of Figure 4.16, with support for only a limited set of devices.

4.2.1.3 Paravirtualization

Up to now we've assumed that the virtual-machine architecture is identical to that of a real machine, and that we run in it an unmodified operating system designed to run on the real machine. While convenient, this assumption has a number of problems. In particular, there are a number of sources of difficulty in implementing such virtual machines:

- Pure performance issues such as the overhead of context switching between virtual machines, the virtual machine monitor, and other contexts such as the host OS of VMware Workstation. Also included here is the cost of emulating privileged instructions.

- The duplication of effort by the OS running in the virtual machine and the virtual machine monitor. For example, both might be running a scheduler (see Chapter 5), and both might be managing virtual memory (see Chapter 7). Both might be interpreting I/O requests and mapping them to devices, whether virtual or real.

- Access to non-virtualizable functions, such as a real-time interval timer.

These issues were first addressed in CMS/CP 67 and later in VM/370. In particular, CMS/CP 67 introduced the notion of a *hypervisor call*, essentially a means for the OS on the virtual machine to communicate directly with the VMM. Among other things, it was used for accessing the real-time interval timer. Implementing the hypervisor call is a bit of an issue — it must be an instruction that is unused by normal operating systems, and thus will generate a trap and be recognized by the VMM as special. The IBM 360 fortuitously had the *diagnose* instruction, which on a real machine was used only in debugging the processor's microcode, never in an operating system. On the x86 architecture the *int* (interrupt) instruction is used for this purpose. It delivers an interrupt identified by its argument to the processor; one simply supplies an argument that is otherwise not used. Utilizing hypervisor calls certainly entails modifying the real-machine operating system as well as the interface presented by the virtual machine, but it allows functionality that would otherwise not be attainable.

The relaxation of virtualization requirements has become known as *paravirtualization*. (Whitaker, Shaw, et al. 2002) describes it as exposing a "virtual architecture that is slightly different than the physical architecture." Though early work was done in the context of CMS/CP 67 and VM/370, we cover it using examples from Denali and Xen.

Denali is designed to run a large number of virtual machines, each with a simple operating system. It is not intended to run existing operating systems designed for real machines, but to run special-purpose OSes on which server applications are hosted. By running each in a virtual machine, the OSes and their applications are isolated from one another and thus less susceptible to attack.

Denali deals with both the context-switch overhead and the multiple device-driver problem by providing a simplified I/O interface to its virtual machines. For example, standard network devices require multiple executions of privileged instructions to send a single frame. Denali's virtual machines see a generic network-interface device and a set of virtual device registers that allow multiple frames to be transferred with a single privileged instruction. Thus the overhead for both context switching and instruction emulation is greatly reduced. Since the network-interface device is generic, virtual machines need support just one device driver, while the VMM supports device drivers for specific network-interface devices.

Interrupts are another source of context-switch overhead. A straightforward virtualization of device I/O would require the VMM to deliver device interrupts to the relevant virtual machine when the interrupts occur. An optimization might be possible if the interrupt is destined for the currently running virtual machine. But Denali is intended to support large numbers of virtual machines concurrently, making it likely that the target of an interrupt is not running at the time the interrupt occurs. So, rather than deliver interrupts one at a time when they arrive, Denali batches them: it holds on to interrupts destined for a particular virtual machine and delivers them all at once the next time the virtual machine runs. This requires that any immediate interaction with the device be done by the VMM. The semantics of an interrupt from the virtual machine's perspective is no longer "something just happened" but becomes "something happened in the not-too-distant past."

Unlike Denali and more like VMware Workstation, Xen (Barham, Dragovic, et al. 2003) is intended to support standard (real-machine) operating systems. Nevertheless, it uses paravirtualization and thus requires some modification of the operating systems that run in its virtual machines. Some of these changes are straightforward: sensitive instructions that are not privileged are replaced with hypervisor calls.

Figure 4.18 shows Xen's basic structure. What it has in common with VMware Workstation is its use of a standard, real-machine operating system to manage devices and perform other control functions. Xen refers to its virtual machines as *domains*; the one special domain in which the real-machine operating system runs is called *domain 0*. This domain has direct access to devices and its operating system includes standard device drivers. The other domains, known collectively as *domain U* (for unprivileged) and individually as *domain Ui*, typically do not have direct access to devices. Unlike VMware Workstation, these other domains are not run as processes under the control of domain 0, but all domains are controlled by Xen's VMM; their executions are scheduled by Xen's scheduler.

As shown in Figure 4.18, the domain-0 OS, on an x86, runs with full privileges in ring 0, while its processes run in ring 3. The other domains run with no privileges — even their operating systems run in ring 1. To perform sensitive operations, they place hypervisor calls. On systems with only two processor modes (e.g., privileged and non-privileged), only the VMM and the OS running in domain 0 run in privileged mode.

Rather than giving the virtual machine the illusion that it is directly controlling a device, Xen eliminates the notion of devices entirely and instead provides direct communication paths between the domain U's and the domain containing the relevant driver, normally domain 0. Thus, for example, a virtual machine does virtual I/O not via a disk driver and a virtual disk, but by transferring blocks of data directly to domain 0 and receiving them from it. Similarly, network code on a virtual machine, rather than using a device driver to control a virtual network-interface device, transfers frames directly to and from domain 0.

The communication takes place via memory, set up by the VMM, that is shared between the two domains. Xen uses what it calls a split device-driver model to make this work. Disk I/O is handled by a block driver split in two parts: a front end running in domain U and a back end running in domain 0. Both parts are generic in that neither depends upon any details of the disk device (or even, in fact, that it is indeed a disk). However, the back end communicates data to the actual device driver that controls the device. The net driver is similarly split into two parts. Thus an operating system running in domain U need only have block and net front ends and is not dependent in any way on the characteristics of actual devices.

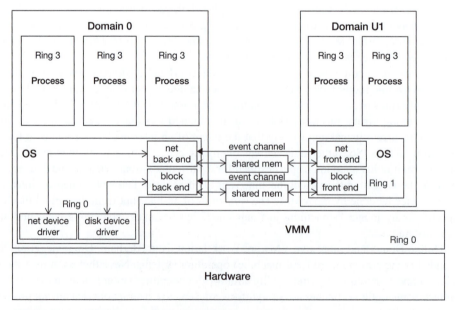

FIGURE 4.18   The structure of a Xen system on an x86.

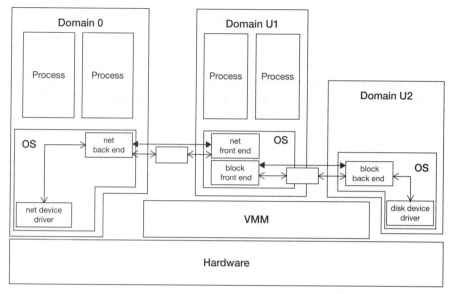

FIGURE 4.19   A Xen system with a driver residing in a separate domain.

Interrupts are similarly replaced with a higher-level concept — event channels. These are a fairly simple abstraction of interrupts. Each domain has some pre-specified number of virtual processors, known as VCPUs, and registers with each of them a set of possible events. Each such event is tied to a source domain, typically domain 0, that triggers it. Associated with each event on each VCPU in the target domain is a *pending bit*, a *mask bit*, and the address of a *handler*. When an event occurs, a VCPU in the target domain that doesn't have the masked bit set is selected. If the VCPU's pending bit is not set, the VMM places an upcall to the event handler and, simultaneously, sets the pending and masked bits. Otherwise it simply sets the pending bit.

Events carry no information other than that they have occurred. They can be used, say, by the net back-end driver to notify the front-end driver that a packet has been enqueued in their common shared-memory. Since there is no notion of queuing events, the front-end driver interprets such an event as notifying it that one or more packets have been enqueued.

Xen provides a number of interesting possibilities for system design. For example, a common source of problems in an otherwise reliable system is a not-so-reliable device driver. In most operating systems device drivers run in the operating-system kernel with full privileges, so that a problem with, say, an uninitialized pointer could cause damage any place in the operating system. So, to protect the operating system, even one running in domain 0, from the actions of a device driver, drivers can be put into separate domains that run at lower privilege levels and, depending on hardware support, have access only to the relevant device control registers and not to the rest of the OS. See Figure 4.19.

4.2.2 Microkernels

The idea behind microkernels is that only the bare essentials should run in privileged mode in the operating-system kernel. All other components should run as normal applications. The reasons for doing things this way involve both security and flexibility.

The need for security makes sense if we assume that people who code OS modules are malicious, incompetent, or both. We want only the most trusted modules running in privileged mode. Modules not coded to the most rigorous standards are dangerous if executed in the kernel, since the entire system is completely unprotected from them. We want to run these modules as user-level applications, within protected processes, so that they have a limited effect if they misbehave — see Figure 4.20.

For example, if you download a new file system from some web site you have no particular reason to trust, you probably don't want to install it in your kernel and thus enable it to control your computer. Instead, it might make sense to give it access to some bounded region of a disk drive, but nothing else, and let it maintain a file system there and respond to the requests of other applications to create and access files.

On the other hand, whether or not you explicitly trust whoever wrote the file system in the operating system on the computer you use, since you allow it to handle all your files, you certainly trust it implicitly — if its coders were malicious, there's no telling what might be happening to your files. Thus, everything else being equal, there's no real additional danger in having the file system reside in the kernel.[8]

The point is that, if properly designed, a microkernel-based operating system lets new functionality be added to an operating system in a reasonably secure way; it provides flexibility by making the system *extensible*. Not only new versions of existing components can be added, but also components that are integrated with the existing components and provide new functionality.

Typical examples involve extending the file-system interface. One is the notion of a *portal*, which is a special kind of file. When a portal is opened it returns not a handle to an ordinary file, but a handle to a process that is communicating with a service on another machine via a network connection. How this can be done is described below.

What parts of an operating system should be in the kernel, running in privileged mode? The kernel is protected from all applications, but has complete control over everything. Thus, what belongs in it are those components that control physical resources used by all. These resources include the processor, primary memory, and many I/O devices. Note that what an application perceives as a resource may actually be controlled by an intermediary sitting between the kernel and the application. For example, the kernel might allocate a certain amount of processor time to a process, but a system-supplied library linked into the process itself might determine how much time each of its threads receives. Similarly, the kernel provides disk devices or portions of disk devices to file systems, but the file systems control the use of their assigned disks.

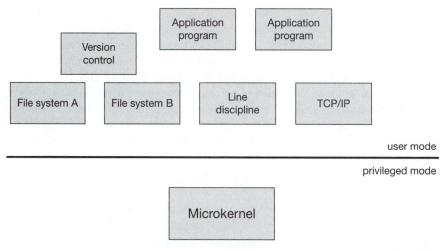

FIGURE 4.20 A system structured as a microkernel.

---

[8] However, putting it in the kernel does violate the "principle of least privilege," which we discuss in Chapter 8.

Getting all this to work requires solutions to two problems. We need some way to link the various components together. When everything is in a single monolithic image, linkages are strictly subroutine linkages. But with microkernels things aren't so straightforward. If an application thread opens a file, the request must be directed to the file-system component, which in turn may need to perform an I/O operation, via the disk-driver component, on one of its disks. The other problem is the efficient transfer of data. In a monolithic system, data can be passed by reference between modules — no copying is required. But if the modules reside in different processes with different address spaces, passing by reference doesn't work, since a pointer in one address space is meaningless in another.

Both to understand the benefits of the approach a bit better and to get some idea of how it might be made to work, let's sketch the design of a hypothetical microkernel-based system. Our design is loosely based on that of the GNU/HURD project,[9] which is built on the Mach 3.0 microkernel (Julin, Chew, et al. 1991) from Carnegie Mellon University.

The kernel, running in privileged mode, contains device drivers, supports threads and a simple form of processes, and manages primary storage and virtual-to-real address mapping. The other functionality discussed in Section 4.1 — terminals, network communication, and the file system — is implemented as separate user-level application processes. Thus the modular structure is similar, if not identical to our simple system; it differs mainly in that the modules are very much isolated from one another, being in separate processes.

The module-linkage problem is solved with a Mach construct known as a *port*, which allows the owner of an object, whether the kernel or a user process, to give others secure references to the object. A port is itself an object managed by the kernel, which provides two sorts of references to it — send and receive rights (see Figure 4.21). Messages are sent to the port by holders of send rights and received by the (single) holder of receive rights. The intent is that the holder of receive rights manages some object and provides send rights for the port to those it wishes to allow access to the object. The receiver interprets the messages as operations on its object.

Returning a response requires a bit more work. The sender of a request has (or creates) its own port, the response port, for receiving responses. It retains receive rights to it, but sends along with its request a copy of the send rights to the response port (see Figure 4.22). The receiver of the request then sends the response back via the send rights to the response port (Figure 4.23).

As an example, suppose the kernel maintains an object representing a disk device, and suppose the file system is running as a user process (Figure 4.24). A port, representing a reference to the disk object, is set up by the kernel, which holds its receive rights but gives send rights to the file-system process. Threads in the file-system process can perform operations on the disk by

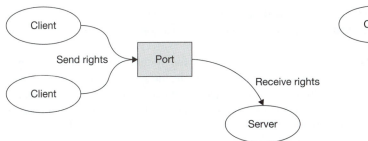

FIGURE 4.21 A Mach port. Two clients hold send rights; a server holds receive rights.

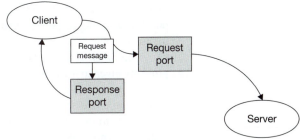

FIGURE 4.22 A client sends a message containing send rights for its response port to the server via its request port.

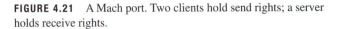

[9] http://www.gnu.org/software/hurd/hurd.html.

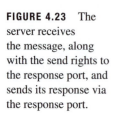

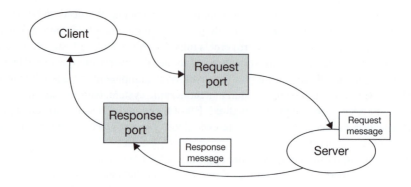

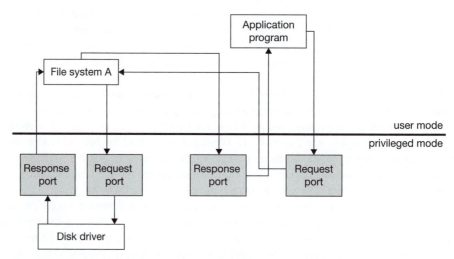

FIGURE 4.24 The use of ports in Mach. The disk driver provides a request port to the file system for access to disk services. The file system, when sending a request, supplies a response port. Similarly, the file system provides a request port to applications through which files may be requested. Applications provide response ports to receive responses, which consist of request ports referring to open files.

sending messages via the send rights on the disk-device port. Each of these threads has its own port for receiving responses, and each includes send rights to that port with the requests it sends to the disk object.

Similarly, if an application process wishes to use the file system, it requires send rights, probably given to it when it was created, to a port representing the file system, whose receive rights are held by the file-system process. In response to a request sent over this port to open a file, the file-system process sets up a port representing the file and sends back to the application process send rights to the file port. Send rights and receive rights to ports are implemented in a similar fashion to Unix's file descriptors and Windows's object handles — an identifier in a process refers to an entry in a process-specific table in the kernel containing a reference to a kernel object.

The mechanism of sending and receiving messages via a port is hidden inside a higher-level mechanism known as RPC (for *remote procedure call*; see Section 9.2). From the point of view of the thread making a request, it is simply making a procedure call — it calls a procedure and a response is returned. Buried inside the procedure is code that sends the request via the port and receives the response via the response port. Things are almost as transparent on the other side.

The object owner provides threads to receive requests coming in via ports. Whenever a request comes in, one of the threads calls a procedure to handle the request, then simply returns to code that sends the result back via the response port. We cover RPC more thoroughly in Chapter 9, where we discuss its use for communication between processes running on different machines.

To make all this reasonably efficient, Mach uses a form of RPC with the oxymoronic name of local RPC — RPC optimized for the case in which the calling and called processes are on the same machine. Passing data from one process to another involves moving it from one address space to another; the caller can't simply pass a pointer to data, since the pointer that points to data in the caller's address space would refer to something completely different in the called-process's address space. The data could be copied from one address space to another, but for moving large amounts of data, as between the disk driver and the file system and between the network driver and the communications module, the time required would be prohibitive. However, such data can be made to appear to be copied from one address space to another by modifying address-translation tables: a new range of virtual addresses is allocated in the recipient, and the mapping tables are set up so that these virtual addresses refer to the data being transferred (we explain this in more detail in Chapter 7). Though often much cheaper than copying the data, this technique, which we call *virtual copy*, is still more expensive than simply passing pointers between kernel modules.

In a normal (local, not remote) procedure call, the calling thread executes the called procedure directly. But with the remote procedure call (even in the local optimization), two threads are involved: the calling thread and a thread in the target process. Thus there's additional overhead in putting the calling thread to sleep, waking up the target thread, then putting the target thread to sleep after it sends the response and waking up the calling thread. This can be speeded up a bit via a technique known as *handoff scheduling*, discussed in Chapter 5.

A system is built from a collection of objects, some inside the kernel, others handled by user applications. Two sorts of objects of particular importance are *tasks* and *threads*. Tasks are what other operating systems call processes; they contain a collection of threads and have an address space. A task is essentially a container for port rights. When created, it contains send rights for a port representing the task object itself, send rights for a *task exception port*, and send rights for a *bootstrap port*. Threads may be created within a task; each thread comes with send rights for a port representing the thread object and send rights to a *thread exception port*. These port rights are added to the task's collection of port rights.

Send rights to ports are much like kernel object handles in Windows (see Exercise 3), though Mach predates Windows. The send rights to the task and thread objects effectively name the associated task or thread. To perform an operation on the task or thread, one sends it a request via its port. So, for example, creating a new thread within a task is an operation on the task, and thus some existing thread sends a *create-thread request* to the task via its port. Without send rights to the task's port, you can't do anything to the task. The creator of the task is given a copy of the task object's send rights, and thus can add threads to it. Threads within a task have access to all the task's send rights, so they can create new threads as well. The bootstrap port is provided so that a task can obtain send rights to other ports. The idea is that associated with the bootstrap port is some sort of object that can receive requests from the task for rights to additional ports.

The task and thread exception ports provide a means for exception handling. If a thread performs an operation that generates an exception, the thread is suspended and an exception message is sent via its exception port. The object with receive rights to the port handles the exception, if possible, otherwise the exception is handled by the holder of receive rights to the task's exception port.

A system built using the microkernel approach might seem to have the same functionality as one built using the monolithic approach of our simple system, but to run more slowly. This may explain why the monolithic approach still seems to be favored in mainstream operating systems, such as Windows and most variants of Unix. The packaging of OS modules into user-level processes does provide some advantages, particularly in security and software maintenance, but it's not clear that these are sufficient to overcome the performance problems.

However, the big promise of microkernel-based systems, according to the developers of HURD,[10] lies in extensibility. A monolithic system, if properly structured, provides some extensibility, as we've discussed: one can add a new kind of disk drive by supplying a driver for it. The file-system module works with the new disk drive by using the standard interface provided by its driver. Similarly, one can add a new file system, a new network protocol, etc. But this sort of extensibility is not for mere mortals. Understanding the intricacies of kernel interfaces is a difficult chore. It takes a great deal of knowledge and experience to understand the kernel well enough to add or replace functionality. A bug in a kernel module can cause the entire system to crash. Furthermore (and with good reason), one must be a privileged user to make kernel modifications.

With a properly designed microkernel-based system, however, one can safely add functionality without needing to understand the operating system completely. An example given by the HURD developers is that of a file system whose contents cannot be modified, but for which modified files are stored elsewhere. This provides the sort of functionality provided by a version-control system, but does so in such a way that a special application is not needed to use the controlled files: all access to these files is handled correctly.

HURD provides this functionality by adding support to the file system for modules known as *translators*. The owner of a file may associate a translator with the file so that when the file is opened, a reference is returned to the translator (send rights to the appropriate port) rather than to the file. The translator module itself is given a reference to the file. Thus, for the version-control application, opening a file read-only causes the translator to redirect access to the most recent version. Opening the file with write access causes the translator to copy it, then redirect access to the copy. Alternatively, the translator might be smarter and make copies only of modified blocks. A new option to open might be devised so that the translator can provide access to older versions of the file.

4.3
CONCLUSIONS

The monolithic approach to operating-system design is still alive and well. Windows, Linux, Macintosh OS X, FreeBSD, and Solaris are all, for the most part, monolithic. Despite its promise of extensibility, the microkernel approach has yet to catch on. The benefits of extensibility have yet to outweigh what are perceived to be inherent performance problems. However, there is a very fine line between microkernels and paravirtualization; much of the innovation that has gone into microkernels might well reappear in the guise of virtual machines.

Windows does employ some ideas that came out of microkernels. It supports local RPC, allowing user processes to communicate with one another efficiently. The graphics subsystem was a user-level process in the earliest versions of Windows NT, but was brought into the kernel in later versions for performance reasons. However, Windows still implements a few subsystems as user-level processes, though their performance is not a major factor in overall system performance.

The Macintosh OS X system has Mach at its core. Despite this, it is not a microkernel system either — it has Unix at its core as well. Mach is used to make it easy to integrate additional functionality into the kernel, but the result is still a monolithic kernel — for performance reasons, all modules are linked together into code that runs in privileged mode. Thus the extensibility made possible by Mach is available only within the kernel.

The virtual-machine idea has been amazingly successful. It started as an interesting idea at IBM, made its way to become a niche product, and is now a critical component of large data-processing centers. Not only is it an essential part of large IBM "mainframe" computers, but, through the efforts of VMware and others, it is used on commodity hardware as well.

---

[10] See http://www.gnu.org/software/hurd/hurd-paper.html.

1. In Unix systems, as discussed in Section 4.1.2.1, the erase character (typically backspace) is processed in the interrupt context. In some other systems, most notably DEC's VMS (the primary ancestor of Windows NT), such processing was done in the context of the thread reading from the terminal. Explain why the Unix approach makes more sense than the VMS approach.

*2. Ideally, data coming from the communications network should be deposited by the network hardware directly into the physical memory locations used by network applications, and outgoing data from an application should go directly into the physical memory locations from which network hardware will retrieve it for transmission. In other words, incoming and outgoing network data should never be copied.

   a. Explain why such a zero-copy approach is not possible with the socket-buffer approach described in Section 4.1.2.2.

   b. Describe how the socket-buffer approach might be adapted to make possible the zero-copy approach.

3. Windows provides a unified interface to kernel objects, something that is lacking in Unix. In particular, processes and threads are instances of kernel objects; user code refers to them via *kernel object handles* — effectively generalizations of file descriptors. Analogous to Unix's *dup* system call is Windows' *DuplicateHandle* system call, which creates a new handle synonymous with its argument and increases the reference count on the associated kernel object. In Windows, one calls *CloseHandle* to remove a handle, thereby decrementing the reference count on the associated object. If the reference count becomes 0, the object is deleted. Thus if a thread has terminated and another thread calls *CloseHandle* on the first thread's kernel object handle (obtained when the thread was created), the first thread's thread control block and stacks are deleted. Suppose, however, that *CloseHandle* is called before thread terminates. Since it's not the case that the thread will be forced to terminate prematurely, how does Windows make sure that the thread terminates only when it is supposed to, yet still arrange that an object is deleted when its reference count reaches 0?

4. What is missing in the address space depicted in Figure 4.10 is a data region. Suppose a thread in the process has called *malloc* to allocate 1024 bytes. Show how Figure 4.10 would be modified to represent the effect of this call. Suppose there is a subsequent call to *malloc*, this time for 4096 bytes. How should the figure be modified to represent the effect of this call?

*5. Again referring to Figure 4.10, we would now like to create additional threads. One issue is representing their user stacks. One approach might be for their stacks to be created via calls to *malloc*. Another approach might be for each of them to be represented by a separate *as_region* structure. Discuss the advantages and disadvantages of both approaches.

6. Section 4.1 implicitly assumes that we are constructing a monolithic kernel. What is it about the design that prevents the kernel from being split up into modules that run in different address spaces? (Hint: this is not a difficult question!) Why is this significant?

7. Explain how it is that both the virtual-machine and the microkernel approaches protect various portions of the operating system from one another?

*8. Assume that in a particular computer architecture there is a special register, accessible only in privileged mode, pointing to an interrupt vector containing the addresses of the routines that are to handle each of the various types of interrupts known to the architecture. For example, if an unmasked interrupt of type *i* occurs, then the current processor context is pushed onto the current kernel stack and control transfers to the routine whose address is in the *i*th component of the vector pointed to by the register.

We would like to virtualize the architecture. Suppose a (real) interrupt occurs while a virtual machine is running.

a. In which stack is the processor's context saved? (It's not sufficient to say "the kernel stack." How is this stack designated?)

b. Suppose the VMM decides that the interrupt should be handled by a virtual machine. Explain how it makes this happen.

*9. In systems using x86 architectures, devices are controlled via registers that are mapped into the address space. So, for example, a disk device might have a memory-address register into which the operating system places the address of a buffer, a device-address register into which the operating system places the disk address of an operation, and a control register into which the operating system places the device command to be performed. All three registers are accessed by loading from and storing to what appear to be memory locations.

How would a virtual machine monitor (VMM) virtualize device I/O in such architectures? Assume that pure virtualization (and not paravirtualization) is being used, and thus unmodified operating systems that normally run on bare hardware are to run in virtual machines. (Hint: the address space is divided into fixed-size pieces called pages, and each page can be separately protected.)

10. The statement is made in Section 4.2.1.2 that a VMware-workstation "application running on a virtual machine hosted on a 733 MHz PC can transmit data at a rate that saturates a 100 million bit/second Ethernet, despite the overhead of the virtual-machine implementation." If you wanted to determine what the overhead of the virtual-machine implementation actually was, what additional experiment might you perform? Would this give you an upper bound or a lower bound on the overhead?

11. A variation of the micro-kernel approach was used by Chorus Systèmes, a French company. Among their ideas was the notion that the various components of a micro-kernel-based system could run as separate processes for development and testing purposes, but, once suitably tested, a production version of the system could be constructed by combining the components and running them all in the kernel in privileged mode. What are the advantages and disadvantages of such an approach?

4.5 REFERENCES

Barham, P., B. Dragovic, K. Fraser, S. Hand, T. Harris, A. Ho, R. Neugebauer, I. Pratt, A. Warfield (2003). Xen and the Art of Virtualization. *Proceedings of the ACM Symposium on Operating Systems Principles.*

Julin, D., J. Chew, J. Stevenson, P. Guedes, P. Neves, P. Roy (1991). Generalized Emulation Services for Mach 3.0 - Overview, Experiences, and Current Status. *Proceedings of USENIX Mach Symposium.* Monterey, CA.

Kroah-Hartman, G. (2003). udev — A Userspace Implementation of devfs. *Proceedings of the Linux Symposium.* Ottawa, Ontario, Canada: 263–271.

Meyer, R. A. and L. H. Seawright (1970). A Virtual Machine Time-Sharing System. *IBM Systems Journal* **9**(3): 199–218.

Popek, G. J. and R. P. Goldberg (1974). Formal Requirements for Virtualizable Third Generation Architectures. *Communications of the ACM* **17**(7): 412–421.

Sugerman, J., G. Venkitachalam, B. H. Lim (2001). Virtualizing I/O Devices on VMware Workstation's Hosted Virtual Machine Monitor. *Proceedings of the 2001 USENIX Annual Technical Conference.* Boston.

Varian, M. (1997). VM and the VM Community: Past, Present, and Future. *http://www.princeton.edu/~melinda/25paper.pdf.*

Whitaker, A., M. Shaw, S. D. Gribble (2002). *Denali: Lightweight Virtual Machines for Distributed and Networked Applications,* University of Washington.

Processor Management

This chapter covers the many aspects of managing processors. We begin by discussing the various strategies for implementing threads packages, not only within the operating system but in user-level libraries as well. Next we cover the issues involved in handling interrupts. Certain things done in reaction to interrupts must be done right away, others must be deferred. Some can be done in a rather arbitrary interrupt context, others in specific process contexts. Finally we cover scheduling, looking at its basics as well as implementations on Linux and Windows.

5.1 THREADS IMPLEMENTA- TIONS

We start this chapter by discussing how threads are implemented. We first examine high-level strategies for structuring the implementation, showing how some of the implementation may be in user-level code while other parts may be in the operating-system kernel. We then sketch a relatively simple threads implementation, first on a uniprocessor, then on a multiprocessor.

5.1.1 STRATEGIES

Since the ultimate goal of the operating system is to support user-level application programs, let's discuss the various strategies for supporting threads in such programs. The primary issues involve where operations on threads, such as scheduling and synchronization, are implemented: in the operating-system kernel or in user-level library code.

5.1.1.1 One-Level Model

The simplest and most direct approach is the one-level model (also called the one-to-one model, since each user thread is mapped one-to-one to a kernel thread): all aspects of the threads implementation are in the kernel (see Figure 5.1). Thread creation, termination, synchronization, and scheduling all take place in the kernel. The thread routines called by user code, such as *pthread_create*, *pthread_mutex_lock*, etc., in POSIX threads and *CreateThread*, *WaitForSingleObject*, etc., in Win-32 threads are all system calls.

A problem with this approach is that operations that should be quick incur the additional burden of a system call. For example, calls to *pthread_mutex_lock* that find the mutex previously unlocked and thus return immediately should take no more than a few machine instructions. But if mutexes are implemented in the kernel, additional work is required to switch to and from the kernel context and vector to the appropriate system-call handler.

The Windows implementation of the Win-32 threads interface is based primarily on this one-level model. However, its implementation of critical sections (which are equivalent to POSIX mutexes) is done partly in user-level library code. The state of the critical section, locked or unlocked, is represented in a user-level data structure. Thus a thread calling *EnterCriticalSection* when the critical section is unlocked can determine this and lock it without making a system call. However, if the critical section is locked, then the thread must make a system call to put itself to sleep.

Similarly, if a thread calls *LeaveCriticalSection*, a system call is necessary only if at least one thread is waiting to enter. However, Windows implements Win-32 mutexes, which are defined as kernel objects, solely in the kernel. Our measurements on Windows NT 4.0 show that taking a critical section when no waiting is necessary is 20 times faster than taking a mutex in similar circumstances. Thus this concern about the cost of system calls is definitely valid.

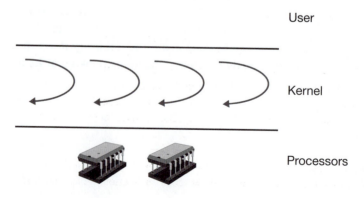

User

Kernel

Processors

FIGURE 5.1 The one-level model for implementing threads: the entire implementation is in the kernel.

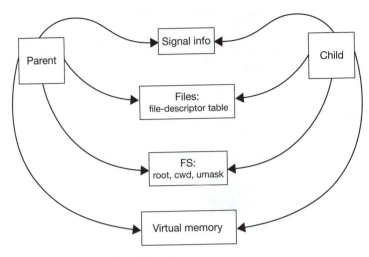

FIGURE 5.2 Variable-weight processes.

Variable-Weight Processes A variant of the one-level model takes advantage of Linux's *variable-weight processes*. Rather than having multithreaded processes, Linux has one thread per process but employs lighter-weight processes that share most of their contexts (see (Aral, Bloom, et al. 1989) for the original description of this approach). Linux, in addition to the *fork* system call, provides the *clone* system call for creating processes. With *fork*, the child process is a copy of the parent. However, with *clone*, the parent process can indicate that the child is to receive a copy of some portions of its context but is to share other portions. In particular, the parent can specify individually for its signal-handling information, file-descriptor table, file-system context (root directory, current working directory, and umask), and entire address space whether it is to be shared with the child or copied into the child. In theory, this provides a fair amount of flexibility. In practice, either everything is shared or everything is copied. See Figure 5.2.

One of the reasons Linux uses variable-weight processes was its designers' hope that a threads implementation would be easy to build on top of them. They reasoned that the kernel needn't support both processes and threads, but just the unified concept of a variable-weight process; threads would simply be the lightest-weight form of such a process. However, it turned out that the peculiar semantics of POSIX threads didn't map very cleanly to variable-weight processes. The initial implementation of POSIX Threads on Linux, known as Linux Threads, was not very elegant and had some performance issues. Some changes were later made and the current version, released in 2004 and called NPTL (native POSIX threads library for Linux), has a more straightforward and efficient implementation (see http://people.redhat.com/drepper/nptl-design.pdf for details on an early implementation).

5.1.1.2 Two-Level Model

While in the one-level model most of the threads implementation takes place in the kernel, in the two-level model a user-level library plays a major role. What the user-level application perceives as a thread is implemented within user-level library code. In the simplest version of the model, the operating-system kernel provides just a single thread per process, and thus the library code must multiplex multiple user threads on this one kernel thread. In other versions of the model, the kernel provides true multithreaded processes, but the user-level library multiplexes even more threads on these.

Single Kernel Thread In this model, also called the *N*-to-1 model, library code provides an implementation of threads much like that sketched in Section 4.1.2. The difference is that the

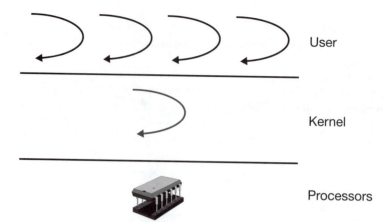

FIGURE 5.3 The two-level model for implementing threads, using one kernel thread.

threads are multiplexed not on a processor but on a kernel-supported thread (see Figure 5.3). Thus when a thread is created, the library code allocates a stack and a control block. The thread is put on a queue of runnable threads and becomes the running thread when its turn comes up. Implementing synchronization constructs such as mutexes is straightforward: if a thread must block it simply queues itself on a wait queue (there's one for each mutex) and calls a context-switch routine to pass control to the first thread on the runnable queue.

The major advantage of this approach over the one-level model is less overhead for operations on threads: no system calls are required and thus there's no need to switch into the kernel context. We've already seen the advantage of this for Win-32's critical sections; here it applies to everything.

However, there's also a major disadvantage. If a user thread makes a system call, such as read, that blocks in the kernel, then the process's only kernel thread blocks. At this point no other user thread in the process can run, since they're all multiplexed on the now-blocked kernel thread.

This is a serious problem. It can be avoided to a certain extent by wrapping potentially blocking system calls with code that checks for blocking. For example, in Unix one might do something like the following:

```
ssize_t read(int fd, void *buf, size_t count) {
  ssize_t ret;
  while (1) {
    if ((ret = real_read(fd, buf, count)) == -1) {
      if (errno == EWOULDBLOCK) {
        sem_wait(&FileSemaphore[fd]);
        continue;
      }
    }
    break;
  }
  return(ret);
}
```

Here *real_read* is the actual *read* system call and *read* is its wrapper. The file has been set up so that if an I/O operation on it cannot take place immediately, then, rather than have the calling thread block, the thread returns immediately with the EWOULDBLOCK error code. Our thread then waits on a binary semaphore (*FileSemaphore* is an array of such, one per active file descriptor). We depend on some other agent (perhaps a signal handler) to perform a *sem_post* when I/O without blocking is possible.

This lets our thread wait for I/O without blocking all the other threads. A minor drawback is that it adds some extra overhead, but its major drawback is that it works only for I/O objects supporting nonblocking I/O, and ordinary disk files are not among those objects. Thus it's not a general-purpose solution, though it's the best solution there is.[1] This approach was used in the earliest implementations of threads on Unix (Doeppner 1987) and also in the early implementations of Netscape Navigator on Unix.

Multiple Kernel Threads   If we build our user-level threads library within a process that already has multiple kernel-supported threads, we gain some benefit at some expense. The result is sometimes known as the *M-to-N* model (see Figure 5.4).

The benefits of the model are that, for the most part, operations on user threads do not require system calls (as in the two-level model with a single kernel thread) and, if there are sufficient kernel-supported threads, a blocking system call by a user threads does not block all user threads in the process (as in the one-level model). We discuss the negative aspects of the model below.

The implementation is similar to that of the two-level model with a single kernel thread except, of course, the execution of the user threads is multiplexed on multiple kernel threads. One important parameter is the number of kernel threads. If there are not enough, we have the problems of the single-kernel-thread approach: the entire process may block because one or more threads are placing blocking system calls.

Note that, without the wrappers discussed above for the single-kernel-thread approach, using too few kernel threads will cause a deadlock. Suppose two threads of our process are communicating using a pipe (this is essentially a kernel implementation of the producer-consumer problem). Assume the pipe is currently full. If one user thread attempts to write to the pipe, it and its kernel thread will block. The other user thread should be able to read from the pipe and thereby allow the first thread to complete its write. But if no other kernel threads are available on which the second user thread can run, we're stuck: the first user thread cannot continue until the second runs, but the second cannot run until the first's kernel thread is no longer blocked. See Figure 5.5.

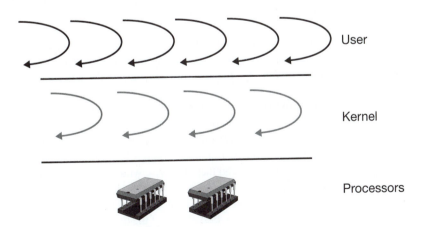

User

Kernel

Processors

FIGURE 5.4   The two-level model for implementing threads, using multiple kernel threads.

---

[1] Another possibility is for the wrapper to send the I/O request to another process via a pipe, then have the single thread in that process perform the I/O. This would require an extra process per active I/O call and would necessitate extra copying of the data being transferred. It's probably not worth the expense.

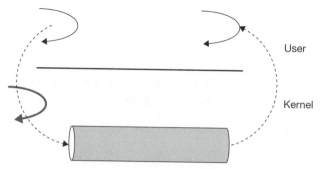

FIGURE 5.5 Deadlock caused by the threads implementation: one user thread is blocked, attempting to write to a full pipe. Another user thread is trying to read from the pipe, but cannot execute because the only kernel thread, currently assigned to the writing user thread, is blocked.

Solaris, which until recently used this model for its threads implementation, automatically created a new kernel thread for the process in this situation. Its general mechanism for doing this was that the operating-system kernel recognized when all of a multithreaded process's kernel threads were blocked. It then notified the user-level threads library, via a signal or similar mechanism, and the threads library in turn requested a new kernel thread if it had runnable user threads that could take advantage of one.

Another kernel-thread-related concern is taking advantage of a multiprocessor. If, for example, we are running a multithreaded program on a four-processor system, we'll need at least four user threads to take advantage of all the processors. But we also need at least four kernel threads: the user-level library is multiplexing user threads on kernel threads, but the kernel is multiplexing kernel threads on processors. A possible strategy might be for a process to have as many kernel threads as there are processors, but this might not be sufficient: a number of the kernel threads might be blocked because their user threads are performing I/O. Perhaps one should give each process a large number of kernel threads, so that one is always available when needed, but even this has the drawback that the excess kernel threads take up system resources. (See http://www .cs.brown.edu/research/thmon/thmon.html for further discussion.)

However, POSIX Threads provides an interface through which a program can advise the user-level threads library on how many kernel threads should be employed. Calls to *pthread_ setconcurrency* tell the threads implementation how many threads are expected to be running concurrently. For the two-level model, this means how many kernel threads should be available for running user threads.

The primary disadvantage of the two-level model is that the actions of the user-level threads scheduler, which is multiplexing user threads on kernel threads, may be at cross purposes with the actions of the kernel scheduler, which is multiplexing kernel threads on processors. As an example, suppose an important, high-priority user thread has just become runnable. The user-level scheduler immediately assigns it a kernel thread that otherwise would be used to run a low-priority user thread. But, immediately afterwards, the kernel scheduler decides that this kernel thread should yield the processor to some other kernel thread of the same process, one that is running a moderate-priority user thread. Thus, despite the best efforts of the user-level scheduler, a moderate-priority user thread is running instead of the high-priority user thread.

There are various ways to try to get around this problem. Solaris lets one *bind* a user thread to a particular kernel thread: the kernel thread is dedicated to running just that user thread and cannot be used for any other purpose. Thus one might bind a high-priority user thread to its own kernel thread, and set things up with the operating system so that the kernel thread also has a high priority. This solves the immediate problem but it also defeats the purpose of the two-level model: the high-priority user thread is now effectively implemented using the one-level model and all operations on it require expensive system calls.

We might provide additional channels of communication between the kernel and the user level so that the user-level scheduler can somehow make its intentions known to the kernel scheduler. But this again requires more system calls, adding to the expense of using threads.

Similar arguments against the two-level model are provided at the previously mentioned http://people.redhat.com/drepper/nptl-design.pdf.

Extremely high-performing threads packages supporting thousands of concurrent threads have been implemented using the two-level model. The Capriccio project at Berkeley (von Behren 2003), a good example of this, supports far more user-level threads than would be possible in the operating system.

5.1.1.3 Scheduler Activations

A third approach, known as the *scheduler activations model* (Anderson, Bershad, et al. 1992), is radically different from the others. With both the one- and two-level models, we think of the kernel as providing some number of kernel-thread contexts for user threads, and then multiplexing these contexts on processors using the kernel's scheduler. But let's change things a bit and separate the kernel-thread context from what's being scheduled in the kernel. We'd like the kernel simply to divvy up processors to processes, and the processes, via their thread libraries, to determine which threads get to use these processors. The kernel should supply however many kernel contexts it finds necessary (see Figure 5.6).

To make some sense of this, let's work through an example. A process starts up that contains a single thread with both user and kernel contexts. Following the dictates of its scheduling policy, the kernel scheduler assigns a processor to the process. If the thread blocks, the process implicitly relinquishes the processor to the kernel scheduler, and gets it back once it unblocks.

Suppose the user program creates a new thread; the user-level library creates the necessary user context. If actual parallelism is desired, code in the user-level library notifies the kernel that two processors are needed. When a processor becomes available, the kernel creates a new kernel context. Then, using the newly available processor running in the new kernel context, it places an *upcall* (going from system code to user code, unlike a system call, which goes from user code

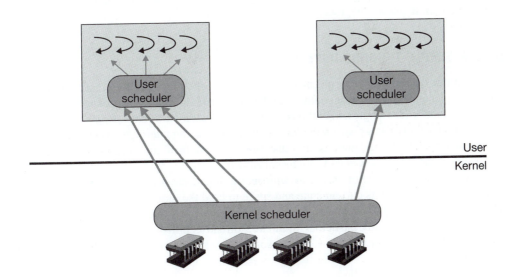

FIGURE 5.6 Scheduler activations: the OS assigns processors to processes; the user-level threads library assigns processors to threads.

to system code) to the user-level library, effectively giving it the processor. The library code then assigns this processor to the new thread.

The user application might later create another thread and ask for another processor, but this machine only has two. However, let's say one of the process's other threads (thread 1) blocks on a page fault. The kernel, using the processor that was previously assigned to thread 1, creates a new kernel context and places another upcall to our process, saying two things:

- The thread using kernel context 1 has blocked and thus it has lost its processor (processor 1).

- Here is processor 1, can you use it?

In our case the process will assign the processor to thread 3. But soon the page being waited for by thread 1 becomes available. The kernel should notify the process of this event — but, of course, it needs a processor to do this. So it uses one of the processors already assigned to the process, say the one the process has assigned to thread 2. The process is now notified of the following two events:

- The thread using kernel context 1 has unblocked (i.e., it would be running, if only it had a processor).

- I'm telling you this using processor 2, which I've taken from the thread that was using kernel context 2.

The library now must decide what to do with the processor that has been handed to it. It could give it back to thread 2, leaving thread 1 unblocked, but not running, in the kernel; it could leave thread 2 without a processor and give it to thread 1; or it could decide that both threads 1 and 2 should be running now and thus suspend thread 3, giving its processor to thread 1 and returning thread 2's processor back to it.

At some point the kernel is going to decide that the process has had one or both processors long enough (e.g., a time slice has expired). So it yanks one of the processors away and, using the other processor, makes an upcall conveying the following news:

- I've taken processor 1.

- I'm telling you this using processor 2.

The library learns that it now has only one processor, but with this knowledge it can assign the processor to the most deserving thread.

If the kernel decides to give the process's only processor to another process, no communication is required until it gets a new processor.

5.1.2 A SIMPLE THREADS IMPLEMENTATION

We begin our discussion of the mechanics of managing the processor by presenting a simple threads implementation, one that could be the basis of a user-level threads package as part of the two-level model with a single kernel thread. We call this a *straight-threads implementation* in the sense that all activity takes place in thread contexts; there are no interrupts to complicate things. To simplify matters further, there is only one processor. We then introduce multiple processors and interrupts and discuss how they can be coped with.

As discussed in Section 4.1.2, to represent a thread we need, at minimum, some sort of *thread object* to hold its current state and space to hold the thread's stack — see Figure 5.7. The object contains such items as the thread's context, ID, and pointers for linking the thread into queues. At any particular moment a thread is either running, ready to run (but not currently running), or waiting for some sort of event to take place, such as a mutex being unlocked.

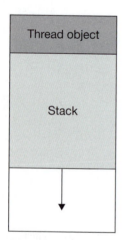

FIGURE 5.7 The basic thread representation: a thread object containing its state and space for the thread's stack.

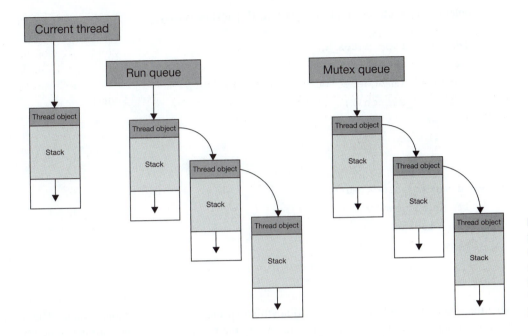

FIGURE 5.8 A collection of threads: one is currently running, three are ready to run, and three are in a queue waiting to lock a particular mutex.

Figure 5.8 shows a collection of threads. Assuming a uniprocessor system, at most one thread is currently running and its thread object is pointed to by the global variable *Current-Thread*. Those threads that are ready to run are organized into a run queue. In our simple system, each mutex has an associated queue of threads waiting to lock it.

The context of a thread is a rather nebulous concept, but, as explained in Sections 3.1.2 and 4.1.3, it contains, at the least, a copy of whatever register points to the thread's current stack frame. This stack frame contains the thread's current register state. This information is not necessarily valid while the thread is running, but must be made valid when the thread is suspended so that it can be resumed. See Figure 5.9.

In Section 3.1.2 we discussed how one thread can yield the processor, switching to another thread. Here is a variation of the code presented there; this time we assume the existence of *swapcontext*, which saves the caller's register context in its thread object, then restores that of the target thread from its thread object:

```
void thread_switch( ) {
    thread_t NextThread, OldCurrent;

    NextThread = dequeue(RunQueue);
    OldCurrent = CurrentThread;
    CurrentThread = NextThread;
    swapcontext(&OldCurrent->context, &NextThread->context);

    // We're now in the new thread's context

}
```

FIGURE 5.9 A thread's context refers to its current stack frame.

The *dequeue* routine performs the role of a scheduler in this simple system: it selects the next thread to run from the run queue. Note that we haven't dealt with the case when the run queue is empty — we take this up in Exercise 5.

Implementing mutexes in our straight-threads package is easy:

```
void mutex_lock(mutex_t *m) {
  if (m->locked) {
    enqueue(m->queue, CurrentThread);
    thread_switch();
  } else
    m->locked = 1;
}

void mutex_unlock(mutex_t *m) {
  if (queue_empty(m->queue))
    m->locked = 0;
  else
    enqueue(runqueue, dequeue(m->queue));
}
```

Note that the *mutex_lock* code doesn't do anything special to make its actions atomic. This is because in our straight-threads system there are no interrupts and all actions are performed by threads, which run until they voluntarily relinquish the processor.

5.1.3 MULTIPLE PROCESSORS

We continue with our straight-threads implementation, but we now allow processors. Thus, say that in Figure 5.8 there are possibly a number of running threads, threads, each on a different processor. Our *thread_switch* routine is no longer sufficient for managing the now multiple processors; we need additional mechanisms to ensure all processors are utilized.

A simple approach is to invent special idle threads, one for each processor. Such threads run only on designated processors (one per processor). The intent is that they run only when no other thread is available to run. To accomplish this, we use the following program:

```
void idle_thread() {
  while(1)
    thread_switch();
}
```

Thus once a normal thread is in the run queue, if there is an idle processor (i.e., one running an idle thread), that processor will soon switch to running the non-idle thread.

How synchronization constructs are implemented has a big impact on a system's performance. There is the cost of just checking to see if the current thread should continue. Such checks, say in the form of locking mutexes, happen so frequently that they are often carefully coded in assembler language to be as fast as possible. Synchronization is important both inside the kernel, where there is direct access to thread-scheduling functionality, and in user-level code as part of threads packages — performing a system call as part of every synchronization operation is usually much too costly.

As an example of the problems faced, let's consider two very simple approaches to implementing a mutex. The first is known as the *spin lock*, in which a mutex is represented simply as a bit indicating whether it is locked or not. So that multiple threads can safely use it concurrently, some sort of interlocked instruction is used to lock the mutex. A typical such instruction is the *compare and swap* (CAS) instruction,[2] defined as follows but executed atomically:

```
int CAS(int *ptr, int old, int new) {
    int tmp = *ptr;
    if (*ptr == old)
        *ptr = new
    return tmp;
}
```

Though CAS is a single machine instruction, it does two loads from memory and one store with the guarantee that, if executed on a multiprocessor system, the effect of concurrent execution of it and an operation on another processor is as if one operation completely takes place before the other. Assuming that a zero value means unlocked and a one value means locked, mutex operations can be implemented as follows:

```
void spin_lock(int *mutex) {
    while(!CAS(mutex, 0, 1))
        ;
}

void spin_unlock(int *mutex) {
    *mutex = 0;
}
```

The invocation of the CAS instruction within the *spin_lock* routine checks to see if the mutex was *unlocked* and, if so, sets its state to *locked*. It returns what the state of the mutex was just prior to the invocation to CAS. The *spin_lock* routine repeatedly invokes the CAS instruction until it reports that the mutex *was* unlocked (but is now locked by the caller). The *spin_unlock* routine simply clears the mutex, setting its state to unlocked.

Providing the atomicity guarantees of CAS slows down the processors considerably, so *spin_lock* is usually implemented by repeatedly checking the mutex's state using normal instructions, then confirming and taking the mutex with CAS, as follows:

```
void spin_lock(int *mutex) {
    while (1) {
        if (*mutex == 0) {
            // the mutex was at least momentarily unlocked
            if (!CAS(mutex, 0, 1)
                break; // we have locked the mutex
            // some other thread beat us to it, so try again
        }
    }
}
```

---

[2] On the x86 architecture, this instruction is *cmpxchg* (compare and exchange), which actually does more than what is shown for CAS. See the Intel documentation for details (http://www.intel.com/Assets/PDF/manual/253666.pdf).

Spin locks are useful only on multiprocessors and, even then, only if locks are held for brief periods — otherwise too much processor time is wasted waiting for the lock to be released. An alternative approach is to use a *blocking lock*: threads wait by having their execution suspended. This involves a thread's explicitly yielding the processor and joining a queue of waiting threads, then being explicitly resumed at some later time. The code below works on uniprocessor systems. It keeps track of which thread has a mutex locked. This is not strictly necessary, but is useful for debugging.

```
void blocking_lock(mutex_t *mut) {
  if (mut->holder != 0)
    enqueue(mut->wait_queue, CurrentThread);
    thread_switch();
  } else
    mut->holder = CurrentThread;
}

void blocking_unlock(mutex_t *mut) {
  if (queue_empty(mut->wait_queue))
    mut->holder = 0;
  else {
    mut->holder = dequeue(mut->wait_queue);
    enqueue(RunQueue, mut->holder);
  }
}
```

This code does not always work correctly on a multiprocessor: there is a potential problem if a mutex is currently locked but its wait queue is empty, the holder of the mutex is unlocking it, and another thread is attempting to lock it. It is possible that the thread locking the mutex will find it locked and be about to queue itself on the wait queue when the other thread unlocks the mutex, finds the wait queue empty, and then marks the mutex unlocked (by setting its holder to zero). Thus the first thread will then join the wait queue, but will be there forever since no thread will ever call the unlock code again.

An attempt at solving this problem is:

```
void blocking_lock(mutex_t *mut) {
  spin_lock(mut->spinlock);
  if (mut->holder != 0)
    enqueue(mut->wait_queue, CurrentThread);
    spin_unlock(mut->spinlock);
    thread_switch();
  } else {
    mut->holder = CurrentThread;
    spin_unlock(mut->spinlock);
  }
}

void blocking_unlock(mutex_t *mut) {
  spin_lock(mut->spinlock);
  if (queue_empty(mut->wait_queue)) {
```

```
            mut->holder = 0;
        } else {
            mut->holder = dequeue(mut->wait_queue);
            enqueue(RunQueue, mut->holder);
        }
        spin_unlock(mut->spinlock);
    }
```

Here we have associated a spin lock with the blocking lock, and use it to synchronize access to the data structures associated with the mutex. This solves the problem described above, but it turns out there is yet another problem.

Suppose a thread calling *blocking_lock* has just enqueued itself on the mutex's wait queue, and is just about to call *thread_switch*. The holder of the mutex now calls *blocking_unlock*, finds the first thread in the wait queue, and moves it to the run queue. This thread is now assigned to an idle processor, even though it is still running on its original processor!

There are a number of ways of solving (or perhaps avoiding) this problem. One approach is for *blocking_lock*, rather than unlocking the mutex's spin lock itself, to pass the address of the spin lock to *thread_switch* and have the spin lock released after the thread has given up its processor. Doing this requires a bit of work — we take it up in Exercise 6.

The blocking approach to mutexes has the obvious advantage over spin locks that waiting threads do not consume processor time. However, it has the disadvantage that suspending a thread, then waking it up are typically somewhat time-consuming operations. This is particularly so for user-level threads that must execute system calls both to suspend themselves and to resume others.

If it is usually the case that lock operations on mutexes succeed, then it makes sense to optimize the lock operation for the case of the mutex being unlocked, at the possible expense of the case in which the mutex is currently locked. Microsoft does this for their implementation of critical sections in Windows, and some implementations of POSIX threads do it for mutexes as well. The basic idea is simple: check if the mutex is unlocked. If it is, then simply lock it and go on. If it's not, then a system call is required to lock it. However, the details are anything but simple. We describe here how it is implemented on Linux, using *futexes* (fast user-mode mutexes). Our approach is based on that of Ulrich Drepper.[3]

A futex is implemented as a simple data structure, accessible to both user-mode code and kernel code. Contained in it is an unsigned-integer state component called *value* and a queue of waiting threads. Two system calls are provided to support futexes:[4]

```
futex_wait(futex_t *futex, unsigned int value) {
    if (futex->value == value)
        sleep();
}


futex_wake(futex_t *futex) {
    // wake up one thread from futex's wait queue,
    // if there is any

    ...

}
```

---

[3] http://people.redhat.com/drepper/futex.pdf.

[4] The Linux implementation uses just one system call, with an additional argument to indicate its function.

A simple approach to implementing mutexes is to represent it with a futex, with the futex's value indicating the state of the mutex: 0 means unlocked and a positive value means locked. Consider the following code, where *atomic_inc* is an instruction that increments its argument by one atomically and returns its previous value:

```
unsigned int atomic_inc(unsigned int *i) {
    // this is performed atomically
    return(i++); // i's original value is returned
}

void lock(futex_t *futex) {
    int c;
    while ((c = atomic_inc(&futex->val)) != 0)
        futex_wait(futex, c+1);
}

void unlock(futex_t *futex) {
    futex->val = 0;
    futex_wake(futex);
}
```

A thread trying to lock the mutex atomically adds one to the futex's value. If the value, before being incremented, was zero, then the mutex has just been locked and nothing more needs to be done. But if the value was positive, then some other thread must have the mutex locked and the calling thread calls *futex_wait* to go to sleep. But it's possible that another thread is concurrently modifying the futex's value (it might be unlocking it or also trying to lock it). So, if the futex's value has changed between being incremented and the call to *futex_wait*, then *futex_wait* returns immediately and the test is tried again.

The code for unlock simply sets the futex's value to zero, meaning unlocked, and then wakes up the first queued thread. This thread returns from its call to *futex_wait* and must go through the while loop of the lock code, thus attempting again to get the lock. If a new thread is not trying to lock the mutex at the same time, it will successfully lock the mutex. Of course if a new thread is trying to lock the mutex, the two will fight it out and one will lock it and the other will go to sleep.

The unlock code is not exactly what we want, since it requires a call to *futex_wake* — a possibly expensive system call — each time it's called. What's desired is for there to be no system call if there are no waiting threads. But, with the current approach, we have no way of knowing if there are any waiters.

The lock code has more serious problems. It's possible for a number of threads to call it at roughly the same time and synchronously go through the while loop a number of times, each first incrementing the futex's value, then detecting, in *futex_wait*, that some other thread has also incremented its value. In actual practice, this turns out to be not improbable, particularly on a multiprocessor. What's worse is that if the threads stay in sync long enough, repeatedly incrementing the futex's value, the value might overflow and wrap to zero, causing one or more to treat the mutex as unlocked, even though another thread has it locked.

That brings us to the following code, which fixes the problems (at the expense of simplicity):

```
unsigned int atomic_dec(unsigned int *i) {
    // this is performed atomically
```

```
      return(i--); // i's original value is returned
   }

   void lock(futex_t *futex) {
     unsigned int c;
     if ((c = CAS(&futex->val, 0, 1) != 0)
       do {
         if (c == 2 || (CAS(&futex->val, 1, 2) != 1))
           futex_wait(futex, 2);
       while ((c = CAS(&futex->val, 0, 2)) != 0))
   }

   void unlock(futex_t *futex) {
     if (atomic_dec(&futex->val) != 1) {
       futex->val = 0;
       futex_wake(futex);
     }
   }
```

In this (correct!) version the futex's value is constrained to be 0, 1, or 2, with 0 meaning unlocked, 1 meaning locked but no waiting threads, and 2 meaning locked with the possibility of waiting threads. In the lock code, CAS sets the futex's value to 1 if it was zero, otherwise leaves it unchanged. Thus if the mutex was unlocked, it's now locked; otherwise it stays locked. So, if the futex's value was zero, the calling thread has locked the mutex and simply returns.

If the futex's value was positive, the calling thread enters a while loop. The if statement checks if there already are waiting threads, or if this thread will be the first waiter. In either case, the calling thread calls *futex_wait* to join the queue. The thread returns from *futex_wait* immediately if the futex's value has changed (due to concurrent actions by some other thread) or returns later when it is woken up by a call to unlock. When threads do return from *futex_wait*, they check whether the futex's value is 0, and, since it's not known whether there are additional waiting threads, they set its value to 2.

The unlock code simply decrements the futex's value. If it was 1 (and thus is now 0), then there are no waiting threads and thus there's no need to call *futex_wake*. Otherwise it calls *futex_wake*, after setting the futex's value to 0.

5.2
INTERRUPTS

Processors normally run within thread contexts. From time to time interrupts occur and are handled in interrupt contexts. For efficiency reasons, these interrupt contexts are fairly minimal and typically use stacks borrowed from whatever context the processor was in when it was interrupted (see Section 3.1.4). The intent is that the interrupt is handled quickly and then control returns to the thread that was interrupted. Of course, one interrupt handler might interrupt another, but the intent and effect remain the same: interrupts are processed quickly so that the processor can get on with its main job of running in thread contexts.

The Unix signal handlers discussed in Chapter 2 are similar to interrupt handlers in that they are executed in a special context containing a stack that's been borrowed from a thread. As we saw there, special consideration is required for common access to data structures from both signal-handling and thread contexts. Similar consideration is required in the kernel for such access from both interrupt and thread contexts.

In some cases, however, it may not be possible for an interrupt handler to do all the desired processing immediately. It might need more time than should be spent in the interrupt context, or the desired actions might need to be performed in the context of a particular thread. In such cases we need some mechanism for *deferred work*: doing work at a later time, perhaps in some other context.

One of an interrupt handler's actions might be to *preempt* the interrupted thread, that is, to make it yield to some other thread. In some systems this preemption might take place as soon as the processor is back in the context of that thread; in other systems the preemption might be delayed until the thread returns to user mode.

In the remainder of this section, we discuss the workings of interrupt handlers: what they can and cannot do. We then cover the various mechanisms for extending their scope via deferred work. Finally, we talk about how they are used to preempt the execution of the interrupted thread, i.e., to force it to yield the processor to another thread.

5.2.1 INTERRUPT HANDLERS

As we discuss in Section 5.3 below, much care is devoted to determining which threads should be running at any given moment. The scheduler, which makes these decisions, takes into account the relative importance of individual threads as well as fairness. Interrupt handlers, on the other hand, are executed strictly in response to interrupts. Though the interrupts coming from the various devices may be prioritized by hardware, any interrupt preempts the execution of any normal thread. Furthermore, on many systems certain interrupts have higher priority than others: while their handlers are running, lower-priority interrupts are masked. Thus interrupt handlers should be quick. They might update a data structure or perform some action on a device, but any processing time they require takes away from what's available to threads and other interrupt handlers.

As discussed in Section 3.1.4, interrupt contexts typically do not have stacks of their own. Interrupt contexts sharing the same stack may not yield to one another, but must run to completion, when not themselves interrupted by higher-priority interrupts. It is similarly usually not a good idea for an interrupt handler using one stack to yield the processor to a thread using another stack: if the processor is switched from the interrupt context to a thread context, not only is the interrupt context put aside, but so is the context it interrupted (there could of course be multiple interrupted contexts: a thread is preempted by one interrupt, which is preempted by another, etc.). Thus, even if the interrupted thread has the highest priority, it would be unable to resume execution until the suspended interrupt handler regains the processor and completes its execution, regardless of how unimportant its interrupt was. For an interrupt handler to run in a context equivalent to that of a thread, we would have to arrange for it to have its own private stack. Such an arrangement can be made (we discuss below how Solaris does this in some circumstances), but in general providing such a stack adds considerable and usually unnecessary expense to interrupt handling.

Some architectures provide separate interrupt stacks: interrupts cause the processor's register state to be saved on this separate stack rather than the current thread's kernel stack. But even in this case, for an interrupt handler to run in a context equivalent to that of a thread, it must have its own private stack, not one it shares with all other interrupt handlers.

5.2.1.1 Synchronization and Interrupts

Interrupt handlers and threads often need to access the same data structures. As we saw with Unix signals in Chapter 2, coordinating this access requires more than the use of mutexes, semaphores, etc. If a thread is accessing a shared data structure, we must make certain it is not interrupted by an interrupt whose handler also uses that data structure. Thus it must mask appropriate interrupts, possibly in addition to locking a mutex.

How interrupts are masked is architecture-dependent, but must be done only in privileged mode. When the processor enters the interrupt context, the interrupt being responded to becomes masked, blocking further occurrences. Many architectures have some notion of a hierarchy of interrupts, so that masking one level masks all interrupts of equal and lower levels; thus when the processor handles an interrupt, all lesser interrupts are masked.

When using multiple threads in user-level programs, we usually assume they are running as if they were on multiple, independent processors, even if we're using a uniprocessor. This is because their execution is being not only multiplexed on the available processors, but also time-sliced: at any moment a thread may be forced to yield the processor to another thread. Furthermore, threads are often assigned priorities: a high-priority thread that becomes runnable will preempt a lower-priority thread, i.e., force it to yield the processor.

This is not necessarily the case within the operating system. As we discuss in Section 5.2.2 below, the operating system might implement time slicing and preemption so that it affects threads only when they are running in user mode. Within the kernel, threads run until they terminate, explicitly block, or return to user mode. Such systems are said to have *non-preemptive kernels*. In such operating systems on uniprocessors, most kernel data structures that are shared by multiple threads need not be synchronized. If threads do not block while using a shared data structure, then the only synchronization necessary is between threads and interrupt handlers. Thus masking interrupts for access to data structures used by interrupt handlers is not merely necessary, it's usually sufficient.

This strategy makes a lot of sense in some circumstances. By limiting time slicing to user mode, the kernel can run more quickly since it needn't suffer the overhead of locking and unlocking mutexes. Many operating systems, among them both Windows and many Unix implementations (including Linux), behave this way when configured for uniprocessor use. (Both Unix and Windows were first written for uniprocessors and had no kernel-level use of mutexes at all. Only later when they were modified for multiprocessors was the use and overhead of mutexes added.)

On uniprocessor systems with non-preemptive kernels, we can use code similar to the following to protect data structures accessed by both threads and interrupt handlers:

```
                              int X = 0;
```

```
void AccessXThread() {              void AccessXInterrupt() {
    int oldIPL;                         ...
    oldIPL = setIPL(IHLevel);           X = X+1;
    X = X+1;                            ...
    setIPL(oldIPL);                 }
}
```

Here *AccessXThread* is called by a thread, while *AccessXInterrupt* is called in the interrupt context. The routine *setIPL* sets the interrupt priority level to its argument (thereby masking all interrupts whose levels are less than or equal to the argument) and returns the previous interrupt priority level. Assuming that the interrupt whose handler invokes *AccessXInterrupt* occurs at priority *IHLevel*, the interrupt will be masked while any thread is within *AccessXThread*, and thus *AccessXInterrupt* will not interfere with *AccessXThread*. Conversely, since all interrupt processing completes before thread processing is resumed, *AccessXThread* will not interfere with *AccessXInterrupt*.

Masking interrupts is important not just for synchronizing access to data structures. Consider the following code, in which a thread starts a disk request, then waits until it completes. It is woken up by code in the disk-interrupt handler.

```
int disk_write(…) {

    …

    startIO();// start disk operation

    …

    enqueue(disk_waitq, CurrentThread);
    thread_switch();
        // wait for disk operation to complete

    …

}

void disk_intr(…) {
    thread_t *thread;

    …

    // handle disk interrupt

    …

    thread = dequeue(disk_waitq);
    if (thread != 0) {
        enqueue(RunQueue, thread);
        // wakeup waiting thread
    }
    …

}
```

This code has a problem if the disk interrupt happens before the thread waiting for it is put on the wait queue — the result will be that the thread joins the wait queue after *disk_intr* has been called. If there are no more disk interrupts, the thread waits forever.

The solution is to replace *disk_write* with the following:

```
int disk_write(…) {

    …

    oldIPL = setIPL(diskIPL);
    startIO(); // start disk operation

    …

    enqueue(disk_waitq, CurrentThread);
    thread_switch();
        // wait for disk operation to complete
    setIPL(oldIPL);

    …

}
```

By masking interrupts before starting the disk operation and unmasking them after the operation completes, we avoid the race in the previous version. However, unless something is done in *thread_switch*, interrupts are never unmasked, and thus *disk_intr* will never get a chance to wake up the waiting thread. This problem is similar to the one with spin locks that we encountered in implementing blocking mutexes in Section 5.1.3: we need to keep interrupts masked until the thread is no longer using the processor. The solution is easier than that with spin locks (though this is the uniprocessor version):

```
void thread_switch() {
    thread_t *OldThread;
    int oldIPL;

    oldIPL = setIPL(HIGH_IPL);
        // protect access to RunQueue by masking all interrupts

    while(queue_empty(RunQueue)) {
        // repeatedly allow interrupts, then check RunQueue
        setIPL(0); // IPL == 0 means no interrupts are masked
        setIPL(HIGH_IPL);
    }
    // We found a runnable thread

    OldThread = CurrentThread;
    CurrentThread = dequeue(RunQueue);

    swapcontext(OldThread->context, CurrentThread->context);

    setIPL(oldIPL);

}
```

Note that the thread's current interrupt priority level (IPL) is kept on its stack as a local variable (*oldIPL*). It is saved in the first executable statement of *thread_switch*, where the IPL is temporarily set as high as possible, so that no interrupt handler can interfere with the run queue while the thread is manipulating it. The call to *swapcontext* switches in the next thread to run, along with its stack and IPL (which is set in the last executable statement of *thread_switch*). This version of *thread_switch* deals with the case of an empty run queue: the processor enters an "idle loop" where it repeatedly checks the run queue for threads.

An alternative approach to handling an empty run queue is not to have one; instead, a system might have a special *idle thread* that runs only when nothing else is runnable. Such a thread repeatedly attempts to yield the processor to the next runnable thread, thus having the same effect as the idle loop above. This approach is much more easily adapted to multiprocessor systems than the idle loop in *thread_switch* — one employs one idle thread per processor. Furthermore, it is clear when monitoring the processor time used by each thread that the system is "idling" when the idle threads are running.

Systems in which time slicing or preemption occur even in the kernel are said to have *preemptive kernels*. In this more general case there are four problems that a thread accessing a shared kernel data structure must contend with:

1. It might be interrupted by an interrupt handler running on its processor that accesses the same data structure.

2. Another thread running on another processor might access the same data structure.

3. It might be forced to give up its processor to another thread, either because its time slice has expired or because it has been preempted by a higher-priority thread.

4. An interrupt handler running on another processor might access the same data structure.

We have just seen how to deal with the first two problems. The third can be solved with mutexes, but in many circumstances, particularly when it wouldn't be necessary to hold the mutex for more than a few instructions, it is cheaper to prevent time-slice expirations and preemption by setting a flag in the thread, marking it as non-preemptible. Problem four requires the use of spin locks, since even if it is waiting for something running on a different processor, an interrupt handler cannot block.

Spin locks by themselves are clearly not sufficient, as seen in the following variation of an earlier example:

```
int X = 0;
SpinLock_t L = UNLOCKED;
```

```
void AccessXThread () {                     void AccessXInterrupt () {
    SpinLock (&L);                              ...
    X = X+1;                                    SpinLock (&L);
    SpinUnlock (&L);                            X = X+1;
}                                               SpinUnlock (&L);
                                                ...
                                            }
```

If a thread calls *AccessXThread* but is interrupted while holding the spin lock *L*, and then if *AccessXInterrupt* is called in the interrupt context, there will be deadlock when it attempts to lock *L*. Furthermore, if one thread has taken the spin lock within *AccessXThread* but is preempted by another thread, and that thread also calls *AccessXThread*, there will again be deadlock. The solution is for threads to mask interrupts before (not after!) they lock *L* and to prevent preemption, as in

```
int X = 0;
SpinLock_t L = UNLOCKED;
```

```
void AccessXThread() {                      void AccessXInterrupt() {
    DisablePreemption();                        ...
    MaskInterrupts();                           SpinLock(&L);
    SpinLock(&L);                               X = X+1;
    X = X+1;                                     SpinUnlock(&L);
    SpinUnlock(&L);                             ...
    UnMaskInterrupts();                     }
    EnablePreemption();
}
```

Many operating systems have variants of their spin-lock routines in which interrupts are automatically masked and preemption is automatically disabled.

5.2.1.2 Interrupt Threads

Solaris avoids many of the interrupt-related problems experienced in other operating systems by allowing interrupts to be handled as threads (Kleiman and Eykholt 1995). This seems contrary to our earlier discussion of how interrupts are handled, but it's actually fairly simple. Each interrupt level has a pre-allocated stack on each processor. When an interrupt occurs, the current context (thread or interrupt) is saved by the hardware on the interrupt stack of the appropriate level. However, no thread control block (known in Solaris as a *lightweight process* or LWP) is set up. If the interrupt handler returns without blocking, the interrupted thread is simply resumed. However, the interrupt handler might block trying to lock a mutex — something not allowed in most other operating systems. If this happens, the interrupt handler becomes a full-fledged thread — a lightweight process is created for it and this interrupt thread is treated just like any other thread, though at a very high priority. The interrupted thread is resumed and continues its execution while the interrupt thread waits. Once the mutex or other synchronization event being waited for by the interrupt thread is available, it joins the run queue and is scheduled in due time (which is probably very soon, given its priority).

Since the interrupt handler may become a thread and thus be allowed to block, it's no longer necessary for threads, when accessing a data structure that might also be accessed by an interrupt handler, to mask interrupts. Thus the system can operate for longer periods of time without having interrupts masked, and its latency in handling interrupts is reduced.

Note that when an interrupt does occur, the interrupt level is raised to that of the interrupt and thus a class of interrupts is masked. The class remains masked even while the interrupt thread is blocked. The previous interrupt level is restored only when the interrupt thread terminates. You might think that this would cause interrupts to be masked for even longer periods of time than in other systems, but the sort of synchronization events waited for by interrupt handlers happen fairly soon. Furthermore, there is never any danger of waiting for user applications to do anything: interrupt handlers wait only for kernel-managed events.

5.2.2 DEFERRED WORK

We've mentioned that an interrupt handler must do whatever it's doing quickly so that it can return the processor to the context it interrupted. This is important for a variety of reasons, not the least of which is that while a processor is in the interrupt context, other important processing (such as responding to other interrupts) cannot be done, since some set of interrupts is masked. So, if there's work to be done that shouldn't or can't be done while the processor is still in the interrupt context, we need a mechanism to do this work later.

For example, on an architecture with an interrupt hierarchy, the processor might be in the interrupt context servicing a high-priority interrupt, responding to a packet that has just been received from the network. A fair amount of processing may be required to deal with the packet fully; indeed, this processing is too time-consuming to be handled with all lower- and equal-priority interrupts masked off, since this would prevent processing of other important interrupts, such as those resulting from disk completions and the arrival of other network packets. Thus we want to do the processing so as not to interfere with other interrupt handling.

A simple approach to handling deferred work is that interrupt handlers add such requests to a *deferred-work queue*, whose entries are processed when the processor returns to the thread context from the interrupt context.

The code below shows an example. *TopLevelInterruptHandler* might be the code invoked by the hardware directly in response to an interrupt. It calls the handler appropriate for the interrupt, here that for packets arriving from the network. This handler does immediate processing and then queues a request for IP protocol processing to be performed later. It then returns to *TopLevelInterruptHandler*, which determines what sort of context it had interrupted and thus should return to. (How this is determined is architecture-specific.) If it was another interrupt context, then it's not yet time to do the deferred processing. But if it is about to return to a thread context, now is the time to do the deferred processing. *TopLevelInterruptHandler* then unmasks all interrupts, so that the deferred processing does not delay handling of further interrupts, and processes each of the queued deferred requests.

```
void TopLevelInterruptHandler(int dev) {
    InterruptVector[dev](); // call appropriate handler
    if (PreviousContext == ThreadContext) {
        UnMaskInterrupts();
        while(!Empty(WorkQueue)) {
```

```
              Work = DeQueue(WorkQueue);
              Work();
          }
      }
  }

  void NetworkInterruptHandler() {
    // deal with interrupt

    ...

    EnQueue(WorkQueue, MoreWork);
  }
```

A more straightforward approach to handling deferred work is to perform it in a special interrupt context, one that's invoked at lower interrupt priority than the others. Handlers for higher-priority interrupts not only queue their deferred-work requests, but also request this low-priority interrupt. When all higher-priority interrupt handling is complete, the lower-priority interrupt handler is invoked and deals with deferred work. This low-priority interrupt is known as a *software interrupt*, since it is invoked by software rather than hardware.

Windows uses this approach to implement its *deferred procedure call (DPC)* mechanism. It assumes the hierarchy of interrupt levels shown in Table 5.1.

An interrupt handler needing to request deferred processing simply schedules a deferred procedure call (DPC), using code similar to

```
  void InterruptHandler() {
    // deal with interrupt

    ...

    QueueDPC(MoreWork);
        /* enqueues MoreWork on the DPC queue and requests
           a DPC interrupt */
  }
```

Table 5.1 Interrupt-request levels in Windows.

Request Level	Use
31	High
30	Power failure
29	Inter-processor
28	Clock
.	
.	
.	
4	Device 2
3	Device 1
2	DPC
1	APC
0	Thread

The handler for DPC interrupts is called only when there are no pending higher-priority interrupts (we explain the role of another software interrupt, the even lower-priority APC, in Section 5.2.3). Its function is roughly described with this code:

```
void DPCHandler(...) {
  while(!Empty(DPCQueue)) {
    Work = DeQueue(DPCQueue);
    Work();
  }
}
```

A drawback of the DPC mechanism is that, even though it allows the preemption of deferred work by all other interrupt handling, such work is still done in preference to normal thread execution, since it is still handled in the interrupt context. Another mechanism, used by a number of past systems and currently by Linux,[5] is to provide one or more special kernel threads to handle such deferred work. Interrupt handlers queue their work requests. Then, rather than having a top-level interrupt handler check a work queue or request a software interrupt, they wake up the appropriate kernel thread. This thread is then scheduled like any other thread. An example is

```
void InterruptHandler() {
  // deal with interrupt
  ...
  EnQueue(WorkQueue, MoreWork);
  SetEvent(Work);
}

void SoftwareInterruptThread() {
  while(TRUE) {
    WaitEvent(Work)
    while(!Empty(WorkQueue)) {
      Work = DeQueue(WorkQueue);
      Work();
    }
  }
}
```

As mentioned in Section 5.2.1 above, operating systems with non-preemptive kernels preempt only those threads running in user mode; threads running in the kernel cannot be preempted. Thus if the clock-interrupt handler determines that the current thread's time slice is over but the thread is in kernel mode, the interrupt handler must arrange for the preemption to take place later, when the thread returns to user mode. Of course, if the interrupt occurs while the thread is in user mode, preemption takes place as soon as the processor returns to the thread context. This can be

---

[5] Linux has three deferred-work mechanisms, all currently built on what it calls *softirq* threads: *bottom halves*, *tasklets*, and *softirqs*. Bottom halves are used by older drivers designed for a single-threaded kernel on uniprocessors that assume no need for synchronization. Tasklets, used by newer drivers, are essentially work requests handled by softirq threads, one per processor. Additional softirq threads may be set up to handle specialized deferred requests independently of tasklets. Two softirq threads are used to handle receiving and transmitting packets on network.

easily arranged using a technique similar to the first one we saw for handling deferred work: a global flag is set indicating that preemption is requested. When the processor is about to return to the thread context in user mode, it checks this flag and, if it's set, calls the scheduler to pass control to another thread:

```
void ClockInterruptHandler() {
  // deal with clock interrupt
  ...
  if (TimeSliceOver())
    ShouldReschedule = 1;
}

void TopLevelInterruptHandler(int dev) {
  InterruptVector[dev](); // call appropriate handler
  if (PreviousMode == UserMode) {
    // the clock interrupted user-mode code
    if (ShouldReschedule)
      Reschedule();
  }
  ...
}

void TopLevelTrapHandler(...) {
  ...
  SpecificTrapHandler();
  ...
  if (ShouldReschedule) {
    /* the time slice expired while the thread was
       in kernel mode */
    Reschedule();
  }
}
```

The *Reschedule* routine puts the calling thread on the run queue and gives the processor to the next ready-to-run thread by calling *thread_switch*. Let's assume that *TopLevelTrapHandler* is the routine called in response to all traps and in turn invokes a specific trap handler, such as one for a particular system call. Thus if our thread was interrupted by the clock while it was performing a system call, it would eventually attempt to return from *TopLevelTrapHandler*, notice that *ShouldReschedule* was set, and call *Reschedule* to relinquish the processor.

The mechanism is essentially the same if the thread was interrupted by the clock while in user mode. However, in this case, *Reschedule* is called from *TopLevelInterruptHandler* in the interrupt context. Though in general an interrupt handler should not call *thread_switch*, in this case there is no further processing to be done in the interrupt context and the handler's next action is to return to user mode. Thus once the interrupted thread regains the processor, it returns to user mode.

Such a non-preemptive approach was employed in early Unix and Windows systems. It can be adapted for multiprocessor systems by having a separate *ShouldReschedule* flag for each processor.

Operating systems with preemptive kernels allow threads to be preempted even while in kernel mode. Thus once the clock-interrupt handler determines that a thread's time slice is over, it must arrange for the thread to yield the processor once the processor is about to return to the thread's context. This can be accomplished using the DPC or similar mechanism, as in

```
void ClockInterruptHandler() {
  // deal with clock interrupt

  ...

  if (TimeSliceOver())
    QueueDPC(Reschedule);
}
```

The result of this code is that *Reschedule* will be called when the processor is finished handling interrupts and is about to return to the normal thread context (in Windows, there is a still lower interrupt level, the APC discussed soon, that is actually considered part of the thread context). Thus once the processor is back in the context of the current thread, it will call *thread_switch* and yield the processor to the next thread.

5.2.3 DIRECTED PROCESSING

An interrupt might indicate that some sort of immediate response is required by a thread. For example, a Unix process might arrange for a signal handler to be invoked in the context of one of its threads once Ctrl-C is typed on the keyboard. A Windows driver might have a callback procedure that must be called, after I/O completes, to copy status information to the address space of the thread that initiated the operation.

The intent of such *directed processing* is that a procedure is executed in a thread's context without affecting the thread, except for perhaps intended side effects of the body of the procedure. It is as if an interrupt takes place while the thread is running, the interrupt handler calls the associated procedure, and when the handler returns, the thread resumes as if nothing had happened.

This is easy to implement for the case in which the thread is actually in the running or runnable state when directed processing is requested: once the thread is made running (if it isn't already), an actual interrupt (at low IPL) is taken on the thread's stack. For cases in which the thread is neither running nor runnable, it first must be made runnable. This is seemingly straightforward: just move the thread from whatever wait queue it is on to the run queue. But what should be the thread's status once directed processing completes? It can't simply be put back on the wait queue whence it came, since whatever it was waiting for might have already happened. Instead, the thread should recheck its reason for waiting and rejoin the wait queue only if necessary. Thus waits should be structured in a manner similar to waits on POSIX condition variables (Section 2.2.3.2), in that waiting threads might resume execution prematurely.

Another issue is synchronization. The intent of directed processing is that the handler executes in the context of the thread. But, as we saw in discussing Unix signals in Section 2.2.5.1, this can result in deadlock problems if the thread is already involved in synchronization actions, such as holding a mutex. Thus either there must be restrictions on the mutexes that may locked by the handler or the interrupt must be masked when the thread is holding certain mutexes, or both.

5.2.3.1 Asynchronous Procedure Calls

Windows implements directed processing with its *asynchronous procedure call (APC)* facility. APCs are similar to DPCs (Section 5.2.2) in that requesters supply procedures and arguments that are queued for later invocation. However, for APCs there is one such queue per thread and the procedure is invoked in the context of the thread. APCs come in two forms — *kernel APC* and *user APC*. The difference between the two has to do with at what point in a thread's execution it is forced to do directed processing. A kernel APC can interrupt a thread at almost any point in its execution, whether it is in user mode or kernel mode. A user APC can interrupt a thread only if the thread is about to return from kernel mode to user mode. Despite its name, it is used by both kernel code and user code.

When an I/O operation completes, there are certain resources, such as buffers and other data structures in kernel memory, that cannot be released until results and status are transferred to the user. To expedite this and make these resources immediately available for further use, Windows device drivers indicate I/O completion with kernel APCs.

Other operations are not quite so urgent and need take place only when a thread is "ready" to handle them, using user APCs. For example, when starting an asynchronous I/O request, a user thread may supply a *completion routine* that is to be called in that thread's context after the I/O request completes. So as to avoid synchronization issues, the completion routine is called only when explicitly allowed by the thread; the thread indicates such permission by putting itself into the *alertable wait state*, in which it is in a wait queue but marked as *alertable*. It does this by issuing certain system calls such as *SleepEx*, which waits for either a user APC to be delivered or a time limit to expire, and *WaitForMultipleObjectsEx*, which waits for either a user APC to be delivered or an object to be signaled. If a user APC is delivered, the thread wakes up from its sleep, executes the queued user APC in user mode, then returns from the system call with an indication that it has just processed an APC.

In both sorts of APCs, the requester supplies a procedure and argument that is queued on a per-thread list of APC requests. For user APCs, all the requester (such as an interrupt handler) must do in addition is to "unwait" the thread if it is in an alertable wait state. This action makes the thread runnable. When the thread is given a processor and returns from kernel mode to user mode, it executes all pending APCs. It is the responsibility of the programmer to make certain that the asynchronously called procedure does not attempt to lock mutexes that conflict with anything else held by the thread. But since the APC is executed only in alertable states, as designated by the programmer, it is relatively easy to ensure that there are no lock conflicts.

Things are different with kernel APCs, which are able to interrupt a thread at almost any point. Getting the attention of a running thread is done with the lowest-priority software interrupt, the APC interrupt. A thread that is in a wait state (not necessarily an alertable wait state) will be unwaited, just as in the case of user APCs. Runnable threads, having been marked as having pending APCs, will execute their asynchronous procedures once they run.

Care must be taken to avoid synchronization problems. There are actually two sorts of kernel APCs — special and normal. *Special kernel APCs* are intended to preempt threads regardless of what they are doing. However, such interrupted threads may incur page faults if they reference user memory. So to prevent deadlock, they run at the APC IPL (see Table 5.1 above); whenever a thread locks a mutex that could be used as part of handling a page fault, it must raise the IPL to at least APC level to prevent an APC from interfering. *Normal kernel APCs* are not quite so urgent; they are run at IPL 0 but are not delivered to a thread if it has a mutex locked.

In addition, a special user APC is run by a thread when it returns from kernel mode to user mode, as with normal user APCs. However, it is not necessary for the thread to be alertable and the procedure (provided by the kernel) is executed in kernel mode. Special user APCs are used only as part of process termination so that the procedure is called after the threads complete their kernel actions but before they go back to user mode.

5.2.3.2 Unix Signals

The Unix signal mechanism must deal with issues similar to those of Windows APCs. Though implemented primarily in the operating system, this mechanism benefits user code and is thus most similar to user APCs. Threads simply check for pending signals on return to user mode from any trap or interrupt and at this point deal with the signal. If the thread is running on another processor when the signal is sent to it, an interprocessor interrupt is directed to that processor. When the processor returns to user mode after handling the interrupt (there was probably nothing to do other than return), it notices the pending signal and the thread now deals with it.

If a signal was sent to a thread while it was blocked, whether or not the thread is immediately awakened depends on a parameter set when the thread entered the sleep state: it may be sleeping *interruptibly*, in which case a signal will wake it up, or *uninterruptibly*, in which case signals can't wake it up. In either case, the thread acts on the signal after it wakes up and just before it returns to user mode. If the thread was sleeping interruptibly when the signal arrived, it is awakened and no further actions are taken to complete the current system call; instead, it does whatever cleanup is necessary. If it received the signal before it made any progress towards completing the system call, it returns with an error: EINTR for interrupted system call.[6] If the system call was partially completed, for example a request to write 10,000 bytes had already written 1000 bytes, then it returns successfully but with an indication of what it accomplished (in this case, writing merely 1000 bytes). But in all cases, just before the thread actually returns to user mode, it takes whatever signal-specific actions have been set up, including terminating the process or invoking a handler — a procedure executed by the thread in user mode.

Invoking the Signal Handler   Unix signal handlers are essentially the user-mode equivalents of interrupt handlers. As with interrupts, when a thread receives a signal it should invoke the handler at the point at which it was interrupted (in this case, by a signal); when the handler returns, the thread should resume its normal processing. It should behave then as if the thread placed a procedure call to the signal handler at the point at which it received the signal. Furthermore, when the thread invokes the signal handler, further instances of that signal are blocked (by setting a mask bit in the process control block). When the handler returns, the signal is unblocked.

To see how this works, we first figure out what must be in place when the handler returns, and then work out how this is set up to begin with. So assume that a thread has received a signal and, as discussed above, has noticed this while it was in the kernel, has invoked its handler, and now is about to return from the handler. In a normal return from a procedure, a certain subset of the registers, having been saved on entry to the procedure, are restored. Then the instruction pointer, referring to the instruction after the procedure call, is loaded and the thread resumes execution in the calling procedure.

However, a normal return from a procedure won't work in this situation, since the signal handler was not invoked in the normal fashion — in particular, the procedure being returned to didn't actually call the signal handler. Why is this an issue? In a normal procedure call, some but not all the registers are saved, then restored. Other registers are supposed to be modified by the called procedure, such as the one used to return the procedure's return value. But in the case of a signal handler, since the thread was not expecting to place a call, it is certainly not expecting to find that certain registers have been spontaneously modified. So we must ensure that the thread saves all its registers on entry to the handler and restores them on return. Furthermore, since the signal being handled is blocked while the thread is in the handler, it must unblock the signal on return. Thus a normal return from a procedure is not sufficient. Rather than return to the procedure that was interrupted, the signal handler returns to different code that restores all the registers (which were previously saved by the kernel, as explained below), unblocks the signal, and then returns to the interrupted procedure.

Here is how this is made to work. Our thread, executing user-level code (Figure 5.10), enters the kernel, where it discovers it is to call a signal handler (Figure 5.11). Since it is in the kernel, its kernel stack contains its user-mode registers; these are the registers that must be restored when the signal handler returns. They are copied onto the thread's user stack, effectively

---

[6] One can specify that, rather than return this error to the user application, the system call should automatically be restarted.

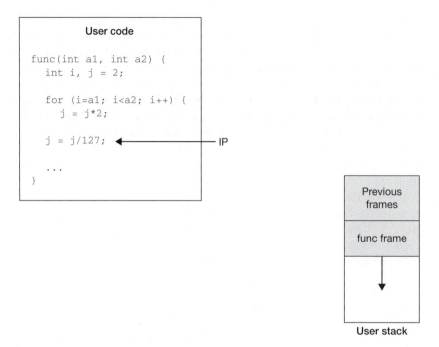

FIGURE 5.10 A thread is executing *func* prior to receiving a signal.

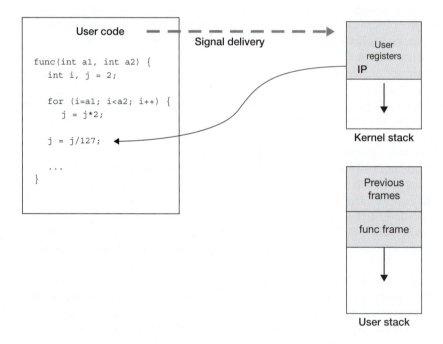

FIGURE 5.11 The thread receives a signal. It discovers the signal while in the kernel and its user registers, including its instruction pointer, are on the kernel stack.

creating a new stack frame. Also pushed on the user stack are the arguments being passed to the signal handler. Finally, the address of a single instruction, a system-call trap, is pushed along with the instruction itself. This is the instruction returned to when the handler returns; the system call, *sigreturn*, instructs the operating system to restore the threads registers and to unblock the signal. The registers being restored are, of course, those pushed earlier by the kernel, which now are near the top of the stack.

Having set up its stack, the thread is just about ready to return to user mode, invoking the handler. The last step is for it to modify the contents of the kernel stack, adjusting the saved user registers so that when they are restored, the instruction pointer refers to the first instruction of the signal handler and the stack and frame pointers refer to the stack frame that's been set up on the user stack (Figure 5.12).

The thread now returns to user mode, executing the signal hander (Figure 5.13). On return from the signal handler the thread executes the *sigreturn* system call (Figure 5.14), causing the thread's entire previous context to be restored and the thread to continue execution in the interrupted procedure (Figure 5.15).

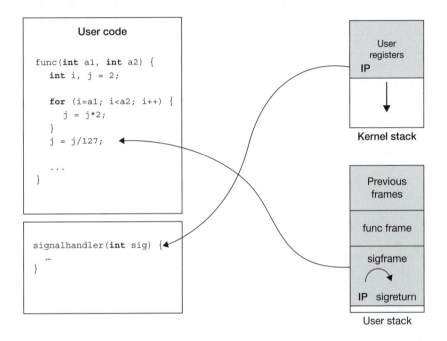

FIGURE 5.12 The thread in the kernel copies its user registers to its user stack, creating a new stack frame called *sigframe*. The arguments to the signal handler (not shown) are also pushed on the stack. The return address — the saved IP — points to a *sigreturn* system call. The saved IP on the kernel stack is set to point to the signal handler.

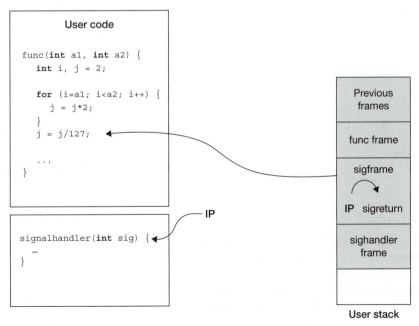

FIGURE 5.13 The thread returns from the kernel to user mode and begins executing the signal handler code.

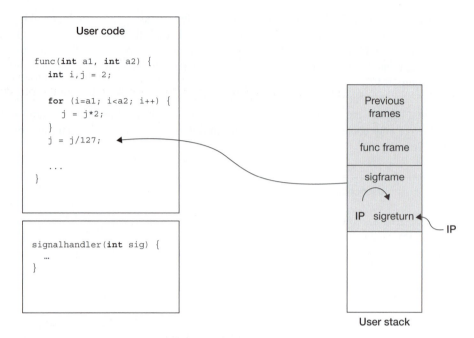

FIGURE 5.14 On return from the signal handler, the thread's instruction pointer points to the *sigreturn* instruction.

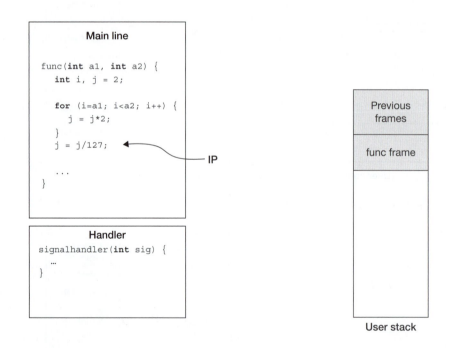

FIGURE 5.15 Finally, the thread executes the *sigreturn* system call, causing the kernel to restore the thread's original registers and unblock the signal.

5.3 SCHEDULING

A common notion of what an operating system does is that it manages resources — it determines who or what is to have which resource when. Processor time is apportioned to threads. Primary memory is apportioned to processes. Disk space is apportioned to users. On some data-processing systems, I/O bandwidth is apportioned to jobs or subsystems.

Our concern in this section is the sharing of processors, a task that's usually referred to as *scheduling* (though certain aspects of memory management in some Unix systems are called "memory scheduling"). The common use of the term *schedule* is that it's something that's prepared ahead of time — we have a schedule for the use of a classroom or conference room; an airline has a flight schedule. Such static schedules make sense if we know or can predict the demands in advance. But the sort of scheduling we're primarily interested in here is dynamic: responding to demands for immediate use of processor time. At any one moment we might have a static schedule for at least the order in which threads wait for processor time, but this schedule changes in response to additional threads becoming runnable and other system events.

A lot goes into determining schedules. At the strategic level, we are trying to make a "good" decision based on some sort of optimization criteria. Are we trying to give good response to interactive threads? Are we trying to give deterministic (and good) response to real-time threads? Are we trying to maximize the number of jobs per hour? Are we trying to do all of the above?

At the tactical level, we need to organize our list of runnable threads so as to find the next thread to run quickly. On multiprocessor systems we need to take into account the benefits of caching: a thread runs best on a processor whose cache contains much of what that thread is using. Furthermore, we must consider the cost of synchronization and organize our data structures to minimize such costs.

5.3.1 STRATEGY

How the processor is shared depends upon what the system as a whole is supposed to do. Listed below are five representative types of systems along with brief descriptions of the sort of sharing desired.

- *Simple batch systems.* These probably don't exist anymore, but they were common into the 1960s. Programs (jobs) were submitted and ran without any interaction with humans, except for possible instructions to the operator to mount tapes and disks. Only one job ran at a time. The basic model is shown in Figure 5.16: a queue of jobs waiting to be run on the processor. The responsibility of the scheduler was to decide which job should run next when the current one finished. There were two concerns: the system throughput, i.e., the number of jobs per unit time, and the average wait time, i.e., how long it took from when a job was submitted to the system until it completed.

- *Multiprogrammed batch systems.* These are identical to simple batch systems except that multiple jobs are run concurrently. Two sorts of scheduling decisions have to be made: how many and which jobs should be running, and how the processor is apportioned among the running jobs.

- *Time-sharing systems.* Here we get away from the problem of how many and which jobs should be running and think more in terms of apportioning the processor to the threads that are ready to execute. The primary concern is wait time, here called response time — the time from when a command is given to when it is completed. Short requests should be handled quickly.

- *Shared servers.* This is the modern version of the multiprogrammed batch system. A single computer is used concurrently by a number of clients, each getting its fair share. For example, a large data-processing computer might be running a number of different online systems each

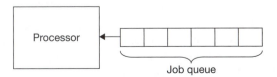

FIGURE 5.16   A simple batch system.

of which must be guaranteed a certain capacity or performance level — we might want to guarantee each at least 10% of available processing time. A web-hosting service might want to give each of its clients the same fraction of total processor time, regardless of the number of threads employed.

- *Real-time systems*. These have a range of requirements, ranging from what's known as "soft" real-time to "hard" real-time. An example of the former is a system to play back streaming audio or video. It's really important that most of the data be processed in a timely fashion, but it's not a disaster if occasionally some data isn't processed on time (or at all). An example of the latter is a system controlling a nuclear reactor. It's not good enough for it to handle most of the data in a timely fashion; it must handle *all* the data in a timely fashion or there will be a disaster.

5.3.1.1 Simple Batch Systems

Much of the early work on scheduling dealt with the notion of jobs — work to be done, usually by a single-threaded program, whose running time was known. In this sort of situation one could conceivably come up with an optimal static schedule.

On a simple batch system (as described above) you might think we can do no better than *first-in-first-out (FIFO)* scheduling, i.e., a simple queue. However, if our sole criterion for goodness of our scheduler is the number of jobs completed per hour, this strategy could get us into trouble: if the first job takes a week (168 hours) to complete, but the following 168 jobs each take an hour, our completion statistics aren't going to look very good, at least not until towards the end of the second week (see Figure 5.17).

From the point of view of the people who submitted the jobs, a relevant measure of "goodness" might be the average amount of time the submitters had to wait between submitting their job and its completion. If all jobs were submitted at roughly the same time, but the long one was submitted first, the average waiting time is 252 hours: the submitter of the first job waited 168 hours, the submitter of the second 169 hours, the submitter of the third 170 hours, and so forth. Summing up these wait times and dividing by the number of jobs (169) yields 252.

A better strategy might be *shortest-job-first (SJF)* (Figure 5.18): whenever we must choose which job to run next, we choose the one requiring the least running time. Thus in the example of the previous paragraph, rather than having to report 0 jobs/hour completed during the first week, we can report 1 job/hour. With both approaches the figure at the end of the second week is .503 jobs/hour. However, the average wait time is now down to 86 hours. Of course, if we continue to get more of these one-hour jobs, the one-week job might never be handled, but if our concern is solely throughput, we don't care.

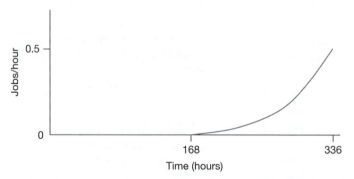

FIGURE 5.17 FIFO scheduling applied to our sample workload.

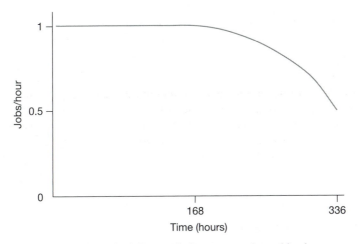

FIGURE 5.18   SJF scheduling applied to our sample workload.

5.3.1.2 Multiprogrammed Batch Systems

Suppose a multiprogrammed batch system runs two jobs concurrently, using two FIFO queues. In one queue are placed long-running jobs and in the other short-running jobs. So, continuing with our example, the 168-hour job is placed in the first queue and the one-hour jobs in the other. When two jobs share the processor, their execution is *time-sliced*: each runs for a certain period of time, known as the *time quantum*, then is preempted in favor of the other.

As with the simple batch systems, the throughput after two weeks is .503 jobs/hour. Computing the average wait time given the time quantum is a bit cumbersome, but consider what happens as the quantum approaches zero: each job experiences a processor that's effectively half its normal speed. Thus the 168-hour job takes two weeks to complete and each of the one-hour jobs takes two hours. The short jobs have an average wait time of 169 hours, while the overall average wait time is 169.99 hours. This is not as good as what we obtained with SJF, but it's better than FIFO and the long job makes progress even if we have a large number of short jobs.

5.3.1.3 Time-Sharing Systems

On time-sharing systems the primary scheduling concern is that the system appear responsive to interactive users. This means that operations that should be quick really are. Users aren't overly annoyed if something that normally takes 2 minutes to run, such as building a large system, takes 5 minutes. But if something that normally seems instantaneous, such as adding a line to a file when running an editor, starts taking more than a second, interactive response is considered poor. Thus in a time-sharing system we want a scheduling strategy that favors short operations at the possible expense of longer ones.

A simple time-sharing scheduler might be time-sliced and employ a single round-robin run queue: a running thread that completes its time slice is put on the end of the run queue and the thread at the front gets to run (see Figure 5.19). To give favored treatment to interactive threads — those that are performing the short operations of interactive users — we might somehow assign them high priorities and modify our queue so that high-priority threads are chosen before

FIGURE 5.19   A round-robin queue.

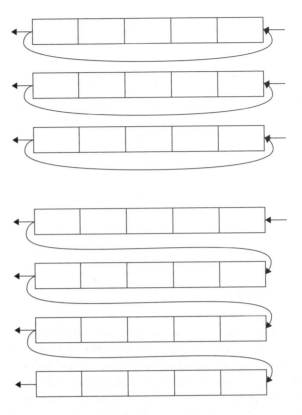

FIGURE 5.20 Round-robin queues of multiple priorities.

FIGURE 5.21 Multi-level feedback queue.

low-priority ones. This could be done by ordering the queue according to priority, or by having multiple queues, one for each priority level (Figure 5.20).

Of course, if computer users are asked to assign the priorities themselves, every thread will be of the highest priority. Thus we need some means for automatically determining "interactiveness" and assigning appropriate priorities. Since threads requiring short bursts of processor time are more likely to be considered interactive than ones requiring long bursts, it makes sense to give the former higher priorities. But how can we determine in advance how big a burst is required? We probably can't, without relying on the honesty of users.

Instead, let's reduce the priority of a thread as it uses more and more time quanta. All threads run at a high priority for the first time quantum of any burst of computation. After each quantum ends, if more processor time is required, the priority gets worse. This can be implemented using a *multilevel feedback queue*, as shown in Figure 5.21. A thread becoming runnable starts at the highest priority and waits on the top-priority queue. Each time it completes a time slice it rejoins the multilevel feedback queue at the next lower queue. Threads in lower queues are not allowed to run unless there are no threads in higher queues.

This general approach makes sense, but it requires a bit more work to be usable. It's based on the implicit assumption that our threads are idle for appreciable periods between bursts of computation. But a thread that we'd like to consider non-interactive might have a large number of relatively brief bursts of computation interspersed with short waits for disk access. Thus the length of the bursts of computation should not be the sole factor in the equation; we need to consider the time between bursts as well.

So, let's modify the multilevel feedback queue by having threads enter the queue at a priority that depends upon what they were doing since they last were in the queue. The priority might be proportional to how long the thread was waiting (for example, for an I/O operation to complete) before returning to the run queue. This approach is conceptually simple and can be roughly summed up by saying that a thread's priority gets worse while it's running and better while it's not. This is the basis of pretty much all thread schedulers employed on today's personal-computer and workstation operating systems, in particular Unix and Windows.

At this point we step back and note that we're using the term "priority" in a rather narrow sense. A thread's priority relates to when it will be scheduled on the processor for its next burst of execution. This is probably not what you have in mind, though, when you use the term "priority." What you probably mean relates to importance: a high-priority task is more important than, and thus, everything else being equal, should be *completed* before a lower-priority task. Thus even in the narrow context of describing operating-system schedulers, a high-priority thread should be given preferential access to resources over lower-priority threads, not just for its next request but at all times.

The user documentation of many operating systems uses this latter sense (importance) when describing thread priorities as seen by user applications, but uses the former sense (short-term scheduling order) when discussing internal priorities. Unix systems provide the *nice* command to modify the importance of a thread, so called because it's generally used to reduce the importance of a thread or process — thus one uses it to be "nice" to everyone else on the system. On Windows, one runs a thread at one of six *base priorities*, defining its importance. These base priorities are a major, but not the sole factor in determining short-term scheduling order.

5.3.1.4 Shared Servers

A problem with the time-sharing approach to scheduling is that the more threads a computation uses, the greater the fraction of available processor time it gets. This is not a big deal on a personal computer, but it is a big deal on a server. Suppose that you and four friends each contribute $1000 to buy a server. You'd probably feel that you own one-fifth of that server and thus when you run a program on it, you should get (at least) one-fifth of the processor's time. However, with the time-sharing schedulers discussed above, if you're running a single-threaded application and each of your friends are running five-threaded applications, their applications will get 20/21 of the processor's time and you will get 1/21 of it. What you (though not necessarily your friends) would like is a partitioned server in which each of you is guaranteed 20% of the server's processing time.

To accomplish such partitioning, we must account for time in terms of the user or application rather than the thread. The general concept is known as *proportional-share* scheduling — everyone gets their fair share of the computer. One interesting approach for this is *lottery scheduling* (Waldspurger and Weihl 1994), in which each user is given a certain number of lottery tickets, depending on the size of her or his share of the computer. In our example, you and each of your friends would be given one-fifth of the lottery tickets. You would give these tickets to your single thread; your friends would distribute their tickets among all their threads. Whenever the scheduler must make a scheduling decision, it essentially runs a lottery in which one lottery ticket is chosen randomly and the thread holding that ticket gets to run. Thus your thread, holding one-fifth of the tickets, is five times as likely to win as any of your friends' threads, which each hold one-twenty-fifth of the tickets.

A deterministic approach with properties similar to those of lottery scheduling is *stride scheduling* (Waldspurger and Weihl 1995). We explain it here, using somewhat different terminology. (Waldspurger and Weihl 1995) use *stride* to mean what we call the *meter rate* below. We start by assuming that we are giving fair treatment to individual threads, and that all threads are equal. Furthermore, let's assume that all threads are created when the system starts, no threads terminate, and no threads block for any reason. We'll relax all these assumptions soon.

To ensure that each thread gets its fair share of the processor, we give each thread a processor meter (rather like an electric meter) that runs, measuring processor time, only when the thread is in the run state — i.e., the thread is running. Time is measured in arbitrary units that we simply call quanta. The scheduler is driven by clock interrupts, which occur every quantum. The interrupt handler chooses the next thread to run, which is the thread with the smallest processor time on its meter. In case of tie, the thread with the lowest ID wins.

No thread will get $i+1$ quanta of time on its meter until all other threads have i quanta on their meters. Thus with respect to the size of the quantum, the scheduler is as fair as is possible.

Let's now allow some threads to be more important than others. To become important, a thread pays a bribe to have its processor meter "fixed." To facilitate such bribes, the provider of meters has established the *ticket* as the bribery unit. It costs one ticket to obtain a "fair" meter — one that accurately measures processor time. If a thread pays two tickets, it gets a meter that measures processor time at half the rate that a fair meter does. If a thread pays three tickets, it gets a meter that measures processor time at one-third the rate of a fair meter, and so forth. Thus the rate at which a thread's meter measures processor time is inversely proportional to the number of tickets used to purchase the meter.

We make no changes to the scheduling algorithm, other than allowing threads to purchase crooked meters. Thus it is still the case that no thread will get $i+1$ quanta of time on its meter until all other threads have i quanta on their meters, but some threads will consume more actual processor time than others. If two threads' meters have the same value, but one thread has paid n tickets for its meter and the other has paid one ticket, then the first thread will have consumed n times more processor time than the other.[7]

Figure 5.22 shows some of the details of slide scheduling in terms of C code. We store with each thread the bribe it has paid (in units of tickets), the meter rate induced by this bribe (*meter_rate*), and the current meter reading (*metered_time*). The meter is initialized with the reciprocal of the bribe, which is the amount added to the meter after each quantum of execution time. The figure also shows how the meter is updated at the end of each quantum, when the next thread is selected for execution. Note that a real implementation of the scheduler would probably use scaled-integer arithmetic, not floating-point arithmetic.

We don't show the implementation of the run queue in Figure 5.22, but it is clearly critical. If it is a balanced searched tree, where the threads are sorted by *metered_time*, then the operations of *InsertQueue* and *PullSmallestThreadFromQueue* are done in $O(log(n))$ time, where n is the number of runnable threads. Though, as discussed in Section 5.3.3, many schedulers have run queues with linear-time operations, this is certainly acceptable, particularly since the number of runnable threads is not likely to be large.

```
typedef struct {
    ...
    float bribe, meter_rate, metered_time;
} thread_t;

void thread_init(thread_t *t, float bribe) {
    ...
    if (bribe < 1)
        abort();
    t->bribe = bribe;
    t->meter_rate = t->metered_time = 1/bribe;
    InsertQueue(t);
}

void OnClockTick() {
    thread_t *NextThread;

    CurrentThread->metered_time +=
        CurrentThread->meter_rate;
    InsertQueue(CurrentThread);
    NextThread = PullSmallestThreadFromQueue();
    if (NextThread != CurrentThread)
        SwitchTo(NextThread);
}
```

FIGURE 5.22 C code showing the slide-scheduler initialization required for each thread, as well as how the current thread's meter is updated at the end of a time quantum.

[7] Rather than normal threads paying one ticket for their meters, it is more useful for normal threads to pay, say, ten tickets for their meters. This allows not only smaller jumps in processor shares but also provides a means for giving some threads less than the normal processor share.

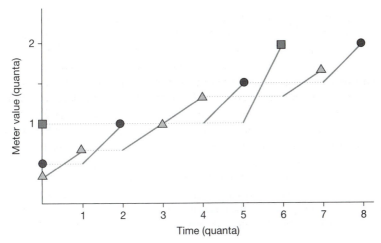

FIGURE 5.23   The execution of three threads using stride scheduling. Thread 1 (a triangle) has paid a bribe of three tickets. Thread 2 (a circle) has paid two tickets, and thread 3 (a square) has paid only one ticket. The solid thick lines indicate when a thread is running. Their slopes are proportional to the meter rates (inversely proportional to the bribe).

An example of the scheduler in operation, adapted from (Waldspurger and Weihl 1995), is shown in Figure 5.23, where we are scheduling three threads that have paid three, two, and one tickets, respectively. Note that the threads' meters can differ from one another by up to one quantum.

Suppose a new thread is created. It pays its bribe and gets a meter, but to what value should the meter be initialized? If it's set to zero, then the new thread gets all the processor time until its meter catches up with the others' meters.

To deal with this problem, we figure out what value the new thread's meter would have had if the thread had been runnable or running since the beginning of time, then set the meter to this value. Thus the thread would join the run queue with no advantage (or disadvantage) over others.

How do we determine this meter value? We could look at the meter of some other thread, but its meter could differ from the desired value by up to an entire quantum. Instead, let's hypothesize a fictitious additional processor as well as a fictitious additional thread that runs only on the additional processor. This thread has as many tickets as all the (real) runnable and running threads put together and, of course, a meter that measures time in steps that are the reciprocal of this total number of tickets. It gets all the processor time of the fictitious processor, but its meter advances at the same average rate as that of any real thread that has been runnable or running since the beginning of time on the real processor. Since its meter advances more smoothly than those of the real threads, the meters of new threads are set to its value upon creation.

Implementing the fictitious thread's meter is easy — just one additional line of clock-tick code is required, as shown in Figure 5.24.

Now suppose a thread blocks, say for I/O or to wait on a semaphore. When it resumes execution, unless we make some adjustments, its meter will have the same value it had when the thread stopped execution. So, like new threads, it sets its meter to the current value of the fictitious thread's meter (though see Exercise 13).

An artifact of stride scheduling, as discussed above, is that processor time is not smoothly distributed among threads that have a large imbalance of tickets. For example, suppose thread 1 has one hundred tickets, and threads 2 through 101 each have one ticket. Thread 1 will execute for one hundred quanta, then each of the other threads will execute for one quantum each, and then the cycle repeats. Though this behavior is not necessarily bad, in some situations (as when some of the one-ticket threads are handling interactive requests) it is. A better schedule might be for thread 1's execution to alternate with each of the other threads in turn, so that thread 1 runs

```
void OnClockTick() {
  thread_t *NextThread;

  FictitiousMeter += 1/TotalBribe;
  CurrentThread->metered_time +=
      CurrentThread->meter_rate;
  InsertQueue(CurrentThread);
  NextThread = PullSmallestThreadFromQueue();
  if (NextThread != CurrentThread)
    SwitchTo(NextThread);
}
```

FIGURE 5.24 Updated clock-tick code that maintains the meter of a fictitious thread that has paid a bribe of the sum of all the bribes paid by the real threads. This meter is used to initialize the meters of new threads and to update the meters of newly awoken threads.

for one quantum, then thread 2 runs for a quantum, then thread 1 runs for a quantum, then thread 3 runs for a quantum, and so forth.

Such scheduling is performed using a variant of stride scheduling called *hierarchical stride scheduling*. Threads are organized into groups. In our example, thread 1 would form one group and threads 2 through 101 would form another. Each group is represented by a balanced binary search tree, with the threads as leaves. Each interior node has a meter whose rate is based on the total number of tickets held by the threads at the leaves of the subtree it is a root of. Thus, for our example, the group of one-ticket threads would be represented by a tree whose root has a meter running at 1/100 speed. The singleton group for the 100-ticket thread would also be represented by a (one-node) tree whose root has a meter running at 1/100 speed.

At the end of a quantum, the group whose root has the least time on its meter is selected to run. Within the group, the thread (leaf) with the smallest time on its meter is selected and removed from the tree (this requires rebalancing and updating the meters of each of the interior nodes on the path back to the root). When the quantum of execution for the selected thread completes, it is reinserted into its tree and the meters of its new tree ancestors are updated.

In hierarchical stride scheduling, adding another thread to a group reduces the shares of the processor given to members of other groups. In some situations this might not be desirable. For example, we might want to partition a processor into n groups, with each group getting some fixed percentage of processor time regardless of how many threads are in it. Thus adding a new thread to a group changes the share of processor time given to threads of that group, but doesn't affect threads of other groups. We take this up in Exercise 14.

5.3.1.5 Real-Time Systems

Scheduling for real-time systems must be dependable. On a time-sharing system or personal computer, it's fine if interactive response is occasionally slow as long as most of the time it's very fast. On real-time systems, though, prolonged periods of faster-than-necessary response do not make up for any period of slower-than-necessary response. In a soft real-time application such as playing music, the faster-than-necessary response doesn't make the music sound any better, while the slower-than-necessary response produces some annoying noises. For a hard real-time application such as running a nuclear reactor, a slower-than-necessary response might necessitate a wide-area evacuation in which earlier quick responses become irrelevant and later quick responses become impossible.

Both Unix and Windows provide real-time scheduling support that both (rightly) characterize as insufficient for hard real-time applications. The approach taken is to extend time-sharing scheduling by adding some very high real-time-only priorities. Runnable real-time threads always preempt the execution of other threads, even those performing important system functions such as network protocol processing and mouse and keyboard handling. This clearly provides fast response, but, as we explain below, not necessarily dependable response.

We shouldn't undervalue fast response — it's definitely important for many applications. So, before we discuss hard real time, what else can be done to improve response times and make them more dependable? Let's start our answer by listing some things that either slow response or make it less dependable.

- *Interrupt processing.* Even though real-time threads have the highest priority, interrupt handling still preempts their execution.

- *Caching and paging.* These techniques serve to make execution normally fast except for occasions when what is needed is not in the cache or in memory.

- *Resource acquisition.* Real-time threads must acquire kernel resources such as memory, buffers, etc., just like any other thread. If a mutex must be locked that's currently held by a lower-priority thread, the waiting thread must wait for the low-priority thread to make progress. This situation is known as *priority inversion*: the high-priority thread, while waiting, is essentially at the other thread's priority.

What can we do about these problems? To minimize the effects of interrupt processing, systems take advantage of the deferred-work techniques we discussed in Section 5.2.2. Where possible, much work that would ordinarily take place within interrupt handlers is deferred and done in contexts that can be preempted by real-time threads.

In general, caching in its various forms is considered so beneficial to overall speed that even systems supporting soft real-time applications use it. However, some hard real-time systems eschew hardware caches so as to insure that performance is uniform. To avoid delays due to paging (see Chapter 7), many systems (including Unix and Windows) allow applications to *pin* portions of their address spaces into primary memory. This means that these portions are kept in primary memory accessed without delays due to page faults, etc. Of course, doing this reduces the amount of memory available for others.

Priority inversion has a straightforward solution — *priority inheritance*. If a real-time thread is waiting to lock a mutex held by a lower-priority thread, the latter's priority is set to that of the real-time thread until the mutex is unlocked. Thus the lower-priority thread runs at the priority of the waiting real-time thread until the real-time thread acquires the lock on the mutex. If the lower-priority thread is itself waiting to lock another mutex, the priority of the holder of that mutex must be raised as well. This is known as *cascading inheritance*.

Let's now look at hard real-time systems. This is an important area of its own and we just scratch the surface here by examining two simple scheduling approaches. Say we have a number of chores to complete, each with a deadline and a known running time. A simple, intuitive approach is *earliest deadline first*: always complete the chore whose deadline is soonest. This certainly makes sense in everyday life. If you have a number of things to do, all else equal you should complete those things first that must be done first. You can work on longer-term projects when time permits, that is when you don't have an imminent deadline for some other project. Of course, this might well mean that your long-term projects get done at the last minute, but at least you meet your deadlines. If you don't end up having time to complete your long-term project, it's not because of poor scheduling, it's because you took on too many projects. In other words, if a successful schedule is at all possible, an earliest-deadline-first schedule will work.

However, things are not so simple if we have multiple processors, or, in the everyday case, if you are managing multiple people who do your work for you. The general multiprocessor scheduling problem is NP-complete. There is a vast literature on efficient algorithms for special cases and approximate algorithms for more general cases; we don't discuss them here, but see, for example, (Garey and Johnson 1975).

An interesting and useful single-processor case is when a number of chores must be performed periodically. Suppose we have a set of n chores such that each chore i must be completed every P_i seconds and requires T_i processing time. Of course, T_i must be less than or equal to P_i. Furthermore, the sum of the chores' duty cycles must be less than or equal to one: a chore's duty cycle is the time required for each instance divided by the length of its period — it's the fraction of the total time that must be devoted to handling this chore. If the sum of all duty cycles is greater than one, then we clearly can't do them all — there's not enough time.

If the sum of the duty cycles is less than or equal to one, then the chores can be successfully scheduled using earliest-deadline-first. However, particularly if we have a large number of chores, this scheduling algorithm is, in general, rather expensive to run: each scheduling decision requires evaluating the current status of all chores. If instead we can assign fixed priorities to the threads running the chores and use a simple preemptive priority-based scheduler, scheduling will be quick and efficient.

An intuitively attractive approach is to give threads whose chores have short periods higher priority than threads whose chores have long periods. Thus if thread T_i is handling chore i, its priority is $1/P_i$. The high-frequency (short-period) threads have more frequent deadlines than the low-frequency (long-period) ones and thus would seem to need the processor more often. This approach is known as *rate-monotonic scheduling* and is particularly attractive because most general-purpose operating systems provide schedulers that can handle it.

The example of this approach in Figure 5.25 shows the schedule for the first 9.5 seconds. During this period, all chores are scheduled before their deadlines. But will this continue to be so if we look beyond the first 9.5 seconds? If all chores start in phase, that is, all periods start at the same time, the answer is yes, in fact, we could have stopped after 2.5 seconds — the period of the longest-period chore. In other words, if a chore will ever fail to meet its deadline, it will fail in its first period.

To see this, consider the following. The highest-frequency (and thus highest-priority) chore runs whenever it's ready. Thus if its duty cycle is less than one, it will be successfully scheduled. The second-highest-frequency chore runs whenever both it is ready and the highest-frequency chore is not running. It's of course necessary that the sum of its duty cycle and that of the first chore be less than or equal to one, but it is not sufficient — the first chore, because of

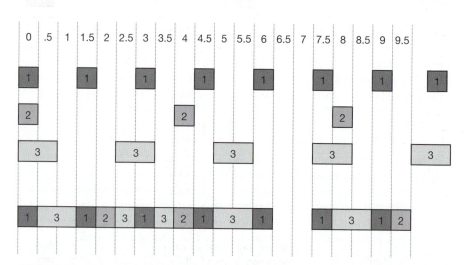

FIGURE 5.25 A successful application of rate-monotonic scheduling. The top three rows show three cyclic chores. The first occurs every 1.5 seconds and requires .5 seconds. The second occurs every 4 seconds and requires .5 seconds. The third occurs every 2.5 seconds and requires 1 second. The fourth row shows the schedule obtained using rate-monotonic scheduling.

its priority, might preempt the second at a time when the second must run to meet its deadline but the first chore could wait and still meet its deadline. This would happen if, during one period of the second chore, the first used up so much time that there was not sufficient time left for the second. So, if we start the schedule so that the first chore uses the largest fraction it will ever use of the second's period, and if the second, nevertheless, is able to meet its deadline, then it will certainly be able to meet its deadline in all subsequent periods. We maximize this fraction by starting both periods at the same moment.

By applying this argument to the third-highest-frequency chore, to the fourth, and so forth, it becomes clear that all we have to consider is an initial time duration equal to the period of the lowest-frequency chore. Thus, in Figure 5.25, it's sufficient to show just the first 2.5 seconds — the period of the lowest-frequency chore.

Note that the above argument applies only if the chores' periods start in phase. As shown in Figure 5.26, it might be possible, if they don't start in phase, to apply rate-monotonic scheduling successfully, even though it would fail otherwise.

Does rate-monotonic scheduling always work in the cases where the sums of the duty cycles are less than one? Figure 5.27 shows a counterexample. We add one more cyclic chore to the example of Figure 5.25, this one with a period of 4.5 seconds. With rate-monotonic scheduling, we see that the new chore cannot meet its deadline. However, as shown in the bottom line of the figure, with earliest-deadline-first scheduling all deadlines are met.

Rate-monotonic scheduling has been studied extensively in the literature, and it's been shown that no algorithm using statically assigned priorities can do better than it (Lehoczky, Sha, et al. 1989). It's also been shown (see (Lehoczky, Sha, et al. 1989) for details) that if the sum of the duty cycles is less than $n(2^{1/n}-1)$, where n is the number of chores, then rate-monotonic scheduling is guaranteed to work. As n gets large, this value approaches $ln\ 2$ (the natural logarithm of 2, roughly .69314718). However, this is a sufficient but not necessary condition — in Figure 5.25 the sum of the chores' duty cycles exceeds the value given by the formula, but rate-monotonic scheduling still works.

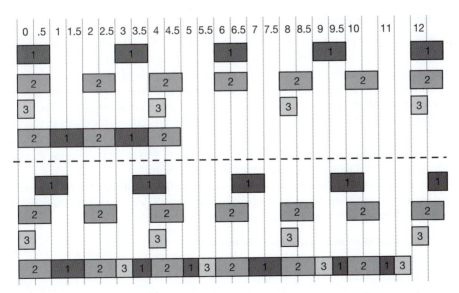

FIGURE 5.26 The effect of phase on rate-monotonic scheduling. The top three rows show three chores. The first requires 1 second every 3 seconds, the second requires 1 second every 2 seconds, and the third requires .5 seconds every 4 seconds. The fourth row shows what happens when rate-monotonic scheduling is used: the third chore can't make its deadline even once. In the bottom half of the figure, we've started the first chore a half-second after the others. The last row shows the rate-monotonic schedule: all three chores consistently meet their deadlines.

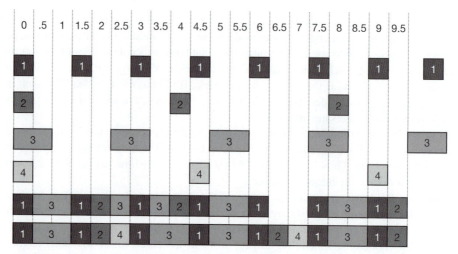

FIGURE 5.27 Rate-monotonic scheduling doesn't work, but earliest-deadline-first does. We've added one more cyclic chore to the example in Figure 5.22, this one requiring .5 seconds every 4.5 seconds. The fifth row is the beginning of a schedule using rate-monotonic scheduling: we can't complete the new chore within its period. However, with *earliest deadline first*, we can meet the deadline, as shown in the bottom row.

5.3.2 TACTICS

In a few special situations, techniques are needed to circumvent the scheduler's normal actions in order to make certain that certain threads run. These situations include using local RPC (Section 4.2.2) for fast interprocess communication, synchronization on multiprocessors, and partitioning multiprocessors. We cover each of these in turn.

5.3.2.1 Handoff Scheduling

In local RPC, a thread in one process places a call to a procedure residing in another process. From the application's point of view, the effect is as if the calling thread actually crosses the process boundary and executes code in the called process. In reality, as implemented in most operating systems, threads can do no such thing; they are restricted to executing within one process. So, two threads must be employed — one in the calling process and one in the called process.

A typical approach is that processes supplying remote procedures for others to call provide one or more threads to execute the remote procedures in response to such calls. This sounds straightforward enough: such threads wait on a queue and are woken up in response to incoming calls. The calling thread then sleeps until the called thread returns.

The problem is the scheduling latency. We'd like the time required to execute a local RPC to be not much worse than the time required to execute a strictly local procedure call. Two things are done in the RPC case that are not done in local procedure calls:

- transferring arguments and results between processes

- waking up and scheduling first the called thread at the beginning of the RPC, then the calling thread on return

We cover the former issue in Chapter 9. The problem with the latter is the time lag between when, for example, the calling thread wakes up the called thread and when the called thread is actually chosen by the scheduler to run. To eliminate this lag, we must somehow circumvent the normal actions of the scheduler and get the called thread to run immediately.

The circumvention method is called *handoff scheduling* (Black 1990a). The calling thread invokes the scheduler, passing the ID of the called thread. The calling thread blocks and the called thread starts running immediately, using the processor originally assigned to the calling thread. For this to be reasonably fair to the other threads of the system, the scheduling state of the calling thread might also be transferred to the called thread. For example, the called thread's initial time slice is set to be whatever remains of the calling thread's time slice.

5.3.2.2 Preemption Control

Does it make sense to use spin locks to synchronize user threads? It certainly does not on a uniprocessor, so let's assume we are dealing with a multiprocessor. If one thread is holding a spin lock while another is waiting for it, we want to ensure that the thread holding the lock is making progress. The worst thing that could happen is for the thread holding the lock to be preempted by the thread waiting for the lock. And this is entirely possible if the time slice of the lock-holding thread expires.

The solution is somehow to convince the scheduler not to end the time slice of a thread that is holding a spin lock. In principle, this is not difficult. A thread could simply set a bit in its control structure to extend its time. This has two difficulties:

1. All threads might set this bit and never clear it. Thus the bit has no real effect.

2. The reason for using a spin lock rather than a blocking lock is performance. If setting a bit in a control structure is expensive (because the control structure belongs to the operating system), this might negate the performance benefits of using a spin lock.

To deal with the first problem, we must provide an incentive not to set the bit for longer than absolutely necessary. To deal with the second, the implementation must be extremely fast. Sun's Solaris operating system provides a mechanism that does both. If a thread executes for longer than its time slice, its scheduling priority becomes correspondingly worse. The system call that implements the operation is in the "fast track," meaning that threads calling it go into and out of the kernel with minimal overhead.

5.3.2.3 Multiprocessor Issues

How should the processors of a multiprocessor system be scheduled? Assuming a symmetric multiprocessor (SMP) system, in which all processors can access all memory, an obvious approach is to have a single queue of runnable threads feeding all processors. Thus whenever a processor becomes idle and needs work, it takes the first thread in the queue.

This approach has been used in a number of systems but, unfortunately, suffers from two serious problems. The first is contention for the queue itself, which processors must lock before accessing. The more processors a system has, the greater the potential delay in dispatching a thread to a processor.

The second problem has to do with the caching of memory in the processors. If a thread that was running on a processor becomes runnable again, there is a good chance not only that some of the memory referenced by that thread is still in the original processor's cache, but also that the thread will reference this memory again soon. Thus it makes sense to run the thread on the same processor on which it ran previously. What a thread has brought into a processor's cache is known as its *cache footprint*. The size of the cache footprint will certainly get smaller with time while other threads are running on the processor, but as long as it still exists, there is a potential advantage to a thread's running on its most recent processor.

To deal with both these problems it makes sense to have multiple run queues, one for each processor. Thus, since each processor uses only its own queue, there is no lock contention. If a thread, when made runnable, is always put on the queue of its most recent processor, it will always take advantage of whatever cache footprint remains.

This might seem to solve all our problems, except that we need to make certain that all processors are kept reasonably busy. When a thread is created, on which processor should it run? If some processors have longer queues than others, should we attempt to balance the load?

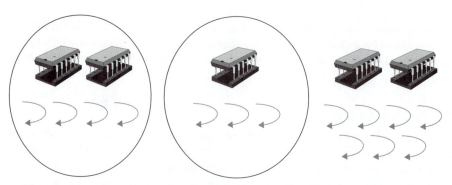

FIGURE 5.28 A system with two processor sets, contained in the ovals. The leftmost contains two processors and four threads; the other contains one processor and three threads. The remaining processors and threads effectively form their own set.

Load balancing will definitely cause some contention when one processor either pulls threads from or gives threads to another's run queue, but, assuming such operations are infrequent, the cost is small. The more difficult issue is the strategy for load balancing, which must take into account not only cache footprints, but also the likelihood of threads' sharing memory and how the processors and caches are organized.

In our usual model of a shared-memory multiprocessor system, any thread may run on any processor. This makes a lot of sense for most personal computers and many servers. But in many circumstances it makes sense to restrict the use of some or all of the processors. For example, a virtual-machine monitor might want to dedicate certain processors to certain virtual machines. A real-time system might need to shelter some applications from the effects of interrupt handling, so it might run their threads on processors that don't handle device interrupts.

A technique for doing this sort of partitioning, pioneered in the Mach microkernel (Black 1990b), involves the use of *processor sets*. Each such set is a collection of processors and threads. The processors may run only those threads in their set; the threads may run on only those processors in their set (see Figure 5.28). Thus for the virtual-machine example mentioned above, a virtual machine, and hence all its threads, might be assigned a processor set that's supplied by the VMM — the processors would be made available for that virtual machine. For the real-time system, critical applications might have their threads put in processor sets that include only those processors not involved with interrupt handling.

Processor sets are explicitly supported by Solaris. Windows has a similar concept that it calls affinity masks.

5.3.3 CASE STUDIES

In this section we examine how scheduling is done in two systems: Linux and Windows. Each has to deal with the following concerns and each does so differently.

- *Efficiency and scaling.* Scheduling decisions — which thread to run next — are made often and thus must be done efficiently. What might be practical for a personal computer with rarely more than two runnable threads doesn't necessarily work well for a busy server with many tens of runnable threads.

- *Multiprocessor issues.* It matters which processor a thread runs on. Processors have caches and if a thread has run recently on a processor, it may make sense for the thread to run on that processor again to take advantage of its "cache footprint" — those storage items it needs to use that might still be in the cache and thus accessed quickly. Another issue is that multiple processors might cause contention on mutexes used to protect run queues and other scheduler data structures, thus slowing down scheduling.

- *Who's next*? Both systems must somehow determine which threads should be the ones that are running at any particular moment. This must take into account the relative importance of individual threads, the resources tied up by threads, and I/O performance.

5.3.3.1 Scheduling in Linux

Until early 2003, Linux employed a rather simple but unscalable approach to scheduling. This was replaced by a new scheduler that was not only more scalable but also more suitable for multiprocessors. The new scheduler was itself replaced in 2007 by an even newer scheduler based on stride scheduling (see Section 5.3.1.4). The general approach in the first two schedulers is to divide time into variable-length cycles and give runnable threads time on the processor each cycle roughly in proportion to their priority and in inverse proportion to how long they've been running recently. Real-time threads, however, compete only with each other on a strict priority basis: lower-priority real-time threads run only when no higher-priority threads are runnable.

Any one thread is governed by one of three scheduling policies, settable by user code. The SCHED_FIFO policy provides soft-real-time scheduling with high priorities and no time slicing: threads run until they terminate, block for some reason, or are preempted by a thread of even higher priority. The SCHED_RR policy provides soft-real-time scheduling that is just like SCHED_FIFO except time slicing is done using user-adjustable time quanta. The imaginatively named SCHED_OTHER policy provides normal time-sharing scheduling and is used by most threads.

In the old scheduler, each thread is assigned a priority as an indication of its importance. For time-sharing threads this priority is based on the thread's "nice" value (see Section 5.3.1.3). For real-time threads it's the thread's priority relative to other real-time threads, but higher than that of any time-sharing thread. For time-sharing threads, this priority is used to initialize the thread's *counter*, a variable that measures how much processor use the thread has had recently and also indicates how much of the processor it should get soon. The next thread to run depends on the result of a per-thread "goodness" computation: for real-time threads, this goodness value is based on its priority, and for time-shared threads it's the thread's counter value.

Every 10 milliseconds a clock interrupt occurs and the value of the counter for the currently running thread is decremented by one. When a (time-sharing) thread's counter becomes zero, its time slice is over and it goes back to the run queue. Thus the length of the scheduling cycle is the sum of the counters of all the runnable threads. At the end of a scheduling cycle, when there are no runnable real-time threads and all runnable time-sharing threads have zero counters, the counters of all time-sharing threads, not just the runnable ones, are set as follows:

```
counter = counter/2 + priority;
```

Thus the counters for the runnable threads are reset to the threads' priorities ("nice" values), while those of sleeping threads increase to a maximum of twice the threads' priorities. Threads that have been sleeping for a while end up with a large share of the scheduling cycle the next time they run. Since such sleeping threads are likely to be interactive threads — they may have been sleeping or waiting for the next keystroke or mouse click — interactive threads get favored treatment for their next burst of processor usage.

What's wrong with this old scheduler? Why was it replaced? There are a number of problems. Determining the next thread to run requires computing the goodness value for all threads on the run queue — it's the first one encountered with the highest goodness value. Thus performance suffers with larger run queues. What's equally bad, if not worse, is that the counter values of all time-sharing threads, not just all runnable ones, must be recomputed at the end of each scheduling cycle. For a server with thousands of threads, this can be time-consuming.

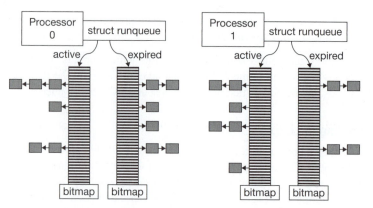

FIGURE 5.29   The run queues of the O(1) Linux scheduler.

In addition, there is no explicit support for multiprocessors. On such a system, the one run queue serves all processors; a thread is equally likely to run on any processor from one execution to the next. Furthermore, with a single run queue there is contention for the mutex protecting it.

The new scheduler, known as the *O(1) scheduler* for reasons explained below, has a roughly similar effect to the old one in determining which thread runs when, but does so more efficiently and takes cache footprints into account when scheduling for multiprocessors.

Each processor has a separate run queue — actually a separate pair of run queues labeled *active* and *expired* (see Figure 5.29). Each run queue is itself an array of queues, one for each priority level, of which there are 140. Attached to each run queue is a bit vector indicating which of the queues are non-empty. Finding the highest-priority runnable thread involves searching the bit vector for the first non-empty queue, then taking the first thread from that queue. Thus scheduling decisions are made in constant time, as opposed to the linear time required by the old scheduler — thus explaining the name of the scheduler.

A processor's active queue provides it with threads to run. When one is needed, the thread from the front of the highest-priority non-empty queue is chosen and runs with a time slice that depends on its priority. When a thread's time slice is over, what happens next also depends on its priority. Real-time threads (necessarily SCHED_RR since SCHED_FIFO threads aren't time-sliced) go back to the active queue at their priority. A time-sharing thread's priority is reduced; if it's still above an interactive-priority threshold, it goes back to the active queue at its new priority. Otherwise it goes to the expired queue. However, if threads have been waiting in the expired queue for too long (how long depends on how many there are), then all time-sharing threads go to the expired queue when their time slice is over.

If there are no threads in the active queue, which means there are no runnable real-time threads, then the active and expired queues are switched. The threads that were on the expired queue now compete for the processor.

When a thread that has been sleeping wakes up, it's assigned a priority that depends both on how long it was sleeping and what it was waiting for. The longer the sleep, the better its priority becomes. If it was waiting on a hardware event such as a keystroke or a mouse click, its priority becomes even better. The assumption is that long-term sleepers or those who had been waiting for such events are the most likely to be interactive threads. Newly awoken threads go on the active queue.

The effect of all this is that real-time threads run to the exclusion of all other threads. Threads determined to be interactive get favored treatment over non-interactive threads.

As we've mentioned, each processor has its own set of queues. Threads typically run on the same processor all the time, thus taking advantage of their cache footprints. Of course, we also need a means for sharing the workload among all processors — the benefits of using the cache footprint do not outweigh those of using multiple processors.

What the O(1) scheduler does is to have a clock interrupt on each processor every millisecond. If the interrupt handler sees the processor's run queues are empty, it finds the processor with the largest load and steals threads from it (assuming not all processors are idle). Every 250 milliseconds the interrupt handler checks for a load imbalance — if its processor's run queue is much smaller than others, it also steals threads from the others.

The result of all this is threefold:

- Threads rarely migrate from one processor to another — thus advantage is taken of cache footprints.

- Queues remain in balance over the long term.

- Processors rarely access one another's queues and thus lock contention is rare.

The Completely Fair Scheduler   Despite the improvements gained with the O(1) scheduler, the Linux developers decided, apparently because of a few examples of anomalous behavior, to replace it with a scheduler based on stride scheduling (see Section 5.3.1.4) and called the *completely fair scheduler* (CFS). (The CFS approach was apparently developed without knowledge of the prior work on stride scheduling, which was described twelve years earlier (Waldspurger and Weihl 1995) — there is no mention of stride scheduling in any of the CFS documentation. Since stride scheduling requires logarithmic time, CFS might be called the $O(\log(n))$ scheduler.)

In support of CFS, the scheduler architecture was changed to allow the use of a number of scheduling policies. Standard Linux supplies two: a real-time policy supporting the POSIX SCHED_RR and SCHED_FIFO classes and a fair policy (stride scheduling) supporting the other POSIX scheduling classes. The policies are ordered so that no runnable threads in a lower policy are scheduled if there are any runnable threads in a higher policy. Thus when the scheduler makes a decision, it first invokes the real-time policy to select a thread; then, if no real-time threads are available to run, it invokes the fair policy. The real-time policy is implemented much as it was in the O(1) scheduler, but without the expired queue.

Threads of all scheduling policies are assigned to individual processors and scheduling is done separately for each processor. Just as in the O(1) scheduler, load balancing is done to even out the number of threads assigned to each processor.

5.3.3.2 Scheduling in Windows

The Windows scheduler is essentially round-robin with multiple priorities, but with a few twists. Its basic strategy is straightforward. Threads are assigned priorities ranging from 0 through 31, with 0 reserved for special idle threads. Priorities of normal threads must be less than 16 and greater than 0; "real-time" threads have priorities from 16 through 31. Normal threads are assigned a fixed base priority, but their effective priority is "boosted" when they wake up after sleeping and is reduced while they are running. The priorities of real-time threads are fixed. Users assign base priorities to threads according to their importance.

Another scheduling parameter is the length of a thread's time quantum — how long it runs until preempted by a thread of equal priority. Normal threads are assigned a default quantum whose value depends on the type of system. Servers typically have longer quanta than interactive computers. But subsystems external to the actual scheduler can change the quanta of individual threads while they are running. In particular, the Win-32 subsystem, which manages windows on the display, increases the quanta of foreground threads — threads belonging to the process of the foreground window. The effect of doing this is to make sure that these threads get a greater portion of the processor's time than do threads of equal priority belonging to background processes. Note that simply assigning such threads a higher priority might prevent background threads from running at all — if that is what is desired, then the user can give such threads a lower base priority.

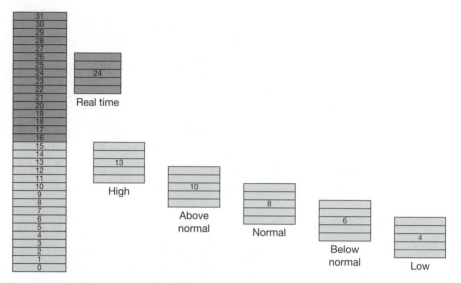

FIGURE 5.30 Priority ranges in Windows.

The base priorities assigned to threads are typically from the middle of ranges labeled *high*, *above normal*, *normal*, *below normal*, and *low*, as shown in Figure 5.30. Real-time threads are typically assigned priorities from the range labeled *real time*, though their priorities do not change. A normal thread's effective priority is some value equal to or greater than its base. When waking up from a sleep, a thread's effective priority is set to their base priority plus some wait-specific value (usually in the range 1 to 6, depending on what sort of event it was waiting for). A thread's effective priority is decremented by one, but to no less than the base, each time a quantum expires on it.

The effect of all this is that threads of the same range share the processor with one another, but threads of lower ranges cannot run at all unless there are no runnable threads in higher ranges.

As described so far, the Windows scheduler handles typical interactive computing and servers reasonably well, but, despite its real-time priorities, it doesn't handle many real-time chores very well. One issue is priority inversion, as described in Section 5.3.1.5. Rather than attempt to detect instances of priority inversion, Windows makes sure that all runnable processes eventually make progress (though threads running at real-time priorities can prevent other threads from running). A system thread known as the *balance set manager*, whose primary job is to assist in managing virtual memory, periodically checks for threads that have been runnable for a certain period of time, but have not actually been running. It increases their priority to 15, the maximum value for normal threads. Once such a thread has run for its time quantum, its priority goes back to what it was.

Another issue is handling applications, such as audio and video, that have rather stringent performance requirements and, if given high real-time priorities, could monopolize the processors. A system running only such applications can be scheduled using rate-monotonic scheduling (Section 5.3.1.5), but such scheduling doesn't take into account the requirements of non-periodic "normal" applications.

Windows, beginning with Windows Vista, handles this with an approach called the *multimedia class scheduler service* (MMCSS) in which thread priorities are dynamically adjusted so that they can meet their constraints without monopolizing the processors. Threads needing this service are called *multimedia threads*. They register for the service by indicating at what real-time priority they should run and how much processor time should be reserved for other (normal) activity — by default, 20%. The service is provided by user threads, running at a high real-time priority (27), that monitor the multimedia threads and boost their priority to the desired range for (by default) 80% of the time, but lower their priorities to the low normal range for 20% of the time. Thus, over a 10-millisecond period, their priorities are in the real-time range for 8 milliseconds, but drop to low values for 2 milliseconds.[8]

Unfortunately, this by itself is not quite enough to guarantee that the multimedia threads get 80% of processor time. Recall that Windows uses deferred procedure calls (Section 5.2.2) to cope with such potentially time-consuming activity as handling network traffic. Since this work takes place in the interrupt context, it preempts the execution of threads, even real-time threads. Thus, despite MMCSS, the multimedia threads may suffer because of network activity. This could perhaps be dealt with by doing network-protocol processing by kernel threads rather than DPCs (though see Exercise 17); Windows handles it by having MMCSS direct the network-protocol code (running as DPCs) to "throttle back" and thus reduce the rate at which network packets are handled.

The Windows scheduler is implemented using an elaborate set of states (Figure 5.31) and queues. Associated with each processor is a set of *ready queues*, one per scheduling priority level. These queues contain threads that are to run on the given processor. In addition, each processor has a *deferred ready queue*, containing runnable threads that have not yet been assigned to a particular processor. There are any number of queues of threads waiting for some sort of event to occur.

To see how this works, let's follow the life of a thread. When it's created and first made runnable, its creator (running in kernel mode) puts it in the deferred ready state and enqueues it in the deferred ready queue associated with the current processor. It's also randomly assigned an *ideal processor*, on which it will be scheduled if available. This helps with load balancing. Its creator (or, later, the thread itself) may also give it an *affinity mask* (Section 5.3.2.3) indicating the set of processors on which it may run.

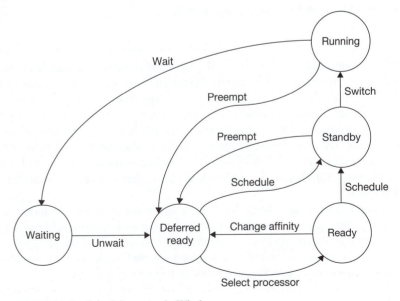

FIGURE 5.31   Scheduler states in Windows.

---

[8] This description is based on http://technet.microsoft.com/en-us/magazine/cc162494.aspx.

Each processor, each time it completes the handling of the pending DPC requests, checks its deferred ready queue. If there are any threads in it, it processes them, assigning them to processors. This works as follows. The DPC handler first checks to see if there are any idle processors that the thread can run on (if it has an affinity mask, then it can run only on the indicated processors). If there are any acceptable idle processors, preference is given first to the thread's ideal processor, then to the last processor on which it ran (to take advantage of the thread's cache footprint (Section 5.3.2.3)). The thread is then put in the *standby* state and given to the selected processor as its next thread. The processor would be currently running its idle thread, which repeatedly checks for a standby thread. Once found, the processor switches to the standby thread.

If there are no acceptable idle processors, then the thread is assigned to its ideal processor. The DPC handler checks to see if the thread has a higher priority than what's running on that processor. If so, it puts the thread in the standby state, and sends the processor an interrupt. When the processor returns from its interrupt handler it will notice the higher-priority thread in standby state and switch to it, after first putting its current thread on its deferred ready list. Otherwise, the DPC handler puts the thread in the ready state and puts it in one of the ideal processor's ready queues according to the thread's priority.

When a thread completes its time quantum (which, as discussed in Section 5.2.2, is dealt with by a DPC), the processor searches its ready queues for a thread of equal or higher priority and switches to it, if it finds one. Otherwise it continues with the current thread.

An executing thread might perform some sort of blocking operation, putting itself in a wait queue. Its processor then searches its ready queues for the next thread to run.

When a thread is made runnable after it has been in the wait state, it's put into the deferred ready queue of the processor on which the thread doing the *unwait* operation was running.

Other operations shown in Figure 5.31 include preempting a thread that's in the state (possible, though unlikely) and changing the affinity mask of a thread that's already been assigned a processor, making the current processor selection unacceptable.

5.4 CONCLUSIONS

Processor management entails multiplexing the available processors to handle all the activities taking place in a computer system — almost everything involves the use of one or more processors. We started our discussion by looking at implementation strategies for threads. From an application's point of view, a thread is the processor; everything having to do with threads is essential to performance. Interrupt processing, though hidden from applications, also has a performance role. By their nature, interrupts displace other activity. Thus we need careful control over when they can occur. In many cases it is important to do only what is absolutely necessary within interrupt handlers, relegating work to other contexts so it can be done with minimal disruption.

Scheduling is a topic unto itself. We briefly examined its theory, in terms of the basic strategies employed in computer systems. In practice, at least for interactive systems, a fair amount of attention is paid to determining which threads are indeed interactive, giving them favored treatment. But a major theme in all the operating systems we have looked at is scalability — the scheduler must perform well, with low overhead, on large, busy systems.

5.5 EXERCISES

1. Suppose you are designing a server that requires many thousands of concurrent threads. Which approach would be the most suitable: the one-level model or the two-level model with multiple kernel threads? Explain.

*2. Implementing POSIX threads on Linux was made difficult because of Linux's use of variable-weight processes. Changes had to be made to the process model to make possible the more efficient NTPL implementation.

    a. One problem was that, since Linux "threads" were actually processes, the only way to wait for the termination of a thread was via the *wait* family of system calls. Explain why this was a problem. (*Hint*: consider how *pthread_join* can be used.)

    b. This problem was overcome in a rather creative but not terribly efficient way. How might you handle this problem if you were implementing POSIX threads?

3. An *upcall* is a mechanism by which kernel code can place a call into user code — it is essentially the reverse of a system call. Explain how it might be implemented. (*Hint*: consider what resources must be available in the user process.)

*4. The following code is an alternative to the implementation of mutexes given in Section 5.1.2. Does it work? Explain why or why not.

```
kmutex_lock(mutex_t *mut) {
  if (mut->locked) {
    enqueue(mut->wait_queue, CurrentThread);
    thread_switch();
  }
  mut->locked = 1;
}
kmutex_unlock(mutex_t *mut) {
  mut->locked = 0;
  if (!queue_empty(mut->wait_queue))
    enqueue(RunQueue, dequeue(mut->wait_queue));
}
```

5. The simple implementation of *thread_switch* in Section 5.1.2 doesn't deal with the case of the run queue's being empty. Assuming that threads are either runnable or waiting on a mutex, what can you say about the system if there are no threads in the run queue?

*6. The final implementation of *blocking_lock* on page 174 requires some changes to *thread_switch*. Show how *thread_switch* must be modified.

*7. Show how to implement semaphores in terms of futexes. Be sure to give the implementations of both the P and V operations.

*8. We have a new architecture for interrupt handling. There are n possible sources of interrupts. A bit vector is used to mask them: if bit i is 1, then interrupt source i is masked. The operating system employs n threads to handle interrupts, one per interrupt source. When interrupt i occurs, thread i handles it and interrupt source i is automatically masked. When the thread completes handling of the interrupt, interrupt source i is unmasked. Thus if interrupt source i attempts to send an interrupt while a previous interrupt from i is being handled, the new interrupt is masked until the handling of the previous one is completed. In other words, each interrupt thread handles one interrupt at a time.

    Threads are scheduled using a simple priority-based scheduler. It maintains a list of runnable threads (the exact data structure is not important for this problem). There's a global variable *CurrentThread* that refers to the currently running thread.

a. When an interrupt occurs, on which stack should the registers of the interrupted thread be saved? Explain. (*Hint:* there are two possibilities: the stack of the interrupted thread and the stack of the interrupt-handling thread.)

b. After the registers are saved, what further actions are necessary so that the interrupt-handling thread and the interrupted thread can be handled by the scheduler? (*Hint:* consider the scheduler's data structures.)

c. Recall that Windows employs DPCs (deferred procedure calls) so that interrupt handlers may have work done when there is no other interrupt handling to be done. How could this be done in the new architecture? (*Hint:* it's easily handled.)

d. If there are multiple threads at the same priority, we'd like their execution to be time-sliced — each runs for a certain period of time, then yields to the next. In Windows, this is done by the clock interrupt handler's requesting a DPC, which forces the current thread to yield the processor. Explain how such time-slicing can be done on the new architecture.

9. Consider the implementation of DPCs given in Section 5.2.2. The intent of the DPC mechanism is to deal with chores generated by interrupt handlers at a lower priority level and thus not interfere with higher-priority interrupts. This mechanism works well; however, if there are a lot of these chores, it could prevent equally important threads from running.

    a. Describe the existing mechanism that ensures that DPC requests are handled in preference to threads. (*Hint:* this is easy.)

    b. Describe (i.e., invent) a mechanism to solve this problem. That is, how can we limit the number of DPC requests that are processed in preference to normal thread execution such that the remaining DPC requests are processed on an equal basis with normal threads? (*Hint:* this is slightly less easy.)

10. Explain why Windows deferred procedure calls (DPCs) may not access user memory, but asynchronous procedure calls (APCs) may.

*11. An operating system has a simple round-robin scheduler used in conjunction with time slicing: when a thread's time slice is over, it goes to the end of the run queue and the next thread runs. The run queue is implemented as a singly linked list of threads, with pointers to the first and last threads in the queue. Assume for parts a and b that we have a uniprocessor system.

    a. The system has a mix of long-running compute threads that rarely block and interactive threads that spend most of their time blocked, waiting for keyboard input, then have very brief bursts of using the processor. Assuming we want the system to have good interactive response, explain what is wrong with the scheduler.

    b. How might the scheduler be improved to provide good interactive response? (*Hint:* a simple improvement is sufficient.)

    c. We add three more processors to our system and add the appropriate synchronization (spin locks) to our scheduler data structures. Describe the performance problems that will arise.

    d. Describe what might be done to alleviate these performance problems, yet still have reasonable parallelism.

*12. Explain why the APC interrupt priority level must be lower than that of a DPC.

*13. Figure 5.24 shows how threads' meters are updated after each clock tick under stride scheduling. *FictitiousMeter* is used to initialize the meters of new threads and of threads rejoining the run queue after having been sleeping. However, when a thread blocks, its meter's value probably is not the same as that of *FictitiousMeter*.

a. Explain why this is so.

b. Why might it be reasonable to keep track of this difference between the thread's meter value and that of *FictitiousMeter* and to add this difference to the current value of *FictitiousMeter* when the thread rejoins the run queue?

*14. In hierarchical stride scheduling, whenever a new thread joins a group, the total number of tickets held by the group increases and thus so does that group's collective share of processor time. A better approach might be to give each group a fixed number of tickets to be evenly distributed among all its members. However, it might be a bit time-consuming to readjust each member thread's bribe whenever a new thread joins the group. Describe how we might modify hierarchical stride scheduling so that each group's share of processor time remains constant despite the addition or deletion of group members, and that such addition and deletion is done in constant time (not counting the time to update the balanced tree).

15. Suppose, in the scheduling scenario in Figure 5.25, each cyclic chore is handled by a thread — one thread per cyclic chore. Show how the scheduling constraints can be satisfied on either Unix or Windows. Note that there are actually two constraints: each chore must finish exactly once per cycle and each chore must start exactly once per cycle. The first constraint is handled by the scheduler, the second by the thread itself (perhaps by waiting on a timer).

16. Why does the Linux O(1) scheduler maintain two queues per processor — the active queue and the expired queue? (*Hint*: consider load balancing and cache footprints.)

*17. Windows performs network-protocol processing in the interrupt context using DPCs. As explained in Section 5.3.3.2, this can cause interference with multimedia applications that, despite running at real-time priorities, are preempted by network-protocol processing. An alternative approach might be to have special kernel threads handle the network-protocol processing and thus do it under the control of the scheduler, which could then give favored treatment to multimedia applications. Explain what the disadvantage of this approach would be. (*Hint*: consider things from the point of view of network performance, even without multimedia applications.)

18. Explain why the Windows scheduler has the *standby* state, rather than simply having a processor run the highest priority thread in its *ready* queues.

5.6 REFERENCES

Anderson, T. E., B. N. Bershad, E. Lazowska, H. M. Levy (1992). Scheduler Activations: Effective Kernel Support for the User-Level Management of Parallelism. *ACM Transactions on Computer Systems* **10**(1): 53–79.

Aral, Z., J. Bloom, T.W. Doeppner, I. Gertner, A. Langerman, G. Schaffer (1989). Variable-Weight Processes with Flexible Shared Resources. *Proceedings of the Winter 1989 USENIX Technical Conference*.

Black, D. L. (1990a). *Scheduling Support for Concurrency and Parallelism in the Mach Operating System.* IEEE Computer **23**(5): 35–43.

Black, D. L. (1990b). *Scheduling and Resource Management Techniques for Multiprocessors.* School of Computer Science, Carnegie Mellon University CMU Thesis CMU-CS-90-152.

Doeppner, T. W. (1987). *Threads: A System for the Support of Concurrent Programming*, Brown University, at http://www.cs.brown.edu/~twd/Threads Paper.pdf

Garey, M. R. and D. S. Johnson (1975). Complexity Results for Multiprocessor Scheduling Under Resource Constraints. *SIAM Journal of Computing* **4**(4): 392–411.

Kleiman, S. R. and J. Eykholt (1995). Interrupts as Threads. *ACM SIGOPS Operating Systems Review* **29**(2): 21–26.

Lehoczky, J., L. Sha, Y. Ding (1989). The Rate Monotonic Scheduling Algorithm: Exact Characterization and Average Case Behavior. *Proceedings of the Real-Time Systems Symposium*, 166–171.

Von Behren, R., Jeremy Condit, Feng Zhou, George C. Necula, and Eric Brewer (2003). Capriccio: Scalable Threads for Internet Services. *Nineteenth Symposium on Operating Systems Principles*. Lake George, NY, ACM.

Waldspurger, C. A. and W. E. Weihl (1994). Lottery Scheduling: Flexible Proportional-Share Resource Management. *Proceedings of the First Symposium on Operating Systems Design and Implementation*. Monterey, USENIX.

Waldspurger, C. A. and W. E. Weihl (1995). Stride Scheduling: Deterministic Proportional-Share Resource Management. Massachusetts Institute of Technology Technical Memorandum LCS/TM-528.

File Systems

The purpose of a file system is to provide easy-to-use permanent storage with modest functionality. Unlike database systems with sophisticated search and access capabilities, file systems typically present files as simple, unstructured collections of bytes and provide tree-structured naming. We use files to hold the programs we run, the source code of programs we're developing, documents we're reading or composing, email messages we've sent and received, data we've collected from an experiment, and the like.

There are few aspects of operating systems that aren't affected by file systems. The performance of the file system is a major factor in the performance of the entire system — most operations performed on computers involve files. How well a computer survives crashes is completely dependent on its file system's ability to handle them. Much of computer security is the security of files.

Thus there are four top criteria for file systems:

- *Easy access*: files should be easy to use. This means that the abstraction of a file presented by the file system should be simple, understandable, and useful.

- *High performance*: access to files should be quick and economical. The file-system implementation should let us exploit the speed of the underlying hardware to its fullest, yet have no undue wastage of space.

- *Permanence*: file systems should be dependable. Data stored in them should be accessible as long as they are needed. System crashes and hardware problems should not cause data loss.

- *Security*: data stored in file systems should be subject to strict access controls. (We cover security in Chapter 8.)

We start by looking at a rather ancient Unix file system, S5FS, which, in a simple, elegant fashion, provides all the basic functionality needed by application programs and the virtual-memory system to store and retrieve data. Files can be accessed with equal ease both sequentially and randomly.

The reasons why S5FS is not the last word in file systems are what make file systems interesting. Disks do not provide uniform access times the way primary storage does — much care is required to get top performance from them. After a crash, whatever damage was done to on-disk data structures must be repaired for the system to return to normal operation. S5FS's elegance and simplicity don't take any of this into account, but it gives us a starting point for discussing more recent file systems that do.

We tackle performance first, starting with techniques used in a somewhat later Unix file system known, not too surprisingly, as the "Fast File System" (FFS). We look at later improvements to this system as well as techniques used in other systems such as Microsoft's NTFS. Finally, we cover an interesting approach known as log-structured file systems that first appeared in a research system but have been adapted for more recent commercial systems from Network Appliance (WAFL) and Sun (ZFS).

We then cover approaches for making file systems resilient to crashes. These range from insuring that what's on disk is always consistent, just in case there's a crash, to providing enough extra information on disk to make possible post-crash recovery.

Among S5FS's shortcomings were its directories, which didn't actually provide all the functionality needed by applications — component names were limited to eight characters. Removing this limitation exacerbated performance problems; we examine these problems and see how other systems have dealt with them using hashing and balanced-tree techniques.

Next we take on the use of multiple disk drives, not only to provide additional space, but also to improve performance and failure tolerance. In particular, we look at an approach known as RAID: redundant array of inexpensive disks.

We then look at a relatively new alternative to disk technology — flash memory. Its characteristics have ramifications for the file systems that use it.

We finish the chapter by looking at additional details of the file systems we've used as examples: FFS, NTFS, WAFL, and ZFS.

6.1 THE BASICS OF FILE SYSTEMS

6.1.1 UNIX'S S5FS

We start with a file system that became obsolete well over twenty years ago — the file system of sixth-edition and some later Unix systems known as the System 5 File System (S5FS). Because of its simplicity and elegance, it is suitable for implementation in student operating-system projects. As a file system for real operating systems, however, it has a number of deficiencies and does poorly on all but the first of the criteria listed above. We use it here as a starting point to discuss how modern file-systems handle these concerns.

The Unix file abstraction is simple — a revolutionary feature in Unix's early days. Files are arrays of bytes. User applications need not know how files are physically represented on disks. Other file systems of the time forced the user to be aware of the *record size* — the amount of data transferred to or from the application in each file request — as well as the *block size* — the unit by which data is transferred to or from the disk. Unix just had bytes. Applications read or wrote as many bytes as necessary. It was up to the file system to implement such requests efficiently using the available disk storage. Rather than making programs allocate space for files before using them, Unix files grow implicitly: writing beyond the current end of a file makes it bigger. Files are named by their paths in a single, system-wide directory hierarchy.

The architecture of the underlying storage medium is, of course, pretty important in file-system design. We assume here that it's a disk organized as a collection of sectors, each of the same size — 512 bytes is typical. As detailed in Section 6.1.2 below, disks are accessed by moving disk heads to the appropriate cylinder and then waiting for the disk to rotate until the desired disk sector is under one of the heads. Thus the time required to access a sector depends on the distance of the current position of the disk heads from the desired sector. One of the things that make S5FS so simple is that it does not take this distance into account when allocating space for files. It considers a disk to be a sequence of sectors each of which can be accessed in the same amount of time as all the others; the only optimization done is to minimize the number of disk accesses. No attempt is made to minimize the time spent waiting for disk heads to be properly positioned (the *seek time*) or the time waiting for the desired sector to be under the disk head (the *rotational latency*).

This simplifies things a lot. All sectors are equal; thus we can think of a disk as a large array. Accessing this array is a bit expensive compared to accessing primary storage, but the design of on-disk data structures needn't differ substantially from the data structures in primary storage. (This, of course, is a simplification used in S5FS; it doesn't apply to all file systems!)

Figure 6.1 shows the basic format of a file system on disk.[1] The first disk block contains a *boot block*; this has nothing to do with the file system, but contains the first-level boot program that reads the operating system's binary image into primary memory from the file system. The next block, the *superblock*, describes the layout of the rest of the file system and contains the heads of the free lists. Following this are two large areas. The first is the *i-list*, an array of index nodes (*inodes*) each of which, if in use, represents a file. Second is the *data region*, which contains the disk blocks holding or referring to file contents.

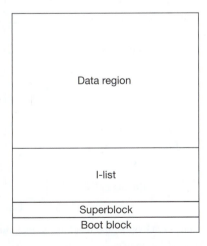

FIGURE 6.1   S5FS layout.

---

[1] Note that one physical disk is often partitioned to hold multiple file-system instances. Thus what is shown in Figure 6.1 is a single file-system instance within a region of a partitioned disk.

Device
Inode number
Mode
Link count
Owner, Group
Size
Diskmap

FIGURE 6.2 S5FS inode.

Each file is described by an inode; thus a file is referred to internally by its inode, which is done via the inode's index in the i-list. As we saw in Chapter 1, directories are otherwise normal files containing pairs of directory-component names and inode numbers. Thus following a path in the directory hierarchy involves reading the contents of a directory file (contained in sectors taken from the data region) to look up the next component of the path. Associated with that component in the file is an inode number that is used to identify the inode of the file containing the next directory in the path.

The layout of an inode is shown in Figure 6.2. What's important to us at the moment is the disk map (Figure 6.3), which refers to the disk blocks containing the file's data. The disk map maps logical blocks numbered relative to the beginning of a file into physical blocks numbered relative to the beginning of the file system. Each block is 1024 (1 K) bytes long. (It was 512 bytes long in the original Unix file system.) The data structure allows fast access when a file is accessed sequentially and, with the help of caching, reasonably fast access when the file is used for paging and other "random" access.

The disk map contains 13 pointers to disk blocks. The first ten of these pointers point to the first 10 blocks of the file, so that the first 10 KB of a file are accessed directly. If the file is larger than 10 KB, then pointer number 10 points to a disk block called an *indirect block*. This block contains up to 256 (4-byte) pointers to *data blocks* (i.e., 256 KB of data). If the file is bigger than this (256 KB + 10 KB = 266 KB), then pointer number 11 points to a *double indirect block* containing 256 pointers to indirect blocks, each of which contains 256 pointers to data blocks (64 MB of data). If the file is bigger than this (64 MB + 256 KB + 10 KB), then pointer number 12 points to a *triple indirect block* containing up to 256 pointers to double indirect blocks, each of which contains up to 256 pointers pointing to single indirect blocks, each of which contains

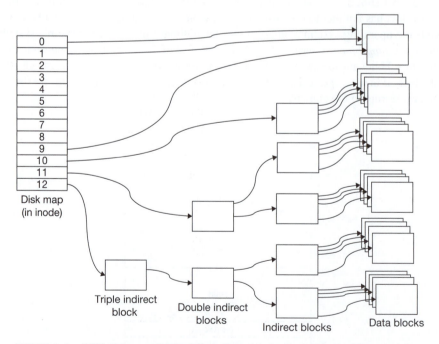

FIGURE 6.3 S5FS disk map. Each of the indirect blocks (including double and triple indirect blocks) contains up to 256 pointers.

up to 256 pointers pointing to data blocks (potentially 16 GB, although the real limit is 2 GB, since the file size, a signed number of bytes, must fit in a 32-bit word).

Sequential access to a file with this scheme is fairly efficient in terms of the number of disk accesses. When a file is opened, its inode is fetched from disk and remains in primary storage until after the file is closed. Thus the addresses of the first ten blocks of each file are available (in the inode's disk map) without further disk I/O.

Accessing blocks of a file beyond the first ten requires additional disk accesses to fetch their addresses, but only one disk access per 256 data blocks is required for the portion of the file mapped by indirect blocks. Beyond that, additional accesses are required for double and triple indirect blocks, but only one access of double indirect blocks per 2^{16} data blocks is required and only one access of a triple indirect block per 2^{24} data blocks is required.

For random access, however, the overhead can be a lot greater. Accessing a block might require fetching three blocks (triple, double, and single indirect) to obtain its address. While this is possible with truly random access, more typically a program fetches data blocks sequentially starting at some specific file location. Thus additional fetches are required to obtain the indirect blocks necessary to get started, but, since these blocks are cached, the addresses of subsequent blocks are available without additional disk I/O.

One interesting attribute of the disk-map data structure is that it allows the efficient representation of sparse files, i.e., files whose content is mainly zeros. Consider, for example, creating an empty file and then writing one byte at location 2,000,000,000. Only four disk blocks are allocated to represent this file: a triple indirect block, a double indirect block, a single indirect block, and a data block. All pointers in the disk map, except the last one, are zero. Furthermore, all bytes up to the last one read as zero. This is because a zero pointer is treated as if it points to a block containing all zeros: a zero pointer to an indirect block is treated as if it pointed to an indirect block filled with zero pointers, each of which is treated as if it pointed to a data block filled with zeros. However, one must be careful about copying such a file, since doing so naively creates a file for which disk blocks are allocated for all the zeros!

The issues involved in organizing free storage on disk are similar to those in organizing the blocks of individual files: we want to minimize the number of disk accesses required to manage free storage. (We'll see soon that there are other concerns as well, but minimizing disk accesses was the primary one in S5FS.) Ideally, whenever a free disk block is required for a file, its address should be available without a disk access. Similarly, freeing a block from a file should not require disk I/O. We can't achieve these ideals, of course, but we can do a lot better than a naive implementation in which a disk access is required for each block allocation and liberation.

Free disk blocks are represented as a linked list (see Figure 6.4); the superblock, which is kept in primary storage while a file system is being used, contains the addresses of up to 100 free disk blocks. The last of these disk blocks contains 100 pointers to additional free disk blocks. The last of these pointers points to another block containing up to *n* free disk blocks, etc., until all free disk blocks are represented.

Thus most requests for a free block can be satisfied by merely getting an address from the superblock. When the last block reference in the superblock is consumed, however, a disk read must be done to fetch the addresses of up to 100 additional free disk blocks. When a block from a file is freed, the disk block's address is simply added to the list of free blocks in the superblock. If this list is full, then its contents are written out to disk in the block being freed and are replaced with the address of this block.

Inodes are handled differently. Rather than keep track of free inodes in a linked list, they're simply marked free or not free on disk, with no further on-disk organization (see Figure 6.5). The superblock, however, contains a cache of the indices of free inodes (recall that inodes are organized as an array on disk — the i-list). Thus when the system creates a file and therefore must allocate an inode, the index of a free inode is taken from the cache and the on-disk copy of

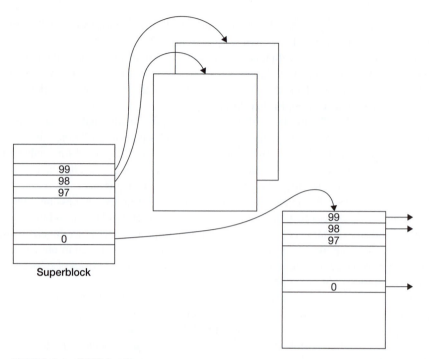

FIGURE 6.4 S5FS free list.

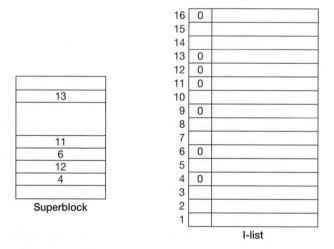

FIGURE 6.5 S5FS free inode list.

the inode is marked as allocated. If the cache is empty, then the i-list is scanned for sufficient free inodes to refill it. To aid this scan, the cache contains the index of the first free inode in the i-list. Freeing an inode involves simply marking the on-disk inode as free and adding its index to the cache, if there's room.

Why are inodes handled this way? In particular, why use a technique that requires a disk write every time an inode is allocated or freed? There are two reasons. First, inodes are allocated and freed much less often than data blocks, so there's less need for a relatively complex technique

Component name	Inode number

Directory entry

.	1
..	1
unix	117
etc	4
home	18
pro	36
dev	93

FIGURE 6.6   S5FS directory.

to minimize I/O. The second reason, as discussed further in Section 6.2 below, has to do with crash tolerance. If the system crashes, information that's been cached in primary storage but is not yet on disk is lost. Though this is definitely a problem for data blocks and the various indirect blocks, it has especially severe consequences for inodes. Thus leaving changes to inode allocation information uncached and caching only a list of some free ones ensures that nothing about the allocated/unallocated state of inodes is lost in a crash.

S5FS directories are implemented exactly as discussed in Section 1.3.5.5. They are otherwise ordinary files whose inodes are marked as being directories. Their contents are represented just like those of other files, though they have a special interpretation: a sequence of component-name/inode-number pairs (see Figure 6.6). The component-name is in a fixed-width field 14 characters long. Thus searching a directory is a simple matter of reading the file block by block, scanning the component-name field for a match and then returning the associated inode number. That the component-name field is fixed-width improves the efficiency of the search, though it definitely limits the possible file names.

6.1.2 DISK ARCHITECTURE

To understand file-system performance, let's first take a careful look at how disk drives work. The typical disk drive (see Figure 6.7) consists of a number of platters, each with one or two recording surfaces (on top and bottom). Each surface is divided into a number of concentric tracks; each track is divided into a number of sectors. All the sectors are the same size. Early disk drives, keeping things simple, had the same number of sectors in each track. This was, of course, a waste of space in outer tracks. Modern disk drives put more sectors in outer tracks than inner ones, thus keeping the bit density roughly constant. The data stored on disks is read and written using a set of read/write heads, one head per surface. The heads are connected to the ends of arms that move in tandem across the surfaces. Only one head is active at a time — the desired one must be selected explicitly. The set of tracks selected by the disk heads at any one moment is called a cylinder.

The data in a particular disk sector can be read or written only when the sector moves under one of the read/write heads. Thus the steps to perform a read or write are:

1. Position the read/write heads over the correct cylinder. The time required for this positioning is known as the *seek time*. The time required to select the head that's positioned over the desired track is assumed to be zero.

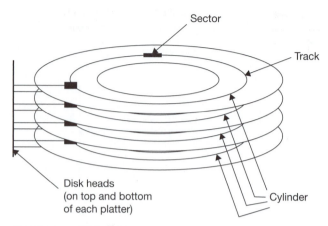

FIGURE 6.7 Disk architecture.

2. Rotate the disk platter until the desired sector is underneath the read/write head. The time required for this is known as the *rotational latency*.

3. Rotate the disk platter further so the head can read or write the entire sector, transferring data between it and the computer's memory. The time required for this is known as the *transfer time*.

The seek time is usually the dominant factor. Back in the days when S5FS was popular and FFS was being developed (the early 1980s), average seek times (i.e., the time required to move from one randomly selected cylinder to another) were typically in the neighborhood of 30 milliseconds. At the time of this writing, average seek times are from 2 to 10 milliseconds. It takes less time to move the disk heads a shorter distance than a longer distance, but the relationship is not linear: we must take into account the time required for acceleration and deceleration of the disk heads and other factors as well. A typical disk drive might have 25,000 cylinders. The time to move the heads one cylinder might be .2 milliseconds, yet the average seek time might still be 4 milliseconds. For our purposes, however, it suffices to say that closer means faster.

Rotational latency times depend on the speed at which disks spin. In the early 1980s this was pretty much always 3600 RPM. Today's spin rates range from 5200 to 15,000 RPM. Assuming that the average rotational latency is the time required for half a revolution, rotational latency has gone from 8.3 milliseconds in the early 1980s to as little as 2 milliseconds today.

The transfer time depends both on rotational latency and on the number of sectors per track: the more sectors on a track, the smaller the fraction of a full revolution the platter must spin to pass one complete sector underneath a head. Since modern disks have more sectors in outer tracks than in inner tracks, the transfer time depends upon which track the sector is in. A typical drive might have 500 sectors in the inner tracks and 1000 in the outer tracks, with a sector size of 512 bytes. Thus at 10,000 RPM, the transfer rate can be as high as almost 85 MB/second, though this rate can be maintained only for as much data as there is in a track. Transferring data that is spread out on multiple tracks requires additional positioning time.

Many disk controllers automatically cache the contents of the current track: as soon as a disk head is selected after a seek to a new cylinder, a buffer in the controller begins to fill with the contents of the sectors passing under the head. Thus after one complete revolution, the entire contents of the track are in the buffers and each sector can be read without further delay.

This form of caching is innocuous in the sense that it can only help performance and has no effect on the semantics of disk operations. Another form of caching — *write-behind caching* — is used by many modern disk controllers (particularly SATA) to cache disk writes, allowing the writer to proceed without having to wait for the data to be written to the actual disk. This can speed things up a fair amount, but can be a problem if, for example, there is a power failure and the data does not actually get to disk. Worse yet, data may be written to disk in a different order from what the writer intended (we discuss the consequences of this in Section 6.2.1). Some file systems (such as ZFS (Section 6.6.6)) cope with this correctly, others do not.

Keep in mind that typical processor speeds in the early 1980s were over a thousand times lower than they are today. Even though disk technology has improved since then, processor technology has improved even more and thus the discrepancy between processor speed and disk speed has increased dramatically.

We now see where we must work so as to improve file access times. The biggest issue is seek time: we need to minimize how often and how far the disk heads move while satisfying disk requests. A lesser but still important issue is rotational latency: we need to position file data on disk so as to minimize it.

6.1.2.1 The Rhinopias Disk Drive

We now specify a disk drive to use as a running example so that we can be specific in examining file-system performance. We want our drive to be representative of drives available today, though it will undoubtedly be obsolete soon. We also need to give it a name: we'll call it the Rhinopias drive. Our drive has the following characteristics:[2]

Rotation speed	10,000 RPM
Number of surfaces	8
Sector size	512 bytes
Sectors/track	500–1000; 750 average
Tracks/surface	100,000
Storage capacity	307.2 billion bytes
Average seek time	4 milliseconds
One-track seek time	.2 milliseconds
Maximum seek time	10 milliseconds

From this information we compute its maximum transfer rate, which occurs when we transfer consecutive sectors from one track, as 85.33 million bytes/sec. Of course, this occurs only on outer tracks. A better figure might be the maximum transfer rate on the average track of 750 sectors: 64 million bytes/sec.

What is the maximum transfer rate when we're transferring data that occupies more than one track? Let's first consider data that resides in a single cylinder. Though we can switch read/write heads quickly to go from one track to another in a cylinder, this requires some time, enough that by the time the drive switches from the read/write head for surface 1 to the head for surface 2, the disk has rotated some distance into the next sector. Thus if we want to access that next sector, we have to wait for the disk to spin almost one complete revolution.

What current disk drives (and thus our Rhinopias drive) do to avoid this problem is a trick called *head skewing*. Sector 1 on track 2 is not in the same relative position on the track as sector 1 of track 1; instead, it's offset by one sector. Thus, after accessing sectors 1 through 750 on one 750-sector track, by the time the drive switches to the disk head of the next track, the disk has rotated so that sector number 1 is just about to pass under the head. Thus to compute the time required to transfer all the data in one cylinder, we must add to the transfer time for all but the last

---

[2] We use the prefixes kilo-, mega-, and giga- to refer to powers of two: 2^{10}, 2^{20}, and 2^{30}. The terms thousand, million, and billion refer to powers of ten: 10^3, 10^6, and 10^9.

track the time required for the disk to rotate by one sector. For the average track, this is 1/750 of a disk rotation time (8 microseconds), which reduces the transfer rate to about 63.9 megabytes/sec from the 64 megabytes/sec of single-track transfers.

In addition, if our data resides in multiple cylinders, we need to factor into the computation the time required to move from one cylinder to the next. With average (750-sector) tracks, each cylinder contains 6000 sectors, or 3,072,000 bytes. After transferring that many bytes at 63.9 million bytes/sec, we must wait .2 milliseconds to move the read/write heads to the next cylinder. During that time the disk rotates almost 25 sectors. To avoid waiting for the disk to make an almost complete rotation to bring sector 1 under the read/write head, our drive uses *cylinder skewing*, which is similar to head skewing: sector 1 of the next cylinder is offset by 25 sectors. Thus by the time the heads reach the next cylinder, sector 1 is just about to rotate beneath them. So, to compute the average maximum transfer rate for data occupying more than one cylinder, we simply factor in the one-track seek time, giving us a rate of 63.7 million bytes/sec. (The rate would be 56.8 million bytes/sec if cylinder skewing were not used.)

6.1.3 PROBLEMS WITH S5FS

So what's wrong with S5FS? Lots, it turns out. Its file-allocation strategy results in slow file access. Its small block size contributes to slow file access. The segregation of inodes from other file-system information contributes even more to slow file access. Its limitations on directory-component names are inconvenient, and its lack of resilience in the face of crashes is a real killer.

Its performance problems are due to too many long seeks combined with too short data transfers. In particular, it does nothing whatsoever to minimize seek time. Consider its segregation of inodes from other file data. When accessing a file, first the inode is fetched, and then there is a long seek to the data region to fetch the file's data and indirect blocks. These blocks are, in general, not organized for fast sequential access. Instead, they're allocated when needed from the free list, which, though it's ordered in some fashion when the file system is created, is pretty well randomized after the file system has been used for a while. Thus successive data blocks of a file are in random locations within the data region. On average, the read/write heads must travel halfway across the data region to go from one file block to the next — and then, after the heads travel such a long distance, they transfer only 512 bytes of data.

To see the effect of all this, let's implement S5FS on the Rhinopias drive and analyze how well it performs. In particular, let's compute how fast a file can be read from disk to primary storage. How long does it take to do each of the seeks required to access each file block? If the data region occupied the entire disk, we could use the 4-millisecond average seek time. But since the data region is smaller than this, that would be a bit pessimistic. So let's be generous and say that the average seek between blocks takes 2 milliseconds. Once the heads are positioned over the desired cylinder, we have to wait the average rotational latency of 3 milliseconds. The time required to transfer one 512-byte sector is negligible in comparison, so every 5 milliseconds 512 bytes can be transferred. This gives us an average maximum transfer rate of 102.4 thousand bytes/sec. This is a remarkable 0.16% of Rhinopias's maximum speed! And note that the speed would have been considerably lower on the disk drives used in S5FS's heyday.

This performance is so terrible that one really wonders why this file system was used at all. It turns out that, though S5FS is amazingly slow by today's standards, the processors on the systems it was used on were also amazingly slow: instruction execution was measured not in billions per second, as is common today, but in tens or hundreds of thousands per second. Thus the data-transfer rate of S5FS was not badly out of line with application requirements. Furthermore, the typical file size was much smaller than it is today: the average Unix file contained just a few thousand bytes. So, though definitely slow, S5FS wasn't out of line in early Unix systems and was certainly usable.

6.1.4 IMPROVING PERFORMANCE

It should be clear from the above discussion that to improve file-system performance we need both to minimize the setup delays of seek time and rotational latency and to maximize the amount of useful data transferred after these delays. In this section we discuss a few techniques for making such improvements, starting with the fairly straightforward and continuing to the quite remarkable. We mention some of the file systems that employ each of these techniques, and discuss these file systems in more detail in Section 6.5.

One approach to improving file-system performance is to take advantage of buffering. We've already mentioned and will continue to discuss the buffering of file-system data by the operating system. But what about buffering implemented in the disk hardware? Rhinopias's user manual (if it had one) would show that it, like other disk drives, has a *pre-fetch buffer* that stores the contents of the current track in a buffer managed by the disk controller. Of course, the buffer doesn't fill until the disk makes a complete rotation while the read/write heads are properly positioned and the appropriate head selected. We can certainly take advantage of this to improve latency for reads, but it provides no improvement for writes.

6.1.4.1 Larger Blocks and Improved Layouts

In a first attempt to improve file-system performance, we might simply try to group file-system data so as to reduce seek time and to use a larger block size so as to maximize the useful data transferred. These were the major innovations of the FFS (sometimes called UFS) system that supplanted S5FS on Unix systems starting in the early to mid-1980s (McKusick, Joy, et al. 1984). The Ext2 file system of Linux is similar to FFS, and we discuss the two together.

Block Size   Increasing the file-system block size seems easy. Simply switching from a 512-byte block to an 8-kilobyte block sounds straightforward, but doing so causes problems: the average space wasted per file due to internal fragmentation (Section 3.3.1) is half a block. Thus if there are 20,000 files, the wasted disk space goes from 5.12 million bytes to 80 million bytes — a fair amount of space, particularly if your disk holds only 60 million bytes (see Figure 6.8).

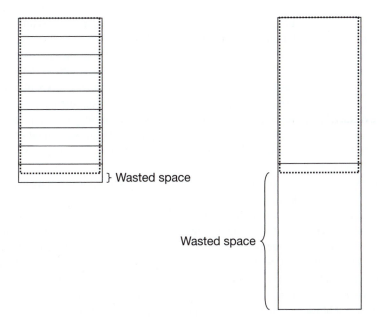

FIGURE 6.8   Wasted space with 512-byte blocks (left) and 8-kilobyte blocks (right).

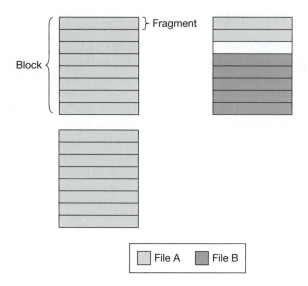

FIGURE 6.9 File A has two full blocks plus a partial block containing two fragments, for a total of 18 fragments. File B has five fragments in a partial block.

FFS used a rather complicated strategy to avoid this problem: files were allocated in blocks except for what would otherwise be the last block, for which a partial block is used. To obtain such partial blocks, blocks are divided into pieces somewhat confusingly called *fragments*, each typically two sectors (1024 bytes) in length. Thus if a file's length is 17.5 fragments (17,920 bytes) and the block size is 8 fragments, two blocks would be allocated to hold its first 16,384 bytes and a partial block consisting of two contiguous fragments would be allocated to hold its last 1536 bytes (see Figure 6.9). Thus the wastage due to external fragmentation would be 512 bytes, rather than the 6656 bytes it would have been if only whole blocks were used. Of course, in S5FS the wastage would have been zero, though remember that the number of seeks required to fetch the blocks of the file is three, whether the file is allocated wholly in blocks or with whole blocks followed by a partial block. S5FS would require 35 seeks to fetch the contents of this file.

The file-system block size is equal to some small power-of-two multiple of the fragment size — in the first version of FFS it could be 2, 4, or 8 fragments, in later versions up to 64 fragments. This block size is a parameter and is fixed for each on-disk instance of the file system.

This block-size strategy doesn't sound complicated, but that's just because we're not finished yet. FFS must keep track not only of free whole blocks but also of each of the various sizes of partial blocks. We discuss how it does this soon, when we talk about optimizing block placement. But for the time being let's assume FFS can handle the partial blocks and examine their use.

Suppose our 17.5-fragment file grows by 513 bytes. Another fragment is required to hold it, since its length is now 18 fragments plus one byte. FFS can't simply allocate another fragment from any place in the file system, because that would yield a file with two partial blocks: a two-fragment one and a one-fragment one.

Instead, we'd like the last portion of the file to reside in a single three-fragment partial block — a block consisting of three contiguous fragments — that can be fetched after just one seek. This is easily done if the fragment following our two-fragment partial block is free: FFS simply allocates it and extends the two-fragment block to be a three-fragment block (Figure 6.10). But if this next fragment is not free, then FFS must find three free contiguous fragments, copy the original two-fragment block into its first two fragments, replace the original partial block in the file's disk map with this new one, and return the original block to free storage. Of course if, for example, our 17.5-fragment file grows by seven fragments, FFS expands its partial block into an (8-fragment) whole block and gives it a new one-fragment partial block (Figure 6.11). Now things are getting complicated — and expensive.

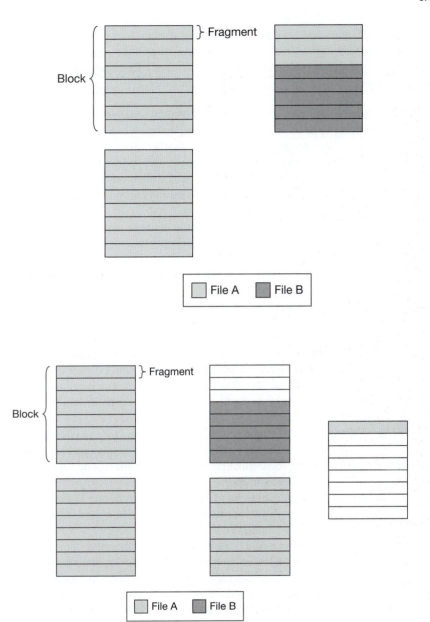

FIGURE 6.10 File A grows by one fragment into an adjacent free fragment.

FIGURE 6.11 File A grows by six more fragments. Its partial block is copied into a full block and its last fragment is in a new partial block.

To reduce the expense, FFS tries to arrange things so there are always free fragments for partial blocks to expand into. One way for FFS to do this, in allocating a partial block for a file, is actually to give the file a whole block starting on a block boundary, and then free the unneeded fragments. Assuming FFS always does this, there is always room to extend partial blocks. Of course, this also defeats the entire purpose of using partial blocks: it's effectively reserving each partial block's expansion fragments, and this isn't a whole lot different from simply allocating whole blocks.

All this begins to make sense, however, if FFS uses a two-policy allocation strategy. As long as plenty of whole blocks are available, when a partial block is needed, FFS allocates a whole block and then frees the unneeded fragments. This is known as the *optimization-for-time policy*. However, once an FFS instance starts running low on whole blocks but instead has lots of short runs of free fragments, it switches to allocating partial blocks containing just the number of fragments needed and pays the price of copying when files grow. This is known as the *optimization-for-space policy*. A parameter in each on-disk FFS instance specifies at what point the allocation strategy switches from one policy to the other.

Reducing Seek Time   Reducing seek time is conceptually straightforward — simply keep the data items that are likely to be accessed in close time proximity close to one another on the disk. Thus the blocks of each file should be close to one another. Since files' inodes are accessed in conjunction with their data blocks, this means keeping data blocks close to the corresponding inodes. Since the inodes of a directory are often examined all at once (for example, when listing the attributes of all the files in a directory), this also means keeping the inodes of one directory close to one another.

One way to do this is to divide the disk into a number of regions, each comprised of relatively few adjacent cylinders. Items that are to be kept close together are placed in the same region. Of course, we've got to be careful or we'll end up attempting to put everything in the same region. Thus, in addition to identifying items that are to be stored in close to one another, we need to identify items that are to be spread out.

FFS and Ext2 both use this region approach; in the former the regions are called *cylinder groups* (see Figure 6.12), in the latter *block groups*. Each group contains space set aside for inodes as well as space for data and indirect blocks. In general, inodes are stored in the same group as the inode of the directory containing them. Data blocks are stored in the same group as their inode. To spread things out, inodes of subdirectories are put in different groups from their parents. Only those direct blocks are stored in the inode's group. The remaining portion of files requiring indirect blocks is divided into pieces (two megabytes each in some versions of FFS), each of which is stored in a separate group.

The result of all this is that the inodes of files within a directory can be examined quickly, requiring no worse than short seeks, except when a subdirectory is encountered. Then a long seek is required to reach its inode. Accessing the blocks of files requires long seeks only every two megabytes: otherwise the seeks are short.

An important part of this procedure for placing pieces of files into cylinder groups is identifying cylinder groups with plenty of free space. The intent is to spread out the allocations so that, for example, the cylinder group assigned to an inode has enough space to hold the first two megabytes of the file, as well as inodes and initial portions of other files in the directory. In FFS this is accomplished by using quadratic hashing, which both quickly finds cylinder groups with sufficient free space and spreads out the allocations so that the cylinder groups are used uniformly. The approach works well as long as roughly only 90% of disk space is in use. So, FFS keeps its last 10% of disk space as a reserve, making it available only to privileged users.

Suppose we stop here, having improved on S5FS by increasing the block size and improving locality. How well have we done? To put things in the most favorable light, let's look at the average

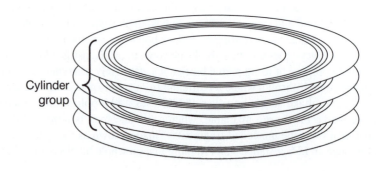

FIGURE 6.12 Four adjacent cylinders forming a cylinder group in FFS.

Cylinder group

maximum transfer speed for a single file, one that fits entirely within a cylinder group. Let's further assume that our Rhinopias disk is configured with cylinder groups of 20 cylinders each, or roughly 60 megabytes for the average cylinder group. We'll have to make an educated guess on the average seek time within a cylinder group: since the one-track seek time is .2 milliseconds and the time required to seek 500 cylinders (halfway across the disk) is only 20 times greater, the time required to seek 10 cylinders is probably fairly close to the one-track seek time — let's say .3 milliseconds.

Once the disk head is positioned over the correct cylinder, we have to wait on average half a rotation for the desired block to come under the disk head — this takes an average wait of 3 milliseconds. The time for one 8-kilobyte block (16 sectors) to pass under a disk head, assuming 800 sectors/track, is .12 milliseconds. Thus, on average, in every 3.42 milliseconds we can transfer one 8-kilobyte block. This gives us a transfer speed of 2.40 million bytes/sec. This is around 3.7% of Rhinopias's capacity — more than 20 times the 0.16% we computed for S5FS, but still pretty miserable.

Reducing Rotational Latency   It should be clear from the above analysis that the major cause of our performance problems is now the rotational latency — we've done a pretty good job of reducing seek delays. Not much can be done to reduce the rotational delay that occurs just after a seek completes. But if there are a number of blocks of the file in the cylinder, perhaps we can arrange them so that, after an initial delay, they can all be read in without further rotational delays.

In our discussion on reducing seek time, the order in which blocks of a file are requested didn't matter much, particularly for files fitting in one cylinder group. But when we discuss rotational delays, order is important. If blocks of a file are requested randomly, nothing can be done. But if blocks are requested sequentially, we can usefully access a number of them in a single disk rotation.

Let's assume that blocks of a file are being requested sequentially. How should we arrange blocks on a track (this will generalize to cylinders) so that they can be read with minimal rotational delay? It might seem obvious at first glance that we should place our blocks in consecutive locations on the track. Thus, after accessing one block, we can immediately access the next (see Figure 6.13). However, this doesn't necessarily work all that well, particularly on early 21st-century systems.

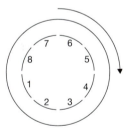

Suppose the block size is 8 kilobytes and each track holds 50 blocks. Two separate disk operations are required to access the two consecutive blocks. The operating system starts the first operation, waits until an interrupt notifies it of completion, and then starts the second. However, some period of time elapses from when the first operation completes to when the second is started. During this time the disk rotates; how far depends upon both its rotation speed and the speed of the processor. Even though there is space between disk sectors and thus between the last sector of the first block and the first sector of the second block, the disk might rotate far enough that by the time the second operation is issued, the read/write head is beyond the beginning of the second block. Thus, to read the entire block, we must wait for the disk to make an almost complete revolution, bringing the beginning of the block to the read/write head. How long does this take? If the disk is spinning at 10,000 RPM, a single revolution takes 6 milliseconds — a significant amount of time; in fact, we'd probably be better off if the second block were on a different cylinder within the cylinder group.

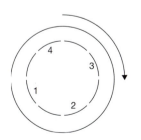

Suppose our processor takes 100 microseconds to field a disk-operation-completion interrupt and start the next operation. (This is a long time by today's standards, but on processors of the early 1980s, it was the time to execute at most 100 instructions.) With 50 blocks/track (16 sectors/block), each block (including the inter-sector gaps) takes 120 microseconds to pass under the read/write head. Thus by the time the second operation starts, the read/write head is near the end of the second block and the disk must rotate roughly one complete revolution to read the entire block.

FIGURE 6.13   Above, a disk surface with consecutive block access; below, block interleaving is used.

To alleviate this problem, FFS used a technique known as *block interleaving*. Rather than placing successive blocks of a file in contiguous disk locations, it places the second block some number of block locations after the first. In our example, if successive blocks from the file are separated by a single block on disk, then the read/write head is positioned to begin a read of the second block after only 20 microseconds after the operation is started — a factor-of-300 improvement over the wait time in the approach where we don't skip a block.

So, what's the average maximum transfer speed of FFS with block interleaving? As earlier, let's consider a 2-megabyte file fitting in a cylinder group. Since each track holds 50 blocks, a Rhinopias cylinder has 400. Thus, in this best case, all the blocks of the file are in the same cylinder. To transfer these blocks, we first have a .3-millisecond seek to that cylinder. Then there's a 3-millisecond rotational delay. At this point, the disk heads are positioned to read the first block without further delay. Simplifying things slightly: with each disk rotation 25 blocks are transferred (since every other block is skipped). Thus 2 megabytes are transferred after 10.24 revolutions of the disk, which takes 61.44 milliseconds. Adding in the initial seek and rotational delays of 3.3 milliseconds yields an effective transfer speed of 32.4 million bytes/second, about 50% of Rhinopias's maximum speed. The good news is that we have a 13-fold improvement over the previous figure. The bad news is that, even in this best-case analysis, we can achieve only 50% of Rhinopias's capacity.

Clustering and Extents   With today's faster processors it should be possible both to respond to a disk interrupt and to start the next operation so quickly that block interleaving is not needed. However, the balance could change if, for example, disk technology improves so that disks spin much faster. A better disk-access strategy is to recognize ahead of time that more than one block is to be accessed and issue one request for all of them. Alternatively, we might do away with fixed-size blocks entirely and allocate disk space in variable-size but generally larger units.

Both Ext2 and later versions of FFS use multiple-block-at-a-time strategies known as *block clustering*. In Ext2's preallocation approach, contiguous disk blocks are allocated eight at a time when the first of each eight file-system blocks is written. The preallocated blocks are available for other files but are not taken back unless there is a shortage of disk space. In FFS, as implemented on Solaris (McVoy and Kleiman 1991), disk-block allocation is delayed until a certain number of file-system blocks, say eight, are ready to be written, and at this point contiguous disk blocks are allocated for them. Both strategies result in an effective block size that's eight times the actual block size, but with minimal internal fragmentation costs.

An approach that actually predates block clustering is *extent-based allocation*. Rather than make any pretense of allocation in fixed-size blocks, files are treated as collections of large contiguous regions of disk space called *extents*. In principle, a large file can consist of a single such extent, thus allowing fast access with a minimum of metadata. However, since extents are of variable size, external fragmentation becomes a problem — a heavily used file system's free space might mostly reside in small pieces, thus making it impossible to allocate large extents. Thus, in the worst case, an extent-based file system might require just as much metadata as a block-based one and have even worse performance problems because file data is widely scattered and in small pieces.

Windows's NTFS is an extent-based file system. Like most such systems, it represents a file's disk space with a *run list* consisting of items describing each successive extent; each item contains an extent's starting disk address and length (Figure 6.14). If the run list becomes so long that it no longer fits in a file record (the NTFS equivalent of an inode: see Section 6.1.5 below), additional file records are allocated for the additional run-list segments and a separate list is maintained that indexes these segments. Thus, for example, a highly fragmented file might have 100 extents. Rather than searching linearly through a 100-element run list to find a particular extent, a top-level run list (referred to in NTFS as an "attribute-list attribute") with just a few entries is searched to find which expansion file record contains the entry for the extent in question.

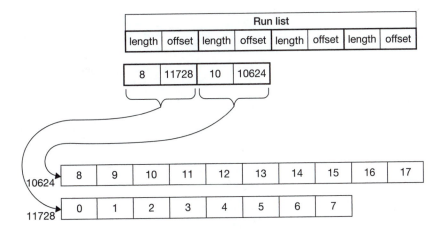

FIGURE 6.14 NTFS uses run lists to refer to multiple extents. The figure shows two: one starting at location 11728 and containing 8 blocks, the other starting at location 10624 and containing 10 blocks.

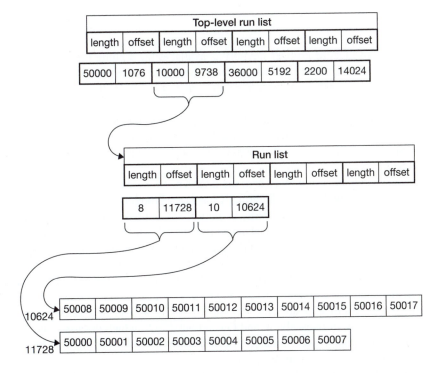

FIGURE 6.15 A two-level run list in NTFS. To find block 50011, we search the top-level run list for a pointer to the file record containing the run list that refers to this block. In this case it's pointed to by the second entry, which contains a pointer to the run list that refers to extents containing file blocks starting with 50,000 and continuing for 10,000 blocks. We show the first two references to extents in that run list. The block we're after is in the second one.

Then the run list in this file record, containing perhaps just 10 entries, is searched. This two-level approach reduces the search time considerably (see Figure 6.15).

NTFS requires active avoidance of fragmentation problems. It uses a defragmenter program to rearrange free and allocated space on disk so that files are comprised of few but large extents and free space similarly is comprised of a small number of large regions. Overall good performance is achieved if the defragmenter is run often enough, which could be anywhere between once a day and never depending upon how full the disk is.

6.1.4.2 Aggressive Caching and Optimized Writes

The file-system layout policies discussed so far have organized disk space primarily to optimize the sequential reading of files (see Figure 6.16). But it's not clear that this is necessarily the

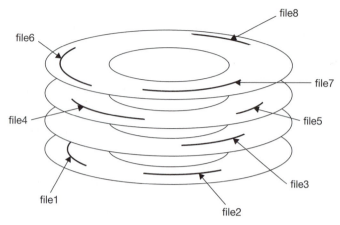

FIGURE 6.16 Files organized for optimal read access using single extents.

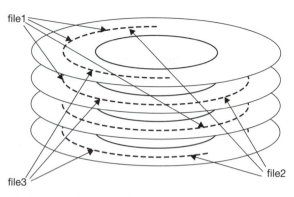

FIGURE 6.17 Portions of files are placed in the log (shown here as occupying most of one cylinder) in the order in which they were written.

best strategy. Suppose lots of primary memory is available for caching file-system blocks. For active files, most reads might well be satisfied from the cache. However, so that our data doesn't disappear if the system crashes, modifications are written to disk. Perhaps what we really want to optimize is writes.

Rather than trying to aggregate the data of any one file for fast read access, let's simply maintain a sequential log of file updates (Figure 6.17). We buffer the updates and write batches of them to disk in the order in which they arrive. Thus we're assured of fast updating, rather than hoping for fast reading.

On the one hand, this is optimal use of the disk: since we are usually writing to contiguous locations, the greatest seek delays we'll normally have are in moving the heads from one cylinder to the next as cylinders are filled. If we write in units of whole tracks and provide sufficient buffering, we minimize the effects of rotational delays. On the other hand, though, the approach looks remarkably stupid, since reading a file would seem to require searching through the update log to track down the blocks of the file and thus would require many expensive disk operations.

The approach becomes a lot less stupid, though, if we take advantage of a large file-system cache in primary memory and either access file blocks from it directly or use it to find them quickly. This is the basis of what are called *log-structured file systems*. Pioneering work on such file systems is described in (Rosenblum and Ousterhout 1992), which discusses the *Sprite File System*. This system is logically similar to FFS in its use of inodes and indirect blocks, but is radically different in most other respects.

To illustrate the utility of the log-structured approach, we adapt an example from (Rosenblum and Ousterhout 1992). Suppose we are creating two single-block files *dir1/file1* and *dir2/file2*. In FFS we'd allocate and initialize the inode for *file1* and write it to disk before we update *dir1* to refer to it. We'd then add the appropriate entry to *dir1* and write the modified block that contains the entry to disk — let's assume we can do this without adding a new block to *dir1*. Finally we write data to *file1*, which requires us to allocate a disk block, fill it with the data being written, write this block to disk, and modify *file1*'s inode to refer to the new block.

Doing all this requires six disk writes, including those to modify the bit maps of free blocks and free inodes (note that we write *file1*'s inode twice — once when it's allocated and once when we add a block to it). Since we're also creating *dir2/file2*, we need six more disk writes. Most of these writes potentially go to scattered disk locations — each requires a seek (see Figure 6.18).

The Sprite File System accomplishes all this with a single, long disk write. However, this write includes some additional data so that the files can be read back again. Here's what's done.

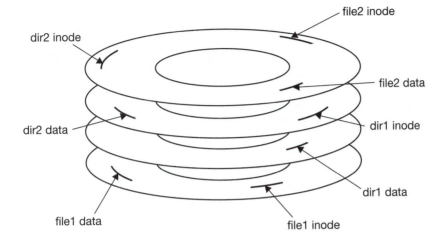

FIGURE 6.18 Creating two files in FFS requires writing each of the blocks shown here, with the inodes for *file1* and *file2* being written twice. Not shown are the blocks containing the free vector, which must be written twice, once for *file1*'s data block and again for *file2*'s data block.

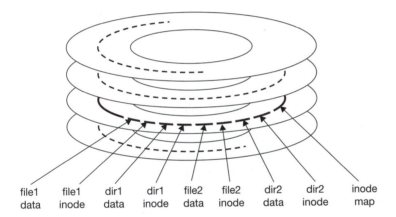

| file1 | file1 | dir1 | dir1 | file2 | file2 | dir2 | dir2 | inode |
| data | inode | data | inode | data | inode | data | inode | map |

FIGURE 6.19 In Sprite FS, everything required to create *file1* and *file2* is added to the log in a single write. Here, again, the log occupies most of one cylinder.

Creating *file1* in *dir1* requires modifying the contents of *dir1* to refer to *file1*. Rather than simply modifying the current block of *dir1* that holds this information, we allocate and write out a new block to replace it. So that this new block can be found, we have to modify the disk map in *dir1*'s inode. However, rather than simply modifying the old inode, we allocate and write out a new one to replace the old.

Of course, we need to keep track of where this new version of *dir1*'s inode is — a new data structure, called an *inode map*, is used for this. The inode map is a simple array that's indexed by inode number; each entry points to the current location of the inode and contains some other information about it. The map's current contents are in primary memory. As it's updated it's written out to disk in pieces, along with other update information. The location of these pieces is recorded in a *checkpoint region* that is stored at a fixed location on disk. There are actually two copies of this region at two different fixed locations; the two alternate between being the current copy and the copy being updated.

So, the single, long disk write contains the data block for *file1*, *file1*'s inode, the modified data block containing the *dir1* entry referring to *file1*, and the modified *dir1* inode. It also contains similar information for *dir2* and *file2*, as well as the pieces of the inode map necessary to locate the new and modified inodes (see Figure 6.19). What's missing is anything recording block allocation — such information turns out to be unnecessary, as we discuss shortly.

First, though, to make sure we understand how everything works, let's go over what must be done to read the data in *file1*. We first find its inode by following the path *dir1/file1*. Some unspecified directory contains the inode number of *dir1*; suppose this number is 1137. We look this up in the inode map, which is in primary memory. The entry there gives us the disk location of the inode for *dir1*. Since we have a large cache, we probably can find this inode there, but if not, we fetch it from disk. The inode's disk map refers us to the block containing the *file1* entry, which contains *file1*'s inode number. We look this number up in the inode map to find the inode's address. We fetch this inode, probably from the cache. Finally, the inode contains the disk map, which refers us to the file's data.

Let's compare this with what it would take to read *file1* in FFS. The only additional steps required in Sprite FS are the two in which it reads the inode map. Since the inode map is in primary memory, reading from it doesn't add to the cost of reading from the file. What if *file1* has multiple data blocks that we want to read sequentially and quickly? If they were produced sequentially (and quickly) on Sprite FS, they'd be in contiguous locations on disk. But if they were produced in some other fashion, they might be in scattered locations. In FFS, they would normally be near one another. However, if the file is in active use, the disk locations of the blocks don't matter, since they'll be accessed directly from the cache.

The next issue in Sprite FS is disk-space management. Sprite FS requires large contiguous regions of free space so that it can write out large amounts of data at once. The larger a free region is, the more such writes Sprite FS can handle without seek delays, and thus the better its performance.

When we initialize a disk for Sprite FS, some small beginning portion will be allocated and the rest will be free, thus giving us a large contiguous block of free storage. As we use the file system, we allocate more and more disk space from the beginning of the free-storage area. As discussed above, many of these allocations will supplant storage previously in use, leaving a lot of garbage blocks within the allocated region of the disk. Somehow we have to identify these garbage regions and consolidate them as free space.

If we can identify the garbage regions, there are two ways we might consolidate them. One is simply to link them together. This is easy to do, but doesn't provide the necessary large contiguous regions of free space. The other way is to rearrange the various regions of disk space, moving all the allocated portions to one end and leaving one large, contiguous free region. This has the desired result but is rather complicated to do. What Sprite FS does is a combination of the two. It divides the disk into large segments, each either 512 kilobytes or one megabyte in length. The live (that is, non-garbage) blocks are identified in a number of segments and are consolidated into a smaller number of segments by moving some of them from one segment to another. Those segments made entirely free are linked together.

Each segment contains a *segment summary* identifying everything in the segment. Thus, say, if a data block is moved from one segment to another, the segment summary identifies the inode number and block number of the file the block belongs to; this makes it possible to modify the appropriate disk map to contain the block's new location. To determine whether a block is live or garbage, the segment summary is consulted to find where the block belongs. If the disk map still refers to the block, it's live, otherwise it's garbage.

Though Sprite FS was strictly a research file system and was never put into widespread use, it demonstrated the feasibility and desirability of the log-structured approach. It influenced the design of many subsequent file systems, including WAFL and ZFS, which we discuss in Sections 6.2.2.3 and 6.5.

6.1.5 DYNAMIC INODES

In describing S5FS we introduced the notion of an inode, a notion used in one form or another in almost all file systems. In many file systems inodes are allocated as in S5FS: from a static array.

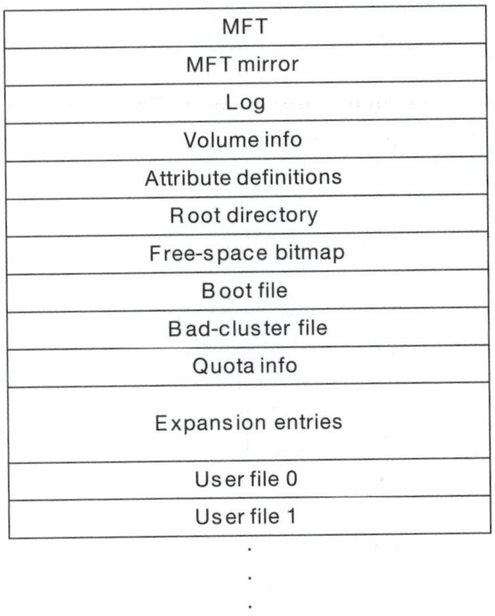

MFT
MFT mirror
Log
Volume info
Attribute definitions
Root directory
Free-space bitmap
Boot file
Bad-cluster file
Quota info
Expansion entries
User file 0
User file 1

FIGURE 6.20 NTFS's Master File Table (MFT). Each entry is one kilobyte long and refers to a file. Since the MFT is a file, it has an entry in itself (the first entry). There's a copy of the MFT called the MFT mirror. Then there are a number of other entries for system files and metadata files, and then the entries for ordinary files.

In FFS, Ext2, and Ext3, this array is broken up into pieces, but is still static. Thus their inodes are still identified by their indices within this array.

This causes two sorts of problems. The first is that in laying out a file system on disk, you have to predict the maximum number of files the system will have — that is, you need to determine the size of this inode array. If your guess is too large, the space is wasted for unneeded inodes. If your guess is too low, eventually you can no longer create files in your file system, even though plenty of disk space is available for file contents. The second problem is that you might want to add more disk space to the file system. The original assumptions about the number of inodes needed might no longer be valid if the file system becomes larger.

What's clearly needed is a means for allocating inodes from the same pool of disk blocks from which everything else is allocated. This doesn't seem like a big deal, but we often still want to be able to refer to an inode by a simple index rather than by a disk address — this facilitates having standard inode numbers for certain key files, such as roots of file systems, as well as making it possible to use fewer bits for the inode number than for general disk addresses.

A simple approach that maintains the notion of an index is to treat the array of inodes as a file. This inode file is represented just as any other file and thus can grow and shrink as needed. Of course, like any other file, an inode is required to refer to it. And this inode, like any other inode, is in the inode file. This might seem like a recipe for infinite recursion, but the inode for the inode file is simply kept at a fixed location on disk, with a backup copy at another fixed location in case of problems with the first copy.

NTFS is organized in this way. It uses the term *file record* rather than inode, and the inode file is called the *master file table* (MFT). Thus the master file table is a file containing an array of file records (see Figure 6.20).

Computer crashes are annoying. For file systems, we'd like to make sure they're merely annoying and not devastating — in particular, that no data is lost. Early versions of S5FS and other file systems were capable of devastation — a system crash could destroy not only what you'd spent the last three hours adding to a file, but its prior contents as well. Though now you should still back up any files you value, modern file systems have made great strides in minimizing data loss from crashes.

6.2 CRASH RESILIENCY

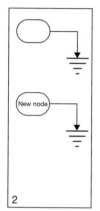

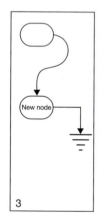

In this section we discuss the problems that bedeviled S5FS and examine how they have been mitigated in modern versions of FFS as well as in recent file systems, including Ext3, NTFS, WAFL, and ZFS.

6.2.1 WHAT GOES WRONG

How do computer crashes take such a toll on file systems? We might expect some ambiguity about the effect of a write that was taking place just as the system crashed, but how could S5FS lose entire files?

The culprits are the metadata structures — those data structures that form the structure of the file system itself. Examples are inodes, indirect blocks, directories, and the like. If these are damaged, then some user data, even though on the disk, could be inaccessible. Worse yet, the metadata structures could become so scrambled that one data item might appear in multiple files, "good" data might appear in free space, etc. Thus making certain that anything survives a crash entails special care of these metadata structures. It was lack of care of such structures that caused files in early S5FS to disappear.

A simple example of the sort of problem we're dealing with is adding an item to the end of a singly linked list. Figure 6.21 shows an apparently safe way of doing this. A list item consists of a data field and a link field; the last item's link field contains 0. To add a new item to an existing list, we first write the new item to disk, ensuring that its link field contains zero. Then we write out a new version of what had been the end of the list, changing its link field to contain the address of the new item. If the system crashes before this write takes place, the worst that could happen, it seems, is that our new item isn't appended to the list: when the system comes back up from the crash, the linked list should be as it was before we tried to add the item.

But things aren't this simple. As discussed in Chapter 4, most operating systems employ caches for file-system data and metadata. Active portions of files are in primary storage; modified data and metadata are not written to disk immediately. This caching is done so that many file operations can take place at memory speed rather than at disk speed. In the event of a crash, however, we have two problems.

The first is that many file modifications are only in the cache and were never written out to disk: when the cache's contents are lost in the crash, the modifications are lost too. Thus the application might have written to the file and received every indication that the operation succeeded (for example, the system call returned with a success status), but nevertheless, after recovery from the crash, the modifications don't appear in the file (Figure 6.22). From one point

FIGURE 6.21 Adding a node to a linked list.

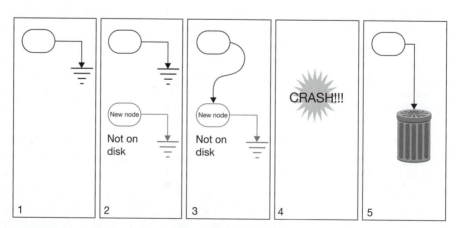

FIGURE 6.22 Adding a node to a linked list via a cache.

of view, this isn't a big deal, since it is equivalent to the system's crashing slightly earlier. From another, though, the application might have printed out a message such as "file successfully modified," leading the user to believe that the file really was modified. If the data involved recorded something such as the hand-in of a homework assignment or the purchase of a stock before its price went up, this could be pretty disastrous.

Things get worse with the second problem: the modifications that were written from the cache to the disk weren't necessarily the oldest ones. Modifications can be written to disk in a different order from that in which they were sent to the cache. This would happen if, for example, a least-recently-used policy is used to determine when data and metadata are written from the cache to disk. It is this sort of problem that can cause the destruction of entire files — not just the loss of the most recent updates.

To see how this could happen, let's take another look at our linked-list example (Figure 6.21). We first allocate a new disk block and modify a cached copy of the block to contain the new item with a zeroed link field. We then modify the cached copy of the disk block containing what had been the last item in the list so that it points to the new item. So far, all changes are in the cache; if the system were to crash, the version of the data structure on disk would be unchanged.

However, suppose the cached copy of the old item (what used to be the last item of the list) is written out to disk and then, before the cached copy of the new item can be written out, the system crashes. When the system comes back up, the former last item of our list now points to what is probably garbage. We have a badly damaged list structure that could cause much harm, particularly if it's metadata. Are metadata really stored in the form of such singly linked lists? Most definitely — disk maps, run lists of extents, and directories contain them.

Our general problem is that the metadata structures on disk at any particular moment may not be *well formed*: they may not be how they are supposed to be. In a well formed linked list, each node is supposed either to point to another node or to have a null pointer. In a well formed directory hierarchy (in most systems), the directories and their hard links form a directed acyclic graph (DAG) — if there is a cycle, the directory hierarchy is not well formed. If a disk block appears in more than one file or in both a file and in free space, then the disk map, free space, or both are not well formed. If a disk block is unaccounted for — if it's not in free space and it's not in a file — then free space is not well formed, since it is supposed to include all disk blocks that are not otherwise used.

If all the metadata structures are well formed, the file system is *consistent*. Thus the problem is that, because of caching, what's on the disk is not only not the current version of the file system, it's not necessarily even a consistent version of the file system. What applications perceive as the file system, which we call the *cache view*, is a combination of what is in the cache and what is on disk.

Our discussion above has focused on metadata. While ordinary data is pretty important too, metadata problems cause more widespread damage than data problems. If user data is inconsistent after a crash, there is clearly trouble, but it's localized to a particular file and does not affect the integrity of the entire file system. Thus file-system crash protection has traditionally focused on metadata without any real concern for data issues, a simplification that aids performance by allowing aggressive caching.

Another class of problems arises from media failures of various sorts. A disk sector can spontaneously go bad. A disk head can collide with a disk surface and destroy a good portion of it. A power glitch can cause a disk controller to write out random bits. These issues have nothing to do with caching and may or may not be easy to detect (a head crash has one positive attribute: it's pretty obvious something has happened). Bad sectors can be isolated and effectively removed from the file system. If the file system is mirrored, new sectors can be allocated and loaded with the copy.

6.2.2 DEALING WITH CRASHES

It is clear what needs to be done to make sure we can recover from crashes:[3] simply make certain that what is on disk is either consistent or contains enough information to make it consistent easily. This is relatively simple if we can ignore caching. We thus begin by assuming there is no cache and examine what can be done, and then we look at the effects of adding the cache.

Performing an update system call, such as *write*, *create*, *delete*, and *rename*, to a file requires a number of disk operations that affect both data and metadata. One approach to making file systems crash-tolerant is to make sure that each of these operations takes the file system from one consistent state to another. The idea is that at all times the file system is consistent and that if there is a crash, what is on disk is a valid file system. This doesn't quite work, however, because in some cases multiple disk writes are necessary to move from one consistent state to another.

We saw an example of this already in adding an item to a singly linked list (see Figures 6.21 and 6.22). Even when we do the disk writes in the correct order — first writing the contents of the node that is to be added, then writing out the new value of the node that points to it — a crash between the two writes would leave the file system in an inconsistent state, since there would be a block that is neither part of a file nor in free space. This isn't so bad, however: other than reducing the amount of available space a bit, we haven't damaged the file system. Furthermore, we can clean this up relatively easily by garbage-collecting these orphaned disk blocks. We'll consider this an *innocuous inconsistency*.

Another situation arises in renaming a file. This involves removing the entry for the file in one directory and putting it in another. We should avoid doing this in just that order, since a system crash between the two operations would make the file not appear in any directory afterwards. The correct way is first to add the file to the new directory, then remove it from the old. If the system crashes between these two operations, the file will be in both directories. This isn't exactly what was intended, but the file system remains consistent and the extra link can easily be removed. (See Exercise 13 for the issue of the file's link count, stored in the inode or equivalent.)

Some operations may require many steps. Writing a large amount of data to a file can require any number of separate disk operations. Similarly, deleting a large file can require many steps as each of the file's blocks is freed. If a crash occurs in the middle of such a multi-step operation, the disk will end up in a state in which only part of the write was completed or only part of the delete was completed — the file still exists, but it's smaller than it was. The file system is still consistent, but the user or application must check after the system comes back up to see how far the operation actually got.

This approach — performing multi-step file-system updates so that the on-disk file system never has anything worse than innocuous inconsistencies — is called the *consistency-preserving approach*. It's the basis of the soft-updates technique we describe below. Another approach, known as the *transactional approach*, treats a sequence of file-system updates as *atomic transactions*. This means that if the system crashes during such a sequence, the effect (perhaps after some recovery operations) is as if the operations either took place completely or didn't happen at all. Thus there's no such thing as a partially completed operation, though there is some uncertainty about whether or not an operation actually happened.

Transactions are standard fare in databases, where there is much concern that a sequence of steps have a well defined effect regardless of whatever else may be going on, including system crashes. For example, what happens when I transfer $1000 from one bank account into another? The expected outcome is clearly that the first account, assuming it has sufficient funds, ends up with $1000 less than it started and the other ends up with $1000 more.

---

[3] Note that by "recover from crashes" we mean bringing the file system's metadata to a consistent state. As discussed above, file systems generally make no attempt to make data consistent after a crash, and recent updates can disappear because of a crash.

A more complete definition of transactions is that they have the "ACID" property:

- *Atomic*: all or nothing. Either all of a transaction happens or none of it does. For example, if the system crashes in the middle of my $1000 transfer, I don't want to end up with the money taken out of the first account but not deposited in the other. At some point in the progress of a transaction we say it is *committed*: the full effect of the transaction is applied to the database or file system if the system crashes after this point, and no part of the transaction is applied if it crashes before this point.

- *Consistent*: transactions applied to a consistent database or file system leave it in a consistent state. In the example, regardless of whether or not the system crashes, my bank-account information should still be well formed.

- *Isolated*: a transaction has no effect on other transactions until it is committed and is not affected by any concurrent uncommitted transactions. This means that if I have $50 in my bank account and someone is in the act of transferring $1000 into it, I can't transfer the $1000 out until the first transaction commits. This is important since the first transaction might not commit — it could be aborted so that no money is deposited into my account. This requirement might also be construed as meaning that (again assuming my account balance is $50) it would be OK to make two concurrent transactions, each transferring all $50 out of it. However, this would violate the consistency requirement — a negative balance is not well formed.

- *Durable*: once a transaction has fully taken place, its effect on the database or file system persists until explicitly changed by some other transaction. If I deposit $1000 in your bank account, the money shouldn't spontaneously disappear sometime later.

Implementing transaction processing may seem at first glance a tall order, but, at least conceptually, it's not all that complicated. There are two basic strategies. In *journaling*,[4] the steps of a transaction are first written onto disk into a special journal file. Once the steps are safely recorded, the operation is said to be *committed* and the steps are applied to the actual file system. If the system crashes after the operation is committed but before the steps have been fully applied to the file system, a simple recovery procedure takes place when the system comes back up in which the steps are applied from the journal so as to perform the operation fully. This is known as *redo* or *new-value journaling*. If the system crashes after the operation has started but before all the steps have been recorded in the journal, crash recovery simply disposes of those steps that were recorded and the file system is left unmodified.

A variant of this approach, known as *undo* or *old-value journaling*, involves storing in the journal the old versions of blocks to be modified. Once these are safely on disk, the file system is updated. If the system crashes before this update is completed, the file system is restored to its previous state by writing back the contents of the journal.

A combination of both variants is used in some systems (for example, NTFS): both the old and the new values of the items being modified are put in the journal. Section 6.6.4 discusses why NTFS employs this combination.

In both redo and undo journaling, it might seem that we're doubling the amount of work: blocks are written not only to the file system, but to the journal as well. However, the techniques discussed in Section 6.1.4.2 to improve file-system performance — writing large amounts of data to contiguous blocks — can minimize the time required for this extra work. So, rather than write each item to the journal as it is produced, we delay until a fair number can be written at once, and then write them to contiguous locations. Of course, we must keep track of when we've written items to the journal and make sure we don't update the file system until afterwards.

---

[4]This is also called *logging*; we prefer *journaling* so as to avoid confusion with log-structured file systems.

What should transactions be in a file system? In other words, how do we decide where one transaction ends and another begins? One possibility is that each file-system system call is a separate transaction. This would be convenient, providing a well defined notion that makes sense to the application programmer, but would make it difficult to batch the writing of updates to the journal. The problem is the wide range in the number of disk operations used in system calls — writing a small number of bytes to an existing location within a file might take one operation, but deleting a large file could require millions of operations. Most system calls involve a small number of disk operations and thus their transactions would have so few steps that we'd get little benefit from batching their steps when journaling them. Others would be so large that the journal might not have enough space for all the steps of their transactions. What's generally done is a compromise: group together a number of short system calls into a single transaction, but split a long system call into a number of transactions. In all cases the transactions obey the ACID rules and, in particular, take the file system from consistent state to another.

The alternative approach to journaling is known as *shadow paging*. With shadow paging, new space is allocated within the database or file system to hold the modifications, but the original versions of the modified items are retained as well. The new versions are not integrated into the database or file system and the old versions continue to be part of it until the transaction is committed. At this point, a single write to disk effectively removes the old versions and integrates the new versions.

Consider a file-system example (Walker, Popek, et al. 1983). Suppose we are modifying a block of a file in an S5FS- or FFS-like file system. We allocate a new block, copy the contents of the old block into it, and then write the new data into it. If the original block is referred to by an indirect block, we allocate another new block, copy the original indirect block into it, and set it to point to our new data block. We then ensure that the changes are written to disk.

At this point, if the system were to crash, the effect would be that this update transaction hasn't happened, since the changes haven't been integrated into the file system. But now we can do this integration with a single disk write: we modify an in-memory copy of the block containing the file's inode so that it points to the newly modified indirect block, and then write the copy to disk, overwriting the original copy. This single write effectively removes the old information from the file system and integrates in the new. Some background cleanup may have to be done to add to the free list the disk blocks that were orphaned by a crash.

Why choose one of the transaction approaches over the other? An early comparison of the two (Brown, Kolling, et al. 1985) argues in favor of journaling: the argument is that, even though journaling requires more disk operations than shadow paging, most operations are either reads that are normally satisfied from the cache or writes that go to contiguous locations in the journal file. Shadow paging requires fewer disk operations, but these operations require more time. We refute this argument in Section 6.2.2.3 below.

6.2.2.1 Soft Updates

At first glance, it would seem that implementing the consistency-preserving approach should be straightforward: simply make sure that writes from cache to disk are done in the same order as the cache was updated. This would be easy if each metadata item occupied a separate block on disk. However, these items are typically small and thus are stored many per disk block so as to maximize the use of disk bandwidth. For example, in S5FS and FFS, multiple inodes are packed into a single block; directories consist of many blocks, but each block consists of a number of entries (each containing a component-name/inode-number pair). Of two cache pages, for instance, each containing a copy of a disk block, one might contain a metadata item that must be written out before a metadata item in the other, and vice versa. Thus there could well be circular dependencies on write order among cache pages.

Before we discuss how to handle these circular dependencies, let's reexamine the ordering constraints for changes to metadata. We must ensure that at all times the metadata on disk forms a consistent file system containing all the files and file data that applications believe should have been there at some point in the very recent past. Thus, assuming we start with a consistent file system on disk, after each write to disk it should still be consistent.

An easy way to prevent circular dependencies is the following: when two metadata items are to be modified and one must be written to disk before the other, write out the first synchronously (i.e., wait for the disk write to complete) immediately after modifying it; then modify the other but leave it in the cache, to be written out sometime later.

For example, Figure 6.23 shows what must happen when a new file is created and added to a directory. The file's inode is initialized, the data block containing the new directory entry is modified, and the directory inode is modified. Assuming each modification is in a separate block, all three blocks must be written to disk. The correct order for the writes would be first the new file's inode, then the directory entry, then the directory's inode. However, if the directory's inode and the file's inode share the same disk block (Figure 6.24), there is a circular dependency: the block containing the inodes must be written first, since it contains the file's inode, but it also must be written last, since it contains the directory's inode. Thus if both the two inodes and the data block are modified in the cache but are unmodified on disk, it is not possible to update the disk in a consistency-preserving order. To avoid this problem, a thread performing such a sequence of operations must, before updating the directory inode in the cache, first add the file inode to the cached block and wait for it to be updated on disk, and then wait for the data block to be written to disk.

This approach was used in early versions of FFS and provided good crash resiliency. But this came at the cost of significant performance loss due to the synchronous writes: the loss of performance in FFS due to such synchronous writes was between a factor of six and a factor of twenty over a version of FFS called Async FFS in which all updates of metadata are deferred and can be done in any order (Ganger, McKusick, et al. 2000).

Eliminating circular dependencies without requiring synchronous writes involves somehow keeping track of the metadata updates individually so they can be written out in the correct order. The *soft updates* technique does this while still maintaining the most recent updates in the cache (Ganger, McKusick, et al. 2000), so that the cumulative effect of changes to files appears in the cache, while the individual updates are listed separately. In this approach, when a cache page is to be written out, any updates that have been applied to it but must not be written out yet due

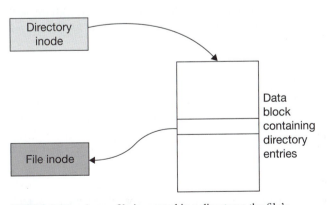

FIGURE 6.23 A new file is created in a directory: the file's inode is initialized, the data block containing the new directory entry is modified, and the directory inode is modified. All three modifications must be written to disk.

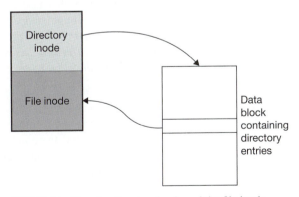

FIGURE 6.24 Here the directory inode and the file inode share the same disk block. Thus it is impossible to write the modifications out so that the file inode is written before the directory-entry block, yet have the directory-entry block written before the directory inode — we have a circular dependency.

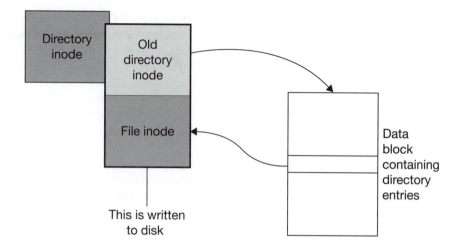

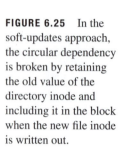

FIGURE 6.25 In the soft-updates approach, the circular dependency is broken by retaining the old value of the directory inode and including it in the block when the new file inode is written out.

to ordering constraints are undone: the cache page is restored to its state before the update was applied. The page is then written out to disk; the update is redone on completion. While the page is in this undone state, it's locked so as to prevent access until the updates are redone. Using this technique on FFS yielded performance almost as good as that of Async FFS, yet with the benefits of correctly ordered updates. Figure 6.25 shows how the circular dependency is broken.

(Ganger, McKusick, et al. 2000) identified three general problems necessitating ordering constraints in the cache.

1. The system might write out a new value for a metadata item so that it points to an item that isn't properly initialized on disk. A crash would thus make the just-written item point to garbage. The pointed-to item should have been written out first, as in our linked-list example. *Thus a constraint is added that the pointed-to item must be written out first.*

2. The system might modify a pointer in a metadata item so as to orphan an item that shouldn't be orphaned. That is, it might remove the last pointer to an item containing data still in use. A crash would cause the permanent loss of the orphaned item, since nothing on disk refers to it. This might happen when we're renaming a file and remove the on-disk directory entry containing the file's previous name before adding an on-disk directory entry with the new name. *A constraint is added specifying that the new directory entry must be written out before the old directory entry.*

3. The system might write out a new value for a metadata item for which on-disk items still point to and depend upon its old value. This could happen in FFS if, in the cache, we delete a file and reuse its inode for a new file, and the new inode contents are the only thing written to disk. Thus there are directory entries on disk for the old file that refer to the new file's inode. A crash would cause the replacement of the old file's contents with those of the new file. *A constraint is added specifying that metadata items containing pointers to the old use of the metadata item must be written out (with null values) before the new contents of the metadata item are written out.*

Thus, subject to the above constraints, the writing back to disk of cached file-system updates can be deferred. And, as explained above, if a single cache page contains a number of updated metadata items, it might be written back several times so as not to update a particular metadata item on disk before its constraints allow.

The soft-updates technique has a few drawbacks. More disk writes may be necessary than with Async FFS so as to maintain ordering constraints, and extra memory is required to represent the constraints and to hold old metadata values. (Ganger, McKusick, et al. 2000) found these problems to be minimal. In addition, after a crash, some disk blocks may be free but not accounted for as free space. While these blocks must be reclaimed, this can be done as background activity after the system restarts.

6.2.2.2 Journaled File Systems[5]

Many file systems use journaling for crash tolerance. Many of these, such as Ext3 and VxFS, use redo journaling. NTFS, for reasons discussed in Section 6.6.4 below, uses a combination of both redo and undo journaling. We use Ext3 to introduce journaling: it's essentially the same file system as Ext2 but with journaling added, much as soft updates were added to FFS. Recall that Ext2 is similar to FFS.

Ext3 uses journaling to protect metadata and, optionally, user data as well. Its approach is to treat all operations on the file system in a specific time interval as one large transaction. As with Ext2 and FFS, disk blocks are cached in memory. No modified blocks are written to the file system or the journal on disk until the transaction is about to commit. A special journal thread performs the commit, writing all modified blocks to the journal. Once they are safely copied to the journal, a *checkpointing* phase begins in which the file system itself is updated: the cached blocks are released to the normal buffer-cache writeback mechanisms (as in Ext2 and the original FFS), which write them to the file system in due course. As soon as all modified blocks have reached the file system, the copies of them in the journal are no longer needed, and the space they occupy is released.

Lots of details need to be filled in to get a really clear understanding of how Ext3 works. A major issue is whether user data is journaled along with metadata. Let's proceed by assuming at first that it is, and then examine what must be done if not. The portion of Ext3 that does journaling is split off into a separate subsystem known as JFS that makes the journaling code usable by other subsystems as well. Thus JFS provides the mechanism for journaling, while Ext3 proper determines what is to be journaled.

The example in Figures 6.26 through 6.28 shows what a transaction consists of. Ext3 provides JFS with what we call subtransactions — sequences of operations that take the file system from one consistent state to another. JFS determines how many of these subtransactions to group into a transaction. Note that no distinction is made as to which thread or process produced the subtransactions; JFS simply groups them together until it has a large enough transaction or until a time limit (five seconds, say) is exceeded. A separate kernel thread, known as *journald* (the *journal daemon*), then wakes up and does the commit processing: it writes the updated blocks of the transaction to the journal. Note that transactions are formed sequentially in time: all subtransactions within the JFS-determined transaction interval are grouped into the same transaction. A new transaction is started as soon as the previous one begins to commit.

In the terminology of the Ext3 implementation, the subtransactions are referred to via *handles* provided by JFS. For example, when Ext3 performs a *write* system call, it splits the transfer into separate pieces along block boundaries. As it processes each piece, it obtains a handle from JFS to refer to the piece. Thus the file-system updates required to add one block to the file system form a subtransaction, or at least part of one: JFS can arrange to group subtransactions together by supplying the same handle for the second piece of a single *write* system call as for the first piece, and similarly for subsequent pieces. Thus one handle can refer to a subtransaction forming some or all of the steps of one system call. JFS combines any number of these subtransactions into a single transaction.

---

[5] Some of the material in this section is based on a presentation by Stephen Tweedie, the developer of ext3. See (Tweedie 1998).

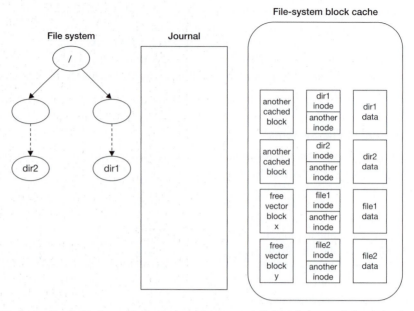

FIGURE 6.26 Journaling in Ext3, part 1. One process has created *file1* in directory *dir1*, another has created *file2* in directory *dir2*. The *journald* thread has yet to begin commit processing, so these operations have so far affected only the cache. Each process has performed two system calls: one to create the file, another to write data to it. Creating a file involves making an entry in the parent directory and allocating an inode. Note that a disk block contains more than one inode. Writing to a file involves allocating a disk block and modifying the inode's disk map. Thus the cached blocks containing directory data, the files' inodes, the files' data, and portions of the free vector are modified. Let's assume that JFS has grouped these into two subtransactions, one for the steps required to create and write to each file. These modified cached blocks must stay in the cache and must not be written to the file system until they've been copied to the journal.

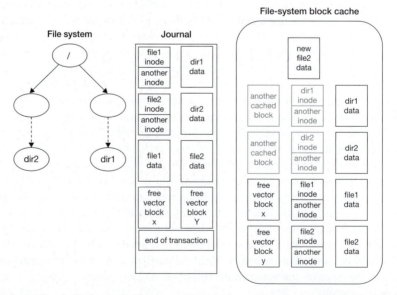

FIGURE 6.27 Journaling in Ext3, part 2. The *journald* thread has written the modified cache blocks to the journal, thus committing the transaction. Note that the unmodified cached blocks can be removed from the cache (i.e., their storage can be reused for other items). However, in the meantime, new data has been written to *file2*. Since the original copy of its data block is involved in the earlier transaction, a copy of that block is made for a new transaction that will include this update.

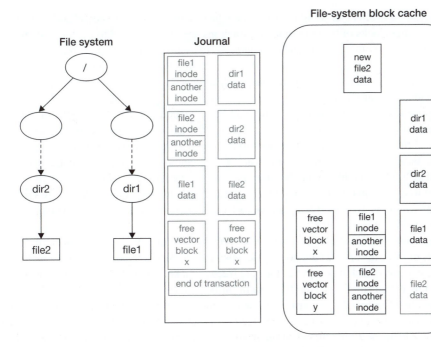

FIGURE 6.28 Journaling in Ext3, part 3. The transaction has been checkpointed, i.e., the cached blocks have been written to the file system, and thus it's now safe to remove the transaction from the journal. The old *file2* data is removed from the cache, since it's superseded by the new data.

The steps of the subtransactions (and hence transactions) are represented by the new contents of blocks and are stored in memory as part of the usual file-system block cache. Thus file-system updates are applied to the blocks in the cache. These modified blocks are written out to the journal as part of commit processing, and are later written to the file system as part of checkpointing. Normally, there's at most one copy of any particular disk block in the cache. Thus if a block contains a number of metadata items, their updates are effectively batched: the block is written out only once each to the journal and the file system, even if multiple items have been modified. This is particularly important for the free-space bitmap, in which each bit in a block is a separate metadata item.

As we've mentioned, when JFS determines it has reached a transaction boundary, it closes the current transaction and wakes up the *journald* thread to begin commit processing. This thread writes all the modified disk blocks to the journal and then writes a special *end-of-transaction record* to make it clear that the entire transaction is in the journal. It then starts checkpointing by linking together the cached copies of the modified blocks in the dirty-block list of the buffer cache, so they'll be eventually written to the file system. Each of these blocks refers back to the transaction it was involved in, so once they all have been written to the file system, the journal space their copies were occupying can be freed.

What if the contents of a block involved in the previous transaction are modified by the current one before it is written to the journal as part of committing the previous transaction? If there is only one cached copy of the block, we have a problem: what is to be written to the journal should be the contents of that block as it was at the end of the previous transaction, yet we also want to modify it to contain the block's new value. To get around this dilemma, Ext3 makes a copy of the block for use by the *journald* thread to write to the journal. The original cached copy can then be modified as part of the current transaction.

The journal contains a sequence of disk-block copies along with their location in the file system. When the system reboots after a crash, recovery involves simply finding all committed transactions (that is, ones with commit records at their ends) and copying their modified disk blocks from the journal to the indicated positions in the file system. If the system crashes in the middle of recovery, no harm is done: copying a disk block to the file system is *idempotent*, meaning that doing it twice has the same effect as doing it once. When the system reboots the second and perhaps subsequent times, the blocks of the committed transactions are simply copied to the file system again.

By journaling both metadata and user data, we're assured that after crash recovery the state of the file system is what it was at the end of the last committed transaction. But journaling user data could cause a significant slow-down, since everything is written to disk twice. So, what happens if only metadata is journaled?

Suppose we've just created a new file and have written a few million bytes of data to it. The transaction containing the new metadata for this file has committed, but the system crashes before any of the file's data has been written to the file system. After the system comes back up, the file's metadata is recovered from the journal. This metadata correctly refers to the disk blocks that should be holding the file's data, but the data never made it to disk. Thus what we find instead are the previous contents of these disk blocks, what they contained before they were last freed. They might well contain sensitive information from someone else's file — information we are not supposed to be able to read.

Unless your goal is to be an information thief, this is not good. We've got to make sure that the old contents of these disk blocks are not visible when the blocks are reused. Some extremely secure systems write zeros to disk blocks when they are freed to make certain there is no information leakage. Since this would slow down the file system further, we'd like to avoid it. Instead, let's simply make certain that the new data is written to the disk blocks before the metadata is committed. So, in Ext3, all the cached copies of newly allocated data blocks related to the current transaction are written to disk by the *journald* thread before it writes the metadata to the journal. Thus if the system crashes as in the scenario described above, after crash recovery the data blocks referred to by the recovered metadata will contain their intended new contents, not their prior contents.

We've solved one problem, but have we created others? We're trying to get the effect of journaling user data without the expense of writing it to the journal — we're simply writing it to the file system. However, suppose the system crashes after we've written the user data to the file system, but before the metadata has been committed in the journal. Since the transaction didn't commit, none of the metadata changes appear in the file system after crash recovery. However, the changes to user data, having been applied directly to the file system, do appear.

So, suppose just before the crash we deleted file A and then created file B and wrote some data to it. As it turns out, the data blocks that were freed when we deleted A were allocated to hold the new data for B. Unfortunately, the system crashed before the transaction containing the operations on A and B could be committed. So, after crash recovery, A still exists and B was never created. However, the data we wrote to B did make it to disk — it resides in the disk blocks that are now still part of file A. For those interested in information thievery, this is further good news.

To avoid this problem, Ext3 allocates new blocks from only those blocks that were free in the most recent committed version of the free vector. Thus a block that has been freed in the current, uncommitted transaction is not a candidate for reallocation until the transaction commits.

But there's another problem, shown in Figures 6.29 through 6.32. Suppose we create a file X in directory A. We then delete X as well as the entire directory A. These operations end up in the same transaction, which is committed but not yet checkpointed.[6] We now create a new file Y and write to it. The data block allocated to hold the data used to be a metadata block[7] containing the entry for file X in directory A — it was freed when A was deleted. The transaction containing this operation on file Y is committed and thus the new contents of Y were written to the file system beforehand. Furthermore, checkpointing of this transaction completes before that of the first transaction and thus Y appears on disk in the file system.

---

[6] Remember that at most one copy of a cached block is in the journal. Thus when a transaction involves multiple operations on the same block, only the final contents of the block appear in the journal.

[7] Note that the contents of directories are metadata, despite residing in data blocks. Thus changes to directories are journaled even though the data blocks of non-directory files are not.

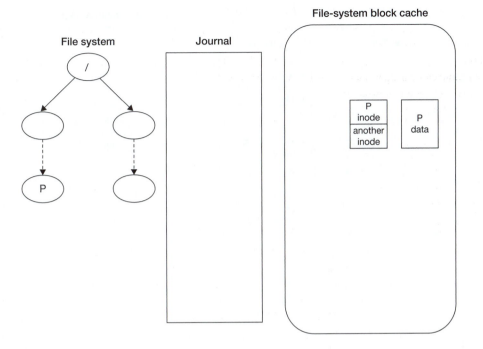

FIGURE 6.29   The need for revoke records in Ext3, part 1. Directory P is empty and we're about to create a subdirectory within it.

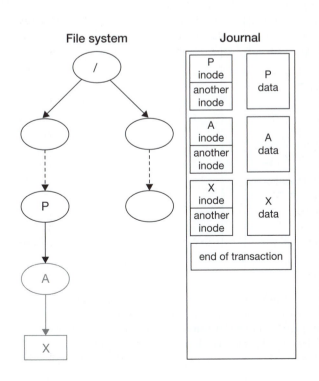
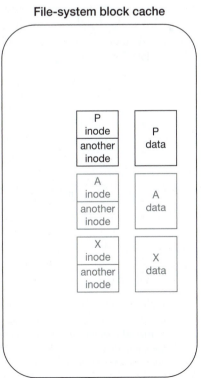

FIGURE 6.30   The need for revoke records in Ext3, part 2. Directory A was created and file X created in it, then both were deleted. These operations become part of the same transaction, which is committed but not checkpointed. However, since it was committed, the blocks occupied by A and X are added to the free vector and available for use.

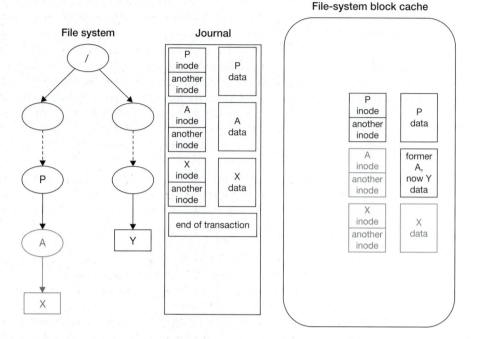

FIGURE 6.31 The need for revoke records in Ext3, part 3. File Y is created and written to. Its data block is the one that formerly held the contents of directory A.

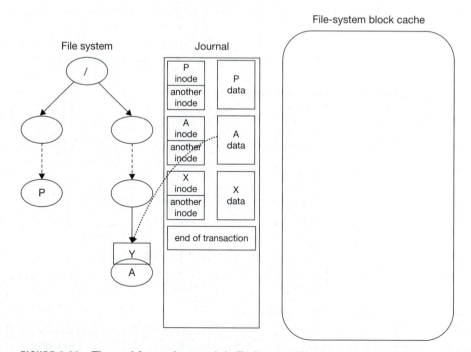

FIGURE 6.32 The need for revoke records in Ext3, part 4. The system has crashed and come back up. The contents of the journal are applied to the file system. In particular, the journaled contents of the block that originally contained the entries of directory A are copied back into their original location, which now is the first data block of Y. Thus Y's previous contents are destroyed.

Now the system crashes. Since checkpointing of the first transaction wasn't completed before the crash, the journal still contains its components and in particular the metadata block from directory A (with the entry for X deleted). Even though this block is subsequently deleted, when the journal is played back as part of crash recovery, the journaled contents of this block are written to the file system, overwriting the data that was written into file Y. Thus when the system returns to normal operation, everything appears fine except that file Y has in it, not the data that was written to it, but what used to be the metadata block from the old directory A.

So a problem again arises from our attempt to avoid journaling user data. If we were journaling user data, this problem clearly wouldn't happen: the journal would contain the new data written to Y, which would be copied to the file system during crash recovery after the old metadata is written there.

We can attack this from a different angle: the problem occurs because we've modified and then deleted a metadata block. Since the metadata block is being deleted, there's no real point to keeping the earlier entry containing the modified block in the journal. However, rather than actually deleting this entry, Ext3 writes a special *revoke* record to the journal indicating that the earlier metadata update should be ignored during crash recovery.

It's a bit disconcerting, though, to assert that something is correct merely because we've dealt with all the problems we can think of. Short of a formal proof, let's try to be a bit more convincing that Ext3's metadata-only journaling actually works. What do we mean by "works" in this case? We certainly want the file system's metadata to be in a consistent state after a crash. This would be guaranteed if all writes to disk were done as part of transactions, but, of course, writes to user data are not. If any particular disk block were always used for user data or always used for metadata, it would be clear that the consistency of metadata is protected by the transactions, but we know that one block might be used for metadata at one moment and for user data an instant later. However, if all blocks being used as metadata within a transaction are modified only via the journal during the transaction, we're assured that if the system crashes before the transaction commits, then the blocks will revert to their pre-transaction contents. But if a block is used and modified both as user data and metadata within the same transaction, then some changes to it are applied directly to the on-disk file system, while others are applied via the journal. By allocating new blocks from only those free at the end of the previous transaction, we make certain that no block is used both as user data and metadata in the same transaction.

What can we say about the state of user data after crash recovery? Since it's not journaled, we can't say it's consistent. However, we would like to say that the contents of any user-data block are relatively recent and were written there by the application program. In other words, we'd like to say that no opportunities for information thievery exist. Thus user-data blocks are initialized before they are linked into a file, and once a disk block is allocated to hold user data, the only writes to it are those containing data provided by the application program. By writing the contents of newly allocated user blocks to disk before the current transaction is committed, we guarantee their proper initialization. The revoke records guarantee that nothing in the journal will overwrite a user-data block during crash recovery.

How does journaling compare with soft updates? (Seltzer, Ganger, et al. 2000) reports that neither is a clear winner over the other.

6.2.2.3 Shadow-Paged File Systems

Shadow-paged file systems are a cross between consistency-preserving and journaled file systems: at all times the on-disk file system is consistent, yet operations are performed in a transactional fashion. Such systems, also called *copy-on-write file systems*, are simpler to explain (and implement!) than the metadata-only journaling used in systems such as Ext3. We examine the approach used in both Network Appliance's WAFL (Write-Anywhere File Layout) and Sun's ZFS (Zettabyte File System — so called because it can handle storage of size greater than 10^{21}

bytes, or a *zettabyte*). An additional feature of shadow paging is that it makes possible convenient "snapshots" of the past contents of a file system.

To accomplish all this, all in-use blocks of the file system are organized as one large tree — the *shadow-page tree*. The root of this tree (called the *überblock* in ZFS and *fsinfo* in WAFL) refers to the inode of the file containing all the inodes (see Section 6.1.5), which in turn refers to all the inodes currently in use, each of which refers, perhaps via indirect blocks, to the contents of all the files — see Figure 6.33. When a node of the tree (a disk block) is to be modified, a copy is made and the copy is modified — the original stays as it was (Figure 6.34). To link the modified copy into the tree, the parent node must be modified so as to point to it. But rather than directly modify the parent, it too is copied and the copy is modified. To link it into the tree, its parent must be modified; this copy-on-write approach continues all the way up to the root (Figure 6.35).

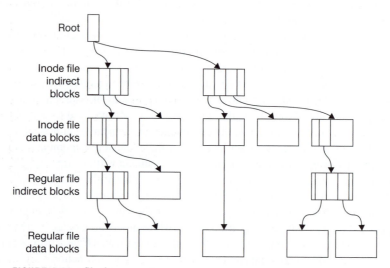

FIGURE 6.33 Shadow-page tree.

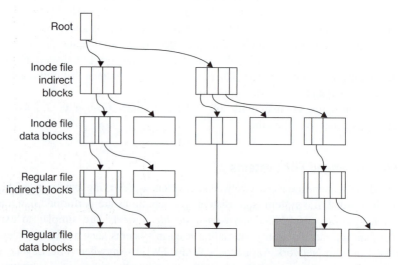

FIGURE 6.34 A leaf node in a shadow-page tree is modified, step 1.

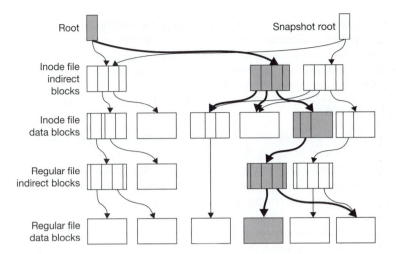

FIGURE 6.35 A leaf node in a shadow-page tree is modified, step 2. Copies are made of the leaf node and its ancestors all the way up to the root. A copy of the old root is maintained, pointing to a snapshot of the old version of the file system.

The root itself is at a known location on disk and is modified directly, in a single disk write. Thus, note two things:

1. If the system crashes after any non-root nodes have been modified but before the root is modified, then when the system comes back up the root refers to the unmodified file-system tree. No changes take effect on disk until the überblock is modified. Thus we have a transaction — the modified copies of the nodes are the shadow pages.

2. A copy of the unmodified root refers to the file-system tree as it was before the modifications took place. Thus we have a snapshot of the earlier state of the file system. Such snapshots can be kept around to let us recover inadvertently deleted files and can also provide a consistent copy of the file system for backup to a tape drive.

Note also that the transactions don't require extra disk writes, as the journaling approach does. As mentioned in Section 6.2.2 above, (Brown, Kolling, et al. 1985) argued that though fewer disk writes are required, those that were necessary were expensive because they are not to contiguous locations. But file-system technology has improved greatly since 1985. In particular, log-structured file systems have shown that we can simply group a bunch of seemingly unrelated file pages together and write them as a sequence of contiguous blocks. This and other techniques are used in both WAFL and ZFS to provide good performance, as we discuss in Sections 6.6.5 and 6.6.6 below.

Naming in file systems is pretty straightforward: files are named by their path names in a basically tree-structured naming hierarchy. We could certainly think of other naming techniques — for example, names could be completely unstructured with no notion of directories — but the organizing power of directories has proven itself over the past few decades and seems here to stay.

We note briefly that file systems are not database systems. File systems organize files for easy browsing and retrieval based on *names*. They do not provide the sophisticated search facilities of database systems. The emphasis in file systems is much more on efficient management of individual files than on information management in general. Thus, by database standards, the organization of file systems only on the basis of file names is pretty simplistic. But implementing such naming well is extremely important to the operating system.

The implementation of a file-system name space has all the requirements of the rest of the file system: it must be fast, miserly with space, crash tolerant, and easy to use. The key components are directories and various means for piecing different name spaces together — that is, the notion of

6.3
DIRECTORIES
AND NAMING

connecting one directory hierarchy to another, such as the mounting that takes place in Unix. File-system naming can be extended into other domains and applications. Unix extends such naming to devices and processes (see Section 6.3.2.2). And, as we explain below (Section 6.3.2.1), NTFS's notion of *reparse points* allows naming to be extended to non-file-system applications.

6.3.1 DIRECTORIES

We begin with directories. Their role is clearly pretty important. Every time we open a file, we must follow its pathname through a sequence of directories, looking up successive components in each. Creating a file involves verifying all but the last component of the pathname, then inserting this last component into the last directory. Deleting entails the lookup work of opening a file, then removing the last component from the last directory. Listing the contents of a directory is another common operation.

As we did with file systems in general, let's start with a simple design intended for small systems: S5FS's directories. We've seen them already, in Section 6.1.1. All entries had the same fixed length and were added sequentially in the order in which they were created. Directories were searched sequentially — this wasn't a performance problem, since most directories were rather small. Listing the contents of a directory was straightforward: you simply read through the directory sequentially, enumerating its contents and sorting them if required.

Deleting directory entries was a bit of a problem if it was subsequently necessary to compact the now smaller directories and free unneeded space. Deleting one directory entry was easy: the slot was simply marked free and made available for the next entry to be added. But suppose you create a directory and insert two disk blocks' worth of entries into it. You then delete half the entries in the first block and half the entries in the second block. To give that space back to the file system, it would be necessary to copy the active entries from one of the blocks into the free space of the other. Doing this so as to be immune from any problems resulting from an untimely system crash was considered too difficult back then. The easy way to avoid problems from crashes was to avoid doing anything complicated. Thus no directory space was given back to the file system unless the entire directory was deleted. Since the space for deleted entries was reused when new entries were added, this simple approach normally worked fine.[8]

The first version of FFS, in 4.2BSD Unix, made one major change to the simple S5FS directory format: variable-length entries were used to support component names much longer than the fourteen-character maximum of S5FS (see Figure 6.36). Everything else was the same: directories were searched sequentially. Since entries were now of variable length, they were added using a first-fit approach; a new block was appended to the end if more space was needed. Directories were still not compacted after entries were deleted, and space was not released to the file system unless the entire directory was removed. To help further with crash tolerance, though directory entries were of variable length and successive entries were in successive locations, no entry was allowed to cross a 512-byte block boundary. This ensured that a directory could be modified with exactly one 512-byte (one-sector) disk write.

Despite or perhaps because of this simplicity, directory operations turned out to be a major bottleneck in 4.2BSD Unix. The operating-system kernel was spending a remarkable 25% of its time dealing with path names (Leffler, McKusick, et al. 1989). This performance issue was mitigated in the next release, 4.3BSD, through caching: recent component-name-to-inode

---

[8] FFS is certainly not the only fi le system whose directories have this problem. For example, storage for directory entries in the operating system used by NASA on its Mars Rovers is also not freed when entries are deleted. This property almost caused the demise of NASA's Spirit Rover (traversing Mars) in January, 2004. Its fi le system ran out of space due to deleted but unfreed directory entries. Fortunately, NASA was able to send it instructions to free the space. (From http://www.wired.com/news/space/0,2697,64752,00.html?tw=wn_tophead_3)

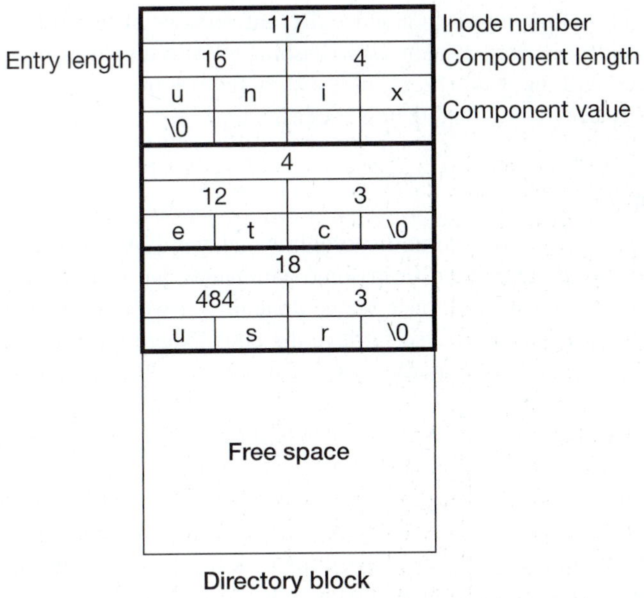

FIGURE 6.36 A 512-byte directory block in FFS. Each entry contains the inode number, the length of the path-name component (not counting the null character at the end), and the length of the entire entry. The latter was always a multiple of four bytes. If it was longer than necessary for the given component, then it was the last entry in the block and the extra space was free space.

translations were stored in a cache that was consulted before the directory itself was searched. This reduced the kernel time spent on path names to 10% — better but still fairly high.

The directory-related performance issues of BSD Unix make it clear that directory implementation plays a crucial role not just in file-system performance, but in overall system performance. Linear-searched, unordered directories simply aren't sufficient for any but the smallest systems. The directory in which I maintain the material for this book contains a few tens of entries — linear directories are fine. However, my department's mail server has over two thousand entries in the directory for everyone's incoming email. Every time a new message arrives for me, the mail-handling program would have to perform a linear search to find my mailbox if this directory were unordered. The comparable directory for a large Internet service provider (ISP) would be considerably larger. Adding an entry to linear directories requires linear ($O(n)$) time as well, meaning that the time required to create all the entries is quadratic ($O(n^2)$) — a search must be done to ensure each entry doesn't already exist as well as to find space for it. Similarly, deleting all the entries in a directory requires quadratic time.

To deal with these problems, we can continue with the strategy taken in 4.3BSD Unix and employ even better caching. We can also adopt strategies developed in the database world for providing efficient indexing for large databases by using better on-disk data structures. Both approaches typically employ more efficient search techniques and are based on either hashing or some variant of B trees (usually B+ trees, explained in Section 6.3.1.2 below).

The use of caches to improve directory performance has the advantage that no changes are required to on-disk data structures. Thus we can continue to use the current disk contents unmodified — which makes moving to a system with enhanced directory performance much more attractive. Furthermore, a cache-based system doesn't need to be crash-tolerant; the cache is simply recreated each time the system starts up.

But a cache-based system won't show any performance improvement the first time each directory is accessed after a reboot. In fact, some approaches might show considerably worse performance with the first access to a directory if the entire directory must be fetched so as to construct the cache. Furthermore, if we use a disk-based approach in conjunction with journaling or shadow paging, we'll get crash tolerance for free (after suitable integration). Thus we have a tradeoff between cache-based and disk-based approaches.

Almost all approaches appear in practice. Recent versions of FFS use an approach called *dirhash*, which is a cache-based system using hashing. WAFL also uses caching and hashing. ZFS uses disk-based hashing, while NTFS uses disk-based B+ trees.

Below we discuss first hashing, then B+ trees.

6.3.1.1 Hashing

We have a number of disk blocks at our disposal in which we'd like to create directory entries. So, given a name (say a component from some pathname), we want to determine in which block to create an entry for it. And, once we've done this, if we're given the name again, we need to find this block again so we can retrieve the entry. There might of course be multiple entries in a block. For now we'll perform a linear search within a block to find the entry we're after.

How do we determine which block to use? In hashing we use a *hash function* that computes an index from the name. Thus if h is our hash function and *comp* is the name, $h(comp)$ is the index identifying the block containing the entry for that name. In standard hashing terminology, all names that have the same image under h, i.e., are hashed to the same value, are called *hash synonyms*. The things indexed by these values, the disk blocks in our example, are known as *buckets* — all hash synonyms are thrown into the same bucket.

Choosing the right hash function is pretty important. We won't go into how this is done, but let's assume our hash function does what it's supposed to do — the hashes of the names are uniformly distributed across the buckets.

If we have a static environment in which nothing is added to or deleted from our directories, then hashing clearly allows us to search directories in constant time: a fixed amount of time to hash a name and identify the block the corresponding entry should be in, then a linear search of a fixed-size directory block. But how do we handle adding and deleting items? If we add an item and there's room for it in the appropriate bucket, it's easy — we simply put the item in that bucket. But what if the bucket (that is, directory block) is full? We could use an approach called chaining in which we create a new block and link it to the first. But if we continue with this approach we will have chains of unbounded length and our search times will be linear again. So what we really want to do is to increase the number of buckets and modify our hash function so that it hashes names to the new set of buckets.

One approach for doing this is *extensible hashing*. It uses a sequence of hash functions $h_0, h_1, h_2, \ldots$, where h_i hashes names into 2^i buckets, and for any name *comp*, the low-order i bits of $h_i(comp)$ are the same in $h_{i+1}(comp)$. Thus if $h_2("Adam")$ is 1, $h_3("Adam")$ is either 1 (001 in binary) or 5 (101 in binary). Suppose at the moment we have four buckets and are thus using hash function h_2 (see Figure 6.37). We now add the name *Fritz*, which should go into bucket 2, but doesn't fit. To accommodate *Fritz* (and future additions), let's double the number of buckets. This requires a new hash function, h_3, which hashes into eight buckets. Then we take bucket 2 and rehash all the names that were in it. Assuming these names are reasonably well distributed, roughly half will stay in bucket 2 under h_3 and half will go into bucket 6. Since the other buckets haven't overflowed, we won't rehash and redistribute their contents until they do.

Now we have a problem: though we've switched from hash function h_2 to h_3, we've gone from four buckets to only five, rather than the eight required by h_3. We add a level of indirection to accommodate this — an array of *indirect buckets*. (This array of indirect buckets is usually called a *directory* in the hashing and database literature, but that name is too confusing to use in our context.) The value produced by the hash function is used to index into this array; each entry in the array points to the appropriate bucket. If another bucket overflows, we simply create a new bucket, rehash the contents of the old using h_3, and update the appropriate indirect buckets as shown in Figure 6.38.

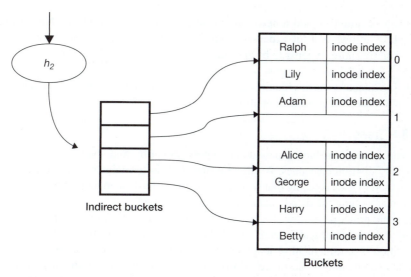

FIGURE 6.37   Extensible hashing example, part 1. Here we have four buckets and hence are using h_2, which actually computes indexes into the array of indirect buckets, which, in turn, lead to the appropriate bucket. Each of our buckets holds two items. We are about to add an entry for *Fritz*. However, h_2(*Fritz*) is 2 and the bucket that leads to it is already full.

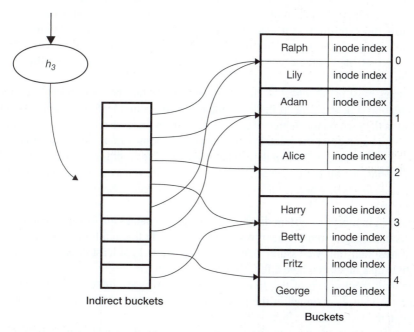

FIGURE 6.38   Extensible hashing example, part 2. Here we've added an entry for *Fritz* to the directory of Figure 6.37. Since the bucket *Fritz* was to go in under h_2 was full, we've switched to h_3, which maps names into eight buckets. However, rather than double the number of buckets and rehash the contents of all the old buckets, we take advantage of the array of indirect buckets. We double their number, but, initially, the new ones point to the same buckets as the old ones do: indirect buckets 0 and 4 point to bucket 0, indirect buckets 1 and 5 point to bucket 1, and so forth. For *Fritz*'s sake we add a new (direct) bucket which we label 4. We rehash *Fritz* and the prior contents of bucket 2 under h_3, with the result that *Fritz* and *George* end up in the bucket referred to by indirect bucket 6, while *Alice* stays in the bucket referred to by indirect bucket 2. Thus, we set indirect bucket 6 to refer to the new bucket 4. If, for example, we add another name that would go into bucket 0, we'd have to add another bucket to hold it and rehash the current contents of bucket 0.

The time required to add a new entry is now constant except when a bucket overflows. Coping with overflows is a bit expensive, but doesn't happen very often. Directory searches are made slightly more expensive by the addition of looking up hash values in the indirect buckets.

Deleting directory entries requires us to determine whether it's possible to combine buckets and thus save space. We leave the details of this to Exercise 15.

6.3.1.2 B+ Trees

Hashing works well if the hash function does a good job of hashing the actual names being used into uniformly distributed values. A different approach is to maintain some form of balanced search tree, thereby guaranteeing that searches can always be done in logarithmic time. The down side is that maintaining the data structure is a bit complicated.

The basic principle of how B+ trees work is fairly simple. Names are in the leaves of the tree and are in lexicographical order. Each level of the tree partitions the names into ranges; each level's partition is a refinement of its predecessor. Thus a search takes us from the root, which partitions the names into broad ranges, down to a leaf, which leads us to a narrow range or an individual name.

At each node the ranges are defined by a number of *separator names*. If the node has p ranges, then p-1 names are used to divide them. For each of the p ranges there is a link either to the root of a subtree that further divides the range or to a leaf. For example, if the node divides the space into three ranges r_1, r_2, and r_3, then all names in range r_1 are less than all names in r_2, which are less than all names in r_3. If the name we are after falls within range r_2, we follow the r_2 pointer. If it leads to the root of a subtree, then we compare our name with the subtree's separators and follow the pointer from the selected range. Otherwise if it points to a leaf, if the name we're after is present, it's in that leaf (see the example of Figure 6.39).

B+ trees must be *balanced* — that is, the distance from the root node of the tree to any particular leaf must be the same as that from the root to any other leaf. Another important aspect of B+ trees is the limit on the degree of each node. If the names we are searching for are of fixed length, then we can require that each B+ tree must be of some *order*, say p, such that each of its nodes must have between $p/2$ and p descendants, inclusive, except for the root node, which may have fewer. Thus, for all but the smallest trees, if there are n leaves, the number of tree levels is between $ceil(log_p(n))$, where $ceil(m)$ is the smallest integer greater than or equal to m, and $2+ceil(log_p(n))$.

However, in most file-system directory applications, names are of variable length. We thus modify this node-degree requirement to say that each node fits in a block and each such block must be at least half full. We assume that each block can hold at least three entries (in practice, an 8-kilobyte disk block can hold a few hundred typical entries).

One final requirement of B+ trees is that their leaves are linked together. Thus one can enumerate the values contained in the leaves in lexicographic order simply by starting at the leftmost leaf and following the links to the others.

When B+ trees are used in file-system directories, their leaves usually don't contain individual directory entries, but are disk blocks containing some number of directory entries, all in lexicographic order. Thus the parent B+-tree node of each leaf specifies the range of names found in that leaf. When doing a search, we descend the tree to a leaf, and then search the leaf sequentially.

As with hashing, the hard part is insertion and deletion. We sketch how do to them here, and then work out the details in the exercises. If we insert a new name and there's room in the appropriate directory block, then things are easy. *Igor*, for example, is easily added to the

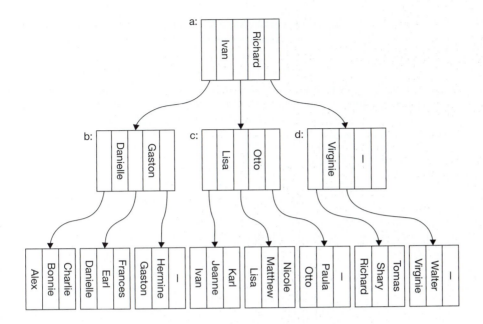

FIGURE 6.39 A B+ tree representing a directory. To simplify the figure, all entries occupy the same amount of space.

example of Figure 6.39. But if there's no room, we need to add a new directory block and fit this block into the search tree.

Adding a directory block requires a bit of work. Suppose we add the name *Lucy*. Since the directory block it should go into does not have enough free space to hold it, we create a new block and move everything greater than *Lucy*, namely *Matthew* and *Nicole*, from the old block to the new one, and put *Lucy* in the old one. We now have two blocks where we used to have one. If the parent node, *c*, of the just-copied block had room for it, we could simply modify *c*'s ranges to refer to the new block as well as the old one and we'd be done — we wouldn't have increased the length of any search path, so the tree would still be balanced.

However, in our case, this parent-node *c* has no room. So we split it into two nodes, *c* and *c′*, and add a range for the new node to the appropriate parent — *c′* in this case. We again have two nodes where we used to have one. So we must go to the parent of *c* and *c′* to accommodate *c′*. As before, if this parent has room, we're done, otherwise we have to split it and continue on.

If we reach the root and have to split it, we create a new root node with two ranges, each referring to one of the halves of the former root. We've thus increased the number of levels in the tree by one, yet maintained its balance. In our example, we have to split node *a* into nodes *a* and *a′*, and thus create a new root, *r* — see Figure 6.40.

When deleting an entry, we must make certain we maintain the invariant that all nodes are at least half full. Let's suppose we remove *Paula* and *Otto* in Figure 6.40. This causes the directory block containing them to become empty. We could simply leave the empty block in the directory — this is what S5FS and FFS do, after all. But it's certainly cleaner and more space efficient to remove it, so let's do so (though note that many systems don't bother rebalancing after a deletion, but simply delete the storage when a block is completely free).

We free the block and remove its range from the parent node that points to it, *c′*. If this node were more than half full, we'd be done. In our case it's not, so we examine the parent's adjacent siblings (there must be at least one — just node *d* in our case). Can we combine the contents of nodes *c′* and *d* to form a single node? If we can't, we would move just enough entries from *d* to *c′* so that it is at least half full (since each node must have room for at least three entries, this is always possible), adjust the ranges in the grandparent (a'), and we'd be done. If we can combine the two nodes, as we can here, we do so, free one of them, and remove its entry in the grandparent (a').

We now check this grandparent node to make sure it still is at least half full. If not, we repeat the above procedure on it and one of its adjacent siblings, working our way up towards the root as necessary. If we reduce the number of children of the root to one, we can eliminate the root and make its child the new root, thereby reducing the number of tree levels by one. The result for our example is shown in Figure 6.41.

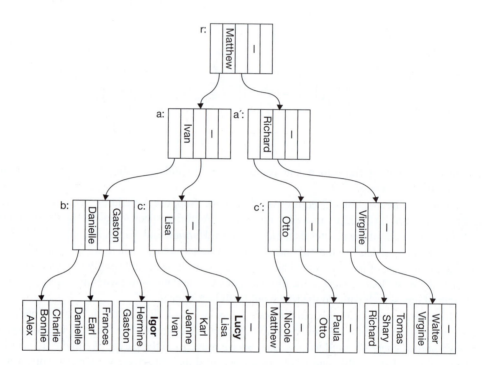

FIGURE 6.40 The result of adding entries for *Igor* and *Lucy* to the example of Figure 6.39.

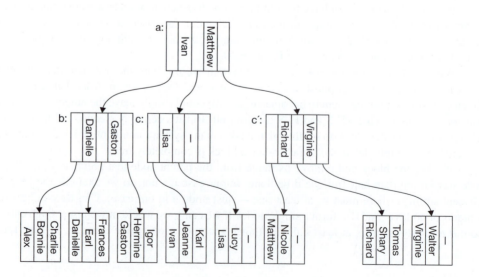

FIGURE 6.41 The directory after removing *Paula* and *Otto*.

6.3.2 NAME-SPACE MANAGEMENT

Let's now focus on the name spaces formed by directories. We have two concerns. One is that we have a number of such name spaces, one for each file-system instance. How do we distinguish them? How might we unify them? Another is whether we can take advantage of file-system name spaces to name things other than files.

6.3.2.1 Multiple Name Spaces

Microsoft systems use a simple approach to managing multiple name spaces: distinguish the name spaces by the "drive" their file system resides on. Thus *A:\x\y* is a file on drive A, while *B:\x\y* is a different file on drive B. A drive might be a region of a disk drive or perhaps all of a CD-RW or diskette, etc.

Alternatively, we might piece together the various directory hierarchies into a single unified hierarchy, as is done in Unix (and, recently, in Windows). We can superimpose the root directory of one file-system instance onto a directory of another, a procedure known as *mounting*. The original contents of the mounted-on directory become invisible; any attempt to access that directory accesses instead the directory mounted on it. Thus a path starting at the root of the mounted-on file-system instance can cross seamlessly into the file-system instance that was mounted upon it. For example, if, in Figure 6.42, the root directory of file system 2 is superimposed (mounted) on the directory */a/c* in file system 1, then we can refer to file system 2's */x/z* as */a/c/x/z* with the path starting in file-system 1.

This notion of mounting is used on Unix systems to tie all the file-system instances into a single unified name space. The file-system instance containing what is to be the root of this name space is called the *root file system*. If the file-system instance containing users' home directories is in file-system instance Z, it might be mounted on the root file system's */home* directory. So, for example, if my home directory is contained in Z at */twd* and I have a file in it called *memo.txt*, I could find it at */home/twd/memo.txt* in the unified hierarchy.

Both Unix (and hence Linux) and Windows support mounting, but they use different strategies for implementing it. In the Unix strategy one issues *mount* requests that tie the root of the file-system instance being mounted to the mounted-on directory. Any attempt to access the mounted-on directory gets the mounted root instead. This is accomplished within the operating system by linking together the cached copies of the file-system instance's inodes, without any changes to the on-disk copies of these inodes.

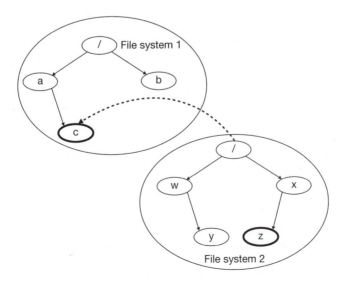

FIGURE 6.42 Mounting file system 2 on file system 1's directory */a/c*.

In a generalization of this approach, called *stackable file systems*, access to the mounted-on directory invokes other code layered on top of it. This has been used to implement "union mounts" in which the roots of multiple file-system instances are mounted on the same directory, so that one sees the union of their name spaces. Another application is the *portal* — access to the mounted-on directory results in, for example, the invocation of code to access some remote service. Portals were implemented in Free BSD Unix, but don't appear to be widely used.

Mounting is implemented in Windows via a mechanism called *reparse points* that, like stackable file systems, supports a number of other applications (unlike stackable file systems, these other applications are actually used). Marking a file or directory as a reparse point indicates that it requires special treatment. For example, if we want it to be a mount point, then its contents should be ignored and another directory, whose name is supplied as *reparse data*, should be used instead.

A file or directory marked as a reparse point contains, in addition to reparse data, a *reparse tag* indicating which subsystem is responsible for interpreting it. When such a file or directory is encountered when the system is following a path, an error is returned to the system code. The system code then examines the reparse tag and then directs further processing to the appropriate subsystem, which uses the reparse data. Applications include standard notions such as hard and symbolic links (known as *junctions* in Windows) as well as more novel ideas such as support for hierarchical storage management (HSM). This latter allows one to mark a file, via a reparse point, as having been moved to offline storage. An attempt to access the file is translated into a request to HSM to fetch the file from the offline store.

6.3.2.2 Naming Beyond the File System

Among the many important ideas popularized, if not introduced, by Unix is the notion of naming things other than files via the directory hierarchy. Earliest Unix used the file system to name devices. For example, */dev/disk1* might refer to a disk device, not the files within it. */dev/mt* might refer to a magnetic tape unit, and so forth. The */dev* directory is where, by convention, devices appeared in the name space. In principle they could appear in any directory. An entry in the name space referring to a device was called a *special file*.[9]

There were two important uses for this idea. The first was that it provided a simple means for referring to a device as a whole. For example, if you want to mount the file-system instance contained in */dev/disk1* on the directory */mnt*, you can do it simply with the following command:

```
mount /dev/disk1 /mnt
```

The other use was to simplify using devices. If, for example, you want to write to the tape drive, you could simply open */dev/mt* as if it were a file, then write to it via the file descriptor. Of course, within the kernel, the *write* system call code would have to call the tape driver rather than the file system. An inode for */dev/mt* would be stored on disk, but rather than representing a file, it would indicate which driver to use to access the tape drive and which tape drive to access.[10]

More recent versions of Unix have expanded the use of the file-system name space to refer to processes as well. A special file system, *procfs*, can be mounted whose files represent processes. This is particularly handy for debuggers, which can "open" a process, read and write its address space, and control its execution (Killian 1984). This idea of using the file system to name pretty much everything was further elaborated in *Plan 9*,[11] an operating system designed by the original developers of Unix after they grew tired of Unix (Pike, Presotto, et al. 1995).

---

[9] Unix distinguishes between block-special and character-special files. The former are accessed via the buffer cache, the latter are not. Disk and tape devices are typically named with two special files, one block-special, the other character-special.

[10] Similar functionality could certainly be obtained with reparse points, though this notion of special files predated reparse points by around 30 years.

[11] Plan 9 is actually short for "Plan 9 from Bell Labs," a name derived from that of the classic B movie "Plan 9 from Outer Space."

Another trend has been to extend naming outside of the file system. On the one hand, this makes names transient, since, if they aren't in the file system, they won't survive crashes. On the other hand, they can be recreated each time the system reboots. Such naming was used with great success in SpringOS, a research operating system developed at Sun Microsystems Laboratories (Radia et al. 1993).

This approach was also adopted in Windows NT, where it's used to refer to objects maintained by the operating system, including those representing I/O devices. For example, *Device\ CdRom0* refers to a CD-ROM device. However, unlike Unix's special files, this name is employed internally and cannot currently be used by applications. An application instead would refer to drive D, which is mapped by the kernel to *\??\CdRom0*. The *\??* directory contains names used in the older DOS operating system and provided backwards compatibility in Windows.

Names are also used outside of the file system by Windows to support its *registry*, which is a simple database providing names and values useful for configuring and maintaining state information for system and user applications. Though it's outside the file system, both the registry and its naming hierarchy are maintained on disk. For details, see (Russinovich and Solomon 2005).

What are the benefits of more than one disk drive?

6.4
MULTIPLE
DISKS

1. You have more disk storage than you would with just one disk drive.

2. You can store data redundantly, so if one drive has a problem, you can find the data on another.

3. You can spread data across multiple disk drives; then, taking advantage of parallel transfers to and from the drives, you can access the data much faster than if it were on a single drive (this assumes there is sufficient I/O bandwidth).

The first point may seem so obvious as to be flippant, but putting it into practice is not straightforward. With two disks, we could have two separate file-system instances, one on each disk. However, this does us no good if we want to handle a really large file, one that is too big to fit on one disk. Or we might want to have within a single directory files whose total size is larger than can fit on one disk.

Thus it's often useful to have one file system spanning two or more disks. However, the disk addresses used within a file system are usually assumed to refer to one particular disk or subdisk; i.e., the disk or subdisk forms an address space. There is no means of directly referring to disk blocks on another disk or subdisk.

One way to get around this problem is to provide an interface that makes a number of disks appear as one. The software that does this is often called a *logical volume manager* (LVM). It provides this sort of functionality by presenting to the file system a large address space, but mapping the first half of the addresses to one disk and the second half to another.

A logical volume manager can also easily provide redundancy: with two disk drives, each holding a separate, identical copy of the file system, writes can go to the LVM and the LVM can direct them to the same block address on each disk. Reads can go to either disk; a reasonable LVM would direct them to the less busy one. This technique is known as *mirroring*.

Parallel access can be provided by putting our file system on multiple disk drives in yet another way, using a technique known as *striping*. Let's say we have four disk drives, each on a separate controller. When we write to disk, we arrange to write four sectors at a time: the first goes to the first disk, the second to the second disk, and so forth. Of course, we'll also read the file four sectors at a time. We get a clear fourfold speedup over a file system on just a single disk drive. The reason for the term "striping" becomes apparent if we depict our file as a matrix that's four sectors wide. Each column of sectors resides on a separate disk; each row represents logically contiguous sectors. If we think of each of the rows as being colored differently, then we have stripes (see Figure 6.43).

	Disk 1	Disk 2	Disk 3	Disk 4
Stripe 1	Unit 1	Unit 2	Unit 3	Unit 4
Stripe 2	Unit 5	Unit 6	Unit 7	Unit 8
Stripe 3	Unit 9	Unit 10	Unit 11	Unit 12
Stripe 4	Unit 13	Unit 14	Unit 15	Unit 16
Stripe 5	Unit 17	Unit 18	Unit 19	Unit 20

FIGURE 6.43　Disk striping: each stripe is written across all disks at once. The size of a "unit" may be anywhere from a bit to multiple tracks. If it's less than a sector in size, then multiple stripes are transferred at once, so that the amount of data per transfer per disk is an integer multiple of a sector.

Striping requires some careful design to be really effective. Let's first discuss the terminology. The two factors normally specified are the *stripe length*, which is the number of disks to which data is written, and the *striping unit*, which is the "maximum amount of logically contiguous data that is stored on a single disk" (Chen and Patterson 1990). This latter term requires some explanation. It's not necessarily the amount of data written to one disk at a time, but is rather an indication of how data is spread across the disks. It can be as small as one bit, in which case we have what is known as "bit interleaving": the first bit of a file goes to the first bit of the first block of the first disk, the second bit of the file goes to the first bit of the first block of the second disk, and so forth until we have one bit on each disk. Then the next bit of the file goes to the second bit of the first block of the first disk, the bit after that goes to the second bit of the first block of the second disk, and so forth — the bits are distributed in round-robin style across all the disks.

If the striping unit is a byte, we have byte interleaving: the bytes of a file are spread out in round-robin style across the disks. Similarly, we might have sector as well as block interleaving. We can think of the stripe unit as the width of the stripe (as opposed to the length, which is the number of disks), so that with bit interleaving the stripes are one bit wide and with block interleaving they are one block wide.

For a given request size and a fixed number of disks, low striping unit values allow us to spread each request across all the disks. This achieves high parallelism for the request, even with a relatively small amount of data to transfer to or from each disk. With large striping unit values, many requests might be for data that resides completely on one disk; thus the data is transferred without the benefits of parallelism.

It might seem that maximal parallelism is the way to go, but suppose we have a number of requests for data at uniformly distributed locations waiting to be served. With a small striping unit, the transfer time for each request is kept small due to the parallel transfer from the multiple disks. However, the positioning delays are not reduced:[12] for each request, all disks must first seek to the proper cylinder, then wait for the desired sector to come by. Thus for each request we

---

[12] In fact, rotational delays could be worse: another striping issue is whether or not the disks rotate synchronously, so that the first sector on all disks rotates under each disk's heads at the same time. This is important if we're concerned about the time to write to or read from all disks in parallel. If they are rotating synchronously, then the effective average rotational delay for all disks is what we expect for a single disk — half the maximum delay. But if they're not rotating synchronously, the effective average rotational delay — the time we must wait for the appropriate sector to rotate underneath the disk heads on all disks — is much closer to the maximum delay.

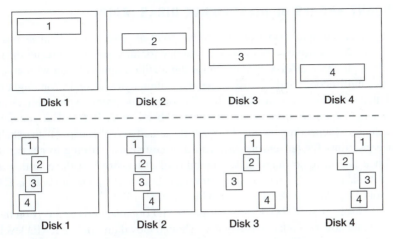

FIGURE 6.44 The top half of the figure shows four disks with a four-sector striping unit. Suppose we have requests for the four data areas shown, each four sectors in length. The four requests can be handled in roughly the time it takes to handle one, since the positioning for each of the requests can be done simultaneously, as can the data transfer. The bottom half of the figure shows four disks with a one-sector striping unit. We have the same four requests, but in this case each is spread across all four disks, one sector per disk. Handling the requests requires first positioning the heads on all four disks for the first, then positioning the heads on all four disks for the second, and so forth. Thus the total positioning delays are four times those in the top half of the figure, which has a larger striping unit.

have to wait a long time for positioning, then wait a brief time for the parallel transfer of the data. The total time to handle all the requests is the sum of all the positioning delays — a large number — plus the transfer delay — a small number.

We might be better off with a large striping unit that causes each request to be handled completely on a separate disk. Thus multiple requests could be handled at once, each on a separate disk, with the total positioning delays being reduced by a factor equal to the number of disks. Though individual transfers would not benefit from parallel access, the total amount of data being transferred would be much increased — the positioning for the multiple requests is done in parallel, as are the data transfers. Thus the total time spent transferring data using a large striping unit would be the same as with a small striping unit, but the positioning time would be dramatically reduced. See the example in Figure 6.44.

The number of requests waiting to be handled is known in the striping literature (Chen and Patterson 1990) as the *concurrency factor*. The larger the concurrency factor, the less important striping is: performance is better with a large striping unit than with a small one.[13]

Thus striping gives us what is in effect a disk with much faster data transfers than ordinary ones, but with no improvement in seek and rotational delays. This "effective disk" is also more prone to failure than the usual sort.[14]

---

[13] Note that this line of reasoning assumes that the requests are to uniformly distributed locations on the disks. If there is locality of reference, the argument is not as strong.

[14] Assuming disk failures are independent and identically distributed (not necessarily a valid assumption), if the probability of one disk's failing is f, then the probability of an n-disk system failing is $(1 - (1 - f)^n)$.

6.4.1 REDUNDANT ARRAYS OF INEXPENSIVE DISKS (RAID)

Let's look at the use of multiple disks from a different point of view — cost. Unless you get an incredibly good deal, N disk drives cost more than just one for all values of N greater than 1. But what if you want to purchase a "disk system" to handle a zillion bytes of data with an average access time of two milliseconds and a transfer rate of 1 billion bytes/second? You might be able to find one disk that satisfies your constraints, but it's going to be pretty expensive (it's called a SLED — single large expensive disk — in (Patterson, Gibson, et al. 1988)). But you could put together a large number (depending on how big a zillion actually is) of cheap, off-the-shelf disks that meet your constraints for far less money. You'd of course use striping to get the desired transfer rate. Since you have so many disks, the odds of at least one of them failing are not insignificant, so it makes sense to have some extra ones. So, what we end up with is RAID: a redundant array of inexpensive disks (Patterson, Gibson, et al. 1988).[15]

(Patterson, Gibson, et al. 1988) defined various RAID organizations or *levels* on the basis of the striping unit and how redundancy is handled. Though they didn't define RAID level 0, the term now commonly refers to pure striping as discussed above — no redundant disks. What were defined in the paper are levels 1 through 5.

RAID level 1 (Figure 6.45) is disk mirroring, as discussed above. Two identical copies are kept of the file system, each on a separate disk. Each write request is applied to both copies; reads go to either one.

RAID level 2 (Figure 6.46) is striping using bit interleaving and some redundancy. Rather than an extra copy of each disk, an error-correcting code (ECC) is used. Such codes let us provide a few extra "check bits" along with each set of data bits. In the case of a single-error-correcting code, if any one bit is modified (due to noise, etc.), whether a data bit or a check bit, we can compute which bit it was and hence correct it. We won't go into any of the details; (Patterson, Gibson, et al. 1988) refers its readers to (Hamming 1950), which describes a code that uses four check bits per ten data bits to correct any single-bit error.

Suppose we have ten disks holding data. We would need an additional four disks to hold check bits so that all one-bit errors can be corrected. Since the striping unit is one bit, as we distribute each set of ten data bits on the ten data disks, we compute the check bits and distribute them across the four check disks. Consider any sector on any of the disks. Each bit in that sector is part of a different 10-data-bit-plus-4-check-bit stripe. If any number of them is modified due to a problem, we can determine which they were and repair them. Thus we can recover even if we lose an entire disk.

In discussing the performance of RAID disks, we need to distinguish between large writes, which have enough data to fill a block in each data disk, and small writes, which have just a block's worth of data. For large writes, performance is good. Since RAID level 2 has fewer check disks per data disk than RAID level 1, it makes more efficient use of space. However, performance for small writes is miserable: to write one block's worth of data, one must first read a block from each of the data disks, then bit-interleave the new data on these blocks, and then write them all out to the data disks along with the new check blocks to the check disks.

The use of sophisticated ECC in RAID level 2 is overkill, since most disk controllers already employ it at the sector level on disk drives. Thus a problem with a particular sector can be resolved by the disk controller. However, if there's a major problem with that sector, it's likely that the controller won't be able to repair the error, but merely identify the sector as bad. If we lose an entire disk drive, it should be pretty clear which one it was.

RAID level 3 (Figure 6.47) is an improvement on level 2 for the (usual) case in which the disk controller does sector-level detection of errors. If there's an error, we don't need to identify

---

[15] Common usage today is that the "I" in RAID stands for *independent*, perhaps because all disks are now inexpensive.

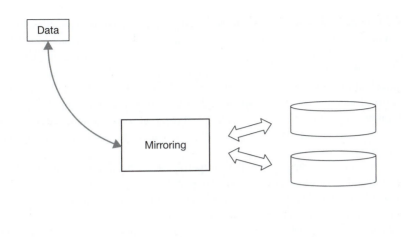

FIGURE 6.45 RAID level 1: disk mirroring.

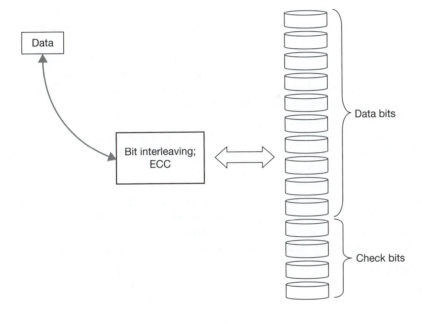

FIGURE 6.46 RAID level 2: bit interleaving with an error-correcting code.

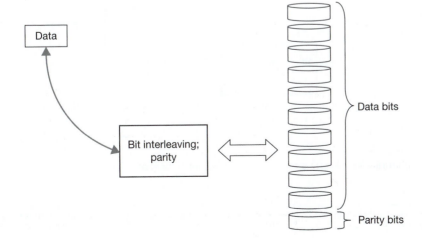

FIGURE 6.47 RAID level 3: bit interleaving with parity bits.

where it is, since that's done for us already, but we do need to repair it. Now, however, no matter how many data disks we have, we need only one check disk. For a system with 10 data disks and a striping unit of 1 bit, for each 10 bits distributed to the data disks, the check bit is the exclusive OR of the data bits. Thus if any of the bits are modified, recomputing the exclusive OR will show that there's a problem, though with only this information we won't know which bit was in error. But since we'll find out from the disk controller that a particular sector is suspect, we'll know which bits might be in error — those that reside in that sector. Since each of these bits resides in a separate 10 data-bit plus 1 check-bit stripe, we can restore it to its correct value as necessary.

Bit interleaving has some convenient properties if we need to compute check bits for an error-correcting code, but otherwise it's expensive, particularly if done in software. RAID level 4 (Figure 6.48) is just like level 3, except block interleaving rather than bit interleaving is used — the striping unit is increased to be equal to the block size.

RAID level 4 is not great at handling write requests of just one block. It's bad enough that modifying one block requires us to modify the corresponding block on the check disk as well,[16] but modifying any block on any of the data disks requires an update operation to modify a check block on the check disk. Thus the check disk becomes a bottleneck.

RAID level 5 (Figure 6.49) fixes this problem: rather than dedicating one disk to holding all the check blocks, all disks hold check blocks (and data) — the check blocks rotate through all the disks. As we go from one stripe to the next, the check block moves to a successive disk. Performance is thus good both for small writes and large writes, and there is no bottleneck disk for the small writes, as in RAID level 4.

It would seem that RAID level 5 is the ultimate, certainly more desirable than the other RAID levels. But there is at least one other concern: expansion. Suppose we decide to add another disk or two to a RAID level-5 system we've been using for a couple of years. Doing this would involve reorganizing the contents of all the disks so as to extend the check-block pattern to the new disk. Adding a disk to a RAID level-4 system involves simply recomputing the contents of the check disk to take into account the new data disk, a much easier job.

The one advantage of RAID level 5 over RAID level 4 is its performance for small writes. But, as we've seen, relatively recent file systems such as WAFL and ZFS really don't have small

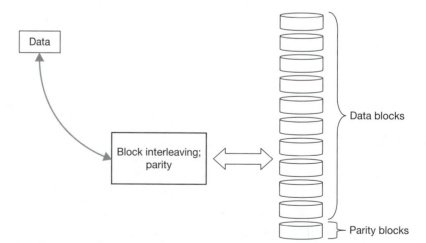

FIGURE 6.48 RAID level 4: block interleaving with parity blocks.

---

[16] You might think that we have to read all the other data blocks in the striping row in order to recompute the check block, but this is not necessary — see Exercise 17.

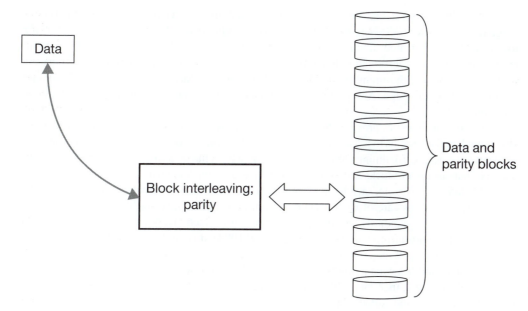

FIGURE 6.49 RAID level 5: block interleaving with parity blocks. Rather than dedicating one disk to hold all the parity blocks, the parity blocks are distributed among all the disks. For stripe 1, the parity block might be on disk 1; for stripe 2 it would be on disk 2, and so forth. If we have eleven disks, then for stripe 11 the parity block would be back on disk 1.

writes. Updates are collected until a large number can be written out, and thus most writes contain a number of stripes. However, other recent file systems, in particular journaled systems such as Ext3 and NTFS, must still make relatively small updates as part of checkpointing. For them, RAID level 5 makes the most sense.

Since the seminal paper on RAID (Patterson, Gibson, et al. 1988) the hierarchy has been extended. RAID level 6 is similar to RAID level 5, except that it provides additional parity blocks allowing it to handle two failures. *Cascaded RAID* combines two RAID architectures into one. RAID 1+0 (sometimes called RAID level 10) does striping across mirrored drives. RAID 0+1 has two striped sets, one mirroring the other.

Up to this point we've assumed that file systems reside on disks — an assumption that has been valid for around 50 years. Flash memory is a relatively new technology providing the functionality needed to hold file systems: it is both writable and readable, and it retains its contents even when power is shut off. Though more expensive than disk technology, it is cheaper than DRAM technology (on which primary storage is built). It provides generally faster access to data than disks do, although it is slower than DRAM, and unlike disks, it provides uniform random access to data. However, writing takes significantly more time than reading, and there is a limit to how often each location can be written to. In this section we explore how flash memory is used both to supplant and augment disk devices for support of file systems.

**6.5
FLASH
MEMORY**

6.5.1 FLASH TECHNOLOGY

There are two sorts of flash devices, *nor* and *nand* — the names referring to how the individual cells are organized. The earlier was *nor*, which is byte-addressable and thus can be used to hold code such as BIOS for direct execution. The more recent is *nand*, which is page-addressable and less expensive. Thus *nand* flash is used in conjunction with file systems; we focus our attention on it. (Wikipedia 2009) provides a general and concise discussion of flash technology.

Nand flash devices are organized into blocks that are subdivided into pages. Block sizes range from 16k bytes to 512k bytes, with page sizes ranging from 512 bytes to 4k bytes. Writing to a block is complicated, involving *erasing* and *programming*. *Erasing* a block sets it to all ones. One can then *program* an individual page by changing some of its ones to zeros. One can perform multiple programming operations on a page, but the only way to change zeros to ones is to erase the entire page. Any particular block can be erased no more than around a hundred thousand times.

These characteristics provide challenges to implementing a file system on flash. The propensity of modern file systems to reuse blocks exacerbates the problem of blocks "wearing out" because of too many erasures. To minimize the effects of wear, a flash file system must avoid reusing blocks and distribute its use of blocks across the entire device, a notion known as *wear-leveling*.

A relatively easy approach to an effective flash file system is to create a layer on top of the flash device that takes care of wear leveling and provides a disk-like (or block) interface. Then one simply places a standard disk file system on top of it. Such layers were formalized in 1994 and are called the *flash translation layer* (FTL) (Intel 1998). It is implemented in firmware within a device controller and maps virtual disk blocks to real device blocks. In broad outline, when the file system modifies what it thinks is a disk block, FTL allocates a new device block, copies the modified block into it, then maps the disk block into the new device block. The old device block is eventually erased and added to a list of available blocks.

The reality is a bit more complicated, primarily because the file systems FTL was designed to support were Microsoft's FAT-16 and FAT-32, which are similar to S5FS, particularly in supporting a single and rather small block size. Thus FTL maps multiple virtual disk blocks to a single device block.

6.5.2 FLASH-AWARE FILE SYSTEMS

Using an existing file system on a flash device is convenient, but the file system was presumably designed to overcome problems with accessing and modifying data on disk devices, which are of no relevance to flash devices. We can make better use of the technology by designing a file system specifically for flash memory. Flash devices that do not have built-in controllers providing FTL or similar functionality are known as *memory technology devices* (MTD).

File systems, regardless of the underlying hardware, must manage space. This certainly entails differentiating free and allocated space, but also entails facilitating some sort of organization. For disks, this organization is for supporting locality — blocks of files must be close to one another to allow quick access. But file systems for flash devices must organize space to support wear-leveling; locality is not relevant.

File systems also must provide some sort of support for atomic transactions so as to prevent damage from crashes. What must be done in this regard for file systems on flash memory is no different than for file systems on disk.

Consider a log-structured file system. Files are updated not by rewriting a block already in the file, but by appending the update to the end of the log. With such an approach, wear-leveling comes almost free. All that we have to worry about is maintaining an index and dealing with blocks that have been made partially obsolete by subsequent updates. Transaction support also comes almost free — the log acts as a journal.

The JFFS and JFFS2 file systems (Woodhouse 2001) use exactly this approach. They keep an index in primary storage that must be reconstructed from the log each time the system is mounted. Then a garbage collector copies data out of blocks made partially obsolete and into new blocks that go to the end of the log, thereby freeing the old blocks.

UBI/UBIFS started out as JFFS3, but diverged so greatly that it was given a new name. (The design documentation of UBIFS is a bit difficult to follow; (Bityuckiy 2005) describes an early version when it was still known as JFFS3 and helps explain what finally went into UBIFS.) UBI (for *unsorted block images*) is similar to FTL in that it transparently handles wear-leveling (Linux–MTD 2009). However, UBI makes no attempt to provide a block interface suitable for FAT-16 and FAT-32; its virtual blocks are the same size as physical blocks. Layered on top of it is UBIFS (the *UBI file system*), which is aware that it is layered on UBI and not on a disk. Any number of UBIFS instances can be layered on one instance of UBI (on a single flash device); all share the pool of blocks provided by UBI.

UBIFS (Hunter 2008) is log-structured, like JFFS, but its index is kept in flash, thereby allowing quicker mounts. Its index is maintained as a B+-tree and is similar to those used in shadow-paged file systems (Section 6.2.2.3), such as WAFL's. So that the index does not have to be updated after every write, a journal is kept of all updates since the index was last modified. Commits are done when the journal gets too large and at other well defined points (such as in response to explicit synch requests) — they cause the index tree to be updated, so that each modified interior node is moved to a new block.

6.5.3 AUGMENTING DISK STORAGE

Flash fits nicely in the storage hierarchy, being cheaper and slower than primary storage (DRAM) and faster and more expensive than disk storage. (Leventhal 2008) describes how it is used to augment disk-based file systems, in particular ZFS. One attractive use is as a large cache. Though the write latency to flash is rather high, the file system can attempt to predict which of its data is most likely to be requested and write it to flash, from where it can be quickly retrieved. (Leventhal 2008) reports that in an enterprise storage system, a single server can easily accommodate almost a terabyte of flash-based cache. This approach works so well that the disk part of the storage hierarchy can be implemented with less costly, lower-speed disks that consume far less power than high-performance disks.

Another use of flash is to hold the journal for ZFS, thus keeping uncommitted updates in nonvolatile storage. In the past this has been done with battery-backed-up DRAM, but flash provides a cheaper alternative. To get around its poor write latency, it can be combined with a small amount of DRAM to hold updates just long enough for them to be transferred to flash. This DRAM requires some protection from loss of power, but only for the time it takes to update the flash. (Leventhal 2008) suggests that a "supercapacitor" is all that is required.

Here we summarize and fill in some of the details about the file systems mentioned earlier in this chapter. Our intent is to give a balanced presentation of all of them and to point out important features that aren't covered above. This section may be skipped by those interested only in file-system concepts and not in further details of existing systems.

**6.6
CASE STUDIES**

6.6.1 FFS

FFS, the Fast File System originally developed at the University of California, Berkeley (McKusick, Joy, et al. 1984), has been the primary file system of BSD Unix starting with 4.2 and continuing with FreeBSD. Its design was the basis for Linux's Ext2 and Ext3. It's been supported in a number of commercial versions of Unix, including Sun's Solaris, and has come to be known as UFS, the Unix File System. A number of improvements have been made to it over the years and it's probably the best studied and best published file system in existence (for example, (Ousterhout, Da Costa, et al. 1985), (McVoy and Kleiman 1991), and (Smith and Seltzer 1996)).

As we discussed in Section 6.1.4, the design of FFS was a response to the problems of S5FS and features better organization of file data and metadata to minimize positioning delays,

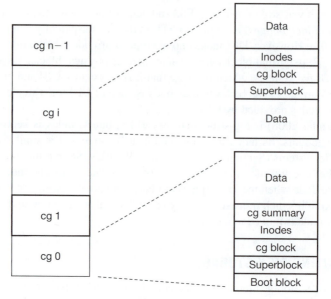

FIGURE 6.50 FFS layout.

as well as a larger block size to improve transfer speed. The key features discussed above include the use of cylinder groups to help localize file allocation, what was at the time a large block size made palatable through the use of fragments, and a file representation based on inodes allocated from a static array. Among the later improvements is the use of block clustering to improve data-transfer bandwidth.

Figure 6.50 shows the on-disk organization of FFS. Allocation information for each cylinder group, including free-fragment bitmaps, is maintained in a *cylinder-group block* (*cg block*) data structure. Though residing on disk, it's cached in memory when used. To facilitate finding space in cylinder groups, a *cylinder-group summary* (*cg summary*) structure is stored in cylinder group 0 and brought into kernel memory when the file system is in use. The cylinder-group summary contains the amount of space available in each cylinder group and thus can be scanned before going to find the space in the cylinder group itself.

Lastly, the *superblock* resides in cylinder 0 and contains all the file-system parameters such as size, number of cylinder groups, and so forth. Just in case a disk problem destroys the super-block, copies of it are maintained in each of the other cylinder groups, in a rotating track position (track 0 in cylinder group 0, track 1 in cylinder group 1, etc., wrapping around at the maximum track number of a cylinder).

FFS's approach to crash tolerance is careful ordering of updates to disk. Initially this was achieved with the aid of synchronous writes of key metadata. As explained in Section 6.2.2.1, more recent versions of FFS employ soft updates to accomplish the same thing without the need for synchronous writes.

6.6.2 EXT3

Ext3 is the third in a sequence of extended file systems for Linux, each moving farther away from the original Linux file system, Andrew Tanenbaum's Minix file system (Tanenbaum 1987). It's become the mainstream file system of Linux, though certainly not its only file system — others with either journaling or other support for crash tolerance include ReiserFS (see Section 6.6.3

below), XFS (Sweeney et al. 1996), originally developed at SGI, and Episode (Chutani, Anderson, et al. 1992), developed at Transarc (a company later acquired by IBM).

Ext2 is based on the original design of FFS. It was later updated to include clustering, as explained in Section 6.1.4.1 above. Other improvements, such as extent-based allocation, either have been made or are being discussed for it (see (Ts'o and Tweedie 2002)).

Ext3 is Ext2 with the addition of journaling (see the discussion of Ext3's journaling in Section 6.2.2.2). Since its on-disk format is essentially the same as Ext2's, one can switch from Ext2 to Ext3 (and back again) without having to convert what's on disk. This adds greatly to its appeal.

A recent addition to Ext3 is a new directory format that, imitating how Ext3 added journaling, is fairly compatible with the old format. This format replaces the sequentially searched directories of previous versions of Ext3 with one based on a combination of hashing and balanced search trees called *HTrees* (Phillips 2001). It's a search tree, though searching is based on the hashed values of component names rather than the actual names. Balancing is not done explicitly; instead, the hash function is relied on to keep things distributed. The leaves of the search tree are the original sequentially structured directory of Ext2. Since each tree node has a fanout in the hundreds, three levels of search tree (in addition to the leaf nodes) are far more than sufficient to handle any reasonably sized directory.

The search-tree nodes are encoded on disk as free space within Ext2 directory blocks. Thus an Ext2 or a non-upgraded Ext3 system will ignore the search tree during directory searches, though the tree might be badly damaged if new entries are added!

6.6.3 REISER FS

The Reiser file system, so called because it's the work of Hans Reiser and a few associates, was one of the more popular Linux file systems, probably second to the more conservative Ext3. It's radically different from Ext3, featuring a fair degree of extensibility as well as a unique structure. We discuss its version 4, which was to have replaced version 3 until development was halted after Reiser's 2008 murder conviction.

The entire file system is organized as a single balanced search tree, essentially a B+ tree, with exactly four levels (see Figure 6.51). It may seem like a tall order to make everything — directory entries as well as all file blocks —accessible via the same search tree, but this is accomplished using some magic in the search key. This key is 192 bits long and is structured depending on what is being searched for. When looking up a directory entry, the key consists of the object ID of the directory and the hashed name of the directory entry. When looking up a location within a file, the key consists of the file's object ID and the starting offset within that file.

The tree nodes are of fixed size, 4 kilobytes, and are made up of smaller units called *items*. For the top three tree levels — the interior nodes — items point to nodes at the next lower level and contain a *left delimiting key*, which is the smallest key of any item in the subtree rooted by the item.

Since Reiser FS uses a B+ tree, the leaves contain the data, both that of ordinary files and that of directories, as well as what in other file systems would be stored in inodes: file owner, permissions, link count, etc. The data of small files is divided into pieces called, strangely, *tails*, each of which is contained in an item; multiple such items are packed into a single 4-kilobyte leaf node. Larger files are divided into extents; the third tree level, known as twigs, may contain extent pointers, which contain both a pointer to a node and a length — the number of 4-kilobyte (leaf) nodes in the extent.

With fixed-height trees, balancing is not an issue. Instead, the concern is wasted space within the tree nodes. For example, three adjacent nodes, each one-third full, can be combined into a single node, freeing up the other two. Checking on every operation to see if such combining is possible is expensive. Reiser FS does such combining only when nodes are actually written to disk or when there is a severe shortage of space — an approach called *dancing trees*.

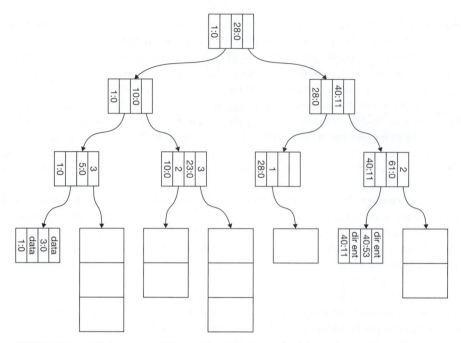

FIGURE 6.51 A Reiser4 tree. To keep things simple, each of the nodes contains at most two items. The leftmost leaf contains data starting at location 0 for each of two small files: one with object ID 1 and the other with object ID 3. Its sibling leaf is referred to by the parent via an *extent pointer*, and is three blocks long. The next three leaves to the right are also extents. The next leaf contains two directory entries, both of the directory whose object ID is 40. One entry's hashed component name is 11, the other's is 53. The rightmost leaf is a two-block extent.

Crash tolerance is achieved using a combination of journaling and shadow paging called *wandering logs*. The concern is that, when updating a file-system block, shadow paging avoids the cost of writing both to the log and to the original location at the expense of moving the block to a new location whose position might harm read performance. Reiser FS uses heuristics to determine which policy makes sense for each update. As part of committing a transaction, both shadow-paged and journaled blocks are written to contiguous locations, as in log-structured file systems. The journaled blocks are linked together, along with the address of their original positions, to form the journal (hence the term "wandering log"). The journal is in turn linked to the file system's superblock. In a crash, each member of the list of journaled blocks is written to its original location upon recovery.

Reiser FS uses *plugins* to achieve extensibility. Every item in the tree has a plugin ID identifying the module that provides its semantics. Plugin modules are provided to define the semantics for standard files, directories, and hash functions, but alternative versions are easily added.

One important aspect of extensibility is Reiser FS's support for *attributes*, a form of metadata. Unlike much metadata we've discussed before, however, attributes are used not for the system's layout of data, but to provide information about data. Attributes are used for the sort of information about a file, such as owner, protection information, and so forth, that often resides in inodes. With the use of plugins, arbitrary additional attributes can be added, along with restrictions implied by the attributes. For example, additional security attributes may be defined; who is allowed to use a file, and under what circumstances, can be governed by these attributes.

6.6.4 **NTFS**

NTFS is the standard file system on Microsoft's larger operating systems. WinFS is a database system that's layered on top of NTFS. Though in many cases users are dealing directly with WinFS, it is still NTFS that manages everything on disk. We discuss NTFS and leave WinFS for database textbooks.

We've already discussed much of the technology used in NTFS. Files are represented using extents. Directories are built on B+ trees. NTFS uses the term *file record* rather than inode and, as discussed in Section 6.1.5, maintains its array of one-kilobyte file records — what it calls the *master file table* (MFT) — in what is essentially a file. It provides four options for using multiple disks (see Section 6.4):[17]

- spanned volumes, in which regions from two different disks are combined to form what appears to be one single region

- RAID level 0 (striping)

- RAID level 1 (mirroring)

- RAID level 5

It provides crash tolerance using journaling, though unlike Ext3's redo journaling (Section 6.2.2.2), it employs a combination of both redo and undo journaling. Thus what are written to the journal are both the old contents and new contents of modified disk blocks.

Why do things this way? The idea behind redo journaling is that all steps of a transaction are written to the journal before the file system is itself modified. Though straightforward, this means that all file-system changes must remain in the cache and not go to disk until the transaction commits. This could be a problem if the operating system needs some of the cache's memory for other purposes. With undo journaling, a cached change may be written to disk and removed from the cache after it has been written to the journal but before all the transaction commits, thus allowing some cache memory to be freed, if necessary. (Why bother with redo journaling at all? Why not employ strictly undo journaling? See Exercise 11.)

Let's look again at the master file table (Figure 6.20). Each non-free entry describes a file in terms of a set of attributes. Some of these attributes are important special cases: a name attribute and a data attribute contain a file's name relative to its parent directory and its contents, respectively. There's also an attribute containing some of the usual attributes of a file, such as access and creation times and link count, and called, fittingly, *standard information*. Directories contain attributes comprising their B+ trees. The reparse information described in Section 6.3.2.1 is contained in another attribute. Files may be given a unique object ID, contained in yet another attribute.

If an attribute's value takes up little space, it's stored directly in the file-table entry. Otherwise the entry contains an extent table, referring to extents containing the attribute's value. This provides an efficient representation for small attributes, particularly for small data attributes. Thus a small file fits entirely within its file record (see Figure 6.52).

Indexing is a notion used in databases in which one finds data items by their attributes, much as one finds items in a book by looking them up in the index. Directories provide an index of files based on the last components of their name attributes. NTFS also maintains an index based on object ID in a special hidden file, implemented using a B+ tree, whose components are, of course, attributes. This is used by system components and applications that need a way to refer to files other than by names.

Multiple data streams allow one to associate data with a file in addition to the normal data. These are essentially a means for adding new attributes of arbitrary length to files. For example,

---

[17] This "volume aggregation" is actually done not by NTFS proper, but by a lower-level module on which NTFS is layered.

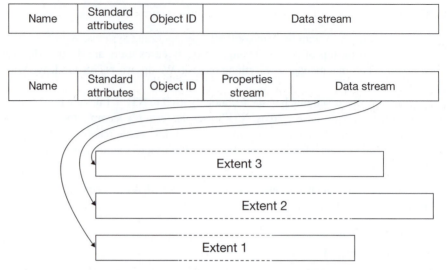

FIGURE 6.52   Two NTFS file records. The top one is for a small file fitting completely within the record. The bottom one is for a file containing two streams, one for some application-specific properties and one for normal data. The latter is too big to fit in the file record and is held in three extents.

many Windows applications support a notion of *properties* with which one can tag a file with a description of the file's contents. In NTFS, such properties are implemented as separate data streams (see Figure 6.52). The standard data stream containing the "normal" file data is unnamed and referred to implicitly simply by using the file name. The other streams are referred to by appending a colon and the stream's name to the file name. For example, the information associated with the file *MyStuff\book.doc* is referred to as *MyStuff\book.doc:information*.

One option for an NTFS file is for it to be compressed. Two techniques are employed for doing this. One is simply not to allocate space for long runs of zeros within files. Such runs are left out of the runlist of extents. Thus when the file system encounters a gap in the runlist, it assumes this missing extent contains all zeros.

The second technique is to use a compression algorithm[18] to compress the data in individual extents. Thus an extent that logically covers, for example, 16 kilobytes of data might be contained in 4 kilobytes of actual disk space. The compression and decompression are performed automatically by the file system.

6.6.5 WAFL

WAFL (for "Write-Anywhere File Layout"), from Network Appliance, runs as part of a special-purpose operating system on a special-purpose file-server computer, or *filer*, whose sole purpose is to handle file requests via such protocols as CIFS and NFS (see Chapter 9). For some details, see (Hitz, Lau, et al. 1994).[19]

WAFL is one of the first commercially available file systems to employ shadow paging and is perhaps the first file system to be structured as a tree with its data blocks as the leaves

---

[18] Microsoft's documentation does not reveal which compression algorithm is used.

[19] This article is somewhat out of date — our discussion is based partly on recent personal communication with George Cabrera of Network Appliance.

and most of its metadata as interior nodes, thus allowing periodic snapshots of the file system (see Section 6.2.2.3). It takes advantage of techniques pioneered by log-structured file systems (see Section 6.1.4.2): file updates are written to consecutive disk locations in batches, minimizing seek and rotational delays. This batching is further capitalized on to work well with RAID level 4, so as to provide the advantages of parallelism and redundancy shared with RAID level 5 while avoiding the latter's problems with adding new disks, and also avoiding the bottlenecks of typical RAID level-4 implementations (see Section 6.4.1).

How does all this work? Let's look at how the shadow-paging tree of Section 6.2.2.3 is implemented in WAFL. The root, rather than being called the überblock as in ZFS (Section 6.6.6), is given the rather unimaginative name *fsinfo*. Nevertheless, it contains the inode for what's called the inode file, containing inodes for all other files (see Section 6.1.5), including certain files that are actually metadata. Among the latter are files containing the free-space map.

As discussed in Section 6.2.2.3, all tree nodes (which are, of course, disk blocks) are treated in a copy-on-write fashion: when one is to be changed, a new copy is made and the copy is modified. Thus when a leaf node is modified, creating a copy entails modifying its parent's pointer to it, and hence the parent too is copied. This propagates all the way up to the root. Rather than actually writing all these changes to disk with each write to a file, the changes are collected into batches that are written out as *consistency points* at least every ten seconds. These changes are collected between disk writes in non-volatile RAM (NVRAM), which is battery-backed-up storage that retains its contents across power failures and other system crashes. Thus no file updates are lost, even if the system crashes. (This property is essential for WAFL to be a server for early versions of NFS, as discussed in Chapter 10.)

The disk space into which these batched changes are written is allocated so as to maximize speed. On a single-disk system, this would mean that contiguous blocks are allocated. WAFL, however, uses RAID 4 and thus the blocks are allocated in stripes across the disks; if multiple stripes are required, they occupy contiguous disk blocks on each of the disks. Since data is written not in single blocks at a time, but in multiples of stripes, the single parity disk of RAID 4 is not a bottleneck: it is written to roughly as often as the other disks (see Figure 6.53).

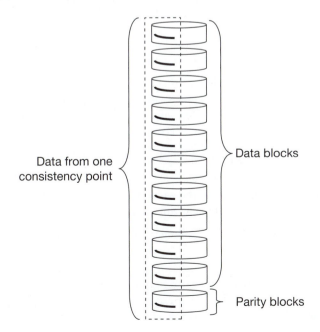

FIGURE 6.53 WAFL writes out changes in batches called consistency points. Each batch occupies some integral number of stripes — thus the parity disk is written to no more often than the data disks.

Normally the original copies of blocks modified at consistency points are freed, but the system administrator can arrange to retain a "snapshot" of the file system: the blocks being modified are not freed but kept, including the prior version of the modified fsinfo node — the root (see Figure 6.35). The administrator establishes a "snap schedule" indicating when such snapshots are made, perhaps hourly or nightly. Up to 255 may exist at any one time.

How is free space managed? Recall that with log-structured file systems (Section 6.1.4.2), free space was reclaimed as a background activity, as part of "log cleanup." Though WAFL is similar to log-structured file systems in the way it writes updates to contiguous locations, it doesn't require such a log-cleanup activity. Instead, since the free-space map is maintained in a number of files, these files are updated just like any other file: modifications are done in a copy-on-write fashion and written to disk as part of consistency points. Thus at each consistency point, the on-disk free-space map is updated.

With all the snapshots, how does WAFL determine what's free and what isn't? Each snapshot, including the most recent one reflecting the current status, has a bitmap indicating which blocks are in use. A summary bitmap, which is the logical OR of all the snapshot bitmaps, then indicates what's really free.

6.6.6 ZFS

ZFS (for "Zettabyte File System"), an open-source file system, was developed at Sun Microsystems for their Solaris operating system (Bonwick, Ahrens, et al. undated technical report: probably 2003) and has since been adopted by Apple for Mac OS X. It provides a robust approach to handling failures and providing good performance, along with much flexibility. Its name refers, indirectly, to the size of the addresses it uses, 128 bits.[20]

Its flexibility is made possible by its layered architecture, shown in Figure 6.54. At the top is the *ZFS POSIX Layer* (ZPL), which converts standard POSIX-style (Unix-style) operations into operations on *objects* within *datasets*, abstracting files and disks. The *Data Management Unit* (DMU) batches these operations into transactions and manages the metadata. Both ZPL and DMU operate in a large virtual address space and are oblivious to physical addresses. The *Storage Pool Allocator* (SPA) provides a malloc-like interface for allocating space (using slab allocation) and is responsible for mapping the virtual address space into actual disk addresses from any number of disks. In doing so, it may employ spanning, mirroring, or various forms of RAID, depending on the configuration.

ZFS is distinguished from the other file systems we have looked at by going well beyond them in the sorts of problems it can handle. In particular,

- Suppose there is a power failure while writing to a set of RAID disks. Perhaps a stripe consists of fifteen disks and writes to seven complete successfully, but writes to eight do not. When the system comes back up, there is not enough information available to recover either the new data that was not written or the old data that was overwritten.

- Suppose an obscure bug in the RAID firmware causes garbage to be written to disk (with correct parity!) on rare occasions.

- Perhaps a system administrator types the wrong command and accidentally scribbles on one disk, replacing data with garbage (again with correct parity).

- Suppose one's 1.6-TB file system is no longer large enough and must be made one terabyte larger.

---

[20] A zettabyte (10^{21} bytes) is actually far less than 2^{128} bytes (which is approximately 10^{36} bytes). It is, however, the smallest numerical prefix such that 64 bits aren't enough to address files of that size.

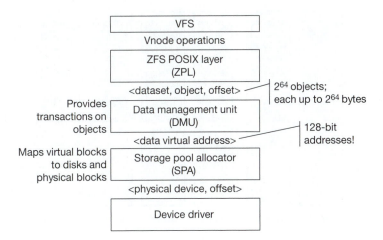

FIGURE 6.54 ZFS's layered architecture.

The DMU layer handles the first three of these problems by adding redundancy to its meta-data. As described in Section 6.2.2.3, the data management unit organizes all of its storage into a tree, headed by the überblock. This tree consists of a number of subtrees, each representing a separate logical file system. Creating a new file system is thus trivial — a new subtree is created and the file system uses the storage provided by the storage pool allocator, in common with all the other logical file systems of the pool. Snapshots may be taken of individual file systems, in a similar fashion as in WAFL.

Suppose, for example, a firmware problem causes the disk controller to write garbage data to a disk. Such errors are not covered by the parity provided with each sector by hardware, since the bad data we're concerned about here is, from the disk drive's point of view, good data that was written purposely. To cope with such errors, DMU maintains a checksum on the data in each block of its storage tree. For all but the überblock, the checksum is stored in the block's parent. Thus, if for some reason a block is inadvertently scribbled on, the checksum will detect the problem. If there is sufficient redundancy in the storage pool, the block can be automatically repaired.

If the only copy of a block is lost (perhaps because it was scribbled on), there is, of course, no way to recover it. This is bad, but it's even worse if the block contains metadata, particularly at the higher levels of the tree. ZFS protects against loss of metadata by allowing for three copies, known as *ditto blocks*, of each metadata block — each pointer to metadata is actually three addresses, one for each copy (see Figure 6.55).

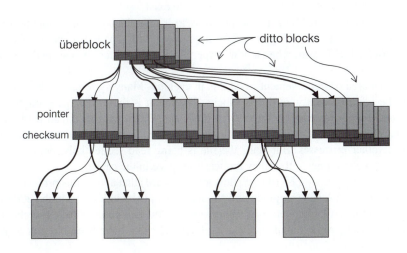

FIGURE 6.55
ZFS's shadow-page tree.

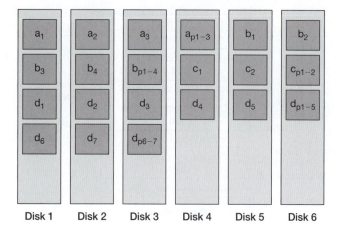

FIGURE 6.56
A RAID-Z layout.

Since all physical storage management is handled in the SPA layer, the DMU is completely independent of concerns such as mirroring and higher RAID levels. An administrator can add another physical disk drive to the set used by SPA, which can then start providing more storage to DMU. No reorganization is necessary at the DMU level, since the SPA level takes care of everything.

A RAID-4 and -5 shortcoming is the cost of small writes. Updates to data occupying a partial stripe on, say, two disks, requires first reading then writing parity information on a third disk. ZFS avoids this shortcoming by using a variant of RAID known as RAID-Z. Rather than use fixed-length stripes, each block forms a stripe, regardless of its length, and each has its own parity. Figure 6.56 shows an example where blocks *a*, *b*, *c*, and *d* on are striped on six disks. Block *a* consists of three sectors and is written to disks 1 through 3, followed by a parity sector written to disk 4. Similarly, block *b* consists of four sectors and is written, along with a parity sector, to the disks; block *c* consists of two sectors and is written with a parity sector. Block *d* consists of seven sectors but, so that there is enough parity to recover on the loss of a disk, has two parity sectors.

Thus small writes are handled efficiently — it's not necessary to read the parity sector before modifying it, since the block's parity depends only on the block itself. The down side is that, to determine the block boundaries (perhaps for recovery purposes), one must traverse the metadata (the shadow-page tree). But, with the use of ditto blocks (as described above), at least one copy of each block of metadata is highly likely to exist.

Another feature of RAID-Z is that it is easy to handle the addition of another disk drive. In Figure 6.57, the example of Figure 6.56 is augmented with a new disk. None of the existing stripes are affected. However, when a new stripe, block *e*, is written, it is striped over all seven drives.

The final area of improvement in ZFS is in caching. Many systems employ LRU caches: they hold the n least-recently-used disk blocks. The intent is that n is large enough so that the cache holds the blocks needed by the current processes. But suppose a thread reads an n-block file sequentially. It fills the cache with the blocks of the file, thereby removing the blocks that are useful to the other processes. But since the file is being read sequentially, none of the blocks are accessed a second time — thus they are wasting space in the cache.

The approach used by ZFS (though developed at IBM) that avoids this problem is *adaptive replacement caching* (ARC) (Megiddo and Modha 2003a) (Megiddo and Modha 2003b). To see how it works, let's first look at a non-adaptive version of it. Suppose we have a cache that holds up to n blocks. Let's reserve half its capacity for blocks that have been referenced just once,

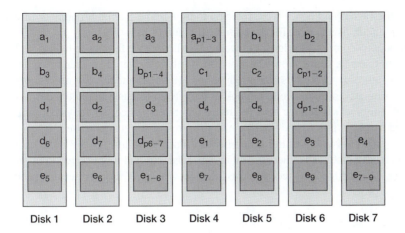

FIGURE 6.57 The RAID-Z layout augmented with a new disk and a new stripe.

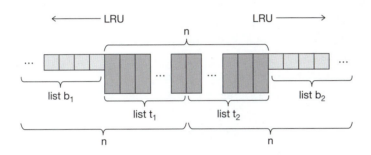

FIGURE 6.58 The adaptive replacement cache (ARC).

and the other half for blocks that have been referenced at least one more time since entering the cache. Both halves of the cache are organized in an LRU fashion. Thus in the example in the previous paragraph, a thread that reads a file sequentially can use no more than half the cache space, since the other half of the cache is reserved for blocks that have been referenced at least twice.

This might be an improvement over a strict LRU cache, but perhaps performance would be better if the cache weren't split in half, but apportioned in some other way. The idea behind ARC is that the portions of the cache used for the two sorts of blocks vary depending on use. If a number of processes are reusing the same set of n blocks and one process is reading a large file sequentially, we'd like to dedicate the entire cache to blocks that have been referenced more than once. On the other hand, if the system is starting up and a set of processes are making their initial references to file-system blocks, we would like to dedicate the entire cache to blocks that have been referenced just once, since none have yet been referenced more than once.

To do all this, ARC maintains, in addition to the n-block cache, two lists of block numbers, each in LRU order (see Figure 6.58). The first list, t_1, refers to blocks that have just entered the cache after being referenced. The second list, t_2, refers to blocks that were re-referenced while in t_1 (or again while in t_2). (Note that t here stands for top and b for bottom.) Thus the maximum total number of block numbers in both lists is n.

So as to determine how many blocks should be in each list, ARC keeps two additional lists of the block numbers of the most recent blocks evicted from the cache. One list, b_1, refers to blocks that have been evicted from the single-reference portion of the cache (and hence were referred to by t_1); the other list, b_2, refers to blocks that have been evicted from the multiple-reference portion of the cache (and hence were referred to by t_2). The maximum number of entries in the combined t_1 and b_1 lists is n, as for the combined t_2 and b_2 lists.

The adaptive part of the algorithm works as follows. A reference to a block in b_1 is taken to mean that more cache space should be available for blocks that have been referenced just once. So, the maximum size of list t_1 is increased by one[21] (up to n) and the size of t_2 is correspondingly decreased. Similarly, a reference to a block in b_2 is taken to mean that more cache space should be available for blocks that have been referenced more than once. So, the maximum size of list t_2 is increased by one (up to n) and the size of t_1 is correspondingly decreased.

A pseudocode version of the general algorithm is as follows. Note that a cache hit means that the referenced block is not necessarily in the cache, but that it is referred to in one of the four lists. LRU(x) refers to the least-recently-used element of list x; MRU(x) refers to the most-recently-used element of list x.

```
cache miss:
    if t₁ is full
        evict LRU(t₁) and make it MRU(b₁)
    referenced block becomes MRU(t₁)
cache hit:
    if in t₁ or t₂, block becomes MRU(t₂)
    otherwise
        if block is referred to by b₁
            increase t₁ space at expense of t₂
        otherwise
            increase t₂ space at expense of t₁
        if t₁ is full
            evict LRU(t₁) and make it MRU(b₁)
        if t₂ is full
            evict LRU(t₂) and make it MRU(b₂)
        insert block as MRU(t₂)
```

6.7 CONCLUSIONS

File systems provide persistent storage. For most computer systems, they provide all the persistent storage, except for that provided by specialized backup devices. Not only must they perform well, in terms of both time and space, but they must also be tolerant of both hardware and software failures.

We started this chapter by studying one of the simplest file systems, S5FS. It served to illustrate all the problems that later file systems have strived to overcome, yet provided an application interface that is almost identical to that provided by modern file systems. Modern systems employ a number of techniques to improve on S5FS. Much was achieved by reorganizing on-disk data structures to take into account disk architecture and to maximize speed of access and transfer. Further progress was made by taking advantage of techniques such as RAID to utilize multiple disks, improving both performance and tolerance of media failures.

While S5FS was notorious for losing data in the event of a crash, modern systems rarely suffer from such problems. Two approaches are used, consistency-preserving updates and transactional updates.

---

[21] The actual algorithm increases the size of the list by an amount proportional to relative sizes of t_2 and t_1.

Whether used on a personal computer or on a large server, a file system must be easy to administer and be sufficiently scalable to handle what are often growing demands. This has been made possible by techniques based on the dynamic-inode approach as well as support for ever larger files and disks.

File-system technology remains an active area of work, with much competition from both the open-source community and makers of proprietary systems.

---

1. Assume we are using the Rhinopias disk drive discussed in Section 6.1.2.1.

   a) What is the maximum transfer rate for a single track?

   b) What is the maximum transfer rate for accessing five tracks consecutively (assume head skewing)?

2. Explain why the typical transfer rate achieved on S5FS is far less than the maximum transfer rate of the disk.

3. How do block-based file systems differ from extent-based systems? What is block clustering?

*4. Assume we're using the Rhinopias disk drive.

   a) Suppose we are using S5FS and we've doubled the block size from 512 bytes to 1024 bytes. Is the maximum expected transfer rate roughly doubled? Explain.

   b) We've done the same with FFS. Is the maximum expected transfer rate roughly doubled? Explain. Assume that we're using two-way block interleaving: when we allocate successive blocks on a track, one block is skipped. Thus, in the best case, every other block of a track is allocated to a file.

   c) Why should we care about the block size in FFS?

5. Explain what is meant by innocuous inconsistency. How does it differ from non-innocuous or real inconsistency?

6. The layout of disk blocks is an important factor in file-system performance. FFS uses the technique of block interleaving to reduce rotational delays. This technique provides a large improvement over the use of consecutive blocks. However, many of today's most advanced file systems, such as WAFL and ZFS, do not use block interleaving.

   a) Explain how block interleaving helps FFS reduce the time required to read from disk.

   b) Explain how WAFL's design provides fast access without the need for block interleaving.

7. Would log-structured file systems (Section 6.1.4.2) have been feasible in the early 1980s when FFS was designed? Explain. (Consider the cost of the resources required.)

8. What approach did the original FFS use for crash tolerance? What impact did this have on performance? How has this been improved in recent versions?

**9. Section 6.2.2.1 covers soft updates and mentions that FFS using soft updates may require more disk writes than Async FFS. Give an example in which more disk writes would occur with soft updates than with Async FFS.

**10. One early application of shadow paging in a file system was in an FFS-like system. All operations between *open* and *close* of a file were treated as part of a single transaction. Thus if the system crashed before the file was closed, the effect was as if nothing had happened to the file since the *open*. This was done by making a copy of the file's inode when it was opened, and applying all changes to copies of blocks being modified (i.e., using copy-on-write techniques). When the file was closed, the reference to its inode in the directory it appeared in was replaced with a reference to the new, modified inode. Thus in a single disk write, all modifications took effect at once.

There are a few problems with this approach. It doesn't handle files that appear in multiple directories. It also doesn't handle concurrent access to the file by multiple processes. Let's ignore both of these problems (they're fixable, but we won't fix them here!). There's a performance problem: the original blocks of the file were allocated on disk so that the file could be accessed sequentially very quickly. But when we make copies of the disk blocks being modified, these copies aren't necessarily going to be near the original copies. Thus writing these blocks might incur long seek delays. For this reason shadow paging wasn't used in file systems until relatively recently. How might these problems be fixed?

**11. NTFS does a combination of both redo and undo journaling. Section 6.6.4 explains why it's useful to have undo journaling. Why is redo journaling also done?

12. NTFS has a feature called data streams. Describe this feature and give an example of how it might be useful.

**13. Explain how renaming a file can be done using the consistency-preserving approach so that a crash will not result in the loss of the file. Be sure to take into account the link count stored in the file's inode. Note that there may have to be a temporary inconsistency; if so, explain why it will not result in lost data.

*14. A defragmenter is often used with NTFS to improve its performance. Explain how a similar tool might be devised for S5FS to improve its performance. Would the use of this tool bring S5FS's performance up to acceptable levels?

15. Hashing is often used for looking up directories entries. Explain the advantages of extensible hashing over simple static hashing.

**16. Section 6.3.1.1 discussed extensible hashing. Show how deletions of directory entries can be implemented so that buckets are combined where possible, allowing the bucket and indirect bucket arrays to be reduced in size.

*17. RAID level 4, in handling a one-block write request, must write to both a data disk and the check disk. However, it need not read data blocks from the other data disks in order to recompute the check block. Explain why not.

*18. We have an operating system whose only file system is S5FS. Suppose we decide to employ a RAID level 4 or RAID level 5 disk system. Can S5FS take advantage of all the features of these systems? Explain. Assume that the block size of S5FS is equal to the disk-sector size.

19. Explain why Ext3 and NTFS use RAID level 5 rather than RAID level 4. Explain what features of WAFL make it particularly well suited for use with RAID level 4.

**20. An issue with ZFS is reclamation of data blocks. With multiple snapshots in use for each file system, it's not necessarily trivial to determine which blocks are actually free. For example, there might be, in addition to the current version of the file system, three snapshots of it. If we delete the snapshot that's neither the most recent nor the least recent, how can we determine which blocks must be deleted and which must remain? To answer this question, let's go through the following steps.

   a) Explain why reference counts are not part of the solution.

b) Suppose each block pointer, in addition to containing a checksum, also contains the time at which the block was created (note that blocks are never modified in place, thus the creation time for a particular file-system block on disk doesn't change). Explain how this information can be used to determine that a block was created after a particular snapshot.

c) Suppose a block is freed from the current file system (but might still be referenced by a snapshot). Explain how it can be determined whether the most recent snapshot is referring to it.

d) If such a block cannot be reclaimed because some snapshot is referring to it, a reference to it is appended to the file-system's *dead list*. When a new snapshot is created, its dead list is set to be that of the current file system, and the current file-system's dead list is set to empty. Let's assume no snapshots have ever been deleted. We say that a snapshot is *responsible for* the existence of a block if the block's birth time came after the creation of the previous snapshot and the block was freed before the birth time of the next snapshot (or of the file system if this is the most recent snapshot). In other words, the only reason the block cannot be reclaimed is because this snapshot exists. Are all such blocks in the next snapshot's dead list (or in the current file system's dead list if this is the most recent snapshot)? Explain.

e) Suppose a snapshot is deleted (the first one to be deleted). How can we determine which blocks to reclaim?

f) We'd like this algorithm to work for subsequent deletions of snapshots. Part d describes an invariant: all blocks for which a snapshot is responsible appear in the next snapshot's dead list (or in the dead list of the file system if it's the most recent snapshot). What else must be done when a snapshot is deleted so that this invariant is maintained (and the algorithm continues to work)?

6.9 REFERENCES

Bityuckiy, A. B. (2005). JFFS3 Design Issues. http://www.linux-mtd.infradead.org/doc/JFFS3design.pdf.

Bonwick, J., M. Ahrens, V. Henson, M. Maybee, M. Shellenbaum (undated technical report, probably 2003). *The Zettabyte File System*, Sun Microsystems.

Brown, M. R., K. N. Kolling, E. A. Taft (1985). The Alpine File System. *ACM Transactions on Computer Systems* **3**(4): 261–293.

Chen, P. M. and D. A. Patterson (1990). Maximizing Performance in a Striped Disk Array. *Proceedings of the 17th Annual Symposium on Computer Architecture*, ACM: 322–331.

Chutani, S., O. T. Anderson, M. L. Kazar, B. W. Leverett, W. A. Mason, R. N. Sidebotham (1992). The Episode File System. *Proceedings of the USENIX Winter 1992 Technical Conference*: 43–60.

Ganger, G. R., M. K. McKusick, C. A. N. Soules, Y. N. Patt (2000). Soft Updates: A Solution to the Metadata Update Problem in File Systems. *ACM Transactions on Computer Systems* **18**(2): 127–153.

Hamming, R. W. (1950). Error Detecting and Correcting Codes. *The Bell System Technical Journal* **29**(2): 147–160.

Hitz, D., J. Lau, M. Malcolm (1994). *File System Design for an NFS File Server Appliance*. Proceedings of USENIX Winter 1994 Technical Conference.

Hunter, A. (2008). A Brief Introduction to the Design of UBIFS. http://www.linux-mtd.infradead.org/doc/ubifs_whitepaper.pdf.

Intel (1998). Understanding the Flash Translation Layer (FTL) Specification. http://www.eetasia.com/ARTICLES/2002MAY/2002MAY07_MEM_AN.PDF

Killian, T. J. (1984). Processes as Files. *USENIX Conference Proceedings*. Salt Lake City, UT, USENIX Association: 203–207.

Leffler, S. J., M. K. McKusick, M. J. Karels, J. S. Quarterman (1989). *The Design and Implementation of the 4.3BSD UNIX Operating System*, Addison-Wesley.

Leventhal, A. (2008). Flash Storage Memory. *Communications of the ACM* **51**(7): 47–51.

Linux-MTD. (2009). UBI — Unsorted Block Images. http://www.linux-mtd.infradead.org/doc/ubi.html.

McKusick, M., W. N. Joy, S. J. Leffler, R. S. Fabry (1984). A Fast File System for UNIX. *ACM Transactions on Computer Systems* **2**(3): 181–197.

McVoy, L. W. and S. R. Kleiman (1991). Extent-like Performance from a UNIX File System. *Proceedings of the Winter 1991 USENIX Technical Conference.* Dallas, USENIX: 12.

Megiddo, N. and D. S. Modha (2003a). ARC: A Self-tuning, Low Overhead Replacement Cache. *Proceedings of FAST 2003: 2nd USENIX Conference on File and Storage Technologies.*

Megiddo, N. and D. S. Modha (2003b). One Up on LRU. *login* **28**(4): 7–11.

Ousterhout, J. K., H. Da Costa, D. Harrison, J. Kunze, M. Kupfer, J. Thompson (1985). A Trace-Driven Analysis of the UNIX 4.2 BSD File System. *Proceedings of the 10th Symposium on Operating Systems Principles*: 15–24.

Patterson, D. A., G. Gibson, R. H. Katz (1988). A Case for Redundant Arrays of Inexpensive Disks (RAID). *Proceedings of the 1980 ACM SIGMOD International Conference on Management of Data*: 109–116.

Phillips, D. (2001). A Directory Index for Ext2. *5th Annual Linux Showcase and Conference*, USENIX: 173–182.

Pike, R., D. Presotto, S. Dorward, B. Flandrena, K. Thompson, H. Trickey, P. Winterbottom (1995). Plan 9 from Bell Labs. *Computing Systems* **8**(3): 221–254.

Radia, S., M. N. Nelson, M. L. Powell (1993). The Spring Name Service. Sun Microsystems Laboratories Technical Report SMLI-93-16.

Rosenblum, M. and J. K. Ousterhout (1992). The Design and Implementation of a Log-Structured File System. *ACM Transactions on Computer Systems* **10**(1): 26–52.

Russinovich, M. E. and D. A. Solomon (2005). *Microsoft Windows Internals*, Microsoft Press.

Seltzer, M. I., G. R. Ganger, M. K. McKusick, K. A. Smith, C. A. N. Soules, C. A. Stein (2000). Journaling Versus Soft Updates: Asynchronous Meta-data Protection in File Systems. *Proceedings of the 2000 USENIX Annual Technical Conference.*

Smith, K. A. and M. Seltzer (1996). A Comparison of FFS Disk Allocation Policies. *Proceedings of the USENIX 1996 Annual Technical Conference*. San Diego.

Sweeney, A., D. Doucette, W. Hu, C. Anderson, M. Nishimoto, G. Peck (1996). Scalability in the XFS File System. *Proceedings of the USENIX 1996 Annual Technical Conference.*

Tanenbaum, A. S. (1987). *Operating Systems: Design and Implementation*. Prentice Hall.

Ts'o, T. Y. and S. Tweedie (2002). Planned Extensions to the Linux Ext2/Ext3 Filesystem. *Proceedings of the FREENIX Track: 2002 USENIX Annual Technical Conference.*

Tweedie, S. C. (1998). Journaling the Linux ext2fs File System. *Proceedings of the 4th Annual LinuxExp*, Durham, N.C.

Walker, B., G. Popek, R. English, C. Kline, G. Thiel (1983). The LOCUS Distributed Operating System. *ACM Symposium on Operating Systems Principles*: 49–70.

Wikipedia. (2009). Flash Memory. *Wikipedia*, http://en.wikipedia.org/wiki/Flash_memory.

Woodhouse, D. (2001). JFFS: The Journalling Flash File System. http://sourceware.org/jffs2/jffs2-html.

Memory Management

In Chapter 5, we discussed the processor resource; in this chapter we discuss the memory resource. Gaining an understanding of memory management takes us deeply into the shared realm of hardware architecture and software architecture. To make sense of the hardware architecture, we need to understand the software requirements. Similarly, to figure out how an operating system manages memory, we need to understand the underlying hardware.

Memory management is much more than dynamic storage allocation. It involves providing an appropriate memory abstraction and making it work on the available physical resources, usually considered to consist of a high-speed cache, moderate-speed primary storage, and low-speed secondary storage. We begin with a brief history of memory management, introducing some of the more important memory management issues and how they were handled early on. We then focus on the concept of virtual memory, covering its basic architectural features and requirements. We look at the operating-system issues of virtual memory and discuss a couple of representative systems. Finally, we cover the issues involving the management of the backing store for virtual memory.

7.1 MEMORY MANAGEMENT IN THE EARLY DAYS

Early approaches to managing the address space were concerned primarily with protecting the operating system from the user. One technique was the hardware-supported concept of the *memory fence*: an address was established below which no user-mode access was allowed. The operating system was placed below this point in memory and was thus protected from the user (see Figure 7.1).

The memory-fence approach protected the operating system, but did not protect user processes from one another. (This wasn't an issue for many systems — there was only one user process at a time.) Another technique, still employed in some of today's systems, is the use of *base and bounds registers* to restrict a process's memory references to a certain range. Each address generated by a user process was first compared with the value in the bounds register

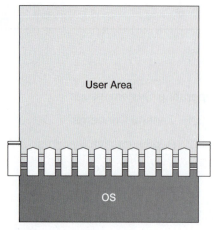

FIGURE 7.1 Memory fence.

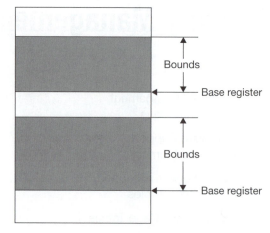

FIGURE 7.2 Base and bounds registers.

to ensure that it did not reference a location beyond the process's range of memory. It was then modified by adding to it the value in the base register, insuring that it did not reference a location before the process's range of memory (see Figure 7.2). A further advantage of this technique was to ensure that a process would be loaded into what appeared to be location 0 — thus no relocation was required at load time.

Another major memory-management issue was fitting a process into the available memory. In the earliest days, either a process fit or it couldn't be run. Early time-sharing systems, however, needed to have many active processes at once. Though each one individually would fit in memory, together they might not. An obvious though rather inefficient approach for handling this was to time-share the memory as well as the processor: when a user paused to think, his or her process was swapped out and that of another user was swapped in. This allowed multiple users to share a system that employed only the memory fence for protection.

Base and bounds registers made it feasible to have a number of processes in primary memory at once. However, if one of these processes was inactive, swapping let the system swap this process out and swap another process in. Note that the use of the base register is very important here: without base registers, after a process is swapped out, it would have to be swapped into the same location in which it resided previously.

Another technique, *overlaying*, was used when a process couldn't fit into memory even if it was the only one there. Say we have 100 kilobytes of available memory and a 200-kilobyte program. Clearly, not all the program can be in memory at once. The user might decide that, while one portion of the program should always be resident, other portions of the program need be resident only for brief periods. The program might start with routines A and B loaded into memory. A calls B; B returns. Now A wants to call C, so it first reads C into the memory previously occupied by B (it *overlays* B) and then calls C. C might then want to call D and E, though there is only room for one at a time. So C first calls D, D returns; C overlays D with E and then calls E.

The advantage of this technique is that the programmer has complete control of the use of memory and can make the necessary optimization decisions. The disadvantage is that the programmer *must* make the necessary decisions to make full use of memory — the operating system doesn't help out. Few programmers can make such decisions wisely, and fewer still want to try.

The notion of virtual memory was invented in 1961 as part of the Atlas Computer project at the University of Manchester in the United Kingdom (Fotheringham 1961). It first appeared in a commercial system, the Burroughs B5000, the following year. Its use has often been disparaged, then adopted in a number of marketplace segments. IBM introduced virtual memory into its "mainframe" operating system, OS/370, in 1972. It was introduced into Unix as part of 3BSD

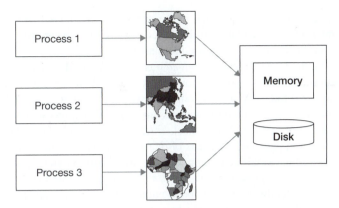

FIGURE 7.3 Address-space mapping with virtual memory.

Unix in 1979 (Babaoğlu and Joy 1981).[1] Microsoft introduced virtual memory into Windows as part of Windows NT 3.1 in 1993. Apple introduced virtual memory into MacOS as part of release X in 2000.

Virtual memory is the support of an address space that is independent of the size of primary storage. Some sort of mapping technique must be employed to map virtual addresses to primary and secondary stores (Figure 7.3). In a typical scenario, the computer hardware maps some virtual addresses to primary storage. If a reference is made to an unmapped address, then a *page fault* occurs that the operating system is called upon to deal with. The operating system might then find the desired virtual locations on secondary storage and transfer them to primary storage. Or the operating system might decide that the reference is illegal and deliver an addressing exception to the process.

As with base and bounds registers, the virtual-memory concept allows us to handle multiple processes simultaneously, with the processes protected from one another. The big advantage is that processes can grow, at least conceptually, up to the size of the address space.

Virtual memory is used in almost all of today's computer systems (except for small embedded systems). Unless otherwise mentioned, we assume the storage-management systems discussed in this text are in some way based on the virtual-memory concept. In the remainder of this chapter we discuss how virtual memory is made to work.

There are two basic approaches to structuring virtual memory: dividing it either into fixed-size *pages* or into variable-size *segments*.

With the former approach, the management of available storage is simplified, since memory is always allocated one page at a time. However, there is some waste due to *internal fragmentation* — the typical program requires not an integral number of pages, but instead memory whose size is, on the average, half a page less than an integral multiple of the page size.

With the latter approach, memory allocation is more difficult, since allocations are for varying amounts of memory. This may lead to *external fragmentation*, in which memory is wasted (as we saw in discussing dynamic storage allocation in Chapter 3) because a number of free areas of memory are too small to be of any use. The advantage of segmentation is that it is a useful organizational tool — programs are composed of segments, each of which can be dealt with (e.g. fetched by the operating system) independently of the others.

**7.2
HARDWARE
SUPPORT
FOR VIRTUAL
MEMORY**

---

[1] 3BSD is the third Berkeley Software Distribution, a series of Unix add-ons and systems from the Computer Systems Research Group of the University of California, Berkeley.

Segment-based schemes were popular in the '60s and '70s but are less so today, primarily because the advantages of segmentation have turned out not to outweigh the extra costs of the complexity of the hardware and software used to manage it.

There is also a compromise approach, *paged segmentation*, in which each segment is divided into pages. This approach makes segmentation a more viable alternative, but not viable enough. Few if any systems use it today. We restrict our discussion to strictly page-based schemes.

So, we assume our virtual-memory systems are based on paging. Somehow we must map virtual addresses into real addresses. The most straightforward way of providing such a mapping is via a *page table*. A page table consists of one entry per page of the virtual address space. Suppose we have a 32-bit virtual address and a page size of 4096 bytes. The 32-bit address is thus split into two parts: a 20-bit *page number* and a 12-bit *offset* within the page. When a thread generates an address, the hardware uses the page-number portion as an index into the page-table array to select a page-table entry, as shown in Figure 7.4.

If the page is in primary storage (i.e. the translation is valid), then the *validity bit* in the page-table entry is set, and the page-frame-number portion of the page-table entry is the high-order bits of the location in primary memory where the page resides. (Primary memory is thought of as being subdivided into pieces called *page frames*, each exactly big enough to hold a page; the address of each of these page frames is at a "page boundary," so that its low-order bits are zeros.) The hardware then appends the offset from the original virtual address to the page-frame number to form the final, real address.

If the *validity bit* of the selected page-table entry is zero, then a page fault occurs and the operating system takes over. Other bits in a typical page-table entry include a *reference bit*, which is set by the hardware whenever the page is referenced by a thread, and a *modified bit*, which is set whenever the page is modified. We will see how these bits are used in Section 7.3 below. The *page-protection bits* indicate who is allowed access to the page and what sort of access is allowed. For example, the page can be restricted for use only by the operating system, or a page containing executable code can be write-protected, meaning that read accesses are allowed but not write accesses.

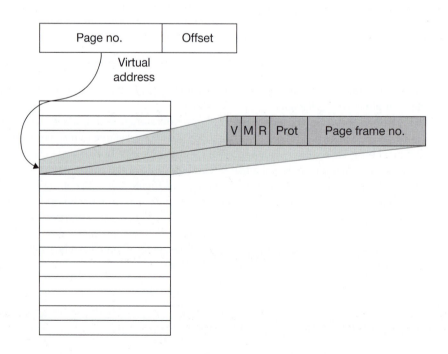

FIGURE 7.4 A simple page table, showing the validity bit (V), modified bit (M), reference bit (R), page protection bits (Prot), and page frame number.

Before we get too excited about page tables, we need to determine what they cost. One measure is how much memory is used merely to hold the page table. In our example, the page table must have 2^{20} entries, each 4 bytes long. Thus the size of the table is 2^{22} bytes — 4 megabytes. Though today this is an almost trivial amount,[2] in the not-too-distant past it was far more than could be afforded, particularly for such a per-process overhead function. If we consider 64-bit architectures (see Section 7.2.5), the cost of memory to hold a complete page table again becomes prohibitive (to put it mildly).

7.2.1 FORWARD-MAPPED PAGE TABLES

Rather than having a complete page table in primary memory, we might have just those pieces of it that are required to map the portion of the address space currently being used. One approach for doing this is the *forward-mapped* or *multilevel* scheme in which the page tables form a tree, as shown in Figure 7.5. Here the virtual address is divided into three pieces: a level-1 (L1) page number, a level-2 (L2) page number, and an offset. Each valid entry in the L1 page table refers to an L2 page table, and each valid entry of the L2 page tables refers to a page frame. Thus a virtual-to-real translation consists of using the L1-page-number field of the virtual address as an index into the L1 page table to select an L2 page table. Then the L2-page-number field is used as an index into the L2 page table to select a page frame. Finally, the offset is used to select a location within the page frame.

The advantage of this scheme is that not all L2 page tables need to be in real memory at once, just those mapping portions of the address space in current use. If the L1 and L2 page numbers are each 10 bits long (as in the most commonly used address-translation scheme of the Intel x86 architecture), then each page table requires 4 kilobytes of storage. Since each page table contains 1024 ($= 2^{10}$) entries, each L2 page table maps 4 megabytes ($= 2^{10} \times 2^{12}$ bytes) of virtual memory. A simple Unix or Windows process would require one L2 page table to map the low-address portion of its address space (text, BSS, data, and dynamic in Unix, assuming they require less than 4 megabytes) and another one to map the high-address portion (containing the stack, also assuming it requires less than 4 megabytes). Thus the total overhead is 12 kilobytes (one L1 and two L2 page tables) — an appreciable savings over the 4 megabytes of overhead required for one-level paging.

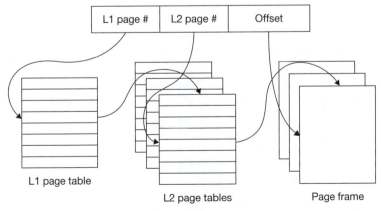

FIGURE 7.5 Forward-mapped page table.

---

[2] At \$12/gigabyte, a reasonable price at the time of this writing, four megabytes is 5 cents' worth of memory — hardly worth worrying about. However, in the early 1980s it was around \$40,000 worth of memory and totally out of the question.

The SPARC version 8 architecture (see Appendix H, page 236 of http://www.sparc.com/standards/V8.pdf) divides the virtual address into four pieces, with a correspondingly greater savings per page.

The down side of forward-mapped page tables is that mapping a virtual address to a real one requires multiple memory accesses: two for the x86, three for the SPARC version 8. This cost is reduced by using translation lookaside buffers (see Section 7.2.4), but is still a concern.

7.2.2 LINEAR PAGE TABLES

Linear page tables are a scheme superficially like complete page tables, except that the page tables occupy contiguous virtual-memory locations rather than real. Additional translation is required to obtain the real addresses of the page-table entries. As with forward-mapped page tables, only a portion of the page tables required for mapping the entire address space needs to be in real memory at once. However, the translation is performed bottom-up rather than top-down and, as we will see, usually requires fewer memory accesses than the forward-mapped scheme.

Figure 7.6 shows a typical linear-page-table scheme. The address space is divided into a small number (four in this case) of regions or *spaces*, each with its own page table. The VPN field of the virtual address is used to select an entry in the appropriate page table, which contains the address of the corresponding page frame. However, since the page table is itself in virtual memory, the address of the page-table entry must be translated into a real address.

One scheme for doing this was used in Digital Equipment Corporation's 1978 VAX architecture; we discuss the details to help put into perspective what might be done to support 64-bit address spaces. Each address space is divided into four spaces and the page size is 512 bytes. Each user process fits in two spaces (thus there were multiple instances of these spaces, one pair for each process) in the lower half of the complete address space, one space (in the upper half) is used by the kernel, and the fourth space is unused. The user spaces are called P0 and P1 space and the kernel space is called S space. We refer to them as **00**, **01**, and **10** spaces, using the high-order bits of their address ranges to name them.

The page tables mapping the **00** and **01** spaces (the user spaces) reside in **10** space (the kernel space). The page table mapping **10** space is in real memory. Thus a virtual address generated by a user-level thread, say in **00** space, is translated by the **00** page table in **10** space. In general, an additional translation, using the **10** page table, is required to translate the virtual address of the

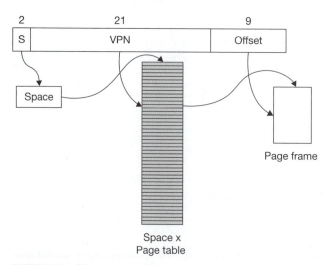

FIGURE 7.6 Linear page table.

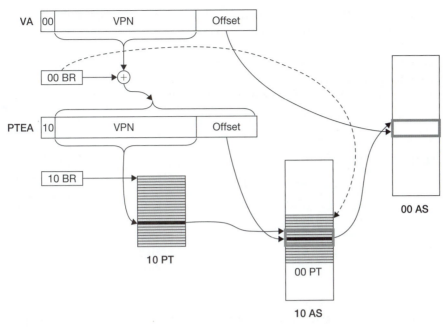

FIGURE 7.7   VAX linear-page-table translation.

00 page-table entry to real memory. However, this translation is usually cached in the translation lookaside buffer (Section 7.2.4) and thus no memory reference is required.

Nevertheless, Figure 7.7 shows the full translation process. Starting with the virtual address (VA) of a location in **00** space, the first step in the translation is to find the entry in the **00** page table (**00** PT) that maps it. This page table resides in **10** space at an address given in a special processor register, the **00** base register (**00** BR). By using the virtual page number field (VPN) from the original virtual address as an index into the 10 page table, we get the virtual address of the **00**-page-table entry in **10** space (this address is called PTEA in Figure 7.7). We now have to figure out the real address of this page-table entry, so we need the **10** page table. Its real address is given in another special processor register, the **10** base register (**10** BR). From the VPN field of PTEA and the contents of this base register, we get the real address of the **10**-page-table entry mapping the page of the **00** page table containing the translation of VA. From this page-table entry and the offset field from PTEA, we get the real address of the **00**-page-table entry. And from this and the original offset field from VA, we finally get the real address we were after in the first place.

It's not immediately clear what the resource requirements are for linear page tables, so let's do some calculations. Suppose a process requires the entire contents of its **00** and **01** spaces, each of which contains 2^{30} bytes. Since the page size is 512 ($= 2^9$) bytes and each page-table entry occupies 4 bytes, the page tables for these two spaces occupy 8 megabytes ($= 2^{23}$ bytes) each. Since these page tables reside in **10** space, there is room for only 64 pairs of them, minus the space occupied by the kernel itself. If the entire **10** space is used, we need 8 megabytes of real memory for its page table alone. (Keep in mind that when the VAX architecture was first released in 1978, the cost of memory was \$40,000 per megabyte, or 3.8 cents per byte!)

To reduce the resource requirements for page tables, the VAX architecture provides **00**, **01**, and **10** *length registers*, each indicating the maximum size of the corresponding space and thus limiting the size of the space's page table. So, if we limit the size of a process's **00** space to one megabyte, the process needs only a 16-page **00** page table in **10** virtual memory, requiring 16 entries in the **10** page table. The same is true if we limit the **01** space to one megabyte. Since the **10** page table must reside in real memory and at least one page of real memory must be allocated for each of the **00** and **01** page tables, the minimum storage needed to hold the translation information

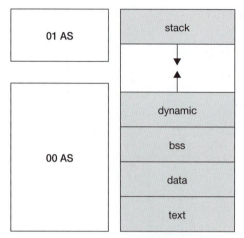

FIGURE 7.8 VAX address spaces with traditional Unix.

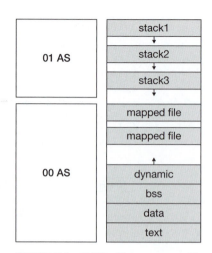

FIGURE 7.9 VAX address spaces with modern Unix.

for such a process is 1152 bytes (at a cost of $43.95 in 1978). Since 32 pages of **10** page-table entries are required for each process of this size, at most 2^{16} such process can exist at once.

Linear page tables made a lot of sense in 1978 for the VAX. But the layout of the address space for Unix processes (and, more importantly for Digital, whose proprietary operating system was VMS, for VMS processes as well) was relatively simple (see Figure 7.8): it consisted of two contiguous regions of allocated virtual memory. Thus the **00** and **01** page tables could be compact: there were no "holes" of unallocated memory separating allocated memory. Since the sizes of these page tables were limited by the length registers, a minimal number of **10** page-table entries were required to map them.

But now consider modern Unix and Windows processes, with multiple threads, each with its own stack, and numerous mapped files (see Section 4.1). There are no longer just two contiguous allocated regions in the address space, but many such regions (see Figure 7.9). If each process has allocated regions scattered randomly (and sparsely) throughout its address space, we won't be able to use the length register to limit the size of the **00** and **01** page tables by any appreciable amount. Thus we need complete, 8-megabyte page tables, each requiring 2^{14} **10** page-table entries occupying four bytes each. Each process now requires 128 kilobytes of real memory for its **10**-page-table space alone. In 1978 terms, this is $5000 per process.

In today's terms, this cost is a bit over a penny per process, so you might think we needn't worry about it. However, as we discuss below (Section 7.2.5), the size of the address space is growing from 2^{32} bytes to 2^{64} bytes, a 4,294,967,296-fold increase. This factor is significant, even when applied to a penny.

7.2.3 HASHED PAGE TABLES

To deal with the problem of sparse but wide allocation of the address space, let's go back to two-piece virtual addresses (page number plus offset), but use a radically different approach for organizing the page table. We fill the table with address-translation information only for allocated portions of the address space, and access this information using a hash function of the virtual address.

Figure 7.10 shows a simple example of such a *hashed page table*; the hash function reduces the page number from the virtual address to two bits. Collisions are dealt with by chaining. Thus each translation requires, in addition to the information in the "normal" page-table entry, a tag

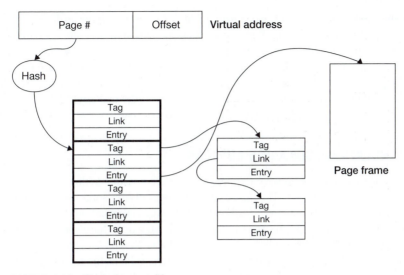

FIGURE 7.10   Hashed page table.

field containing the page number of the entry (so we can determine if this is the translation for a given virtual address), and a link field referring to the next hash synonym.

This approach clearly does a good job of handling a number of small regions in a sparsely allocated address space. However, the overhead of two additional words per entry probably makes it infeasible when there are large regions of allocated memory, each requiring many page-table entries.

This problem can be greatly ameliorated by grouping pages together, as in a technique known as *clustered page tables* (Talluri, Hill, et al. 1995). Multiple consecutive pages are grouped together into *superpages*, and each group has a clustered-page-table entry, as shown in Figure 7.11.

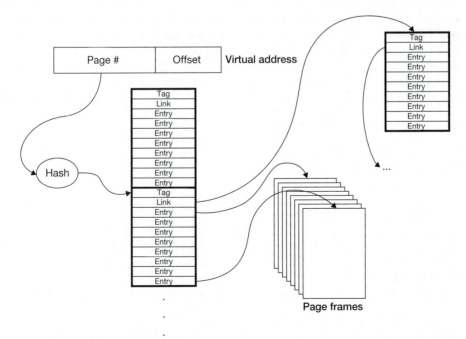

FIGURE 7.11   Clustered page table.

Yet another variation of the hashed page table is the *inverted page table*, in which the page table is indexed by page-frame number (rather than by page number) and each entry identifies which page from which address space occupies that page frame. As in hashed page tables, a hash function of the virtual address chooses an entry in this table. Hash synonyms are linked together. The advantage of this approach is that the table size is a fixed fraction of the size of primary memory (since there's one entry per page frame). However, the operating system must maintain elsewhere a complete description of what's in each address space.

7.2.4 TRANSLATION LOOKASIDE BUFFERS

Even if just one memory lookup were required to translate a virtual address to a real address, the time spent would be exorbitant. Thus most architectures rely on some sort of cache, normally called a *translation lookaside buffer* (TLB), to speed address translation. In some architectures, such as the MIPS family of processors, the TLB is the only hardware-supported address-translation mechanism: if a translation is not found in the TLB, then a trap to the operating system occurs and the operating system must take over. In others, such as the Intel Pentium family, if a translation is not found in the TLB, then the hardware automatically looks it up in the page table. Only if the translation is marked invalid is there a trap to the operating system. The Intel Itanium has two modes: TLB only or TLB with hardware-accessed page table.

Figure 7.12 shows an example of TLB architecture, in this case a "two-way set-associative" cache for a computer with a 4k page size. When a virtual address is to be translated, six middle bits are used to index into the 64 slots of the TLB. Each such slot contains two entries, each of which is a translation of some virtual address to a real address. Both entries are checked to determine if either is the translation of the given virtual address. If one of them is, then it contains the appropriate page-frame number. The high-order 14 bits of the virtual address for which an entry in the TLB is the translation is given in its *tag* field. The next 6 bits are implicit from its position in the table. Thus determining whether a virtual address is in the TLB involves comparing the high-order 14 bits of the virtual address with the tag fields of the two entries in the slot selected by the address's middle 6 bits.

If the virtual address is not in the cache, then, depending on the scheme used, either the hardware searches the page table for the translation or the operating system is invoked to find the translation. In either case, once a translation is found, it's inserted into the cache, replacing one of the two entries in the appropriate slot (which entry is replaced is typically chosen randomly). This insertion is performed automatically by the hardware if it looks up the address, or explicitly by the operating system if it looks up the address.

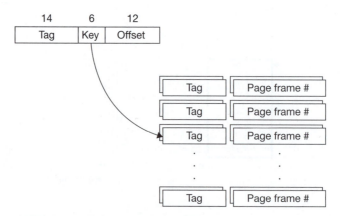

FIGURE 7.12   Translation lookaside buffer.

An important issue is that modifying a page-table entry does not automatically cause the TLB to be updated. Thus a change to a page-table entry might have no effect on address translation if the old information is still in the TLB. It's up to the operating system explicitly to "flush" entries of the TLB if they've been made obsolete in this way. Computers supporting such TLBs have TLB flush instructions designed to do this.

If a context switch is being made from one address space to another, then the entire contents of the TLB become obsolete and thus must be flushed. Note that this adds considerably to the expense of a context switch, since once the new context is entered, there are no translations in the TLB and address translation must be done by page-table lookup (involving expensive memory references) until new translations are inserted into it.

However, some TLBs, for example that of the Intel Itanium, include not just tag bits in the TLB entries, but also address-space identification information. Thus each entry identifies both which virtual address it is a translation for and which address space it belongs to. It's not necessary to flush the TLB after a context switch. Translation still proceeds slowly if there are no entries for the new address space in the TLB, but if a thread running from this address space has been recently active on this processor, then there is some chance that some of the address space's translations are still in the TLB.

A trickier issue arises on multiprocessors. If two or more processors are executing threads of the same address space, and if one of the threads (perhaps because of a page fault) causes the address space's page table to be modified, then it must flush the appropriate entries not only in its own TLB, but in the TLBs of the other processors running threads from this address space.

Algorithms for dealing with this problem are known as *TLB shootdown algorithms* and work roughly as follows. The processor modifying the page table forces an interrupt on each of the other processors using the address space, then waits until they all notify it, by setting bits in shared storage, that they've responded to the interrupt and are idling in wait loops waiting on another bit to be set by the first processor (and thus are not using the affected address space). At this point the first processor makes its changes to the page table and sets the bit being repeatedly tested by the other processors. All then flush the appropriate entries in their TLBs and proceed.

7.2.5 64-BIT ISSUES

Four gigabytes is no longer a lot. At the time of this writing (spring 2010), that much primary memory costs $50 and continues to decrease in price. It is not uncommon for computers to have more real memory than virtual memory. With multithreaded processes requiring multiple stacks, combined with the use of large files mapped into the address space, four gigabytes of virtual memory is often no longer sufficient. Current 64-bit architectures thus extend the approaches used by 32-bit architectures, exacerbating all the problems.

The problems are the space required to hold translation information and the time required to access it. With 8-kilobyte pages, a complete page table (with 8-byte entries) occupies 16 petabytes (2^{54} bytes). While two or three levels of page tables are sufficient to handle 32-bit forward-mapped translation, four to seven are required for 64-bit translation. Thus a fair number of memory accesses are required in the event of TLB misses.

Two current 64-bit architectures are the x64 and the IA-64. Both support Unix and Windows implementations. The x64[3] is a mostly straightforward extension of the 32-bit x86 architecture employing forward-mapped page tables, which are searched automatically by the hardware following a TLB miss. It supports two 64-bit paging modes: one with 4-kilobyte pages, the other with 2-megabyte pages. Any one address space can be composed of both page sizes, just as long as the start address of each page is an integral multiple of the size of that page. Current implementations

---

[3] See http://support.amd.com/us/Processor_TechDocs/24593.pdf for technical documentation.

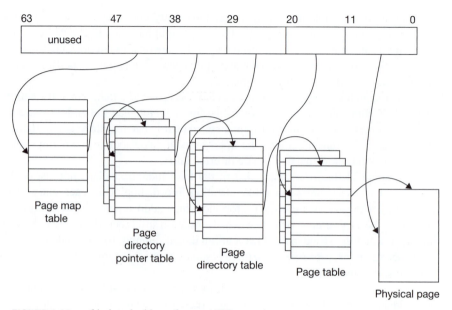

FIGURE 7.13   x64 virtual address format (4KB pages).

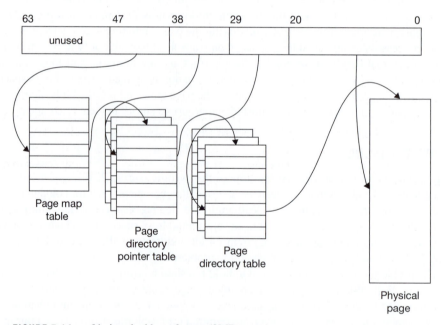

FIGURE 7.14   x64 virtual address format (2MB pages).

of the architecture are limited to no more that 48-bit addresses. With this limitation, four levels of page tables are used with 4KB pages (Figure 7.13) and three levels are used with 2MB pages (Figure 7.14). The small page size minimizes internal fragmentation, at the expense of an extra level of page tables. The large page size reduces the number of levels, at the expense of internal fragmentation. It also reduces the number of TLB entries needed for a range of addresses. An operating system might use the larger page size for its own address space, so as to leave more of the TLB for user processes. Both Linux and Windows do this, and they also let user processes specify the use of the larger page size when mapping files into their address spaces.

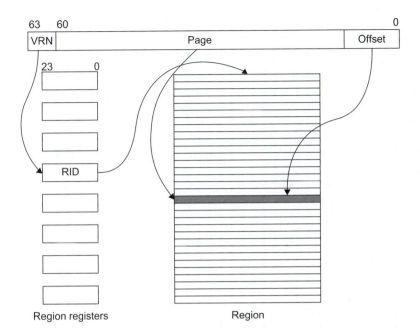

FIGURE 7.15 IA-64 virtual address format. The virtual region number (VRN) selects a region register, which contains a region ID (RID) identifying a region.

The IA-64 page-translation architecture[4] is a major departure from the x86 approach. Its 64-bit addresses are divided into two pieces: the most significant three bits contain the *virtual region number (VRN),* selecting a *region,* and the remaining 61 bits form the virtual address within the region (Figure 7.15). A variety of page sizes are supported: most, but not all, powers of 2 between 4 kilobytes and 4 gigabytes. As with the x64 architecture, any one region may be composed of pages of various sizes, as long as the start address of each page is an integral multiple of that page's size. The three VRN bits don't identify a region directly, but do so indirectly by selecting one of eight region registers, each of which contains a 24-bit region identifier. Thus the effective size of the address space is 2^{85} bytes! However, since privileged instructions are required to modify the region registers, user-level programs are limited to easy access to only a 2^{64}-byte address space. Furthermore, current implementations limit each region to no more than 2^{51} bytes. No current operating system takes advantage of the region registers to provide a larger address space.

The IA-64 has three options for page translation. Its TLB can be configured simply to trap into the operating system on a miss, thus not mandating any paging technique. Alternatively, it can be configured to use a per-region linear page table (Section 7.2.2) or a hashed page table (Section 7.2.3) to load translations automatically. Given its variety of page sizes, the hashed page table is effectively a clustered page table (Section 7.2.3). When a linear page table is used, the TLB itself is relied upon to map it into real memory. Both the Linux and Windows IA-64 implementations use linear page tables.

7.2.6 VIRTUALIZATION

Let's return to virtual machines, introduced in Chapter 4. How can we virtualize virtual memory? First, we need to introduce some terminology. Normally we think of translating virtual addresses in virtual memory to real addresses in real memory. What on a virtual machine is considered to

---

[4] See http://www.intel.com/design/itanium/arch_spec.htm for technical documentation.

be virtual and real memory might more accurately be called, from the real machine's perspective, *virtual virtual memory* and *virtual real memory*. Thus an operating system running on a virtual machine arranges for the translation of virtual virtual addresses to virtual real addresses. Since virtual real addresses are virtual as far as the real machine is concerned, the virtual machine monitor (VMM) must somehow arrange to translate them into real addresses.[5]

In an architecture with page tables, the operating system on the virtual machine sets up page tables to do the virtual-virtual to virtual-real mapping. The VMM has set up page tables to do the virtual real to real mapping. When the virtual machine is running, what we really want is the composition of the mappings done by the two sets of page tables — a mapping from virtual virtual to real.

One way of doing this is the *shadow page-table* approach. The VMM maintains for each virtual machine a set of page tables (the shadow page tables) that actually is the composition of the virtual-virtual to virtual-real translation and virtual to real translation. Thus the operating system on the virtual machine maintains a set of page tables mapping what it considers virtual memory to what it considers real memory. Whenever it establishes or modifies such a set, the VMM is notified and makes the appropriate changes in the shadow page tables (Figure 7.16). When the real processor is running a program that is expecting the virtual virtual address space, it uses the shadow page table.

Though laborious, shadow page tables are required if the operating system on the virtual machine is to behave as if it were running on a real machine. But they are costly in time and space. What would be nice is if the hardware were aware of the two levels of translation (virtual virtual to

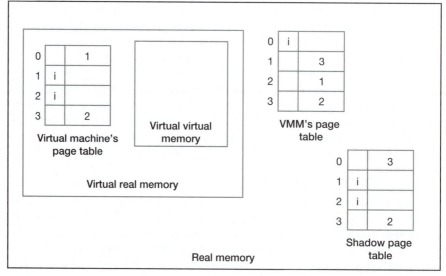

FIGURE 7.16 A shadow page table. Here the address space has four pages. A virtual machine, running in virtual real memory, has set up a page table mapping virtual virtual addresses into virtual real addresses. The VMM has its own page table mapping virtual real addresses into real addresses. It has set up a shadow page table providing the composition of the other two tables, mapping virtual virtual addresses into real addresses. In each page table, the rows are labeled with the page number, the first column indicates whether the translation is invalid (i) or not, and the second column is the translation (page-frame number).

---

[5] We resist the temptation to talk of real virtual addresses and real real addresses.

virtual real and virtual real to real) and could be convinced to compose the two itself. Recent additions to the x86 architecture by Intel do exactly this: using a feature called *extended page translation* (EPT), the hardware is given pointers to two sets of page tables (in the x86, both sets are two-level page tables) and does the composite translation without the need for a shadow page table.

We explore other issues in virtualizing address translation in the exercises.

The operating system's job with respect to virtual memory is, simply put, to make sure that programs execute at a reasonable speed even though they are using virtual memory. This means that the OS must determine which pages should be in primary memory and get them there. In this section, we first describe how this is done overall, then go into the details of some of the more important issues.

7.3

OPERATING-SYSTEM ISSUES

7.3.1 GENERAL CONCERNS

The virtual-memory duties of the operating system are traditionally broken down into three areas:

- The *fetch policy*: when to bring pages from secondary storage into primary storage and which ones to bring.

- The *placement policy*: where to put the pages brought in from secondary storage.

- The *replacement policy*: which pages to remove from primary storage and when to remove them.

To make some sense of what these entail, let's look at a scheme with a simple approach to each of the policies. Though this approach is much too inefficient for any real system, it will get us started in our general discussion. The classic early paper on which much of this discussion is based is (Denning 1970).

A simple fetch policy is a form of lazy evaluation known as *demand paging*: don't fetch a page until a thread references something in that page. Thus we start a program with no page frames allocated for it. As the program executes and references pages with invalid translation entries, it faults to the operating system, which fetches the desired pages. Note that if the cost of fetching *n* pages is *n* times the cost of fetching one page, this approach is optimal. However, as we discuss below, this is rarely the case.

It might seem that the placement policy is hardly worth thinking about: since all pages and page frames are the same size, it doesn't really matter where a page is placed in memory, just as long as it starts on a page boundary. This is certainly the case with our usual notion of primary storage: it is random-access memory, with all locations taking equal time to access. However, we have to modify this point of view when we take into account the use of memory caches.

For a replacement policy, let's simply keep track of the order in which pages are brought into primary memory. Then, when we've run out of page frames and need to remove something to make room for a new page, we simply remove the page that has been in primary memory the longest. This is known as the first-in-first-out (FIFO) approach. It has its obvious drawbacks, not the least of which is that the page that's been in memory the longest might be a really important page that's referenced a lot. However, it's simple to implement and is useful as a basis of comparison for other techniques (it makes almost any other technique look good).

To get an idea of how well our paging scheme will perform, let's consider what happens in response to a page fault. The steps are

1. Trap to operating system because reference to page results in a page fault.

2. Find a free page frame.

3. Write page out to secondary storage if there are no free page frames.

4. Fetch desired page from secondary storage.

5. Return from trap.

How expensive are these steps? Clearly step 1 (combined with step 2) has a fairly large cost — a reference to memory might take, say, 10 nanoseconds if there is no page fault. If there is a page fault, even if no I/O is performed, the time required before the faulted instruction can be resumed is probably some number of microseconds. If a page frame is available, then step 2 is very quick, but if not, then we must do step 3, which may result in an output operation that could take milliseconds. Then, in step 4, the thread must wait for an input operation to complete, which could take more milliseconds.

Even in the best of circumstances, then, a thread takes a major performance hit once it causes a page fault. So the best thing we can do is to reduce the number of such faults. An obvious thing to do is *prepaging*: fetch pages before they are referenced. However, it's not so obvious how to do this. In some cases it might be clear which pages a thread will be referencing soon, but in most cases the only way to determine this is to let the thread run and find out which pages it references. But it's often a reasonably good bet that if a thread has referenced one page, it will likely be referencing the next page in its address space soon. It's no certainty, of course, but if it doesn't cost much to fetch subsequent pages after one page is fetched, we might as well do so. This form of prepaging is known as *readahead* and takes advantage of the fact that reading adjacent pages from a disk costs little more than reading just one page (see Figure 7.17).

If a thread does suffer a page fault, it will help matters considerably to make certain a page frame is already available for it to use: we don't want the thread to have to wait for an I/O operation to complete for a page frame to be freed. So, rather than force the faulting thread to free a page frame, such freeing can be done as a background activity by some other thread, one dedicated to the virtual-memory system. We'll call this the *page-out thread*.

We've already seen that the FIFO approach to determining which pages to remove from primary memory isn't very good. But how can we do better? If our operating system were omniscient, it would free that page whose removal would cause our program the smallest slowdown. Certainly we'd like to remove those pages that will never be referenced again. (Belady 1966) proved that the page to remove is the one whose next reference is the farthest in the future. This technique is known as *Belady's optimal replacement algorithm* and has a lot to be said in its favor except that it cannot be implemented in practice.

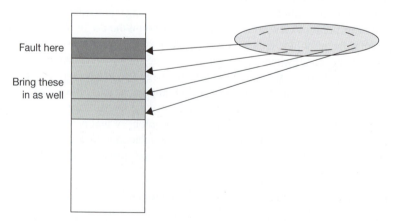

FIGURE 7.17 Prepaging using readahead.

The best we can do is to make a good guess. What seems reasonable is that Belady's page, the page whose next reference is farthest in the future, is the page whose most recent reference was the farthest in the past. This clearly isn't always true, but it has the advantage of being something we have a hope of implementing and something that might work reasonably well in practice. This approach is known as *least-recently used* (*LRU*) and has applications in other areas as well.

An exact implementation of LRU would require the operating system to keep track of all references to page frames and to be able to order them by time of last reference. Without rather expensive hardware support, doing this would be so time-consuming as to negate any possible benefit. However, we can approximate LRU without undue expense.

Rather than ordering page frames by their time of last reference, let's use a coarser approach and divide time into discrete periods, each long enough for there to be thousands of references. Most virtual-memory architectures support a reference bit in their translation entries, set to 1 by the translation hardware each time the entry is used (i.e., when the corresponding page frame is referenced). At the end of each period we can examine the reference bits and determine which page frames have been used. At the same time we zero these bits, so we can do the same thing in the next period. This coarse measure of LRU works well enough, particularly when we remember that LRU itself is just a way to get an educated guess about which page is least likely to be used in the near future.

Rather than implement the approximate LRU algorithm exactly as we've described it, many systems use a continual approach known as the clock algorithm. All active page frames are conceptually arranged in a circularly linked list. The page-out thread slowly traverses the list. In the "one-handed" version of the clock algorithm, each time it encounters a page, it checks the reference bit in the corresponding translation entry: if the bit is set, it clears it. If the bit is clear, it adds the page to the free list (writing it back to secondary storage first, if necessary).

A problem with the one-handed version is that, in systems with large amounts of primary storage, it might take too long for the page-out thread to work its way all around the list of page frames before it can recognize that a page has not been recently referenced. In the two-handed version of the clock algorithm, the page-out thread implements a second hand some distance behind the first. The front hand simply clears reference bits. The second (back) hand removes those pages whose reference bits have not been set to one by the time the hand reaches the page frame (see Figure 7.18).

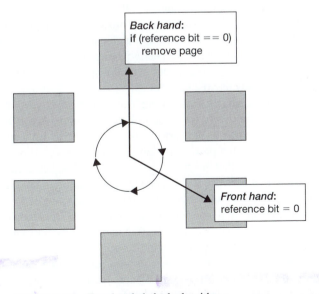

FIGURE 7.18 Two-handed clock algorithm.

An important factor is how quickly the list of pages is traversed. What's normally done is to make this a function of the number of page frames on the free list: the fewer free page frames there are, the faster the active page frames are traversed. If there are plenty of free page frames, the active ones aren't traversed at all.

Our final general concern has to do with the competition for page frames: to what extent should processes compete for them? For example, all processes might compete for page frames from a global pool. Alternatively, we might give each process a certain number of page frames for its private use, avoiding competition but with no chance for additional page frames.

The second approach, known as the local approach, clearly has the disadvantage that a process needing more memory would not be able to get it, even if it is available. The first approach, known as the global approach, avoids this drawback, but has one of its own.

Consider the following extreme example. We have a computer with two page frames of real memory whose operating system used the global approach to page-frame allocation. We have two processes, A and B, competing for page frames.

1. Initially A has a page in frame 1 and B has a page in frame 2.

2. Process A references another page, causing a page fault.

3. Process B's page in frame 2 is removed from memory and frame 2 is given to process A.

4. Process B now runs but, of course, immediately has a page fault.

5. Process A's page in frame 1 is removed and frame 1 is given to process B.

6. Process A now runs, but faults on the page that was in frame 1.

7. Process B's page in frame 1 is removed from memory and frame 1 is given to process A.

8. Ad infinitum . . .

What we have is the situation known as *thrashing*: neither process can make progress, since whenever either tries to run, it has a page fault and handles it by stealing a page from the other. The situation of the example is an extreme case, but it illustrates the general problem. If demand for page frames is too great, then while one process is waiting for a page to be fetched, the pages it already has are stolen from it to satisfy the demands of other processes. Thus when this first process finally resumes execution, it immediately faults again.

A symptom of a thrashing situation is that the processor is spending a significant amount of time doing nothing — all the processes are waiting on page-in requests. A perhaps apocryphal but amusing story is that the batch monitor on early paging systems would see that the idle time of the processor had dramatically increased and would respond by allowing more processes to run, thus aggravating an already terrible situation.

(Denning 1968) is a classic paper proposing a compromise between global and local allocation that avoids thrashing. In this paper he described his *working-set principle*: in the typical process, the set of pages being referenced varies slowly over time and is a relatively small subset of the complete set of pages in the process's address space. This set of pages, determined over some suitable time interval, is called the process's *working set*. The key to the efficient use of primary storage is to ensure that each process has enough page frames to hold its working set. If we don't have enough page frames to hold each active process's working set, then demand for page frames is too heavy and we are in danger of entering a thrashing situation. The correct response in this situation is to remove one or more processes in their entirety (i.e., swap them out), so that there are enough page frames for the remaining processes.

Certainly a problem with this principle is its imprecision. Over how long a time period should we measure the size of the working set? What is reasonable, suggests Denning, is a time roughly half as long as it takes to fetch a page from the backing store. Furthermore, how do we determine which pages are in the working set? We can come up with an approximate working set using techniques similar to those used above for approximating LRU.

The working-set principle is used in few if any systems — the concept of the size of the working set is just too nebulous. However, it is very important as an ideal to which paging systems are compared. The term *working set* is frequently used (and abused) in describing many of today's systems.

7.3.2 REPRESENTATIVE SYSTEMS

In this section we briefly describe the memory-management subsystems of two representative systems: Linux and Windows. Note that many of the details mentioned here may have been changed subsequent versions of these systems, so what's described isn't necessarily how it's done on the version of the system the reader may be using.

7.3.2.1 Linux

Linux, like all operating systems, has evolved over the years. Its earliest virtual-memory design was rather simple and not terribly efficient, but it has now become competitive in performance with other operating systems designed for the same hardware. What we discuss here is based on Linux version 2.6.7.

This 32-bit version of the operating system is, of course, limited to four gigabytes of virtual memory. It is organized as shown in Figure 7.19: the lower three gigabytes are used by the current process, while the operating system (including thread kernel stacks) fits in the upper gigabyte. Thus the operating system always has direct access to the address space of the current process. This is important since it facilitates accessing arguments that are passed to the operating system in system calls.

We normally think of memory management from the application's point of view, where it's virtual memory that's allocated. It's up to the operating system to allocate real memory — it manages a pool of page frames that it divvies out when needed. Since the operating system itself runs in virtual memory, when it allocates memory for its own use, it must allocate both virtual memory and real memory. Until relatively recently, Linux handled this by the simple expedient of permanently mapping all real memory into the gigabyte of virtual memory used by the operating system. Thus by allocating real memory, it is also allocating virtual memory. When it

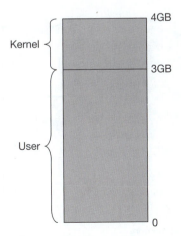

FIGURE 7.19 Linux address-space layout.

allocates page frames for user-process address spaces, these pages are mapped both into the user address space and into the operating-system address space.

Two implications of this scheme are that there is sufficient real memory so that pages needed by the operating system are always mapped to real memory and there is no more than one gigabyte of real memory. With more than one gigabyte of primary storage, not all of it can be mapped into the kernel's virtual memory. So, the upper 128 MB of kernel virtual memory was cut out and used as the *kmap region*: the first 896 MB of primary storage is still permanently mapped into the operating-system virtual memory, but any beyond that is temporarily mapped, when necessary, into the kmap region. The operating system's data structures are allocated from the first 896 MB (the permanently mapped pages) to insure that they are always mapped. Page frames from user processes may come from anywhere, since they are rarely accessed directly by the operating system. When the operating system must do so, it temporarily maps them into the kmap region (see Figure 7.20).

But there's more! One aspect of the evolution of any operating system is that its design must not only accommodate advances in hardware technology, but also must continue to support, for a reasonable period, obsolete and outdated hardware. Linux's original virtual-memory subsystem assumed that no system would have more than a gigabyte of primary storage, but as memory has become cheaper, this assumption is no longer valid, and Linux must support systems with many gigabytes of memory. On the other hand, it must continue to support older devices and buses, some of which could handle only 24 address bits, and thus it cannot reference memory addresses greater than 2^{24}.

The text, data, and BSS (space for uninitialized data — see Section 1.3.2) of the operating system itself occupy page frames that are permanently mapped into its address space. The remaining page frames are divided into three zones, based on their address:

- *DMA*, for those whose addresses are less than 2^{24}. These page frames are used for buffers accessed by direct-memory-access (DMA) devices that can handle only 24-bit physical addresses.

- *Normal*, for those whose addresses are between 2^{24} and $2^{30}-2^{27}$. Operating-system data structures must reside in pages in this range; user pages may be in this range.

- *HighMem*, for page frames whose addresses are greater than $2^{30}-2^{27}$. These are used strictly for user pages.

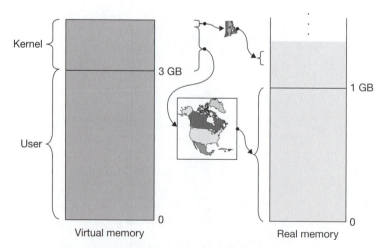

FIGURE 7.20 Mapping real memory into Linux's kernel.

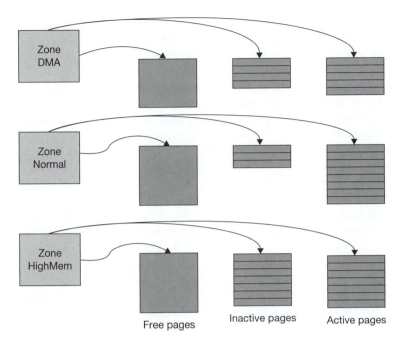

FIGURE 7.21   Linux's memory zones.

Page frames needed for user processes (and for pages to buffer blocks from files) are taken from the HighMem zone. If this zone has none, they are taken from the Normal zone; if this zone has none, they are taken from the DMA zone. Page frames needed for kernel data structures are taken from the Normal zone, but if it has none they may be taken from the DMA zone. Of course, page frames needed for devices that can access only the DMA zone are taken only from it.

Each zone's page frames are divided into three lists (see Figure 7.21):

- *free*: those page frames that are not currently in use and thus are not mapped into any process's address space, nor are being used by any operating-system subsystem; free pages are not kept as a simple linked list but are organized using the buddy system (Section 3.3.2) to facilitate allocation and liberation of contiguous runs of pages. This is important primarily for data structures in the kernel, where contiguity of real addresses implies contiguity of virtual addresses.

- *inactive*: those page frames that, though perhaps mapped into a process address space or being used by some subsystem, haven't been used recently.

- *active*: those page frames that are in active use.

The technique for managing these lists evolved from the two-handed clock algorithm (Section 7.3.1), implementing what is essentially a global page-replacement policy (Section 7.3.1). A kernel thread, known as *kswapd*, is responsible for most of the work. It periodically wakes up and scans the zones. It scans each zone's active list for page frames to move to its inactive list, and scans each zone's inactive list for page frames to move either to its free list, if they haven't been subsequently referenced, or back to the active list if they have. If a page is "dirty" (i.e., has been modified since it was last fetched), kswapd starts the operation to write it out when it is about to be freed. In addition, a number of kernel threads, known as *pdflush* threads, periodically write out modified pages.

However, Linux departs from the standard clock algorithm and manages the zones somewhat independently. Before scanning the pages of the zones, it checks the zones to see if they are low on free pages. If HighMem is low, it then scans all zones. However, if HighMem is not low but Normal is, then it scans just Normal and DMA; if only DMA is low, then it scans only DMA. The rationale is that the lower zones probably run low on free page frames before the upper zones do.

Another concern has to do with pages used to cache blocks from files. As discussed in Chapter 4, files are accessed in two ways: either explicitly via *read* and *write* system calls or implicitly using *mmap*. In both cases, Linux keeps track of which pages hold which blocks from which files. Blocks accessed via *mmap* are in pages mapped into one or more process address spaces. Blocks accessed via *read* or *write* are in pages referred to by kernel *buffer headers*, which form a cache of recently used blocks — the *buffer cache*. If a block is accessed both ways, the page holding it is both mapped into process address spaces and referred to by a buffer header.

The concern is that, if there is a lot of explicit I/O, the buffer cache might monopolize most of the available page frames — pages are consumed rapidly to hold blocks coming from files, but these blocks are used essentially just once and are freed by kswapd more slowly than they are consumed.

Linux's solution is that kswapd favors page frames holding pages that are mapped into process address spaces over page frames being used just by the buffer cache. Ordinarily, when scanning page frames in the zones, kswapd does not move page frames holding mapped pages to the inactive list. Only when it can't otherwise inactivate sufficient pages does it inactivate mapped pages.

7.3.2.2 Windows

Windows's approach to virtual-memory management differs considerably from Linux's. Its basic design and terminology is derived from that of the much earlier VMS operating system of Digital Equipment Corporation.[6] As with Linux, we look at the 32-bit version of the system. Further information on the Windows virtual memory system can be found in (Russinovich and Solomon 2005).

The standard layout of virtual memory in Windows divides the address space evenly between user and operating system, with each user process residing in the lower two gigabytes of address space and the operating system in the upper two gigabytes. However, the system can be set up so that the user's portion is anywhere between two and three gigabytes, with the kernel's portion accordingly smaller. Unlike Linux, not all of the operating system's pages are permanently mapped to primary storage. Much of the operating system resides in pageable memory, and thus it must be prepared to handle page faults when accessing its own code and data structures. Of course, certain portions (for example, page-fault handlers) do occupy non-paged memory.

Windows uses a simple but effective page-replacement approach that balances local and global replacement. In rough terms, each process is guaranteed a certain number of page frames. If more are needed, it competes for them with all other processes and the operating system.

Each process has a *working set* of pages in primary storage. However, unlike Denning's original use of the term (Section 7.3.1), a working set here is simply the set of pages that reside in primary storage, not the set of pages the process must have in primary storage so that it can execute efficiently. Each process has a *minimum working-set size* that is the number of page frames the operating system guarantees it will have while it is running. It also has a *maximum working-set size* that is nominally a limit on the number of page frames a process may have, but may be exceeded as long as the system has plenty of spare page frames. Thus when a process encounters a page fault, it can add another page frame to its working set as long as one is available.

Maintaining working-set sizes within reasonable bounds is the job of a kernel thread known as the *balance-set manager*. The balance set is the set of pages that are not in working sets. Thus

---

[6] This operating system is now owned by Hewlett Packard and called OpenVMS.

this thread examines working sets and, if necessary, moves some of their contents to the balance set. It uses a one-handed variant of the clock algorithm (Section 7.3.1), scanning each process's working set while testing and clearing hardware reference bits. Each time it finds that a page has not been referenced since its previous pass, it adds to the page's *age*, a value maintained for each page frame. The age is then used to determine which pages should be removed from the working set.

Pages removed from working sets by the balance-set manager continue to exist in memory, though any reference to them causes a fault. They are collected in two lists, the *standby page list*, for those that do not need to be written back to their backing store, and the *modified page list*, for those that do. If a thread in a process references a page in either of these lists, the page-fault handler puts the page back into the process's working set.

Two threads, called *modified-page writers*, are responsible for cleaning the dirty page frames of the modified page list. Page frames containing data backed by files are written back to their files by one of these threads. However, doing this involves the execution of file-system code that may itself reside in pageable memory. So, to avoid deadlock that could result when a page-in request requires a page-out to be satisfied, the other page-writer thread handles page frames containing private data, i.e., pages backed not by the normal file system but by the special system paging file. The code this thread executes is not in pageable memory. See Exercise 17.

Page frames are allocated from either the *free-page list* or the *zeroed-page list*. The latter, as its name implies, contains free page frames whose contents are all zeros. Such zeroed pages are required not only to satisfy the requirements of C and C++ that the values of uninitialized global variables be zero, but also to deal with security concerns — the leftover pages of one process should not be viewable by another. A special *zero-page thread* runs in the background, takes page frames from the free page list, zeros them, and puts them on the zeroed page list.

If the free-page list and zeroed-paged list are empty when a page frame must be allocated, page frames are allocated from the standby list.

Page frames are added to the free-page list when they are truly free: when their contents contain no useful information. This happens when a process terminates and its private pages are released, or when a file is deleted and thus any page frames containing its blocks are no longer needed. No thread (or other agent) moves page frames containing useful pages to the free-page list.

Figure 7.22 shows the states a page frame can be in and the transitions among them. Page frames in the active state hold pages that are in either a process's working set or the system's

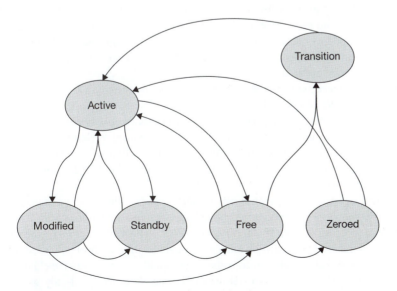

FIGURE 7.22 Page-frame states in Windows.

working set. The balance-set manager takes page frames out of this state and puts them into either the standby or modified states, corresponding to their being on the standby or modified lists. The two page-writer threads take page frames in the modified state and put them in the standby state. The zero-page thread moves page frames from the free state to the zeroed state. When the contents of a page frame are no longer useful the page frame is moved, by whatever thread discovers or causes the uselessness, to the free state.

Page frames in the modified and standby states contain useful pages that are part of processes' balance sets. Threads referencing them incur page faults but, as part of handling the faults, immediately put the pages back into their processes' working sets, changing the page frame state to active.

When a thread references a page that isn't in memory, i.e., doesn't have a page frame, then either a zeroed or free page frame is taken. If the page frame can be initialized immediately (for example filled with zeros or copied from another page frame), then it is put into a working set and marked active. However, if data must be read from a device, the page frame is put in the transition state until the operation completes, then is set to the active state and moved to a working set. This state is needed for the situation in which two or more threads fault on the same page. The first thread starts the input operation and puts the page frame in the transition state. The subsequent faulting threads, finding the page frame holding the desired page in that state, simply wait for the operation to complete; they do not attempt to fetch their own copies into other page frames.

A feature found in Windows but not in Linux (though present in some other Unix systems) is swapping. So that more primary storage can be made available to running processes, idle processes may have all their page frames removed; i.e., their working sets are reduced to null. This is done in stages by a system thread called the *swapper* that is periodically woken up by the balance-set manager. It identifies threads that have been idle for extended periods (15 seconds) and adds the page frames of their kernel stacks to the standby and modified page lists. Once all the threads of a process have been so identified, the process is marked as swapped and all its working set is removed.

7.3.3 COPY ON WRITE AND FORK

Fork, as introduced in Chapter 1, is seemingly expensive to implement, since a child process's address space must be a copy of the parent's. Can this be done without actually copying the address space? What can make things perhaps worse is that the typical use of *fork* in Unix involves execution of an *exec* system call shortly afterwards, which replaces the entire contents of the just-copied address space with a new image, fresh from disk. Thus most of the work involved in copying the address space was for naught, since most of the address space was never accessed before it was replaced.

Before we proceed, we must ask the question: is *fork* strictly a Unix problem? Although, for example, native Windows applications use neither *fork* nor any operation that requires the copying of the address space as in *fork*, Windows still supports *fork* because it supports a POSIX environment in which a subset of Unix functionality can be used, including *fork*. Future versions of Windows might support a snapshotting capability that would involve copying issues similar to those in *fork*. Thus the issues involved in implementing *fork* affect Windows just as much as they affect all the various versions of Unix.

To avoid the expense of copying an entire address space within *fork*, we can take advantage of a basic principle known as *lazy evaluation*: *put off work as long as possible, because if you wait long enough, it could well turn out that you never have to do it*. In the context of *fork*, where this principle actually works, it means that you avoid doing any copying until it is absolutely necessary.

What is done is that, rather than copy the parent's address space into the child's, the two processes actually share their address spaces. However, the pages are made read-only, so that a protection fault occurs when either process attempts to modify a page. When such a modification attempt occurs, the operating system makes a copy of the page for the modifying process and has it modify the copy. Thus only those pages that are modified are copied. Thus if an *exec* comes shortly after a *fork*, the child process modifies few if any pages and thus little page copying need be done.

This notion of making pages read-only so they can be copied in response to writes is known as *copy on write* (*COW*). As an optimization, it has wide application in virtual-memory systems, but it does not come without cost. A fair amount of bookkeeping is required to keep track of what has and has not been copied. To see what all the issues are, let's first look at the details of mapped files.

As we discussed in Chapter 4, a file may be mapped into a process in two ways: a shared mapping and a private mapping. With both sorts of mappings, the pages of the process's address space are initialized from the file. With shared mappings, pages modified by the process are written back to the file, but with private mappings, they are not.

The executable code of a typical process is a mapping of the corresponding portion of the executable file. Since it's read-only, it doesn't really matter whether it's a private or a shared mapping. However, the process's data section is definitely a private mapping of the data portion of the executable file. BSS, dynamic, and stack regions can be thought of as private mappings of files whose contents are zeros, though in practice the pages are filled with zeros directly. A process can explicitly map any number of additional files into its address space, either shared or private.

This all seems pretty straightforward until we consider the effect of a *fork*. The semantics of this with respect to mapped files is that a file that's mapped shared in the parent is also mapped shared in the child. It might seem, then, that all we have to say is that a file mapped private in the parent is also mapped private in the child.

But things aren't quite so simple. Those pages from the mapped file that were modified by the parent before the *fork* must appear, as modified, in the child. Thus the child's pages aren't necessarily initialized from the file; rather, some are initialized from the parent's address space. However, any modifications to pages made by the parent after the *fork* don't affect the child. And, of course, either process may perform another *fork*, compounding the problem. Thus we have some careful bookkeeping to do.

Consider a process with a "fresh" address space, for example, in Unix, right after a call to *exec*. Everything in the address space is a mapping of some sort of object (either a file or, in the case of the BSS, dynamic, and stack regions, an artificial object that supplies zeros). When pages are referenced for the first time, they are initialized from the object. For pages in regions whose object is mapped shared, changes are sent back to the object.

What about the pages in the regions whose objects are mapped private? Once a page has been modified, it is no longer associated with the original object. However, it requires some sort of object — if for no other reason than there should be someplace to store changes made to the page, just in case the page must be freed but is referenced again sometime later. Let's invent a new object called a *shadow object* (using a term from Mach (Rashid, Tevanian, et al. 1987), which was probably the first operating system to handle this problem). A shadow object holds those pages that were originally copy-on-write but have been modified. As we discuss below, backing store can be associated with shadow objects so their pages can be paged out and later paged in.

Consider a page in an address-space region into which an object was mapped private, such as the data region. To find the current object associated with that page, you first look in the shadow object. If the page is there, then it is associated with the shadow object; otherwise it has not been modified and it is still associated with the original object (see Figure 7.23).

Now suppose the process forks. The initial contents of all the pages in the child's address space should be the same as the contents of those pages in the parent at the time of the *fork*.

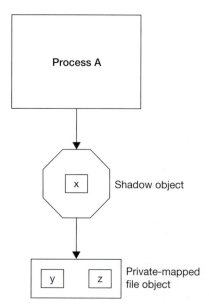

FIGURE 7.23 Process A has a private mapping of the file and has modified page x but neither page y nor page z.

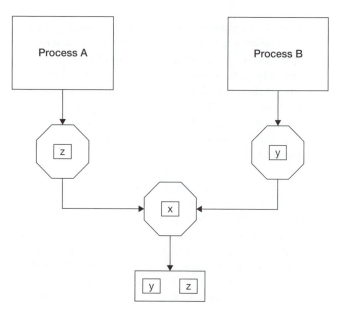

FIGURE 7.24 Process A forks, creating child process B. Shadow objects are created to contain the further modified pages of A as well as of B. B modifies page y and A modifies page z.

Thus both the parent's private objects as well as its shadow objects are mapped into the child. However, any further changes to pages in a private-mapped region of either process affect only that process. So, at the time of the *fork*, we give each process a new shadow object for each of its private-mapped regions to hold any newly modified pages. To find the current object associated with a page in either process, you look first in the newest shadow object for the region in that process, then in the original shadow object of the parent, and finally in the original object (see Figure 7.24).

Of course, if either process forks again, then another pair of shadow objects is created, as shown in Figure 7.25. Thus, in principle, there could be an arbitrarily long chain of shadow objects. In practice, long chains are unlikely, since most *fork*s are followed fairly quickly by *exec*s. In addition, a few simple operations can be used to shorten lengthy chains in some circumstances. We explore these operations in Exercise 21.

In Chapter 4 we introduced the notion of *local RPC*, in which data must be copied from one process's address space into another's. If there is a lot of data to copy (at least a page or so), it makes sense to do it lazily, with the hope that neither the sender nor the receiver will modify the data. Thus, using techniques similar to those just described for optimizing *fork*, we have what's known as a *virtual copy* operation: rather than copy the data, it is mapped into the receiver's address space and the underlying pages are marked copy-on-write.

We might apply our shadow-objects technique to handle any modifications to virtually copied pages, but there's a complication that didn't come up with *fork*. Suppose that the pages being virtually copied are coming from a region of a process into which an object is mapped shared. If the virtually copied pages are modified in the sending process, they must of course be physically copied. However, unlike the case in which the original object was mapped private, here the changes must be retained in the share-mapped object. So the copy of the page, rather than being placed in a shadow object belonging to the sender, is put in the shadow object belonging to the receiver (see Figure 7.26).

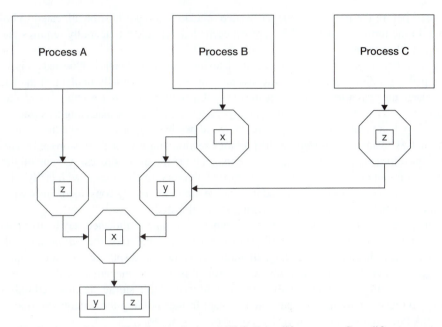

FIGURE 7.25 Process B forks, producing child C. B modifies page x; C modifies page z.

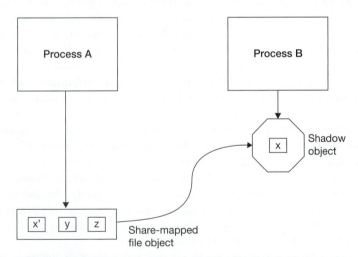

FIGURE 7.26 Process A has share-mapped a file, then performs a virtual copy of the mapped portion of its address space into Process B. If A modifies page x, the page is first copied to B's shadow object and then is modified in the file.

7.3.4 BACKING STORE ISSUES

Pages from share-mapped files are backed by the original file, and thus space for them is managed by the file system. The private pages of a process are those that are backed by no named file. Such pages may have been initialized from a file, as when a file is private-mapped into the process. Or they may have been initialized with zeros. In many systems they are called *anonymous mappings*, since there is no named file to back them.

Unmodified private pages don't require additional backing storage — they can simply be reloaded from their original source. But once such a page is modified, if its page frame is ever reused before the page is no longer needed, backing storage must be allocated to hold its contents. In the terms of Section 7.3.3 above, each shadow object potentially requires backing storage to hold its pages.

There are two concerns here: where is the backing store and when is it allocated? It is usually on disk, perhaps a disk shared with a file system. Some systems actually implement the backing store as a large file or as a set of files, using the file system to manage its space. Other systems reserve disk space for it outside of a file system, using specialized methods for managing its space.

As for when to allocate backing store, there are two basic approaches. The first is an extension of the lazy evaluation concept of the previous section: allocate backing store only when it's needed. Thus, for example, one might private map a huge file into a process. Or one might allocate a huge amount of dynamic storage — in virtual memory. In either case, with lazily allocated backing store, no resources other than address space are immediately consumed. Only when it is necessary to write the pages out is the backing store allocated.

For example, suppose that a gigabyte of dynamic storage is allocated, say by using *malloc* in a C program. As long as there is sufficient room in virtual memory, the *malloc* succeeds. No real resources are allocated. If this range of addresses is then used sparsely — for example for a hash table, in which the total size of the items inserted is just one megabyte — then at most one megabyte of backing store must be allocated to hold it. And this storage is allocated only if it's necessary to reuse for some other purpose the page frames holding these items. So our system might work fine even with just a megabyte or so of backing store.

But suppose there is competition from other processes for the backing store. Even though there is sufficient backing store for our process, others make larger demands, perhaps exceeding the available storage. Our process may have been running for some time when the contents of one of its pages must be written out to backing store. However, at this moment there is no space left in the backing store. The operating system is in a bind. It cannot continue until it writes out the contents of our page, since it needs the page frame for some other process. However, there's no space for it. Two likely outcomes are either to terminate our process, since it's the immediate problem, or to give up entirely and terminate the operating system. Neither is pleasant.

The alternative approach might be characterized as *eager evaluation*: backing store is allocated along with virtual memory. Thus if our process allocates one gigabyte of virtual memory, the operating system allocates one gigabyte of backing store just in case it needs it. If there isn't sufficient backing store, we find out about it at the moment we attempt to allocate storage, rather than at some random moment in our process's execution, as with lazily allocated backing storage. With such early notification of insufficient space, our process might be able to revise its strategy and settle for a smaller amount of storage. If the allocation succeeds, our process is guaranteed that backing store will be available for it whenever needed.

The negative side of eager allocation is, of course, that we may end up with much more backing store than we will ever need — there must always be enough to back up all private pages, regardless of whether they are ever modified, let alone written out.

Most modern systems provide both eager and lazy allocation. In the terminology of Windows, a process can do lazy allocation by *reserving* address space. Such address space cannot be used, but the reservation ensures that no other thread uses the locations for something else. When the space is actually to be used, pages are *committed*, meaning that backing store is also allocated. This is how Windows handles thread stacks. One megabyte of address space is, by default, reserved for each stack, but only a limited amount of space is actually committed. If the thread needs more stack space beyond the original committed pages but within the reservation, the system commits further pages, assuming backing-store space is available. This, of course, means that a thread may have to be terminated in the middle of its execution if it tries to grow its stack but no more backing store is available, but this is considered a reasonable alternative to actually committing one megabyte of stack for each thread. In most Unix systems stack space is reserved but never committed until used.

Normal allocation of memory, such as via *malloc*, and allocation of address space for private-mapped files are done with eager allocation as the default in Windows and most Unix systems, though both provide means for lazy allocation of memory.

Memory management, though not as crucial to system performance as it once was, is still an important concern. Virtual memory was introduced mainly to allow large programs to run on systems with small amounts of primary storage. (It is rumored that virtual memory was a major factor in the sale of add-on primary storage for many systems, as people came to realize that though their large programs could run with small amounts of primary storage, they ran very slowly.) Today virtual memory is important because it enables multiple programs to coexist in a system without interfering with one another. The isolation provided by virtual memory is exploited by recent virtualization technology, which is finally getting the attention of hardware designers who have enhanced their architectures with such improvements as extended page translation.

7.4 CONCLUSIONS

---

1. In the discussion of base and bounds registers in Section 7.1, it was said that "without base registers, after a process is swapped out, it would have to be swapped into the same location in which it resided previously." Explain why this is so. Then, explain how modern virtual memory systems avoid this problem.

2. Early memory-management systems included implementation of a memory fence between user and kernel space, the use of base and bounds registers on a per-process basis, and over-laying. Describe the features that each of these systems was meant to achieve. Explain how modern VM systems provide all these features.

3. In Section 7.2 we discuss three schemes for structuring virtual memory: the use of fixed-size pages, variable-size segments, and a hybrid approach. Explain the advantages of segmented schemes and why modern systems largely do not use them.

4. Virtual memory gives each process the illusion that it has the entire address space at its disposal. How large is the address space for a 32-bit CPU? What about a dual-core 32-bit CPU? What about a 64-bit CPU?

5. **a.** Suppose we have a 30-bit page number and 4-byte pages. How large is the complete page table for such a virtual memory system?

   b. What are the tradeoffs involved in having smaller pages versus larger pages?

   c. Why does Linux choose to use large pages for its kernel address space, and smaller pages for the user address space?

6. Suppose we have a uniprocessor machine. Why is it important to flush the TLB after a context switch between processes?

7. Consider the following extreme example. We have a computer with four page frames of real memory. We wish to execute a single process which in total requires five pages. The program proceeds by sequentially referencing its five pages in order repeatedly. That is, first page 1 is referenced, then 2, then 3, etc. Is LRU the best replacement policy for this system? Explain. If not, what *is* the best replacement policy? For the purpose of this example, assume that the operating system itself occupies no pages of memory.

7.5 EXERCISES

8. When a Unix process invokes *fork*, why should shared mappings not be marked copy-on-write?

9. What are the benefits of inverted page tables as opposed to normal page tables? Why have they fallen out of favor?

*10. Suppose the x64 architecture supported 4KB and 4MB pages. Could the two different page sizes coexist in the same address space as the 4KB and 2MB page sizes do in the actual architecture? Explain.

**11. As mentioned in Section 7.2.5, the IA-64 implementations of both Linux and Windows use linear page tables. Both operating systems use a three-level forward-mapping scheme to map the pages of the page table (this is used strictly by the operating system — the IA-64 TLB relies on its own entries to find page-table entries; if it can't map a page-table entry, it traps to the operating system).

Suppose a thread is accessing a region sequentially, one page at a time, and TLB entries are inserted only when required. Assume that initially no relevant translations are in the TLB (though assume that the translation for the page containing the code being executed is in the TLB) and that the page size is 8K. Linear page-table entries are eight bytes long. Assume all desired translations are in valid entries of the linear page table.

  a. How often will there be a TLB miss, requiring the TLB to load an entry from the linear page table? Stated another way, will there be a miss on each access to a new page, on every fourth new page, on every 64th new page, etc.?

  b. How often will there be a trap to the operating system?

  c. How many memory accesses, other than those needed to fetch instructions, are required to get translation information when a gigabyte if memory is accessed sequentially?

12. Figure 7.5 shows a forward-mapped page-translation approach known as segmented paging. This is what's commonly used on x86 architectures, where 12 bits are used for the offset and 10 bits each for the L1 page number and the L2 page number. There's a special hardware register, known as CR3, that is set by the operating system to point to the L1 page table, known as the page-directory table. The hardware, when doing an address translation, looks in this register to find the address of the page-directory table. Any attempt to store to or load from this register directly while in user mode causes a trap to the operating system.

Suppose we have a virtual-machine monitor for the x86, supporting virtual machines that are intended to behave just like real x86 machines. We'd like to run in a virtual machine an operating system Z that provides a separate virtual address space for each of its processes. Our x86 system is rather old and does not support extended page translation. Thus the VMM must support shadow page tables (Section 7.2.6).

  a. Suppose Z, the operating system on the virtual machine, running in virtual privileged mode, sets CR3 to point to a new page-directory table. How will the VMM be notified that this action has taken place?

  b. What should be the VMM's response to Z's setting of CR3?

  c. What other actions might Z do that affect the translation of virtual virtual addresses to virtual real addresses?

  d. How might things be set up to ensure that the VMM finds out about these actions?

13. Consider an architecture that does address translation using a software-managed TLB, with no page tables. Explain how a VMM might virtualize address translation.

14. Suppose a large amount of thrashing is going on in a system. What would be the first thing you would do to alleviate the situation?

*15. In the Fortran programming language, arrays are stored in column-major order, meaning that adjacent entries in each column are stored in adjacent memory locations. For example (using C notation for matrices), Matrix[i][j] is stored just before Matrix[i+1][j]. However, most scientific programs written in Fortran access arrays using loops similar to the following (again, using C notation rather than Fortran):

```
int Matrix[M][N];
for (i=0; i<M; i++)
    for (j=0; j<N; j++)
        Matrix[i][j] = somefunction(i, j);
```

For example, if M is 6 and N is 4, the elements of the matrix are stored in the order below:

0	6	12	18
1	7	13	19
2	8	14	20
3	9	15	21
4	10	16	22
5	11	17	23

This caused no problems until such programs were run on machines supporting virtual memory, where performance (particularly for large values of M and N) turned out to be much worse than on machines that didn't support virtual memory. Explain why performance was worse. (*Hint*: consider the page-replacement policy.)

16. Explain what the problem is with the one-handed clock algorithm, and explain how the two-handed clock algorithm solves this problem. What factor in this algorithm would let it be adjusted for use in systems of arbitrary-sized memory?

**17. Section 7.3.2.2 discusses virtual-memory management in Windows. It mentions a potential deadlock situation in which one of the two modified-page-writer threads invokes pageable file-system code.

   a. Describe a scenario in which such a deadlock might happen.

   b. Explain how dividing the duties of the modified-page-writer threads — so that one handles page frames containing file data and the other handles page frames containing private data — avoids deadlock.

**18. Many operating systems allow programs to do file I/O in two different ways: programs may use explicit system calls (*read* and *write* in Unix, *ReadFile* and *WriteFile* in Windows) and they may map files into the address space (*mmap* in Unix, *MapViewOfFile* in Windows). In the former approach incoming data is read from disk and stored in a buffer in the operating system, from where it is copied to the program. Outgoing data is copied from the program to the operating system's buffer, then, perhaps sometime later, written to the disk from the buffer. In the latter approach, the virtual-memory system fetches data from the file and writes modified data back to the file, while the program merely accesses and modifies what's in its address space.

   a. Describe the problems that might occur if one program accesses a file via explicit system calls, while another program accesses the same file by mapping it into its address space.

   b. Explain how to fix things so that the problems mentioned in part **a** don't occur.

*19. Many Unix operating systems provide the *madvise* system call with which a thread can tell the operating system how it will be referencing memory. For example, a thread can specify that its references to a particular region of memory will be random, meaning that there's no predicting whether any particular page will be referenced or not at any given moment. It can also specify that its references to a particular region of memory will be sequential, meaning that pages are going to be accessed in sequential order.

Explain how the operating system might use this information. In particular, how might it affect page-ins and page-outs?

20. Unix process X has private-mapped a file into its address space. Our system has one-byte pages; the file consists of four pages, which are mapped into locations 100 through 103. The initial values of these pages are all zeros.

X stores a 1 into location 100.

X forks, creating process Y.

X stores a 1 into location 101.

Y stores a 2 into location 102.

Y forks, creating process Z.

X stores 111 into location 100.

Y stores 222 into location 103.

Z adds the contents of locations 100, 101, and 102, and stores the result into location 103.

What value did Z store into 103?

**21. Section 7.3.3 discusses the use of shadow objects.

  a. Give an example showing how the chain of shadow objects may grow arbitrarily long.

  b. Describe the circumstances under which such a chain may be made shorter.

7.6 REFERENCES

Babaoğlu, Ő. and W. Joy (1981). Converting a Swap-Based System to Do Paging in an Architecture Lacking Page-Referenced Bits. *Operating Systems Review* **15**(5): 78–86.

Belady, L. A. (1966). A Study of Replacement Algorithms for a Virtual-Storage Computer. *IBM Systems Journal* **5**(2): 78–101.

Denning, P. J. (1968). The Working Set Model for Program Behavior. *Communications of the ACM* **11**(5): 323–333.

Denning, P. J. (1970). Virtual Memory. *Computing Surveys* **2**(3): 154–189.

Fotheringham, J. (1961). Dynamic Storage Allocation in the Atlas Computer, Including an Automatic Use of a Backing Store. *Communications of the ACM* **4**(10): 435–436.

Rashid, R., T. J. Tevanian, M. Young, D. Golub, R. Baron, D. L. Black, W. Bolosky, J. Chew (1987). Machine-Independent Virtual Memory Management for Paged Uniprocessor and Multiprocessor Architectures. *Proceedings of the 2nd Symposium on Architectural Support for Programming Languages and Operating Systems*, ACM: 14.

Russinovich, M. E. and D. A. Solomon (2005). *Microsoft Windows Internals*, Microsoft Press.

Talluri, M., M. D. Hill, Y. Khalidi (1995). A New Page Table for 64-bit Address Spaces. *Symposium on Operating Systems Principles*, ACM: 184–200.

Security

Security is clearly an important area. Even when we restrict its scope to computer systems, it's a very broad area. In this chapter we cover a rather narrow but essential aspect of computer security — operating-system support for security. This entails not just making the operating system itself secure, but facilitating the writing of secure applications.

8.1 SECURITY GOALS

The ultimate security goal for any system is that the system does exactly what it's supposed to do — no more and no less. We can divide this rather concise specification into three related areas: confidentiality, integrity, and availability. *Confidentiality* is prevention of unauthorized or unintended disclosure of information. *Integrity* involves making sure that information (including executable code) stored on a system isn't tampered with, augmented, or deleted, either without authorization or unintendedly. *Availability* is the assurance that a system can always perform its intended function.

A system without proper integrity controls certainly can't provide confidentiality — the confidentiality controls could be tampered with because of the lack of integrity. Similarly, a system without good confidentiality controls might well not be able to provide integrity: passwords for system accounts might be easily stolen, thus enabling attackers to tamper with the system.

We ordinarily think of confidentiality and integrity in terms of the accessibility of files. If I want to share information, I put it in a file that is accessible to others. If I have information I consider private, I put it in a file whose access protections prevent others from reading it. I put important data and code that must not be tampered with in files whose access protections prevent others from modifying them.

The approach outlined in the previous paragraph is the basis of security in many if not most current operating systems. However, it doesn't really work. Among the problems is that people don't access files — programs do. I specify file permissions in terms of people. Trina may read and write that file; Andy may only read it. I set things up this way because I trust Trina. But do I trust all the programs she runs? She may download a program from the web that, as a hidden side effect, copies all files accessible to her to some location in a distant country and then wipes out the local files' contents.

Another problem is that my real concern is protecting information, not files. Let's say that a group of my colleagues and I are putting together secret plans for a start-up company. We are careful to protect all files containing these plans. However, one of us is a bit careless and lets some sensitive information end up briefly in a temporary file that is accessible to the world and the world reads it. What I'd really like to do is simply specify that certain information is confidential and not have to worry about getting all the file permissions right (an amazingly difficult task to do correctly all the time).

Furthermore, in addition to being concerned about leaking sensitive information, I might also be concerned about contamination due to bad data or perhaps viruses. When I receive e-mail attachments or when I surf the web, I want to make certain that these attachments and web pages cannot affect the files and other objects in my computer.

One approach to dealing with security problems is to rely on the operating system only for standard file protection, and to depend on applications for more sophisticated security. This has been the approach used in many web browsers that attempt to enforce a number of security-related rules. The result has been complicated programs and rules that aren't fully understood or appreciated by users. Furthermore, these browsers have been notable for their lack of security.

It makes more sense for the operating system to provide protection that can be relied upon by applications. Despite the use of type-safe, managed programming languages such as Java and C#, large, complex applications such as web browsers appear to be more susceptible to corruption than operating systems. Operating systems are large and complex too, but they are isolated from application-level attacks. An operating system can monitor and limit an application much more effectively than can the application itself. To do this, however, an operating system must provide a suitable security architecture.

For example, Microsoft provided an elaborate security architecture within Internet Explorer, but found that it was not sufficient. What was needed was a means "to limit the ability of an exploit running in the browser to create unwanted startup files, modify user data files, make annoying changes to browser configuration settings, or drive the behavior of other programs running on the desktop."[1] They therefore introduced "Protected-Mode Internet Explorer" as part of Windows Vista, which takes advantage of new security features provided by the operating system (as described in Section 8.2.2 below).

8.1.1 THREATS

What are the threats to a computer system? Why do we devote an entire chapter of an operating-systems text to security? The two primary concerns are gaining access to a system and exploiting such access.

How does one gain (illicit) access to a system? The most straightforward approach is to learn someone's user name and password and log in as that person, via either a direct connection or a network. How this is done is usually outside the realm of the operating system. People often have obvious user names with easily guessed passwords. The solution is pretty straightforward — even if your user name is obvious, don't have an easily guessed password.

A system must have some means for determining if the password presented by a user is correct. An obvious approach is to have a file containing each user's password. Such a file, of course, must be well protected. Since people often use the same password on many different systems, discovering someone's password on one system could compromise that person's accounts on other systems. Early Unix systems pioneered the use of one-way functions to encrypt passwords. Such functions are easily computable, but their inverses are not. Furthermore, if f is a one-way function and p and q are passwords, then if $f(p) = f(q)$, it is highly likely that $p = q$. So, if p is your password, then $f(p)$ would be stored in the password file rather than p. When you log in and supply a string q as your password, $f(q)$ would be computed and compared with $f(p)$. If they are equal, then the system assumes you have typed in the correct password. Since f^{-1} is not easily computable, the contents of the password file can be made public without compromising your password.

This was the theory. Unfortunately, it was susceptible to a *dictionary attack*: if most passwords are words from the dictionary, then one could compute f of each word in the dictionary and

---

[1] From "Windows Vista Integrity Mechanism Technical Reference," http://msdn.microsoft.com/en-us/library/bb625964.aspx.

compare the results with what is in the password file and determine, for each password image in the file, what the password is.

To stymie such an attack, some randomization was added. For a password p, rather than storing $f(p)$ in the file, the two-part value $(f(append(p, salt)), salt)$ is stored, where *salt* is a random value. This would require that one launching the dictionary attack would have to do it for all possible salt values. However, (Feldmeier and Karn 1989) showed that doing this is easy, and did it for the 12-bit salt values that were in use in standard Unix systems: they produced a list of what they found to be the 732,000 most common passwords and concatenated each with the 4096 possible salt values, yielding a table that they claimed covered around 30% of all passwords.

The way to counter this sort of attack is to make sure that your password does not exist in the dictionary or on any list of common passwords, perhaps by including in it numbers and punctuation.

Your password might well be remarkably obscure and unguessable, but this is of no avail if someone can steal it. Of course, everyone knows that you should never write down a password (though some argue that any password you can remember isn't good enough), so how can it be stolen? Well, when you type your password into the computer to identify yourself, how can you be sure the program receiving your password is a system program and not someone's application that's designed to look like the system program, but instead steals your password? For example, if, on a Windows XP system, you see the screen shown in Figure 8.1, you might reasonably believe that it is indeed the Windows XP operating system that is asking for your password. But any program can produce this screen image (we've done so here, for example). How can you make certain that the screen really is produced by Windows XP and that it is Windows XP that receives the password you type in?

What can be done (and is done in Windows) is for the operating system to reserve a particular key sequence that goes only to certain system programs and never to application programs — such a sequence is known as a *secure authentication sequence* (SAS). In Windows it is ctrl-alt-delete.[2] When it is typed, the entire display contents is replaced with a special image and one is guaranteed that what is typed subsequently is received by a designated system program.

FIGURE 8.1 Is this log-in prompt real or fake? Used with permission from Microsoft.

---

[2] Ctrl-alt-delete is available in Windows for this purpose because it had never been available for application use in earlier Windows versions or in MS-DOS. This is because prior to its current use, it was used to command MS-DOS to reboot. Unix has no such input that has always been unavailable to application programs, so creating one might "break" applications that have depended on it for some other purpose.

A more serious threat is the *Trojan horse*, by which a legitimate user of a system is convinced to run a program that does something other than (or something in addition to) what it is supposed to do. Let's say you receive a program as an email attachment that purports to upgrade your CD drive to a DVD drive. Do you run it? Probably not — it is pretty obviously a Trojan horse. But suppose a window pops up on your screen and asks you to download a program that will upgrade your web browser to the latest version. Now it is not so clear whether this is a Trojan horse or not. Ideally, we would like some completely reliable means for determining whether the software we are about to run is legitimate (and, while we are at it, bug-free). Since no such means exists, we should be prepared to cope with running programs that intend to do harm. How we can cope is covered in Section 8.2 below.

Trojan horses are a special case of a general class of threats by which authenticated users are somehow tricked into executing "malware." Included here are viruses and many web exploits. A virus is a program that is attached to a *host* — otherwise unmodified executable code or data that arrives at a computer via legitimate means, as in an email message. Executing the program, or running a program that utilizes the data, executes the virus program too. It may do some damage to the current system, but it also propagates itself to others, for example by causing mail containing itself to be sent to the contents of the current user's address book.

Worms are threats that enter a computer system without the active help of a logged-in user. They typically exploit bugs in server applications to gain access. A common example of such a bug is the buffer-overflow problem, in which the server provides a fixed-size buffer to receive arguments of arbitrary length. The attacker exploits this by sending a carefully prepared argument that overwrites the buffer and adjacent locations with executable code, perhaps to the extent of overwriting the return-address field in the current stack frame with an address that points to this code. Thus when a program returns from the current procedure, it begins to execute the code provided by the caller.

Such buffer-overflow problems have been exploited since the 1980s, if not earlier, and continue to be a problem. They have been found and exploited even in network device drivers, allowing successful attacks that begin with the reception of a malformed packet.

Finally, an attacker may gain access to a system via a *trap door*. This is code provided with a system that allows those in the know to gain privileged system access. For example, you might sneak into the system-development process and arrange for your version of the login program to be shipped with all copies of the system. Your version does what it is expected to do, but it also gives anyone who supplies the user name serenus_sammonicus and password abracadabra full superuser (or administrator) access.

Device drivers provide a means for installing trap doors. They are often provided, in binary form, by hardware vendors. They are installed in the operating-system kernel and run in privileged mode. Not all device functions are handled by open, close, read, and write system calls — for example, a DVD device driver might accept a command to eject the DVD. This sort of extra functionality is provided in Unix via the *ioctl* system call, which takes a command argument indicating what is being requested. One might provide a driver that does everything it is supposed to do, but, if given an obscure, undocumented command, takes advantage of its running in privileged mode to give its caller superuser powers.

A particularly scary trap door was created by Ken Thompson, the co-developer of the original Unix system, who modified the C compiler so that whenever it compiled the login program it inserted such a trap door automatically (Thompson 1984). The C compiler was further modified so that whenever it compiled a new C compiler, it automatically produced code in the new C compiler that inserted the trap door whenever the login program was compiled. We trust that the C compiler no longer does this.

Once an attacker is executing code on a system, what can it do? This depends, of course, upon the access rights it has obtained. On most systems, a Trojan horse has whatever access rights are normally given to the user it has tricked, and thus it can do whatever that user can do.

This includes reading, modifying, and deleting files and sending information over the network. Viruses and worms can use the latter ability to propagate themselves.

A more dangerous form of attack is the installation of software such as spyware that records and sends on all information typed into the computer. Even worse is the installation of a *rootkit*, which not only gives the attacker complete control of the system with access rights to everything ("root" or superuser privileges in Unix terminology; "administrator" privileges in Windows terminology), but hides any trace of the attacker's existence.

An attacker who cannot gain access to a system can still cause a security problem by preventing the system from performing its intended chores. In particular, it could launch a *denial-of-service* (DOS) attack, using up system resources and preventing real work from being done. For example, it can bombard a system with malformed network packets requiring substantial processor time and system memory to handle them. Dealing with such an attack involves apportioning system resources so that at most only a reasonable fraction of the system is tied up in coping with it.

What must be done to make a system secure? For starters, we need rules about who is allowed to do what to the system objects we'd like to protect: files, devices, etc. We also need to determine who is allowed to perform operations that affect the system as a whole, such as setting the time-of-day clock, halting the system, backing up files, etc. And, of course, we must enforce all of these rules.

8.2 SECURITY ARCHITECTURES

A system's security architecture encompasses all such security-related issues. In this section we cover a few general frameworks for security architectures and look in detail at how things are done in Unix and Windows.

A common theme in all such architectures is access control. There are certain entities — originally called *objects*, but now, to avoid confusion with the objects of object-oriented programming, sometimes called *resources* — that must be protected. There are other entities — by convention called *subjects* — that are the active agents from which the objects are protected. Threads of control and processes are examples of subjects. The files, web sites, and so forth that they might access are objects. Since a thread can perform operations on other threads and processes (such as terminate them), threads and processes are objects as well.

The most familiar approach for controlling subjects' access to objects is *discretionary access control* (DAC): the owner of an object controls access to it. The ways in which a subject is allowed to access a resource — for example, read-only, read and write, write-only — are called its *access rights*. We think of subjects as running on behalf of human *users* and of resources as being owned by such people. Thus the owner of an object indicates the access rights not in terms of subjects, but in terms of users. A subject's access rights depend on the user on whose behalf it is running. The collection of access rights possessed by a particular subject is called its *protection domain*.

In addition to human users, most systems have abstract users such as "the system." So the term *security principal* (or just *principal*) is often used as the abstraction of the human user. Thus subjects run on behalf of principals, principals own objects, and access to an object is specified in terms of principals. Users and principals are also organized into groups, so that access can be specified for a group of users. Thus a group is also a security principal.

Lampson introduced the notion of an access matrix (see Figure 8.2) to represent how objects may be accessed (Lampson 1971). Each row of the matrix corresponds to a protection domain and each column to an object. Each entry is labeled with the access rights the protection domain has for the object. We think of a subject as executing within a protection domain and thus the domain represents the subject's access rights to each object in the system.

This access matrix sounds pretty simple, but it's been misunderstood and abused almost ever since it was published. What exactly are the rows? Do they correspond to subjects, or do they correspond to principals? Lampson didn't say, leaving things fairly abstract. On the one

FIGURE 8.2 An access matrix with principals labeling rows. Itay's protection domain is read-write access for file /a/b/c and read-write access for process 112. The access-control list for file /a/b/c is read-write for Itay, read for Colin, and read for Owen.

	/a/b/c	/x/y/z	Process 112
Itay	rw		rw
Colin	r		
Panda		rw	
Owen	r		

FIGURE 8.3 An access matrix with subjects labeling rows. Process 112 has a read-write capability for file /a/b/c and a read-write capability for itself.

	/a/b/c	/x/y/z	Process 112
Process 112	rw		rw
Process 13452	r		
Process 23293		rw	
Process 26421	r		

hand, it's convenient to think of each row as being the protection domain of a principal. That way we can easily represent the matrix by storing it by columns, one column per object. If the empty entries are eliminated, then such columns are known as *access-control lists* (ACLs), listing each principal's access rights to the associated object (Lampson called them *access lock lists*, a phrase never used again). With further compression and restrictions on the access rights, such columns become the permission vectors of Unix file systems.

However, associating rows with principals rather than with subjects means that all of a principal's subjects must run in the same protection domain. While this is indeed the case in traditional Unix and Windows systems, it is far from ideal, as we discuss below. So, why not associate rows of the matrix with subjects rather than with principals? Individual access-control entries would have to specify access permissions in terms of subjects rather than principals (see Figure 8.3). This would mean that an access-control entry might have to say, for example, that process 23293 has read-write access to a file rather than saying that user tom has such access. In addition to the obvious conceptual advantages of dealing with "tom" rather than "process 23293," process IDs tend to be more dynamic than users. If process 23293 terminates, all access-control entries that refer to it must be nullified. When process 23294 is created, a whole bunch of new access-control entries may need to be created for it. One way around this is to design a system so that processes tend to be long-lived and persistent. Another way is to forget about the notion of access control lists and represent the access matrix via rows rather than columns. Thus one associates with each domain (subject in this case) the list of all its access rights to objects. Such a list is called a *capability list*, or *c-list*. We explore the use of capability lists in Section 8.2.3 below.

An important design principle that is easily exploited in systems using capability lists is the *principle of least privilege* (Saltzer and Schroeder 1975). This is the notion that a protection domain should be as small as possible — that subjects should run with no more access rights than necessary. This principle makes a lot of sense. Suppose a subject turns out to be running faulty code, or what it is running turns out to be a Trojan horse. If its protection domain is everything accessible by some principal, then everything the principal has access to is in jeopardy. Keeping protection domains small limits the scope of the potential damage. However, even though the principle was stated well over thirty years ago and has been widely accepted as a good idea, few systems provide general support for it.

One thing that has happened in the past thirty or so years is that the meaning of the term *privilege* has narrowed a bit. Rather than including access rights to objects, it now commonly means the ability to perform operations that affect the system as a whole. Most systems provide, as a privilege, the ability to bypass access-rights checking. While some systems provide fine-grained representation of privileges, in many systems it is either all or nothing (e.g., superuser privileges in Unix and administrator privileges in older Windows systems). This is further confused in Linux, which uses the term *capability* to refer to what other systems call privileges[3].

8.2.1 ACCESS CONTROL IN TRADITIONAL SYSTEMS

Unix and Windows provide contrasting approaches to discretionary access control. Though they have similar notions of a process's security context, they have different ways of representing it. We introduced Unix's permission vectors in Section 1.3.5.6. Windows's ACLs, though more powerful, are considerably more complex. Both provide means for a modicum of least privilege — primarily for servers — but do so in radically different ways.

A process's security context in both operating systems includes a user identity, a set of group identities, and a set of privileges. Both also include a primary group identity, a notion very important in Unix but much less so in Windows, as we explain soon. In Windows this security context is aggregated as a process's *access token* and, as discussed below, can be manipulated and copied to others.

Unix's objects[4] are tagged with security information including an owner, a group, and a permission vector. Only an object's owner (or a process with the appropriate privilege, such as superuser) may modify the permission vector. As we know from Chapter 1, the permission vector gives permissions for the object's owner, group, and the rest of the world. Thus objects must have owners and groups to be referred to by the permission vector.

Window's objects are tagged with *security descriptors*[5] that include an owner, a group (not used by Windows proper, but only by its rarely used POSIX subsystem), and two ACLs.

---

[3] In Linux's defense, this use of "capability" comes from what was ultimately a failed attempt at a POSIX standard — POSIX 1003.1e.

[4] This discussion applies only to named objects. For example, standard Unix pipes are objects, but don't have names. There is some variation in how named objects are treated. Processes have identifiers (process IDs), but also appear in the naming hierarchy within the /proc directory. The various versions of Unix have different approaches to structuring this name space. Each named aspect of a process has a name in the /proc directory with owner, group, and permission-vector information. Many Unix systems support what is known as "System V IPC," which has a naming structure independent of the file-system naming hierarchy. Ownership and permissions are specified in a manner similar, but not identical, to other named objects. To simplify our discussion, we assume that all objects are named in the file-system naming hierarchy and have owners, groups, and permission vectors as described in Chapter 1.

[5] Windows uses security descriptors consistently for all named objects.

In similar fashion to Unix, an object's owner may modify the ACLs, but others may as well, depending on the ACL. One of the ACLs is the *discretionary access-control list* (DACL), which specifies access permissions as one might expect. The other — the *system access-control list* (SACL) — specifies which actions by whom should be recorded in a system audit file.

The protection domain of a process in both Unix and Windows is determined by its user and group identities in conjunction with its privileges. With some exceptions discussed below, these identities and privileges are set up when a user logs in. What happens is that once the system authenticates a user, her or his initial process is set up with the user identity and all the group identities, as well as (in the usual case) a minimal set of privileges. All other processes are descendants of the initial one and inherit its security context.

The security context is set up once and for all at login time primarily because it is a relatively time-consuming task. But a consequence of this is that removing someone from a particular group does not take effect until the next time that person logs in. In most environments this is not a big deal, but in some it is a serious problem.

We ordinarily think of user identities and group identities as having common names, such as "tom" or "inGroup." But for a number of reasons (see Exercise 1), such names are not used within the operating system and must be translated into other identifiers. For example, traditional Unix systems maintain files (/etc/passwd and /etc/group) that map user and group names to integer user and group IDs.

An issue is the scope of these IDs. If we are interested in accessing files only on a local system, it makes sense for the scope of user and group IDs to be just that system. But suppose we have a distributed file system: it might make sense for the scope of these IDs to encompass all the computers using it. This would require a common administration for all systems to ensure that all are using the correct IDs. In practice, this is done by having systems share a common database; many NFS/Unix systems use network information system (NIS), while Windows systems use active directory (AD).

If two separately administered systems are merged, there are likely to be collisions in the ID spaces used by the two. Windows avoids this problem by using globally unique values of variable length called security IDs (SIDs).

The general architecture of Windows access protection in Figure 8.4 has a subject with its access token, an object with a security descriptor, and the security reference monitor (SRM), which is a kernel module responsible for all access descriptions. The SRM has access to an audit log to which it can write its access decisions for auditing, as specified in objects' SACLs.

Security descriptors attached to each object include the SID of the object's owner and two ACLs, as mentioned above. The DACL consists of a list of access-control entries (ACEs), each of which contains the SID of a security principal (such as a user or a group), a bit vector indicating what sort of access is described (such as reading, writing, executing, deleting, etc.),

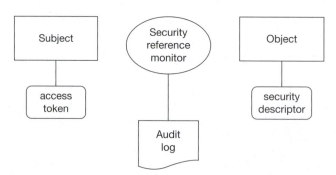

FIGURE 8.4 Windows access-protection architecture.

a field indicating whether the access is allowed or denied, and some flags that we explain soon. Unlike Unix permission vectors, DACLs allow one to specify rather intricate access rules. As in Unix, a subject requests a set of access types, such as read-write, from the SRM. The SRM takes the subject's request along with the subject's access token and consults the object's DACL. A number of complications to this are discussed later in this section, but a simplified version of the decision algorithm, covering most uses, is as follows:

```
accesses_permitted = null
walk through the ACEs in order
    if access token's user SID or group SID match ACE's SID
        if ACE is of type access-deny
        if a requested access type is denied
           Stop — access is denied
        if ACE is of type access-allow
            if a requested access type is permitted
                add access type to accesses_permitted
            if all requested accesses are permitted
                Stop — access is allowed
    if not all requested access types permitted
       Stop — access is denied
```

An empty DACL grants no access whatsoever; if there is no DACL (as opposed to an empty one), all accesses are granted to all.

Consider the example in Figure 8.5. On the top is a DACL with two ACEs. If Colin is a member of inGroup and desires read or write (or both) access to the DACL's object, he will be granted it, since the allow entry provides all he asks for and it precedes the deny entry. Note that if the ACEs are ordered as in the DACL on the bottom of the figure, then Colin's request will be denied — the order of ACEs in a DACL is important. However, the tools provided in Windows to examine DACLs do not let one see the order in which they appear. Thus Colin cannot determine by looking at the tools' views of DACLs what sort of access he gets. Fortunately, he can use the tool to ask what his effective access will be.

SACLs are structured just like DACLs, except their ACEs indicate whether a reference to the indicated access by the indicated principal should be written to the audit log. (This happens regardless of whether the DACL permits the action or not.)

Most Windows users are probably barely aware that access control exists, much less understand it (the same can probably be said of many Unix users, despite Unix's simpler model). Thus it is important that the DACLs assigned to objects by default make sense. Windows's rules for this are almost as complicated as the rules for DACL evaluation.

A new object may get its DACL in one of four ways; all of the applicable approaches in the list below are used.

- The creating thread may provide a set of ACEs to assign to the new object.

- Objects (such as directories) that "contain" other objects are known as *container objects*. Some of the ACEs in such objects are marked as inheritable, meaning that they are copied to new objects created within them.

- Subjects may have a default DACL in their access tokens. If there is no other source of ACEs for a new object and the creator has such a DACL, then its entries are copied to the object.

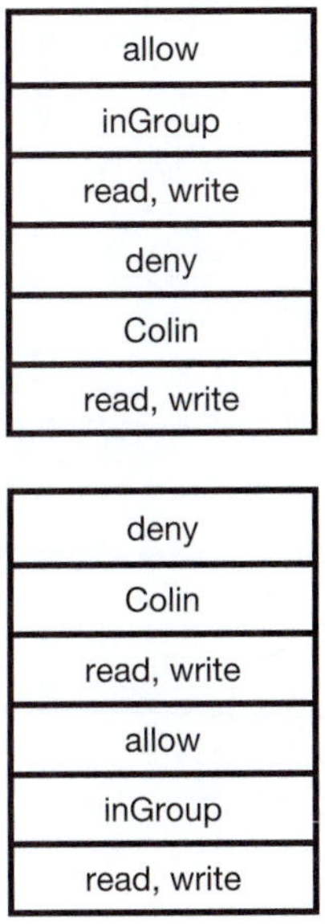

| allow |
| inGroup |
| read, write |
| deny |
| Colin |
| read, write |

| deny |
| Colin |
| read, write |
| allow |
| inGroup |
| read, write |

FIGURE 8.5 Windows DACL example.

- If none of the other three rules apply, the object gets no DACL (as opposed to an empty DACL) and thus gets no access protection.

During the 1990s the Unix community tried to adopt a standard approach, POSIX 1003.1e, for access control that included an ACL model not terribly dissimilar to that of Windows. While this effort was ultimately abandoned, much of what was done has influenced modern Unix systems and there is support for ACLs in both Linux and Solaris, among other Unix systems.

The basic security model of both Unix and Windows gives user processes protection domains that are as large as possible — allowing access to everything permitted by the discretionary access-control policies. Though neither system provides much support for allowing clients (e.g., ordinary users) to reduce their protection domains, both provide means for servers, particularly system servers, to do so.

It would be nice to give object owners a bit more discretion about the use of their objects. A principal might want to allow others to access a file, but only if they do so using code it provides. For example, suppose whenever you run a particular application, a log record is to be written to a file. The record must be of a particular format, and it must be written only as a side effect of running the application.

The file must have appropriate access protection so that others cannot write to it arbitrarily. However, when you (and others) run the application, it must be able to append records to the file. One approach might be to have some sort of server that is accessed via a named pipe, so that whatever is written to the pipe is received by the application, checked for the proper format, and then, if appropriate, written to the file. But how can the server be certain that the data sent to it comes from the application and not from some impostor who is trying to trick it?

As another example, suppose we are designing a print server. Applications send it file names and it prints the files. The problem is making sure it can read the files whose names it is given. One approach might be to have it run as some all-powerful user (such as Unix's superuser) who is able to bypass access control and read everything. But then how do you make certain that callers can't trick it into printing files that the callers aren't allowed to read? One easy way around this problem is to send the server not the name of the file, but the contents of the file. For the sake of an example, assume this approach is not feasible, perhaps because we do not have enough storage space to hold additional copies of files to be printed. We discuss yet another approach based on transmitting file descriptors in Exercise 4.

Finally, suppose we have a file whose contents are sensitive, such as a file containing all users' passwords. We would like to enable users to change their passwords in the file, but to make certain that they cannot change other users' passwords. Clearly we need a service running in a protection domain that has write access to whatever objects contain password information. Its clients do not need to give it access to additional files, but they do need to identify themselves securely. One approach might be to require callers to supply their old passwords along with their new ones, but many will feel this should be unnecessary, since they've already authenticated themselves with the system and thus their identities should be known.

Unix systems use the *set-user-ID* approach, named after the system feature that makes it possible.[6] Roughly speaking, what this approach does is that when an executable file marked set-user-ID is *exec*'d, its process runs as if it were the owner of the file.

The details are considerably more complicated. A Unix process actually has three user IDs (principals) associated with it: the real user ID, the effective user ID, and the saved user ID. Similarly, it has three group IDs: the real group ID, the effective group ID, and the saved group ID. (It also has an additional list of runtime groups, as discussed above.) Normally, all the user IDs are identical and all the group IDs are identical. However, when a process execs a file marked

---

[6] This feature was patented by Dennis Ritchie, its inventor, but was later put in the public domain by his employer, AT&T. See http://www.textfiles.com/law/softpat.txt.

set-user-ID, both the effective user ID and the saved user ID become the ID of the owner of the file. The real user ID does not change. When the process attempts to open files, the effective user ID determines its permissions. Thus the process runs as if it were the owner of the *exec*'d file. (We discuss the role of the saved user ID soon.)

For example, the *passwd* command on traditional Unix systems is owned by root and is marked set-user-ID.[7] When one runs the command (by typing its name into a shell), the effective and saved user IDs of the process *exec*'ing the file containing *passwd* are changed to root. Thus the process is able to read and modify the file containing the password database. Of course, the *passwd* program must determine who the invoker is and change the password of that principal only. To do this, it issues the *getuid* system call, which returns the real user ID of the process, which is the user ID of the invoking principal.

As another example, let's look at something similar to the print service, but simpler. Many Unix systems support the *wall* (write-all) command, which writes a message on the screens of all logged-on users of a computer; this message may be supplied by giving the name of a file that contains it. Superuser powers are required to write a message to all screens, and thus *wall* is a set-user-ID program owned by root. To prevent people from using *wall* to display the contents of someone else's mailbox to all users, we need to make certain that any file given to *wall* is actually readable by the invoker.

One technique for doing this is to use Unix's *access* system call, which tests to see if a file is accessible based on the caller's real IDs (as opposed to effective IDs). It might be used as follows:

```
// possible code from wall:
if (access(CallersFile, R_OK) == 0) {
   // ... fail
}
fd = open(CallersFile, O_RDONLY);
CopyFileToTerminalWindows(fd);
```

The above code checks, by calling *access*, to see if *wall*'s invoker has read permission for the given file. Assuming it does, then *wall* opens the file (using its effective user ID of root).

This looks reasonable, but suppose you invoke *wall* from the shell as follows:

```
% wall FileContainingInnocuousMessage
```

You arrange that the following code is executed at the same time that *wall* is executing the code above:

```
unlink("FileContainingInnocuousMessage");
symlink("/var/spool/mail/andy",
   "FileContainingInnocuousMessage");
```

If this code runs at just the right moment, it will *unlink* (i.e., remove) the file just after *wall*'s call to *access* has confirmed its readability. Moreover, if the call to *symlink* occurs before *wall*'s call to *open*, what *wall* will be opening, and hence copying to everyone's terminal windows, is the contents of Andy's mail file. This is known as a "time-of-check-to-time-of-use" (TOCTTOU) vulnerability, and is clearly a problem.

---

[7] In networked environments in which the password database is maintained by a server for the entire network, the *passwd* command works differently. The assumption here is that the password database is stored in a local file.

Eliminating the problem involves the heretofore-unused saved user ID. What *wall* needs to do is to open the file with the access checks done using its real user ID (i.e., the invoker's user ID). The *seteuid(uid)* system call sets the caller's effective user ID to the argument if the argument is the caller's real, effective, or saved user ID. Thus by calling *seteuid(getuid())*, *wall* sets its effective user ID to be the same as its real user ID. If it then calls *open*, it will succeed only if the file is readable by *wall*'s invoker. Since *wall*'s saved user ID hasn't changed (and is still zero), it can now go back to running as root by calling *seteuid(0)*.[8] The complete sequence is:

```
seteuid(getuid());
fd = open(CallersFile, O_RDONLY);
seteuid(0);
CopyFileToTerminalWindows(fd);
```

There is also a set-group-ID feature that takes advantage of a process's real, effective, and saved group IDs. It works analogously to the set-user-ID feature and can be used along with it.

Windows, which does not support set-user-ID, has a different approach to solving these problems. As mentioned above, a Windows process's credentials (user ID and group IDs) are stored in a kernel data structure called an *access token*. Rather than having users invoke new instances of programs that manage protected files, it employs server processes that receive requests to perform operations involving such files. So that they can act on behalf of their clients, these servers actually receive the clients' credentials in the form of copies of their access tokens, and can use them (instead of their own) when accessing files and other objects. This approach, called *impersonation*, is enabled by clients who, as part of opening or creating a communication channel to a server, specify a *security quality of service* indicating the extent to which the server may use their access tokens. This use ranges from not at all, to providing the client's identity, to granting the server complete use of the client's token when accessing objects.

Thus, for example, to change your password, you execute a program that sends a pass-word-change request to a system-service process known as the *local security authority subsystem* (LSAS), over a channel for which you have requested a security quality of service of identifi-cation-only. LSAS runs with administrator privileges and can modify the password database. It actually requires you to type in your old password, presumably to keep someone from changing your password while you go off for a cup of coffee. However, LSAS is assured, since it has your identification-enabled access token, that it's really you.

A local print server could be constructed that prints files given their names. You send it a file name over a channel for which you have specified a full-impersonation security quality of service. On receipt of your message, a thread running in the server can request to impersonate the client at the other end of the communication channel. At this point, all access attempts (such as opening files) are done using the client's access token rather than that of the thread's process. When the thread is finished with the request, it reverts back to its original (its process's) access token.

Both the set-user-ID and the impersonation approaches allow object owners to provide access to their objects via owner-provided code, running in protection domains consisting of the union of what the object owner can access and what the client can access. This model works well as long as the object owners are trusted. In the examples given, and as used in most real systems, the object owner is essentially the operating system, so it pretty much has to be trusted.

---

[8] How does one change the saved user ID? In some Unix systems, such as Solaris and MacOS X, calls to *seteuid(uid)* change the real, effective, and saved user IDs to the argument, assuming that one of the old user IDs is equal to the argument. In Linux, *setuid* behaves this way only if the original effective user ID is root. Otherwise it changes only the real and effective user IDs, and thus non-root callers cannot change the saved user ID.

Is such trust a good idea? Though I must trust the operating system, perhaps there is a bug in a server's code that, in certain circumstances, causes it to destroy all files in its protection domain. Perhaps a server has been taken over by an attacker. The program I've just downloaded from a website not only provides an exciting game, but also copies my confidential files to another website.

Putting things another way, suppose you are told that the program you are about to run may have been sabotaged and there's some chance it will maliciously modify some of your files. It would be foolish to run the program in a protection domain in which all of your files are accessible. Yet, to a certain extent, this is what you do whenever you run a program on a computer that is connected to the Internet. To be safe, you really want to run the program in the smallest protection domain possible, one that provides just the access rights required for just those files the program is supposed to access. Thus if your program does turn out to have been sabotaged, you have minimized the extent of the damage.

We return to the *principle of least privilege* introduced in Section 8.2 above. We discuss in Section 8.2.3 below how it is well supported in capability-based systems, but how might it be done within the discretionary access control approaches of Unix and Windows?

A simple approach used in Unix is to reduce a program's name space. Rather than having the entire file-system naming tree be available to a subject, one can arrange so that just a subtree is. This approach is used for FTP (file transfer protocol) servers in order to restrict anonymous clients to retrieving files from a small subtree. Thus even if its clients can somehow subvert the program and gain superuser powers, all they can use them for is to get access to the objects they've been given access to anyway.

Implementing such a restriction is not as simple as it might seem. An easy approach (which is still available for use) is to associate with each process a process-specific root directory, such that all references to the "/" directory refer to this root, and references to ".." within this directory refer to itself. The default value is the normal root directory, but one can change it by calling the *chroot* system call, giving it the path name of what is to become the process's root.

Such use of *chroot* might seem to be foolproof. However, if the caller of *chroot* is holding a file descriptor of a directory outside of the subtree to which it is supposedly restricted, it can access any file within the complete tree. For example, suppose we have restricted a process to using a subtree, but that process then executes the following code:

```
chdir("/");
pfd = open(".", O_RDONLY);
mkdir("Houdini", 0700);
chroot("Houdini");
fchdir(pfd);
for (i=0; i<100; i++)
  chdir("..");
chroot(".");
```

The first call to *chdir* sets the process's current directory to the root of the subtree it has been restricted to. It then opens that directory and holds onto the file descriptor. It creates a new directory, *Houdini*, that is a subdirectory of its process-specific root, and calls *chroot* to set its process-specific root to that directory. It now has a file descriptor for a directory that is outside the subtree to which it is currently restricted. It sets its current directory to be that directory, then follows the path upwards in the tree, changing its current directory one tree level at a time. Since the path "/.." leads one to "/", and assuming that the initial process-specific root had a path-length no greater than one hundred from the real root, when our process completes the *for* loop, its current directory will be the real root of the file system. It now simply calls *chroot* again to set its root to be the real root.

Even if we solve this problem, there are others. Unix set-uid programs such as *su* use the /etc/passwd and /etc/shadow files to determine if the caller is providing the correct password. As shown in Figure 8.6 and Figure 8.7, one might be able to use chroot to trick su into looking at the caller's version of /etc/passwd and /etc/shadow, rather than the system's versions. Thus unrestricted use of chroot might actually reduce security rather than improve it.

Tightening things up to produce an implementation that really does restrict a process to a subtree is not difficult (see Exercise 5). The FreeBSD *jail* facility does exactly this. Thus if it is convenient to set up a server so that all the objects it needs (and only those objects) appear in a subtree, then this is a viable technique for helping to secure servers.

An even more effective approach is to run each server in a separate virtual machine, with a limited file system made available that provides only what the server needs. Not only does the server run in a limited name space, but even if it subverts the entire operating system it cannot access more than it is supposed to.

Chromium OS (Google1) (Google2), an operating system being developed at Google that incorporates a Linux kernel, uses isolation as one of its major defenses. Among its features is its ability to isolate groups of processes within various namespaces, including:

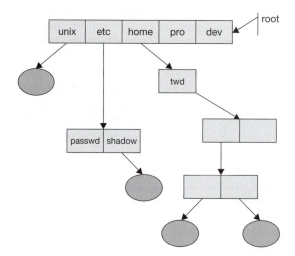

FIGURE 8.6   Before calling *chroot*.

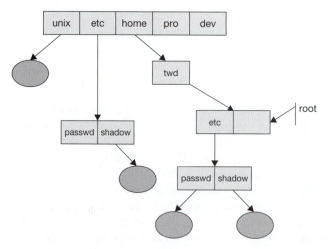

FIGURE 8.7   After calling *chroot*.

- *Process-ID name spaces.* A group of processes within such a namespace are aware of one another's existence, but not of any other processes running on the system. The first process in the namespace is assigned process ID 1, the second 2, and so forth. Process IDs refer only to processes in the namespace, thus it is impossible to refer to others.

- *IPC (interprocess communication) namespace.* Certain Unix IPC objects are assigned names that are independent of the file-system namespace. Analogous to process-ID namespaces, groups of processes in an IPC namespace may refer only to IPC objects within the namespace.

- *VFS namespace.* Processes and groups of processes may have private file namespaces. A good example of this is the /tmp directory, which is normally viewable by all. Giving a group of processes a private namespace mounted at /tmp makes the group's view of /tmp completely different from those of other groups.

- *Network namespace.* Network devices and processes can be assigned to network namespaces, such that only those processes in the namespace can access the devices in the namespace, and processes in the namespace can access only those network devices.

Chromium OS also supports a new Linux feature known as *control groups,*[9] which allow processes to be placed in groups that are tightly controlled in their use of resources, in particular processor and memory. This provides a means for the operating system to defend against denial-of-service attacks, by ensuring that particular services (those undergoing attack) cannot use all the available system resources.

Windows uses a different approach to limit what servers may access. Rather than segregate a server's allowed objects into a subtree, it simply marks them and restricts servers to accessing only such marked objects. It does this by adding to a server's access token a list of additional SIDs (security identifiers) that identifies the application that is running (as opposed to identifying the user running the application, as normal SIDs appearing in the access token do). These SIDs are known as *restricting SIDs*, and typically there is only one. Access-control entries are added to the ACLs of all objects the application is to access (essentially "marking" them), giving permission to a restricting SID. When a thread in such a server process attempts to open an object, an access check is performed twice on the ACL: the first time with the subject's normal SID, the second with its restricting SID. Access is granted only if both access checks are successful.

Figure 8.8 shows the use of restricting SIDs to reduce a protection domain. Here the print service runs as the system administrator and hence would normally be able to access all files. In

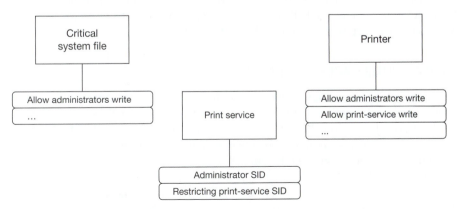

FIGURE 8.8   Using restricted SIDs to reduce a server's protection domain.

---

[9] See http://lxr.linux.no/#linux+v2.6.30/Documentation/cgroups/cgroups.txt.

particular, it has write access to some critical system file, as well as to the printer. By adding a print-service SID to its access token as a restricting SID and adding an ACL entry to the printer (but not to the critical system file), we allow the print service to access the printer, but not any files that lack ACL entries allowing the print service access.

Finally, we discuss privileges. Traditionally in both Unix and Windows systems there are unprivileged users, who are subject to DAC policies, and privileged users, who can do anything they please. In Unix, there is exactly one privileged account, known as either *root* or *superuser*, which has a user ID of 0. In Windows, any account may be marked as an administrator, giving it full privileges. Though in a few instances giving a user (or a subject) such privilege is warranted, in most cases it is not. A user or subject who merely needs to be able to set the system's clock does not require the ability to read and modify any file in the system unimpeded.

Standard procedure in Unix systems is for all users to use unprivileged accounts and for administrators to use the "su" command (supplying an appropriate password) to create a process running as superuser when required. This two-level approach is not great, but it is a lot better than if administrators were always to have superuser privileges.

More recent Unix systems use a new subsystem known as *sudo*, which allows the caller to execute a single command, provided he or she gives the correct password, and the user ID of the caller as well as the command are in a list of allowed callers and commands. This allows fairly fine-grained control of commands, though not of objects accessed. In addition, its implementation requires no new kernel functionality — it is built on the set-user-ID facility.

Prior to Windows Vista, the situation in Windows was much worse. Rather than an "su" command, Windows has a "run-as" command that allows one to run a command as another user, such as administrator. Though this might seem similar to su, in practice it's either unknown or cumbersome, so most administrators (and all home-computer users) always use an account with full administrator privileges.

Windows Vista introduces the notion of *user account control* (UAC) to improve its notion of accounts with administrator privileges. Such accounts are given two access tokens, one without special privileges, the other with administrator privileges. Normally the user's subjects use the unprivileged access token. But when a subject attempts to perform an operation that requires privilege, such as modifying a file that the user would not normally be allowed to touch, the user is asked if she or he really wants to perform the action. If so, the subject resumes execution using the privileged access token. So, if the program the user downloaded from the web tries to do something requiring administrator privileges, the user can stop it.

A relatively recent addition to both Unix and Windows is a finer granularity of privileges, rather than "all or nothing." In both systems the intent is to provide a restricted environment for servers, keeping in step with the notion of least privilege.

8.2.2 MANDATORY ACCESS CONTROL

Rather than leaving access permissions to the discretion of object owners, we might want to enforce a system-wide policy on information access. Since such a policy does not leave security to the discretion of object owners, it is known as *mandatory access control* (MAC). The standard example of this, primarily because early research in the area was driven and funded by them, is protection of classified information by the U.S. military. This form of MAC is known as *multi-level security* (MLS).

National-defense documents are labeled with security classifications coming from a hierarchical set including *unclassified*, *confidential*, *secret*, and *top secret*, with unclassified being the lowest level and top secret being the highest.[10] Individuals are given security clearances

---

[10] Classifications higher than top secret exist, some of whose names are top secret.

indicating the maximum classification of documents they are allowed to see. Thus if I have a secret clearance, I may look at unclassified, confidential, and secret documents, but not top-secret documents.

However, even if I am cleared for secret, I'm not allowed to see all secret documents, only those for which I have a "need to know" (essentially the principle of least privilege). Furthermore, in addition to the hierarchical categories, there are independent, non-hierarchical categories known as *compartments*. The names of these compartments can be used to label documents in addition to their hierarchical labels, and individuals are cleared for individual compartments. For example, I might be cleared for top secret, compartment A. I'm not allowed to access documents that are labeled compartment B, even if they are also labeled merely secret.

Note that even if am cleared only for secret, I can produce a document labeled top secret, though I can't look at it after producing it. This doesn't sound all that sensible, though it's a bit more reasonable if I phrase it as contributing to a top-secret document, rather than producing it all by myself.[11]

Our goal is to reproduce this system of classification in a computer system and enforce it. This requires establishing access-control rules that are governed by system-wide policy — *mandatory access control* (MAC). This approach was the subject of a rigorous study by Bell and LaPadula starting in 1973 and is thus known as the Bell–LaPadula model (Bell and LaPadula 1973).

In the Bell–LaPadula model, objects are labeled with a security classification and subjects are labeled with a clearance. There are two basic properties, given rather unimaginative names by Bell and LaPadula:

1. *simple security property*: no subject may read from an object whose classification is higher than the subject's clearance.

2. **-property*: no subject may write to an object whose classification is lower than the subject's clearance.

These properties are more conveniently known as the *no-read-up* and the *no-write-down* properties.

If this model is adhered to strictly, we get an information black hole: information tends to move to higher security levels and thus can never be seen again by subjects at lower levels. This makes it difficult to implement national policy: decisions based on highly classified information must, at some point, be passed on to the troops so they know where they are going. Thus Bell and LaPadula make the distinction between trusted and untrusted subjects. The latter must obey the rules; the former, who are assumed to be both trusted and intelligent, are not bound to the rules and thus may release information that would otherwise be classified.

While trusted subjects must run programs that have been carefully vetted to be trustworthy, virus-free, etc., untrusted subjects may run ordinary, off-the-shelf programs. Suppose an untrusted subject at the top-secret level runs a program that has been infected with a virus, one that turns the program into spyware. Let's refer to this subject as agent X. It gathers all sorts of sensitive information that it would like to transmit to the spymaster, who's accessible via e-mail. However, e-mail may be used only by subjects running at the unclassified level. Thus agent X cannot send e-mail containing the information it's gathered to the spy master.

However, agent X has a confederate, agent Y, who is running at the unclassified level. Unfortunately for them, due to the no-write-down and no-read-up properties, agent X cannot pass

---

[11] William Safire, the late *New York Times* columnist and formerly a speech writer for Richard Nixon, reported that he once drafted a statement for Nixon that he thought might be considered a bit sensitive, so he labeled it "[President's] eyes only, not for distribution" and gave it to the President for review. He tried to get it back for revision a bit later, but was told no, he wasn't cleared for eyes only. (See http://www.pbs.org/wgbh/pages/frontline/newswar/interviews/safire.html.)

on its information to agent Y: X cannot put information into a file that is accessible to Y. Similarly, X cannot write to an interprocess communication channel (such as a pipe) that is readable by Y.

Bell and LaPadula prove there can be no leakage of information from a higher level to a lower level, as long as information travels through *overt* channels — those that are accounted for by the model. However, they don't cover *covert* channels (Lampson 1973), those not accounted for in the model.

For example, X and Y know that an invasion is planned; will it be tomorrow? X finds out the answer and thus needs to communicate one bit of information to Y. X and Y agree on the following technique: if the invasion is not tomorrow, X does nothing. But if the invasion is tomorrow, X uses all available processor resources for 10 minutes. Y can thus determine, by monitoring system load, whether the invasion is imminent, and then send appropriate e-mail to the spy master.

What can be done to prevent this? Remove all covert channels, of course. (Lampson 1973) provides advice on doing this, though it readily admits that it is probably not possible to identify, let alone remove, all of them. Exercise 7 covers eliminating this particular covert channel.

As we have just seen, the Bell–LaPadula model is susceptible to viruses and other attacks on the integrity of information. If our concern is with integrity and not with confidentiality, we might replace the no-read-up and no-write-down properties with *no-write-up* and *no-read-down* variations. Biba proposed this approach shortly after the Bell–LaPadula model was published (Biba 1977). He pointed out that in many cases unclassified information is important; tampering with it could have grave implications for national security. He gives as an example a database containing interstate transportation routes. Clearly, its contents are not secret. However, tampering with the database maliciously could cause serious problems in coping with certain national emergencies.

One might argue that the obvious solution is to protect both confidentiality and integrity, and thus enforce no-read-up, no-write-down, no-read-down, and no-write-up. This would mean no communication at all between security levels. This is not really feasible and thus hasn't been done.

An important implementation issue is the location of the code that enforces security. The part of a system (comprising both hardware and software) on which security depends is known as the *trusted computing base* (TCB). Pretty much by definition, this is the part that *really* has to be secure. For example, that part of the hardware that enforces the distinction between privileged mode and non-privileged mode is part of it, as well as those parts of the operating system responsible for memory mapping and access control. Many approaches to security mandate, as part of the TCB, a *security reference monitor* (SRM), which is a single module responsible for all access decisions. The intent is that keeping the code that handles such decisions compact means not only that the code can be readily verified, but that it is relatively easy to check that all code paths dealing with access decisions go through it.

The U.S. Department of Defense released *The Trusted Computer System Evaluation Criteria* (called the *Orange Book* because of the color of its cover) in 1983 and a revised version in 1985. As the title implies, it provides criteria for evaluating the security of a computer system. The intent is that one submits a system for evaluation and gets back a grade indicating how secure it is. We briefly summarize the criteria here; those interested in the details should consult the actual document (Department of Defense 1985).

The lowest grade is D — *minimal protection*. This might also be thought of as a grade of F, as it means that the system flunked.

Next is C — *discretionary protection*. It requires a minimal level of security and is divided into two classes, C1 and C2. To be in class C1, a system must provide controls so that users can protect private information and keep others from accidentally reading or destroying information. The model is of cooperating users processing information at the same levels of security. Most Unix and Windows system should fit within this class easily.

To be in class C2, a system must meet all the requirements for class C1 and, in addition, users of the system must be individually accountable for their actions through login procedures, auditing, and resource isolation. A security reference monitor must be supported. Unix and Windows systems may relatively easily aspire to be in this class.

The first serious security grade is B — *mandatory protection*. It is divided into three classes. To be in class B1, a system must meet all the requirements for C2. In addition, it must have an informal statement of the security policy and must provide subject and object labeling and mandatory access control over named subjects and objects. The capability must exist for accurately labeling exported information (e.g., Top-Secret printouts must be clearly labeled as such).

To be in class B2, a system must meet all the requirements for class B1 and, instead of an informal statement of the security policy, there must be a clearly defined and documented formal security policy. The discretionary and mandatory access controls of B1 must extend to all subjects and objects, much more thorough testing and review is required, and very stringent configuration management controls are necessary.

To be in class B3, a system must meet all the requirements for class B2. In addition, its trusted computing base (TCB) must be small enough to be subjected to rigorous analysis and test. All accesses of subjects to objects must be mediated, the system must be tamper-proof, a security administrator must be supported, audit mechanisms must be expanded to signal security-relevant events, and detailed system recovery procedures must be in place.

Grade A is given for *verified protection*. Only one class is defined. The only difference between this class, A1, and B3, is that the formally specified design must be formally verified.

Note that in the Orange Book, "mandatory access control" means multi-level security following the Bell–LaPadula model. This model was adhered to not just because computer viruses were little more than a theoretical possibility when the Orange Book was written, but also because, despite Biba's work, confidentiality was considered much more important than integrity.

What are the security requirements for users of personal computers — those who surf the web and receive email with attachments (and open them)? Would PCs benefit from any of the Orange-Book requirements? The threats that most individuals are concerned about have to do with confidentiality — theft of credit-card numbers, bank passwords, etc. But these threats are related more to integrity issues than to confidentiality issues: attackers install spyware, viruses modify key files, etc. Most people have no use for the strict security levels of Bell–LaPadula. However, whether they know it or not, they are concerned about the installation of malware on their computers. This gives us a potential application of the Biba model.

Microsoft has adapted the Biba model for Windows, starting with Vista, calling it the *Windows integrity mechanism*.[12] Their intent is to protect system and user data from possibly untrustworthy subjects, regardless of the subjects' user credentials. In particular, they are targeting web browsers, a popular outlet for malware.

Both subjects and objects are assigned integrity levels, chosen from the following set:

- untrusted level
- low integrity level
- medium integrity level
- high integrity level
- system integrity level

A subject's integrity level is included in its access token, while objects' integrity levels are included in their SACLs (Section 8.2.1). In keeping with their threat model, the default policy

---

[12] See http://msdn.microsoft.com/en-us/library/bb625964.aspx.

is *no-write-up* — read-down is always permitted; higher-integrity subjects are assumed to be careful about what they read. In a departure from the usual meaning of mandatory, object owners are permitted to change the integrity level of their objects (but only to lower levels). In addition, they may specify that an object requires *no-read-up*, i.e., that lower-privilege-level subjects may not read the object's contents. This is particularly important for process objects, so as to keep untrustworthy subjects from reading their address spaces and obtaining such items as recently typed-in passwords.

The default integrity level for both subjects and objects is medium. However, when a new process is created, its integrity level is the minimum of those of the creator and of the file containing the program being executed. Thus Internet Explorer is set to run at the low integrity level. A similar rule is used for file creation, allowing the creator of a file to read it and modify it.

A few years after the publication of the Orange Book, Clark and Wilson published a paper (Clark and Wilson 1987) arguing that its confidentiality-based multi-level security is irrelevant for commercial systems. For such systems, it is not just that integrity is more important, but that what is meant by integrity is not merely constraints on who may modify data, but also on what procedures are used to modify data. Information flow is not the issue, but instead how information is modified and manipulated.

They use as an example accounting systems, in which even authorized users are not allowed to make arbitrary changes to data. A typical such system is based on "double-entry bookkeeping." If a withdrawal is made in a money account, there must be a matching entry in an accounts-payable account indicating the purchase. Thus update operations must be part of *well formed transactions*. The state of the system can be verified: if there's money withdrawn from the money account but no corresponding accounts-payable entry, then there was a fraudulent withdrawal.

Separation of duty is another important component of commercial systems. The same person should not be able to perform all the steps involved in a purchase: requesting a purchase order, authorizing the purchase order, recording the arrival of the item, recording the arrival of the invoice, and authorizing payment. Requiring these steps to be distributed among multiple people reduces the possibility of fraud.

Finally, entering new information into the system is a common operation in commercial systems and thus must be handled as part of the security model. The Biba model handles this outside the security system by relegating such work to "trusted subjects" and a "security officer."

The military models (Bell–LaPadula and Biba) are focused on the clearances of the principals whose subjects are accessing objects. The Clark–Wilson model is focused both on how data items may be manipulated (i.e., using what programs) and on who may cause such manipulation.

Much of what Clark and Wilson wanted can be captured by combining two approaches to mandatory access control that became popular in the 1990s: *type enforcement* (TE) and *role-based access control* (RBAC). The former approach assigns types to subjects and objects and has strict rules on what the various types of subjects can do to the various types of objects. The latter assigns access rules not in terms of principals, but in terms of the various roles that principals play in a system. The two are combined in *SELinux*, an extension to Linux (and other Unix systems) developed at the U.S. National Security Agency (NSA) (see (Loscocco and Smalley 2001)).

SELinux bases its approach primarily on type enforcement. It labels all subjects and objects with a security context consisting of a *user*, a *domain*, and a *role*. The domain is the type of the subject or object; the administrator provides rules indicating what each subject domain (or subject type) may do to each object domain (or object type). Any form of access not explicitly allowed by the rules is not allowed. SELinux's use of the terms domain and type as synonyms is a bit confusing. To help clear things up a bit, we use *domain* when referring to subjects and *type* when referring to objects.

A domain (referring to subjects) is essentially a restricted execution environment. The rules specify which users running which programs may form subjects of a given domain. Subjects executing within a particular domain are restricted in what types of objects they may access and as to how they may access them.

For example, the Unix file /etc/passwd contains account information intended to be viewable by all users. (This example is adapted from (Mayer, MacMillan, et al. 2006) and based on the actual rules supplied with the SELinux distribution.) However, the /etc/shadow file contains sensitive information (such as the images of passwords) that is not intended to be viewable by all. Subjects of "normal" users run in the domain *user_t*. Publicly readable files such as /etc/passwd might be given the type *public_t*. To allow such files to be read by normal users, an SELinux system might include the rule:

```
allow user_t public_t : file read
```

This rule states that any subject executing in the *user_t* domain may have read access to files of type *public_t*. (This doesn't imply that they actually will be granted read access; keep on reading . . . .)

Assume that subjects permitted to modify password and other account information run in the *passwd_t* domain, and that the /etc/shadow file is of type *passwd_data_t*. To allow these subjects to access such files, an SELinux system might have the rule:

```
allow passwd_t passwd_data_t : file {read write}
```

This rule states that any subject executing in the *passwd_t* domain may have read and write access to files of type *passwd_data_t*.

Again, any access not explicitly permitted by rules such as the above is not permitted. Thus the rules designate exactly the access permitted to a domain. But that's not enough — we see from our discussion of the Clark–Wilson model that it is important to restrict what programs may be run in a domain. We do this by placing restrictions on the programs used to enter a domain. By default, no programs are allowed to enter a particular domain. Continuing with our example, among the small set of programs that should be allowed access to the /etc/shadow file is the *passwd* program, used to change one's password. Assuming *passwd* (and similar programs) have the type *passwd_exec_t*, we provide a rule allowing subjects executing programs of that type to enter the *passwd_t* domain:

```
allow passwd_t passwd_exec_t : file entrypoint
```

This rule states that the *passwd_t* domain is allowed *entrypoint access* to files of type *passwd_exec_t*, meaning that the domain can be entered if this program is being run. Thus any program for which a domain does not have *entrypoint* access cannot be used to enter the domain.

What we have yet to permit is for normal users to actually execute the passwd program, and for subjects in the *user_t* domain to be allowed to switch to the *passwd_t* domain, even when they are running the approved program. The following two rules provide the appropriate permissions:

```
allow user_t passwd_exec_t : file execute
allow user_t passwd_t : process transition
```

Last, in addition to allowing a transition from *user_t* to *passwd_t*, we provide a rule that makes it happen:

```
type_transition user_t passwd_exec_t : process passwd_t
```

This rule states that whenever a subject in the *user_t* domain executes a program of type *passwd_exec_t*, it should attempt to switch to the *passwd_t* domain. Of course, the attempt will not be successful unless explicitly permitted, by rules such as those above.

To show a bit more of SELinux, consider the accounting example used by Clark and Wilson. To keep this relatively simple, we look at just the process of issuing a purchase order. We must enforce a separation of duty: one person requests a purchase order and another approves it. SELinux does this by role-based access control. We also need to make certain that accounting data is accessible only through approved programs. SELinux does this by type enforcement.

So that we can control access, we set the type of all files containing accounting data to be *account_data_t* and provide two domains for subjects accessing these files — the *account_req_t* and *account_approv_t* domain. Included in the set of rules for our system are

```
allow account_req_t account_data_t : file {read write}
allow account_approv_t account_data_t : file {read write}
```

These specify that subjects in the *account_req_t* and *account_approv_t* domains have read and write access to file objects in the *account_data_t* domain. Assuming there are no other such *allow* statements, no other subjects may access these files.

Next we need to indicate the programs that subjects may use to access accounting data. Assume that *requestPO* is the program one runs to request a purchase order and *approvePO* is the program one runs to approve a request for a purchase order. We need to provide domains for the files containing these programs — the domain of *requestPO* is *account_req_exec_t*; the domain of *approvePO* is *account_approv_exec_t*. We provide the following rules:

```
allow account_req_t account_req_exec_t : file entrypoint
allow account_approv_t account_approv_exec_t : file entrypoint
```

These state that a subject may enter the *account_req_t* domain if it is running a program whose domain is *account_req_exec_t*, and similarly for *account_approv_t* and *account_aprov_exec_t*.

Now we need to give subjects a means for entering the *account_req_t* and *account_approv_t* domains. Assume that users' subjects are normally executing in the *user_t* domain. To allow such subjects to enter the account domains, we provide the following rules:

```
allow user_t account_req_t : process transition
allow user_t account_approv_t : process transition
```

This says that subjects in the *user_t* domain may switch to the account domains (assuming that all other rules are obeyed). We want to restrict such transitions so that only designated individuals can do them. This is where *role-based access control* (RBAC) comes in.

Assume that the normal user role is *user_r*. Let's define two new roles for users: *POrequester_r* and *POapprover_r*. We then provide rules stating that users in the former role may have subjects in the *account_req_t* domain, and similarly for the latter role:

```
role POrequester_r types account_req_t
role POapprover_r types account_approv_t
```

These rules allow users in the indicated roles to have subjects in the indicated domains. If there are no other such rules, then only users in these roles may be in these domains — which is our goal.

Finally, suppose that user andy is to be authorized to request purchase orders and user trina is to be authorized to approve them. To allow them to take on their roles, we include the following statements:

```
user andy roles {user_r POrequester_r}
user trina roles {user_r POapprover_r}
```

What's more, we need:

```
allow user_r {POrequester_r POapprover_r}
role_transition user_r account_req_exec_t POrequester_r
role_transition user_r account_approv_exec_t POapprover_r
```

The first says that a subject in the *user_r* role may switch to the *POrequester_r* and *POapprover_r* roles. The next one says that if a subject in the *user_r* role executes a file of the *account_req_exec_t* domain, then it automatically switches to the *POrequester_r* role (assuming this is permitted — otherwise it fails). And similarly for the third rule.

We are still not finished — we must allow andy and trina to execute the programs they need to run:

```
allow user_t {account_req_exec_t account_approv_exec_t} : file
execute
```

This gives subjects executing in the *user_t* domain permission to execute files in the *account_req_exec_t* and *account_approv_exec_t* domains — i.e., permission to execute the *requestPO* and *approvePO* programs.

As of this writing, SELinux is included in standard Linux distributions, though its use is optional. NSA provided a reference policy as a basis for Linux security; after further work by NSA and others, it is now known as the *strict policy*. It includes domains for all standard system applications, so that they run with the fewest privileges necessary. Normal users are assigned the *user_r* role; those authorized to run privileged commands are assigned the *staff_r* role. Neither of the roles is authorized to run privileged commands; however, those in the *staff_r* role may transition to the *sysadm_r* role, which is authorized to run privileged commands (but has nowhere near the power of root in a normal Unix system). Users in the *user_r* role may not transition to any other role.

In practice, the strict policy has been difficult to live with. Many applications simply do not work because of differences between the local system environment and that expected by the policy. Furthermore, the policy consists of over 20,000 rules, which is testimony to just how complicated access control is in a real system.

A compromise policy that is easier to live with is the *targeted policy*, so called because it targets just those applications that are "network facing," i.e, subjects servicing Internet clients. These applications are handled just as they are in the strict policy, but all other applications are lumped into a single domain — *unconfined_t* — that has no restrictions other than those imposed on a normal Linux system (without SELinux). Even so, the targeted policy has around 11,000 rules.

SELinux works best for systems running a fixed set of applications, such as servers. Though additional policy rules can be loaded into the kernel dynamically when new software is installed, designing the rules is far from trivial. It is not really the intent that new domains can be installed on the fly.

8.2.3 CAPABILITY SYSTEMS

Up to this point the systems we have discussed utilize the *who-you-are approach* to security: subjects carry a security context that identifies them, and this context is used to determine their access to objects. For lack of a better term, we refer to such systems (including Unix systems) as being *ACL-based*.

Capability systems provide a much different approach to security that might be thought of as the *what-you-have approach*. Rather than objects' having a list of subjects' access rights (ACLs), subjects have a list of capabilities (*C-lists*) — see Figure 8.9. These systems are often thought of as more or less the dual of ACL-based systems, since they effectively represent the access matrix by rows (with subjects) rather than by columns (with objects), but this view dramatically oversimplifies matters. (Miller, Yee, et al. 2003) provides a rigorous description of what capability systems are and discusses how they have been misrepresented.

In a "pure" ACL-based system, a subject's *authority* to access objects depends entirely on its user and group identities. This is because ACLs (and Unix-style permission vectors) determine access permissions as a function of user and group identities. Most real systems, and certainly Unix and Windows, are not "pure" ACL systems. Subjects obtain file descriptors or file handles when they open objects, and these are effectively capabilities. Since one subject may communicate such a capability to another, a subject's authority is not based on just its user and group identities, but may be augmented by capabilities it has received from others.

In a "pure" capability-based system, a subject's authority to access objects depends entirely on the capabilities it possesses — its user and group identities are irrelevant. This property makes it easy to take advantage of the principle of least privilege. One gives a subject just the privileges it needs to perform its task, with no possibility of its gaining more.

An oft-cited example illustrating the danger of separating authority from naming is the *confused deputy problem* (Hardy 1988). As originally stated, the deputy is a compiler that charges for use. One sends the deputy the names of an input file and of an output file, and makes certain that the deputy (i.e., compiler) has read access to the input file and write access to the output file. It compiles the contents of the input file and writes the result to the output file. For its own billing purposes, it records what's been done in a billing file. Of course, only the compiler has

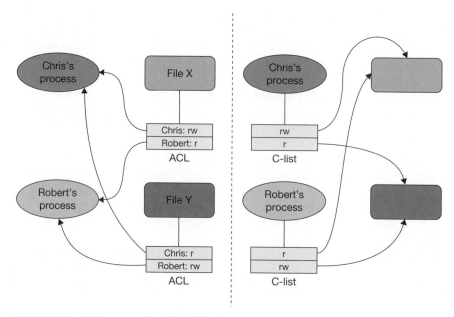

FIGURE 8.9   ACLs are used on the left, C-lists on the right.

write access to the billing file. Confusion occurs when the caller provides as the output file the name of the billing file. The compiler, which has write access to both, blindly writes the compiled program to the billing file, destroying all billing information.

We have seen how to solve this problem in both Unix and Windows. In both, the process running the compiler would temporarily switch to the caller's credentials to make sure the caller has access to the output file. However, this leads to what we might call the *malicious deputy problem*: the deputy has access to everything accessible to the caller and can do what it pleases with it.

Using a capability system, one could give the compiler capabilities for the input and output files, and nothing else. Since the caller does not have a capability for the billing file, it cannot pass one to the compiler.

Note that both Unix and Windows have sufficient support for capabilities that can be used to solve both the confused deputy and malicious deputy problems: capabilities are file descriptors in Unix and file handles in Windows. One simply passes file descriptors or handles for the input and output files to the deputy. It is not clear why neither system has taken advantage of such capability support.

The basic structure and organization of a pure capability-based system is necessarily different from an ACL-based system. Some issues immediately come to mind: subjects are given capabilities when they are created. How does the first subject (or the subject representing one's login session) get capabilities? As new objects are created, how can capabilities for them be made available to others? Since the operating system seems to deal strictly with capabilities, what happens with object names? Is that concept irrelevant?

To deal with these issues, we need some more machinery. For capabilities to persist across system crashes, we might use a special sort of object that holds capabilities (and persists). Such an object could play the role of a directory, maintaining an association between names and capabilities. However, unlike normal directories, none of the objects referred to have ACLs — having an appropriate capability for the directory implies that one has the authority to use any of the capabilities contained therein. So that the subjects can transfer capabilities in a controlled fashion, a special sort of capability is required to read capabilities from and write capabilities to such objects — read-capability and write-capability capabilities. See Figures 8.10 and 8.11.

In this scheme, rather than, say, use an ACL to allow a particular group access to a file, one would put a capability for the file in a directory for which group members have read-capability capabilities (see Figure 8.12). Such capabilities would have names, akin to traditional file names, but the naming hierarchy would necessarily be structured differently to take into account the difference between grouping capabilities into a directory and independently assigning access permissions to files.

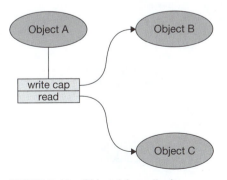

FIGURE 8.10 Object A has a "write-capability" capability for object B, allowing it to copy capabilities to B.

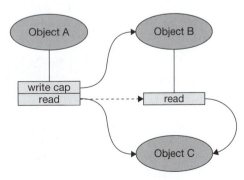

FIGURE 8.11 Object A has copied its "read capability for object C" to object B.

This use of capabilities clearly makes it easy to set up very restricted protection domains. For example, in Figure 8.13 we have downloaded a program from an untrusted source. In Figure 8.14 we have set up a minimal protection domain in which it can run, giving it no means for doing harm to the rest of the system.

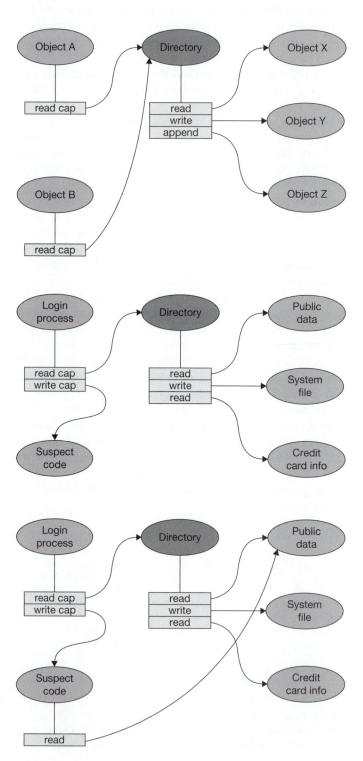

FIGURE 8.12 Here we have a directory object that provides capabilities to other objects. Object A may use its read-capability capability to fetch capabilities from the directory object.

FIGURE 8.13 Here we want to run a program that we've recently downloaded from the web. We create a process in which to run it, giving our login process a write-capability capability to it.

FIGURE 8.14 We give the new process a read capability for some public data, but no capability for anything else (and particularly no capability for getting other capabilities from the directory).

When a person logs onto such a system, her or his login process (running, perhaps, a shell) must possess a read-capability capability to a directory object containing or referring to all capabilities the user may have. How does it get this capability? Since our system does not use user identities to determine authority, we cannot use some sort of "super-authority" such as the Unix superuser or the Windows administrator. We might hypothesize some sort of kernel facility for constructing processes with pre-existing capabilities. A more appealing possibility, however, is that one's login process never terminates — it persists across reboots. Thus as part of creating an account, a login process is created containing the necessary capabilities. When the user logs in, she or he is merely reconnected to that process.

With such a facility, objects can be made accessible to users at the discretion of object owners — i.e., discretionary access control (DAC) is possible (see Exercise 10). But users, via the shell program running in their login process, can create subjects to run programs and insert into them only the capabilities needed. Subjects other than those corresponding to login processes generally do not have read-capability capabilities for directory objects.

Can mandatory access control (MAC) be done in capability systems? It's been "proven" impossible twice (Boebert 1984) (Gong 1989), yet in both occasions what was actually proven was a less than total understanding of how capability systems work. If we want to implement multilevel security (MLS) as in the Bell–LaPadula model, then we must ensure that information can be restricted so as not to flow from more secure levels to lower levels. This can be done by careful placement of capabilities — subjects in lower security levels must not have write capabilities for objects in higher security levels. In one of the impossibility proofs, it was thought that subjects in higher security levels could communicate read capabilities for high-security objects to lower security levels. But this can be prevented by having no write-capability capabilities between higher-level subjects and lower-level objects.

The other impossibility proof held that it was impossible to retract a capability once granted — an ability required for B-level certification by the Orange Book. At first glance, this would seem a legitimate gripe — capabilities are granted with no strings attached. However, with a bit more machinery, one can add a level of indirection to capabilities, so that capabilities do not necessarily refer directly to an object, but to an intermediate object controlled by the owner of the target object, who can disable the intermediate object at any time, thus retracting the capability that indirectly refers to the target object (see Figure 8.15).

KeyKOS (Bomberger, Hardy, et al. 1992) was a commercial capability-based operating system whose development started in the late 1970s and continued until 1990. It was designed essentially as a microkernel system on which one built the OS interface seen by applications. One of these OS interfaces was Unix, which might seem to have defeated the purpose of a capability-based system, but another was KeySAFE, a system that was designed to satisfy "high B-level" requirements.

Given that high B-level requires subject and object labels and that all access be mediated by a security reference monitor, it might seem rather difficult for a pure capability-based system to comply, when such things seem antithetical with the principles of a capability system.

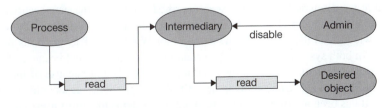

FIGURE 8.15 A capability with a string attached.

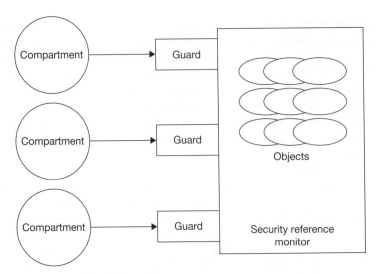

FIGURE 8.16 KeySafe architecture.

The KeySAFE design shows how these notions can be built on top of a capability-based system, justifying KeyKOS as a microkernel.

The idea behind KeySAFE is to use capabilities to provide controlled isolation. Processes of the same user running at the same security level are grouped together into a *compartment*, as shown in Figure 8.16, collectively forming a subject. These processes possess a capability for a *guard*, which provides their only access to the security reference monitor. Associated with the guard is the compartment's security label, identifying the user and security level.

The security reference monitor is the custodian of objects, maintaining their security labels, which include both ACLs and their security levels. For a process to obtain a capability for an object, it must send a request via the capability for its guard. The guard, being part of the security reference monitor, then determines whether access should be allowed using the compartment's label and the object's label. If access is permitted, it returns a capability for an intermediate object, the front-end object, that acts as the interface to the requested object. If at some point the compartment's access to the object is revoked, the front-end object is invalidated, preventing processes in the compartment from further access to the object.

8.3 CONCLUSIONS

Security has proven to be one of the most difficult and error-prone aspects of computer systems. In this chapter we've restricted our discussion to operating-system support for security. We have looked at the various threats that systems must defend against and the various architectures that have been proposed for providing these defenses. In Unix systems, most of the security architecture we discussed (with the exception of SELinux and the new security features being put to use in Chromium OS) has been in place for decades. In Windows, the current model came into widespread use only with the adoption of Windows NT as the basis for all Windows systems. In both systems, many of our current problems are due not because of inadequacies of the security architectures (though they certainly do exist!), but because of inadequate use of what has been provided. Unix systems haven't always provided reasonable default permissions for files. It has been too often the case in Windows systems that most users have full administrative rights and thus all security controls are for naught. Despite its being first espoused forty years ago, the principle of least privilege has yet to be put into common practice. It is much too easy in most systems, Unix and Windows, to run a program of unknown provenance in one's own full protection domain — there is no easy way to run it in a restricted domain. One of the major challenges of computer systems is to provide strong and workable security.

---

1. In most systems today, one identifies oneself using a simple name such as "tom" or "twd."

   a. Such simple names are generally not used within the operating system to identify users, but are translated into some sort of numeric ID. Explain why.

   b. It may be `necessary, when logging in, to specify some sort of domain, such as "cs," in which to look up your user name. Thus I might log in as "cs\twd." What is the rationale for using such domains?

   c. Suppose it is necessary to combine two systems so that each user in one can log into the other. Unfortunately, the intersection of the sets of user names of the two systems is not null. Say, there are two different people with user names of "tom," one in one system and one in the other. The system administrator decides to resolve the problem by renaming one "tom1" and the other "tom2". That was easy. However, the administrator now realizes that the real problem is that the space of numeric user IDs, the ones used internally by the two systems, are the same in both systems. Thus there is a user 17 in one system and also in the other system, but they refer to different people. Suggest a means for assigning user IDs in the future so that collisions will not be a problem in the event that systems are merged.

2. Tenex was an operating system for DEC PDP-10 computers used in the late '60s and early '70s. It had a number of features, including one that allowed user code to be invoked in response to each page fault. It stored passwords in plain text (i.e., unencrypted) in a file that was adequately protected. A user could supply his or her password not only when logging in, but also from a program so as to switch from one protection domain to another. The system code that checked for a correct password would do so one character at a time, moving from left to right, stopping when it encountered an incorrect character. It was soon discovered that it was relatively easy to figure out any user's password. Explain how. (*Hint*: a few guesses were required.)

3. By default, Windows allows users to access directories even though they do not have explicit permission to follow a path through the directories' parents. In Unix, there is no getting around the requirement that you must have execute permission in each directory in order to follow a path through the directories. The sorts of permissions one can specify for Unix files and directories are read, write, and execute. Windows allows one to specify read, write, execute, and delete, and does so via ACLs rather than via permission vectors.

   a. Describe a situation in which, in order to provide the desired access control for a file in Unix, one must take advantage of the requirement for execute permission in all directories in its path.

   b. Explain why this can't be done in Windows. Describe an access-control situation that Windows can handle but Unix cannot.

4. Many Unix systems allow a thread to transmit a file descriptor via a Unix-domain socket. The intent is that the receiver gains, via the received file descriptor, the same access rights to the file that the sender had via the original file descriptor. Thus, for example, if the sender had opened a file for reading and writing and then transmitted the file descriptor to the receiver, the receiver now has the file open for reading and writing.

   a. Show, in terms of the open-file structures described in Chapter 1, what actually happens when a file descriptor is transmitted from one process to another.

   b. Show how this technique could be used to implement a print server.

5. We showed in Section 8.2.1 that Unix's *chroot* system call is not sufficient to restrict a process to a subtree of the directory hierarchy. Describe what easily enforced additional measures can be taken to restrict a process to a subtree securely.

*6. A security problem popular in the late 1960s and early 1970s was the *mutually suspicious users problem*. User A has a proprietary program. User B has proprietary data. B wants to run A's program on B's data, but wants to make certain that A doesn't get a copy of the data. A wants B to use A's program (for a fee), but doesn't want B to get a copy of it. The solution is to set up a protection domain that has read access to B's data, execute-only access to A's code, write access to a solutions file that can be read only by B, and no other access rights.

   a. Can such a protection domain be established in Windows? Explain.

   b. Can such a protection domain be established in Unix? Explain. (Hint: consider the *chroot* system call. Also, your solution might take advantage of a trusted third party to set things up.)

7. Section 8.2.3 discusses covert channels and describes one involving the processor utilization. Describe the measures that can be taken to eliminate such a covert channel.

8. In normal Unix systems (and Windows systems), one's access rights for a file are checked only when the file is opened. However, in SELinux, they are checked at every access to the file. Explain why this change was made.

9. In the SELinux example in Section 8.2.2, roles are established for users participating in an accounting activity. Suppose user john attempts to run the program *requestPO*. Assuming no SELinux rules other than those given in the text, explain what prevents user john from using this program to request a PO.

*10. We would like to add discretionary access control to a capability-based system. As described in Section 8.2.3, such a system might support persistent processes — processes that survive crashes and retain their capabilities indefinitely. Assuming such a facility, describe how you might add support for discretionary access control. You may also assume the system provides directory-like objects that contain name-capability pairs: one can search such an object for a particular name; if the name exists, and one has the read-capability capability for the object, then one can retrieve the associated capability.

11. It is sometimes said that an *access matrix* such as Figure 8.2 can represent everything there is about access control in a system. Furthermore, it said that representing such a matrix by columns (i.e., storing the entries along with the object heading the column) and representing the matrix by rows (i.e., storing the entries along with the subject heading the row) are equivalent. Such columns are known as *access-control lists* and such rows are known as *capability lists*. Taking this discussion one step further, it might be argued that a capability system can be represented as an access matrix. This turns out not to be a valid characterization. Explain why not.

8.5 REFERENCES

Bell, D. E. and L. J. LaPadula (1973). Secure Computer Systems: Mathematical Foundations, Mitre.

Biba, K. J. (1977). Integrity Considerations for Secure Computer Systems, Electronic Systems Division, Hanscom Air Force Base.

Boebert, W. E. (1984). On the Inability of an Unmodified Capability Machine to Enforce the *-Property. *Proceedings of the 7th DoD/NBS Computer Security Conference*: 291–293.

Bomberger, A. C., N. Hardy, A. P. Frantz, C. R. Landau, W. S. Frantz, J. S. Shapiro, A. C. Hardy (1992). The KeyKOS NanoKernel Architecture. *Proceedings of the USENIX Workshop on Microkernels and Other Kernel Architectures*: 95–112.

Clark, D. D. and D. R. Wilson (1987). A Comparison of Commercial and Military Computer Security Policies. *1987 IEEE Symposium on Security and Privacy*: 184–194.

Department of Defense (1985). *Trusted Computer System Evaluation Criteria.* http://csrc.nist.gov/publications/history/dod85.pdf.

Feldmeier, D. C. and P. R. Karn (1989). UNIX Password Security — Ten Years Later. *Proceedings of the 9th Annual International Cryptology Conference on Advances in Cryptology,* Springer-Verlag Lecture Notes In Computer Science. **435**.

Gong, L. (1989). A Secure Identity-Based Capability System. *Proceedings of the 1989 IEEE Symposium on Security and Privacy*: 56–65.

Google1. Chromium OS. from http://www.chromium.org/chromium-os.

Google2. Chromium OS System Hardening. http://sites.google.com/a/chromium.org/dev/chromium-os/chromiumos-design-docs/system-hardening.

Hardy, N. (1988). The Confused Deputy: (or Why Capabilities Might Have Been Invented). *ACM SIGOPS Operating Systems Review* **22**(4): 36–38.

Lampson, B. W. (1971). Protection. *Proceedings of Fifth Princeton Symposium on Information Sciences and Systems.* Princeton: 18–24.

Lampson, B. W. (1973). A Note on the Confinement Problem. *Communications of the ACM* **16**(10): 613–615.

Loscocco, P. and S. Smalley (2001). Integrating Flexible Support for Security Policies into the Linux Operating System. *Proceedings of the FREENIX Track of the 2001 USENIX Annual Technical Conference.*

Mayer, F., K. MacMillan, et al. (2006). *SELinux by Example: Using Security Enhanced Linux,* Prentice Hall PTR.

Miller, M. S., K.-P. Yee, J. S. Shapiro (2003). Capability Myths Demolished, Johns Hopkins University.

Saltzer, J. H. and M. D. Schroeder (1975). The Protection of Information in Computer Systems. *Proceedings of the IEEE* **63**(9): 1278–1308.

Thompson, K. (1984). Reflections on Trusting Trust. *Communications of the ACM* **27**(8): 761–763.

CHAPTER 9   Introduction to Networking

Computer networks are essential components of modern computer systems. Though the architecture of networks and the protocols used for communication are not directly related to operating systems, we cover them for two reasons. The first is that distributed file systems, which are important components of operating systems, depend on them. Much of their design is governed by what standard network protocols do and do not provide. The second is that network protocols are usually implemented in the operating system. Doing this well presents a number of challenges to the operating-system designer.

We first look at network protocols, concentrating on the Internet's TCP/IP. We then look at remote procedure calls, a notion introduced in Chapter 4. Together these give us the foundations for the next chapter, on distributed file systems.

9.1 NETWORK BASICS

What exactly is a computer network? For our purposes, it's a way to interconnect computers so they can communicate data with one another. Examples range from a home network interconnecting two or three computers to the Internet, interconnecting most of the computers on earth (and perhaps beyond).

To better appreciate how networks work, let's look at their components. We say that two computers are *directly connected* if they can send each other data without involving any other parties. They might be connected by cable or by radio. And a number of computers might be directly connected, since they are connected to a broadcast medium: anything sent by one can be received by all. We call such directly connected networks *base networks*.

Base networks can be combined to form larger *composite networks*. A computer that is attached to two separate base networks can *forward* data from one to the other. Thus a computer on the first network can send data to one on the second by sending it to the computer in the middle, which will forward it to the intended recipient. We can extend this forwarding technique to allow communication among computers on any number of base networks, as long as there is a forwarding path from one network to another.

In general, a message going from one computer to another goes through a sequence of intermediate base networks, each with a computer in common with the networks immediately before and after it. Two approaches are commonly used to arrange this sort of communication. One, known as *circuit switching*, is to set up this network sequence before communicating, forming a path known as a *virtual circuit*. This is much like placing a telephone call. First you dial the other party's number; once connected, you can talk or send as much data over the connection as you like. In ages past such a telephone connection really was made by an electric circuit between the two parties. Today's virtual circuit is implemented by arranging for each computer in the path to forward messages on to the next one. The computers in such a setup are called *switches* and are often specialized for this chore.

A real circuit has a definite bandwidth that's constantly available to the two parties communicating over it. A virtual circuit makes an approximation of this constant bandwidth by reserving capacity on each of the switches and on the "wires" that connect them. Thus messages sent over a virtual circuit have a high probability of reaching their destination. Furthermore, since they all take the same path, they arrive at the destination in the order they were sent. This reserved capacity is both a feature and a problem: a feature because you can be sure that the capacity is always available; a problem because you must pay for it even when you're not using it.

The other approach is known as *packet switching*: data is divided into pieces called packets that are sent independently across the composite network. Each packet is tagged with the address of its destination. The computers it passes through on its way to the destination are known as *routers* (and, like switches, are often dedicated to this purpose). With packet switching, no path is set up through the routers ahead of time. Instead, each router forwards packets on the basis of its latest information on the best route to the destination. Since this information can change over time, consecutive packets might take different routes to the destination and may well arrive out of order. In general there is no reservation of capacity in the routers (particularly since it's not necessarily known ahead of time which routers will be used). The collective routers of the network make a "best effort" to get each packet to its destination. Due to overloaded routers and other problems, some packets may not make it to their destinations. So, unlike circuit switching, with packet switching there is no guaranteed capacity but, on the other hand, you aren't paying for capacity you aren't using.[1]

The Internet is essentially a large version of the networks described above. In general, packet switching is used for communicating data over the Internet, though some portions, typically long-haul networks provided by phone companies, use circuit switching.[2] Thus from the point of view of messages being sent over it, the Internet is simply a large collection of routers. The circuit-switched components are usually made to appear to the packet-switching world as point-to-point links.

In this book we ignore the details of computing routes. However, this is where the Internet can no longer be thought of as simply a large network. It consists of a number of networks, each with separate administration. These *autonomous systems* each handle its own internal routing, using a variety of routing protocols. Routing among autonomous systems is currently handled by a rather complicated protocol known as BGP (border gateway protocol[3]).

9.1.1 NETWORK PROTOCOLS

We've defined networks as collections of interconnected base networks. But we need to look at many more details to see how we communicate over them. In particular, we need to address the following concerns:

- The base networks are not homogeneous; different sorts have different characteristics such as the packet sizes that can be transmitted, the size of network addresses, bandwidth, and so forth.

- Routes through the network must be computed and utilized.

---

[1] An analogy made by an early packet-switching proponent concerns a long-distance car trip, say from New York to San Francisco. With circuit switching you reserve a route before you leave, make sure that no one else is on it, then drive unimpeded across the country. With packet switching you just start driving, making decisions at each interchange on which road to take next. The circuit-switching approach would be exorbitantly expensive (though fun, since you could probably drive as fast as you'd like). The packet-switching approach will get you there much less expensively.

[2] The telephone network, often used as the prime example of circuit switching, is moving towards packet switching, particularly in voice-over-IP (VoIP), which routes telephone calls over the Internet.

[3] Its official specification is at http://www.ietf.org/rfc/rfc1771.txt.

- Data passing through the network can be lost or reordered.

- Too much traffic can overwhelm the routers and switches.

These concerns and others were addressed by a committee operating under the auspices of the International Organization for Standardization (known as ISO[4]) in the 1970s by defining a network model consisting of seven layers, known as the *Open Systems Interconnect* (OSI) model (Figure 9.1). Each layer is built on top of the next lower layer and provides certain types of functionality. Protocols can then be designed and implemented to provide the functionality of a particular layer.

Here's a brief description of the OSI model's layers.

1. The *physical layer* corresponds to the "wire." Concerns here have to do with electromagnetic waves and the medium through which they are propagating.

2. The *data link layer* provides the means for putting data on the wire (and for taking it off). An example is the Ethernet. Concerns here include how to represent bits as electromagnetic waves. Data is represented as sequences of bits known as *frames*. If, as in the Ethernet, the physical layer can be shared with potentially more than one other computer, some means for sharing must be provided; doing this properly is known as *medium access control* (MAC). The MAC address is used to indicate who should receive a frame. Important parameters include the form of the MAC address and the maximum and minimum frame sizes.

3. The *network layer* sees to it that the data travels to the intended destination (perhaps via a number of intermediate points). It deals with data in units known as *packets*. Some notion of a network address is needed here to identify other computers.

4. The *transport layer* is responsible for making sure that communication is reliable, i.e., that what's sent is received unchanged.

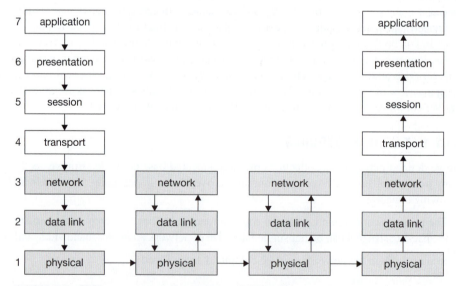

FIGURE 9.1   ISO's open systems interconnect (OSI) model.

---

[4] One might think it should be known as IOS, but it's supposed to be an international organization, and IOS would make sense in English, but, for example, not in French. So, "ISO" is chosen as its abbreviation: the three letters are derived from "isos," which means "equal" in Greek. (See http://www.iso.org/iso/about/discover-iso_isos-name.htm.)

5. The *session layer* builds on the reliable connection provided by the transport layer. Among the services provided here can be *dialog control*, which indicates whose turn it is to transmit, and *synchronization*, which tracks progress for error recovery. For example, if the transport connection fails, a new one can be established under the same session as the original.

6. The *presentation layer* deals with the representation of data. It copes with the different ways machines represent basic data items (such as integers and floating-point numbers) and provides a means for communicating more complicated data items, such as arrays and structure.

7. The *application layer* is not necessarily where the application resides, but rather where high-level software used by the application for network access resides. For example, the HTTP protocol used for web browsing can be considered to reside here.

The bottom three layers (layers 1–3) are sometimes called the *communications subnet*. Data that must pass through a number of machines on its way to the destination is forwarded by an implementation of protocols in these lower layers on each intermediate machine.

The distinctions among the top three layers are in general pretty much ignored. Many applications use remote-procedure-call and similar protocols that are built on top of the transport layer and incorporate all the functionality of layers 5 through 7.

The OSI model is useful in helping us understand a number of networking issues, but as a model it's not strictly followed in practice, where "practice" means the Internet. The Internet's model is considerably simpler and more specific: while the OSI model was intended as the basis of any number of network protocols, the Internet model was designed as a model for the Internet, period.

The OSI model can be considered an *a priori* model in the sense that it came first, with the idea that protocols were to follow. With the Internet model, the reverse happened: first there were protocols, then a model to describe them. This is an *a posteriori* model: the model came after the protocols.

The protocols used on the Internet are known as the *Internet protocols* (also called TCP/IP). They don't fit precisely into the OSI model (for example, there is no analog of the session and presentation layers), but the rough correspondence is shown in Figure 9.2.

There was much speculation in the 1980s that protocols designed to fit in the OSI model not only would be competitors of the Internet protocols, but would replace them. Today one hears very little of the OSI protocols (though the OSI seven-layer terminology is much used); whatever competition there was between the OSI protocols and the Internet protocols was definitely won by the latter.

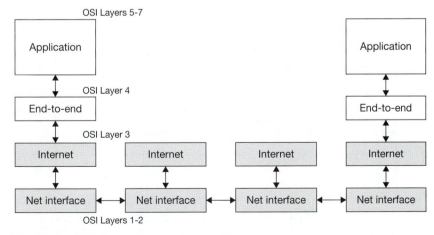

FIGURE 9.2 The Internet's networking model.

9.1.1.1 The Internet Protocol (IP)

What we called a "base network" earlier is abstracted by OSI layers 1 and 2. Thus the peculiarities of a particular base network are handled by protocols at OSI layer 3. The Internet has exactly one protocol defined for this layer, the *internet protocol* (IP). It is, however, evolving. Version 4 is currently in use (versions 1 through 3 were never in common use), but may be replaced by version 6 (version 5 was never in common use either). Here we discuss version 4.

First, we say a few words about what's called a *protocol data unit* (PDU). This is the information sent as one unit by a protocol at a particular level. The PDU of IP, sitting at the network layer, is known as a *packet*. In general, PDUs contain control information as well as data. This control information is usually segregated from the data and placed at the beginning, where it's called a *header*; however, sometimes some or all of it may be at the end of the PDU, where it's called a *trailer*. What's important is that the data portion of a PDU is the PDU of the next-higher-layer protocol. In particular, the data portion of an IP packet is the PDU of the transport layer (where the PDU is called a *segment*). Similarly, the network-layer packet is the data portion of the data-link-layer PDU (a *frame*).

IP forms packets from the segments given it by the transport protocol. Ordinarily IP simply takes the segment as is and puts a header in the front (see Figure 9.3, where the transport layer's segment is called data). However, if the resulting packet would be too large for the data-link layer to handle (for example, Ethernet's *maximum transfer unit* (MTU) is 1500 bytes, meaning that its frames cannot be larger than that), IP breaks the segment into some number of *fragments*, so that each, when combined with IP and Ethernet headers, is no larger than the MTU, and transmits each as a separate packet. When forwarding packets on a router, IP ordinarily simply takes them and forwards them on to their destination. However, if the packet is too large for the outgoing data-link layer, it again breaks the packet data into appropriately sized fragments and forwards each separately. It's the responsibility of the ultimate destination's IP to reassemble the fragments into the segment expected by the transport protocol. The *fragment offset* field of the IP header (Figure 9.3) indicates the byte offset relative to the beginning of the original segment of the data portion of a fragmented IP packet. The *identification* field identifies the original segment of which this is a fragment.

IP's primary job is forwarding: getting packets to their destination. Each packet contains the source and destination addresses. Based on the destination address, IP either keeps the packet, sending it up to the higher-level protocol, or forwards it on to the next hop in its route.

Determining the route is the tough part. Routing information is not maintained by IP, but supplied either by a separate routing protocol or by an administrator. In either case, routes are stored in a table for IP's use. If the destination is another host on a directly connected network, IP

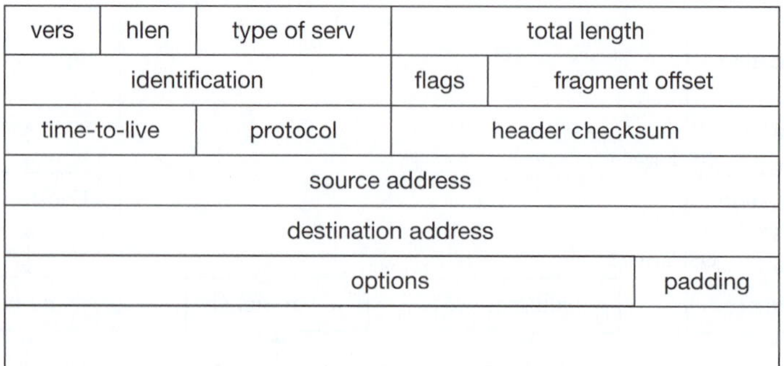

vers	hlen	type of serv	total length	
identification			flags	fragment offset
time-to-live		protocol	header checksum	
source address				
destination address				
options				padding
data				

FIGURE 9.3 IP packet showing header.

forwards it directly to that host. Otherwise it checks the routing table for either an entry containing a route to the given address or, if that's not present, an entry giving a route to the base network of the destination. If neither is present, then there should be a default entry giving a route to a router with more information. Ultimately this leads to one of a set of routers (originally called *core routers*) without default entries in their tables, but with routes to all known base networks.

Internet addresses are structured 32-bit values usually written in *dot notation*, in which each byte, from most significant to least, is written in decimal and is separated from the next by a dot. For example, 0x8094400a is written as 128.148.64.10. The original idea was that these addresses were split into three fields: a class identifier, a network number (identifying a base network), and a host number (Figure 9.4). Three classes of addresses, known as A, B, and C, were defined, each providing a different split between the bits identifying the network and the bits identifying a host on that network. Each network uses just one class of addresses — networks are referred to as class-A, class-B, or class-C. A fourth class of addresses, class D, was also defined, as explained below.

Class-A networks have 7 bits to identify the network and 24 to identify the host on that network. Thus there could be up to 2^7-2 class-A networks (the all-zeros and all-ones addresses are special), each with $2^{24}-2$ hosts. Class-B networks have 14 bits to identify the network and 16 bits to identify the host. Class-C networks have 21 bits for the network and 8 bits for the host. Thus there could be $2^{14}-2$ class-B networks, each with $2^{16}-2$ hosts, and $2^{21}-2$ class-C networks, each with 2^8-2 hosts. Class-D addresses are used for multicast: one-to-many communication. Not counting the multicast addresses, this scheme allows a total of 2,113,658 networks and 3,189,604,356 hosts.

There are two problems with these address classes. The first is that the numbers are too big. The other is that they're too small. They're too big because they require huge routing tables and too small because there aren't enough usable addresses.

Since the core routers must have routes for all networks, their routing tables potentially have 2,113,658 entries. What's more, the routing protocols require that the core routers periodically exchange their tables. The memory and communication costs for this were prohibitive in the 1980s (though they are not that bad now).

Making the problem of not enough network addresses even worse was that a fair portion of the class-A and class-B addresses were wasted. This was because few if any class-A networks had anything close to $2^{24}-2$ hosts on them, or could even contemplate having that many. Even with class-B networks, $2^{16}-2$ hosts were far more than was reasonable.

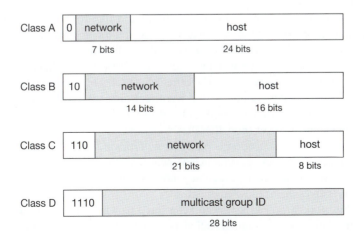

FIGURE 9.4 Class-based Internet addresses.

To cope with these issues, the definition of "network" was changed. The network portion of an address was reinterpreted as identifying not a base network, but a collection of networks, perhaps all those of one institution. So, instead of holding routes to base networks, the core routers hold routes to these aggregated networks. Depending on how you look at it, this either allows smaller routing tables, since each entry is a route to a number of base networks, or allows more base networks.

What didn't happen was an increase in the size of a network address. Thus the bits needed to distinguish the base network from the others within an aggregate network had to be taken from the bits previously dedicated to identifying a host. What had been the host number was split in two and now identified both as a base network (known as a *subnet*) and a host. Which bits are in each portion are indicated by a *subnet mask*, which needs to be known only by the hosts on the subnet. The beauty of this technique is that the core routers (and any other part of the Internet) don't need to know about the subnet mask of an aggregate network. Only when packets reach the aggregate does the subnet become relevant.

Despite the improvements from subnetting, however, full routing tables were still too large and too many network addresses were still being wasted. It became clear that the class-based network addresses weren't such a good idea. So, at least in assigning new addresses, the class-based approach was eliminated and a new approach was introduced, *classless Internet domain routing* (CIDR, pronounced "cider"), in which any number of subnets could be combined into a single aggregate network. Thus, rather than a class-dependent fixed boundary between the network and subnet/host portions of the address, the boundary could be anyplace. This was accomplished by giving routers extra information: a small integer indicating how many of the most significant bits are the network number.

So, for example, one might assign a company 32 consecutive class-C networks: 198.17.160.000 through 198.17.191.255. Instead of having 32 routing-table entries, these would be aggregated and represented as the single entry 198.17.160.000/19, meaning that the 19 most-significant bits represent the (aggregate) network number. A subnet mask would still show which of the remaining 13 bits indicate the subnet and which indicate the host, but, as before, this subnet mask needs to be known only locally.

IP version 6 promises to solve some of IP's addressing problems (while perhaps adding others) by using 128-bit addresses. If all are usable, there are enough for over $6 \cdot 10^{22}$ unique addresses per square foot of the earth's surface, or over a billion unique addresses per cubic mile of a sphere with radius equal to the mean distance from the Sun to Pluto. It probably won't be necessary for all addresses to be usable.

9.1.1.2 The Transport Level

Despite the uncertainties of Internet communication, we'd like to make certain that data is communicated acceptably well. What this means depends on the application. For our concerns here — primarily distributed file systems — "acceptably well" means that data is communicated reliably: nothing is lost, nothing is garbled, the receiver receives exactly what the sender sent. We might also, of course, want communication to be extremely fast, but this is of secondary importance. Alternatively, if the data being communicated were real-time video, absolute reliability is of secondary importance to minimal delay — it is OK to lose packets here and there as long as most of them are arriving at the receiver soon after they were sent.

Attaining reliable communication is pretty straightforward. The sender sends data to the receiver. The receiver sends back an acknowledgment that it's received the data. If the sender doesn't get an acknowledgment in a reasonable amount of time, it resends the data, and does so repeatedly until it receives the acknowledgment.

To make this work, we need a way to keep track of what's been sent and what's been received. Note that, in general, communication is in both directions, so each party is both a sender and a receiver.

The two primary Internet transport protocols are UDP (user datagram protocol) and TCP (transmission control protocol). UDP provides no reliability other than a checksum on the data. It's useful for applications in which reliability is not important and for those that provide their own implementation of reliability. TCP, on the other hand, does provide reliable communication. Furthermore, it copes with network congestion problems.

Both TCP and UDP augment the network addresses in their headers with 16-bit *port numbers* indicating which entity on the sending machine sent the segment and which entity on the receiving machine is to receive it. It would be convenient to have some sort of permanent assignment of port numbers to applications, but 16 bits isn't a whole lot, so, except for the first 1024, these port numbers are assigned dynamically.

TCP keeps track of what has been sent as well as what has been successfully received by using *sequence numbers*. Each byte[5] of data, as well as instances of certain control information, is numbered with consecutive 32-bit sequence numbers. Data is grouped into segments, each containing the sequence number of the first byte of data (or an instance of control information) and the number of data bytes and control information instances (though the latter is always 1). The receiver responds with a segment containing an acknowledgment sequence number that indicates that all bytes and control information with sequence numbers less than it have been successfully received.

Since there are only 2^{32} sequence numbers, however, what happens when we use them all up? It takes a little less than two and a half hours at 4 million bits/second (the speed my ISP promises me over broadband cable) to transmit 2^{32} bytes. Clearly we must allow sequence numbers to wrap around: the sequence number immediately after $2^{32}-1$ must be 0. But this presents a problem if different segments take different routes over the Internet. For example, we might transmit a segment whose data starts with sequence number 1000. For some reason this segment gets lost. The sender, after not receiving an acknowledgement in due time, retransmits the segment. It then sends just under 2^{32} more bytes of data and, around two and half hours later, it again sends a segment whose data starts with sequence number 1000. At around this time the original segment finds its way to the destination. How is the receiver to distinguish this late-arriving segment from the most recently transmitted one?

It can't. The only way to deal with this problem is to make sure it cannot happen. Built into the Internet is what's called the *maximum segment lifetime* (MSL): the maximum time a segment can exist on the Internet before being discarded. MSL is set (pretty much by fiat) at two minutes. It's not strictly enforced — there really isn't a mechanism for doing so[6] — but in practice it's rarely exceeded. Thus, at a communication bandwidth of four megabits/second, this "duplicate sequence number" problem won't happen. However, at 100 megabits/second ("Fast Ethernet" speed), 2^{32} bytes are sent in less than six minutes, and at a gigabit/second, 2^{32} bytes are sent in less than 35 seconds. To cope with these speeds, the protocol can be augmented by effectively increasing the number of sequence-number bits through time stamps. For our purposes, we assume bandwidths are small enough that sequence-number wraparound can't happen in less than some reasonable multiple of the maximum segment lifetime.

However, there is still another problem, known as session reincarnation. Which sequence number is used to start a connection? Making it always zero is another source of duplicate sequence numbers. Suppose we start transmitting segments and then for some reason quit

---

[5] The TCP documentation uses the term *octet* rather than byte to mean an eight-bit unit of data. This is because when TCP was introduced, some computers had bytes of length other than eight bits. This doesn't seem to be the case anymore, so we use byte to mean an eight-bit unit.

[6] TCP segments have a *time-to-live* field indicating their remaining lifetime. In principle, routers examine this field, subtract the amount of time the segment has spent in the router, and discard the packet if the value is zero. In practice, since the units of the fields are seconds, it has become a limit on the number of routers the packet may go through — a maximum hop count. Thus there's nothing preventing a router from holding a packet for two and a half hours and then forwarding it.

while some of the segments are still in transit. Then we start again, "reincarnating" the session. If we start with the same sequence number as we started with previously, the late-arriving segments from the previous session may be mistaken for segments belonging to the current session. So, when starting a new session, we need to choose an initial sequence number that we know is not in a previously transmitted segment that's still out on the Internet.

It might seem reasonable to keep track of the last sequence number used and use one greater than that for the next connection to a particular destination. But this would mean keeping track of sequence numbers of all recently terminated connections. This probably wouldn't be all that unreasonable today, but was considered so in 1981. It also wouldn't completely solve the problem, as explained below.

What was done instead was to guess the maximum speed at which sequence numbers are being consumed and then assign initial sequence numbers assuming that any previous connection ran at that speed. The speed chosen was 250,000 bytes/second. So, for example, a connection starting at time 0 was given an initial sequence number of 0. If that connection terminated for some reason and a new connection was made 1000 seconds after the first one started, since the old connection must have transmitted less than 250,000,000 bytes, the new one was safely given an initial sequence number of 250,000,000. This approach is known as using an *initial-sequence-number* (ISN) *generator*. Of course, if the actual communication speed was greater than 250,000 bytes/second, or if the ISN generator wrapped around completely (it had a period of 4.55 hours) while a connection was still active, there still might be a duplicate sequence-number problem. However, in 1981, communication that fast and that long-lasting didn't happen, so this approach worked.

There were other problems, though. If a system crashed and then restarted, the ISN generator would be restarted as well. One might think that the generator could be based on a time-of-day clock that survives crashes, but this has problems as well. So, the suggestion was to wait an MSL after rebooting before starting up TCP. In practice, machines took far longer than an MSL to reboot, so such a delay was not needed. A more serious problem has to do with sequence-number-guessing attacks — see RFC 1948.[7]

Let's look at how TCP actually works. Figure 9.5 shows a typical TCP segment, including its header. There's no need for IP addresses, since these are in the IP header; but the header does contain the sending and receiving port numbers. The *flags* field contains various control bits. Two of these bits — the SYN and FIN flags — appear in the sequence number space and thus are sent

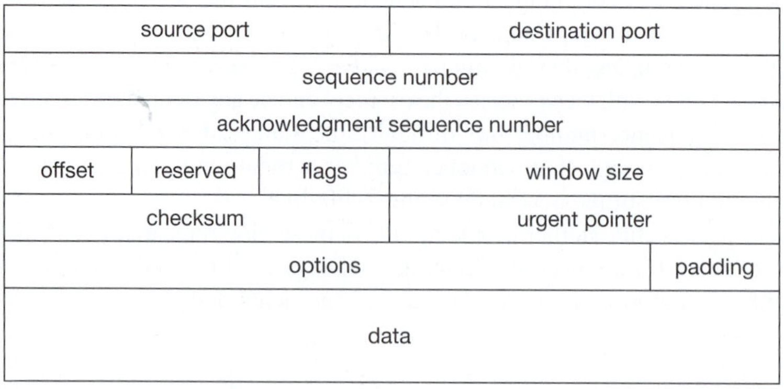

source port		destination port	
sequence number			
acknowledgment sequence number			
offset	reserved	flags	window size
checksum		urgent pointer	
options			padding
data			

FIGURE 9.5 TCP segment with header.

reliably if set. If the ACK flag is set, then the *acknowledgment sequence number* field contains an acknowledgment as described above: all data bytes and control bits with sequence numbers less than this have been received. The RST (reset) bit, used to indicate something has gone wrong, generally means that the connection is being unilaterally terminated. The PSH (push) bit indicates that the segment should be passed to the application without delay. The URG (urgent data) bit indicates that the *urgent pointer* field is meaningful. If the URG bit is set, then the urgent-pointer field contains the sequence number of the end of "urgent data" that should be delivered to the application even before data with earlier sequence numbers. (The urgent data begins at the beginning of the first segment with the URG flag set.)

The *checksum* field is a checksum not only on the TCP header, but on the TCP data and on the address portions of the IP header as well. If a receiver determines the checksum is bad, it discards the packet and relies on the sender to retransmit it. The *options* field contains variable-length optional information that we won't discuss. Finally, the *window-size* field indicates how much buffer space the sender has to receive additional data. We discuss this in more detail below.

TCP's actions are controlled by the rather elaborate state machine shown in Figure 9.6. Here the edges between states are labeled with the event causing a state transition as well as the action performed when changing states. An entity using TCP starts with its connection in the *closed* state. If it's a server, it performs what's called a *passive open* and goes to the *listen* state, where it's ready to receive connections from clients.

It's the client that actually initiates a connection. It starts a "three-way handshake" in which both parties come up with a suitable initial sequence number and reliably communicate it to the other. The client performs an *active open*, in which it sends a special *synchronize* segment to the server and goes to the *syn-sent* state. This synchronize segment has the SYN bit set in the header's flags and contains the client's initial sequence number — thus the SYN bit itself has this number. When the synchronize segment reaches the server, it responds with its own synchronize segment and goes to the *syn-received* state. Its synchronize segment has the SYN and ACK bits set in the flags, contains the server's initial sequence number, and acknowledges the client's initial sequence number (that is, its acknowledgment-sequence-number field contains a value

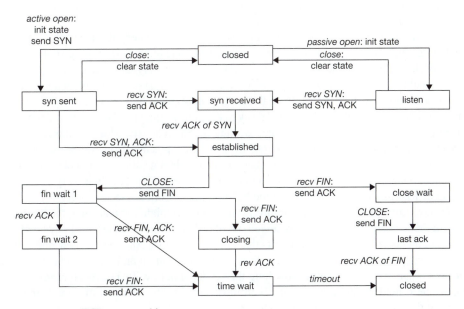

FIGURE 9.6 TCP state machine.

that's one greater than the client's initial sequence number). When this reaches the client, the client goes to the *established* state and responds by sending back a segment that acknowledges receipt by having the ACK bit set in the flags and one greater that the server's initial sequence number in the acknowledgment-sequence-number field. Finally, on receipt of the acknowledgment segment, the server goes to the *established* state.

Once in the established state, both parties may send segments containing data. We discuss this below, but first let's continue with the state machine by looking at how a connection is terminated. One party in a TCP connection shouldn't terminate a connection unilaterally, because it doesn't know if the other party has more to send. Thus safe termination is done by a very polite sequence of messages that go essentially like this: "I have no more data to send to you, but I will happily receive more data from you." "Thank you for saying that, I do indeed have more data for you." "I now have no more data for you, please let me know when you've received everything I've sent." "I have received everything you've sent; it's been nice communicating with you."

In terms of the state machine, here is what happens: One party (it could be either client or server) receives a *close* request from its application, meaning that it has no more data to send. This party goes to the *fin-wait-1* state and sends a *finish* segment to the other, which is a segment in which the FIN bit is set in the header flags. This bit is sent reliably and hence is given the next sequence number. On receipt of the segment, the other party goes to the *close-wait* state and sends back an acknowledgment. On receipt of the acknowledgment, the first part enters the *fin-wait-2* state. At this point communication is one-way — from the second party to the first — and can continue indefinitely.

At some point the second party receives a *close* request from its application. It sends a *finish* segment to the first party and goes to the *last-ack* state. The first party, on receipt of the *finish* segment, sends an acknowledgment back to the second party. At this point we have a problem. Suppose this acknowledgement is lost — that is, suppose it never makes it to the second party. After a while, the second party will time out (how long this takes to happen we discuss below) and, assuming that its finish segment never made it to the first party, will retransmit the segment. If the first party, after sending the acknowledgment, disappeared (i.e., closed its connection and removed all trace of it), the retransmitted finish segment will be rejected at the first party's site, since there is no trace of the connection it was terminating. The first party's site will respond with a *reset* segment, i.e., one with the RST bit set, which tells the second party that there's a problem. This is reflected to the application as an error, giving it reason to believe that the first party may have crashed before receiving all the data that was sent.

So we see that the first party shouldn't go away — it should keep its side of the connection active long enough for it to receive a retransmitted acknowledgment. How long should it wait? One approach might be for the second party to acknowledge receiving the acknowledgment, but then that would have to be acknowledged as well, and so forth, resulting in an endless sequence of acknowledgments. Instead, let's rely on the maximum segment lifetime (MSL) again. Now the first party waits long enough for the second party to time out waiting for the acknowledgement and retransmit the finish segment. The mandated waiting time is twice the MSL — four minutes. It's not perfect — there is no perfect solution — but it works well in practice. However, since connections are identified by the addresses and port numbers of their endpoints, this solution does mean that a new connection from the first party to the second can't be created until the first party goes into the *closed* state, four minutes after it receives the finish segment from the second party.

We now turn our attention to reliability. Some segments might not make it to the destination. Others might be delayed, and thus be received out of order. Thus the sender must pay attention to acknowledgments and retransmit segments that appear to be lost. And the receiver must hold on to early-arriving segments, delaying their delivery to the application until they can be delivered in the correct order. We discuss below how long the sender should wait. The receiver must reserve buffer space to hold incoming segments, both those arriving in order and those arriving out of order, until they are consumed by the application.

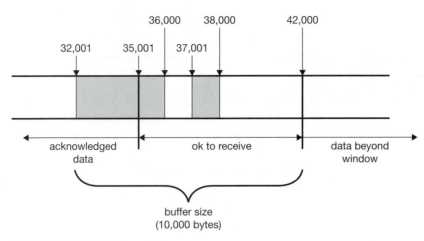

FIGURE 9.7 TCP receive window.

Since the receiver can reserve only a limited amount of buffer space and it would waste network bandwidth for the sender to transmit segments that the receiver has no room for, we need a means for the receiver to tell the sender how much buffer space it has. Such a means is known as *flow control*.

Through the *window-size* field of the header, each side of a TCP connection tells the other how much buffer space it has. For example, one side might indicate that it has 10,000 bytes reserved. If the other side has sent 8000 bytes of data that have yet to be acknowledged, then it knows that really only 2000 bytes are available, so it must not send any more than that.

Let's look at things from the receiver's point of view by describing its *receive window* (see Figure 9.7, where the shaded regions represent received data that have not yet been consumed by the application). Let's say the receiver has 10,000 bytes of buffer space for incoming data. It's already received and acknowledged 15,000 data bytes with sequence numbers from 20,001 through 35,000. Moreover, the application has consumed the first 12,000 bytes of these. Thus 3000 bytes of data in its buffer have been acknowledged but not consumed — it must hold on to this data until the application consumes it. It's also received data with sequence numbers 35,001 through 36,000 and 37,001 though 38,000 that it hasn't yet acknowledged (and, of course, it must not acknowledge data in the latter range until the data in the range 36,001 through 37,000 arrives). Thus there are an additional 2000 bytes of data in its buffer, leaving room for 5000 more bytes. If it receives new data with sequence numbers in the range 20,001 through 36,000 or in the range 37,001 through 38,000, it may assume these are duplicates and discard them. However, new data in the ranges 36,001 through 37,000 and 38,001 through 42,000 are not duplicates and must be stored in the buffer. If it receives anything whose sequence number is greater than 42,000, it must discard it because it doesn't have room for it.

Now for the sender's point of view — we look at its *send window* (see Figure 9.8). It has sent out and received acknowledgments for bytes with sequence numbers from 20,001 through 34,000. The sender has also sent out but hasn't received acknowledgments for data bytes with sequence numbers from 34,001 through 39,000. It must retain a copy of these data bytes just in case it has to resend them. The most recent segment the sender has received from the other side indicates the receive window is 8000 bytes. However, since it knows 5000 bytes' worth of data have been sent but not acknowledged, it knows that it really can send no more than 3,000 additional bytes of data — up through sequence number 42,000.

If the sender doesn't receive an acknowledgment for a range of data bytes, it must resend them. How long should it wait before deciding to resend? This *retransmission timeout period* (RTO) must be chosen with care. If it's too short, data is retransmitted needlessly and thus makes

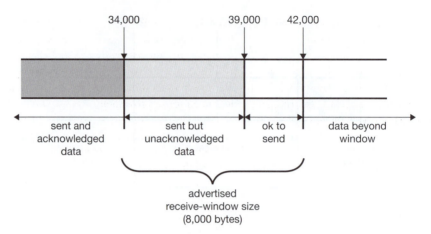

FIGURE 9.8 TCP send window.

for unnecessary network congestion. But if the RTO is too long, then there are needless delays in getting the data to the receiving application.

The approach suggested in the TCP specification RFC 793[8] is to keep track of the average time between sending a segment and getting its acknowledgment — this is known as the *smoothed roundtrip time* (SRTT). If an acknowledgement hasn't come after a period significantly longer than SRTT, then the corresponding segment is retransmitted. What's "significantly longer"? The specification suggests an initial period of four times the average deviation of the roundtrip time.[9]

How long should the sender wait for an acknowledgment after retransmitting a segment? If there's still no acknowledgment even after waiting the RTO period after the retransmission, it could well be that some problem in the communication path has made the original RTO too short. So an *exponential backoff* approach is used: the sender doubles the RTO after sending the first retransmission. If it times out again, it doubles the RTO again and continues to double as needed up to some maximum value before deciding that the connection is dead and giving up.

A more general question is: how fast should the sender be sending segments? It might seem reasonable for it to transmit as fast as its directly attached network will accept them. But suppose some router between it and the destination computer can't handle the segments that quickly. This router is likely to drop the packets it can't handle right away — to simply get rid of them. The sender, oblivious to the problems at this router, continues to transmit at top speed, but perhaps most of these packets are being dropped. At some point the sending TCP times out waiting for the acknowledgments and retransmits the dropped segments. But the router is still overloaded and drops them again. Furthermore, retransmitting these dropped packets adds to the router's overload. Thus, though the sender's transmission speed is high, real throughput is low — most of the segments have to be retransmitted a number of times.

The problem is clearly that the sender is sending too quickly. Its retransmissions are adding to network congestion and aggravating an already bad situation. Even though successive retransmissions have an exponentially increasing interval between them, once an acknowledgment is received, transmission reverts to the original speed and the problems continue — the

---

[8] http://www.ietf.org/rfc/rfc0793.txt.

[9] Why is it *average deviation* rather than *standard deviation*? Because standard deviation involves computing square roots and the use of floating-point arithmetic. This was considered too expensive for systems of the 1980s — in particular, floating-point arithmetic was completely avoided in the OS kernel so as to eliminate the need to save floating-point registers.

sender continues to be oblivious to network congestion. The only throttle on its speed is the send window — it can't transmit more data than what the receiver is prepared to receive.

What's more, it's not just one sender who's doing this, but all senders — each is transmitting as fast as it can, retransmitting again and again all the segments that were dropped by overloaded routers. In the early days of the Internet, this was pretty much how things were done. The result was a dramatically congested Internet and a clear need for improvement.

Such an improvement was devised by V. Jacobson (Jacobson 1988) in the *slow-start* procedure. It's useful to think of a network connection as being an oil pipeline. It is has a finite capacity that's determined by its length and diameter. In a real pipeline, back pressure prevents us from sending too much oil. What we need, then, is some analog to this back pressure to prevent senders from sending data too quickly. As we've seen, the only indication the sender gets that something's wrong is a retransmission timeout, indicating that a segment probably did not reach its destination. We've been inclined to think of these RTOs as caused by acts of God — lightning, solar activity, or some other seemingly random event that has caused our segment to disappear. But, in fact, segments normally disappear not because of acts of God but because of acts of routers.[10] So, let's use RTOs as back pressure.

If we start transmitting at high speed, an RTO will tell us that going too fast, but this comes at the expense of having to retransmit a fair number of segments. Furthermore, we don't get an indication of how fast we should be transmitting, other than slower than we have been.

The slow-start approach involves carefully and deliberately discovering the current pipeline capacity. The current estimate of this capacity is the *congestion window*, a quantity indicating how many unacknowledged bytes may be in the pipeline. It starts with a value of one segment. Each time an acknowledgment is received, indicating that the pipeline's capacity hasn't been exceeded, the congestion window is increased by one segment. Though this is called slow-start, the rate of increase is actually quick — as a congestion window's worth of segments is acknowledged, the congestion-window size doubles.

Of course, once the congestion-window size surpasses the pipeline's capacity, some overloaded router will drop a packet and eventually there will be a retransmission timeout. So the RTO indicates that our transmission rate has exceeded the capacity of the pipeline. Halving the congestion-window size reverts to a value giving us a transmission rate that's probably somewhat less than capacity, but not more. At this point slow-start increases the congestion-window size linearly rather than exponentially, dropping it again by a factor of two whenever there is an RTO.

One might think the result would be the saw-tooth pattern shown in Figure 9.9, but there are additional factors. The congestion window gives us the capacity of the pipeline, but we still need

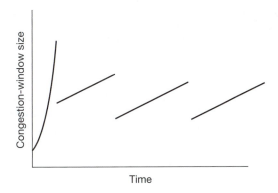

FIGURE 9.9 Idealized congestion-window size vs. time using the slow-start approach.

---

[10] This is not the case on wireless links, where electromagnetic noise can indeed cause packets to be lost.

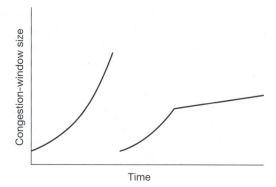

FIGURE 9.10 Actual congestion-window size vs. time, taking into account the need to reestablish ack clocking.

to know the rate of flow through it — how quickly may the sender put segments into it? A neat trick known as *ack clocking* provides the answer. In a real pipeline, oil flows out at the same rate it flows in. The sender does know how fast segments are being received by the receiver — each acknowledgment indicates something came out at the other end. So, receipt of an acknowledgment means that more may be transmitted and thus transmission speed is determined by the rate at which acknowledgments are received.

However, this strategy leads us to a small problem. Slow start involves increasing the congestion-window size until there's an RTO. But by the time the timeout occurs, all the segments that were in the pipeline have been received, and thus there is no source of acknowledgment to drive ack clocking. So, even though a reduced congestion-window size has been determined, the sender must go through slow start once again to reestablish ack clocking — rather than increasing the congestion-window size until it gets another RTO, it stops once it reaches half its previous value. Thus the actual plot of congestion-window size is not as in Figure 9.9, but as in Figure 9.10.

What's needed is a way to determine that a segment has been dropped without waiting for an RTO. A simple addition to the TCP protocol provides this. When a segment is received whose sequence number is greater than expected, it's pretty clear (to the receiver) that one or more segments are late or lost. So the receiver repeats its most recent acknowledgment. When the sender receives two identical acknowledgments in a row, the segments are clearly reaching the receiver — something is inducing the acknowledgments — yet at least one segment didn't make it. If the sender receives three identical acknowledgments in a row, it's really clear that a segment was lost. So the sender can immediately retransmit that segment, halve the congestion-window size, yet still retain ack clocking.

The full procedure as just described is known as *slow start with fast retransmit*.[11] It's been in use on the Internet since the early 1990s. Further improvements for even better congestion control have been added over the years — see (Floyd 2001).

9.2 REMOTE PROCEDURE CALL PROTOCOLS

An important special case of communication is the client-server relationship in which a client sends requests to a server and receives responses in return. An example of particular importance for the next chapter arises when the server is a file server providing file access to its clients. Clients place requests to look up names in directories, read blocks of file, write blocks to files, etc.

The idea behind *remote procedure calls (RPC)* is to treat requests as if a thread on the client computer were invoking a procedure on the server and to treat responses as the procedure's

---

[11] It is fully described in RFC2001 (http://www.faqs.org/rfcs/rfc2001.html).

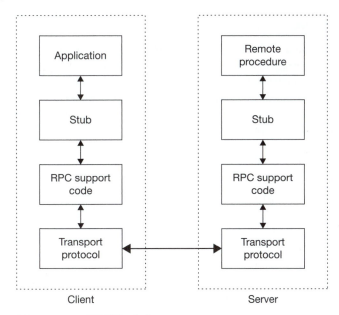

FIGURE 9.11   RPC block diagram.

return. In effect, the client thread travels to the server computer, carrying with it the arguments. It executes the procedure on the server, passing it the arguments. On return, the thread travels back to the client, carrying with it the procedure's return value as well as the values of any output arguments. The classic paper describing how to implement RPC is (Birrell and Nelson 1984).

Remote procedures are typically implemented as shown in Figure 9.11. The actual code for the procedure resides on the server and, in general, is no different from the code of a local procedure. What makes it usable by remote clients is a pair of *stub routines*, one on the client and one on the server. A client thread placing a call to a remote procedure actually calls the client-side stub, which puts a description of the request and the arguments into one or more packets and transmits them to the server. On the server a thread receives these packets, determines which remote procedure is being called, and calls the appropriate server-side stub; the server-side stub extracts the arguments and calls the procedure with them. On return from the procedure, the server-side stub puts the results into one or more packets and sends them back to the client-side stub. The client-side stub extracts the results and returns them to the original caller.

The process of putting data, either arguments or return values, into a packet to be transmitted is called *marshalling*.[12] The reverse, extracting the data from packets, is called *unmarshalling*.

In addition to the concerns about reliable data transmission discussed in the previous section, RPC protocols must deal with passing data between machines that represent data differently, as well as providing correct operation in spite of computer crashes and communication breakdowns.

Though a number of RPC protocols have been developed over the past few decades, two of particular importance are Open Network Computing RPC (ONC RPC), developed by Sun Microsystems in the 1980s, and what we call Microsoft RPC.[13]

---

[12] From the verb "to marshal," which, according to the Oxford English Dictionary, means "to arrange or organize in a body or procession."

[13] Microsoft RPC has a long history. It goes back to the Network Computing Architecture RPC (NCA RPC), developed by the Apollo Computer Corporation in the mid-1980s, a company that was later acquired by Hewlett Packard. NCA RPC was the basis of the Distributed Computing Environment RPC (DCE RPC) of the Open Software Foundation (OSF), now part of the Open Group. DCE RPC is the basis for Microsoft RPC.

9.2.1 MARSHALLING

Marshalling and unmarshalling data are not as trivial as they might seem. Marshalled data, produced from a data representation in a language system on one sort of machine, must be unmarshalled into the representation of that data in a possibly different language system on a possibly different sort of machine. This requires a detailed description of the data's type, including size — information that is not available in standard programming languages such as C.

To make this more concrete, consider the C declarations below:

```
typedef struct {
    int     comp1;
    float   comp2[6];
    char    *annotation;
} value_t;

typedef struct {
    value_t element;
    value_t *next;
} list_t;

bool add(int key, value_t element);
bool remove(int key, value_t element);
list_t query(int key);
```

We've declared a simple database interface with three procedures. From this declaration, we would like to be able to create automatically a set of client and server stubs to do the appropriate marshalling and unmarshalling for remote access to the database. But, as we will soon see, this declaration does not contain enough information to do this. Here we rely on our knowledge of the programmer's intent to show how marshalling and unmarshalling are done; happily, both ONC RPC and Microsoft RPC provide a separate language for describing remote procedural interfaces so that stubs can be generated automatically.

Our database consists of a collection of elements of type *value_t*, each identified by an integer key. The *add* routine adds a new element with a particular key, returning false or true depending on whether or not an identical key/element was already there. The *remove* routine removes a particular key/element combination. The *query* routine returns a list of all elements with a particular key.

Figure 9.12 illustrates placing a call to *add,* and Figure 9.13 illustrates the return from *add*. To marshal *add*'s arguments the client-side stub must put them into a form such that they can be unmarshalled when they reach the server. The first argument, *key*, should be easy — it's just an integer. How should the stub marshal it?

There are two issues: how big the integer is and how it is represented. Though older versions of C allowed the size of *int*s to depend on the architecture, modern C compilers set the size to 32 bits. But the representation still depends on the architecture, which might be big-endian (the byte with the lowest address contains the most significant bits) or little-endian (the byte with the lowest address contains the least significant bits).

One approach to dealing with these two possibilities is to choose one, say big-endian, as the standard and have the marshalling code in the client-side stub convert to that standard if necessary. Then the unmarshalling code in the server-side stub knows the representation of the incoming integer and converts, if necessary, to its architecture's representation. This approach is simple, though perhaps a bit inefficient if both sender and receiver are little-endian. It is what is used in ONC RPC, however.

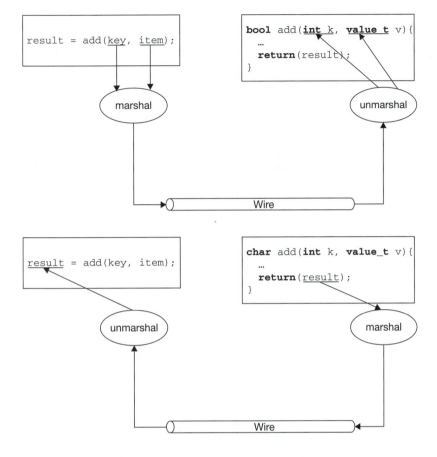

FIGURE 9.12   Placing a remote procedure call.

FIGURE 9.13   Returning from a remote procedure call.

An alternative approach is for the sender to marshal the data using its own representation, but also to supply a code indicating what that representation is. Then the receiver can determine if conversion is necessary. This approach is used in Microsoft RPC.

Marshalling the second argument in the *add* routine above is a bit more complicated, since it's a structured type. But this is handled simply by marshalling each of the components in turn. The second component is itself a structured type, a fixed-length array. Since the length (six) is known by both parties, each element is marshalled in turn. Each of the elements is a float, which has similar issues to those involved in the int. The solution is the same: either use an agreed-upon standard representation, or send it using the sender's representation, along with a code indicating what that representation is.

The third component of the structure, *annotation*, presents a problem: not enough information is provided in the C declaration to marshal it. Though it's probably clear to the human reader that *annotation* is a null-terminated character string, the declaration allows other possibilities. For example, it might be a pointer to a single character, in the same way as an *int ** would be a pointer to a single integer. If the stub is to be produced automatically, more information about *annotation* is needed. An interface language might have an explicit string type that could be used to indicate unambiguously that *annotation* is a null-terminated string. In any event, to marshal *annotation*, the stub must compute its length and send it along with the bytes of the string. Figure 9.14 shows the marshaled arguments of *add* (a standard data representation is assumed).

Unmarshalling the arguments is now straightforward. The server-side stub expects an integer as the first argument and thus takes the first four bytes of the marshalled arguments. If the standard data representation differs from that of the server, the stub performs the necessary conversion. It expects the second argument to be of type *value_t*. The initial component of the

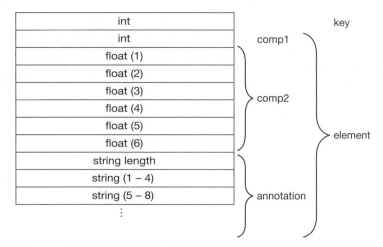

FIGURE 9.14   The marshalled arguments of *add*.

	array length
0: value_t	next: 1
1: value_t	next: 2
2: value_t	next: 3
3: value_t	next: 4
4: value_t	next: 5
5: value_t	next: 6
6: value_t	next: -1

FIGURE 9.15   A marshalled linked list.

structure is an integer, so it interprets the next four bytes of the marshaled data as an integer. Similarly, it expects the next component to be a fixed-length array of floats, and interprets the 28 bytes as that array. Finally, it expects a string and expects that the next four bytes will be the length of that string. It then creates a null-terminated string from that number of remaining bytes.

The *query* routine from our database interface returns a linked list. While at first glance the pointers in such a data structure might seem difficult to marshal, remember that the desired result of unmarshalling the marshalled linked list is a copy of the original list. One approach to doing this, used in Microsoft RPC, is to marshal the list as an array and marshal the pointers as array indices, as in Figure 9.15.

The linked list in Figure 9.15 can be easily reconstructed by the receiver. It might either allocate storage for all of it at once, converting the indices into pointers, or allocate storage for each *value_t* separately, linking them together with pointers.

9.2.2 RELIABLE SEMANTICS

What does it mean for an RPC protocol to be reliable? We'd like it to mean that whenever a call is placed, the remote procedure is executed *exactly once* and the results are returned. But what if there are short-term problems, such as a network outage or a server crash (and restart)? Ideally, these problems shouldn't affect anything — the call to the remote procedure should still return (eventually) with the results, as in Figure 9.16.

To achieve this reliability, it makes sense to layer RPC on top of a reliable transport protocol such as TCP. Thus an RPC request is sent over a TCP connection, and the response comes back over that connection. TCP handles all the details of ensuring that everything gets where it's supposed to and gets there in the correct order. As long as the TCP connection is operational, the RPC exchanges running on top of it are perfectly reliable.

But what happens if we lose the TCP connection? This might happen because a temporary communication problem makes the connection time out, or the server might crash, then restart. Can we simply create a new TCP connection and resume the RPC activity?

Consider an example from the client's point of view. It sends a request, but before it receives a response, perhaps even before its TCP gets an acknowledgment, the connection times out. The client might successfully create a new connection to the server, but should it retransmit its original request or not?

Maybe the original request was received by the server and acted upon, but either the server crashed before the response could be transmitted, or a network problem terminated the connection while the response was in transit. Or perhaps such a problem occurred before the request arrived at the server in the first place. Thus the client is in a quandary: it doesn't know whether or not the server has acted on the original request (see Figure 9.17).

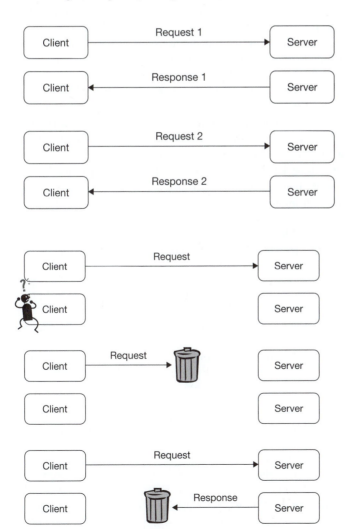

FIGURE 9.16 How RPC is supposed to work: requests are followed by responses.

FIGURE 9.17 Uncertainty when a request is not followed by the response: was the request lost or the response lost?

There are two rather obvious things for the RPC client to do. One is to give up and admit to the application that it doesn't really know what happened. Thus, rather than guaranteeing that it executes the remote procedure exactly once, it has to fall back on guaranteeing *at most once*. Alternatively, the client portion of RPC might try again, and, if necessary, continue trying again, until it finally gets a response from the server. This, of course, has the danger that the server might end up executing the remote procedure more than once. Thus the reliability guarantee drops from exactly once to *at least once*.

In many cases, this at-least-once semantics isn't a problem. Some procedures are *idempotent*, meaning that the effect of executing them twice in succession is no different from the effect of executing them just once. Consider a request that writes data to a certain location in a file. Performing it twice is inefficient, but the net result is just the same as doing it once (see Figure 9.18). But certainly not all procedures are idempotent — consider one that transfers money from one account to another.

One possibility for getting around this uncertainty of whether or not the server has executed the remote procedure is that the server keeps track of the requests it has executed. Of course, if it receives a repeat of a request, it can't simply ignore it, since the client is probably still waiting for the response. So, the server might hold onto responses from past requests and resend a response if it receives a retransmission of the request. This is the approach NFS uses with ONC RPC. But note that it requires the server to hold state information in addition to what's held by the transport protocol, and also requires this state information to continue to exist even if the transport connection is lost.

So, since the functionality of the reliable transport protocol must be augmented by RPC, why not dispense with the transport protocol entirely, run RPC on an unreliable protocol, such as UDP, and have RPC do all the work of providing reliability?

This was the preferred approach in the early days of RPC, where UDP was often used as the transport, and it is still used in some situations today. For the next part of our discussion, we assume that UDP is the transport. This allows us to see more clearly what the issues peculiar to RPC are. We then go back to TCP and discover that, even though some RPC problems are less likely to occur on TCP than on UDP, they are still possible.

One reason for using UDP rather than TCP is that, in principle, RPC can provide reliability more efficiently on its own, because it can take advantage of its own simplicity. A simple exchange of a request from a client followed by a response from the server in general requires four packets if TCP is used: the request, followed by an acknowledgment from the server, and then the response, followed by an acknowledgment from the client. But over UDP only two packets are needed, because the acknowledgments are not necessary. Rather, the response serves as the

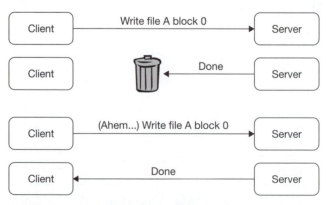

FIGURE 9.18 An example of the use of an idempotent procedure.

acknowledgment of the request; if the client is single-threaded, i.e., it has just one request in progress at a time, then the client's next request serves as the acknowledgment of the response.

However, the important case is the multithreaded client. For example, in most implementations of NFS (see Chapter 10) the client is the operating system, acting on behalf of all threads on the machine — many requests are in progress at once. A great deal of work has been done to make the multithreaded case just as efficient (in terms of the number of messages exchanged) as the single-threaded case. The focus of all this attention is the server's response to the client's request: making its transmission reliable is the key to reliability of RPC.

So let's fill in a few more details of an RPC protocol layered on top of UDP, in an environment in which clients have multiple requests in progress at once. We follow the design of ONC RPC, as used with NFS.

Requests and their matching responses are identified by unique integers called transmission IDs (XIDs). It's not necessary that they form a sequence, just as long as each request/response pair is uniquely identified.

A client's task is simple. It sends a request. If it doesn't get a response in due time, it resends the request. If it receives a response for which it doesn't have a matching, unresponded-to request (which is thus probably a retransmission of a previous response), it ignores it.

The server's task is a bit more complicated. It differentiates between idempotent and non-idempotent procedures, and maintains a cache, called the *duplicate request cache (DRC)*, of copies of responses to recently executed non-idempotent procedures. Responses stay in this cache for a certain period of time, say a minute or so. When the server receives a request to execute an idempotent procedure, it simply executes it and returns the response. Since the procedure is idempotent, there's no harm if the request is a duplicate. When it receives a request to execute a non-idempotent procedure, it first checks if the request is in the cache, i.e., if the request is a retransmission of one received earlier. If so, it doesn't execute it again, but simply returns (retransmits) the response it returned the first time. Otherwise it executes the request and sends back (and saves a copy of) the response.[14]

This design is simple and the protocol is efficient. Unfortunately, it doesn't always work. Suppose a request is sent by the client but gets delayed somewhere in the network. The client, not receiving a response soon enough, retransmits the request. This time the request gets to the server right away and is answered quickly. The client receives the response and then sends its next request. This reaches the server, which handles it and sends back a response. At this point, the first transmission of the client's original request finally makes it through the network and arrives, very late, at the server. If it's an idempotent request, the server executes it, since it has no information about whether it is a duplicate. If it's a non-idempotent request, the server first checks the DRC. But the request may have been delayed long enough so that the other instance of it is no longer in the DRC. Thus the server executes it.

Does this cause any harm? It clearly is a problem in the non-idempotent case, but it's also a problem in the idempotent case. For example, suppose the original request was to write a current account balance ($10,000) into the beginning of a file. The second request was to write the new balance ($5) into the same location. Thus the final result should be a balance of $5. However, the delayed first request overwrites the location with old data — $10,000.

Particularly in environments in which ONC RPC is commonly used, we often assume that the network and its routers are well behaved and that such a scenario will not happen. But in general, on the other hand, we have to assume that routers are conspiring against us to do whatever it

---

[14] The actual algorithm used in early NFSv2 differed slightly from this. The non-idempotent requests used in NFSv2 fail if executed more than once in succession (for example, consider the effect of unlinking a file twice). Thus the duplicate request cache is examined *after* execution of a non-idempotent request, not before, and only if the request failed. See Exercise 12.

takes to invalidate the assumptions made about the network. Such malicious routers are known as *Byzantine routers*.[15]

Similar symptoms observed by (Juszczak 1989) were due not to Byzantine routers, but to a bug in the implementation of the protocol in which the servers were, essentially, not thread-safe. (Juszczak 1989) suggested a fix in which the headers of both idempotent and non-idempotent requests (enough to identify duplicates) are cached in the duplicate request cache along with the complete responses to non-idempotent requests. As Figure 9.19 shows, when the server receives a request, it immediately checks if it is a duplicate of a request still in the cache. If not, the request is performed. If so, and if the original is still in progress, the duplicate is discarded, i.e., the client must have timed out and retransmitted prematurely. Otherwise, the request was executed, but evidently the client did not receive the response.

If the request succeeded the first time it was executed, but was non-idempotent, then, as in the original approach, the original reply is sent back without re-executing the request. But, if the original request was unsuccessful (and no doubt will still be unsuccessful if re-executed) or if it was successful and idempotent, then it makes more sense to simply discard it without re-executing it. The rationale, backed up by experience, is that the response really did make it to the client (or is on its way), but that the client has prematurely retransmitted the request. Thus the client will soon (if not already) receive the response and be happy. However, if the response really was lost (which is considered unlikely), the client will repeatedly retransmit the request until it does get a response. At some point the original request will have timed out of the cache, and the request will be treated as a new request (and a response will be sent to the client).

This fixed the implementation bug and made the bank-balance scenario outlined above less likely, but did not prevent it completely. The protocol was still susceptible to Byzantine-router problems — if the delayed request arrives after the other instance has been removed from the cache — but, in the environments in which the protocol is used, such problems are exceedingly rare. (We have more to say about this later in this section.)

A final issue is the effect of a crash. Client crashes are bad news for client applications, but are not a real concern to RPC. On the other hand, a server crash is a concern. If a server crashes

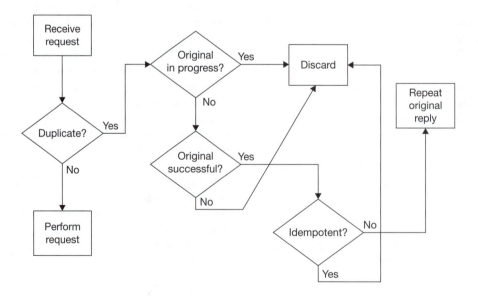

FIGURE 9.19 Juszczak's algorithm for handling possibly duplicate incoming RPC requests (adapted from (Juszczak 1989)).

---

[15] It's unlikely that routers have really been programmed to be nasty, but heavy network loads and imperfect routing algorithms can make them look that way. Routers generally don't act Byzantinely when the communication paths between clients and servers are few and simple. The problem comes up (occasionally) when clients communicate over the Internet with distant servers.

after the client sends a request but before the response arrives, the client has the same uncertainty mentioned at the beginning of this subsection about whether or not the request actually took place on the server. Furthermore, since any state information kept by the server in volatile storage is lost after a crash, there is no direct way to find out.

Let's now bring back TCP. Its performance is better than in the 1970s and 1980s — there is much less reason than in the past to avoid it because of its performance. In fact, because it provides congestion control (see Section 9.1.1), it's a better overall "network citizen" than is UDP and is in general preferred to UDP.

Because TCP is a reliable transport, and thus data is sequenced, using it might seem to eliminate the need for a duplicate request cache and also nullify any problems from Byzantine routers. If RPC could depend on never losing its TCP connection, then TCP's sequencing would indeed make all this so. But if the underlying TCP connection fails for some reason and a new one is created, TCP's sequencing information is lost.

For example, suppose a client sends a request and the server sends back a response. But the response is lost when a router that's forwarding it crashes. The TCP connection is lost as well, so the server's TCP doesn't retransmit the response. The client creates a new connection. Since it's still waiting for the response, it retransmits the request. If the server doesn't have a duplicate request cache, it cannot determine that the retransmission is a duplicate. And, even if it has such a cache, if the original request is no longer in the DRC, it still cannot determine whether the retransmission is a duplicate, just as in the UDP case.

As another example, suppose a client sends a request, but the underlying TCP connection to the server times out before it receives a response. The client creates a new connection and then retransmits its request over it. Assuming the request is idempotent, there should be no danger from its being executed twice on the server. However, the server end of the original TCP connection has not timed out and is still in the established state (this is unlikely, but possible). The original request turns out to have been delayed at a Byzantine router. It finally arrives at the server over the old connection, long after its retransmission, and perhaps long after the retransmission has been removed from the duplicate request cache and after other requests from the same client have been received. The server thus does not detect the original request as a duplicate and happily executes it.

Despite its vulnerability to problems with duplicates, ONC RPC using Juszczak's DRC algorithm has worked well in practice — in most environments these problems simply don't occur. We call this form of ONC RPC the *original ONC RPC* in order to distinguish it from what we discuss next.

What is needed to make the original ONC RPC reliable in the face of dropped TCP connections and Byzantine routers is a way to detect a duplicate request that isn't so dependent on the replacement policy and the finiteness of the duplicate request cache. So, let's modify the caching approach a bit. To distinguish the new approach from the old, servers have *reply caches* rather than duplicate request caches. A client establishes a *session* with a server, and associated with each session is a separate reply cache, holding a single request and its complete response. Each request contains a sequence number assigned by the client. If the client is single-threaded, i.e., has only one request in progress at a time, then requests should be arriving at the server in sequence-number order. If a request arrives with the same sequence number as the previous one, the response to that first request must not have arrived at the client and thus the server repeats its previous response, which is guaranteed to be in the reply cache. If a request arrives with a sequence number less than that of the previous one, it must be a duplicate whose response has already been received by the client, and thus can be ignored — it may have come via a Byzantine router.

To handle clients that have multiple concurrent requests, the client and server agree ahead of time to a maximum number of concurrent requests, say n, and have the server give the client n slots in its reply cache (see Figure 9.20, where client 1 has specified a maximum concurrency

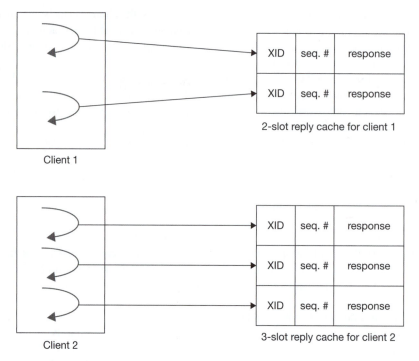

FIGURE 9.20 Session-oriented ONC RPC.

of 2 and client 2 has specified a maximum concurrency of 3). The client then has effectively n channels through which it can send requests, and only one request at a time is active on each channel. The client provides a slot number and sequence number with each request, and the server holds onto its most recent response for each channel. The server determines how to respond to a request, just as in the previous paragraph.

Versions of ONC RPC that use sequence numbers and channels as just described are called *session-oriented ONC RPC*. It is used in NFS starting with version 4.1 (see Section 9.5.1).

9.3
CONCLUSIONS

This chapter has covered some of the details of the TCP/IP protocols so as to understand how the reliable communication required for RPC protocols is made to work. The intent has been to remove the magic behind reliable communication and, perhaps, motivate the reader to take a course on network protocols. Similarly, we explained RPC in depth, since it is used to support distributed file systems, the topic of the next chapter.

9.4
EXERCISES

1. Network address translation (NAT) is a means by which a collection of computers appears to the rest of the Internet to have one IP address. The computers of the collection actually have their own IP addresses and are all connected to one local area network, which in turn is connected to the Internet via a special router known as a *NAT box*. All communication to computers of the collection is addressed to the NAT box. For example, see Figure. 9.21, where the NAT box is connected to the Internet with an interface whose IP address is 128.148.64.10. It is also connected to the LAN with address 192.168.1.1. Each of the computers in the collection, C1 through C5, is connected to the LAN with an IP address from the range 192.168.1.101 through 192.168.1.105. No router on the Internet is aware of IP addresses of

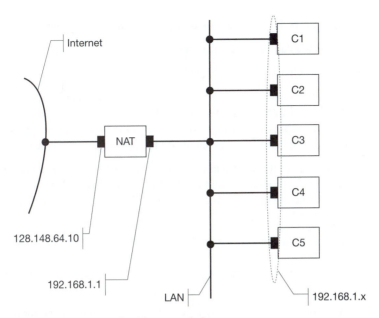

FIGURE 9.21 Network address translation.

the form 192.168.x.y, thus none of the computers in the collection may be contacted directly. When an application on computer C3 attempts to connect to a computer in the Internet, it sends its packets to the NAT box. The NAT box modifies the headers of such packets so that their source address is 128.148.64.10, then sends them on. When it receives packets from the Internet, it determines which computer of the collection they should be forwarded to, changes the destination address in the header to that computer (e.g., 192.168.1.103), and forwards them.

   a. Assume that C3 is establishing a TCP connection to 128.147.13.5. When packets are sent back from that address, how does the NAT box determine that they should be forwarded to C3? (*Hint:* some state information must be set up in the NAT box when the C3 initiates the connection. What state information is necessary?)

   b. Suppose that running on C4 is a server application that receives connection requests on port 1234. Explain how the NAT box can determine that requests for this service should go to C4.

2. How many packets are needed to initiate a TCP connection? Explain.

3. Safely terminating a TCP connection requires the cooperation of both communicating parties.

   a. Explain why it's not good for one party to terminate a connection unilaterally.

   b. Consider the correct shutdown sequence for a TCP connection. That is, one side sends a FIN, and the other side must acknowledge the FIN packet, and then send its own FIN, which must be acknowledged as well. Explain why the first party must wait a few minutes after transmitting the acknowledgment of the final FIN before it may consider the connection to be closed.

4. In Section 9.1.1.2, we state that "attaining reliable communication is pretty straightforward." There are, however, some extreme cases that must be dealt with to ensure reliability.

   a. Explain why TCP packets need to have a maximum lifetime.

   b. Explain why TCP connections cannot always have initial sequence numbers of 0.

5. Consider the size of the receive window used for one end of a TCP connection.

a. What problems are caused if it is too small?

b. Are there any problems if it is too large?

c. Two important parameters of a TCP connection are its bandwidth — the average number of bytes/second transmitted over it, and its delay — the average time required to receive an acknowledgment for a segment, measured from the moment the segment was sent. In terms of these two quantities, what should be the size of the receive window? Explain.

6. The window-size field of the TCP header is used by one end of a TCP connection to inform the other of the size of its receive window. A common special case of TCP is when data is being sent in only one direction, such as when a file is transferred. Let's say a file is being transferred from A to B.

a. In such a one-way transfer, all segments from B to A (containing acknowledgments and window sizes) have the same sequence number, since no data is being transferred in that direction. If such segments arrive out of order, how can A determine which contains the most recent window size?

b. Suppose A's send window is full: A may not send more data at the moment, though it has data to send. At some point B's receive window will open up (because its application has consumed data). May B immediately send a segment containing an updated window size? Explain.

c. A's send window is still full. Are there potential problems if A repeats its most recent transmission to B so as to solicit a response containing the most recent window size? Explain.

d. How should A find out that B's receive window is no longer full?

7. Suppose we have a 10 Gbit/second network with a round-trip time of 100 milliseconds; the maximum segment size is 1500 bytes. How long will it take a TCP connection to reach maximum speed after starting in slow-start mode?

8. Explain how ack clocking serves to help senders determine how fast to send data. Explain how the modification to the TCP protocol described at the end of Section 9.1.1.2 (repeating the most recent acknowledgement) allows ack clocking to work even though packets are being lost and thus cannot be acknowledged.

*9. You'd like to transmit one hundred one-megabyte files from computer A to computer B over the Internet. Assume that the latency from A to B is very small, and that the bandwidth on the intermediate connection from A to B is quite large. Also assume the routers on the path from A to B have a large amount of buffer space.

Three possible approaches are:

i) Use 100 separate TCP connections that are set up and used sequentially: the first is made, the first file is completely transmitted, and then the connection is torn down, then the second connection is set up and the second file is transmitted, etc.

ii) Use 100 separate TCP connections, all set up and used in parallel (i.e., all 100 files are opened, 100 connections are made, and then all files are transmitted concurrently).

iii) Send all 100 files sequentially, but over the same connection.

Which of the three approaches should be the fastest? Explain.

10. A simple technique for marshalling a pointer is to transmit just the target of the pointer. Thus to marshal an *int **, the sender transmits the pointed-at *int*. The receiver unmarshals by allocating storage for an *int*, copying the received *int* into the storage, and providing a pointer to that storage as the unmarshalled result. Does this marshalling/unmarshalling technique work for all uses of pointers? Explain.

11. A remote procedure may be declared to have no return value, i.e., it returns *void*. Would it be safe for clients to treat such procedures as asynchronous requests, i.e., once the call is placed, the client application may immediately proceed to its next instruction?

12. Suppose we have a remote procedure that is called to delete the file whose name is supplied as an argument.

    a. Explain why it is not idempotent.

    b. Assuming there is no duplicate request cache, will the file system be damaged if a client retransmits its request to delete a file after the response to its previous request was lost (and the retransmitted request is executed)? Explain.

    c. Explain how the scenario of part b might harm a client application program.

*13. An RPC request is said to have "at-least-once" semantics if, once the request returns to the calling application, it is guaranteed that the remote procedure was executed at least once on the server. This makes sense for idempotent procedures. The other extreme is "at-most-once" semantics, where the remote procedure is guaranteed not to be executed more than once. This makes sense for a non-idempotent procedure (though one certainly hopes that most of the time it is in fact executed once).

    Of course, what we really want is "exactly-once" semantics: a guarantee that the remote procedure is executed exactly one time.

    a. Explain how exactly-once semantics can be achieved if we can guarantee that the server never crashes.

    b. Is exactly-once semantics possible if we no longer have the no-crash guarantee? What additional mechanisms would be needed? Explain.

Birrell, A. D. and B. J. Nelson (1984). Implementing Remote Procedure Calls. *ACM Transactions on Computer Systems* **2**(1): 39–59.

Floyd, S. (2001). A Report on Some Recent Developments in TCP Congestion Control. *IEEE Communications Magazine* **3**(4): 84–90.

Jacobson, V. (1988). Congestion Avoidance and Control. *Proceedings of SIGCOMM '88*, ACM.

Juszczak, C. (1989). Improving the Performance and Correctness of an NFS Server. *Proceedings of the Winter 1989 USENIX Technical Conference*: 53–63.

9.5 REFERENCES

CHAPTER 10 Distributed File Systems

Distributed file systems straddle the boundary between what is covered in a course on operating systems and what is covered in a course on distributed systems. They provide common file access to a collection of computers; all computers in the collection can access files as if they were local, even though the files don't reside in their local file systems. The need for such a distributed system grew out of the switch in the 1980s from multiuser time-shared systems to networks of workstations (or personal computers). A community of people using a time-sharing system shared a single file system, all files were accessed identically by programs, and files were shared trivially. Furthermore, the file systems were easily administered — they were all attached to one machine and could be easily backed up. A *distributed file system* provides all the benefits of the file system on a time-sharing system and opens them up to users of a collection of personal computers.

The history of distributed file systems goes back to the late 1970s and early 1980s. The first commercially successful distributed file system came as part of the Apollo Domain system, released in 1982, soon followed by Sun's Network File System (NFS). What motivated both these systems was the desire not only to share files, but also, since disks were fairly expensive, to support relatively cheap, diskless workstations.

To a certain extent, the ideal distributed file system behaves as if all parties were on the same computer — in other words, as if it really weren't a distributed system. Programs designed to work using a local file system should work just as well using a distributed file system. Coming close to this ideal is possible, but most existing systems do not — they make tradeoffs so as to improve performance and reduce complexity.

Things get complicated when we consider failures: client crashes, server crashes, and communication failures. In the single-computer case, either the entire system is up or the entire system is down; we typically do not worry about file-system semantics on "partially up" or "partially down" systems, since these cases simply don't arise. In a distributed file system, though, what should happen if a server crashes but its clients remain up? Or suppose clients and servers are up, but the network connections between them are down. Or suppose a client crashes while the rest of the system remains up.

The most obvious benefit of the distributed file system is that files are shared. If I want to let you work with one of my files, I simply give you its pathname. You see everything I've done to the file. If you make any modifications to it, I see those modifications. Neither of us needs to have to worry about synchronizing the contents of multiple copies of a file. Without the distributed file system, we'd have to exchange files by e-mail or use applications such as the Internet's FTP (file transfer protocol).

A related benefit of a distributed file system is that my programs can access remote files as if they were local. The remote files have no special application-program interface; they are accessed just like local ones. With this property, known as *access transparency*, programs need not be aware whether a file is remote or local.

Lastly, a distributed file system is easier to administer than multiple local file systems. Typically in such a system a small number of server machines provide files to a large number of clients. Rather than having to back up files on each of the clients, only the servers' files need to be backed up.

Another term for distributed file system is *network attached storage (NAS)*, referring to attaching to the network servers that provide file systems. A similar-sounding term that refers to a very different approach is *storage area network (SAN)*. Here the intent is to make available over the network not file systems but storage devices. For example, an organization might own a few large-capacity RAID devices (Section 6.4.1), each providing many terabytes of storage. The total capacity might be split into a number of logical storage devices, each assigned to a specific server. Some of the servers might be file servers, which use their logical storage devices to hold a file system. Others might be database systems, which use their logical storage devices to hold databases. The capacity can be shuffled among logical devices as needed to meet new requirements; the redundancy provided by RAID is shared by all. See Figure 10.1.

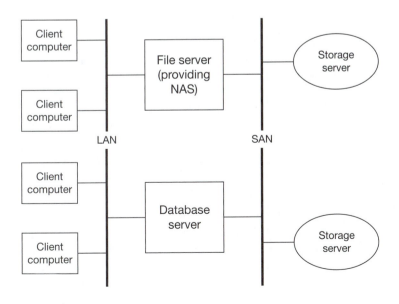

FIGURE 10.1 The relationship between *network attached storage* (NAS) and a *storage area network* (SAN).

10.1
THE BASICS

The ideal distributed file system shouldn't give its users any unpleasant surprises: it should behave as much as possible as if it and its users were all on the same computer. The semantics of file operations should be exactly the same for distributed file systems as for local file systems. When multiple applications access the same file, the result should be the same on the distributed system as if all parties, clients and server, were on the same system. Failures, such as communication problems and crashes of client and server computers, should be minimally disruptive. And to top it all off, performance should be good.

Designing such a system entails determining how its various components are distributed — what resides on the servers, what resides on the clients. We categorize this information as follows:

- the *data state*: this is the contents of files.

- the *attribute state*: this is information about each file, such as its size, most recent modification time, access-control information, etc.

- the *open-file state*: this is the information indicating which files are open or otherwise in use, as well as describing how files are locked. For example, in both Unix and Windows systems, opening a file adds to its reference count, and a file cannot be deleted unless its reference count is zero. A range of bytes of a file can have a shared (or read) lock or an exclusive (or write) lock applied to it.

As shown in Figure 10.2, each of these components might be kept on the server or on the clients, either in volatile storage (which is lost if a machine crashes) or in non-volatile storage (which isn't lost after a crash). We think of the data state as permanently residing on the server's local (disk) file system, but recently accessed or modified information might reside in volatile storage in server or client caches (or both). Some systems even cache data on client disks. Similarly, the attribute state resides permanently on the server's local file system, but might be cached on servers and clients. The open-file state is transitory; it changes as processes open and close files. Thus it makes sense for this to reside in volatile storage, but, as we discuss below, for crash-recovery purposes some systems keep a portion of it in non-volatile storage.

Three basic concerns govern this placement:

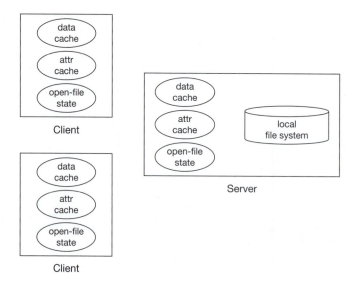

FIGURE 10.2 Possible locations for caches and open-file state in a distributed file system.

- *access speed*. Access is slow if the information resides on the server, yet is accessed and modified by clients. Caching such information on clients improves performance considerably. Information stored in volatile storage can be accessed and modified much more quickly than information stored in non-volatile storage.

- *consistency*. If clients cache information, do all parties share the same view of it?

- *recovery*. If one or more computers crash, to what extent are the others affected? How much information is lost?

Though the factors affecting access speed are straightforward, those affecting consistency and recovery are not. So, before discussing the tradeoffs among these concerns, we first spend some time discussing consistency and recovery, giving a quick overview of what is relevant to distributed file systems and focusing on data consistency.

Suppose a single thread is performing operations on files. We want the order in which these operations occur on the files to be the same as was executed by the thread; i.e., we want the operations to be *time-ordered*. If things were otherwise we'd consider the file system broken and wouldn't use it. If no operations are performed by other threads, any read of a particular location of a file by a thread retrieves the result of the thread's most recent write to the location. We call this property *single-thread consistency*.

It's not a big stretch to extend this form of consistency to an entire client computer: the operations on the file system by the computer are time-ordered, and thus, in the absence of operations by other computers, any read of a particular file location by a thread on the computer retrieves the result of the most recent write to the location by any thread of the computer. This we call *single-client consistency*.

It's a bigger step to extend consistency to the threads on all the client machines of a distributed system. But if all operations on a file system are time-ordered, and thus any read of a particular file location by any thread on any computer retrieves the result of the most recent write to that location by any thread on any computer, the file system is said to have *strict consistency*.

It may be difficult if not impossible to time-order the operations coming from many client computers. If operations are executed on different client computers, how do we know which happened first? In general, if this cannot be determined, it probably doesn't matter. What is important is that all parties agree on whatever order is selected and that the selected order be one that could have happened. Suppose Ted is updating a file on one computer and Alice is reading that file on another computer. If they do these operations at about the same time, and if the clocks on the various computers either are not synchronized well enough or do not have enough resolution to order the two events, then it really is not clear which happened first and either order makes sense — neither Ted nor Alice will be surprised by either outcome. Assuming that the system remains single-client consistent, this weakening of strict consistency is known as *sequential consistency* (Lamport 1979).

But suppose Ted's and Alice's computers are a foot apart and Alice reads the file immediately after Ted tells her he's modified it. Both Ted and Alice will be unpleasantly surprised if Alice gets the old version of the file. To rule out such surprises, we might insist that our system be strictly consistent.

On the other hand, if Ted and Alice are savvy computer users they would realize that expecting deterministic results from concurrent operations on remote files without some form of synchronization might not be realistic. So Ted might apply a write lock to the file before modifying it, and Alice might apply a read lock before reading it. Though this file system is not strictly consistent, it is said to have *entry consistency* (Bershad and Zekauskas 1991) if some *acquire* operation (such as taking a lock) can guarantee the client that the most recent contents of file locations are protected by the lock, and if some *release* operation can make the client's changes available to others.

What sorts of consistency do distributed file systems provide for data? NFS, as discussed in Sections 10.2 and 10.5 below, provides single-client consistency but not strict consistency. If applications lock the files they are using, they get entry consistency, but this is strictly up to the applications. CIFS, as discussed in Section 10.3, provides strict consistency. DFS, as discussed in Section 10.4, also provides strict consistency.

All systems must provide strict consistency for the lock-state portion of open-file state — locks make no sense otherwise. But, as described in Section 10.2, NFS versions 2 and 3 get away with not even sharing the reference state of files, let alone doing so consistently. Most systems keep the attribute state strictly consistent, but NFS provides at best entry consistency.

What happens if there is a failure? In a non-distributed system a failure takes down the application and everything else. In a distributed system failure of a client computer takes down its application. But if the server or other clients fail, the application is not necessarily affected at all. Another way of putting this is that for non-distributed systems, either the entire system is up or the entire system is down. When the system comes back up after a crash, people do not expect the cache and the open-file state to be as they were before the crash — all application processes must be restarted anyway.

But with a distributed file system, partial crashes can happen and must be dealt with. One or more clients might crash; the server might crash; there might be times during which certain computers cannot communicate with one another due to network problems. In some cases, complete recovery is possible. In others, for instance when a client crashes, problems are restricted to the crashed computer — no other computer is adversely affected. In still other cases, problems can occur that would not have happened if a local file system were being used.

For example, an application that has locked a file might discover that, because of a combination of server crashes and network problems, not only has it lost its lock on the file, but the file has been locked by another application. Ideally, of course, such "surprises" will not happen. But, as explained in the following sections, these surprises, though rare, are unavoidable. The best we can ask for is that applications are notified when they occur.

In the sections below we look at a few representative distributed file systems, discussing the tradeoffs taken among speed, consistency, and recoverability. We start with NFS version 2, a relatively simple yet successful system. As already noted, it has a fairly relaxed approach to consistency but handles failures well. Next we cover CIFS, which provides strict consistency but is essentially intolerant of server failures and network problems. We then discuss DFS, which provides strict consistency and is tolerant of server failures and network problems, but requires the cooperation of applications in coping, and finally NFS version 4, which does as good a job with failures as is probably possible.

A final concern, independent of the others, is the file-system name space. If all parties are on one computer, there is probably just a single directory hierarchy and thus one name space. But for the distributed case, the one-name-space approach doesn't necessarily make sense. Both NFS and CIFS allow each client to set up its own name space, and both also provide a means for all clients to share the same name space. DFS uses a model in which one global name space is shared by all in the distributed system.

| 10.2 **NFS VERSION 2** | NFS — Network File System — was developed by Sun Microsystems in the mid-1980s. Its design is simple[1] yet successful; it and its descendants have been widely used ever since, uniquely among distributed file systems of its time. In this section we focus on NFS version 2. Version 1 was used strictly within Sun. At the time of this writing, version 3 is in common use while version 4 (discussed in Section 10.5) is beginning to be adopted. |

[1] This characterization applies only to version 2 of NFS!

NFSv2 servers are passive parties that give their clients a simple file store. They respond to client requests, but take no actions on their own. NFS clients actively maintain caches of information obtained from servers, performing read-aheads and write-behinds as necessary. The approach to consistency is rather relaxed but works well in practice. Here's how things work. An NFS server gives its clients access to one or more of its local file systems, providing them with opaque identifiers called *file handles* to refer to files and directories. Clients use a separate protocol, the *mount protocol*, to get a file handle for the root of a server file system. They then use the *NFS file protocol* to follow paths within the file system and to access its files, placing simple remote procedure calls to read them and write them. A third protocol added later, the *network lock manager protocol* (NLM), can be used to synchronize access to files. All communication between client and server is with ONC RPC (see Section 9.2).

Here we call the combination of the mount protocol and the NFS file protocol *basic NFS*; basic NFS plus NLM we call *extended NFS*. We begin by discussing basic NFS.

All open-file state information resides on the clients. Servers are thus called *stateless* since they are essentially unaware of what files clients have open, though they necessarily do hold data and communications state.

Figure 10.3 summarizes the information maintained on clients and servers. Clients maintain caches of file data and attributes as well as hold all open-file information (except for locks, which are maintained on the server via the NLM protocol). No other open-file information is held on the server.

To see how NFSv2 operates, let's work through an example. Suppose a Unix thread executes the following instructions, accessing a file system on an NFSv2 server.

```
char buffer[100];
int fd = open("/home/twd/dir/fileX", O_RDWR);
read(fd, buffer, 100);
...
lseek(fd, 0, SEEK_SET);
write(fd, buffer, 100);
```

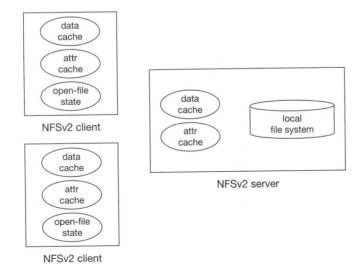

FIGURE 10.3 Distribution of components in NFSv2.

Our thread opens a file, reads the first 100 bytes, then writes 100 bytes at the beginning of the file, replacing the previous data there. The kernel data structures representing the open file are just what they would be if the file were local (see Section 1.3.5.2). The only difference from the client operating system's point of view is that the actual operations on the file are handled by the NFSv2 client code rather than by a local file system such as FFS.

The NFSv2 server has its own directory hierarchy and exports a number of subtrees of this hierarchy to its clients. The client's operating system has mounted one of them (see Section 6.3.2.1) on the local directory /home/twd. It did this by first placing a remote procedure call, using the mount protocol, to the server, and obtaining a file handle for the root of this subtree. As Figure 10.4 shows, any attempt to access the directory /home/twd is now interpreted as an attempt to access the remote directory represented by the file handle.

Thus to follow the path /home/twd/dir/fileX, our thread, executing in the client operating system, goes as far as /home/twd and discovers that a remote file system is mounted there. It places a remote procedure call to the NFSv2 server's *lookup* routine, passing it the file handle for the remote file system's root as well as the pathname /dir/fileX. The server returns a file handle for fileX.

The client operating system records the fact that fileX is open, just as it would for a local file (see Section 1.3.5.2). However, rather than representing the file with an inode or equivalent, it uses the file handle together with a communication handle representing the remote server (see Figure 10.5).

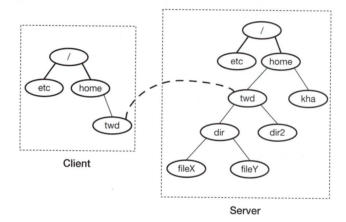

FIGURE 10.4 The client has mounted the server's */home/twd* on its own */home/twd*.

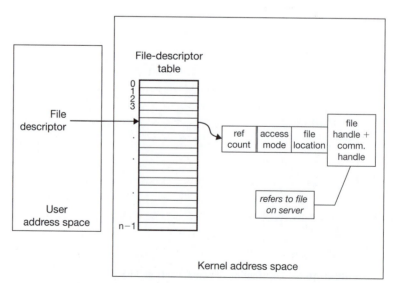

FIGURE 10.5 Open-file data structures on client (compare with Figure 1.6).

When the thread performs the *read*, it first checks its local cache within the client operating system. If the data is not there, it places a remote procedure call to the server's read routine, passing the file handle, the offset within the file (0), and the length (100). The server returns the 100 bytes from that location.

The *lseek* call sets the local file offset to 0, but does not cause a request to be sent to the server. When the thread calls *write*, the data is first copied to the local cache. Sometime later a kernel thread places a remote procedure call containing the file handle, the current offset (0), the data, and the length to the server's *write* routine. The server returns an indication of successful completion of the operation.

This is remarkably simple and straightforward, though we've omitted a few details (to be covered in Section 10.2.3). But let's look at the ramifications of this simplicity. We have already noted that the server maintains no open-file state: the client obtains a file handle for the file, but the server has no record that some client is using the file.

Consider the following code fragment:

```
int fd = creat("/home/twd/dir/tempfile", 0600);
char buf[1024];
unlink("/home/twd/dir/tempfile");
...
write(fd, buf, 1024);
...
lseek(fd, 0, SEEK_SET);
read(fd, buf, 1024);
close(fd);
```

The file /home/twd/dir/tempfile is created, then its directory entry is immediately removed. If this were done on a local file system, the file itself would continue to exist, even though there no longer is a directory entry referring to it — that the file is open makes it continue to exist. This code sequence is rather common in Unix programs, since it is a standard technique for creating a temporary file, one guaranteed to disappear once the process terminates: as soon as the file is closed, there is no longer a reference to it and the operating system deletes it.

Since NFSv2 servers do not keep track of whether files are open, the unlink request in the code above removes the last link to the file and leaves it with no other references — the file is then deleted, much to the client's surprise.

NFSv2 relies on the client to keep track of such state information and to modify its requests to the server accordingly. In our example, the client would realize that asking the server to *unlink* an open file isn't in its best interests. So, rather than doing that, it sends it a *rename* request, changing the file's name to a special name that does not show up in normal directory lookups (in Unix, this is accomplished by using "." as its first character). Thus the file no longer exists under its original name, yet the client's file handle still refers to it. When the client process closes the file, it sends an unlink request to the server, removing the file's special name from the directory and thus finally deleting the file.

This solution is clearly not perfect: it works only if the file is open on the same machine as the one doing the unlink. In practice this is the only case that matters, so it does well enough. But what happens if the client renames a file, but crashes before the file is closed? Then the renamed file is not deleted and remains on the server. The server must periodically check for such orphaned files and delete them.

The NFS Mount Protocol, described in Section 10.2.2 below, lets clients access subtrees of server directory hierarchies. Clients may place these subtrees in their own directory hierarchies wherever they please, but it's usually more convenient to handle this automatically so that all clients have the same file-system name space. Most organizations using NFS define such a name space in an organization-wide database. Each client, using software known as the *automounter*, consults this database and mounts server-provided subtrees into its own directory hierarchy as necessary.

10.2.1 RPC SEMANTICS

The NFSv2 protocols are layered neatly on top of the original ONC RPC (Section 9.2). RPC, aided by the duplicate request cache and relying on the idempotency of most of the remote procedures, is completely responsible for ensuring that client operations have an exactly-once effect. Neither client nor server code does anything further to make this happen. Of course, as we saw in Section 9.2.2, original ONC RPC does not do a perfect job. It's designed for a well behaved environment, free of Byzantine routers.

Let's quickly review how the original ONC RPC operates. If UDP is the transport protocol, the client RPC layer repeatedly retransmits each request (with suitable delays in between) until it gets a response. If TCP is the transport protocol, the client RPC layer doesn't retransmit unless there's a loss of connection, in which case a new connection is made and the client retransmits over it. With both transports, the effect is that requests are received by the server's RPC layer at least once. Most requests are for idempotent procedures, and thus can be safely executed many times in a row. The server uses its duplicate request cache to handle duplicate non-idempotent requests.

What's particularly nice about this approach is that client applications need not be aware that they are using a distributed file system and need do nothing special to cope with crashes or network problems. The client RPC layer eventually makes the desired result happen: if the server crashes while an application is attempting to read from a file, the read system call simply appears to be slow, but it eventually returns with the desired data (assuming the server recovers from the crash).

As an option, a client can set things up so that system calls on files of a particular remote file system eventually time out if the server has crashed or there's a network problem. In practice this is done only rarely, because few applications do anything intelligent in response to such timeouts.

10.2.2 MOUNT PROTOCOL

This is by far the simplest of the NFSv2 protocols. Its primary job is to provide clients with file handles for roots of exported file systems. It also provides limited security by giving these file handles only to certain specified clients.

What are file handles? Servers give them to clients to identify files on the server. From the client's point of view they are completely opaque: their contents have no meaning other than as interpreted on the server.

From the server's point of view, however, file handles play a role similar to that of Unix inodes: they uniquely identify files. While a file might have multiple pathnames, it has only one file handle. A file handle must identify a file even if the file has been renamed; it must continue to be valid until the file is deleted. After a file has been deleted, its file handle must be invalid, so that clients can reliably determine that a file no longer exists.

So, what does a file handle contain? For a Unix server that actually identifies files by their inodes, the file handle contains an identifier for the file-system instance (the server might have many) as well as the inode number. Thus it identifies a particular file within the file system.

But this isn't enough: if a file is deleted, its file handle must become invalid. The problem with using the combination of inode number and file-system identifier as a handle is that, though this combination will be invalid immediately after the file is deleted, the inode number might be reused for a new file. Thus the handle becomes valid again and refers to a different file from what the holder had intended.

To get around this problem, we need a way to distinguish between different uses of the same inode number (or similar identifiers). What is done is to tag each inode with a generation number, a 32-bit field that takes on a different value each time the inode is reused — a random value works well here. The file handle contains a copy of the value that is current when the handle is created. If the corresponding file is deleted and its inode reused, the generation number in the file handle no longer matches that of the inode and the handle is rejected — the error message is "stale file handle."

10.2.3 NFS FILE PROTOCOL

The NFS File Protocol does most of NFS's work. It's responsible for communicating file data between client and server and for maintaining client caches and keeping them reasonably consistent. Its basic operation is remarkably simple. Client application processes make system calls on files. For get-type operations — fetching data, file attributes, etc. — if the relevant information is in the cache, the call completes immediately. Otherwise the NFS client code places an RPC to the server both to obtain the needed information for the cache and to return it to the application. For most put-type operations, such as file writes, the information is stored in the local cache, and sometime later NFS client code updates the server via an RPC.

Assuming the communications protocol is providing exactly-once semantics for each client's RPC requests, the client caches are single-client consistent. But what happens if more than one client is using a file? The basic premise of NFSv2 is that file sharing takes place primarily for read-only files, such as binaries. Writable files are generally used by only one client at a time. So, with this premise as justification, NSFv2 uses an approximate approach to consistency. For cases in which the premise is unjustified, the separate Network Lock Manager protocol comes into play, as described in Section 10.2.4 below.

In the NFSv2 approximate approach to consistency, cached information is assumed to be valid for a certain period of time after it's put in the cache. NFS client code periodically checks with the server for changes to files that are at least partially cached on the client. If so, regardless of the extent of the changes, the cached information for the file is invalidated and subsequent get-type requests result in RPCs to the server.

To aid in doing this, clients maintain a separate cache of file attributes — information obtained from the server about the files they are accessing (see Figure 10.6). This information is essentially anything the server can provide, including access permissions, file size, creation time, access time, and modification time. This cached information is used to satisfy requests by processes for file attributes (via the *stat* and *fstat* system calls in Unix). It is also used in determining whether the cached data from a file is up to date. Cached attributes are valid only for a brief period of time, ranging from a few seconds to a minute, and cached file data are valid only while

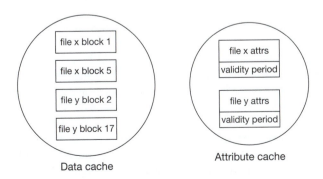

Data cache   Attribute cache

FIGURE 10.6 An NFSv2 client's data and attribute caches.

the file's attributes are valid. If an attempt is made to access cached data beyond the attributes' validity period, a "GETATTR" RPC request is sent to the server asking for the file's current attributes. On return, the new attributes are cached; if they indicate that the file hasn't been modified since the previous attributes were cached, the cached data are still used. Otherwise the file's cached data are flushed — this means that modified file blocks are sent to the server via WRITE RPC requests and unmodified blocks are removed from the cache.

This attribute caching helps keep caches "sort of" consistent, but does not give any useful guarantees. Many NFS implementations go a step farther and provide *close-to-open consistency*: when a file is closed, all changes are sent to the server. When a file is opened, the remaining validity time for its cached blocks is ignored and a GETATTR is sent to the server. The blocks are flushed if the new attributes indicate recent changes. This procedure helps prevent surprises: if a file is shared by multiple clients but is open on at most one at a time, the clients' caches will be consistent.

Given the near lack of state information the NFS File Protocol keeps on the server, dealing with client and server crashes is straightforward — nothing needs to be done! However, care must be taken with certain operations so that crashes don't cause undue surprises. If a client application performs a synchronous request, such as writing to a file synchronously, the request really needs to be performed synchronously — the application should not be notified of its completion until after the server file system has been updated. Otherwise, in the event of a client or server crash, the user of the application may be under the false impression that the file has been modified.

In fact, all RPC calls that update the server must be synchronous: a client that receives a "successful-completion" response assumes its job is done — the server has been updated and the client can move on. So the modifications really must have been committed on the server. Otherwise, if the server crashes before the updates have been committed, they are lost forever.

This synchronous-update requirement slows file updates on NFSv2 systems, since, for example, all WRITE RPC requests must be synchronous. Some implementations handled this by providing a non-volatile cache into which updates could be committed on the server. The cache survived crashes and its contents were written to the file system as part of crash recovery.

One of the major improvements in NFSv3 was to weaken the requirement for synchronous updates. Writes in NFSv3 may be asynchronous, meaning that the server may return a response even though the data has not been written to disk. But when the client sends a COMMIT RPC request, the server may not respond until the data from all previous writes to the file are safely on disk.

10.2.4 NETWORK LOCK MANAGER

The final component of NFSv2, forming extended NFS from basic NFS, is its Network Lock Manager (NLM) protocol, which enables clients to lock files. While in the rest of NFSv2 the open-file state resides in the clients, NLM maintains lock state on the servers, as well as on the clients. Its operation is simple: clients place RPC calls to the server requesting locks on files and the server grants or refuses these requests on the basis of state information it maintains locally. But this shared lock state adds a new wrinkle to NFS: significant work must be done to recover from both client and server crashes.

NLM supports the standard Unix notion of file locks: locks are *advisory*, meaning that applications are free to ignore them, and are *byte-range*, meaning that they are applied to a range of locations within a file. They come in two forms, *shared locks* and *exclusive locks*. The latter are essentially write locks: no two may have overlapping ranges on the same file at the same time. The former are essentially read locks: they may overlap with each other, but not with exclusive locks.

The lock state is shared consistently by keeping most of it on the server, which keeps track of the locks applied to all its files. An application process applies locks to remote files just as it does to local ones — it issues a system call and is notified whether or not it was successful. The local (client) operating system places a LOCK RPC request to the server, which locks the file if possible, updating its own lock-state information, and sends back a success/failure response. If successful, the open-file state on the client is updated to indicate that a portion of the file has a lock applied to it.

The hard part of maintaining lock state is coping with crashes. NLM avoids much of the potential complexity of crash recovery by simply ignoring the difficult cases. In practice this has worked reasonably well, primarily because NFSv2 is used in well behaved environments that lack Byzantine routers and other networking problems.

The first issue in crash recovery is determining that there's been a crash. This is fraught with difficulty since a false determination causes big problems. NLM avoids these problems by being extremely conservative. A computer is deemed to have crashed only when it comes back up and announces it is restarting. Otherwise it is assumed to be running fine (despite, say, being unresponsive for the past hour).

Thus NLM clients keep on disk a list of which servers they are holding locks from, and servers keep on disk a list of which clients are holding locks on their files. When a client restarts, it notifies the servers in its list that it is restarting, and the servers release all the client's locks.

Recovering from a server crash involves recovering the lock state of all the clients. This would be trivial if the state had been stored on disk along with the client list, but for performance reasons it is not. Instead the lock state is kept in volatile memory and thus disappears with a server crash. To recover it, servers rely on their clients.

As when clients restart, when a server restarts it notifies all the clients in its list of lock holders. These clients then have a certain period of time, the *grace period* (typically 45 seconds), to reclaim the locks they held before the server crashed. During this period the server accepts no new lock requests.

NLM's approach to recovery is not perfect. We take this up again in Section 10.5.2 below, when we discuss NFSv4.

CIFS is Microsoft's distributed file system. Its long history goes back to the mid-1980s, when it was developed by IBM and was known as the SMB (Server Message Block) protocol, running on top of NetBIOS (Network Basic Input/Output System). Microsoft took over further development of SMB, and renamed it CIFS in the late 1990s. Though it still can run on top of NetBIOS, NetBIOS is often layered on top of TCP and, with some simple extensions, SMB can run directly on top of TCP (without NetBIOS). The term SMB is still used to refer to the RPC-like communications protocol on which CIFS is layered.

10.3 COMMON INTERNET FILE SYSTEM (CIFS)

The CIFS approach is to provide strict consistency among clients and servers, allowing client-side caching for efficient handling of the two most common file usages — when a number of clients are sharing a file read-only and when a file is being used exclusively by one client. One way to characterize the differences between CIFS and NFSv2 is that CIFS is always strictly consistent and usually fast, while NFSv2 is always fast and usually strictly consistent. Though keep in mind that by "fast" we mean only that client-side caching is used.

Unlike basic NFS (see Section 10.2), CIFS servers hold open-file state from their clients. Thus if a client crashes, this state must be cleaned up. On the other hand, if a server crashes, clients make no attempt to recover their state when it comes back up: operations on files that were open at the time of a crash will fail.

CIFS requires the transport protocol to be reliable and regards the transport connection as the sole indication of the health of the computer at the other end. So if the connection is lost, perhaps because of a network timeout, CIFS considers the other computer to have crashed.

This approach to failure allows CIFS to be simpler than NFSv2 and other distributed file systems. A request is not retried if the connection is lost: the application must assume the worst, that the server has crashed and there's no hope of recovery. Whether or not the remote procedure is idempotent doesn't matter.

The organization of the CIFS namespace is similar to that of NFS. Servers export *shares*, subtrees of their own hierarchies. Clients may place them in their local namespaces as desired — Windows clients typically assign drive letters to them (creating a local *forest*). Alternatively, much as NFS defines a namespace shared by all clients by using the automounter and a distributed database, Windows uses a distributed database called "active directory" to define a namespace shared by all clients.

To get a better idea of how CIFS works, consider the code below, which is similar to the code we examined in Section 10.2 when looking at NFSv2.

```
char buffer[100];
HANDLE h = CreateFile(
    "Z:\dir\file",                    // name
    GENERIC_READ|GENERIC_WRITE,       // desired access
    0,                                // share mode
    NULL,                             // security attributes
    OPEN_EXISTING,                    // creation disposition
    0,                                // flags and attributes
    NULL                              // template file
);
ReadFile(h, buffer, 100, NULL, NULL);
. . .
SetFilePointer(h, 0, NULL, FILE_BEGIN);
WriteFile(h, buffer, 100, NULL, NULL);
CloseHandle(h);
```

In this code a thread opens an existing file (despite the name of the system call!), requesting both read-write access and that the file not be shared with others until the returned handle is closed (it does this by supplying a "share mode" parameter of 0 — we discuss share modes later in this section). It reads 100 bytes from the beginning of the file, then, after resetting the file pointer, writes 100 bytes to the beginning of the file. Finally it closes the handle, allowing others to open the file.

Here, in outline form, is what takes place for all this to happen. At some point before this code is executed, the client must have created a transport connection with the server. Then, so that the server can do access checking, the client identifies itself to the server (and proves its identity). Next the client identifies to the server the "disk share" it wants to access. This is a subtree of the server's file system that the server is willing to export. If the client is allowed access to the share, the server returns a *tree ID (TID)* identifying the share. Our client associates this exported file system with the drive letter "Z." Note that this is much as in the NFSv2 mount protocol, via which the client obtains a file handle for the root of a server file system (see Section 10.2.2).

At this point our client thread can issue the *CreateFile* system call to open the file it wants. It passes to the server the *UID*, identifying the user, the *TID*, identifying the share, and the path (in this case \dir\file) to follow in that share. In addition it passes the *desired access*, which the server checks to make certain it's allowed, the *share mode*, which the server must honor, and the other parameters (except for the template file, which is ignored when opening an existing file, but may be used as a source for the attributes if creating a new file). If successful, the server returns a *file ID (FID)*, which the client subsequently uses to identify the file.

As in NFS, read and write system calls by client threads don't necessarily send requests to the server immediately; they might instead be satisfied by a local cache. But when the client operating system fetches data from the server or sends modified data back to it, it sends read and write requests that identify the file by the file ID. The file pointer, used by the application thread to identify file position, is maintained on the client side; read and write requests sent to the server contain an explicit file location.

Unlike NFSv2 servers, CIFS servers must be aware of what their clients are doing. In general, they keep track of not only the reference counts on files, but also the *share modes*. These indicate in what ways a file may have concurrent opens. The default, a share mode of 0, is that concurrent opens are not allowed. But a thread can specify, for example, that others can open the file for reading or that others may open the file for writing, or perhaps for both. Thus when a thread tries to open a file, the open succeeds only if the desired access does not conflict with the share mode of all the other current opens of that file.

CIFS supports "byte-range" locks that are similar to those supported by NFSv2 in that application threads can lock portions of a file. However, CIFS's locks are mandatory — they must be honored by all threads on all clients, unlike the locks supported by NFSv2 (and NFSv3). From the client application's perspective, locks are associated with the combination of the file handle and the process: all threads of one process using the same file handle share the lock on a byte range of a file. Even if this file handle is shared with threads of a different process, these latter threads do not share the lock. If another handle for the file is created in the original process (by opening the file again), threads using that second handle don't share the lock. Thus the server must keep track of not only which file handle a lock is associated with, but also with which process on which client machine.

10.3.1 SERVER MESSAGE BLOCK (SMB) PROTOCOL

The Server Message Block (SMB) protocol plays the role of RPC for CIFS. Like RPC, it's a request-response protocol: clients (and sometime servers) send requests; servers (and sometimes clients) send responses. However, unlike a true RPC protocol, it's not extensible. It consists of a predefined set of requests and responses, all in a fixed format. Nevertheless, it suffices for CIFS (after all, it was designed for CIFS!).[2]

As the name SMB implies, requests and responses are sent as message blocks, each containing a standard header along with some arguments and data. A client first sets up a session with a server that has already established the client user's identity. The client and server must first negotiate which version of the SMB protocol they are using and then, via a log-on procedure, establish the user's identity (thus setting the UID) and prove it to the server. After the session is established, the client may request access to one or more server shares, obtaining a TID for each. With such a TID, the client may open a file, thus obtaining a FID.

Each client operating system must identify which user process is sending a request by supplying a process ID (PID) unique to the client. PIDs are necessary for correctly implementing locks, but are also used to match responses to requests. The idea is that a process has only one outstanding request at a time — which made sense before processes were multithreaded, but not since. To allow the client OS to sort out responses to multithreaded processes, yet another ID is used: a multiplex ID (MID), which, along with the PID, performs the function of ONC RPC's XID.

The set of IDs form the context for a request and are included in special field in the header, as needed. For many of the details of SMB see (Storage Networking Industry Association 2002).

Table 10.1 (adapted from (Storage Networking Industry Association 2002)) shows a typical exchange of messages. A fair number of messages must be exchanged before the client can get any data from a file, and most of these messages simply add one more ID to the context. So, rather

---

[2] Microsoft RPC is actually layered on top of SMB, primarily so that it can exploit the authentication and resource (share) identification provided by SMB. However, CIFS does not use Microsoft RPC.

Table 10.1 SMB message exchange in CIFS.

Message	Meaning
SMB_COM_NEGOTIATE -> server	Client gives server list of SMB versions it is willing to use.
client <- SMB_COM_NEGOTIATE	Server chooses one and informs client. It also sends the client a security challenge.
SMB_COM_SESSION_SETUP_ANDX -> server	Client sends encrypted challenge to server, along with user's identity.
client <- SMB_COM_SESSION_SETUP_ANDX	Server verifies identity and fills in UID field.
SMB_COM_TREE_CONNECT_ANDX -> server	Client identifies the share it wants to use.
client <- SMB_COM_TREE_CONNECT_ANDX	Server fills in security fields and TID field.
SMB_COM_OPEN_ANDX -> server	Client sends path name of file.
client <- SMB_COM_OPEN_ANDX	Server performs access checks (based on UID) and, if ok, responds by filling in FID field.
SMB_COM_READ -> server	Client requests data from file.
client <- SMB_COM_READ	Server returns data.
SMB_COM_CLOSE -> server	Client closes file.
client <- SMB_COM_CLOSE	Server returns success.
SMB_COM_TREE_DISCONNECT -> server	Client disconnects from share.
client <- SMB_COM_TREE_DISCONNECT	Server returns success.

than require these messages in sequence, SMB lets them be batched: a client sends a sequence of requests in a single message and the server responds to all of them in a single response message. This batching ability is given the ungainly name of "andX." Thus in the sample exchange in Table 10.1, the requests starting with the session setup request through the read request can all be sent in one message. If they all succeed, the server sends back a single response containing all the IDs that have been established and the data requested by the read. If any of the requests fails, the server handles no further requests from the message and returns the cumulative result of all requests up through the failing one. Any request (or response) may be at the end of a batch; only those requests (or responses) whose names end with "_ANDX" may come before other requests (or responses) in a batch.

10.3.2 OPPORTUNISTIC LOCKS

One way to achieve strict consistency is to perform all operations at the server without caching data at clients. This is CIFS's default approach, but definitely not the only one possible. Local caching of a file's data at a client is safe, with respect to consistency, either if the client is the only one using the file or if all clients using the file are doing so read-only. The hard part is limiting such caching to just those two cases.

CIFS relies on the server's knowledge of clients' open-file states to determine when it is safe for a client to do local caching. If a client opens a file for reading and writing that is not otherwise open, the server may notify the client that caching is safe. If another client wants to open the file (assuming the share mode permits it), the server must notify the first client that caching is no longer safe and that the client must send all changes it's made to the file back to the server. Then both clients may use the file, but no local caching is permitted on either.

When a client opens a file, as part of the open SMB request it may ask for an *opportunistic lock* (or *oplock*). There are two categories of such locks: level I and level II. The former allow exclusive access; the latter allow shared access. The server may or may not grant the request depending on whether and how the file is open by others. If the client obtains a level-I oplock, then it is assured that no other client has the file open and thus it can safely cache file data (and metadata) locally. If it obtains a level-II oplock, then it is assured that no other client has the file open in a mode that allows changes, and thus it can safely cache blocks from the file, but any changes it makes must be sent directly to the server, and the server will then revoke all level-II oplocks on the file. Thus if a file is being used for both reading and writing, a level-I oplock is needed, but if it's being used just for reading, level II suffices. Note that the client application is oblivious of oplocks — it simply opens files and performs operations on them. It's the client's operating system that's responsible for local caching and thus must request oplocks.

To revoke an oplock, the server sends the client an oplock-break SMB request. If a level-I oplock is being revoked, the server will give it a level-II oplock if possible. The client must send back all changes to the server, then signify it's done so by sending a response to the oplock-break request. Since there is nothing to send back when a level-II oplock is being revoked, no response is required.

The CIFS protocol doesn't allow a client to request a level-II oplock. Instead, it must request a level-I oplock, but it might, at the server's discretion, get a level-II one instead. This might seem a bit strange; the rationale is that though files are often used read-only, rarely are they opened that way. Thus most opens are read-write, even though writing may well not be done. So, if one client has a file open read-write but doesn't write, and another client opens the same file read-write but doesn't write either, then if both clients request level-I oplocks, they will end up with level-II oplocks.

If a client closes a file for which it has an oplock, will its cache still be useful if it opens the file again a short time later? The SMB close request releases all oplocks associated with the file, so there's no guarantee that cached data is valid if the file is reopened — since the client no longer has an oplock, the server isn't obliged to notify the client if any other client opens the file. However, the client might cheat a bit: rather than sending an SMB close request to the server when its user application closes the file, it can keep quiet in hopes that some local application opens the file again. If this indeed happens and the client still holds the oplock, then the client is guaranteed that its cache is still valid. On the other hand, if another client opens the file, the server will revoke the original client's oplock, thus telling it that its cache is no longer valid. At this point the client might tell the server that the file is really closed.

For level-II oplocks, such a delayed-close strategy might seem easy: the client holds a level-II oplock when the application closes the file. Shortly thereafter an application opens the file again. Since the client already has a level-II oplock, not only is the cache still valid, but no sort of request needs to be sent to the server. However, as we just mentioned, few applications open files read-only. Thus the second open will probably be for read-write use (even though the file might never be written to). Since the only opportunity the client has to request an oplock is when the file is opened, the client must request a level-I oplock on the off chance that the application might actually write to the file. Thus an SMB open request must be sent to the server, and the server might grant the level-I oplock or might simply let the client keep the level-II oplock. But the cached file blocks at the client are still valid, so despite the need to send a request to the server, the delayed-close strategy is a win.

The delayed-close strategy for level-I oplocks works a bit differently. If an application closes a file and then it or some other client application opens it again, a level-I oplock need not be requested of the server, since the client already has one. Thus, until the level-I oplock is revoked, there's no need for the client to notify the server of any changes to the open state of the file, nor any need to write back modified file blocks (other than to reduce loss in the event of a client crash). However, if the server does revoke the level-I oplock, the client must not only send back to the server all modified file blocks, but also update it to the file's current open state by sending it whatever SMB open and close requests will get it there.

Not all clients are capable of doing this sort of batching, so there are actually two kinds of level-I oplocks — *exclusive* and *batch*. If a client holds an exclusive oplock, it must send the server an SMB close request along with all modified blocks when the application closes the file. It must then obtain a new oplock if the file is reopened, at which time it may not use any previously cached blocks from the file. If a client holds a batch oplock, then it uses the delayed-close strategy mentioned above. Only on older systems do clients still use exclusive locks.

10.4 DFS

DFS, the Distributed File System of DCE, is no longer in common use but is worth discussing because of its interesting approach to caching and failure recovery. It is derived from an earlier distributed file system, AFS.[3] Both systems addressed the need for client caching of files in a day when primary storage was expensive: they use client disks to cache files from the server. AFS caches files in their entirety; DFS caches data from files in 64KB blocks. Like CIFS, DFS provides strictly consistent sharing of files. However, unlike CIFS, clients always use their caches, even if multiple clients are making changes to the same file. Further unlike CIFS, DFS attempts to recover from server crashes.

The DFS server coordinates its clients' use of their caches by passing out *tokens,* each of which grants the client permission to perform a certain operation (such as read or write) on a range of bytes within a file. Since all operations are done in the client's cache, the tokens control the use of the cache.

Suppose an application on client A opens a file for reading and writing. Client A's DFS cache manager (running as part of the operating system) sends an open request to the DFS server (using DCE RPC) asking for *open_read* and *open_write* tokens for the file. (See Figures 10.7 through 10.12.) The server sends back a response containing the tokens, keeping as part of its token state that such tokens are at client A. In response to the application's first read of the file, client A's cache manager requests data from the server, along with a *data_read* token giving it permission to use this data in its cache. It fetches not just the data needed but 64KB data blocks, thus performing aggressive read-ahead. If the client application performs a write system call, the client's cache manager first obtains a *data_write* token from the server, granting the client permission to modify a range of bytes in its cache.

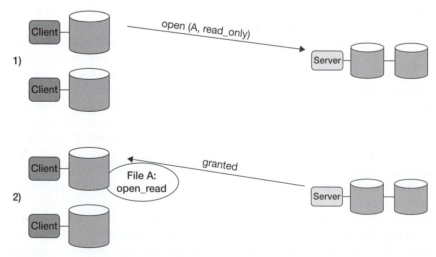

FIGURE 10.7　A DFS client opens a file read-only.

---

[3] AFS stands for Andrew File System, so called because it was developed at Carnegie Mellon University: both Mr. Carnegie and Mr. Mellon had the first name Andrew.

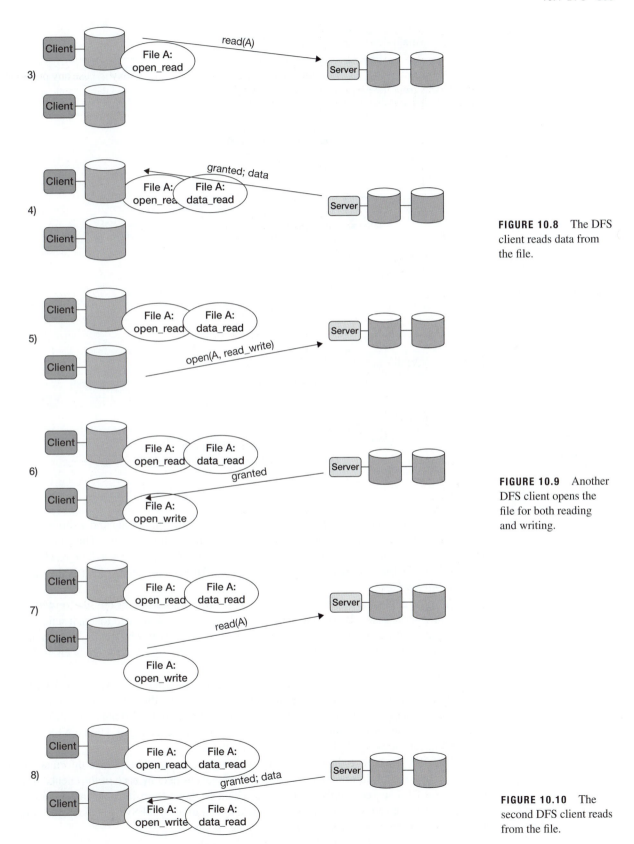

FIGURE 10.8 The DFS client reads data from the file.

FIGURE 10.9 Another DFS client opens the file for both reading and writing.

FIGURE 10.10 The second DFS client reads from the file.

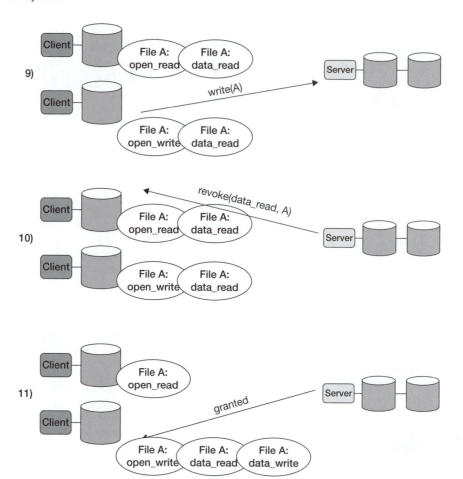

FIGURE 10.11 The server revokes the first client's *data_read* token.

FIGURE 10.12 The DFS client gains permission to write to the file.

Suppose an application on client B opens the same file for reading and writing. Client B's cache manager obtains *open_read* and *open_write* tokens, as did client A's. The application now performs a read system call for a portion of the file for which client A has a *data_read* token (but not a *data_write* token). This isn't a problem, so the DFS server sends client B the data along with a *data_read* token.

Now the application performs a read system call for a portion of the file for which client A has a *data_write* token. Before the DFS server can grant B a *data_read* token, it sends a revoke request to client A revoking its *data_write* token. Client A responds by both giving up the token and sending back the modified file data from its cache. The server now sends client B both a *data_read* token and the data.

This is all straightforward, though perhaps laborious. Like both NFSv2 and CIFS, DFS handles the common cases efficiently: if only one client is modifying a file and no clients are reading it, or if a number of clients are reading a file but none are modifying it, all file data resides in client caches and just a minimal number of messages are exchanged. Unlike NFSv2 but like CIFS, all client caches are strictly consistent with the server.

The DFS server, like the CIFS server, maintains a fair amount of state information about its clients. In DFS, this information consists of all the tokens held by each of the clients. If a client crashes, the DFS server simply removes the client's tokens from its state information. If the server crashes, then a procedure almost identical to that used by NFSv2's network lock manager (Section 10.2.4) recovers the server state from the clients.

Providing strict consistency is relatively easy when, as in CIFS, no attempt is made to recover from server crashes. Recovering from server crashes is relatively easy when, as in NFSv2, no attempt is made to provide strict consistency. DFS tries to do both and has to make some compromises.

The primary issue is client behavior while the server is not responding. If the server is actually down and the client's tokens will not have timed out by the time the server comes back up, then it would be reasonable to let client applications continue to function, where possible, using their local caches. But it could be that the server is not down, just unreachable because of network problems. If so, it's possible that the server, not being able to contact our client, has assumed it to have crashed; our client's tokens might then be unilaterally superseded by the actions of another client, one that can communicate with the server.

Because of this uncertainty, DFS forces system calls on open files to fail once the client determines that the server is not responding. When the server does respond, perhaps having just recovered from a crash, then if the client's tokens are still valid, system calls on open files succeed again.

This approach has the advantage of adhering to POSIX file semantics as long as system calls succeed. However, unlike NFSv2, where client applications can be oblivious to periods of server unresponsiveness, DFS requires the client to be prepared for system calls to fail while the server is unreachable and to retry them explicitly. Furthermore, contact with the server might be lost after an application has performed its last write to a file, but before it has closed the file and before the data has been transferred to the server. Thus the only system call left that can fail, and thus tell the application that something is wrong, is the close. It's therefore important that applications check for errors from close when using files from a DFS server. However, few applications do this, since with other file systems it seems inconceivable that close could actually fail.

10.5 NFS VERSION 4

NFSv4 is a major revision of NFS. Its designers' goals were to provide better performance, stronger consistency, and stronger security than in prior versions, to support not only Unix clients but also Windows clients, and to work well on the modern Internet, particularly where clients and servers may be behind firewalls. A side effect of all this is that the three separate protocols of prior NFS versions (mount protocol, file protocol, and network lock manager) are all combined into a single protocol.

NFSv4 dispenses with the mount protocol by having servers combine their exported file systems into a single "pseudo file system" and supplying an RPC request to obtain the root of that file system. Figure 10.13 shows the file system of a server that exports a few of its subtrees to clients; Figure 10.14 shows the pseudo file system that is made available to clients — note that anything not exported by the server is not seen by clients.

NFSv4 reduces network traffic by using *compound RPC*, which allows a number of RPC requests to be encoded in a single message and their responses to be returned in a single message, much as is the case with CIFS's andX facility.

We focus here on consistency and failure handling. Of particular interest is NFSv4's support for *mandatory locks* (it supports advisory locks as well) and *share reservations* — the same thing as share modes in Windows (see Section 10.3). The network lock manager of prior NFS versions supported only advisory locks. Mandatory locks are expected by Windows applications and supported by some versions of Unix. Share reservations are not really usable by Unix applications — there is no standard API for them — but they are required by Windows applications.

NFSv4's consistency model essentially combines the rather weak consistency of prior NFS versions and the strict consistency of CIFS. If clients use locks or share reservations appropriately when accessing files, NFSv4 guarantees entry consistency (Section 10.1). If locks are not used, consistency is the same as that in prior NSF versions. As a performance optimization, NFSv4 uses a technique similar to CIFS' opportunistic locks called *open delegation*. It allows a server

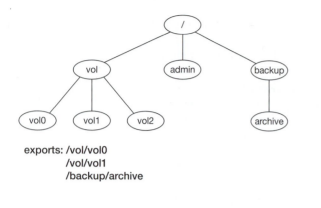

exports: /vol/vol0
         /vol/vol1
         /backup/archive

FIGURE 10.13 The directory hierarchy of an NFSv4 server that exports three subtrees.

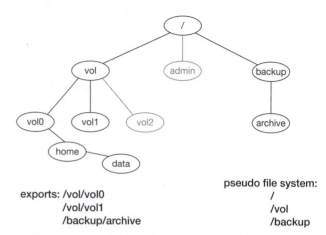

exports: /vol/vol0
         /vol/vol1
         /backup/archive

pseudo file system:
      /
      /vol
      /backup

FIGURE 10.14 The pseudo file system that clients of the server of Figure 10.13 see. /admin and /vol/vol2 are not seen.

to delegate to a client the chores of managing opens, locks, and caching for a file while no other clients are performing conflicting operations.

The big difference between NFSv4 and CIFS is NFSv4's tolerance for failures. Prior versions of NFS were failure-tolerant as well, but NSFv4 is a step more so, since its servers hold much more state information than those of prior versions.

CIFS depends on the transport protocol to insure that requests are properly ordered, without duplicates. NFS, on the other hand, effectively has the notion of a session layer above the transport, and it's this session layer that insures proper ordering of requests.[4] Thus if the transport connection is lost, CIFS has no additional information to insure proper request ordering and must delete all client state on the server, causing any current and subsequent client requests to fail. NFS doesn't depend on the transport protocol for proper ordering and thus can recover from a loss of transport connection (and can run on unreliable, connectionless transports such as UDP).

In prior versions of NFS, this connection layer doesn't require any state information on the server other than the duplicate request cache, and thus clients do nothing explicit to set up the session or take it down. But NFSv4, as we discuss in Section 10.5.1 below, requires more substantial session-oriented state information. Though clients explicitly establish sessions, there is no explicit action to take them down. Instead, as explained below, servers remove session state when the client appears to be no longer active, but clients can recover it.

10.5.1 MANAGING STATE

NFSv4 servers maintain a hierarchy of state. At the top is the inventory of active clients. Each client identifies itself to the server, providing a unique *client ID*. In response the server puts together client-ID state, which includes a *lease period*: if the server doesn't hear from the client during this period, it concludes that it has crashed or has otherwise lost interest, and thus the server can rid itself of the client-ID state and all subordinate state. A client renews its lease by making any sort of NFSv4 request to the server. If it has nothing else to say, it can send a special *renew* request that does nothing but renew the lease.

When a client does open a file, there are additional concerns. To support share reservations, each time some client opens a file the server must put together an *open-state* record containing the access modes and the share reservation. The server returns the client a *state ID* to refer to it,

---

[4] The session layer is implicit in NFS through version 4.0 and is made explicit starting in version 4.1.

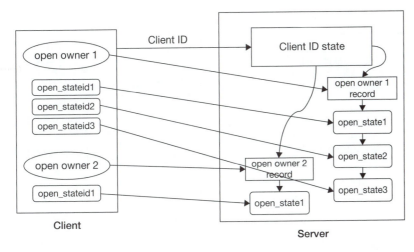

FIGURE 10.15   Open state in NFSv4.

which, along with the NFS file handle, plays the role of a Unix file descriptor or a Windows file handle and is included with subsequent file operations to identify the caller's open state.

The open-state records and state IDs form the elaborate data structure shown in Figure 10.15 in which the client has a number of files open, each with its own open-state record. We explain this figure more fully below, where we explore the notion of an *open owner.*

10.5.1.1 Mandatory Locks

NFSv4 supports not only advisory byte-range locks but mandatory ones as well. The latter are a rarely used feature of Unix, partly because it hasn't been supported by NFS in the past, partly because using it is somewhat obscure (it is enabled by turning on a file's set-group-ID access-permission bit and turning off its group-execute permission bit. On Linux one must additionally turn on this facility for an entire file system by setting a mount flag). Adding to the confusion is the fact that Windows' semantics for mandatory byte-range locks (it doesn't support advisory locks) are different from Unix's. In both systems, byte-range locks belong to a process. Thus, for example, in Unix, suppose a process P1 opens file F, producing file descriptor FD1, and then forks a child process P2. If P2 places a mandatory exclusive byte-range lock on byte 0 of the file via FD1, then only P2 may access that byte — not P1, even though they share the same open-file-table entry for the file. Now suppose P2 opens the same file again, this time producing file descriptor FD2. Even though P2 had locked byte 0 via FD1, it can still access that byte via FD2 — what matters is that the process has the file locked; it doesn't matter which file descriptor is used.[5] However, things are different in Windows, where the lock is associated not just with the process but also with the Windows file handle. Thus in a Windows version of this example, the process is not allowed to access byte 0 via FD2 until the lock placed via FD1 is removed.

When a server receives a read or write request from a client, it needs to know which locks held by the client actually apply to this particular request. For a Unix client, the answer would be all locks held by the client process for the file in question, but for a Windows client, it would be just those locks held by the client process that were placed using the same Windows file handle as was used for the read or write request. But the server doesn't necessarily know which requests came from which processes or which requests were made through which Windows file handles.

---

[5] Another property is that all byte-range locks of a file are removed if any of the process's file descriptors for the file are closed. So suppose P2 in our example wasn't aware that FD1 and FD2 refer to the same file. If it then locks the file via FD2 and closes FD1, it might be surprised to discover that the file referred to by FD2 no longer has a lock.

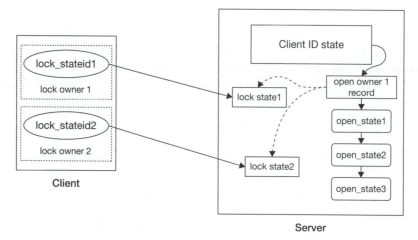

FIGURE 10.16   Lock state in NFSv4.

Rather than give the server this information (which would have to include whether Unix, Windows, or some other lock semantics are being used), the NFSv4 client instead assigns *owners* to locks. When it issues a read or write request, it lets the server know which locks apply by telling it who the owner is. So, for Unix clients, all locks taken by a particular process might be given the same owner, or perhaps all locks taken by a particular process on a particular file might be given the same owner (it doesn't matter which, since the read or write request identifies the file). For Windows clients, all locks taken by a particular process via a particular Windows file handle are given the same owner. The server doesn't need to know what the client's lock semantics are; it just needs to keep track of lock owners.

A *lock owner* on a client is simply a unique (to the client) integer. When the client requests a lock requiring a new lock owner, it passes the corresponding integer to the server. In response, the server establishes *lock state* to represent this lock owner and returns to the client a *lock-state ID* referring to the state. Henceforth the client uses this lock-state ID rather than the lock-owner integer. When the client requests additional locks for the same lock owner, it passes the corresponding lock-state ID to the server. When, for example, the client sends a write request to the server, it includes a lock-state ID to tell the server which locks should apply (a special lock-state ID is sent if no locks apply). Thus the server's lock state represents all the locks held by a particular client lock owner. See Figure 10.16.

10.5.1.2 Maintaining Order

NFSv4's state hierarchy of client ID, open state, and lock state presents challenges. Client crashes must be detected and no-longer-useful state removed from the server. Not only must server crashes be detected, but clients must reestablish their state on the servers. And lastly, everything must function correctly in spite of Byzantine routers.

Establishing the client-ID state is far from immune to problems with late-arriving duplicates. If the server receives a request to establish a client ID that already exists, it might decide that the client has crashed and has restarted. Even a request to establish a client ID that doesn't exist might be a long-delayed duplicate from a client that is no longer active. Setting up the state again might tie up resources needlessly.

Open requests (with share reservations) and mandatory lock requests are particularly sensitive to Byzantine routers. Suppose, for example, a portion of a file is locked, then unlocked, and then a much-delayed duplicate of the lock request arrives at the server. If the server doesn't realize it's a duplicate and locks the file again, then, since the client doesn't know the file is locked, the file might stay locked for an arbitrarily long period of time.

An explicit session layer, introduced in NFSv4.1, simplifies matters tremendously. As part of session setup, clients and servers agree upon the maximum number of concurrent requests and then use session-oriented ONC RPC (Section 9.2.2). This is a big deal since it means that, *in the absence of server crashes*, open requests, lock requests, data-transfer requests (reads and writes), etc. have exactly once semantics — there are no problems with Byzantine routers and duplicates that cross transport-connection boundaries.

10.5.2 DEALING WITH FAILURE

NFSv4 deals with failure issues not handled by its predecessors. Though it uses basically the same strategy for recovery from server failures as the network lock manager of v2 and v3, there is more state to recover and there are more operations that depend on this state. Not only locks but all open state must be recovered. Because locks may be mandatory and share reservations definitely are mandatory, it's particularly important that crashed clients be detected quickly and restarted servers recover their state quickly. But in addition there's a new problem: when a server restarts, the client with the most recent lock state might be temporarily unreachable, but a client with older, superseded lock state might try to reclaim that state on the server.

Leases provide the basic defense against client crashes. Clients are expected to renew their leases; if a client ID's lease time expires, the server assumes it has crashed and may dispose of all its state, thus closing all files and breaking all locks. This might be considered pretty drastic if the client hasn't really crashed but there is merely a temporary network problem. It's also very different behavior from that experienced by NFSv2 and v3 clients: they never had to worry about the server's closing their files, since the server never knew they were open in the first place. However, such behavior is unavoidable when unresponding clients hold lock state or share reservations.

A client might crash, reboot, and recontact the server well before its original lease has expired. The fact that the client is reestablishing its client ID might be a clue to the server that it has restarted, but there are reasons other than crashing that a client might do this. So included with the client-ID state on the server is a 64-bit *verifier* that is supplied by the client when it establishes its client ID and is different each time the client reboots. Thus, if the server receives a set-up-client-ID request from a client for which it still has state, if the verifier supplied with the request is different from what's included with the saved state, then the server knows the client has restarted and the saved state should be discarded. But if the verifiers are the same, then the saved state is still valid.

Clients find out about server crashes when RPC requests that depend on open and lock state return error codes indicating that the state no longer exists. For a period before then (while the server was down) such calls might have timed out, but the only way for a client to distinguish a server problem from a temporary communications problem is for the server to give a positive indication that it has no record of the client. The problem might turn out to be not that the server crashed, but that the client's lease expired, but from the client's point of view, lease expiration is just as bad, if not worse.

As with the network lock manager in v2 and v3, when a server restarts, it establishes a grace period during which clients may recover their states. How long should the grace period be? A client won't discover that the server has crashed until it sends it a request. But the client isn't required to send the server a request until just before its lease expires. So, in case a client renewed its lease just before the server crashed, the server's grace period should be at least as long as the lease period.

Suppose a client discovers that its server state has disappeared. Its first response is to reestablish its client-ID state, along with a new verifier. Then, as with the network lock manager, it tries to reclaim its previous state.

Now the server has decisions to make. If it is not in its grace period following a restart, then the reason the client's state no longer exists is probably that it was discarded after the client's lease expired. This could be due to incompetence on the client's part, but is most likely the result of a network problem. If the server can determine that no conflicting opens or locks have been given to other clients since the lease expired, then it may allow the client to reclaim its state. But, in general, the server probably can't determine this, so it must refuse the reclaim request and the client must report an error back to the application (and thus the application must be prepared to cope with the bad news).

If the server is within its grace period, then the reclaim request is probably for state held when the server crashed, and thus it should be granted. However, the client might have been disconnected from the server because of a network problem. In the meantime, the client's lease expired, the server granted a conflicting lock to another client, and then the server crashed. Finally, the network problems experienced by the first client have been solved and it is now trying to reclaim its (ancient) state. But it really should be the second client whose state is reclaimed.

The general problem for the server when it receives a reclaim request is to make sure that the state being reclaimed hasn't been superseded by more recent operations by other clients. The NFSv4 specification (RFC 3530[6]) requires servers to err on the side of safety: if they aren't sure, they must refuse the reclaim request.

The only way for a server to be absolutely sure is to record all share reservations and locks in stable storage, so that they can be recovered after a crash. This is probably too time-consuming for most servers. At the other extreme, a server could simply refuse to accept reclaims, on the grounds that it doesn't have enough information to determine if any of them are for the most recent state.

A reasonable compromise is for the server to keep enough information on stable storage to determine which client IDs hold state. Then, during the grace period, it can refuse all reclaim requests from clients who didn't hold state at the time of the most recent crash.

RFC 3530 suggests servers record the following information on stable storage for each client ID:

- client ID.

- the time of the client's first acquisition of a share reservation or lock after a server reboot or client lease expiration.

- a flag indicating whether the client's most recent state was revoked because of a lease expiration.

In addition, the server stores on stable storage the times of its two most recent restarts. Doing this requires minimal server overhead, yet allows it to determine whether a client definitely held valid server state at the time of the last server crash. We take this up in Exercise 9 below.

10.6 CONCLUSIONS

Distributed file systems are normally made as transparent as possible to users and their applications; as we have seen, much has been done to make accessing remote files indistinguishable from accessing local files. The major problem is coping with failure, both of communication and of machines. NFS has been successful because of its compromises. Prior to version 4 it provided semantics that were "pretty close" to local Unix file semantics, with a response to failure that "pretty well" insulated the client from server and network problems. CIFS, and to a certain extent DFS, were based on the premise that providing semantics that are exactly the same as local semantics is more important than insulating the client from server and network problems. NFSv4 is attempting to come as close as possible to achieving local-file-system semantics while still insulating clients from server problems (and vice versa).

---

[6] http://www.faqs.org/rfcs/rfc3530.html

1. Suppose we have a file server that connects to a storage server via a storage area network (SAN) — see Figure 10.1. The storage server provides a collection of disk blocks for use by the file server. The file server uses these disk blocks to store files, and provides these files to its clients. Since its clients are fully capable of implementing a file system from the disk blocks provided by the file server, is the file server really necessary? Can't the clients deal directly with the storage server? Explain.

2. An approach for implementing file locking in distributed file systems is to maintain the locks on the server in volatile storage (i.e., storage whose contents disappear in the event of a crash). Thus, after a server crash, the server must recover its prior state by obtaining information from its clients about who had which files locked. If servers maintained locks in non-volatile storage, then, it would seem, state recovery after a crash would not be necessary. Explain why neither NFS nor DFS maintains such lock information in non-volatile storage. (*Hint*: consider, among other things, client crashes.)

3. In most operating systems file access permissions are checked only when the file is opened and not with each read or write. Thus if you open a file successfully for both reading and writing, obtaining file descriptor *f*, and if you subsequently change the file's access permissions to read-only, you can still write to the file using *f*.

   a. Explain why supporting this feature is difficult in distributed file systems whose servers do not hold open-file state, such as NFSv2.

   b. How might you "approximate" this feature so that it's supported on NFSv2 for what's probably the most common case: the file's owner is accessing the file?

4. As discussed in Section 10.2.2, file handles in the Unix implementation of NFSv2 contain inode numbers. Suppose we have a user-mode implementation of an NFS server and inode numbers are not available to it (this would be the case with CD-ROM file systems). Instead, the file handle for a file contains the file's directory-path name. Will this cause any problems? Explain. (*Hint:* consider the client's data cache.)

5. Suppose we wish to add to basic NFSv2 a remote procedure for appending data to the end of a file.

   a. Explain why such a remote procedure is needed: why can't its effect be obtained through the use of the *stat* procedure (which, among other things, returns the size of a file) and the *write* procedure?

   b. Assuming a well behaved network and a server that never crashes, will there be any problems if an append request or response is lost? Explain.

   c. Suppose the network is not so well behaved and the server is not so reliable. Will there now be problems if the request or response is lost? Explain.

6. Suppose a CIFS server crashes and restarts.

   a. How do its clients discover that the server has restarted?

   b. Explain why the clients cannot simply resume their operations, as in NFSv2.

   c. The clients can recover from the server crash by rebooting. Can a less drastic approach be taken? Explain.

7. Suppose two CIFS clients are running applications that simultaneously open the same file for both reading and writing, with share modes that allow this to take place. The applications on both clients first issue a number of read requests, then, more or less simultaneously, both issue write requests to the file. Explain how this is handled by the CIFS protocol: what

SMB messages are exchanged? When may clients use data in their local caches? Be sure to explain in what order events must take place.

*8. If a DFS client application pays attention properly to the return codes of all I/O system calls and does appropriate retries in case of communication timeouts, is it assured that all its updates are correctly stored on the server?

*9. This question concerns lock recovery in NFSv4 (Section 10.5.2).

a. Suppose the server holds no state information in stable storage; thus all such information is lost if it crashes. Give a scenario in which a client locks a portion of a file, loses contact with the server, then regains contact and reclaims its lock. However, while the client was out of touch with the server the locked portion of the file was modified by another client. All parties honor all the rules, including the use of the grace period. (Hint: consider not only server crashes, but also network partitions (in which two machines cannot communicate because the network connection between them is temporarily inoperative, but each can communicate with others).)

b. Suppose locks are kept in stable storage on the server and thus survive crashes. Explain how you would modify the lock-recovery technique used above so that your scenario would be handled sensibly.

c. As mentioned in Section 10.5.2, recording all locks in stable storage is too time-consuming. Explain how the solution given in Section 10.5.2 (from RFC 3530) deals with the scenario of part a.

*10. Consider the following sequence of events in NFSv4:

i. Client A requests an exclusive lock on all of file X and the client receives the server's response of "success."

ii. Client A requests that the lock be "downgraded" to a shared lock. The server responds "success," but the response is lost.

iii. Client B requests a shared lock on all of the same file. The client receives the server's response of "success."

iv. The server crashes.

v. The server restarts and starts its grace period.

vi. Client B quickly recovers its shared lock.

a. The server is still in its grace period as client A attempts to reestablish its lock state. What does it do and what are the responses? (Hint: we may have a big problem here.)

b. What might be done to fix this problem with the protocol?

10.8 REFERENCES

Bershad, B. and M. Zekauskas (1991). Midway: Shared Parallel Programming with Entry Consistency for Distributed Memory Multiprocessors. Carnegie Mellon University Technical Report CMU-CS-91-170.

Lamport, L. (1979). How to Make a Multiprocessor Computer That Correctly Executes Multiprocess Programs. *IEEE Transactions on Computers* **C-28**(9): 690–691.

Storage Networking Industry Association (2002) Common Internet File System (CIFS) Technical Reference. http://www.snia.org/tech_activities/CIFS/CIFS-TR-1p00_FINAL.pdf.

Index of URLs

Index

Note: Bold page number ranges indicate chapters; bold single numbers, either alone or as the first number in a range indicate first use or definition of a term. URL locations in the book chapters have "URL" in a sub-entry.